SECONDARY SCHOOL READING INSTRUCTION

THE CONTENT AREAS

SECONDARY SCHOOL READING INSTRUCTION
THE CONTENT AREAS

THIRD EDITION

BETTY D. ROE

Tennessee Technological University

BARBARA D. STOODT

University of North Carolina at Greensboro

PAUL C. BURNS

Late of University of Tennessee at Knoxville

HOUGHTON MIFFLIN COMPANY   BOSTON

Dallas   Geneva, Illinois   Lawrenceville, New Jersey   Palo Alto

To Mike

and

To Linda and Susan

Source for list of highest frequency words for ten occupations on pp. 299–300: R. Rush, A. Moe, and R. Storlie, *Occupational Literacy Education* (Newark, Del.: International Reading Association, 1986), p. 65. Reprinted with permission of the International Reading Association and the author.

Printed in the U.S.A.

Library of Congress Catalog Card Number: 86-81608
ISBN: 0-395-35806-X

EFGHIJ-H-89

CONTENTS

PREFACE

AUDIENCE AND PURPOSE

This book has been written primarily for secondary school content teachers—those who are preparing for certification in teacher-training programs and those who are experienced and wish to learn how to help their students read content assignments with more understanding. Neither group is likely to have background knowledge in reading; this book has thus been written at an introductory level, with the needs and concerns of these teachers in mind. The text also contains much information that is useful for reading specialists who work cooperatively with content teachers in helping secondary students with reading difficulties and for secondary school administrators who must know about the reading needs of secondary school students if they are to set school policies appropriately.

The aim of this book is to help prepare secondary classroom teachers to teach the content of their subject areas more efficiently. Because most secondary content material is written at a fairly high level and requires large amounts of reading, teachers who know how to teach the reading skills necessary for understanding their content will enhance their success in the classroom.

REVISIONS IN THIS EDITION

The information from the second edition has been expanded and updated in this revision. For example, the section on minimum competency testing has been expanded. Teacher education considerations have also been included. The coverage of individual content area techniques has been expanded. Coverage of computer literacy and agriculture has also been added to the text.

The skills chapters have been greatly strengthened. The vocabulary chapter has been restructured to include material on word recognition skills that some secondary students need to acquire, as well as material on understanding figurative language. The comprehension chapter has been restructured and updated to cover information from recent research, including topics such as metacognition and teacher modeling.

COVERAGE AND FEATURES

The first chapter of the text introduces the topic of secondary school reading instruction and clearly presents the need for such instruction. Following this introduction, separate chapters are devoted to the development of vocabulary, comprehension skills, and reading-study skills in the secondary classroom. Chapter 5 serves as an overview to content reading; Chapters 6 and 7 describe in detail instructional strategies for individual content fields, both academic and vocational. These chapters include skills and activities specific to each content area, as well as to the common needs in all content areas, and present varied examples of material from content area textbooks. Because a typical secondary classroom may include readers of widely differing backgrounds and abilities, assessing pupil progress and adjusting reading assignments to fit all students are treated extensively in Chapters 8 and 9. Chapter 10 discusses the reading process underlying the practical suggestions in this text. The final chapter describes various plans for providing reading instruction in the secondary school, particularly total school reading programs, which involve all personnel in a school. Answers to the Self-Tests that appear at the end of each chapter are included in the text appendix.

From the beginning it was our intent to include an abundance of practical activities and strategies for improving students' reading performances, including representative secondary school textbook pages with accompanying original "how to" materials such as illustrative lesson plans, worksheets, and activity lists. This text should, then, continue to be a valuable reference book for both the new and the experienced teacher.

To help the content teacher gain a more complete understanding of reading instruction, this book contains many instructional aids:

Overviews, which are designed to provide information about the chapter content and to motivate the reader, begin each chapter.

Purpose-setting Questions, part of the opening material in each chapter, help to increase comprehension by focusing on important ideas.

Key Vocabulary, also part of the chapter openers, presents terms that represent important but often unfamiliar concepts.

Chapter Summaries pull together and review the chapter's major points.

Self-Tests (objective) and *Thought Questions* (essay) provide questions to help students determine their own levels of mastery.

Enrichment Activities supply additional self-improvement opportunities; these activities are useful in promoting a task-oriented reading of the chapter and in reinforcing ideas presented in the chapter.

ACKNOWLEDGMENTS

We are indebted to many people for their assistance in the preparation of our manuscript. Although we would like to acknowledge the many teachers and students whose inspiration was instrumental in the development of this book, it is impossible to name them all. Grateful recognition is also given to the following reviewers, whose constructive advice and criticism helped greatly in the writing and revision of the manuscript: Deborah Gaddy, North Carolina State University; Bruce Lloyd, Western Michigan University; Mary Jane Quirin, National University; Sherrie Shugarman, University of Dayton; Lawrence Smith, State University College of New York at Buffalo; and Edward Sullivan, Providence College. In addition, appreciation is expressed to those who have granted permission to use sample materials or citations from their respective works. Credit for these contributions has been given in the notes in the text.

Betty D. Roe, Tennessee Technological University

Barbara D. Stoodt, University of North Carolina at Greensboro

SECONDARY SCHOOL READING INSTRUCTION
THE CONTENT AREAS

CHAPTER
O   N   E

READING IN THE

SECONDARY SCHOOL

OVERVIEW

This chapter opens with a discussion of the nature of reading. The relationship of
reading instruction to the secondary school curriculum is then discussed. The discussion includes consideration of the roles of the various school personnel responsible for reading instruction. Reading achievement levels of students and minimum competency requirements for teachers are also addressed.

PURPOSE-SETTING QUESTIONS

As you read this chapter, try to answer these questions:

1. What occurs during the reading process?
2. What are the major phases of a secondary school reading program?
3. What are some faulty assumptions about teaching reading in secondary
   schools?
4. What responsibilities for reading instruction in secondary schools do content
   area teachers have as they try to make their particular content more
   accessible?
5. What responsibilities for reading instruction in the secondary school belong to
   the administrator, the reading consultant, the special reading teacher, and
   the librarian or media center specialist?
6. What are some concerns about reading achievement levels of secondary
   school students?

KEY VOCABULARY

As you read this chapter, check your understanding of these terms:

word identification   corrective/remedial
   skills   reading
study skills   capacity level
content area reading   recreational reading
comprehensive reading   special reading
   program   teacher
developmental reading   reading consultant

WHAT IS READING?

Reading is understanding written language.

Reading is a complex mental process.

Reading is thinking.

Reading comprehension is the reconstruction, interpretation, and evaluation of what the author of written content means by using knowledge gained from life experience.[1]

All of the preceding explanations of reading are accurate. Despite continuing disagreement about the precise nature of the reading process, there are some points of general agreement among reading authorities. One point of agreement is that "reading comprehension is the real purpose of reading instruction."[2] In fact, *reading comprehension* and *reading* frequently are considered synonymous because reading usually means comprehending written language. When understanding breaks down, reading actually has not occurred.

Many reading authorities agree that during reading the eyes sweep across a line of print in jerks (*saccadic movements*) and stops (*fixations*), sending messages to the brain during the stops. When the brain associates meaning with these sensory-perceptual messages, reading occurs. The word identification skills of sight words, context clues, structural analysis, and phonic analysis facilitate understanding by helping readers associate printed words with the words in their oral and listening vocabularies. Readers who lack word identification abilities will not be able to make these associations; thus, they may require assistance with reading.

During the reading process, there is an interplay between the reader's pre-existing knowledge and the written content. Competent reading is an active process in which the reader calls upon experience, language, concepts, and schemata to anticipate (predict) and understand the author's thoughts, concepts, and language.[3] (*Schemata* are theoretical constructs of knowledge related to experiences.) Thus, readers both bring meaning to print and take meaning from print.

The nature of the reading process alters as students mature. In the early stages of reading, word identification requires a reader's concentration. Eventually, however, as reading competence develops, readers are able to use their reading ability (ability to interpret written language) for pleasure, appreciation, knowledge acquisition, and functional purposes. Thus, reading competence has many faces. A competent reader locates materials and ideas that enable the reader to fulfill a particular purpose; the purpose may be to follow directions, to complete a job application, or to appreciate a Shakespearean play. In addition, competent readers adjust reading style as they move from narrative to expository content. Finally, they read at levels of understanding that begin with the literal level, progress to the interpretive level, and culminate in the critical and creative levels.

The terms *literal, interpretive (inferential), critical,* and *creative* refer to the levels of reasoning that are commonly associated with reading comprehension. *Literal understanding* refers to the reader's recognizing or remembering ideas and information that are explicitly stated in printed material. *Inferential comprehension* occurs when the reader synthesizes ideas and information from printed material with knowledge, experience, and imagination to form hypotheses. This level of comprehension requires that the reader use ideas and information that are not stated on the printed page. It requires the reader to read between the lines, to use deductive reasoning, and to make assumptions based on the facts given. *Critical comprehension (evaluation)* requires that the reader make judgments about the content of a reading selection by comparing it with external criteria. The reader may have developed these criteria through experience, through reference to resource materials, or through access to information provided by authorities on the subject. *Creative understanding (reading beyond the lines)* has to do with the reader's emotional responses to printed material (appreciation) and his or her ability to produce new ideas based upon the reading experience. Creative understanding is built upon literal, inferential, and critical understanding. The reader's intellectual understanding provides a foundation for his or her emotional reaction. For example, readers may respond to an author's style, or they may identify with certain characters, story incidents, or the author's use of symbolism.

Reading is not a single skill; rather, it is a composite of skills and abilities. Reading is a unitary process that is greater than the sum of its individual parts. The various skills and abilities that constitute the reading process occur almost simultaneously. As competent readers function, it is thus impossible to observe discrete reading skills and abilities. However, a number of writers have attempted to identify the various elements of the reading process by developing theoretical constructs of reading. Chapter 10 contains information about these theoretical models.

THE SECONDARY SCHOOL READING PROGRAM

In recent years the need to provide well-conceived secondary school reading programs has grown as the population in secondary schools has increased and the importance of comprehensive curricula has been recognized. Comprehensive programs for reading instruction at the secondary level are described in detail in Chapter 11. This section serves as a brief orientation to the program.

How Does Reading Instruction Fit into the Secondary School Curriculum?

This section is designed to explain the general relationship of reading skills to content reading and to show the content area teacher's position in the overall picture. It also attempts to show the general organization and approach of this text. The concepts discussed here are analyzed in greater detail in later chapters.

Word identification skills include sight words, contextual analysis, structural analysis, and phonic analysis. The goal of word identification instruction is to develop students' independence in identifying words.

Sight words are words students have memorized and are able to identify immediately. Secondary students usually have a good store of sight words that help them read content materials with understanding. Each time a content teacher introduces a new technical or specialized term that is important to the understanding of the content area, the teacher hopes to turn the new word into a sight word for the students; the study of the subject would be inefficient if many of the important words had to be analyzed carefully before recognition occurred. The content teacher can help impress new words on the students' memories, and thus turn them into sight words, by writing the words on the chalkboard, pronouncing them, and discussing them with the students. Knowledge of sight words also enables students to use contextual analysis.

Contextual analysis is use of the context in which an unknown word occurs in order to identify the word. Contextual analysis skills are powerful tools for secondary students to use in reading content area materials, and content area teachers will benefit greatly from helping students become aware of the context and its usefulness in word identification. Contextual analysis not only plays a role in word identification, but it is also an important tool for determining word meaning.

Structural analysis involves the use of word parts such as affixes, root words, syllables, and smaller words that are joined to form compound words to help in the identification of unfamiliar words. Structural analysis is extremely helpful in analysis of content area words because in many cases certain prefixes, suffixes, and root words appear repeatedly in the related technical terms of a discipline. Learning to recognize these word parts can be very helpful in decoding the vocabulary of the discipline. Structural analysis also plays a part in the determination of word meaning, as well as word identification. Morphemes, the smallest meaningful units of a language, include prefixes, suffixes, and root words. Analysis of the meanings of morphemes of technical, or general, terminology can help students determine word meanings, a skill that is at the heart of content area instruction.

Phonic analysis involves breaking words into basic sound elements and blending these sounds together to produce spoken words. Phonic analysis is not generally stressed by the content area teacher, but lies in the province of the special reading teacher.

Word identification skills help students pronounce words, but word meanings must be understood before reading comprehension can occur. Many of the words that content readers encounter represent labels for key concepts in the content areas. A reader learns word meanings through experience, word association, concept development, contextual analysis, structural analysis, and use of the dictionary. Content teachers can help students comprehend content materials by teaching students the meanings of key vocabulary terms.

To read with comprehension, readers must also be able to perceive the internal organization of reading materials, understand the various writing patterns used to structure content materials, and understand the material at the appropriate cognitive level.

A reader's perception of the internal organization of a selection is based on the skill of identifying main ideas and supporting details, as well as on familiarity with various organizational writing patterns. Sentence comprehension is vital to the recognition and understanding of main ideas and supporting details. The concepts of main ideas and supporting details can be applied directly to the teaching of paragraph comprehension. The internal organization of longer units of writing is based on the understanding of paragraphs and their relationships.

Main ideas and supporting details may be organized according to different writing patterns. These patterns may include cause-effect, comparison-contrast, sequence of events, and so forth. Readers understand content better when they are able to follow the particular writing pattern and organization used. Content area teachers need to be familiar with the types of writing patterns encountered frequently in their particular disciplines, so that they can help students to understand these writing patterns better.

Comprehension is also developed and approached through four cognitive levels—literal, inferential or interpretive, critical, and creative. Modeling and judicious use of questioning techniques serve as two major vehicles for developing understanding at these four levels. Since most content area teachers use commercial materials, such as textbooks, to teach their subject areas, they need to be familiar with the types of questions used in these materials. Some textbooks focus too heavily on literal-level questions, therefore not providing the means for encouraging higher-level thinking about the content and certainly failing to offer enough challenge for better students. Other textbooks may be too heavily laden with higher-order questions, without laying the groundwork with literal understanding, thereby overtaxing the abilities of poorer students.

Content reading requires a flexible use of reading rate. The concept of rate can be examined best as it relates to comprehension. Rate is governed by purpose for reading, level of comprehension desired, familiarity with content, and type of content. Content area teachers need to help students learn to vary their reading rates to fit particular instructional materials and different purposes for reading.

Content reading and study skills become more important as students progress through school. Students are expected to become more independent in applying their reading skills in work-study situations. Study skills also represent the application of reading skills to learning. Study skills are closely aligned with content reading because both are concerned with acquiring knowledge from written material. There are three basic types of study skills: those that involve locating information through reading; those that are concerned with understanding and remembering content; and those that are concerned with the organization of information once it has been located and read. Content area teachers need to help students learn to use these study skills efficiently, so that they can study the content assignments more effectively. Teaching study skills in the situations in which they are expected to be used is more effective than teaching them in isolation.

Content reading involves a special application of reading skills to content materials. Successful content reading is based on the application of vocabulary, comprehension, and study skills, an understanding of the ways that knowledge is organized in content materials, and a purposeful reading of these materials to acquire knowledge. Content teachers can improve their students' understanding of content by helping them read their textbooks more effectively.

Phases of the Reading Program

The total, or comprehensive, reading program should be composed of at least four interrelated phases.

1. *The content area phase.*   This program is for all students enrolled in a content area course. Here the student is helped to comprehend the specific subject matter. Reading skills required for effective reading of the content area material are considered. Within each content area—English, mathematics, social studies, science, and so forth—reading materials with which students can experience reading success must be utilized. Such materials might include multilevel texts, materials from library sources with lower levels of reading difficulty, films, and tapes.
2. *The developmental phase.*   This program is for average and above average readers who elect to enroll in it. A special reading teacher, who directs the program, helps students to further develop comprehension skills, vocabulary knowledge, rate of reading, and study skills.
3. *The corrective or remedial phase.*   This program is for disabled readers—students who are reading at a level that is one or more years below their *capacity*, or *potential reading level*. These students usually need to work on basic word recognition and comprehension skills. As these skills improve, the students learn how to apply general study skills. This part of the program also is directed primarily by the special reading teacher.
4. *The recreational phase.*   Since the ultimate goal of all reading instruction is to develop good reading habits that will last a lifetime, this program is an important, though frequently neglected, aspect of the comprehensive reading program. All personnel involved with reading responsibilities should take an active part in encouraging recreational reading.

Although English teachers and reading specialists have particularly strong reasons for motivating students to read for pleasure, all content area teachers should share the responsibility of motivating students to read recreationally. There are three major reasons for this:

1. The content area teacher may have a special rapport with several students who do not like to read and with whom no other secondary teacher has this special relationship.
2. A certain content area may be the only one that holds a student's interest at a particular time. For example, a physical education teacher might be able to motivate a particular boy or girl to read books on sports.
3. Particular subject matter becomes more real as a reader experiences events through imaginative literature. For example, the topic of the American Revolution, which might take up only one chapter in a social studies textbook, will be more meaningful to a student who reads Esther Forbes's *Johnny Tremain* and becomes involved in Johnny's experiences of that period's political intrigue and his preparation for war. Science teachers can enrich their own programs as well as encourage students' individual reading interests by supplementing course material with readings in science fiction (such as Ray Bradbury's *R Is for Rocket*) and nonfiction (such as *Your Trip into Space* by Lynn Poole). Teachers of industrial arts and agriculture can use literature to sustain student interest; for example, Henry Lent's *O-K for Drive Away* is a good book about automobiles and automobile makers, and Henry Billings's *All Down the Valley* is an interesting story of the TVA. Extra effort by each content area teacher may lead to enduring reading habits and tastes in the students. Joseph Sanacore suggested a plan by which all content teachers can incorporate recreational reading into their classes over the period of a year according to a carefully planned schedule.[4] Individual teachers have also developed their own plans for promoting recreational reading.

Some Faulty Assumptions About Teaching Reading

There are several faulty assumptions about the teaching of reading that should be considered.

1. *Teaching reading is a concern only in the elementary school.*   The idea that a child who has completed the sixth grade should have mastered the complex process of reading fails to take into account the fact that learning to read is a continuing process. Children learn to read over a long period of time, attempting more advanced reading skills as they master earlier prerequisite skills. Even after encountering all reading skills, the reader continues to refine these skills. No matter how old a person is, or how long he or she has been out of school, that person can continue to improve reading skills.
2. *Teaching reading in the content areas is separate and distinct from teaching subject matter.*   Teaching reading and study skills is an integral part of

teaching any subject matter. A teacher is obligated to teach students how to use the printed materials that are assigned. When a teacher uses printed materials to teach a content area, that teacher is using reading as a teaching and learning aid and should use it for maximum effectiveness. Teaching reading in subject matter areas is a complementary learning process, inseparable from the particular subject matter. Teachers' efforts to teach reading in various content areas are an important element in the success of any junior or senior high school reading program.

3. *Reading needs in the secondary school can be met through remedial work alone.* Some schools fail to make an essential distinction between *developmental reading,* which is directed to meet the needs of all students, and *corrective* or *remedial reading,* which provides specific assistance to disabled readers. Not only should developmental (as well as remedial) classes be made available, but within each class, content teachers can promote developmental reading by helping students learn the concepts and vocabulary of that content area, and they can enhance their students' reading comprehension by assisting them in interpreting and evaluating the text material.

   Additionally, teachers can help students develop better reading study skills and other specialized skills associated with the particular content areas. For example, reading and understanding written directions are skills that are needed in every secondary classroom. Other universally needed skills include reading to discover main ideas, details, and inferences. Even more important than absorbing the vast amount of printed material that they encounter every day is the secondary school students' development of critical reading skills. Before they leave secondary school, students should know how to sort out fact from opinion, truth from half-truth, information from emotion.

4. *A reading specialist or an English teacher should be responsible for the teaching of reading.* While the reading specialist has distinct responsibilities in a secondary reading program, his or her efforts are negligible without the help of classroom teachers. Reading as a tool for learning is no more important in the English class than it is in most other classes, and English teachers do not necessarily have any better preparation for teaching reading skills than do other teachers. Responsibility for teaching reading cannot be delegated solely to English teachers. All content teachers (science, health, social studies, mathematics, English, computer science, home economics, business education, industrial arts, agriculture, physical education, music, art, and others) have a responsibility to teach the language and organization of their particular content areas, and to do so they must help the students read that content.

5. *The teaching of reading and the teaching of literature are one and the same.* Reading skills are important to the study of literature, as they are to the study of every content area. It should be understood, however, that the teaching of literature, even in junior high school, should not be composed merely of having students read stories and then giving vocabulary drills and exercises to find details and main ideas. It is dangerous to assume that a student improves content reading skills only by practicing with selections of literature.

Personnel Responsible for Reading Instruction

Content Area Teachers

The responsibility of the content area teacher is to help students read their textbooks and supplementary materials more effectively, in order to learn the content more effectively. Content teachers need to know what reading skills are necessary for successful reading of the materials in their particular disciplines, and they need to be capable of assisting students in applying these skills as they complete their content area assignments. In most cases, such as in the teaching of technical vocabulary, reading instruction and content instruction are identical. Content teachers may often find that brief instruction in a particular reading skill will pay large dividends in the students' understanding of an assignment.

Content area teachers are not expected to be *primarily* engaged in teaching reading skills, however. Students who have significantly impaired reading skills are helped by a special reading teacher outside the content class. The content teachers do have to make adjustments for these students and their reading levels when making content assignments. Providing alternate materials and teaching methods for these students is necessary if their content learning is to be successful.

Following are the requirements for content area teachers if they are to meet their responsibilities to their students and the reading program:

1. Knowledge of the reading skills that are needed by secondary students in order to read content materials in their disciplines
2. Knowledge of assessment measures that can help them identify students who cannot read the standard assignments, can read the assignments only with much assistance, or can read the assignments with ease
3. Ability to identify specific learning problems that should be referred to a specialist in order to provide appropriate help for students requiring it
4. Knowledge of ways to help students learn specific skills needed for their content areas
5. Knowledge of study aids and procedures that can help students be more successful in content area reading
6. Knowledge of effective ways to differentiate assignments for students reading at different levels of proficiency
7. Willingness to cooperate with other school personnel, such as the special reading teacher, in helping students reach their full potential in reading to learn content

Special Reading Teacher

The special reading teacher works directly with students. He or she has a graduate degree in reading or the equivalent, has several years of teaching experience, and is certified as a reading specialist.

While the specific responsibilities of the reading specialist may vary from locale to locale, the following are fairly typical:

1. Knows reading skills, formal and informal instruments for assessing reading (being able to administer and interpret them), and a variety of methods and materials for reading instruction.
2. Plans and teaches reading classes for average readers, accelerated readers, and disabled readers.
3. Works with paraprofessionals and parents who may assist with the reading program
4. Works with content area teachers whose students are in reading classes; assists all content area teachers in selecting instructional materials to meet the needs of students; when called upon, helps content teachers develop and utilize reading instruction within content classrooms; provides suggestions on establishment of learning centers within content classrooms, especially involving use of tape-recorded instruction for the severely disabled reader.
5. Assists the reading consultant as a demonstration teacher and resource person.

Reading Consultant

The reading consultant works with administrators and other school personnel to develop and coordinate the school-wide reading program. This person is freed from classroom teaching or instruction of special reading classes. He or she has a high degree of professional skill and knowledge, has had years of formal study in reading and related areas, has had several years of successful teaching experience, and meets certification qualifications as a special teacher of reading.

Again, whereas the specific responsibilities of the reading consultant may vary somewhat from locale to locale, the following are typical:

1. Studies the population to be served—both students and teachers
2. Assists principal/supervisor/administrator in planning a comprehensive reading program that includes (a) development of basic skills, (b) correction/remediation, (c) content area reading and study skills, (d) development of interests and tastes in leisure reading
3. Orients beginning teachers to philosophy, procedures, and materials for school reading program and keeps all school staff informed about new developments in reading
4. Evaluates the program through supervisory activities and research, making recommendations for changes as needed
5. Provides in-service instruction, conducting workshops, seminars, conferences, and minilessons on such topics as readability formulae, informal reading inventories, construction of teaching or study guides, and so forth
6. Evaluates and recommends reading materials
7. Works as resource person with special cases where difficulty or complexity requires a high degree of professional competence
8. Keeps the community informed about purposes and progress of the reading program

Principal or Administrator

A most significant prerequisite for a good secondary reading program is administrative direction. The administrator alone possesses the prestige and authority to carry through a sound reading program. He or she must encourage the staff and insure that the reading philosophy is implemented in logical and innovative ways. He or she needs to provide the impetus for defining the reading program's philosophy and must facilitate that philosophy by extending it to the entire school.

Example 1.1 presents an administrator's self-evaluation checklist. It suggests the responsibility of the administrator in the reading program.

EXAMPLE 1.1 ADMINISTRATOR'S SELF-EVALUATION CHECKLIST —

(Please respond *yes* or *no* to these items)

General Goal Focusing
1. The teachers and I have in mind basic goals of the reading program. _____
2. The teachers and I keep in mind the interdependent instructional reading phases. _____
3. To keep knowledgeable about reading and students,
   a. I read books on the role of the administrator and reading. _____
   b. I take formal course work in reading and attend reading workshops and conferences. _____
   c. I visit often with outstanding reading teachers. _____
   d. I study the reading materials used in the school. _____
   e. I maintain a professional reading library. _____
4. The teachers and I have arrived at basic principles of reading instruction. _____
5. I help stimulate reading improvement opportunities by
   a. evaluating the present program with teachers. _____
   b. observing classrooms for reading instruction practices and noting such items as the following _____

       How are the students prepared for reading?
       How is the reading interpreted?
       How are skills/abilities extended?
       How are interests extended?

   c. providing for intervisitation demonstrations, videotaping. _____
   d. focusing upon reading topics of interest in faculty meetings, workshops, etc. _____

Resource Commitment
6. I make a real effort to reduce teacher-pupil ratio. _____
7. I try to meet and exceed requirements about library resources. _____
8. I try to involve parents, aides, and students in the reading program. _____

9. I make decisions about reading materials for school use only after tryouts on a limited scale and by following selection guidelines. _____

10. I recognize organization is a technique or a system—not a "method of instruction"—and that organization can only facilitate—or hinder—effective instruction. _____

Program Monitoring

11. The teachers and I maintain appropriate record forms for indicating reading progress of each student. _____

12. The teachers and I understand and use reading survey tests, diagnostic reading tests, informal reading inventories, and other assessment techniques. _____

13. The teachers and I have provided corrective/remedial services for appropriate students. _____

14. I am prepared to answer the questions about reading most frequently asked by parents and others. _____

15. The time allocated for reading instruction is sufficient to the task. _____

16. I attempt to designate space for a central resource center. _____

17. The teachers and I review results of our efforts to improve reading instruction. _____

18. I use the data from reviewing sessions to make needed changes. _____

Hiring Personnel

19. I hire classroom teachers who are informed about reading problems in their special areas. _____

20. I hire reading personnel who have adequate expertise in reading. _____

Interpersonal Relationships

21. The teachers perceive me as a facilitator, rather than as a dictator. _____

22. The teachers feel free to come to me when problems related to the reading program develop. _____

23. I communicate well with parents concerning their children's reading difficulties and the steps being taken to help them. _____

24. Students are not afraid to approach me with problems related to their reading program or other areas. _____

Several points may be made to elaborate upon the preceding checklist. The administrator should consider important ultimate goals of a comprehensive reading program:

1. The student likes to read and has acquired an abiding interest in reading a wide variety of worthwhile material.

2. The student makes efficient use of skills to identify words and increase meaning vocabulary (understanding of words) through reading.

3. The student makes efficient use of skills needed to read informative (content) reading materials.

4. The student can understand literally; can interpret, evaluate, and react to printed ideas; and can organize and remember what he or she reads.
5. The student can adjust reading rates to the purpose and nature of the reading material.

There are nine major functions of the administrator in the reading program:

1. *Knowing about reading and students.*   Where knowledge needs to be supplemented, there are various resources; for instance, books such as *The School Reading Program: A Handbook for Teachers, Supervisors, and Specialists,* by Richard J. Smith, Wayne Otto, and Lee Hansen (Boston: Houghton Mifflin Company, 1978), are helpful. Other ways to increase knowledge are suggested in Example 1.1 (see 3b–3e). The administrator should arrive at some basic principles or understandings about reading, such as (a) reading is a complex act with many factors that must be considered; (b) reading depends upon the interpretation of the meaning of printed symbols—it is not just "decoding"; (c) there is no one correct way to teach reading—the teacher is the focal point; (d) learning to read is a continuing process; (e) reading and other language arts are closely interrelated; and (f) reading is an integral part of all content area instruction.
2. *Stimulating improvement opportunities.*   This can be accomplished through the four procedures suggested in Example 1.1 (5a–5d). Reading topics of interest to many teachers—such as methods of grouping students, classroom analysis of reading needs, methods of improving comprehension and recall, methods of teaching word recognition skills, teaching study and research skills, methods of individualizing instruction in the various content areas, and planning a balanced reading program—certainly provide critical issues for consideration at faculty meetings, workshops, and conferences.
3. *Enhancing teaching/learning environment.*   Three major contributions that can be made by the administrator in this area involve items 6–8 in Example 1.1.
4. *Selecting effective materials.*   Publishers and their representatives are in the business of making money; they produce material that they believe will sell well. Valid standards and procedures for selection of superior materials are needed to avoid ill-considered purchases. One of the residual results of the influx of federal money through various programs is storerooms filled with materials and devices that never should have been bought. The best way to avoid such problems is to pre-evaluate materials. Decisions to purchase should rarely be made by a single individual. Tentative decisions should be reached by a group that includes representatives who know (a) what the local resources are, (b) what alternatives are available, and (c) what opinions and preferences the potential users have. Final decisions should come only after tryouts on a limited scale.

   Aids are available for material evaluation and selection. For example, EPIE Reports Numbers 62, 63, and 64 contain guides to instructional materials in the field of reading and contain analyses of commercial reading materials. These reports are available through EPIE Institute, 463 West Street, New York, N.Y. 10014.

5. *Creating appropriate organizational plans.* In organizing for reading instruction, the administrator should be aware of important guidelines: (a) there are vast differences among the instructional needs of students of similar age/grade placement; (b) organizational patterns should be flexible and altered as better ways are discovered; (c) more emphasis should be placed on methods of providing for individual differences by teachers than on methods of grouping; and (d) organization is a technique or system—not a "method of instruction"; therefore organization can only facilitate, or hinder, effective instruction.

6. *Helping collect and interpret test data.* Appropriate reading progress forms need to be maintained by the school in the student's cumulative folder. The administrator realizes that reading survey tests should show in a general way how well students are performing (they indicate the range of reading achievement in the class), while diagnostic reading tests locate specific strengths and weaknesses and possibly suggest causes. The administrator should be sensitive to the fact that the best tests are those for which the sample population used to standardize the test is like the class to be tested; he or she should also be aware that a test score on a standardized reading test frequently reflects the student's frustration level (material is too advanced), rather than instructional level (teaching may be effective) or independent reading level (student can read on his or her own). The administrator values informal reading inventories, informal skills checks, and interest inventories. (See Chapter 8 for a detailed description of such assessment tools.)

7. *Providing corrective/remedial services.* The administrator (a) is sensitive to basic principles of corrective reading instruction; (b) helps identify students reading below capacity level; (c) focuses on possible instructional weaknesses throughout the curriculum, such as failure to adjust content material to the students' reading levels and ineffective motivation for developing reading interests; (d) provides appropriate materials; and (e) wisely utilizes the reading specialist and the reading consultant for this specialized service.

8. *Communicating about the reading program.* The administrator should be aware of frequently posed questions and be prepared to answer them reasonably. How is reading taught in the school? Is my youngster reading at grade level? What can I do to help my child like reading? What about those machines? What can we parents do to help our poor reader? Does my child have dyslexia? Should I hire a tutor for my disabled reader? What special programs do you have for poor readers? How fast should my teenager be able to read?

9. *Hiring capable personnel.* All teachers are expected to understand about reading difficulties that may occur in their content area assignments and to adjust assignments to fit the students' reading capabilities. The administrator should give special consideration to candidates with courses in reading methods.

Teachers who are hired specifically as reading personnel are expected to meet the criteria established by the Professional Standards and Ethics Committee of the International Reading Association.[5]

Teachers should exhibit personnel characteristics that enhance effectiveness with students; empathy, patience, and positive attitudes are important.

Robert Wilhite[6] questioned principals in DuPage County, Illinois, about their views of the principal's ideal leadership role. All of the respondents felt evaluation of the reading staff was part of their role. Ninety-six percent felt that ensuring funding and hiring specialized reading personnel were their responsibility. Eighty-seven percent judged both evaluation of the reading program and establishment of guidelines for hiring specialized reading personnel to be part of their job. Participation in planning in-service programs and planning and implementation of the reading program were seen as the principal's responsibility by eighty-three and seventy-eight percent of the respondents, respectively. Seventy-four percent felt that promotion of staff involvement in reading for the content areas and provision of guidelines for staff communication with the community were their responsibility. Very few felt that participation in the daily operation of the reading program (26%) and selection of equipment and instructional materials for reading (35%) were the principal's responsibility. This study shows that, although principals do view reading-related activities as a part of their responsibility, they may not want to be directly involved on a day-to-day basis. It would be interesting to discover if the instructional programs in which the principals felt the need to participate more had superior results when compared to the other programs.

Stephen Ward and Eugene Bradford[7] found that achievement of junior high students is positively influenced when they are taught under the supervision of an administrator (often an assistant principal) who is eligible for certification in reading or who has earned additional college credits in reading. If the teachers of these students perceive the supervisor to have reading expertise, the effect on students' reading achievement is also positive.

Librarian or Media Center Specialist

The librarian or media center specialist provides assistance to the special reading teacher and the content area teacher alike by locating books and other printed materials on different subjects and reading levels, making available audiovisual aids that can be used for motivation and background building, and providing instruction in location skills related to the library. The librarian may set up special displays of printed materials on specific subjects at different reading levels on request of the teachers and may provide students with direct assistance in finding and using appropriate materials. Recreational reading may be fostered by the librarian's book talks or attractive book displays on high-interest topics.

Teamwork

The content area teacher is a part of a team of personnel who are all concerned with the development of reading skills of secondary school students. The content area teacher is concerned with the level of reading proficiency largely because it can enhance or adversely affect the learning of content. Content area teachers may ask for the reading consultant's assistance when determining which approaches will best meet the special reading needs of students in their content classes. They may send students who are reading far below the level of the instructional materials assigned for the grade to the special reading teacher for diagnosis and remedial instruction; they should work closely with the special reading teacher in planning reading assignments for students who are currently enrolled in special reading classes for remedial assistance; they should consult with the special reading teacher about instructional materials that will meet the reading needs of their students; and they may ask the special reading teacher to demonstrate lessons in some aspects of reading. Content area teachers should expect to work hand-in-hand with the librarian and/or media center specialist when assembling materials for teaching units and when teaching library skills. Content magazines, reference materials, and recreational reading materials should be a part of the library's yearly budget allocation, and content teachers should be the ones who recommend appropriate materials.

The principal sets the tone of the school's reading program. The content area teacher should be able to approach the principal for funding for instructional materials that are needed to meet the diverse reading needs of the students in content classes and for help with organizational arrangements, such as special grouping practices that he or she may wish to use to enhance the content area reading program.

When the principal or administrator, reading consultant, special reading teacher, and librarian or media specialist work with one another and with the content area teachers to produce a good reading program for a school, success for the program is likely. Each staff member needs to understand his or her own job and the jobs of colleagues. This understanding will help enhance cooperation.

READING ACHIEVEMENT LEVELS AND MINIMUM READING COMPETENCY

In recent years concern has been voiced repeatedly about the reading achievement levels of secondary students. As this issue has gained attention, an adjunct concern has arisen with respect to how well prepared secondary teachers are to tackle reading problems that their students have. These issues are considered below.

Reading Achievement Levels

The wide range in reading ability among junior and senior high school students presents secondary school teachers with one of their most vexing problems. For example, in a group classified as seventh graders, there may be boys and girls whose reading skill equals that of many tenth or eleventh graders. Some twelfth graders may have a fifth- or sixth-grade reading ability, while others may read at the level of college seniors. Teaching reading in the secondary schools includes both strengthening the skills of students who are reading well for their grade placement *and* teaching skills to students who are reading at a level significantly below their grade placement.

The reading ability of students in classes above the sixth grade commonly has a range of at least eight school years. Complicating this problem is the large extent of retardation in reading among secondary school students. In 1973 the U.S. Department of Health, Education, and Welfare supplied data that indicated that approximately 1 million teenagers could not read most of the material in newspapers, job application forms, and directions for performing various tasks.[8] Nearly 20 percent of all junior and senior high school students may be in need of small group or individual remedial work to correct specific reading disabilities.[9] Teachers in secondary schools should know that grade placement may mean nothing in terms of reading ability.

The National Assessment of Educational Progress (NAEP) is a study to determine competence in a number of learning areas. The subpopulations that formed the basis for the first reports were students of ages nine, thirteen, and seventeen, and adults between the ages of twenty-six and thirty-five. Findings included the following information:

1. Relatively few young Americans could read and interpret graphs, maps, or tables.
2. Less than one-half of the nation's seventeen-year-olds and young adults could accurately read all parts of a ballot.[10]

Recently, the Commission on Reading of the National Academy of Education reported that in the year 2000 an individual will need a higher level of literacy than that individual would have needed to get by in 1950.[11]

On the other hand, there are some counterpoints to the issue of reading achievement of secondary school students. Roger Farr's historical analysis of reading achievement over several decades suggests that in 1976 secondary students were reading about the same as or better than students were reading in 1944–1945.[12] Reading scores from the National Assessment of Educational Progress have improved somewhat in the past several years. The latest NAEP results reveal that nine-, thirteen-, and seventeen-year-old students' reading skills improved from 1971 to 1984. As a matter of fact, between 1980 and 1984 reading skills of seventeen-year-old students improved for the first time since the assessments began. The 1984 results indicate that almost all thirteen- and seventeen-year-old students have rudimentary reading skills (those necessary to perform simple, discrete reading tasks), and almost 99 percent of the seventeen-year-olds and about 94 percent of the thirteen-year-olds have basic reading skills (those necessary to comprehend specific or sequentially related information). Unfortunately, however, only about 39 percent of the seventeen-year-olds and about 10 percent of the thirteen-year-olds have skills described as adept (those necessary for finding, comprehending, summarizing, and explaining fairly complicated information), and only about 5 percent of the seventeen-year-olds and 1 percent of the thirteen-year-olds have skills described as advanced (those necessary for synthesizing and learning from specialized reading materials).[13]

John Bormuth[14] pointed out additional trends in literacy in this country. Since 1947 the percentage of young people enrolled in colleges has risen and the percentage of workers employed in white-collar jobs has also risen. Thus, the populations being tested now often contain greater numbers of students in the lower range of academic achievement. Any apparent decline in scores (such as the SAT decline during the 1970s) must be viewed with this fact in mind. Any stabilization of scores (such as that of the SAT scores in 1980 and 1981) or increase in scores (such as that indicated by the current NAEP trend) may be viewed as even more meaningful.

However, whether students as a group are reading better now than they did in the past is not the prime issue for the secondary school classroom teacher. The important facts remain that there is, indeed, a very wide *range* of achievement levels in many classrooms and that many secondary students are not reading as proficiently as they should be in order to understand and learn from content materials.

Finally, while the data reported thus far in this chapter refer to overall national samples, it is true that certain groups of students in various parts of the country fall well below the norms on standardized reading tests. For example, Bernice Cooper's 1974 studies of reading achievement in Georgia indicate an apparent lag in achievement in reading skills from elementary school years to secondary school years.[15] In Cooper's study, which involved thirty thousand students in the fourth through the twelfth grades, black children showed a mean comprehension deficiency of 1.2 grade levels in the fourth grade and a deficit of 5.3 grade levels by the twelfth grade; white children lagged 0.2 grade levels in the seventh grade and 2.2 in the twelfth. Cooper cited the need for sustained, sequential reading instruction throughout the secondary school years. The latest NAEP results indicate that black and Hispanic thirteen- and seventeen-year-old students showed greater improvements in reading achievement than did white students in the same age groups, although they still fell behind whites in the same age categories.[16]

In spite of acknowledged inadequacies of assessment tests, a fair-minded interpretation of the data surely should give teachers reason to be concerned. About 20 percent of the students in a typical middle-class suburban high school are likely to read below their grade level; in a typical inner-city high school, at least 50 percent of the students may read below grade level.

Minimum Competency Programs

A development stemming from students' failure to achieve minimum reading competencies is the requirement by some state boards of education that students acquire certain abilities before they can be awarded a diploma certifying that they have graduated from high school. Several states now have published minimum requirements for graduation.

In 1983 the Minimum Competency Programs and Reading Committee of the International Reading Association (IRA) sent a questionnaire designed to determine the extent of minimum competency testing and programs in reading in the United States to the chief officer of each State Department of Education. Responses were obtained from all fifty states. They show that twenty-nine of the states required minimum competency testing in reading, and two other states were planning implementation of such programs that year. Nineteen states indicated no plans to implement minimum competency testing in reading. Fifteen of the states required minimum competency for graduation. Twenty-two of the states conducting minimum competency testing required remedial programs for students who fail, but only fifteen of them had funding provided for the programs.[17] (For further discussion of these ideas see Chapter 8.)

Teacher Education Considerations

A move to require reading courses for certification in secondary education has occurred only recently, and content area teachers have not yet enthusiastically incorporated the procedures that are taught in such courses.[18]

Richard Farrell and Joseph Cirrincione sent a questionnaire to every state director of teacher certification in the United States, designed to determine if instruction in reading methods was a requirement for teacher certification in grades seven through twelve and, if so, for which academic content areas this requirement was in effect. Thirty-one states reported that instruction in reading methods was required for all academic content teachers; one state required instruction for English and social studies teachers; five states reported that the requirement applied to only English/language arts teachers; and fourteen states reported no required reading methods instruction for content area teachers.[19] According to this study, states that required reading instruction for *all* secondary teachers are as follows:

Alabama	Louisiana	New Mexico	Vermont
Arizona	Michigan	North Carolina	Virginia
California	Mississippi	Ohio	West Virginia
Colorado	Missouri	Oregon	Wisconsin
Florida	Montana	Pennsylvania	Wyoming
Hawaii	Nevada	South Dakota	
Idaho	New Hampshire	Tennessee	
Indiana	New Jersey	Utah	

The District of Columbia fell into the same category.

Ezra Stieglitz[20] found that content area teachers who complete a course in content area reading "have more positive attitudes toward issues in content reading and use the instructional practices more than do teachers who have not taken such a course" (p. 696), and content teachers, in general, considered content reading methods courses to be worthwhile. Mark Christiansen[21] also found that a large majority of prospective secondary teachers felt that a course in reading instruction should be required of all prospective secondary teachers.

On a final note, a study revealed the following possibly typical facts about the secondary reading program of one state:

1. On the secondary level, only 3 percent of the schools indicated that reading skills are taught as part of the prescribed curriculum.
2. In 36 percent of the schools, little emphasis is placed on reading skill instruction in content subjects.
3. Another 32 percent of the schools responded that reading skills are taught "as the need arises."
4. About one-third of the secondary schools do not provide content teachers with any formal help in the teaching of reading.[22]

SUMMARY

Knowledge and understanding of the reading process enables teachers to develop effective reading instruction. Reading is a complex process with many facets.

Of the four phases of the reading program, the content area phase is the primary focus of this text. The developmental phase and the corrective or remedial phase are generally the responsibility of the special reading teacher. Responsibility for the recreational phase should be assumed by all personnel who are involved with students' reading development.

There are a number of misconceptions about the teaching of reading at the secondary school level. These faulty assumptions include the notions that (a) teaching reading is a concern only in the elementary school; (b) teaching reading in the content areas is separate and distinct from teaching subject matter; (c) reading needs can be met through remedial work alone; (d) a reading specialist or English teacher should be totally responsible for the teaching of reading; and (e) the teaching of reading and the teaching of literature are one and the same.

Among the personnel responsible for the development of reading ability at the secondary school level are the school administrator, the special reading teacher, the reading consultant, the librarian or media center specialist, and the content area teacher. This book focuses primarily on the content area teacher. It takes the point of view that it is essential for all content teachers to have an understanding of reading, since such understanding helps to facilitate the teaching of their particular subjects.

Factors that influence secondary reading programs include the wide range in reading ability among junior and senior high school students; dissatisfaction with school reading achievement and the resulting trend toward minimum competency testing that is presently in vogue; and many secondary teachers' lack of preparation in the study of reading.

SELF-TEST

1. What is a good definition of reading? (a) Reconstructing, interpreting, and evaluating what the author of written content means by using knowledge gained from life experience (b) Pronouncing a series of words correctly (c) Looking at all of the words on a page in rapid succession (d) None of the above
2. Which of the following statements is correct? (a) Readers bring meaning to print. (b) Readers take meaning from print. (c) Both of the above (d) Neither of the above
3. Which personnel are primarily responsible for finding subject matter materials appropriate to varying levels of reading ability? (a) Administrators (b) Reading consultants (c) Special reading teachers (d) Content area teachers
4. What type of reading program reflects the fact that learning to read is a continuing process? (a) Developmental (b) Corrective/remedial (c) Content area (d) Recreational
5. Which is a true statement? (a) Reading instruction is the concern of only the elementary school. (b) Teaching reading is an integral part of teaching any subject. (c) Only a remedial reading program is needed in secondary schools. (d) Reading and literature instruction should be considered synonymous.
6. To whom does responsibility for encouragement of recreational reading belong? (a) English teacher (b) Special reading teacher (c) Content area teacher (d) All of these
7. What percentage of 17-year-olds have reading skills described as advanced by the NAEP? (a) 99 percent (b) 50 percent (c) 5 percent (d) 1 percent
8. What range of reading ability commonly appears in classes above the sixth grade? (a) Two years (b) Four years (c) Six years (d) Eight years

THOUGHT QUESTIONS

1. Do you agree with the list of seven requirements for content area teachers presented on page 9? Be specific. Why or why not?
2. Which "faulty assumptions" seem most evident in your school situation?
3. Do you believe that it is possible to increase learning in the content areas by providing appropriate help to students in their study of the printed materials? Give as many examples as possible.
4. In your content area, how might recreational reading be promoted most effectively?
5. Do you believe that at least one reading course should be required as a part of certification of *every* secondary school teacher? Why or why not?
6. In your opinion, what factors account for many secondary school graduates not reading well enough to cope with some basic reading requirements? Give reasons for your answer.
7. In your opinion, what factors account for the wide range of reading ability of secondary school students? Defend your answer.
8. How does the principal of a secondary school influence the reading program?

ENRICHMENT ACTIVITIES

*1. What do you think are the most important things about reading that a content area teacher should know? Interview a content area teacher on the same question. Compare your findings with your own views.

2. Keep a log of your reading activities for a week. What do your findings suggest about reading to meet the daily needs of young adults?

*3. Interview three students, one of each of the following types: (a) accelerated reader, (b) average reader, and (c) disabled reader. Try to get each student's perspective as to the effect of his or her reading ability in terms of school achievement, self-image, and life goals. Share your findings with the class.

4. Visit a secondary classroom. Try to identify the range of reading abilities. Compare your impressions with those of the teacher.

*5. List the personnel in your school who are concerned with reading instruction. Briefly describe the responsibilities of each.

*6. Go over the administrator's checklist with a secondary school principal. Share his or her reactions to it with the group.

7. Interview a reading consultant and a special reading teacher. What are their functions and roles? Share your findings with the class.

*Starred activities are designed for in-service teachers, student teachers, and practicum students.

NOTES

1. William D. Page and Gay Su Pinnell, *Teaching Reading Comprehension* (Urbana, Ill.: National Council of Teachers of English, 1979), p. 39.

2. William D. Page, "Reading Comprehension: The Purpose of Reading Instruction or a Red Herring," Vol. 19, *Reading World* (March 1980), 223–231.

3. Ann Brown and Sandra Smiley, *The Development of Strategies for Studying Prose Passages* (Champaign, Ill.: University of Illinois, Center for the Study of Reading, October 1977), p. 12.

4. Joseph Sanacore, "How the Principal Can Promote Free Reading in the Content Areas," *Journal of Reading*, 27 (December 1983), 229–233.

5. Professional Standards and Ethics Committee, *Guidelines for the Professional Preparation of Reading Teachers* (Newark, Del.: International Reading Association, May 1978).

6. Robert K. Wilhite, "Principals' Views of Their Role in the High School Reading Program," *Journal of Reading*, 27 (January 1984), 356–358.

7. Stephen D. Ward and Eugene J. Bradford, "Supervisors' Expertise in Reading Affects Achievement in Junior High," *Journal of Reading*, 26 (January 1983), 362.

8. *Literacy Among Youth 12–17 Years* (Washington, D.C.: U.S. Government Printing Office, 1973).

9. For a historical perspective on selected comments about the reading ability of school students during the period from 1906 through 1951, see Maurice Wolfthal, "Reading Scores Revisited," *Phi Delta Kappan*, 62 (May 1981), 662–663.

10. J. Stanley Ahmann, "A Report on National Assessment in Seven Learning Areas," *Today's Education*, 64 (January–February 1975), 63–64.

11. Richard C. Anderson et al., *Becoming a Nation of Readers: The Report of the Commission on Reading*. Washington, D.C: The National Institute of Education, The National Academy of Education, 1985.

12. Roger Farr et al., *Then and Now: Reading Achievement in Indiana (1944–45 and 1976)* (Bloomington, Ind.: Indiana University, 1978).

13. *Reading Today*, 3 (December 1985/January 1986), 1, 18–19. (The full NAEP report can be found in *The Reading Report Card: Progress Toward Excellence in Our Schools*, National Assessment of Educational Progress, 1985.)

14. John R. Bormuth, "Trends, Level, and Value of Literacy in the U.S.," *Slate Newsletter*, 4 (August 1979), 2.

15. Bernice Cooper, "An Analysis of the Reading Achievement of White and Negro Pupils in Certain Public Schools of Georgia," *School Review*, 72 (Winter 1974), 462–471.

16. *Reading Today*, 3 (December 1985/January 1986), 1, 18–19.

17. Linda B. Gambrell, "Minimum Competency Testing Programs in Reading: A Survey of the United States," *Journal of Reading*, 28 (May 1985), 735–738.

18. Ned Ratekin et al., "Why Teachers Resist Content Reading Instruction," *Journal of Reading*, 28 (February 1985), 432–437.

19. Richard T. Farrell and Joseph M. Cirrincione, "State Certification Requirements in Reading for Content Area Teachers," *Journal of Reading*, 28 (November 1984), 152–158.

20. Ezra L. Stieglitz, "Effects of a Content Area Reading Course on Teacher Attitudes and Practices: A Four Year Study," *Journal of Reading*, 25 (May 1983), 690–696.

21. Mark A. Christiansen, "How Prospective Secondary Teachers Feel About Taking a Required Course in Teaching Reading: A Survey Report," *Journal of Reading*, 29 (February 1986), 428–429.

22. Edward B. Fry and Lillian R. Putnam, "Should All Teachers Take More Reading Courses?" *Journal of Reading*, 19 (May 1976), 614–616.

SELECTED REFERENCES

Allington, Richard, and Michael Strange. *Learning from Texts: An Introduction for Content Area Teachers*. Boston: D. C. Heath, 1980. Chapter 1.

Anderson, Richard C., et al. *Becoming a Nation of Readers: The Report of the Commission on Reading*. Washington, D.C.: The National Institute of Education, The National Academy of Education, 1985.

Burmeister, Lou E. *Reading Strategies for Middle and Secondary School Teachers*. 2nd ed. Reading, Mass.: Addison-Wesley, 1978. Chapters 1 and 2.

Cheek, Earl H., Jr., and Martha Collins Cheek. *Reading Instruction Through Content Teaching*. Columbus, Ohio: Charles E. Merrill, 1983. Chapter 1.

Christiansen, Mark A. "How Prospective Secondary Teachers Feel About Taking a Required Course in Reading: A Survey Report." *Journal of Reading*, 29 (February 1986), 428–429.

Criscoe, Betty L., and Thomas C. Gee. *Content Reading: A Diagnostic/Prescriptive Approach*. Englewood Cliffs, N.J.: Prentice-Hall, 1984. Chapter 1.

Cunningham, James W., et al. *Middle and Secondary School Reading*. New York: Longman, 1981. Chapter 1.

Dillner, Martha H., and Joanne P. Olson. *Personalizing Reading Instruction in Middle, Junior, and Senior High Schools: Utilizing a Competency-Based Instructional System.* 2nd ed. New York: Macmillan, 1982. Chapter 1.

Dupuis, Mary M., and others. "Changing Attitudes Towards Content Area Reading: The Content Area Reading Project." *Journal of Educational Research,* 73 (November/December 1979), 66–74.

Farrell, Richard T., and Joseph M. Cirrincione. "State Certification Requirements in Reading for Content Area Teachers." *Journal of Reading,* 28 (November 1984), 152–158.

Forbes, Roy H. "Test Score Advances Among Southeastern Students: A Possible Bonus of Government Intervention." *Phi Delta Kappan,* 62 (January 1981), 332–334, 350.

Gambrell, Linda B. "Minimum Competency Testing Programs in Reading: A Survey of the United States." *Journal of Reading,* 28 (May 1985), 735–738.

Karlin, Robert. *Teaching Reading in High School: Improving Reading in Content Areas.* 4th ed. New York: Harper & Row, 1984. Chapters 1 and 2.

Lamberg, Walter J., and Charles E. Lamb. *Reading Instruction in the Content Areas.* Boston: Houghton Mifflin, 1980. Chapter 2.

Monteith, Mary K. "How Well Does the Average American Read? Some Facts, Figures and Opinions." *Journal of Reading,* 23 (February 1980), 460–463.

O'Rourke, William J. "Research on the Attitude of Secondary Teachers Toward Teaching Reading in Content Classrooms." *Journal of Reading,* 23 (January 1980), 337–339.

Palmer, William S. "Toward a Realistic Rationale for Teaching Reading in Secondary Schools." *Journal of Reading,* 22 (December 1978), 236–239.

Patberg, Judythe P., et al. "The Impact of Content Area Reading Instruction on Secondary Teachers." *Journal of Reading,* 27 (March 1984), 500–507.

Professional Standards and Ethics Committee. *Guidelines for the Professional Preparation of Reading Teachers.* Newark, Del.: International Reading Association, May 1978.

Seifert, Mary. "Research: High Schools Where Scores Haven't Declined." *Journal of Reading,* 22 (November 1978), 164–166.

Shepherd, David L. *Comprehensive High School Reading Methods.* 3rd ed. Columbus, Ohio: Charles E. Merrill, 1982. Chapter 1.

Singer, Harry, and Dan Donlan. *Reading and Learning from Text.* Boston: Little, Brown and Company, 1980. Chapter 1.

Stieglitz, Ezra L. "Effects of a Content Area Reading Course on Teacher Attitudes and Practices: A Four Year Study." *Journal of Reading,* 26 (March 1983), 690–696.

Vacca, Richard T., and Jo Anne L. Vacca. *Content Area Reading.* 2nd ed. Boston: Little, Brown and Company, 1986. Chapter 1.

CHAPTER
T   W   O

VOCABULARY

OVERVIEW

This chapter focuses on words and word meanings. Fluency in word recognition and in understanding words contributes to increased reading comprehension. Research reveals that word knowledge can be developed through association, conceptual development, use of context, structural analysis, and use of reference materials. Concepts and words are interrelated because so many of the words we know are labels for our concepts. Studying word meanings creates a foundation for understanding content area concepts. Vocabulary teaching strategies and a direct vocabulary instruction program are included in this chapter.

PURPOSE-SETTING QUESTIONS

1. What is the content teacher's role in teaching word identification?
2. What is the relationship between concepts and knowledge of word meanings?
3. What are the benefits of a conceptual approach to teaching word meanings?
4. What are the major approaches to acquiring word meanings?
5. What is the relationship between experience and word meanings?

KEY VOCABULARY

As you read this chapter, check your understanding of these terms:

concept	structural analysis	attributes
categorization	association	structured overview
context	analogy	hierarchy

AN INTRODUCTION TO VOCABULARY

Obviously, words are an important aspect of the reading process. Students must be able to identify words and associate meanings with them or reading cannot occur. Meaning is the essence of the reading process. For effective reading, students must be able to recognize many words instantly, and they must be able to decode words that they do not recognize instantly. Students who do not recognize important words in a reading assignment will find it difficult, if not impossible, to acquire new concepts and ideas from the written content. But, they must go beyond mere recognition and associate appropriate meanings with the words they decode in order to comprehend content reading materials. A significant number of the words encountered in content reading materials represent technical words that are associated with a specific subject. This chapter explores both word recognition skills and meaning association skills.

WHAT ARE WORD RECOGNITION SKILLS?

Word recognition skills are also called word analysis skills, decoding skills, and word perception skills. These skills enable students to change printed words into spoken words. Competent readers recognize many words instantly because they have memorized them as a result of seeing them many times in reading materials. Readers also use word recognition skills to pronounce and identify words that they do not recognize instantly. After repeatedly identifying words, readers memorize the words and they become a part of students' sight word vocabularies. Specifically, word recognition skills include memory (sight words), use of context clues, structural analysis, phonic analysis, and use of the dictionary and thesaurus.

Sight words are those words that readers have committed to memory so well that they can identify them without thinking. These words are instantly, automatically recognized. Efficient reading depends on having a large store of words that are recognized automatically. Students particularly need to know as sight words those words they encounter frequently. Can you imagine stopping to analyze the word *and* everytime you encountered it in reading a selection? Having a vast store of sight words saves time for students, and these words create a context that readers can use to identify other words.

Reading teachers should be familiar with such common sight word lists as the *Dolch Basic Sight Word List*. The 220 words in this list represent approximately 60 percent of all running words in primary grade materials.[1] The Ekwall list of basic sight words includes words that range in difficulty from a grade level equivalent of 1.9 to 3.9.[2] Fry's list of "instant words" contains 300 words that are not usually mastered until at least third grade.[3] Johns developed a useful list of basic sight words for older, disabled readers.[4]

Context clues are the word recognition skills most often used by competent readers. Mature readers automatically reread a sentence or two when they encounter a word they fail to recognize immediately. Context clues are clues to the meanings and pronunciations of unknown words that are derived from the surrounding words, sentences, and paragraphs. Readers use the meanings of the surrounding words, sentences, and paragraphs to determine the meanings and pronunciations of unfamiliar words.

Structural analysis is the process of examining word structure for clues to meaning and pronunciation. In applying structural analysis, readers use prefixes, suffixes, root words, word endings, contractions, compound words, and syllabication as word recognition aids.

Phonic analysis is an approach to decoding that relies on sound-symbol relationships. This approach is used to teach beginning readers word recognition and involves learning such elements as consonants, vowels, consonant blends, digraphs, and diphthongs.

Both the dictionary and the thesaurus are reference works that students can use to help themselves determine the meanings and pronunciations of words. Many content textbooks include glossaries that can be used like dictionaries.

WHY TEACH WORD RECOGNITION SKILLS?

One of the critical aspects of understanding content textbooks is knowledge of content vocabulary. Students who have developed strategies for associating meaning with unknown words can read content area materials more effectively. Word recognition skills enable readers to identify words and associate meanings with them. Students will find it necessary to decode words in the following categories:

1. Printed words that are in their listening vocabularies but that they have not seen in print
2. Printed words that they have never heard in speech
3. Printed words that are not familiar to them, although the concepts associated with the words are familiar
4. Printed words that they do not recognize and for which they do not know associated concepts
5. Printed words that they have seen and heard, but for which they do not know the meanings

In discussing a system for classifying vocabulary, Michael Graves[5] points out some important ideas regarding the varying difficulties in learning different types of words. He notes that teaching students to read words that are in their oral vocabularies and teaching them new meanings for words they know are relatively easy tasks. On the other hand, teaching new words that represent concepts that can be demonstrated or concepts that are concrete is somewhat more difficult. Teaching new words that represent new and abstract concepts is most difficult.

Content teachers can use the material in the word recognition sections of this chapter to help students learn and remember words that are important for the understanding of content area reading materials. Although some secondary students have difficulty recognizing general vocabulary words, content teachers are not expected to teach word recognition skills for these words. Secondary students who cannot decode words or who read at a primary reading level will require the services of special reading teachers. Therefore, content teachers should refer these students to special reading teachers for assistance.

In class, content teachers should emphasize context, structural analysis and the use of the dictionary and thesaurus. These word recognition strategies are the ones that secondary teachers report are most relevant and effective with their students.[6]

HOW DO WE TEACH WORD RECOGNITION SKILLS?

Readers of content materials use sight words, context clues, structural analysis, and the dictionary and thesaurus to recognize words. Content teachers should examine content reading materials to identify potentially difficult words prior to giving reading assignments. The appropriate word recognition skill for a given word will depend upon that word. Therefore, teachers will find it most useful to determine the appropriate word recognition approach after identifying difficult words. Example 2.1 shows a page from a content textbook with the difficult-to-recognize words identified. Figure 2.1 shows the appropriate skill for use with each word.

EXAMPLE 2.1 IDENTIFYING DIFFICULT WORDS IN CONTENT ──────

Introduction

As mentioned in Chapter 1, we will use the computer language BASIC in this book. It is one of the most commonly used programming languages today. Different computers have different versions of BASIC; whenever possible, we will use a general form that will work on most computers. Where there are significant differences, we will give the necessary changes for the *Apple, IBM,* and *TRS-80* microcomputers. For other machines, differences can be explored in the Lab Activities that appear throughout the book.

In the first two sections of this chapter, you will learn how to use the computer as a calculator. Certain words in the BASIC language can be used to give the computer instructions, or *commands,* that it will perform as soon as you press the < RETURN > or < ENTER > key after typing the command. When a computer is used in this fashion, it is said to be in *immediate mode.* Later in the chapter, you will see how to store instructions in the computer's memory as a *program,* a technique that makes the computer a much more useful and powerful tool than a simple calculator. In the final section of this chapter, a short introduction to *graphics* is presented for the *Apple, IBM,* and *TRS-80* microcomputers.

EXAMPLE 2.1 (continued)

2-1 The PRINT Command

One of the most useful words in the BASIC language is PRINT. The PRINT command allows the computer to communicate with you. It can be used to display on the screen any combination of letters, numbers, and symbols (such a combination is called a *string*), or to evaluate <u>numerical</u> expressions and show the results on the screen. When strings are <u>used with</u> the PRINT command, they must be enclosed in quotation marks, as in the following example:

Example 1

a. PRINT "HELLO THERE"   ⟵——— command
    HELLO THERE   ⟵——— output

b. PRINT "NOW WE CAN COMMUNICATE"   ⟵——— command
    NOW WE CAN COMMUNICATE   ⟵——— output

The result, or *output*, of a PRINT command appears on the screen beneath the command on the next line. PRINT causes the computer to display on the screen exactly what is typed inside the quotation marks, including spaces, as you can see in Example 2 on the next page. (The small shaded rectangles in that example are used to represent spaces in this book.)

Source: David L. Myers, Valarie Elswick, Patrick Hopfensperger, and Joseph Pavlovich: *Computer Programming in BASIC* (Boston: Houghton Mifflin Company, 1986), p. 17.

Generally speaking, words that students must continually recognize in print are taught with sight word strategies. Words that can be recognized through meaning clues are taught via context, words that can be analyzed through the chunks forming them are taught through structural analysis, and words that cannot be solved with the aforementioned clues must be located in reference materials such as a glossary, dictionary, or thesaurus. How to teach each of these strategies to content area students is discussed in the sections that follow.

Sight Words

At the middle, junior, and senior high school levels, the focus of sight vocabulary instruction should be on the technical words that appear in content reading material. Content teachers will find it useful to create core lists of sight words for

Text: *Computer Programming in BASIC*					
Word	Page	Sight Word	Context	Structural Analysis	Glossary, Dictionary
commands	17	X	X		
immediate mode	17		X		X
graphics	17	X			
output	17			X	
versions	17		X		
numerical	17			X	

Figure 2.1 Skills for Difficult-to-Recognize Words

their subject areas. For example, suppose a unit or chapter on the study of light (in a science class) includes these words:

concave	retina
convex	sensory
gland	translucent
membrane	opaque
optical	diffuse
refract	transparent

The teacher could display the words, each in the context of a sentence, on the chalkboard, on a chart, or using an overhead projector. The words could then be pronounced, by either students or the teacher, and discussed, considering the context. Some attention could be given to certain parts of a word, for example, the prefixes *con, trans,* and *re.* Comparison and contrast may be used; that is, the pronunciation or meaning of a new word can be compared to a similar known word or contrasted with a dissimilar word (comparison of *translucent* and *transparent,* for example). Where appropriate, real objects or pictures of objects can be used to provide the context for presenting a word; for example, *opaque* and *transparent* may be demonstrated through use of appropriate materials. Later, after the students have read the related material, the teacher can present the words again for further clarification and explanation. During the course of study of the material, the teacher may feel that it is important to isolate certain words for additional practice. There are several ways in which this may be done. A few are listed below.

Activities

1. Use flash cards. Print words or phrases on individual cards and have students take turns checking one another's recognition of the words. The word or phrase cards can be flashed quickly, with known ones in one stack and unknown ones in another. Further study of unknown words can be provided for those who need it.

2. Use mechanical devices. One common mechanical device is a tachistoscope, which reveals printed material on a screen for brief periods of time. If a tachistoscope is not available, teachers or students can make their own for use with vocabulary terms. An illustration of this device is shown in Figure 2.2. A strip of cardboard with the words on it is pulled through an opening cut in the holder. As a word is exposed, the student pronounces it.

   Another device designed to teach vocabulary is the *Language Master Machine* (N.Y.: Bell and Howell). It can be particularly helpful if the teacher prepares the cards to be used by the students.

3. Use games. Games such as word bingo can be used for practice with sight words. In word bingo, the teacher or a leader calls out a word, and the students who recognize that word on their cards may cover it. When a student covers all the words on his or her card, he or she says, "cover," and the teacher

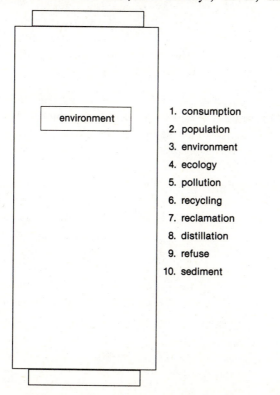

environment

1. consumption
2. population
3. environment
4. ecology
5. pollution
6. recycling
7. reclamation
8. distillation
9. refuse
10. sediment

Figure 2.2   Teacher-made Tachistoscope

congruent	chord	tangent
diameter	free	equidistant
radius	segment	intersect

Figure 2.3   Bingo Card

or leader checks the card to see if all the covered words were called. A sample card is provided in Figure 2.3.

Other card games in which students accumulate "books" of matching cards can be developed into word recognition games. (An original deck is formed by printing the sight words on blank cards.) The rules of a familiar game such as "Go Fish" can be used, except that to claim a book the student must pronounce the word on the matching cards.

4. Encourage reading a wide variety of materials. Providing students with a wide variety of easy reading material on the topic under consideration and encouraging voluntary reading of such books, magazines, and newspapers is one of the most effective ways of helping students develop a store of sight words. Since a number of repetitions of a word are generally necessary before that word actually becomes a sight word, the most useful practice with potential sight words presents the words in context. It is only in context that words can be pronounced or understood with certainty (especially such words as *desert*).

5. Employ other activities. Some activities that can be used to provide reinforcement include matching words to definitions or pictures, completing sentences with new sight words, having vocabulary check tests, and doing creative work to portray new words. These varied activities are illustrated in Example 2.2.

EXAMPLE 2.2   SAMPLE SIGHT WORD ACTIVITY

1. Match each term in Column 1 with the appropriate meaning in Column 2.

Column 1	Column 2
1. decimeter	a. 1000 grams
2. kilogram	b. 1/10 meter
3. hectoliter	c. 10 millimeters
4. centimeter	d. 1/10 kiloliter

2. A dekagram is (a) 10 grams (b) 1000 grams (c) 1/20 g.
3. A gram is the weight of a _____ of water.
4. If [ ] represents 100 sq meters or 1 are, then draw a square to represent a hectare.

Context Clues

Context clues are clues to word pronunciation that are derived from meaning. Students use context clues to infer word pronunciation. This is the word recognition skill most frequently used by mature readers.

Students' ability to use context clues may be assessed with a cloze procedure, which is discussed in Chapter 8. In this procedure, the teacher selects and prepares a passage that does not include too many unknown words. A textbook selection that students can read comfortably without teacher assistance is appropriate for teaching this technique. The cloze procedure is used in the following manner:

1. First, students read the entire passage silently.
2. Then, they reread, filling in words for those the teacher has deleted.
3. Next, the teacher discusses with the students their reasons for choosing the replacement words.
4. Finally, students compare their finished products with the original.

In this assessment, synonyms are acceptable as well as the actual words. (However, only the latter are considered correct when checking for reading levels.) A score of 75 percent or better on filling-in the omitted words indicates satisfactory performance on contextual clue usage.

The following activities are useful practice for students learning to use context clues to recognize words.

Activities

1. Point out the values of context clues and some techniques for using them, using sentence and paragraph examples from the students' content materials. The teacher and students can cooperatively circle unknown words and discuss how students might arrive at the meanings and pronunciations of the strange words. The purposes are to help students become aware of clues that are present in text and to help them learn to search for those clues and synthesize the clues to determine the meanings and pronunciations of the words. From such discussion, summary charts can be cooperatively developed to provide ideas for systematic context analysis. An example is suggested below:
   a. Read the entire sentence or paragraph.
   b. Try to think of a word that would make sense in place of the strange word.
   c. Try to pronounce the unknown word. Does the pronunciation match a word you know?
   d. See if there are other words that give you an idea about this strange word.
   e. Use other word analysis skills to help you unlock the word.
2. Prepare and use cloze exercises. One way of introducing the cloze procedure discussed above is to play a tape recording of a text passage in which key words have been omitted. The teacher can provide a copy of the script to the students and have them fill in the blanks as they listen to the tape.

3. Prepare exercises in which the meaning of the sentence indicates the word to be recognized. Give possible meanings in multiple-choice form.
   a. If a contract runs out before an agreement is reached, there will be a work stoppage, or _____. 1. strike, 2. picket, 3. union
   b. A court order that prevents a union from continuing with a strike is an _____. 1. fringe benefit, 2. grievance, 3. injunction
4. Use nonsense words to illustrate how familiar words can be figured out if their printed forms are not familiar. For example: The Red Cross will sponsor beginner, advanced beginner, and *goblegook* swimming classes at the pool.
5. Use tachistoscopic materials. Read a sentence to students, substituting a blank for an unknown word. Ask students to identify a word that would fit in the context of the sentence in the position of the missing word. Tachistoscopically expose the word for 100th of a second. After it is flashed, students should indicate whether their predictions were confirmed or disproved. Programs such as this are available from EDL (Educational Developmental Laboratories, New York, N.Y.).

Structural Analysis

Structural analysis is the procedure of examining meaningful elements within a word. One exception to this statement is syllabication, which is considered to be a part of structural analysis, even though syllables are not always meaningful elements or morphemes.

Most students in the secondary school developmental reading program have adequate mastery of simple prefixes and suffixes, compound words, and the altering of base words before adding suffixes. Such students, usually, are competent in the basic subskills of syllabication and accent. However, some of them can profit from a brief review of structural analysis skills.[7] The teacher can provide practice with these skills using words from the students' content textbooks.

Activities such as the following are useful for reviewing and reinforcing structural analysis skills.

Activities

1. Have students divide words into structural components. Use words from the content area textbook.

Prefix	Root	Suffix
in	sol	uble

2. Provide practice with a worksheet like that in Example 2.3.

EXAMPLE 2.3 COMPOUND WORD WORKSHEET ————————

Directions: For each of the words in Column 1, find a word in Column 2 that when combined with the word in Column 1 forms a compound word. Connect the words you combine.

Column 1	*Column 2*
rip	line
sea	water
sun	length
wave	point
end	stock
air	saw
coast	rise
high	plane
live	lands

3. Have students divide words into syllables by drawing a line between the syllables. Remind students that each syllable must have one vowel sound.

cylinder	oblique
pyramid	radius
solution	lateral
altitude	hexagonal
sector	conical

Compare/Contrast Strategy

Patricia Cunningham developed the "Compare/Contrast Strategy" for decoding words when the context is not sufficiently rich to reveal the pronunciation.[8] Students who are acquainted with some high-frequency, one-syllable words and who know initial consonant sounds, including most blends and digraphs, are prepared to learn the compare-contrast strategy.

With this strategy, the student compares the parts of unknown words with the word parts of a known word. For example, the teacher may display known words such as *black, hold, kind, rain,* and *run* and ask students to decode *slack, gold, bind, main,* and *runt.* In order to do this, the student identifies the places where the words are alike and where they are different.

Polysyllabic words can also be identified using this strategy. Students use known words like *in, at, then, it,* and *is* as a basis for decoding longer words. Through comparison and contrast, the preceding words can help students pronounce such words as *scatter, Berlin, realism,* and *ginger.* You may wish to study Cunningham's research as a basis for developing this strategy with students.

Phonics

Phonic analysis is a laborious, distasteful task for some secondary students. The primary use of phonics in the secondary school is to help students pronounce technical words that are new to them. Some authors help readers by writing diacritical markings and/or phonetic spellings in parentheses following words that may be unfamiliar. For example, "Tracheae (TRAY kee eye)"[9] is provided for the readers of a biology book. Students who understand diacritical markings and phonetic spellings can translate the symbols and respellings into words.

Activity
Create an activity like the one presented here. Have students pronounce the words in Column 2. Then have them write the words represented by the phonetic spellings and diacritical markings in the correct blanks in Column 1.

Column 1
1. Appoints members of Supreme Court

   _____

2. Passes city laws and ordinances

   _____

3. Determines zoning and prepares budget

   _____

4. Enforces federal laws

   _____

Column 2
a. (si-tē kaun-səl)
b. (pre-zə-dənt)
c. (sə-prēm kort)
d. (kaun-tē soo-pər-vi-zər)

Using the Dictionary, Glossary, and Thesaurus

In order to make efficient use of dictionaries, glossaries, and thesauri, students must know the following:

1. Alphabetical order beyond the first letter of a word
2. How to use guide words
3. How to locate root words, variants, and derivatives
4. How to interpret accent marks
5. How to use the pronunciation key and interpret phonetic spellings

Content teachers may find it useful to review these skills with students. Activities such as the following will be helpful.

Activities
1. Teach students to use the pronunciation key and dictionary abbreviations. Have them use these skills in functional situations, looking up the pronunciations or spellings of words they really need to use in reading and writing situations.

2. Have students complete exercises like the following:
   a. Look up the word *hemisphere*. What are the two guide words on this page?
   b. On what page are the guide words *skeletally* and *skin* found?
   c. Locate the phonetic spelling of the word *sedimentary*.

WHY TEACH CONCEPTS AND WORD MEANINGS?

The number of word meanings a reader knows is an excellent indication of that individual's ability to understand content. Edgar Dale states that to know a content subject one must "learn its key concepts; that is, its language."[10] Researchers report that vocabulary training improves reading comprehension.[11] When vocabulary is limited, understanding is limited. Individuals who have large vocabularies are well informed and use with precision a wide variety of words. Words are labels for thoughts, ideas, concepts, and for the relationships among them; thus, words permit the manipulation of ideas. There is a high correlation between vocabulary, concepts, and thinking. A. V. Mazo and J. K. Sherk say that vocabulary is an important means by which we learn. "That is to say, vocabulary is central to concept formation, acculturation, articulation, and apparently, all learning."[12]

Vocabulary and concepts are very important aspects of secondary reading instruction, because each content area includes unique concepts, which have particular labels. Mathematics includes concepts such as *fractions, integers, decimals,* and *percentages*. Concepts in the area of science are *virus, bacteria, protozoa,* and *algae*. Students must understand content concepts, so teachers must provide instruction in these concepts. One cannot assume that students know basic concepts or that they will look in a dictionary for definitions of words they do not know.

Planned, direct vocabulary instruction in content classes is essential for students because knowledge of word meanings is basic to understanding content materials. Unfortunately, systematic vocabulary instruction is seldom provided beyond the primary grades.[13] The process of teaching word meanings involves developing content area concepts. Content area words usually are labels for concepts that students must know in order to understand content materials.

Concept development and vocabulary are interrelated; many of the words in a person's vocabulary are verbal labels for that individual's concepts. People learn new vocabulary as they grasp the concepts the words represent. A person's grasp of concepts depends on his or her experiences and development.[14] In developing students' knowledge of word meanings, the teacher must build on their backgrounds of experiences. Instruction should create a conceptual base that is related to students' backgrounds of experiences.

Words also function to organize the world of experience, to make it conceptually manageable. The words a person uses are determined in part by his or her environment. For instance, Eskimos have no words for coconut because the coconut does not exist in their environment; hence, they do not have a concept to label with a word. On the other hand, Eskimos have *many* words that tell about the concept *snow*, which is an important aspect of their environment. Among other things, these words describe when the snow fell and its exact condition.

Many words are generic in that they denote a group of referents. The word *measurement* can denote the referents *meter, ounce, gram,* and *inch;* each of these words itself represents a concept. A word also can refer to a series of related experiences. The word *butterfly* represents many different referents: Monarch, Painted Lady, or Kallima. The word *butterfly* might also make one think of the opera *Madame Butterfly.* The linguistic context of a word helps a reader identify the specific instance of the concept to which an author is referring.

A concept is a generalized idea about a class of objects. Concepts are the products of experience; they are the abstracted and cognitively structured mental experiences acquired by individuals in the course of their lives.[15] The process of conceptualizing involves grouping into categories specific things or instances that have common features. The learner compares and contrasts items with which he or she is familiar and assigns specific instances to the appropriate categories. For example, John Kennedy, Lyndon Johnson, Dwight Eisenhower, and Harry Truman can be classified as specific instances of the concept that is labeled "U.S. Presidents."

Concepts provide a mental filing system that enables a person to sort out and organize relationships among specific items and instances. Thus, concepts are a means of identifying things. They reduce the need for us to learn things over and over by letting us organize objects and events according to previously acquired concepts. We may be able to determine the category to which an object belongs without knowing precisely what the object is called. An individual who has a concept for "tree" can categorize a newly perceived species as a "tree," even though he or she does not know whether the tree is an elm or a mimosa.

The best way to learn and remember a word is to learn and understand the concept the word represents. The definition of a word is based on a critical set of attributes (features) that designate the essence of the word's concept. When we use a word to denote a concept, we attend to the significant features of the concept. When classifying the concept of erosion, for example, we attend to the following attributes: a natural process including weathering, dissolution, abrasion, and corrosion of earth or rock material. These features represent a large part of the meaning of the word *erosion.*

Words, like concepts, are not isolated, unrelated entities, but are often aspects of a system. Many concepts and the words that label them can be organized into hierarchical relationships.[16] For example, waterways are navigable bodies of water used for travel or transportation. Lakes, rivers, and canals are types of waterways. The Mississippi River is a specific waterway. Notice that as the concept of waterway is broken down into hierarchical levels, the levels describe aspects of "waterway" that are increasingly specific. Grouping and organizing conceptual information into chunks like this aids understanding and remembering.

A schematic diagram of this hierarchical relationship is presented in Example 2.4. This example illustrates only one aspect of a hierarchy.

EXAMPLE 2.4 A HIERARCHY

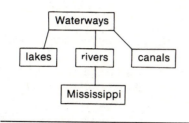

Both concepts and vocabulary are acquired and refined gradually. A young child's understanding of a concept is generally more global, less differentiated than that of an older person, who has more experience. As a person grows older, nuances and subtle distinctions are added to the concepts conveyed by words. The development of these distinctions probably continues throughout an individual's lifetime.[17] A young child's concept of *dog* is usually based on a specific dog that the child has seen. As the concept of dog evolves, the child may think of a dog as an animal that barks, bites, and eats bones. As the child acquires additional experience, this concept may be refined to include different breeds of dogs, personality differences among dogs, and the kinds of work that dogs do.

Because concept development is gradual, and because the focus of content reading is concept acquisition, content teachers can play an important role in helping students acquire and refine concepts. They can help students consciously develop the conceptual skills necessary for successful reading. Content teachers also can guide students in refining the distinctions that are made regarding content area concepts.

WHICH WORD MEANINGS AND CONCEPTS DO WE TEACH?

The words that should be included in vocabulary instruction fall into three categories. The first category, *general vocabulary,* consists of common words that have generally accepted meanings. These words appear in both content reading materials and general reading. Words such as *neutral* and *mobilize* are in this group. The second category of words, *special vocabulary,* comprises words that have both general and specialized meanings. The word *matter* is in this group: in general use, *matter* has meaning in the sentence, "What is the matter?" The word *matter* also has a technical meaning in science content. *Technical vocabulary,* the third category of words, includes words representing a specific concept that is applicable in a content subject. *Photosynthesis* is an example of a technical word used in scientific content.

Content teachers cannot teach all of the unknown words that students might encounter in a chapter or unit. If a selection has twenty-five or thirty unfamiliar words, and a teacher spends only one minute per word, twenty-five to thirty minutes would be taken up with vocabulary development. Because time and energy constraints make this kind of time utilization impossible, teachers should focus on words that are essential to comprehension of the major points in the selection and words that are labels for key concepts. Research indicates that learners most easily learn and retain words when they are "usable." Usable words are those that are frequently used in conversation, on the media, and in reading materials and those that are keys to understanding other words.[18]

Teachers should examine textbook reading assignments carefully to determine whether the author has assumed that students know certain concepts they actually do not know. After carefully determining which concepts are necessary for student comprehension of the selection, the teacher can develop those concepts in class. Teachers should also call students' attention to the way authors of content textbooks use words and language to express concepts. Example 2.5 shows some questions a teacher can ask students to help them see how the author of a business education textbook expresses concepts.

EXAMPLE 2.5 BUSINESS CONCEPTS

How does the author help you understand the nature of the business cycle?

If prosperity is the high point in the business cycle, what do you think the low point in the business cycle is called?

A *cycle* is a repeating period or time. The term we use to describe how the economy moves from good times to bad times and back again is **business cycle.** Sometimes this series of changes is like a roller coaster. For a while, everything seems to be going very well. Jobs are plentiful, and anyone who wants to work can find a job. People feel good about the economy and are willing to spend their money. Because people are buying, business is good. And when business is good, we say we are enjoying prosperity. **Prosperity** is the high point of a business cycle. Sometimes it's called a *boom.* Employment is way up, the demand for goods and services is high, and businesses are turning out goods and services as fast as they can.

Source: Betty J. Brown and John Clow: *General Business: Our Business and Economic World* (Boston: Houghton Mifflin Company, 1982), p. 144.

Example 2.6 is an adaptation of a worksheet created by Patricia Anders and Candace Bos for use by the teacher in analyzing important vocabulary in a chapter on geology.[19] The teacher can create similar worksheets for aid in identifying significant vocabulary in the reading selections he or she assigns prior to teaching the selections. Students can use the worksheets as they study the chapters, identifying the important concepts to which specific words are related.

EXAMPLE 2.6   VOCABULARY WORKSHEET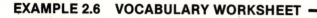

Text: Geology							
Topic: Earth Materials Chapter 6							
	Important Ideas						
Important vocabulary	interfaces between earth materials	abundant elements	rare metal deposits	predominant minerals	atom & molecule	element & compound	
interface							
minerals							
isotopes							
silicates							
carbonates							
sulfates							
halides							
oxides							

Source: William Matthews III, Chalmer Roy, Robert Stevenson, Miles Harris, Dale Hesser, and William Dexter: *Investigating the Earth,* 4th ed. (Boston: Houghton Mifflin Company, 1984), pp. 145–159.

Assessment plays an important role in identifying vocabulary that should be included in an instructional program. The content teacher may choose to construct a vocabulary inventory to assess student knowledge of the key concepts in a chapter. A vocabulary inventory is an informal, teacher-made test; it may consist of matching words with synonyms or may simply provide students with a list of words in order to identify known and unknown vocabulary. Words that are known can be eliminated from further study so the teacher and students can concentrate on unknown words. Or known words can be used to provide the context or synonyms that will help students learn unknown words.

A teacher may also use assessment strategies at the end of a chapter or unit of study to determine whether students have learned the important concepts in the chapter. If assessment indicates that students do not understand key concepts, these concepts need to be retaught. The strategies suggested later in this chapter may be used as either teaching or reteaching activities.

Teachers should use assessment activities primarily when they are unsure of students' vocabulary and concept knowledge. If a teacher observes that students know the meanings of most of the words in a selection, instruction can proceed without formal assessment. On the other hand, if observation indicates that students do not know the meanings of many of the words, vocabulary instruction should proceed without formal assessment. The rest of this section suggests activities that content teachers may use as models for developing their own assessment approaches for vocabulary.

Edgar Dale suggests four methods of testing vocabulary:

1. Identification—the student responds orally or in writing by identifying a word according to its definition or use.
2. Multiple choice—the student selects the correct meaning of the tested word from three or four definitions.
3. Matching—the tested words are presented in one column and the matching definitions are presented out of order in another column.
4. Checking—the student checks the words he knows or doesn't know.[20]

When being tested with the first method, identification, the student responds orally or in writing to a list of words supplied by the teacher. The list should begin with easy words and move to more difficult ones. The student may self-check his or her responses in this testing situation, thereby getting immediate feedback. This technique is particularly useful for alerting students to their own vocabulary strengths and weaknesses. The following example of an identification vocabulary test uses words that are drawn from a science book.

_____ observe
_____ describe
_____ hypothesis
_____ molecules
_____ atoms
_____ substance
_____ interact

_____ chemical change
_____ element
_____ compound

The second method of testing vocabulary, multiple choice, presents words in context. After students complete the exercise, the teacher should discuss their responses with them. Following is an example of a multiple-choice exercise:

Susan broke a window. "You're a big help," her mother said. Susan's mother was being _____. (appreciative, sarcastic, ironic)

The third method of evaluating vocabulary development is to use matching exercises. The following set of words comes from a social studies textbook.

1. Census
2. Human geography
3. Suburb
4. Urban
5. Population distribution

a. A town near a large city
b. The study of where people live and carry on their activities
c. A count of people
d. Areas where people live close together in villages, towns, and cities
e. Where people live on the surface of the earth

The fourth method of vocabulary evaluation is self-checking by the student; it is useful for alerting both students and teachers to vocabulary strengths and weaknesses. Dale suggests the following code for self-checking:

+ means "I know it well, I use it."
√ means "I know it somewhat."
− means "I've seen it or heard it."
○ means "I've never heard of it."[21]

The following list of words for self-checking was taken from a mathematics book.

_____ commutative
_____ metric
_____ symmetrical
_____ pentagon
_____ hexagon

WHEN DO WE TEACH WORD MEANINGS?

Many content teachers recognize the crucial importance of developing word meanings. Unfortunately, balancing vocabulary instruction with content instruction creates the problem of finding time for both. Research shows that devoting a short amount of time to vocabulary instruction and study skills results in improved knowledge of content.[22]

Word meanings can be worked on at various times during content instruction. If a chapter includes words and concepts that have little, if any, meaning for students, these words and concepts should be introduced as a part of the readiness instruction for the chapter or unit of study. Teachers may choose to devote fifteen minutes of each class period to vocabulary instruction, or they may devote longer periods of time less frequently.

Follow-up vocabulary instruction is an option that is useful when the majority of concepts in a selection are familiar or when the content teacher is helping students develop independence in acquiring word meanings. Using vocabulary activities or assessment strategies after students have read a selection, the teacher can extend and refine students' understanding of certain words. These activities include crossword puzzles, identification of concept attributes, and word sorts. (Each of these activities is explained later in this chapter.) These activities also help the teacher make certain that students have understood the words used in a selection.

HOW DO WE TEACH WORD MEANINGS?

A review of research and expert opinion concerning words and the way their meanings are acquired reveals principles to guide vocabulary instruction. Teachers can use these principles as they develop instruction to expand students' understanding of words. In addition, instruction based on these precepts helps students develop independence in acquiring word meanings. The following is a summary of instructional principles for vocabulary.

1. Word meanings are best learned through conceptual development. This approach stresses in-depth understanding as opposed to surface understanding. For example, developing a concept of *river* would include linking it to *waterway, transportation, tributaries,* and *recreation*. Of course, the word *river* can be used to describe something that flows like a river, as in "a river of lava flowed down the mountain."[23] Existing concepts can be used as a basis for acquiring new concepts. For example, a student who knows what a horse is can relate the new concept of *unicorn* to *horse* in order to understand the new concept.

2. Word meanings should be learned in context. The contextual setting gives students clues to word meanings. The teacher should provide examples in which the new word is used correctly, and students should have opportunities to apply the word's meaning.[24]

3. Vocabulary instruction should be based on learner-generated word meanings. Learner involvement increases understanding and memory; thus, when students use their experience and background knowledge to define words, they learn better. The words they are learning serve as labels for concepts. There-

fore, students who have many concepts and experiences to associate with words will have larger vocabularies.[25]

4. Vocabulary instruction should focus on usable words. Teachers should ask themselves whether the words they are teaching will be important five years hence. They should also consider whether knowing the word or words taught will help students figure out other related words.[26]

5. Students should learn transferable skills because these skills will make them more independent. Due to the large number of words students must know in order to read content area materials with understanding, students need the independence that will permit them to progress on their own. For example, knowledge of how to use context clues will help students independently determine word meanings.[27] Structural analysis skills can also increase students' independence.[28]

6. Vocabulary instruction should involve strategies that encourage students to elaborate word knowledge. The harder students work when generating word meanings and concepts, the more likely they are to remember the words and their meanings. By working through activities in in-depth vocabulary study and making word webs, students develop a greater depth of understanding than they would by copying definitions from a reference book. The activities suggested in this chapter are designed to encourage students to interact with word meanings.

7. Students should learn to use the dictionary, thesaurus, and glossary to develop understanding of word meanings when they cannot figure out meanings from experience, context, or structural analysis.

Many fine programs exist for developing word meanings with the use of computers. The specific software the teacher selects will depend on the type of computer available. Software and computers are changing and improving at a very rapid rate; therefore, it is most difficult to recommend specific materials. We do recommend that teachers establish criteria for the software they wish to use and then compare the materials available with their criteria. Many computer dealers and/or salespersons will lend computer software for examination prior to purchase; it is wise to take advantage of this opportunity.

Conceptual Approach

Words are labels for concepts; thus, if one truly knows a word, one has a concept for the word. Word meanings can be developed and reinforced through activities that use a conceptual approach to give students experience in thinking about the basic concepts of a content subject. Concepts are taught through activities that encourage students to label and to think of likenesses, differences, and organization; these elements are the bases for categorizing information. In content reading, categorization is concerned with identifying common features among concepts and developing a sense of the hierarchical relationships among these features.

Victor Rentel synthesized basic ideas regarding concept development; he recommended the following guidelines for teaching concepts.[29]

1. *Establish a label for the concept.*   Associate a word or words with the concept. For example, the word *democracy* can be associated with a specific form of government. The activities suggested in both the "Experience" and the "Association" sections of this chapter are useful at this level of concept development.

2. *Emphasize the attributes of the concept.*   Identify and stress the characteristics of the concept that make it similar to or different from other concepts. For example, to develop an understanding of the attributes of democracy, compare and contrast *democracy* with *communism.* Activities for use in developing this level of understanding are introduced on pages 52 and 53.

3. *Provide examples of the concepts.*   These examples should include both positive and negative instances of the concept. At this level, students could identify some governments that are *democratic* and some that are not democratic; they should be prepared to explain why a particular government represents a positive or a negative example of the concept. Activities for identifying the attributes of a concept will help students develop this understanding. (See page 54.)

4. *Encourage and guide students to discover the essence of a concept by categorizing it and relating it to other concepts.*   Students can develop an understanding of democracy by categorizing various forms of government. The structured overviews that are introduced on pages 56 and 57 are useful activities for developing this understanding.

5. *Provide opportunities for application of the concept.*   Students should develop ways to apply a particular concept. For instance, students could apply their understanding of the concept of government to classroom or school government.

Experience

Words are labels for concepts, and experience plays an important role in concept development; thus, experience is related to both concepts and word knowledge. "One of education's hazards lies in the way in which words are learned. Often they are floating items unattached to real experience, and as a result the knowledge is merely verbal. The shell of meaning is there, but the kernel is missing."[30] Word meanings depend on the experiences that support them; therefore, real and vicarious experiences should be used to support vocabulary instruction.

Understanding depends upon having a large store of information about the world that is derived from experience. As a person reads, words trigger thoughts of related experiences that are stored in the reader's brain, and understanding is facilitated. For example, a girl reading about the term *intersect* in a mathematics book will understand the word better if she has seen a street intersection. If a topic is entirely removed from a reader's experience, comprehension will be limited. Students cannot possibly have had direct experience with every concept they encounter in reading; the teacher can help students relate experiences to the content of reading materials and can also build experience through field trips, films, filmstrips, resource persons, and pictures.

Teachers can anticipate the vocabulary that students will encounter on a field trip, when viewing a film, or when listening to a speaker. They can write such words on the chalkboard, pronounce them, and discuss the meanings. This gives students opportunities to associate the visual forms of the words with the pronunciations and with the meanings. This practice will help students retain these words. For example, students who are visiting a local courthouse may encounter such terms as *attorney, litigation, defendant, and prosecutor.*

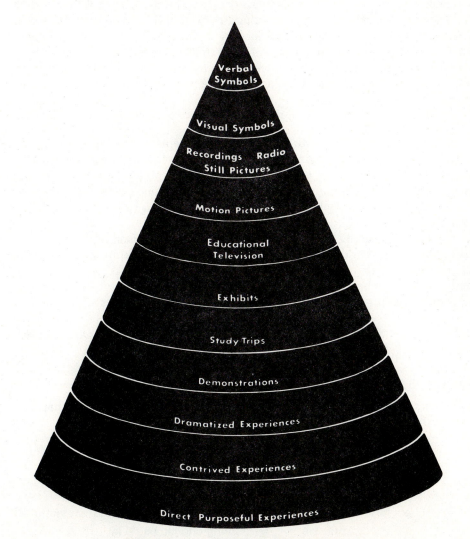

Figure 2.4   Dale's Cone of Experience
Source: From *Audiovisual Methods in Teaching*, 3rd ed. by Edgar Dale. Copyright © 1946, 1954, 1969 by Holt, Rinehart & Winston, Inc. Reprinted by permission of CBS College Publishing.

Also, teachers can point out relationships between concepts and experiences. For example, the girl reading about *intersect* might not recognize that a street intersection is related to the term in her mathematics text. Teachers can help students find a point of contact between experience and the concept being developed.

Concept development is a product of combining experience and thought and cannot be accomplished through memorization and drill. When teachers see that students lack the experiences necessary to understand basic concepts and words, supplemental activities should be planned. Although direct experiences such as field trips are valuable for developing concepts, they are not always possible. Also valuable are vicarious experiences such as dramatization, demonstrations, exhibits, television programs, films, recordings, radio programs, and pictures. Edgar Dale summarizes degrees of abstractness of experiences in his "Cone of Experience," which is presented in Figure 2.4. Note that as experiences move away from direct experience they become increasingly abstract; verbal symbols (spoken words) and visual symbols (printed words) are most abstract.

Association

Association strategies help students develop concepts and word meanings by presenting unknown words in connection with known words that have similar meanings. These activities are effective because it is likely that items that are presented together will be remembered together. Through assessment the content teacher can identify known and unknown words to be used in association activities.

Association teaching strategies include matching exercises, analogies, crossword puzzles, and in-depth word study. They can be used before students read a content chapter or unit to reinforce important vocabulary terms. Association activities also can be used at the end of a unit of study to check student knowledge of word meanings. In the following pages are six examples of association activities.

Example 2.7 illustrates a matching exercise that was prepared for a science text chapter on rockets.

EXAMPLE 2.7 SCIENCE ASSOCIATION WORKSHEET ──────

Directions: Draw a line to connect the words in Column A with the words that have almost the same meaning in Column B.

A	B
combustion	draws forward
thrust	burn
propellant	supplying oxygen
oxidizer	pushing force
propels	burning chemicals

Analogies can be used as an association activity to show a relationship or similarity between two words or ideas. Barbara Bellows suggests that "an analogy is a comparison of two similar relationships. On one side the two objects or concepts are related. On the other side the objects are related in the same way. Like a mathematical equation, an analogy has equal or balanced sides."[31] Analogies help students build associations for words.[32]

Content teachers may construct analogy exercises for students to complete. After learning how to form analogies, students may construct their own. This is a very important form of vocabulary study for college-bound students because analogies are frequently used to evaluate the word knowledge of students who are taking college-entrance examinations such as the SAT and the ACT. Unfortunately, many secondary students are unfamiliar with the format of analogies, so teachers should explain that the colon (:) represents the words *is to*, and the double colon (::) represents the word *as*. Teachers can provide examples of analogies for the entire class to work through in preparation for analogy activities. When working through an analogy example, students should identify the relationship, complete the analogy, and explain their reasoning.

The relationships usually expressed by analogies are:

a. opposites	g. homonyms
b. origin	h. number
c. synonyms	i. classification
d. plural	j. process
e. part-to-whole	k. degree
f. function	l. characteristic

Example 2.8 is an analogy worksheet that was prepared for a chapter in a science textbook.

EXAMPLE 2.8   SCIENCE ANALOGY WORKSHEET

Directions: Select the answer that completes each analogy. Identify the relationship expressed in the analogy and be prepared to explain your answer.

1. water : dehydration :: vitamins : (mumps, deficiency, diseases, jaundice, appendicitis)
2. taste buds : tongue :: villi : (mouth, stomach, small intestine, colon)
3. pepsin : protein :: ptyalin : (oils, fats, starch, sucrose)
4. liver : small intestine :: salivary glands : (mouth, stomach, small intestine, colon)
5. mouth : large intestine :: duodenum : (esophagus, jejunum, ileum, caecum)
6. protein : organic compound :: magnesium : (peptide, vitamin, mineral, salt)
7. pancreas : pancreatic fluid :: stomach : (water, saliva, gastric juices, intestinal fluid)
8. saliva : ptyalin :: pancreatic fluid : (trypsin, anylase, lipase, peptones)

Crossword puzzles are another approach to developing word associations. Content teachers may construct crossword puzzles for students to complete, or students may illustrate their word knowledge by making up their own puzzles. Example 2.9 is a crossword puzzle that was devised to accompany a chapter in a mathematics textbook.

EXAMPLE 2.9   MATHEMATICS CROSSWORD PUZZLE

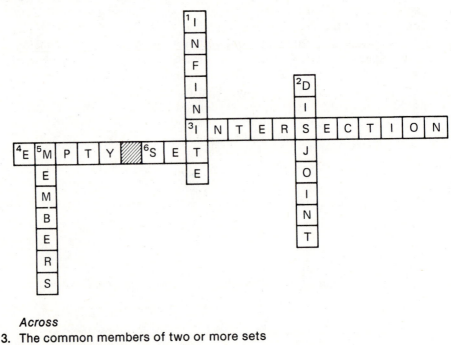

Across

3. The common members of two or more sets
4. A set that has no members is an _____ set.
6. A collection of objects or things

Down

1. A set whose members cannot be counted is an _____ set.
2. Sets that have no members that are the same are _____ sets.
5. Things or objects that belong to a set

In-depth study of a word is another way to increase knowledge of word meaning through association. This strategy involves studying all of the aspects of a word by defining the word and related words.[33] The content teacher may either identify specific words for students to study or ask students to select words that they need to study in greater depth. Students may use their textbooks, a dictionary, and a thesaurus to obtain the needed information. The in-depth study is developed by defining the word and then listing various forms of the word, its synonyms, and its antonyms. Example 2.10 shows an in-depth study of the word *economy*, selected from a social studies textbook.

EXAMPLE 2.10 IN-DEPTH WORD STUDY ━━━━━━━━━━

Economy: "The management of the resources of a country, community, or business: *the American economy.*"[34]

Related words and meanings

economy: (a second meaning) The careful or thrifty use or management of resources; freedom from waste, thrift.

economics: The science of the production, distribution, and consumption of wealth.

ecology: The branch of biology that deals with the relation of living things to their environment and to each other.

Word forms

economic, economical, economically, economics, economize, economization, economizer

opposing concepts	related concepts
liberal	frugal
generous	thrift
wasteful	save
careless	accumulate
bounteous	amass
beneficence	chary
munificence	miser
improvident	parsimonious
lavish	penurious
extravagance	curtail
impoverish	retrench

The association activities that follow are helpful for associating words with their meanings. These activities can be used for review and reinforcement after students have read a textbook chapter. Example 2.11 is based on a chapter entitled "States of Matter" in a general science textbook. Example 2.12 is based on a chapter on disease in a biology textbook.

Students can also play the game "Concentration" to reinforce word meanings. Blank playing cards or 3" × 5" index cards are used for the game cards. The teacher prepares the cards by writing words on half of the cards and definitions on the other half of the cards. The number of words selected for each game depends upon the reading level of the class, but the usual number is ten to sixteen

EXAMPLE 2.11   SCIENCE ASSOCIATION WORKSHEET ━━━━━

Directions: Write *S* on the line beside a set of words if they have the same meaning. Write *D* on the line if the words have different meanings.

_____ hardness—rigidity
_____ brittle—will shatter
_____ tensile strength—can be pulled apart easily
_____ matter—gas
_____ malleability—lumpiness
_____ ductility—can be drawn into wires

EXAMPLE 2.12   SCIENCE ASSOCIATION WORKSHEET ━━━━━

Directions: Write a word from the list below on the line beside its meaning.

_____ the science of disease
_____ departure from a state of health
_____ noninfectious disease
_____ biologically inherited disease
_____ signs of illness
_____ germ disease
_____ resistance to disease

pathology   hereditary disease
disease   symptoms
immunity   infectious disease
deficiency disease

words. These words may be chosen from any content area. After the cards are prepared, the teacher places the cards face-down in three rows and four columns (see Example 2.13, which follows). The students (or teams of students) take turns selecting two cards and determining if the word and the meaning selected are a match. When a student or team does not make a match, the cards are turned face-down again. The game ends when all of the cards are matched. The winner is the person or team with the most pairs.

Attributes and Examples

Activities that emphasize the attributes of a concept develop Rentel's second principle of concept development. These activities should point out how concepts are alike and how they are different and usually are completed by students who have

EXAMPLE 2.13 "CONCENTRATION" CARD GAME ─────────

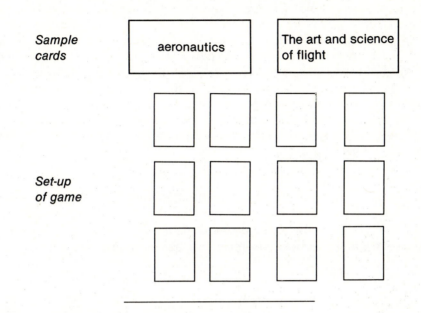

Sample cards

aeronautics

The art and science of flight

Set-up of game

some knowledge of the concepts involved. Example 2.14 was prepared by the teacher; the students complete it by placing an *X* in each appropriate cell. Example 2.15 was also developed by the teacher; in this case, the students must identify the significant attributes to be compared and then make the comparisons.

EXAMPLE 2.14 PHYSICAL EDUCATION ATTRIBUTES ─────────

	bases	yards	rules	ball	field	official
football		X	X	X	X	X
baseball	X		X	X	X	X

EXAMPLE 2.15 MATHEMATICS ATTRIBUTES ─────────

rational numbers	
irrational numbers	

Rentel's third principle of concept development requires students to identify examples and nonexamples of a concept. This is similar to a categorization task because students must understand the attributes that distinguish a particular concept from other, similar concepts. Teachers can provide students with association and attribute activities to develop knowledge of the concept before assigning activities that require students to identify examples and nonexamples. In the content classroom, students can be asked to refer to their text or reference materials to find examples and nonexamples of a particular concept. For example, a home economics teacher might identify the concept of *protein* and an art teacher the concept of *Impressionism*. After identifying examples and nonexamples of the concept, students would be prepared to explain why they chose each.

Example 2.16 is based on the identification of examples and nonexamples (positive and negative examples).

EXAMPLE 2.16 MATHEMATICS EXAMPLES WORKSHEET ───────

Directions: Place a + on the line before each positive example and a − on the line before each negative example. Be prepared to explain your answers.

The concept is triangle.
_____ scalene
_____ adjacent
_____ isosceles
_____ equilateral
_____ left
_____ vertical
_____ acute
_____ right
_____ obtuse

────────────

Categorization and Concept Relationships

Rentel's fourth principle of developing concepts encourages the use of activities for categorizing concepts and examining relationships among concepts.

Categorization This task requires students to sort concepts into categories that are based on common characteristics. Jean Gillet and Charles Temple identify two types of sorts: open-ended and closed-ended. "In closed-ended sorts, the category or the common property of the members of the category is stated at the beginning of the sort."[35] The category that has been identified gives students the basis for including or excluding a class of concepts.

"In open-ended sorts, no category is stated in advance and no exemplars are used."[36] The student seeks relationships among the concepts, grouping the concepts together and defining the relationship that has served as a basis for inclusion or exclusion of concepts.

Examples 2.17 and 2.18 present closed-ended sort categorization activities: the feature that all words in a group must share is stated in advance. When students sort words with no stated sorting criteria, the activity is an open-ended sort. Examples 2.19 and 2.20 present open-ended sort activities.

EXAMPLE 2.17 CLOSED-ENDED SORT FOR HOME ECONOMICS CONTENT

Directions: Sort the list of words into the following categories: protein, carbohydrates, calcium.

fish	nuts
spaghetti	cheese
eggs	sugar
potatoes	cereal
bread	apples
kale	broccoli
peaches	milk

EXAMPLE 2.18 CLOSED-ENDED SORT FOR SOCIAL STUDIES CONTENT

Directions: Draw a line through the name in each group that does not belong. The common characteristic of each group is identified by the word in parentheses.

1. Bob La Follette, Jane Addams, Upton Sinclair, Theodore Roosevelt, Jacob Riis (progressives)
2. Edward Bok, Joseph Pulitzer, Carl Schurz, Samuel Gompers, Ole Rölvaag, Benjamin West (immigrants to the United States)

EXAMPLE 2.19 OPEN-ENDED SORT FOR BIOLOGY CONTENT

Directions: Draw a line through the word in each group that does not belong and identify the common characteristic (category) of the remaining items.

1. intestinal juice, gastric juice, maltose, pancreatic juice
2. anylase, gastric proteinase, lypase, polypeptides, peptidases, disaccharidases
3. fats, amino acids, maltose, glycerol, simple sugars

EXAMPLE 2.20   OPEN-ENDED SORT FOR SECRETARIAL OFFICE PROCEDURES ─────

Directions: Classify the following list of words into groups and identify the common characteristic of each group.

sales invoice	multicopy
purchase order	purchase invoice
bills	horizontal spaces
sales order	binding space
credit memorandum	credit approval
purchase requisition	vertical line
business firm heading	

───────────────

Structured Overview   A structured overview is a graphic organizer that illustrates the hierarchical relationships among the key concepts in a content textbook, chapter, or unit.[37] Structured overviews are based on Ausubel's theory that students should be presented with an orderly arrangement of the concepts needed in order to learn new concepts.[38] This graphic organization gives students a structure for incorporating new concepts. Thus it helps students anticipate the words and concepts in a content selection.

Barron recommends the following steps for devising structured overviews:[39]

1. Identify the words (concepts) that are important for students to understand.
2. Arrange the words (concepts) into a structure that illustrates the interrelationships among the concepts.
3. Add to the structure words (concepts) that the students understand in order to show the relationship between the learning task and the discipline.
4. Analyze the overview. Are the major relationships shown clearly? Can the overview be simplified and still communicate the important relationships?

The relationships in a structured overview are usually arranged in the following manner:

Example 2.21 is a structured overview that was prepared for social studies content. It presents some of the important concepts involved in Franklin D. Roosevelt's "New Deal." With further study, students could add concepts to this structured overview. Example 2.22 presents an overview for a biology chapter.

EXAMPLE 2.21   STRUCTURED OVERVIEW FOR SOCIAL STUDIES CONTENT

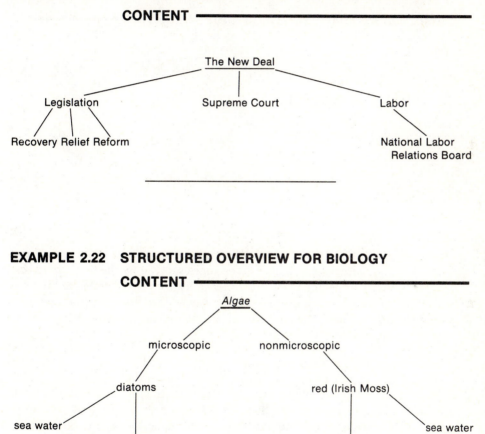

EXAMPLE 2.22   STRUCTURED OVERVIEW FOR BIOLOGY CONTENT

Post-structured overviews are used after a textbook, a chapter, or a unit has been read. They are usually constructed by students to summarize and graphically illustrate conceptual relationships. The students can use Barron's four steps as a guide in developing post-structured overviews.

Hierarchy   The hierarchical relationships of concepts can also be examined through illustrating the movement of a concept from the abstract to the concrete. The development of a hierarchy gives students an opportunity to relate their experiences to a concept because the concrete levels are based on the relating of an abstract concept to personal experience. Example 2.23 illustrates a hierarchy for the concept of transportation.

EXAMPLE 2.23   TRANSPORTATION HIERARCHY ———————

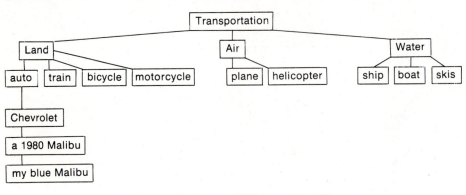

This example illustrates a movement from the abstract to the concrete. *Transportation* is an abstract term that is made more specific by the terms *land, air,* and *water.* Each succeeding level of the hierarchy is more concrete than the previous level; the final level refers to a specific car within the individual's personal experience. Hierarchical development and concreteness are determined by the individual's experience.[40]

Application

Rentel's principles for developing concepts include having students apply their conceptual knowledge by asking them to define words in different ways. This activity should be used after students have studied associations, attributes, examples, nonexamples, and categorization and have developed conceptual understanding of a word. Example 2.24 illustrates this activity with the word *magnanimous,* which was selected from English content.

EXAMPLE 2.24   DEFINING WORDS IN DIFFERENT WAYS ———————

1. Use the word in a sentence that shows its meaning.
   Magnanimous people make good friends.
2. Give a synonym for the word.
   magnanimous—generous

3. Give an antonym for the word.
   magnanimous—penurious
4. State a classification for the word.
   Magnanimity can be classified as a quality of mind and soul.
5. Provide an example of the word, such as by drawing or locating a picture to illustrate the word.
6. Make a comparison of the word with another word.
   Magnanimity is like generosity, but it implies more noble unselfishness.

Many of the activities in this chapter encourage students to process words in ways that help them remember the words. These activities should also increase students' interest in words. The following activities can also be used to build students' interest in words, and they encourage students to process words. These activities may be adapted to any content area.

Activities
1. Using *The Book of Lists* by David Wallenchinsky, Irving Wallace, and Amy Wallace as a model, have students create a class book of lists for any content area.
   a. Home economics students could create lists of foods that are hard to pronounce, words that describe furniture, French words related to food, Italian words related to food, etc.
   b. Social studies students could make lists of words that describe rivers, historical figures, or historical events; lists of names of cities or countries that are hard to spell; etc.
   c. Mathematics students could make lists of terms that are hard to pronounce, words that have a high number of vowels, words with a numerical root (such as *bi, tri*), etc.
2. Explore the creative ideas about words in the book, *The Joy of Lex*, by Gyles Brandreth (New York: Quill). Develop activities based on the concepts in this book.
3. Have students create crossword puzzles, as described earlier.
4. Have students invent vocabulary games using *Trivial Pursuit* as a model.

Context

Context plays an important role in helping readers acquire word meanings. One of the ways we acquire vocabulary is through encountering a particular word in a variety of contexts. Each experience with a word helps us refine our understanding of the word. Readers use context to narrow a word's reference and to specify its meaning. Many authors, especially authors of technical materials, deliberately use context to help readers understand the meaning of the key words in a selection.

Because students do not automatically use context for word meanings, teachers should give guidance in identifying and using contextual clues. Students must be taught to consciously and systematically use contextual material to learn an author's intended word meaning.

Learning to use meaning clues consists basically of developing a mind set or an attitude. It is important to develop an attitude of expectancy about what is being read. For example, consider the following sentences: *Billy looked at his toy airplane and put his hands on the wings. As he lifted the plane off the airstrip, a new pilot was born.* The words *airplane* and *wings* in the first sentence allow the reader to anticipate the meanings and use of *airstrip* and *pilot* in the second sentence. If the words in the first sentence were familiar to the reader and the words in the second were not, identification of the latter words would be facilitated by anticipation based on meaning clues.

Use of meaning clues and contextual analysis are quite similar, but contextual analysis involves rereading or prereading. Contextual analysis involves identifying unfamiliar words or phrases by examining their *semantic* and/or *syntactic* environment or context.

Example of semantic clue: The harshness in his voice and the scowl on his face told that father was in a *captious* mood.
Example of syntactic clue: His *truculent* criticism of the article revealed his deepest feelings.

In the first example, the meaning of *captious* is suggested by some accompanying semantic indications: *harshness in his voice* and *scowl on his face.* In the second example, the reader who finds the word *truculent* unfamiliar can tell by its position in the sentence that the word is not a noun or a verb. Its position shows that it describes a type of criticism; therefore, it is an adjective.

Many students do not use context clues for the following reasons:

1. They stop when they meet an unknown word, forgetting that clues may be provided by succeeding words in the sentence or even by succeeding sentences.
2. They rely too much on other ways of analyzing words, such as looking at configuration (shape of the word) or beginning or ending sounds.
3. They wait for the teacher to provide the contextual signals.

Students need to be encouraged to keep reading backward and forward to where clues may be, to generate hypotheses, to test alternate possibilities, to demand sense, and to recognize a wide variety of language clues. To refine word meaning, readers must frequently use context clues in combination with concept development and dictionary meanings.

The list below suggests different types of contextual aids to understanding word meanings. These kinds of aids are often encountered by students, who should be given extensive practice in using them if contextual analysis is to become an important means of word analysis.

Type	Example
1. Definition	A *micrometer* is an instrument used with a telescope or microscope for measuring minute distances.
2. Restatement	A cockroach has two *antennae*, or feelers, at its head.
3. Example	"The ship plows the sea" is an example of a *metaphor*.
4. Comparison/contrast	A *machete*, like a sword, can be very dangerous. In bright light, the pupils of the eyes contract; in the dark, they *dilate*.
5. Description	A *ginkgo* is a tree of eastern China that has fan-shaped leaves and provides much shade.
6. Synonyms/antonyms	The *mercury* in the thermometer was dropping—the *quicksilver* was contracting. The *acid*, not the *base*, reddened the litmus.
7. Familiar experience of language	*Artificial respiration* was applied to the nearly drowned man.
8. Association	He ate as *ravenously* as a bear.
9. Reflection of mood	All alone, Jim heard the creaking sound of the opening door and saw a shadowy figure standing suddenly before him. Jim was literally *stupefied*.
.0. Summary	Even though he was sixty-five years old, he continued to love sports. He played a skillful game of tennis and seldom missed his daily swim. He was very *athletic*.

Several procedures are useful for providing instruction in contextual clue usage.

Activities
1. Encourage students to find in their text materials examples of the types of contextual aids presented above.
2. Present exercises like the following to groups of students who need practice.
   a. Partial indication of word:
   An agreement was impossible; an im—as—e had been reached. (part spelling)
   An agreement was impossible; an i——————e had been reached. (first/last letter)
   An agreement was impossible; an i—————— had been reached. (first letter)

An agreement was impossible; an ————————— had been reached. (number of letters)

An agreement was impossible; an _____ had been reached. (space)

b. Multiple-choice:

The vase was _____. (fractious, fragile, fragment)

c. Scrambled sentences:

germs. us the protects epidermis from

d. Nonsense words:

Betty's *dreb* expression showed she was not cheerful today.

3. Encourage students to compose exercises for others to complete. Individual students (or groups of two or three) can make up sets of sentences, the teacher can compile and duplicate them, and other students can then work together in small groups to solve them. References to specific classroom activities or classmates can personalize and add some zest to what could be drab and humorless exercises.

4. Relate contextual clue usage to special types of words that need attention; these types include homonyms (That is the only *course* he could take. The dress was made from *coarse* material.), synonyms (*drill—bore*), antonyms (*talkative—taciturn*), and homographs. Homographs are words that look alike but have different meanings and pronunciations. (Did you *record* the science experiment? Jim broke Tom's *record* for the most interceptions in one game.) Multiple meanings of words can cause confusion. The word *base* may appear in mathematics class, but the student may know the word as used in "the *base* of the lamp" or "Jim is stationed at the air *base*." Figurative language (similes, metaphors, personification, hyperbole, euphemism) is used a great deal in literature, both prose and poetry, and also requires special instruction.

As suggested throughout this section on context clue usage, certain factors operate within context reading:

1. *Reasoning ability.* The student must utilize a series of reasoning steps when meeting a strange word. Certain questions must be considered: What else has been said that might reveal the meaning of the word? What words might fit here? Why?

2. *Store of word meanings.* As knowledge of word meanings expands, use of context clues becomes more helpful. Attention to the special types of words suggested above is one way to develop a larger vocabulary.

3. *Extent of information about a topic.* To encourage best utilization of context clues, teachers must build background before students read about topics with which they have had little experience. A reader who knows a great deal about the topic of cars, for example, will be better able than a reader with less background to determine both the pronunciations and meanings of words like *generator, transmission, chassis, accelerator, gasket, lubrication, ignition system,* and even more technical terms like *fore, stroke, displacement, valve, compression, drive shafts, axle, distributor, plug thread, exhaust system.*

4. *Knowledge of other words in the selection.* Teachers must choose reading material carefully; they must "match" students and material. A student cannot be expected to use context clues effectively if his or her word recognition for a selection is less than 95 percent—if the student finds more than one unknown word in twenty running words.

Structural Analysis

By using *structural analysis* to teach new words before students read a selection, the content teacher can prepare students to use this technique on their own. In structural analysis, the clues within a word are used to understand the word's meaning. Structural analysis is also called *morphemic analysis* because it utilizes morphemes, which are the smallest meaningful units of language. For example, *cat* is one morpheme; the word *cats* has two morphemes—*cat* plus *s*, which indicates plural. Free morphemes can stand alone; bound morphemes must be affixed to free morphemes. A word that results from affixing a bound morpheme to a root or base morpheme is called a derivative or a variant. Combinations of free morphemes—such as *book* and *store* (bookstore)—are called *compound words*.

Structural analysis is especially valuable when it is used in combination with context. Context can help students determine the correct meaning of the affix (sequence of letters added to a root word to change its meaning and/or part of speech) and the sense of the word. For example, the suffix *ways* in the word *sideways* can mean "course," "direction," or "manner."

Instructional strategies are concerned primarily with two aspects of structural analysis. The first is combining the meanings of prefixes, root words, and suffixes to obtain the meaning of words. The second is joining the meanings of two (or three) known words that form compound words.

The most useful affixes for instruction are those that have single, invariant meanings.[41] However, many affixes have multiple meanings, so all affixes that occur frequently should be taught. For example, although the prefix *ante* has several meanings, it occurs so frequently in content reading that it should be taught to students. When a multiple-meaning affix occurs, students can use context to determine which meaning is appropriate.

The following section of this chapter includes lists of affixes that are useful for content teachers. In using these lists, teachers should remember that there is no value in having students memorize lists of affixes and their meanings: the fact that students have memorized the affixes is no guarantee that they can or will use them. A better strategy for teaching word meaning is to have students structurally analyze words as they occur in reading selections.[42] This functional approach leads to more effective use of structural analysis.

Affixes and Roots

Prefixes and suffixes are affixes. A prefix is placed before a root word, and a suffix is placed after a root word. Prefixes simply change the meanings of the root words, but suffixes may change the parts of speech of root words in addition to modifying the meanings.

Of the twenty thousand most commonly used words in English, four thousand—or 20 percent—have prefixes. Fifteen prefixes make up 82 percent of the total usage of all prefixes. They are listed below.

ab (from)—abnormal
ad (to)—adhesion
be (by)—belittle
com, con, co, col (with)—
   conjunction
de (from)—decentralize
dis, di (apart)—dissect
en (in)—enact

ex (out)—extract
in, il, un, ir (not)—
   inadequate
pre (before)—predict
pro (in front of)—proceed
re (back)—rebuttal
sub (under)—subway
un (not)—unannounced

Other common prefixes and their meanings include:

ante (before)—antedate
anti (against)—antidote
auto (self)—autobiography
bi (two)—bisect
bene (well)—benefactor
circum (around)—
   circumnavigate
contra (against)—contradict
equi (equal)—equilateral
fore (before)—forepayment
inter (between)—interurban
mono (one)—monologue

non (not)—non-union
out (beyond)—outweigh
peri (around)—perimeter
poly (many)—polygon
post (after)—postscript
retro (backwards)—
   retrogressive
semi (half)—semicircle
super (above)—superimpose
syn, sym (with)—synthesis
trans (across)—transform
tele (afar)—telescope

Common suffixes and their functions are listed below. The most common suffixes are starred.

Noun Suffixes
-ness* (state of being)—arbitrariness
-ment* (agency or instrument)—government
-ance* (quality, state of being)—disturbance
-tion* (state of being)—irrigation
-ant* (person or thing acting as agent)—descendant
-ion (results of)—fusion
-sion (the act, quality, result of)—explosion
-ation (the act of)—formation
-ity or -ty (state or condition)—electricity, unity
-ence (quality, state of being)—congruence
-hood (condition, state of being)—neighborhood

-ship (condition, state of being)—hardship
-or (state, quality, agent, doer)—elector
-ism (state of being)—nationalism
-ist (state, agent, doer)—scientist

Adjective Suffixes

-able* or -ible* (capacity, fitness, tending to, able to)—serviceable, divisible
-al* or -ial* (belonging to, pertaining to)—coastal, remedial
-ful* (full of)—fearful
-ive* (having nature or quality of)—productive
-ous* (abounding in, having)—mountainous
-ic (of, relating to)—volcanic
-ish (of the nature of)—mannish
-less (without, free from)—selfless
-ary (pertaining to, place for)—tributary

Verb Suffixes

-ize (to acquire, become like)—Americanize
-fy (to make, add to, form into)—magnify
-ate (acted upon, function, affected)—emancipate
-en (made of or belonging, cause to be)—soften

Adverb Suffixes

-ly (in manner of)—rapidly
-wise (with regard or respect to)—lengthwise
-ways (course, direction, manner)—sideways
-ward (toward, position)—southward

The most important affixes and roots for the content area teacher to consider are those that are important to the particular subject. For example, a science instructor might find the following affixes occurring commonly in the reading material:

homo- (same or like)—homochromatic
hetero- (other or different)—heterogeneous
hydro- (water)—hydrocarbon
equi- (equal)—equidistant
aqua- (water)—aqualung
pro- (forth)—progenitor
inter- (between or among)—intercellular
bi- (two)—biped
-ology (study of)—biology
-ism (state or condition)—alcoholism

On the other hand, a mathematics instructor might well find the following list of affixes more appropriate to develop:

hemi-, demi- (half)—hemisphere, demitasse
uni-, mono- (one)—unitary, monologue
bi- (two)—bisect
tri- (three)—triangle

quadra-, tetra- (four)—quadrilateral, tetrameter
penta-, quin- (five)—pentagon, quintet
hex-, hexa- (six)—hexagonal
sept-, hepta- (seven)—septuagenarian, heptameter
octa- (eight)—octagon
nona- (nine)—nonary
dec- (ten)—decade
centi- (hundred)—centimeter

One source of important morphemes in the content areas of English, social studies, science, and mathematics may be found in Appendix C of Lou E. Burmeister's, *Reading Strategies for Middle and Secondary School Teachers* (Reading, Mass.: Addison-Wesley, 1978).

The content teacher should give some attention to structural analysis of words in assignment-readiness lessons or during the structured overview. During a course of study, a teacher may find it helpful to isolate particular skills for additional practice. Several ways in which this may be done are listed below.

Activities

1. From a list of words, have students cite prefixes, the meanings of the prefixes, and the meanings of the words.

	Prefix	*Prefix meaning*	*Word meaning*
bisect			
circumference			
encircle			
enclose			
perimeter			
polygon			
semicircle			

2. Develop cards for sets of words that use a particular prefix, suffix, or root word.

photo	graphy

bio-
biblio-
ortho-
carto-
geo-
steno-

3. Have students build new words, making as many new words as possible by adding various prefixes and suffixes to the given root word.

> *construct*
> construction   reconstruct
> constructing   reconstruction
> constructed   reconstructing

4. Consider content area words in terms of Greek or Latin word roots. Sample questions that might be used to develop vocabulary in a science class follow:
   a. If *thermos* means hot, what is a *thermostat?* a *thermometer?*
   b. If *hydro* means water, what do these words mean: *dehydrate? hydrophobia?*
   c. How is *hydroplane* related to *hydrant?*
   d. If *tele* means far, what is the meaning of these words: *telescope? television?*
   e. If *zoo* means animal, what is the meaning of *zoology?* Who is a *zoologist?*
   f. If *tome* is the act of cutting, what is an *appendectomy?*
   g. If *micro* means *small,* what is a *microscope?*
   h. Why would you call *dynamite* and a *dynamo* first cousins?

5. Create a web of words structured upon a root word. Webs may be developed by groups of students or by students working alone.[43]

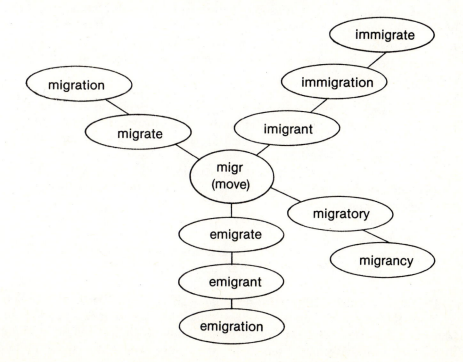

Compound Words

Compound words are made up of two (or occasionally three) free morphemes that have been joined together to form a new word. The original pronunciations of the component words are usually maintained, and the meanings of the original words are connected to form the meaning of the new word. An example from industrial arts is the word *hammerhead* (striking part of a hammer). Students can be asked to define selected compound words whose component words are part of their vocabularies. Examples from a physical education class might include *hammerlock, armdrag,* and *bootleg* (type of football play). Students can also be asked to underline or circle component parts of compound words, as in *whipstitch*. Or they may become more aware of compound words if they are given an opportunity to put together familiar compound words.

Using the Dictionary and Thesaurus

Although context and structural analysis are helpful and valuable aids in developing word meaning, there are times when students must use a dictionary to learn the precise meaning of a word. In suggesting that students use a dictionary or thesaurus, we are not recommending that teachers have students write lists of definitions. This activity can kill students' interest in words and usually does not lead to a real understanding of the terms. Teachers also should understand that it is important that students understand key terms and concepts, but not necessarily every single word in a selection. The unknown words that interfere with comprehension should be the ones targeted for dictionary study.

The following guidelines are useful for using the dictionary in content classrooms:

1. Help students use the context in which the word appears to select the appropriate dictionary definition. That the dictionary incorporates multiple meanings for words can create a problem for students. When a student does not have a meaning for a word, he or she may find it nearly impossible to choose the appropriate meaning from those provided in the dictionary. With practice, most students will learn how to use content context to identify the appropriate meaning.
2. Identify only a few key concepts for dictionary study. It is perfectly legitimate for teachers to tell students the meanings of unknown words. Secondary students generally are more willing to use the dictionary when they need it if they have not been forced by the teacher to use it.

The thesaurus also is helpful for developing an understanding of words. Some students find it easier to understand and remember the synonyms provided in a thesaurus than to remember dictionary definitions. Of course, a thesaurus usually does not include technical terms. The dictionary format of recent editions of the thesaurus makes it easier for students to use as a reference.

Figurative Language

All figures of speech are forms of rhetoric. They are used to persuade or otherwise affect others. Figurative language is language than enhances the vividness of a scene and expresses ideas with greater precision. Notice the difference between the following sentences.

> The man was bigger than the boy.
> The man was a giant next to the shivering boy.

The second sentence is more interesting and the idea is expressed more effectively. The first sentence is literal, while the second sentence relies on picturesque, imaginative language to heighten the comparison. In figurative language the meanings of words and phrases are extended through the connotative meanings attached to the words and phrases. Students use figurative expressions daily in their own language, so they should not have to memorize lists of figurative expressions. Rather they should consider how authors use words to convey special meanings in figurative language.

Figures of speech are found in the textbooks of all content areas. Example 2.25 shows a gloss of figurative language.

EXAMPLE 2.25   A Gloss of Figurative Language in a Geology Text ——

9–5 Island Arcs and Volcanoes

This figurative language helps the reader visualize the volcanic islands.

This simile is based on concepts developed earlier in this text. Note how the figurative language helps the reader understand the continental volcanoes.

There are volcanoes, faults, and earthquakes on the ocean floor as well as on land. Oceanic volcanoes are common. Iceland is a volcanic island. There are isolated volcanoes out in the Atlantic, Pacific, and Indian oceans, far from large land masses. Curved chains of volcanic islands—the Aleutians, the Philippines, the East Indies (Indonesia) and others—<u>form great arcs</u> along the western margin of the Pacific Basin (Figure 9–10). The Antilles in the Caribbean Sea form another island arc. The continental volcanoes seem to be aligned, just like the chains of volcanic islands. Many of the volcanoes are still active and occasionally spew out masses of lava, gases, and vast clouds of ash.

Source: W. Matthews, C. Roy, R. Stevenson, M. Harris, D. Hesser, and W. Dexter: *Investigating the Earth,* 4th ed. (Boston: Houghton Mifflin Company, 1984), p. 225.

The following examples of figurative language were taken from current secondary textbooks:

"We cannot see the folding, bending and squeezing of solid rock happening."[44] (science text)

"He wrung his hands in an agony of apprehension and swayed backwards and forwards in his chair."[45] (literature text)

"The marketplace does have a shady side."[46] (consumer economics text)

Personification, simile, metaphor, and hyperbole are the most common figures of speech; although metonymy, synecdoche, litotes, allegory, and euphemism are types of figurative language, they occur less frequently. The following are examples of each type of figurative language:

1. *Personification* Human or personal qualities are given to inanimate things or ideas. A ship is called "she," and we speak of "Mother" Earth. Personification is used in the following sentence: "The moon smiled down on the lovers."

2. *Simile* A direct comparison is made between things. The words *like*, *as . . . as*, and *so . . . as* are frequently used in making the comparisons in similes. Similes are useful because they help us illustrate our thoughts and ideas. An example of a sentence containing a simile is, "The thunder reverberated like an entire corps of bass drums."

3. *Metaphor* This figure of speech helps writers and speakers create clearer pictures through a direct comparison. This comparison does not use clue words such as *like* or *as*. An example of a sentence containing a metaphor is, "Her blistering remark burned in Jim's mind."

4. *Hyperbole* This is an exaggeration used for effect. The speaker or writer deliberately stretches the truth, as in "I haven't seen you for a million years."

5. *Metonymy* This is the use of the name of one thing for another that it suggests. We often use metonymy without recognizing it. For instance, "tickle the ivories" means "play the piano."[47] In this instance we use the name of the material (ivory) to represent the object made from the material (piano keys).

6. *Synecdoche* This is a figure of speech in which a part is used for the whole. For example, "We need your glove in the lineup" means "We need you in the baseball game."

7. *Litotes* This figure of speech is the opposite of hyperbole. Litotes make an assertion about something by denying its opposite. For instance, "This achievement is of no small importance" means that it is an important achievement. Saying that "Susan is not unhappy with her new job" suggests that Susan is indeed pleased with her new position.

8. *Allegory* An allegory is a story told in symbols. It can be considered an extended metaphor. Allegories often deal with the moral and spiritual nature of human beings. Fables and parables are short allegories. For example, the Aesop's Fable, "The Fox and the Grapes," is a fable and an allegory.

9. *Euphemism*   Most figures of speech rely on comparison, but euphemism is based on contrast. Euphemism is used to express disagreeable or unpleasant facts indirectly. Death is often described as "passing away," "going to one's reward," or "the final rest."

10. *Allusions*   Allusions may refer to Greek and Roman mythology, historical characters, or literature. Allusions are based on the assumption that the reader knows the characters, that the allusion will cause the reader to make associations, and that the allusions will clarify a point. For instance, a person may be declared "a silent Sphinx" or said to have a "Cheshire cat grin" or to be "carrying coals to Newcastle."

Instruction in figurative language should focus on how authors use words to convey special meanings. Teachers should be aware that figurative language presents particular difficulty to students who are learning English as a second language. All teachers will find strategies such as the following activities useful in developing students' understanding of figurative language. Teachers may also find the following references useful: Maxine Bortner and John Gates, *A Dictionary of American Idioms,* rev. ed. (Woodbury, N.Y.: Barron's Educational Services, Inc., 1975); Richard Boning, *Interpreting Idioms* (Baldwin, N.Y.: Barnell Loft, Ltd., 1979).

Activities

1. Have students create simple drawings to illustrate figures of speech.
2. Have students paraphrase figures of speech to illustrate their understanding of figurative language. For instance, have them paraphrase "It's no easy feat to become president of the United States."
3. Have students identify figures of speech in literature according to the categories of figurative language given above.
4. Create a gamelike activity by writing figures of speech on index cards and having students classify them appropriately.
5. Have students write the literal meanings for figurative expressions. For example, ask them to write a literal meaning for "Keep a stiff upper lip."
6. Give students a list of clichés and have them replace the clichés with more creative expressions. For example, ask students to think of replacements for the following similes: "as white as snow," "as quick as a wink," "as black as night," and "as cute as a button."
7. Have students practice using various figures of speech in their writing. Direct them to use specific figures of speech when writing class assignments.

A TEACHING PLAN

The preceding sections of this chapter have presented theory as well as practical examples for developing word meanings in content classes. This section suggests a model that a content teacher could use for the actual teaching of key vocabulary. Content teachers should examine this model and use any or all of it as it fits with their individual instructional approaches.

As a tenth-grade history teacher prepared to introduce a new chapter on World War I, she first identified the key concepts in the selection. She found the following key concepts: *Triple Entente, Triple Alliance, Central Powers, Allies, balance of power, Fourteen Points, Polish Corridor, Allied Expeditionary Forces, Big Three, reparations.*

Second, the teacher used assessment strategies similar to those suggested in the assessment section of this chapter to identify the known and unknown words in this group.

Third, before introducing the chapter, the teacher explained words the students did not know and understand. She used concept development strategies and context clue strategies similar to those suggested in this chapter to help her students acquire the meanings of unknown words. She referred students to a dictionary or glossary for several of the most difficult key concepts. Structural analysis was most useful in teaching the meanings of the words *expeditionary* and *reparations* because these words are composed of affixes and root words.

Fourth, students read the chapter, making certain to use the word meanings they had acquired to aid comprehension.

Finally, the teacher asked her students to create a post-structured overview to show their understanding of the key concepts and the relationships among the key concepts.

SUMMARY

Knowing word meanings is an important aspect of comprehending content materials. Many of the words used in content materials are labels for concepts. Thus, vocabulary and concept development are interrelated. The best way to know a word is to understand the concept it represents. The important words in content materials fall into three general categories: general vocabulary, special vocabulary, and technical vocabulary. Because content materials frequently contain a high proportion of unknown words, teachers may find it impossible to teach students every unknown word. It is important for teachers to focus on key vocabulary.

Assessment strategies can be used to identify known and unknown words. This information is useful for planning instruction. Word meanings can be taught in the following ways: through concept development including experience, association, attributes, examples, categorization, and relationships; through context; through word structure; and through use of the dictionary and thesaurus.

SELF-TEST

1. Why is experience an important factor in vocabulary instruction? (a) Experience helps the reader identify main ideas. (b) Experience helps students understand the concepts that support vocabulary development. (c) Experience provides a purpose for reading. (d) All readers have experience that is directly related to the subjects in their textbooks.

2. Why is it impossible for content teachers to teach all of the unknown words in a content chapter? (a) There may be a large number of new words in a selection. (b) Teachers are not interested in doing this. (c) The students usually know all of the terms. (d) All of these

3. How is the relationship between concept development and vocabulary development best described? (a) No relationship (b) A labeling relationship (c) A spiral relationship (c) None of these

4. Which of the following processes operate in concept development? (a) Comparisons (b) Petrology (c) Concretion (d) Signaling

5. Which of these activities enhance concept development? (a) Categorizing (b) Finding connections (c) Finding common properties (d) All of these

6. A check ($\sqrt{}$) in the code suggested by Edgar Dale means what? (a) I know the word well and use it. (b) I know it somewhat. (c) I've seen it or heard of it. (d) I've never heard of it.

7. What is general vocabulary, as it is defined in this chapter? (a) Common words with generally accepted meanings (b) Words with both general and specialized meanings (c) Technical vocabulary (d) All of these

8. When should word meanings be taught in content instruction? (a) As readiness for reading a chapter (b) As a follow-up to reading a chapter (c) In the middle of a content chapter (d) Both *a* and *b*

9. Which of the following is not a recommended approach to teaching word meanings? (a) Through concept development (b) Through association (c) Through phonics (d) Through structural analysis

10. Which of the following describes an open-ended sort of categorization? (a) Examples are provided. (b) Categories are provided. (c) Neither examples nor categories are given. (d) Essential characteristics are given.

11. Why does a word in isolation lack a clear-cut meaning? (a) Words in English derive meaning from interaction with other words. (b) Words are hard to define. (c) A dictionary is necessary to determine the meaning of a word. (d) The teacher must check the meaning a student gives to a word.

12. Which of the following is not a principle of vocabulary development? (a) Stress learner involvement. (b) Focus on usable vocabulary. (c) Teach unique words. (d) Use reference materials.

13. Which answer best describes figurative language? (a) Literal language (b) Picturesque, imaginative language (c) Language based on artists' illustrations (d) Language rarely found in English

THOUGHT QUESTIONS

1. Why is experience of paramount importance in vocabulary instruction?
2. How are words defined?
3. Why did Edgar Dale say that "to know a content subject one must learn its key concepts; that is, its language"?
4. What are concepts? Explain them in your own words.

5. Identify the principles of developing vocabulary. Describe each briefly.
6. Think of a way to apply each principle of developing vocabulary in your content area.

ENRICHMENT ACTIVITIES

1. Prepare a categorizing worksheet, as illustrated in this chapter, for a chapter from a content area textbook of your choice.
2. Prepare an assessment using words from a chapter in a content area book; use one or more of the four methods of testing vocabulary that are described in this chapter.
3. Prepare a crossword puzzle for a set of important terms associated with a unit of work in your content area.
4. Select a chapter in a content area book and identify the vocabulary that you think you would teach to a class. Plan ways to teach the chosen terms. Following is a list of content areas and the key concepts that might make up one chapter in each area.

   Auto mechanics: thermostat, radiator, carburetor, ammeter, armature, commutator, generator, oscilloscope, polarize, camshaft, valve-tappet

   Music: choreographer, prologue, prompter, score, overture, prelude, libretto, aria

   Health: bacteria, virus, protozoa, metazoa, fungi, carbuncle, psoriasis, shingles, scabies, eczema

   Foreign language: masculine, feminine, gender, predicate, cognates, singular, consonant

   Art: introspective, murals, appreciation, technique, expression, properties, exhibitions, contemporary, interpret

   Driver education: awareness, controlled emotions, maturity, irresponsible, behavioral patterns, compensate, fatigue, carbon monoxide, medication, alcohol, depressants, visual, auditory

   Psychology: learning curve, plateau, hierarchies, massed practice, feedback, frame, negative transfer, retention, overlearning

   Government: delinquent, incorrigibility, omnibus, exigency, indeterminate, adjudicated, arbitrariness, interrogation, formulation, juvenile

5. Develop a worksheet for in-depth study of a word.
6. Make a structured overview for a selection in a content area textbook.
7. Prepare an analogy exercise sheet (similar to the one on p. 49) for a chapter or unit in a content area text.

NOTES

1. E. W. Dolch, "A Basic Sight Vocabulary," *The Elementary School Journal*, 36 (1936), 456–460.
2. E. E. Ekwall, "Basic Sight Words," *Locating and Correcting Reading Difficulties*

(Columbus, Ohio: Charles E. Merrill, 1981), pp. 170–171.

3. E. Fry, "The New Instant Word List," *Reading Teacher*, 34 (December 1980), 284–289.

4. Jerry L. Johns, "A Supplement to the Dolch Word Lists," *Reading Improvement*, 7 (Winter 1971–1972), 91.

5. M. Graves, "Selecting Vocabulary to Teach in the Intermediate and Secondary Grades," in *Promoting Reading Comprehension*, ed. James Flood (Newark, Del.: International Reading Association, 1984), pp. 245–260.

6. Peter A. Dewitz, Mary Jo Jenning, and Judythe P. Patberg, "The Effects of Content Area Reading Instruction on Teacher Behavior," in *Reading in the Content Areas: Application of a Concept*, ed. Judythe P. Patberg (Toledo, Ohio: University of Toledo, 1982). Nicholas P. Criscuolo, Richard T. Vacca, and Joseph J. Lavorgna, "What Reading Strategies Make Sense to Content Area Teachers?" *Reading World*, 19 (1980), 269–270.

7. Wilma H. Miller, *Diagnosis and Correction of Reading Difficulties in Secondary School Students* (New York: The Center for Applied Research in Education, 1973), p. 140.

8. Patricia Cunningham, "Investigating a Synthesized Theory of Mediated Word Identification," *Reading Research Quarterly*, 11 (1975–76), 127–143.

9. E. Hanson, J. D. Lockard, and P. F. Jensch, *Biology: The Science of Life* (Boston: Houghton Mifflin Company, 1980), p. 135.

10. Edgar Dale, *The Word Game: Improving Communications*, Fastback 60 (Bloomington, Ind.: Phi Delta Kappa Educational Foundation, 1975), p. 5.

11. Isabel Beck, Charles Perfetti, and Margaret McKeown, "Effects of Long-Term Vocabulary Instruction on Lexical Access and Reading Comprehension," *Journal of Educational Psychology*, 74, No. 4 (1982), 506–521. Edward Kameenui, Douglas Carnine, and Roger Freschi, "Effects of Text Construction and Instructional Procedures for Teaching Word Meanings on Comprehension and Recall," *Reading Research Quarterly*, 17, No. 3 (1982), 367–388. Robert Crist and Joseph Petrone, "Learning Concepts from Contexts and Definitions," *Journal of Reading Behavior*, 9 (1981), 301–303.

12. A. V. Mazo and J. K. Sherk, "Some Generalizations and Strategies for Guiding Vocabulary Learning," *Journal of Reading Behavior*, IV (Winter 1971–72), 78.

13. Wesley Becker, "Teaching Reading and Language to the Disadvantaged—What We Have Learned from Field Research," *Harvard Educational Review*, 47 (1977), 518–543.

14. Eileen Carr and Karen K. Wixson, "Guidelines for Evaluating Vocabulary Instruction," *Journal of Reading*, 29 (April 1986), 588–595. Camille Blachowicz, "Vocabulary Development and Reading: From Research to Instruction," *The Reading Teacher* 38 (May 1985), 876–881.

15. John Carroll, "Words, Meanings, and Concepts," *Harvard Educational Review*, 34 (Spring 1964), 1, 180, 181, 193–194.

16. Richard C. Anderson, "Vocabulary Knowledge," in *Comprehension and Teaching: Research Reviews*, ed. John Guthrie (Newark, Del.: International Reading Association, 1981), pp. 77–117.

17. Ibid.

18. M. Haggard, "Vocabulary Acquisition During Elementary and Post-Elementary Years: A Preliminary Report." *Reading Horizons*, 21 (Fall 1980), 61–69.

19. Patricia L. Anders and Candace S. Bos, "Semantic Feature Analysis: An Interactive Strategy for Vocabulary Development and Text Comprehension," *Journal of Reading*, 29 (April 1986), 610–616.

20. Edgar Dale and Joseph O'Rourke, *Techniques of Teaching Vocabulary* (Palo Alto, Calif.: Field Educational Publications, 1971), p. 20.

21. Ibid.

22. Barbara D. Stoodt and Elvira Balbo, "Integrating Study Skills Instruction with Content in a Secondary Classroom," *Reading World*, 18 (March 1979), 247–252.

23. Blachowicz, pp. 876–881.

24. Joan Gipe and Richard Arnold, "Teaching Vocabulary Through Familiar Associations and Contexts," *Journal of Reading Behavior*, XI, No. 3 (Fall 1979), 281–285. M. C. Wittrock, C. Marks, and M. Doctorow, "Reading as a Generative Process," *Journal of Educational Psychology*, 67 (1975), 484–489.

25. Blachowicz, pp. 876–881. Elaine Kaplan and Anita Tuchman, "Vocabulary Strategies Belong in the Hands of Learners," in *Classroom Strategies for Secondary Reading*, 2nd ed., ed. W. John Harker (Newark, Del.: International Reading Association, 1985), pp. 80–83.

26. Carr and Wixson, pp. 588–595.

27. Ibid.

28. Lee Deighton, *Vocabulary Development in the Classroom* (New York: Teachers College Press, 1970), p. 17.

29. Victor M. Rentel, "Concept Formation and Reading," *Reading World*, 10 (December 1971), 111–119.

30. Edgar Dale, *Audiovisual Methods in Teaching*, 3rd ed. (New York: The Dryden Press, 1969), p. 33.

31. Barbara Bellows, "Running Shoes Are to Jogging As Analogies Are to Creative/Critical Thinking," *Journal of Reading*, 23 (March 1980), 507–511.

32. Matthew F. Ignoffo, "The Thread of Thought: Analogies as a Vocabulary Building Method," *Journal of Reading*, 23 (March 1980), 519–521.

33. Timothy P. Warner, "Vocabulary: Make It a Stimulant, Not a Depressant," *Journal of Reading*, 15 (May 1972), 590–592.

34. William Morris, ed., *The American Heritage Dictionary* (Boston: Houghton Mifflin Company, 1969), p. 413.

35. Jean Gillet and Charles Temple, "Developing Word Knowledge: A Cognitive View," *Reading World*, 18 (December 1978), 132–140.

36. Ibid.

37. Richard Barron, "The Use of Vocabulary as an Advance Organizer," in *Research in Reading in the Content Area: First Year Report*, ed. Harold Herber and Peter Sanders (Syracuse: Syracuse University Press, 1969), pp. 29–39.

38. David Ausubel, *Educational Psychology: A Cognitive View*, 2nd ed. (New York: Holt, Rinehart and Winston, 1978), pp. 523–525.

39. Barron, "Use of Vocabulary," pp. 29–30.

40. Dale D. Johnson and P. David Pearson, *Teaching Vocabulary* (New York: Holt, Rinehart and Winston, 1978), pp. 45–46.

41. Deighton, p. 26.

42. Richard T. Vacca, *Content Area Reading* (Boston: Little, Brown and Company, 1981), p. 78.

43. Dale, *The Word Game*, p. 10.

44. W. Matthews, C. Roy, R. Stevenson, M. Harris, D. Hesser, and W. Dexter, *Investigating the Earth*, 4th ed. (Boston: Houghton Mifflin Company, 1984), p. 184.

45. P. McFarland, F. Feagin, S. Hay, S. Liu, F. McLaughlin, and N. Willson, *Focus on Literature: Viewpoints* (Boston: Houghton Mifflin Company, 1978), p. 281.

46. J. Morton and R. Rezny, *Consumer Action* (Boston: Houghton Mifflin Company, 1978), p. 101.

47. Edgar Dale and Joseph O'Rourke, *Techniques of Teaching Vocabulary* (Addison, Ill.: Field Educational Publications, 1971), p. 234.

SELECTED REFERENCES

Afflerbach, Peter P., Richard L. Allington, and Sean A. Walmsley. "A Basic Vocabulary of U.S. Federal Program Applications and Forms." *Journal of Reading*, 23 (January 1980), 332–336.

Anders, Patricia L., and Candace S. Bos. "Semantic Feature Analysis: An Interactive Strategy for Vocabulary Development and Text Comprehension." *Journal of Reading*, 29 (April 1986), 610–616.

Atkinson, Rhonda Holt, and Debbie Guice Longman. "Sniglets: Give a Twist to Teenage and Adult Vocabulary Instruction." *Journal of Reading*, 29 (November 1985), 103–105.

Barrett, Mary T., and Michael Graves. "Vocabulary Program for Junior High School Remedial Readers." *Journal of Reading*, 23 (November 1981), 145–151.

Bellows, Barbara. "Running Shoes Are to Jogging As Analogies Are to Creative/Critical Thinking." *Journal of Reading*, 23 (March 1980), 507–511.

Blachowicz, Camille, L. Z. "Making Connections: Alternatives to the Vocabulary Notebook." *Journal of Reading*, 29 (April 1986), 643–649.

————. "Vocabulary Development and Reading: From Research to Instruction." *The Reading Teacher*, 38 (May 1985), 876–881.

Brandreth, Gyles. *The Joy of Lex.* New York: Quill, 1983.

Carr, Eileen M. "The Vocabulary Overview Guide: A Metacognitive Strategy to Improve Vocabulary Comprehension and Retention." *Journal of Reading*, 28 (May 1985), 684–689.

Carr, Eileen, and Karen K. Wixson. "Guidelines for Evaluating Vocabulary Instruction." *Journal of Reading*, 29 (April 1986), 588–595.

Clark, Wilma. "Twenty Hours of Activities in Vocabulary Building for High Potential Students." *English Journal*, 70 (September 1981), 16–21.

Daines, Delva. *Reading in the Content Areas: Strategies for Teachers.* Glenview, Ill.: Scott, Foresman and Company, 1982. Chapter 6.

Dale, Edgar, and Joseph O'Rourke. *Techniques of Teaching Vocabulary.* Palo Alto, Calif.: Field Educational Publications, 1971.

DuBois, Diane, and Carole Stice. "Comprehension Instruction: Let's Recall It for Repair." *Reading World*, 20 (March 1981), 173–184.

Duffelmeyer, Frederick A. "The Effect of Context Clues on the Vocabulary Test Performance of Word Dominant and Paragraph Dominant Readers." *Journal of Reading*, 27 (March 1984), 508–513.

Early, Margaret, and Diane J. Sawyer. *Reading to Learn in Grades 5 to 12.* New York: Harcourt Brace Jovanovich, 1984. Chapter 12.

Frager, Alan M. "An 'Intelligence' Approach to Vocabulary Teaching." *Journal of Reading*, 28 (November 1984), 160–165.

Grubaugh, Steven, and Roy Molesworth, Jr. "Teaching Vocabulary and Developing Concepts in Health." *Journal of Reading*, 23 (February 1980), 402–432.

Guthrie, John, ed. *Comprehension and Teaching: Research Reviews*. Newark, Del.: International Reading Association, 1981.

Haggard, Martha Rapp. "The Vocabulary Self-Collection Strategy: An Active Approach to Word Learning." *Journal of Reading*, 26 (December 1982), 203–207.

Henry, George H. *Teaching Reading as Concept Development: Emphasis on Affective Thinking*. Newark, Del.: International Reading Association, 1974.

Ignoffo, Matthew F. "The Thread of Thought: Analogies as a Vocabulary Building Method." *Journal of Reading*, 23 (March 1980), 519–521.

Kaplan, Elaine M., and Anita Tuchman. "Vocabulary Strategies Belong in the Hands of Learners." In *Classroom Strategies for Secondary Reading*. 2nd ed. Ed. W. John Harker. Newark, Del.: International Reading Association, 1985, pp. 80–83.

Memory, David M. "Planning Content." In *Inservice Education for Content Area Teachers*. Ed. Mary Dunn Siedow, David M. Memory, and Page S. Bristow. Newark, Del.: International Reading Association, 1985, pp. 75–95.

Nelson-Herber, Joan. "Expanding and Refining Vocabulary in Content Areas." *Journal of Reading*, 29 (April 1986), 626–633.

Powell, William R. "Teaching Vocabulary Through Opposition." *Journal of Reading*, 29 (April 1986), 617–621.

Robinson, H. Alan. *Teaching Reading and Study Strategies*. 2nd ed. Boston: Allyn and Bacon, 1978. Chapter 5.

Shepherd, David L. *Comprehensive High School Reading Methods*. 3rd ed. Columbus, Ohio: Charles E. Merrill, 1982. Chapter 2.

Vacca, Richard T., and Jo Anne L. Vacca. *Content Area Reading*. Boston: Little, Brown and Company, 1986. Chapter 3.,

Wallenchinsky, D., I. Wallace, and A. Wallace. *The Book of Lists*. New York: Dell, 1984.

CHAPTER
T H R E E

READING COMPREHENSION

OVERVIEW

Reading comprehension—understanding written content—is the essence of the reading act. This chapter focuses on reading comprehension instruction for secondary students, addressing the aspects of reading comprehension, which include predicting, inferencing, metacognition, schemata, and organizational patterns. Strategies for developing reading comprehension are also explored.

PURPOSE-SETTING QUESTIONS

As you read this chapter, try to answer these questions:

1. In your own words, how would you explain reading comprehension?
2. Why should content teachers be concerned about reading comprehension?
3. What are the major components of reading comprehension for secondary students?
4. Which teaching strategies will help secondary students comprehend?
5. How is metacognition related to the reading comprehension process?

KEY VOCABULARY

As you read this chapter, check your understanding of these terms:

comprehension	structure
interpretation (inference)	main idea
literal	critical (evaluative)
schemata	metacognition
visualization	

WHAT IS READING COMPREHENSION?

The ultimate goal of secondary reading instruction is developing reading maturity. Reading comprehension is a major aspect of reading maturity and of fluent reading. Although there are many aspects of reading that are controversial, the importance of reading comprehension is not questioned: it is universally agreed that students cannot learn unless they can comprehend reading material, and they cannot remember what they have read unless they have understood it. Content reading is the application of comprehension skills to content reading materials.

Reading comprehension is a covert process because it cannot be observed directly. When we examine reading comprehension, we are dealing largely with the product of this process. Students can discuss reading content, answer questions, and verbalize how they have arrived at answers, but their actual mental process is not observable. A good way to explore the process of reading comprehension is through self-examination of one's own reading experiences. The passage that follows will help you think about your own reading comprehension experiences because it illustrates a reading incident experienced by a mature reader.

As the reader sat down with a cup of coffee and the newspaper, her eyes fell on the front-page headline that read: BRRR BOWL . . . ZIP WIN WARMS FANS. The reader knew from this headline that she was reading sports news because her schemata (background knowledge) provided the information that the word *Zip* referred to the University of Akron football team, which is called "The Zips," an abbreviation for "Zeppelins." The team is so named because zeppelins are made of rubber, and Akron, Ohio, is the "rubber capital of the world." Knowing that she was reading sports news gave this reader a mental set (expectation) to read quickly and superficially because she was not an enthusiastic sports fan. However, this story was about an important local game and would provide information to discuss with friends and relatives. Obtaining such information was one of her reasons for reading about the topic.

Recognizing that she was reading sports news also created in the reader a mental set for the way that sports news is organized. The headline stating that the "Zip win warms fans" indicated that the University of Akron team had won the game. "Brr bowl" and "warms fans" also indicated that the game was played in very cold weather. This was about all of the information that the reader wanted regarding the game. However, she remembered that she had overheard a conversation about the fact that the team was playing in championship competition, so she established another purpose for reading the article: to find out what title the Zips were competing for. She skimmed the first two paragraphs of the story and learned that the team had played in the National Semifinal game for the NCAA Division II teams. At this point, she decided that she would like to find out how close the score of the game was, so she scanned the third paragraph for numerals indicative of a game score: it said there that the score was 29 to 26 in an overtime game. The reader had satisfied her purposes for reading and decided that she was disappointed that she had missed such an exciting game.

Although this is an account of just one reading experience, with only one type of content that was read for rather specific purposes, examining it gives us considerable insight into reading comprehension. Notice that the reader did not read the first word in the headline first. Her eyes moved to a meaningful word, *Zip*, a noun that enabled her to predict the type of content. The fact that this was sports news created a mental set for the type of reading in which the reader knew she should engage. Reading this one word also enabled the reader to predict the topic of the article. Reading a few more words enabled the reader to use her store of information (schemata) to predict accurately a large portion of the article, which covered one-third of the front page of the newspaper. Detailed reading confirmed the predictions that the reader made on the basis of her sampling of text information and her schemata. The reader used her knowledge of the organization of sports information to achieve her three reading purposes. She inferred that the quickest way to determine the score of the game was to scan the article for numbers. She responded critically to the information—she regretted missing the game.

This reader used schemata (background information), semantic and syntactic knowledge, and thinking skills to comprehend. She used strategies for understanding that included establishing purposes for reading; relating schemata to reading content; thinking at literal, inferential, critical, and creative levels; reading for main ideas and details. She integrated previous knowledge regarding the Zips, football, and the weather with new knowledge acquired from reading. This brief analysis reveals some of the complexities of reading comprehension and shows how the reader brought to written content knowledge and skill that enabled her to comprehend what she read.

The following sections of this chapter examine aspects of comprehension, the structure of selections, and approaches teachers can take to help students comprehend content materials. Although most secondary students can read, they may not have learned how to use their reading skills to understand the different types of content found in textbooks. The pages that follow explore general comprehension; later chapters address the demands of specific content area materials.

Reading comprehension is a complex, interactive process. The reader uses his or her schemata (abstract knowledge structures),[1] purposes, skills, and experiences as he or she interacts with written language to construct meaning.[2] Whether we are aware of it or not, new information interacts with old knowledge in comprehension. "To say that one has comprehended a text is to say that he or she has found a mental 'home' for the information in the text, or else that he or she has modified an existing mental home in order to accommodate that new information."[3]

The major aspects of comprehension include prediction, schemata, inferencing, and metacognition. An overview of these aspects is provided in the following paragraphs. Each of these topics is later explained in greater depth.

Prediction strategies are very important in reading comprehension: they enable readers to anticipate both the way an author will present ideas and the actual ideas that will be presented. Prediction also helps readers build expectations about the author's message and allows the interpretation of content within an appropriate frame of reference. Research shows that good readers predict more frequently than poor readers.[4] Research also shows that prediction strategies facilitate comprehension.[5]

Schemata also play an important role in reading comprehension. As the fluent reader processes text information, familiar ideas trigger certain schemata, which represent knowledge about a topic, thing, place, idea, and so forth, that comes from prior experience and learning. A schema is a package of knowledge coupled with information about how this knowledge can be used.[6] Research shows that experience is a powerful determinant of reading comprehension.[7]

Inferencing (reading between the lines) is one of the central processes in reading comprehension. In fact, readers infer throughout the reading comprehension process. Readers employ several types of inferences as they comprehend.[8] For instance they infer which schemata are related to the reading selection, and they infer the relationship between the ideas in the reading selection and the ideas in their existing schemata.

Metacognition is knowing when one has understood. Readers use metacognition skills to monitor their understanding. Readers can take steps to correct the gaps in their understanding when they are aware of these failures to understand.

In addition to the aspects of comprehension, the structure of reading selections plays an important role in readers' comprehension. The common structural elements are discussed in the latter part of this chapter.

A number of processes are involved in reading comprehension. However, these processes should not be viewed as sequential steps because they often occur instantaneously and simultaneously. Following is a model of reading comprehension based upon the processes involved:

1. The reader orients him- or herself to the material to be read. He or she acquires a mind set for reading to understand and identifies the type of content and the topic. Readers should have guiding purposes for reading;[9] they should recognize whether they are reading narrative or expository text, and they should grasp the topic of the selection. Reading a narrative requires different skills than reading exposition. Students have to learn how to comprehend different types of content.

2. The reader activates schemata related to the topic and the type of content. In order to activate schemata, the reader must infer the schemata that are most relevant to the reading selection. A schema is a package of knowledge coupled with information about how this knowledge can be used.[10] Schemata are acquired from experience; therefore, if a reader has no experience related to a subject, he or she would not have schemata related to that subject. The reader must invoke schemata to decide how his or her schemata are related to the text.[11] For example, a student who is reading about railroads would activate his or her schemata regarding railroads. This enables the reader to relate the ideas he or she reads to his or her prior knowledge.

3. The reader uses schemata to hypothesize about text organization and meaning. Using his or her background experiences as organized into schemata, the reader forms hypotheses that predict the way an author will present ideas and the actual ideas that will be presented. Prediction also helps the reader create expectations about the author's message. Anticipating the author's ideas increases comprehension.[12] As the reader proceeds through the reading selection, he or she confirms and discounts predictions. The reader may need to modify existing schemata to incorporate new information for future reference.

4. The reader processes content, giving more weight to important ideas and information than to less important ideas. Important text elements are more likely to be learned and remembered than less important elements.[13]

5. The reader relates the new meaning derived from reading to his or her existing knowledge regarding the topic[14] and self-monitors (i.e., uses metacognition) his or her understanding.[15] If the reader finds that this understanding is not adequate for his or her purposes, he or she will infer that it is necessary to reread and/or rethink parts of the selection in order to achieve greater understanding.

Prediction

Efficient readers predict the words and ideas that will follow what they have already read, forming hypotheses about what the text will say and reading to see if these hypotheses are confirmed. When their hypotheses are not confirmed, students must read carefully to learn what the author does say. Prediction helps students look for the author's meaning; it also helps them concentrate on important ideas and eliminate unrelated ones. The predictions they have made based on their schemata enable them to sort out the important from the unimportant ideas. Thus, schemata are necessary to prediction.

Students who have many experiences as a foundation for schemata will be able to anticipate the author's ideas and words better than students whose experiences are very limited. In addition, students must make inferences to identify the schemata that are related to the content they are reading. You may refer to later sections of this chapter regarding activating schemata.

Schemata

The various suggestions for developing schemata that are presented in this section are also helpful for motivating students to become active readers. Schemata are related to an individual's experiential background, and when a student is acquainted with a topic he or she is usually more motivated to read related content.

A *schema* is a cognitive structure or organization of the knowledge one has related to an idea, thing, or concept. "A schema, quite simply put, is an abstraction of reality."[16]

Schemata are the products of individual experiences; therefore, they vary from individual to individual. We use schemata to cluster the memory representations of experience and knowledge about a certain topic.[17] Anyone who flies frequently has schemata of airplanes, the procedures involved in flying, and of airports—the airport's counter for purchasing tickets and checking baggage, the boarding gate, and the baggage-claim area, for example. These schemata have been developed from experiences. When an individual enters a new airport, he or she uses schemata to identify the specific locations of the ticket window, baggage-claim area, and boarding gate, which are located in different places in every airport. Thus, old knowledge about airports is integrated with newly acquired knowledge. We regularly revise schemata to incorporate new information. For example, most of us revised our schemata of airports to accommodate the addition of security procedures that require the x-raying of carry-on baggage.

Content Schemata

Content schemata help a reader make sense of written content by providing a context or frame of reference. For instance, a home economics student who has cooking experience has schemata that will help him or her comprehend a cooking text. Content schemata help us anticipate an author's ideas and provide a cognitive framework for relating what we know to what we read. By using content schemata, readers can organize, understand, and remember content.

Since they involve knowledge of the world, content schemata are extremely important for the comprehension of content materials. Students who have not had experiences in a certain area lack the schemata necessary to understand content topics in that particular area. One has only to reflect on how different a sports-loving student's comprehension of the sports section of the newspaper is from his or her understanding of a chapter of ancient history to see how important schemata are for comprehension: when reading the sports section, a fan can use schemata that he or she has developed from years of experience. This same student may not have had experiences that would develop his or her schemata for ancient history. Consequently, to aid comprehension, teachers must help students develop schemata for content topics.

Textual Schemata

Textual schemata are composed of a reader's knowledge of the structural characteristics of written content. "Textual schemata provide the general outline for material which we read. For example, we expect a newspaper article to have a special form, and that form is quite different from a research article."[18] In a well-written research article, we know where to find the review of related literature, the methods used, and the results of the study. Readers use their knowledge of a particular form of writing to predict, follow, and organize the materials they read. Research by Oaken, Wiener, and Cromer shows that organization of content is an important component of reading comprehension.[19] Rothkopf also identified the important role of text organization in comprehension.[20] A content teacher can help students understand reading material by teaching them to perceive text organization and the thought relationships reflected in the organization of various types of texts.

Expository content materials are structured by sentences, paragraphs, and passage organization. Literature, which is the content material of English classes, is structured by plot, theme, setting, characters, and episodes. Students are more familiar with the textual schemata of literature than with the textual schemata of expository content; therefore this chapter concentrates on developing the textual schemata of expository content in order to help teachers increase students' reading comprehension.

Readers can have schemata about anything in the world; however, schemata of discourse are of particular interest with regard to the development of reading comprehension. We develop schemata of different types of discourse as a result of experience with different types of discourse. Textual schemata for stories are called *story grammars* and are composed of the structural components of a story. Although they have been described in different ways by different researchers, one example of a story grammar is this: story→setting + theme + plot + resolution.[21] The structure of expository discourse is concerned with the organization of subordinate ideas and superordinate ideas. Thus sentences, paragraphs, and overall structure of a selection are important aspects of comprehension. Research indicates that teaching schemata of content organization does improve comprehension.[22]

Activating Schemata

Activating schemata involves recalling existing schemata that are related to a specific subject and relating these schemata to the content being read. When students activate appropriate schemata, they are in a better position to anticipate the author's ideas and information. Readers do not automatically use schemata to increase understanding. Activating appropriate schemata enables students to make inferences regarding content (to fill in missing ideas and information) when the author does not concretely explain ideas. Teachers can use a variety of activities to encourage students to activate appropriate schemata. Strategies for activating schemata are discussed later in this chapter.

Inferencing

Harris and Hodges define inferencing as "the process of inferring beyond the literal meaning of a communication; inferred meaning; reading between the lines."[23] Classically, in cognitive psychology and artificial intelligence, inference is thought of as filling in the missing connections between the surface structure fragments of the text by recourse to context and knowledge about the world."[24] In order to make inferences, the reader must use the explicit information and ideas provided in a reading selection and relate these data to his or her schemata. With the knowledge stored in his or her schemata, the reader is able to fill in missing pieces of information and to go beyond the information in the selection.

Therefore, the reader's prior knowledge, which is the basis of these schemata, is an important component of the inferencing skill.[25] The reader starts reading a selection using the schemata triggered by the title, pictures, or statements made in the early part of the selection. As the reader progresses through a reading selection, he or she raises questions regarding the content, answers the questions by relating the new facts to information stored in his or her schemata, and incorporates an increasing amount of the content from the reading selection into his or her understanding.[26] This process is demonstrated in the following paragraph.

An excerpt from an earth science text reads, "When water boils, bubbles appear and rise to the surface. These bubbles are made up of water vapor, which is an invisible gas. You see the holes where the water isn't in its liquid form."[27] A reader who is studying this selection should activate his or her schemata regarding water and the water cycle. The reader might raise questions like the following:

1. Do the bubbles rise to the surface because they are lighter than water in its liquid form?
2. What makes the water change form during boiling?
3. Why is water vapor important?
4. Will water vapor change back to liquid water?

The reader determines the answers from the text and other sources and incorporates information into his or her schemata.

Poor readers do not routinely and spontaneously make inferences.[28] However, research shows that inferencing ability is amenable to instruction. C. J. Gordon found that inferencing ability increased with direct instruction and practice.[29] Raphael and Pearson successfully improved the inferencing abilities of a group of students with a strategy that guided the students to consciously classify the information they needed to answer questions.[30] The students were given statements and questions about those statements and were asked to determine whether the needed information was provided "right there" or whether it was necessary to "think and search" or to find the information "on their own."[31] An example of this type of exercise follows.

"Water vapor condenses when it is cooled, but at ordinary temperatures it requires solid surfaces to condense on."[32]

1. Why does water vapor require solid surfaces to condense on?
2. What kind of solid surfaces does it need to condense on?
3. What causes water vapor to condense?

Metacognition

Monitoring one's own cognitive processes and products and regulating these processes is called metacognition.[33] The ultimate goal of reading instruction is to develop independent readers who comprehend. To reach this goal, readers must not only recognize that their purpose determines how they should read, which may range from deep, active reading to skimming, but they must also monitor their own comprehension; in other words, they must be conscious of when they have comprehended and when they have not. When they are aware that they have lost understanding, they must "debug" the process, as demonstrated in the following example.

A student read a selection that introduced sampling in a mathematics text. Her purpose was to understand sampling as a basis for statistical analysis. She asked herself questions to ascertain whether she had met her purpose. She realized that she understood the overall process but that she could not define the terms *variance, population,* and *population parameter.* Thus, she was aware of what she understood and what she did not understand and was able to reread to find this information. Such self-regulation requires awareness of one's cognitive processes.

Competent readers, aware of the reading demands of given assignments, identify important parts of the text and focus on them rather than on insignificant parts. The example presented in the preceding paragraph demonstrated this process; the reader recognized the importance of focusing on the terms related to the process she was learning. Readers who consciously coordinate thought and reading are using metacognitive skills.[34] Poor readers do not seem to be aware that they have failed to comprehend.[35] They read assignments but do not think about their understanding of what they have read. Competent readers have better developed metacognitive skills, and they are active comprehenders.[36]

Teachers can use several strategies to teach students to monitor their own reading comprehension, thereby helping students acquire metacognitive skills. Generally speaking, each of these strategies is designed to cause students to read actively, to become involved with the content.[37]

One strategy is modeling the metacognitive process. A demonstration of the modeling process is given later in this chapter. Teachers often find it helpful to use content in their own subject areas to demonstrate metacognition since they have a larger background of experience with that content. A transparency of a reading selection can be prepared for use on an overhead or opaque projector, which can project text material for the class. Then the instructor can proceed through the content discussing his or her thoughts.

Instructing students to make summaries of the content they read can also help them develop metacognitive skills. Exact specification of summarization rules is very helpful to students. See Chapter 4 for additional information regarding summaries.

Content Organization

An author uses specific patterns of organization to structure the ideas presented in a reading selection. The five patterns that reading researchers have emphasized are time order (chronological), list structure, comparison-contrast, cause-effect, and problem solution.[38] However, further analysis reveals that these patterns are often used in combination with other patterns, including narrative, description, example, process, definition, and classification.[39] When readers explore organizational structure they are getting to the gist of the text. They are actually processing the text mentally in a condensing procedure in order to summarize the material.[40] Readers also can use structure to preview a selection to identify the author's major ideas and purposes before reading. Using structure in this manner helps readers recall important ideas.

Research reveals that students who understand the various patterns of discourse have increased recall and understanding of content. In addition, researchers report that readers who use the author's top-level organizational structure (the basic structure of the text) as an aid to comprehension tend to perform better on recall, summarization, and other comprehension tasks than readers who do not use this structure.[41] However, one study also showed that 80 percent of the college freshmen examined were not aware of organizational patterns in textbooks.[42] This is a disappointing figure when one realizes that students can learn to effectively use structural (content) schemata.[43] Researchers have also found that training students to recognize organizational patterns aids in their identification of main ideas.[44] In the following sections, organizational patterns of both selections and paragraphs are explored further. Examples of the most common organizational patterns follow.

1. *Sequential or chronological order:* Paragraphs in sequential or chronological order present information in the order of its occurrence because this order clarifies the ideas presented. The reader should use the time or sequential order pattern to organize the information presented for recall. Some words that may signal this organization are *after, also, along, before, begin, beyond, during, first, finally, next, now, second, then, third, until,* and *when.* The following is an example of a paragraph based on chronological order:

   The Federalist Party disappears. During Jefferson's administrations the Republican Party grew stronger. The Republicans elected the next two Presidents—James Madison, who served from 1809 to 1817, and James Monroe, who was President from 1817 to 1825. During these years, on the other hand, the Federalist Party became weaker and weaker. Finally, in Monroe's first term, it disappeared, and Monroe was re-elected without opposition. Because there was only one political party, the years of Monroe's presidency are called the *Era of Good Feeling.*[45]

2. *Comparison and contrast:* An author can use comparison and contrast to clarify certain points. The reader should keep the following questions in mind: What is the author's main idea? What similarities and/or differences does he or she use to illustrate the point? Students can make tables to list the similarities and differences. Some words that may signal this pattern are *although, but, yet, nevertheless, meanwhile, however, on the other hand, otherwise, compared to, despite,* and *similarly.* Following is an example of a paragraph that uses the comparison and contrast pattern:

   Some individual health policies are filled with loopholes. The average individual health policy pays out only 50 per cent of the premiums in benefits—compared to 90 per cent for group insurance plans. Sales commissions, other costs, and profits eat up the remainder of the premiums of individual plans.

Mail-order health plans are usually the worst buy. This insurance is advertised in newspapers, on television, and by direct mail. Consumers Union says that some of these policies return only a third of their premiums in benefits.[46]

3. *Cause and effect:* Authors use this pattern to help readers understand relationships among facts and ideas. The reader must be able to identify both the causes and the related effects. Authors may imply rather than state causes and effects. The following words may signal cause and effect: *because* or forms of the verb *cause, since, so, that, thus, therefore, if, consequently, as a result.* An example of a cause and effect paragraph follows:

When your body produces an antibody in response to an invading pathogen, the antibody protects you against a disease. It works for your benefit. Antibodies can also be produced in response to other materials such as pollen, the yellow powder produced by the male reproductive organs of some plants. If you have an **allergy**, your body is extra sensitive to certain substances. It works against you. Antibodies react with the pollen, dust, or other substance. A chemical called **histamine** (HIHS tuh meen) is produced. Histamine causes the symptoms of allergy, including sneezing, coughing, and itching. Antihistamines, the major medicines for relieving symptoms of allergies, block some of the effects of histamine.[47]

4. *Definition or explanation:* With this pattern, which is also known as the main idea and supporting details pattern, paragraphs are developed to explain a concept or to define a term. The reader should be alert for paragraphs of definition and note them for future reference because they are basic to understanding in many of the content areas. An example follows:

Gravitational force pulls together masses of gas and dust into these clouds in many places in space. **Gravitational force** is the attraction that pulls things toward one another. You experience gravitation every day. Because of it, your pencil falls to the floor when you let it go. Gravitation brings a pole-vaulter back to Earth and makes it hard for you to learn to ride a bike. The particles in the dust cloud attract each other because of gravitation. As time passes, all the matter in the cloud is crowded into a smaller space. When the particles begin to squeeze each other, the temperature in the dense part of the cloud rises higher and higher. The cloud begins to glow with a reddish color, like a burner on an electric stove or the wires in a toaster.[48]

5. *Enumeration or simple listing pattern:* Paragraphs in this pattern list pieces of information (facts, ideas, and so forth) either in order of importance or simply in logical order. The reader must determine the relative importance of the items listed. Clues to this pattern are the words *one, two, first, second, third, to begin, next, finally, most important, when, also, too,* and *then.*

Chemical energy is a stored form of energy. Fuels such as coal, oil, and natural gas have chemical energy. When they are burned, the energy is released as heat and light. Batteries also have chemical energy. Cars, portable radios, and other battery-operated devices convert chemical energy to electric energy. Food, too, has stored energy. Your body changes the chemical energy in food to heat and mechanical energy.[49]

Organization of Selections

Just as sentences are organized into paragraphs, paragraphs are organized into selections—longer units of discourse. In content reading, we are concerned largely with expository discourse, which is explanatory in nature. The patterns used to organize paragraphs are also used to organize selections (and portions of selections). At times three or four paragraphs are used to create a comparison pattern or one of the other organizational patterns. These patterns can be identified and interpreted in the same ways as they are for paragraphs; the major difference is in the length of the unit.

Well-written expository content—such as chapters in content textbooks—begins with an introductory section, which previews the topic to be discussed. This introduction can be compared to an inverted triangle, because it starts with a broad, general idea of the topic and narrows the topic to a more specific point. This section may be developed in a variety of ways, including comparison, cause and effect, and so forth.

The second part of a selection is the body, which develops the ideas that have been introduced in the first section. Each of the paragraphs that make up the body usually has a main idea and details that relate to the topic presented in the introductory section. These paragraphs may be developed through any organizational pattern.

The chapter or selection usually concludes with a summary paragraph that pulls together the ideas presented in the body. A triangle can be used to illustrate this section, which begins with a specific idea and broadens as it develops. The

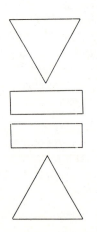

Introductory Section

Body

Summary Section

Figure 3.1

pattern of the summary is the reverse of that in the introductory section. A diagram of a selection based on this pattern is shown in Figure 3.1.

Content teachers can use a textbook chapter to show students the introductory section, the body, and the summary section. Students should be encouraged to read the book's preface, because it usually identifies the author's organization. Then they can compare the author's organization as it is stated in the preface with the actual development of a chapter. Students should also learn to use the table of contents to help with their understanding of selection organization.

Content teachers can ask students to use the summary section of a chapter as a study outline, to which important details can be added. The table of contents for a chapter can be used in the same way.

Identifying the specific patterns of organization is not so important to readers as understanding the concept of text organization. The most valuable instructional use of textual schemata is to teach students to anticipate and follow the author's organization as they read. This will help them organize content so they can connect it to previous knowledge, aiding comprehension and memory.

Paragraph Comprehension

Paragraphs are groups of sentences that are interrelated. Because paragraphs are very important components of content materials, paragraph comprehension is essential for content students. The reader who comprehends successfully must adjust his or her thinking to the organization of the selection being read and must be able to follow the author's line of thought. "One key factor in the comprehension of text or narrative is paragraph structure. A story that is intriguing and a text that is understandable are composed of paragraphs that are clear and simple."[50] Stories should not be complicated by tangled paragraphs, and information should not be buried in badly composed paragraphs.

Paragraph structure is important to reading comprehension because well-developed paragraphs are easier to understand. A well-developed paragraph focuses on a single major topic; a logical, reasonable sequence of sentences is used to structure the paragraph. The sentences have coherence: they are related to the paragraph topic and to each other.[51] In contrast, a poorly organized paragraph does not establish a focus, and some sentences may introduce new ideas or information. Thus, these sentences do not have coherence with the other sentences in the paragraph and may not be presented in a logical order.

Following are examples of a well-developed paragraph and a poorly developed paragraph.

Paragraph A

Flowers bloom throughout the world. They grow on high mountains at the edges of the snow. Other flowers grow in the shallow parts of oceans. Even hot, dry deserts have bright blossoms. The only places where flowers do not grow are the ice-covered areas of the Arctic and Antarctic and the open seas.

Paragraph B

Flowers are the reproductive parts of flowering plants. Flowers bloom throughout the world. They grow on high mountains and in the oceans. Many flowers have a smell that attracts birds and insects. Flowers bloom in the hot, dry desert during the rainy season. The only places flowers do not grow are the Arctic, Antarctic, and the open seas.

If you identified Paragraph A as the well-developed paragraph that is easier to understand, you are correct. Notice that this paragraph sticks to the subject—the fact that flowers grow throughout the world. The ideas are presented in a logical order, and the sentences have coherence. No loosely related ideas are introduced that divert the reader's attention.

Main Ideas and Details

The writing in most content area materials is structured around or built upon details and main ideas. The main idea of a paragraph is the big idea that the author develops and supports with details throughout the paragraph. Details are the smaller pieces of information or ideas that are used to support the "big idea." Pearson says that "the term main idea is but a main idea for a polyglot of tasks and relations among ideas."[52] Through research, Cunningham and Moore established the notion that the term *main idea* is not a single concept. They prefer to use *main idea* as an umbrella term to encompass nine specific types of main ideas that they have identified in their research.[53] These nine types of main idea tasks are the following:

1. Gist
2. Interpretation
3. Key word
4. Selective summary/selective diagram
5. Theme
6. Title
7. Topic issue
8. Topic sentence/thesis sentence
9. Other (unclassified responses)

The common thread holding these various types of main idea tasks together is the fact that each addresses important information. This significant research has expanded our concept of main idea. The types of main idea tasks can be used to guide students in identifying and stating main ideas.

Main ideas and organizational patterns are interrelated. Paragraphs can have organizational patterns such as cause and effect, contrast, or sequential order and express main ideas. For example, a paragraph in a cause and effect pattern has a main idea and supporting details that are expressed through cause and effect. The main idea of such a paragraph could be "causes and effects of erosion." The details would be the specific causes and effects. Similarily, in a paragraph with a comparison and contrast pattern, the details might be the contrasting points and the main idea the overall comparison.[54] Helping students identify this organizational pattern as comparison and contrast will help them generate (state) the main idea and comprehend the selection better.

Researchers have found that instructions that require students to generate the main idea of a selection or paragraph lead students to recall and understand the content better.[55] Therefore, whenever possible, students should be asked to write the main idea in their own words. Palinscar and Brown found that students who learned to summarize main ideas improved their ability to answer questions and to identify important information.[56] You may wish to refer to the summarization strategies suggested in Chapter 4. Strategies for teaching main idea are presented later in this chapter.

READING COMPREHENSION SKILLS

A skill is an acquired ability to perform a task well.[57] We support the notion that reading comprehension skills can and should be taught because students who have such skills read with greater understanding than students who lack these skills. This section explores research in the area of reading comprehension skills.

In a 1956 study, William Gray and Bernice Rogers provided a view of the mature reader that represents the most intensive study of mature readers available today; their findings are supported by more recent research.[58] Gray and Rogers identified the significant characteristics of mature reading skills and then, using these characteristics, developed and validated a scale for evaluating mature reading. Their scale assessed six major categories of information:

1. Interest in reading
2. Purposes for reading
3. Nature of material read
4. Reading comprehension
5. Thoughtful reaction to and use of the ideas read
6. Personal adjustment to reading

The scale was used to analyze case-study data for eighty adults; this analysis revealed that most of the adults demonstrated low levels of reading maturity —limited reading interests and low levels of reading comprehension. Overall, they showed a lack of breadth, interest, self-direction, and quality in personal reading. This discouraging picture of adult readers has been supported by Sharon.[59] Lyle reports similar results in research that correlates reading skill with income level.[60]

Frederick Davis studied secondary students' reading comprehension skills in order to identify the specific skills that constitute the reading comprehension process. He isolated the following skills:[61]

1. *Knowledge of word meanings:* using context to find appropriate word meaning; understanding figurative language

2. *Reasoning in reading:* the ability to think at different levels of reasoning regarding written content
3. *Concentration on literal sense meaning:* the ability to answer questions concerned with information directly stated in a selection
4. *Following the structure of a passage:* the ability to follow the structure of a passage, including identifying the main idea
5. *Recognizing the mood and literary techniques of a writer*

Thomas Barrett developed a popular Taxonomy of Reading Comprehension, which provides still another view of reading comprehension skills.[62] It includes the following levels and skills:

1. *Literal recognition or recall:* This aspect of comprehension is concerned with recognizing and recalling explicitly stated ideas and information. It includes recalling or recognizing details, main ideas, sequence, comparison, cause and effect, and character traits.
2. *Inference:* This type of comprehension requires that the reader not only synthesize previous knowledge with his or her literal comprehension of the content but also use thinking skills to hypothesize ideas that have not been stated in the content. This type of comprehension involves inferring details, main ideas, sequence, comparison, cause and effect, character traits, outcomes, and meanings for figurative expressions.[63]
3. *Evaluation:* This level of comprehension requires that readers make judgments about reading content by comparing it with criteria developed through experience, knowledge, reference materials, and resource persons. Readers are required to judge reality and fantasy, fact and opinion, adequacy and validity of content, appropriateness, and worth of content.
4. *Appreciation:* This type of comprehension is concerned with the reader's emotional reaction to various elements of content: plot, theme, characterization, story incidents, author's use of language and imagery.

Reading comprehension skills as identified and defined by many authors and researchers include specific skills that are applied at the literal, inferential, evaluative, and appreciation levels.[64] Reading comprehension skills are also related to units of writing including phrases, clauses, sentences, paragraphs, selections and/or stories. These elements are discussed later in this chapter.

Barak Rosenshine summarized a number of reading comprehension skill hierarchies in an effort to identify the most significant comprehension skills. He found consensus regarding seven skills, shown in the following list:[65]

1. Recognizing sequence
2. Recognizing words in context
3. Identifying the main idea
4. Decoding detail

5. Drawing inferences
6. Recognizing cause and effect
7. Comparing and contrasting

Rosenshine pointed out that these skills are not in a hierarchical order. Although there is some agreement among reading authorities regarding the identification of reading comprehension skills, "comprehension skills are simply not taught in hierarchical fashion."[66] In the actual reading process, skills and processes are used simultaneously. However, teachers find it necessary to focus on one skill at a time to help problem readers improve their comprehension. The balance of this chapter deals with instructional strategies and activities that teachers can use to help students develop and refine reading comprehension abilities, skills, and knowledge.

READING COMPREHENSION INSTRUCTION

Various researchers have identified the aspects of mature reading comprehension—the skills and abilities that readers need in order to comprehend and the knowledge that will help them read with understanding. Unfortunately, research has also demonstrated that many young people do not exhibit good reading comprehension; there is a clear need for teaching students how to comprehend content materials.

The following modeling strategy for teaching one part of reading comprehension, inferencing, was synthesized from the research presented in the first half of this chapter. This modeling technique can also be used in teaching each of the other aspects of reading comprehension. The subsequent sections of this chapter introduce other instructional strategies teachers can use to help students develop the various aspects of reading comprehension and reading comprehension skills.

Modeling as a Method of Teaching Reading Comprehension

Modeling is a "thinking aloud" strategy. Teachers verbalize their own thoughts while reading aloud. Davey calls these activities "think-alouds."[67] This strategy can be used to demonstrate the comprehension process or to demonstrate specific reading comprehension skills to students. Modeling is a powerful teaching technique.

Example 3.1 presents a "think-aloud" for inferencing, which is based on "The Landlady" by Roald Dahl.[68]

EXAMPLE 3.1 "THINK-ALOUD" FOR INFERENCING ━━━━━━

While the teacher reads the story or selection aloud, the students should follow along, reading the selection silently, listening to the teacher verbalize his or her thoughts.

Story Summary for the Beginning of the Story

Billy Weaver was searching for cheap lodging in London. The Bell and Dragon was recommended, but while on his way to this hotel, he noticed a BED and BREAKFAST sign in the window of a warm, inviting looking house. The house was so attractive and well cared for that he thought this lodging would be too expensive for him. He was about to turn away and go on to the hotel when..."Each word was like a large black eye staring at him through the glass, holding him, compelling him, forcing him to stay where he was and not to walk away from that house, and the next thing he knew, he was actually moving across from the window to the front door of the house, climbing the steps that led up to it, and reaching for the bell."

Modeling Dialogue

Teacher　From the title, I predict that this story will be a character sketch about an unusual landlady. The story seems quite ordinary until the part about each word staring at him like a large black eye. These visual images are unusual and they seem kind of mysterious. It seems that the author is preparing us for something unusual to happen. I expect strange things to happen because in other stories that I have read or seen on television, this kind of language usually signals unusual events and mounting suspense.

Teacher　The next hint of something unusual comes when the author says, "But this dame was like a jack-in-the-box. He pressed the bell—and out she popped! It made him jump." It seems to me that the landlady knew that Billy was at the door before he rang the bell. Billy seems to be feeling that something is strange, because he jumped. I can almost feel how tense he was because he did not know what was going to happen.

Teacher　The next hint of the unusual occurs in the following paragraph. Billy says, "I saw the notice in the window," and the landlady responds, "Yes, I know." Billy says, "I was wondering about a room," and the landlady replies, "It's all ready for you, my dear." She had a round pink face and very gentle blue eyes. Did you notice that she talked as if she knew he was coming? I would be very alert at this point for additional unexplained comments or events. This story is getting more and more mysterious. This is like a television show that I saw.

Teacher　Then they discuss the price. It was fantastically cheap—less than half of what Billy had been willing to pay. The landlady said, "If that is too much, then perhaps I can reduce it just a tiny bit." This sounds as if she is really determined to get Billy to stay with her no matter how low she has to make the price. This makes me even more suspicious. I would expect her to want more money for such a nice place. I am curious as to why she is so willing to cut her price.

Teacher   The author mentions twice that the landlady is strange. Billy thinks that she is "slightly off her rocker" and that she is "slightly dotty." He still thinks that she is harmless, though.

Teacher   When the landlady has Billy sign the guest book, he notices the other names and realizes that he knows the names for some reason that he cannot identify. However, the landlady assures him that he could not possibly know the preceding boarders. But his memory will not let go, and he finally remembers that the preceding boarders disappeared under strange circumstances. Then Billy does grow more tense. The fact that the landlady tries to divert his attention to the tea and to discuss other things makes me even more apprehensive. My experiences reading other stories and watching television and movies lead me to think that this is a strange situation and that Billy may be in danger.

Developing Active Reading

Active readers are motivated: they read with interest because they have a desire for knowledge that sustains them as they read and search for information. Active readers comprehend better than inactive readers.[69] Problem-solving strategies, controversial issues, and prereading questions help students to read actively.

Active reading strategies are used before students read a chapter or a unit in a textbook. They may be simple activities, such as having students in literature class read part of a story, develop hypotheses about the ending, and then read the rest of the selection to test their hypotheses against the way the author developed the story.

Another active reading strategy is to use a problem-solving approach. The teacher develops problem situations that will lead students to an understanding of significant points that relate to the content area. Reading to solve problems may be based on the textbook and/or related materials; if related materials are used, the teacher should prepare for students a bibliography of reference materials. After introducing the problem, the teacher should give students an opportunity to participate in a discussion period during which students may ask questions that will clarify the problem-solving reading activities. The teacher may help by developing questions that will guide the students' reading. Following are examples of problems that could be used in problem-solving reading activities.

Problem-Solving Activities
Social Studies

1a. When studying a Civil War unit, give students a quotation from a southern sympathizer and a quotation from a northern sympathizer. Then ask students to read to determine which point of view they believe is correct and why.

b. Ask students why people from the South refer to the "War between the States," while people from the North call it the "Civil War."

Science

2a. During a unit on environmental disease present the following problem: The water purification, sewage disposal, trash, and garbage collection procedures in Greensboro, North Carolina, were completely disrupted for a two-week period due to a tornado and resulting fires. What diseases would become rampant? Why?

b. Ask students what emergency measures could be taken to control the diseases identified in question *a*.

Industrial Arts

3. While studying a unit on lumber types and uses, give students the following problem: After showing them pictures of various buildings and pieces of furniture, ask them to identify the best type of wood for each item and to explain why they think that particular type would be best for the purpose.

Home Economics

4. When studying a unit on nutritional needs for individuals with various diseases, pose the following problem to students: Plan menus for individuals who have diabetes, an allergy to milk, and an allergy to wheat.

Controversial issues provide material for the problem-solving approach in content area reading.[70] Issues may be selected from newspapers, news magazines, and television programs. Teachers should use the same steps in developing these problems as they use in problem-solving activities. Following are examples of controversial issues the teacher may select:

1. The president's economic changes at the beginning of a new term of office. (economics class)
2. The moral and/or scientific issues in genetic engineering. (science class)
3. The role of computers in education and other facets of life. Will computers stop humanism? (social studies class)

Teachers can also use guiding or purposing questions to activate reading comprehension. These questions are presented to the students before they read a selection; after they finish reading the assignment, they should answer the guiding questions. When the entire class or group has completed the questions, the teacher should lead a discussion of the questions and students' responses, asking students to explain the reasoning behind their answers.

Following are some examples of motivating (purposing) questions:

1. What is this section about? In order to find this information the student reads titles, headings, and subheadings.
2. What is the main idea of the selection?
3. What is the author's point of view? This includes identification of the author's bias, sources, and so forth.

4. Do you agree with the author?
5. How do ideas in this selection relate to what you already know about this topic?

Strategies for Developing Schemata

Strategies for helping students develop schemata should be initiated prior to actual reading. The purposes of these strategies are to increase knowledge and experiential background and to make students aware of the relationship between their own knowledge and the text. Traditional activities like films, filmstrips, pictures, models, reference materials, and resource persons can be used to build background, enrich and elaborate schemata, and prepare a student for reading a text assignment. Before and after developing these experiences, the teacher should lead discussions about the experiences and relate them to text materials to help students integrate old and new knowledge.

A very simple approach to schemata development is to direct students to read the table of contents for a new chapter and then discuss the logic for chapter organization. They might suggest alternative ways of organizing the chapter and might also write down everything they know about each topic in the chapter. These lists will help teachers identify areas that need more background development.

Brainstorming, which is another easy and effective prereading activity for schemata development, can be diagnostic in nature because it indicates areas in which students need more information in order to comprehend. Teachers can brainstorm with an individual, a small group, or an entire class. To use this strategy, the teacher may write on the chalkboard a chapter or unit topic such as *heredity*. Then students say the first words that come to mind, and the teacher lists these terms on the chalkboard. A secondary biology class brainstormed these terms for the word *heredity*:

genes	sex
parents	diseases
eye color	DNA
height	RNA
recessive	mutation
dominant	pedigree
plants	animals
chromosomes	hybrid

The teacher and students should examine the brainstormed words to consider whether they are all relevant to the selection. If any words are removed from the list, students must be able to explain why. After reading the chapter, students should reexamine the list to determine any changes that should be made.

To vary the brainstorming activity, teachers can ask students to categorize the words on the brainstormed list. For example, the list of words associated with *heredity* could be divided into categories of terms that are related to plants, to animals, and to both plants and animals.

A preview guide is a written activity that is usually prepared by the teacher to help students relate past experiences to content materials. This guide may take several forms. One simple approach is to ask students to write down what they know about a topic. For example, the social science teacher who is introducing the topic of *communism* might ask each student to write everything he or she knows about communism. After reading the content selection, each student should look at the ideas he or she wrote down earlier to determine which ideas are accurate and which need to be revised.

A more formal preview guide is composed of statements or questions related to the major concepts that the teacher wishes the students to understand and remember after reading the selection. The students' responses show what information they already know about the topic that they can connect with new information in the reading selection. After reading the selection, students check the accuracy of their responses to the preview guide questions. Example 3.2 shows a preview guide that is based on a social studies textbook chapter discussing the topics of cities and suburbs.

EXAMPLE 3.2 PREVIEW GUIDE

Directions: Before you read the chapter, put an X in the *Yes* or *No* column to show what you believe is true. After reading the chapter, check your answers to see if they are correct.

Yes	No	
____	____	Between 1940 and 1960, millions of Americans moved to the suburbs.
____	____	Transportation is not an important factor for suburbanites.
____	____	The influx of people has changed the nature of the suburbs.
____	____	Moving to the suburbs makes people very happy.
____	____	Commuting is one of the problems of the suburban dweller.
____	____	Loneliness is not a problem in suburbia.
____	____	A revolution in building made the suburbs possible.

Encouraging students to raise questions about the content they are about to read or that they are reading will lead them to activate their schemata. Answering the questions they raise regarding the content will encourage them to incorporate new information into their existing schemata.

Strategies for Activating Schemata

Some of the suggestions in the preceding section can be used to both develop schemata and activate schemata. In addition, the activities included in the active reading section will cause readers to activate their existing schemata.

Encouraging students to raise questions regarding content and to relate the content they are reading to the things they already know about a subject area will help to activate schemata. Suggestions regarding questioning strategies are provided later in this chapter.

Teachers can use guiding or purposing questions to activate schemata. Such questions should be presented to students before they read a selection.

Strategies for Developing Prediction Skills

Prediction exercises help students develop their expectations for reading content and help them create a mind set for following the author's presentation of ideas and information. Therefore, prediction activities are related to activating schemata. Advance organizers and purposing questions can be used for this purpose.

Advance Organizers

Advance organizers, based on David Ausubel's concept and research, are short reading passages that precede a longer selection and deal with the same topic as the selection that is to be read.[71] They give students a conceptual framework for the content and help students predict the author's ideas as these ideas are related to the students' existing schemata.

A teacher often must write advance organizers for students, although some more recently published textbooks include advance organizers for each chapter. You have probably noticed that each chapter in this text begins with an overview—an advance organizer designed to aid *your* comprehension of this book.

It is worth a teacher's effort to construct advance organizers for textbook chapters. These passages are especially valuable when the teacher explains the relationship between the advance organizers and the chapters.

Purposing Questions

Purposing questions can be used to build readers' anticipation of the author's ideas. These questions indicate the important ideas in a selection and give students a structure for organizing content during reading. Students can relate the important ideas indicated by the purposing questions to the message of a selection.

Purposing questions should be broad and should guide a reader through an entire selection. If the questions are too specific, students might read only until they have found ideas to answer the questions. Teachers may formulate two or three purposing questions for a selection.

A good source for purposing questions are the questions that many textbooks provide at the end of each chapter. Reading these questions before reading the chapter gives students a sense of the important ideas suggested by the questions. Another source for purposing questions are a textbook's chapter titles and subheadings. These headings point out the important ideas in a chapter; students can turn these ideas into questions, thus devising purposing questions that they can answer as they read. Finally, students may read the first paragraph of a selection and then formulate questions that are based on the information provided in that paragraph.

Strategies for Developing Metacognition

Teachers can create worksheets to help students develop metacognitive skills. Mary Heller[72] suggests a worksheet like that in Example 3.3, which is based on social science content. The students fill in the topic, purpose, and section A before reading a selection. They complete sections B, C, and the answer to the purpose question after reading the selection.

EXAMPLE 3.3   SOCIAL SCIENCE WORKSHEET ——————————

Topic: Imperialism

Purpose: To understand how imperialism relates to me.

A What I already knew	B What I now know	C What I don't know
Imperialism is extending power. Britain is an imperialist country.	Power can be extended through economic, military, and political means. U.S. used "dollar diplomacy" in Latin America.	Other countries that U.S. practices imperialism on. Does imperialism cause war? Is imperialism good or bad?

Answer to purpose question: The U.S. practices imperialism and sends U.S. tax money to Latin America.

——————————————

Self-questioning is another strategy that facilitates development of metacognitive skills. A number of researchers have demonstrated the value of self-questioning as well as the fact that students can acquire this skill.[73] Teachers may initiate self-questioning instruction through teaching students to ask questions such as, "What is the main idea in this paragraph (selection)?" or "Is there any-thing I don't understand in this paragraph?" They may extend instruction by teaching students about the different levels of questioning (literal, inferential, critical, and creative) and teaching them to generate questions at each level. Whole-class practice of question-generating skills will help students refine these skills.

Hori[74] used the ReQuest procedure to teach students in grades seven through nine to generate literal, inferential, critical, and creative questions in five daily sessions. He found that the trained group was significantly more successful in forming questions than the untrained group. A worksheet like that in Example 3.4 is also useful in guiding students to generate questions.

EXAMPLE 3.4   WORKSHEET FOR GENERATING QUESTIONS ———

Directions: Read the assigned selection, then write a question at each level indicated and answer the remaining questions.

1. Literal-level question:
2. Inferential-level question:
3. Evaluative-level question:
4. Creative-level question:
5. Give an example of the concept presented:
6. What is the main idea of the selection?
7. List the things that you do not understand:

_____

Strategies for Teaching Organizational Patterns

Organizational patterns are used to structure both selections and paragraphs. Content teachers can help students improve comprehension by explaining the common organizational patterns, pointing out the signals to these patterns, describing how to interpret these patterns, and providing examples of the pat-terns from content textbooks. Students should have opportunities to identify and interpret examples of the common organizational patterns. Students often enjoy these activities when they are introduced in a game format. For example, they can have a "treasure hunt" for organizational patterns, using materials from text-books, newspapers, and magazines.

During the early stages of teaching students to read different organizational patterns, teachers should identify the predominant pattern in a content selection. This will help students develop and use schemata for different organizational patterns and will encourage them to anticipate the author's organization of con-tent. Students can identify and discuss the predominant organizational pattern of a selection before reading it. They can skim the selection to determine its organi-zation.

Students can write examples of each type of organizational pattern. This activity will give them an opportunity to practice both writing skills and reading skills.

Teachers can present students with examples of organizational patterns and have the students label the examples by pattern. The students should identify the words or phrases in each example that helped them identify the organizational type.

Sentence Comprehension

Sentences are the basic language units used to organize discourse. Thus, it is important to understand sentences in order to comprehend content reading materials. Secondary students have had much experience with sentences; however, as reading material becomes more sophisticated, sentences are longer and more complex. Increasing sentence comprehension helps students understand and identify details, and this skill helps them understand and identify main ideas of paragraphs.

Sentence comprehension activities are useful for teaching students to comprehend details and for helping students who have difficulty with reading comprehension. These activities can be used after students have read a content selection and should include sentences that have been selected from the content chapters.

Paraphrasing, which is an excellent sentence comprehension strategy, involves restating information in an equivalent statement. In order to paraphrase a sentence, the reader must understand the thought being expressed. Paraphrasing may be *semantic*, in which synonyms are substituted for words in the original sentence, or it can be *syntactic*, in which the order of the words in the sentence is changed. Syntactic and semantic paraphrasing may be combined. Teachers should explain paraphrasing and demonstrate the various types of paraphrasing before asking students to paraphrase content materials.

Following are examples of paraphrasing of the sentence, *Each of the thirteen colonies had its own local government.*

1. Each of the original thirteen colonies had its own local administration. (semantic)
2. A local government was in each of the thirteen colonies. (syntactic)
3. A local administration was in each of the original thirteen colonies. (combination)

Sentence-combining activities involve the combination of two short sentences to form a new and usually longer sentence. For example:

Linda could see something. (sentence 1)
She saw that Susan did not understand the story. (sentence 2)
Linda could see that Susan did not understand the story. (combined sentence)

Practice in sentence combining significantly increases students' comprehension.[75] It also acquaints students with a variety of options in ordering words to express meaning. Following are some sentence-combining strategies:

1. Model the sentence-combining process for students *before* asking them to use it. Discuss the combinations. Point out any problems and reasons for these problems.
2. Select sentences from content materials and ask students to combine them.
3. Provide students with a long sentence and ask them to identify the short sentences that compose it. For example, the sentence, *In the Progressive Era, women became more and more active in civic affairs through the settlement movement,* could be broken into the following shorter sentences:
   a. Women were active in the Progressive Era.
   b. Women were active in civic affairs.
   c. They were active through the settlement movement.

Questioning is another strategy for increasing sentence comprehension. When using this strategy, teachers select a sentence from content materials and ask students to answer questions about *who, what, when, where, why,* and *how*. For example:

During the reign of Yang Ti, the Grand Canal was built to link the Yangtze River and the Hwang Ho.
What—the Grand Canal was built
Why—to link the Yangtze River and the Hwang Ho
When—during the reign of Yang Ti
Where—between the Yangtze and Hwang Ho rivers
Who and how are not applicable for this sentence.

Intersentential Processes

Intersentential processes are the ways in which sentences in a paragraph are related.[76] In order to fully understand one sentence in a paragraph, a person usually must read the other sentences in the paragraph because they are related in consistent, identifiable ways and provide a context for each other. Richard Larson has identified sixteen types of relationships among sentences.[77] The following is a list of the types that occur most frequently. An example of each type is given.

1. **Restatement**   Different words are used to restate previously stated ideas. *Georgia has a mild climate. Most of the state has warm summers and short, mild winters.*
2. **Expansion**   A sentence expands on previously stated ideas. *Genealogy is the study of family relationships. Careful genealogical research may enable a person to trace his or her descent from early ancestors.*

3. **Enumeration**   A sentence lists specific information implied in a previous sentence. *Genes determine the characteristics that living things inherit from their parents. Genes determine such features as sex, height, and hair color.*

4. **Example**   A sentence supplies an example to clarify a previous sentence. *The U.S. Constitution protects the individual rights of every person. For example, the* writ of habeas corpus *protects the rights of a person when he or she is arrested.*

5. **Definition**   This sentence gives the meaning of a previously used word. *Detergents and soap have many everyday uses. A detergent is any substance that cleans.*

6. **Description**   A previously stated idea or object is described. *Grapes are one of the oldest cultivated plants. Grapes are the smooth-skinned, juicy fruit of a woody vine.*

7. **Qualification**   A sentence qualifies a previous sentence. *In the event of fire, students should exit immediately. However, teachers should check to see if the classroom door is hot before opening it.*

8. **Evaluation**   A judgment is made about previously stated information. *Detergents can penetrate soiled fabrics better than soaps can. Unfortunately, detergents can also harm the environment.*

9. **Cause and/or effect**   Reference is made to causes or effects related to a previous sentence. *Greek tragedy was solemn, poetic, and philosophical. These qualities were due to the fact that tragedy was often associated with religious celebrations.*

10. **Comparison or contrast**   Comparison or contrast are used to clarify or emphasize ideas in another sentence. *A steel-string guitar makes a loud, piercing sound. A classical guitar makes a softer, more muted sound.*

11. **Conclusion**   This sentence shows how previously stated information has led to knowledge or judgment. *Dogs are friendly, obedient animals that serve people in work, play, and sport. Dogs have been known as "man's best friend" for thousands of years.*

Content teachers can ask students to use these intersentential relationships to analyze the relationships among sentences in a paragraph. Examining intersentential processes will help to improve students' paragraph understanding and will also help in the identification of details and main ideas.

Teaching Main Ideas and Details

The ability to identify the main idea of a paragraph or selection and its supporting details has a high priority in most reading programs. These are very important skills for content readers because the majority of content is organized around main ideas and details. The major points regarding main idea instruction are summarized in the following guidelines.

Instructional Guidelines for Main Ideas

1. Use expository content to teach main ideas.
2. Remember that the main idea may be stated in the selection or it may be unstated and implied. When the main idea is not stated, the details will indicate what the main idea is. The reader must use the details, his or her experience, and thinking skills to infer the main idea.
3. State the type of main idea (gist, topic, etc.) that students are expected to identify.
4. State the length of the statement that you expect students to produce.
5. Teach students to generate main idea statements. This is more effective than having them draw lines beneath or circle main ideas. There will be times, especially in remedial instruction, when multiple-choice items may be used. However, the teacher's goal should be student generation of main idea statements.
6. Teach students to identify types of organizational patterns as a means of helping them identify main ideas.
7. Remind students that content that precedes a particular paragraph may help them identify the main idea of the paragraph they are working on.
8. Help students discriminate between topic and main idea. These terms are not synonyms. A main idea is often a statement made about the topic of a selection or paragraph.
9. Use activities to teach main ideas and supporting details but be certain to transfer these concepts to content textbooks. Use content textbooks for practicing this skill.

Activities like the following will help students learn how to determine main ideas and details. These activities will give them opportunities to practice this skill before having to apply it in their content textbooks.

One useful activity is for the teacher to identify the main idea of a paragraph in a content textbook and then to ask students to refer to that paragraph and list each detail that supports the main idea.

Reading workbooks and reading activity books usually include main idea activities for students to complete. These activities may be helpful for some students; however, the content teacher is concerned primarily with teaching students to function with content reading materials. The most valuable activities for this goal are those that require students to apply reading skills to actual content materials. The following strategies are designed to be used with text materials either during or after reading the content. These strategies should help students improve their ability to identify details and main ideas in content reading materials.

Main Idea Activities

1. Model the procedure of finding main ideas for students before asking them to locate main ideas themselves. See the examples of modeling that are included in this chapter.

2. Students can ask themselves these questions: What is this sentence, or paragraph, about? What do most of the key words seem to point to? What words occur most frequently? What do these frequently occurring words relate to? What idea is related to most of the supporting details? What sentence would best summarize the frequently occurring ideas? Is the main idea stated or implied? Where is the main idea located in the paragraph (at the beginning, in the middle, or at the end)?

3. Teach students to look for words and phrases that often indicate the main idea; for instance, *first, last, the most important factor, the significant fact*.

4. Prepare blank diagrams in which students can place main ideas and supporting details. Following are two examples: the first example is a generic diagram; the second is a diagram that has been developed for the following paragraph.

A mutation is a change in a gene, which is the part of the cell that determines the inherited characteristics of the offspring. The changed gene is then passed on to succeeding generations. Some mutations produce only a slight change in the offspring, while others produce more drastic changes.

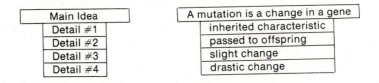

5. Have students create their own diagrams for main ideas and supporting details.

6. Encourage students to write, in their own words, concise statements of main ideas.

Details can be introduced by teaching students to locate key words in sentences. Teachers can direct students to compose telegrams conveying crucial information.[78] Through telegram exercises, students will learn to focus on key words, which are generally nouns and verbs, although other parts of speech can be important in specific messages. For the message "Mother has had a heart attack and is very ill. Please hurry home," students would probably select the following words: "Mother ill. Hurry home." Telegram activities should be used with sentences selected from content textbooks.

Activities for locating key words in sentences can be expanded for finding the key words in a paragraph. Once the key words in the sentences of a paragraph have been identified, the student can relate these words to determine what larger idea they point to. Students can sum up the relationships among the key words.[79] Then they can select the sentence that best states the main idea. If no one sentence sums up the main idea (some main ideas are implied), students can compose a sentence that states the main idea. Following is a paragraph with the key words underlined.

A <u>dog</u> is a <u>useful</u> animal. It <u>guards</u> our <u>homes</u> from burglars and <u>alerts</u> us when <u>guests</u> are coming. The dog will <u>warn</u> members of the <u>household</u> if <u>fire</u> breaks out in the home. Some dogs serve as <u>seeing-eye</u> dogs for <u>blind</u> people. Perhaps most important of all, dogs are loyal, loving <u>companions</u> who provide many hours of <u>pleasure</u> for their owners and families.

The main idea of this paragraph is the first sentence, "A dog is a useful animal." The key words of each sentence clearly point to this idea.

The telegram strategy is useful for teaching students to identify important details, which is an important skill for readers of content materials. Important details develop and support the main idea. Sometimes authors include details that are interesting but that do not give additional information about the main idea. Categorization activities can help students separate important from unimportant details. For instance, students can write down the details they have identified in a paragraph and then categorize these details as either important or unimportant to the main idea. They should then verbalize their reasons and the teacher can clear up misconceptions.

Important Details	Unimportant Details

Levels of Reasoning

A large part of reading comprehension involves thinking about what one has read. Therefore, the teacher must stimulate students' thinking, encouraging the development of thinking skills by using tools such as questions.

Several factors contribute to the development of thinking skills. In order to understand the content they are reading, readers must have complete concentration, not allowing their minds to wander. Readers also need to learn to demand meaning from content. Some students are accustomed to reading words without realizing that they must think about the ideas behind those words. A teacher can help students concentrate on looking for meaning as they read by asking them, "What is the author telling you?" Also, students should ask questions as they read. Current research indicates that strategies requiring students to generate responses while reading tend to facilitate comprehension.[80] Andre and Anderson found that high school students who generated questions for paragraphs as they read performed significantly better on comprehension tests than students who read and reread the same material.[81]

An important factor in developing reasoning skills is providing an environment in which thinking can flourish. Such an environment is created by teachers who accept student answers that differ from their own; different points of view are tolerated and encouraged. Student answers and ideas are accepted, clarified, and expanded, often by the teacher's asking, "Why do you think that?" Plenty of time should be provided for students to think; when a student must answer questions quickly, the quality of his or her answers may be lowered.

All questioning should be carefully planned so that teachers ask questions related to important ideas and concepts in the reading selection. Poorly chosen questions and questions that emphasize insignificant details are detrimental to the growth of thinking skills. For example, the question "What color was Mary's dress?" is an unimportant question that may prevent the reader from identifying the significant information in the selection. Teachers who are preparing to develop questions related to a reading selection should ask themselves the following questions:

1. What are the important ideas in this selection?
2. What ideas do I want the students to remember from this selection?
3. What thinking skills have the students in this group already developed?
4. What thinking skills do the students in this group need to develop?

Both novice teachers and experienced teachers who are unsure of their questioning skills may wish to tape some of their lessons and classroom discussions in order to critique their questioning skills.

Either teachers or students may develop questions to be asked before, during, and after reading. Questions used at each of these points serve an important function in developing students' understanding. Questions asked before reading begins are purposing questions, which help focus students' thinking so that they actively anticipate, understand, and recall more ideas from reading. Reading that lacks purpose tends to be random and less meaningful. The purposing questions should be discussed after the selection has been read. Questions asked by either students or teachers during reading may serve to refocus students' thinking, to stress the importance of certain ideas, or to focus students' attention on the content. These questions may be answered and discussed during or after reading. Follow-up questions posed after reading improve understanding and encourage thinking. They allow students to see how other people react to and understand a selection. The sharing that occurs in a discussion of the selection increases student thinking.

Following is a framework for developing thinking at four levels: literal, interpretive, evaluative (critical), and creative. All of the types of questions discussed above may be implemented at each of these four levels to help develop thinking skills.

Strategies for Developing Literal Thinking

This level of reasoning is concerned with ideas that are stated directly in the reading content. A reader must reproduce the author's ideas to achieve literal understanding and should be concerned with the question, "What did the author say?"—what is actually stated in the lines of print? Literal comprehension includes identification and recall of stated main ideas and details. A thorough understanding of the meanings of words, sentences, and paragraphs is necessary to thinking at the literal level. Questions at this level can be answered by quoting the content. The literal level of comprehension is the basic level—the one on which the other levels of understanding depend.

The main types of literal level thinking are recognizing and recalling stated main ideas; recognizing and recalling stated details; recognizing and recalling stated sequence; following stated directions; recognizing stated causes and effects; and paraphrasing content. Literal questions are factual questions and are as varied as the content on which they are based.

Following are some examples of literal level questions that are asked about a story entitled "A New England Nun," which is a high school literature selection.[82] This story concerns a young woman who was engaged for fourteen years to a man, yet, after waiting all those years for her fiance, decided to break the engagement just before the wedding. Literal questions include

1. What activities gave Louisa pleasure?
2. How would you describe Joe in a short paragraph?
3. Who was the "New England Nun"?
4. What events led to the broken engagement?

Literal comprehension of content materials can be developed by asking students questions that are answered in the content materials. Activities requiring students to paraphrase definitions, directions, and main ideas help to develop literal-level reasoning.

Teachers should model the process of answering questions *before* asking students to answer them. For example, for the first question based on "A New England Nun," the teacher might say, "The activities that gave Louisa pleasure are directly stated in this story. The text states that she enjoys cleaning, baking, sewing, and gardening."

Strategies for Developing Interpretive Thinking

This level is also called *inferential thinking* and is concerned with deeper meanings. Interpretive thinking is difficult to define because it involves many types of thinking. It is based on literal-level thinking, and all higher levels of thinking represent refinements of interpretive skills. Essentially, interpretation involves relating facts, generalizations, definitions, values, and skills.[83] Interpretive questions emphasize finding relationships among elements of the reading content.

In order to understand content at the interpretive level, the reader should examine the author's words, reading between the lines to arrive at understandings that are not explicitly stated in the text. Readers should combine information from their own experiences with information from reading content. The main types of inferential thinking are recognizing relationships; drawing conclusions; making generalizations; predicting outcomes; and understanding figurative language.

An inferential question does not always have one correct answer. When evaluating student answers, the teacher should be concerned with the logical thinking processes that the student has used to arrive at a synthesis of ideas. The student should be asked to support and explain his or her answers. This is a very important comprehension strategy that is also very easy to use.

Interpretive questions based on "A New England Nun" follow:

1. Why do you think this story is called "A New England Nun" when it is about a woman who is engaged?
2. What caused the broken engagement?
3. What was the result of the broken engagement for Joe, for Lilly, and for Louisa?
4. Why did the author tell the reader about Caesar in such detail?

The teacher could model the process of interpretive thinking by thinking aloud as he or she reasons to an answer for one of the above questions. For instance, for question 4, the teacher might say, "The author describes Caesar as a vigorous, active animal who delighted in running free and exploring. The author also describes the way that Louisa restrained Caesar from exploring and running free by chaining him up. The vivid descriptions lead to comparing Joe with the dog. They are both vigorous and healthy and enjoy freedom and exploration, but Louisa tries to restrain Joe the same way that she restrains Caesar."

To understand implied relationships such as comparison, contrast, cause and effect, and sequence, students should be encouraged to use their experiential background to interpret written content. Content activities like the following can help students develop their ability to make inferences:

Comparing and contrasting two historical figures
Comparing and contrasting two cities
Citing examples of concepts and ideas students are reading about
Asking students to identify generalizations in their content textbooks

Strategies for Developing Evaluative or Critical Thinking

On the third level of thinking, critical reading requires that the reader make judgments about the quality, value, and validity of the content he or she is reading. To make judgments, the reader compares content with external criteria derived from experience, research, teachers, and experts in the field. Critical reading depends upon a person's ability to read well at the literal and interpretive levels. The critical reader must be able to recognize the author's purpose and the author's point of view. He or she must be able to distinguish fact from opinion. The reader should test the author's assertions against his or her own observations, information, and logic. In order to read critically, the reader must begin with an understanding of what the author is saying. One cannot read critically if one cannot grasp the author's ideas.

The critical reader should be logical and objective in evaluating content, suspending judgment while gathering the necessary data on which to base an evaluation. Suspending judgment requires that the reader avoid jumping to conclusions. The critical reader must have background experience that provides a basis for making judgments. The critical reading task should be approached with an open-minded, problem-solving attitude. The critical reader should constantly ask questions about the material he or she is reading.

Critical reading questions based on "A New England Nun" follow:

1. Does this story portray an accurate picture of life in the late 1800s?
2. What was the real reason Louisa broke the engagement?
3. Which incident in this story most accurately reveals Louisa's character? Why did you select this incident?
4. Do you think Louisa acted suitably when she broke the engagement? Why or why not?

To model answering a critical-level question, the teacher might say, "To answer question 1, we must think about what we already know about life in the late 1800s in Massachusetts. The majority of people at that time lived a rural existence, farming and preserving their own foods, making their clothing and cleaning their own homes. This is certainly the picture that the author creates. In addition, the author shows that many people were leaving their established lives to move to the frontier, which creates hardships. This fact of life in the 1800s is an important aspect of the story. The life-style, foods, clothing, conversation, and issues portrayed in this story coincide with those described in your social studies text."

A study by Willavene Wolf and others groups critical reading skills required by nonfiction materials into three general categories: semantics, logic, and authenticity.[84] Semantics skills include understanding the denotative and connotative uses of words, the use of vague and precise words, and the use of words in a persuasive manner. Logic skills include understanding the reliability of the author's argument; understanding the reliability of the author's statements; recognizing the use of propaganda; discriminating fact from opinion; and recognizing the various forms of persuasive writing. Authenticity skills include determining if adequate information is included, comparing this information to other relevant information, examining the author's qualifications, and using authoritative sources. Teaching suggestions for these areas are given below.

Semantic Activities

1. Students should be made aware that authors use "loaded" words to influence their readers. For example, many readers have unpleasant reactions to the words *un-American, communist,* and *radical,* while reacting favorably to words like *freedom, peace,* and *human rights.* Ask students to find examples of the use of "loaded" words in newspapers, magazines, and textbooks.

2. Some words are used in very vague, general ways and the critical reader should be alert for these so as not to be influenced by them. (For example, the expressions "everyone is doing it" and "they say.") Students should locate examples of vague uses of words.

Logic Activities

1. Have students create syllogisms that state an author's premises and conclusions. The following example is based on a chapter from a social studies textbook:
Premises:
People with undesirable characteristics are rejected. Some "new" immigrants had undesirable characteristics.
Conclusion:
Those "new" immigrants were rejected.
2. Have students verify the facts found in local newspaper stories.
3. Although authors may not state whether they are giving facts or opinions, sometimes there are indicators of opinions, such as the following qualifying words: *think, probably, maybe, appear, seem, believe, could,* and *should.* Have students examine sentences with the purpose of locating "opinion words." The following sentences might be used:
   a. I believe this is the best cake I have ever eaten.
   b. This symptom could mean that you are getting the flu.
   c. Jane will probably come home for vacation.
4. Making a diagram of the facts and opinions presented by an author will help the reader examine ideas critically. The following diagram is based upon information taken from a social studies textbook.

Facts	*Opinions*
"old" immigrants from British Isles, Germany, Scandinavia	"old" immigrants acceptable
"new" immigrants from Slavic countries, Italy, Greece	"new" immigrants unacceptable, ignorant, greedy, diseased, criminals, insane, wild-eyed, bad smelling

5. Recognizing propaganda is one of the logical skills required by critical readers. Discussions of propaganda techniques and techniques for analyzing propaganda could be held in class. Make sure that students realize these propaganda techniques rarely occur in isolation. Many advertisements include a combination of two or more types of propaganda.
   a. *Bad names*—Disagreeable words are used to arouse distaste for a person or a thing. An example of bad names propaganda is an advertisement for weight reduction headlined with "Why be fat?"
   b. *Glad names*—This device is the opposite of bad names. Pleasant words are used to create good feelings about a person or a thing. For example, a face

cream advertisement claims that it will make your skin as "smooth as velvet."

c. *Plain folks*—This kind of propaganda makes an effort to avoid artificiality and sophistication. Political candidates use this technique when they shake hands, kiss babies, and play with dogs. They are trying to appear neighborly and familiar.

d. *Transfer*—This type of propaganda attempts to transfer to a person or thing the reader's respect for the flag, the cross, or some other universal symbol. The flag is sometimes pictured in the background of an advertisement to achieve this type of effect.

e. *Testimonial*—This technique is like transfer except that a famous person gives a testimonial for a product or a person. Positive feelings for the famous person are supposed to be transferred to the product. For example, a famous actor may appear on television on behalf of a political candidate. Another example of a testimonial is advertising that features a famous athlete who claims to shave with a certain brand of razor blade.

f. *Bandwagon*—This type of propaganda is an attempt to convince the reader that he or she should accept an idea or purchase an item because "everyone is doing it." It is the kind of thinking behind a slogan such as "twenty million people can't be wrong."

g. *Card stacking*—This technique utilizes accurate information, but generally there is information omitted so that only one side of a story is told. For example, a cigarette may be advertised as smooth tasting and long lasting, but the bad effects of smoking are not mentioned.[85]

6. After learning to identify propaganda techniques the reader should analyze the propaganda with the following questions:
   a. What technique is used?
   b. Who composed the propaganda?
   c. Why was the propaganda written?
   d. To what reader interests, emotions, and prejudices does the propaganda appeal?
   e. Will I allow myself to be influenced by this propaganda?

Authenticity Activities

1. The writer's conclusions should be based on adequate information. Occasionally a reader must seek additional data before evaluating the validity of an author's writing. Assign students an article to read, having them check other sources of information on the topic to evaluate the validity of the information given in the article.

2. Ask students to evaluate the author's qualifications for writing on the topic at hand. Questions like the following could help in this evaluation:
   a. Would a lawyer be qualified to write a book on writing contracts?
   b. Would a football player be qualified to be an author of a book on foreign policy?

c. Would a chef be a qualified author for a book on menu planning?

d. Would a physician be qualified to write a book on music theory?

Strategies for Developing Creative Thinking

Like critical thinking, creative thinking goes beyond the lines of print. However, creative thinking serves a different function from critical thinking. Creative reading is a deliberate effort to go beyond the information read to find new ways of viewing ideas, incidents, or characters that may stimulate novel thinking and production. Creative thinking occurs after the reader has read and understood a selection. Thus it requires understanding at the literal, interpretive, and critical levels. Because creative thinking requires that the reader become involved with the content, it is similar to appreciation. The resulting productivity may take the form of a new idea, a new story, a design, a painting, an improved product or method, or an invention.

A creative thinker may be able to come up with several ways of solving a math problem or several ways to perform an experiment in science class. A creative thinker may be able to turn a situation from a literature selection into a puppet show, a skit, a painting, or a piece of sculpture. He or she may be able to make a table in wood shop that has special useful features never before considered or may develop a recipe in home economics that surpasses those suggested in the book. To do these things, a creative thinker translates things that are already known into new forms. Creativity is stifled if all school activities must be carried out according to the precise specifications of the teacher and if deviations from prescribed forms are invariably discouraged, rather than rewarded for inventiveness.

Teachers should use stimulating content and questions to encourage students to use their own knowledge, attitudes, and values creatively. Creative activities related to "A New England Nun" follow.

Activities

1. Write a new ending in which Louisa does not break the engagement.
2. Paint, draw, sketch, or model Louisa's home as you envision it.
3. Rewrite this story, setting it in modern times. One student created a story in which Louisa "jilted" Joe because he did not want her to be a professional woman. Lilly was portrayed as a woman who preferred homemaking to a profession.
4. Reread the introduction to the story. Analyze how history would have changed if more early pioneers had been timid.
5. Write about how you would feel if you were each of these characters: Louisa, Joe, and Lilly.
6. Dramatize the scene you think might have occurred when Louisa told Joe that she would not marry him.

A model for classroom discussion is presented in Example 3.5. This model is based on a chapter in a consumer economics textbook.[86]

EXAMPLE 3.5   A MODEL FOR CLASSROOM DISCUSSION AND QUESTIONING

Chapter Synopsis

The title of this chapter is "The Shady Side of the Marketplace." Various fraudulent practices are discussed in this chapter. Fraud is defined as "getting money through some kind of deception." The authors present four examples of fraud, including "bait-and-switch advertising," "referral selling," "the free gimmick," and "the fear sell." The authors imply that the desire to get something for nothing is a major reason that people are defrauded, although they include fear as another contributing factor in some swindles. Customers also practice fraud when they shoplift, when they fail to speak up about undercharges, and when they steal things from hotels.

A Model for Discussion at Different Reasoning Levels

The teacher identifies the following important ideas that represent focal points for the discussion.

1. A definition of fraud.
2. The four basic types of fraud.
3. The causes of fraud.

After identifying these important points, the teacher writes questions on the chalkboard that would help students understand and discuss these points. The questions are at the levels of reasoning discussed earlier in this chapter (literal, inferential, critical, and creative). Preparing questions ahead of time helps the teacher guide a productive discussion; nevertheless, teachers should allow for changes in discussion as they become necessary to address students' needs. Students should also be encouraged to raise questions regarding content they are reading.

   Before students read the selection silently, the teacher introduces the chapter "The Shady Side of the Marketplace" by asking the students to explain the chapter title. Discussing the title gives the students an opportunity to use their background experiences and encourages them to anticipate the ideas they will be reading.

Student   Shady means dishonest to me, so I think this chapter is talking about dishonesty in stores because the marketplace probably refers to stores.

Teacher   That is a very good answer. This title is a good example of figurative language. Can you think of some dishonest or fraudulent business practices that have been reported in the news during the last week?

Student #1   I heard about some contractors stopping at people's houses and telling them that they would fix their roofs. But they got their pay in advance and never came back to do the work.

Teacher   That is a good example of fraudulent business.

Student #2   I heard that people were going around selling magazines, but the people who subscribed never received the magazines.

Teacher   Certainly, that is dishonest business. Fraud is getting money through some kind of deception. Can anyone tell me what "deception" means?

Students   Telling a lie. Tricking a person.

Teacher   Both of those explanations are good. You should write the terms *fraud* and *deception* and their meanings in your notebooks. Then read Chapter 7 silently to find out why some people are easily cheated (inferential level). Also identify the most common kinds of fraud that the author describes. (literal level)

(Reading takes place.)

Teacher   Now that you have had an opportunity to read this chapter, tell me why some people are easily cheated. (inferential)

Students   Because they want something for nothing.

Teacher   Why does wanting something for nothing make people easy to fool?

Students   Because they are willing to believe schemes that will give them something for almost nothing.

Teacher   Is there anything else that makes people easy to fool?

Students   (Silence.)

Teacher   Look back at the four examples of fraud. See if you can locate anything else that makes people susceptible to fraud.

Student   Oh, fear.

Teacher   What kind of fear? (inferential)

Student   Danger, like fear of carbon monoxide killing you.

Teacher   Can you think of other fears that the author did not mention? (critical)

Student   Some people are afraid they won't have enough money to pay for things they need.

Student   Some older people get confused and afraid.

Teacher   What kinds of fraud were described in the textbook? (literal)

Students   Bait and switch, referral selling, the free gimmick, the fear sell.

Teacher   How can you as a customer prevent a seller from swindling you? (critical level)

Students   We don't know.

Teacher   Look back in your textbook at the four examples. What could you do in the situation described on page 102 to avoid being cheated? For instance, the woman could have gone to some department stores and compared prices as well as performance of the sweeper.

Students   She could have read the contract before she signed it. She could have checked with discount stores and catalogs to see what they charged for the vacuum cleaner.

Teacher   Look at Example 2 on page 103 and think of a way to avoid the swindle. (critical)

Students   They should have shopped around for the carpet because they probably paid too much for it. The store used "bait and switch," which probably means the store can't be trusted. They would have to pay finance charges, which means they would end up paying more than the carpet was worth.

Teacher   Good! Now look at Examples 3 and 4 and think of ways to avoid being cheated.

Students   Alice should have had an inspector check the furnace. She could have gotten three estimates from different companies that had been in business for a long time. She could have checked with the Better Business Bureau. Ed should ιave read the contract and figured out how much the encyclopedias would cost. His kids were too young to use the encyclopedias anyway.

Teacher   These are fraudulent practices used by sellers. How do customers swindle business people? (literal)

Students   Shoplifting, stealing towels and blankets at motels, and not telling anyone when they aren't charged enough.

Teacher   Write a paper explaining how you would prevent customers from cheating you if you owned a business. (creative)

Writing Strategies for Comprehension Development

Research has demonstrated that writing improves reading comprehension.[87] Writing is a way of understanding because it is a mode of language processing along with listening, speaking, and reading. When students must process information or communicate information and facts, they can do so by writing. When you ask students to write, you are forcing them to shape and form their responses to the text—to bring these thoughts to conscious awareness.[88] Students who put the concepts they are reading and studying into their own written language are able to understand more fully and evaluate their own learning. Writing serves as a catalyst for further study and reflection on a topic; therefore, teachers of all subject areas should incorporate writing into their instructional programs. The following factors should be considered when incorporating writing into content area instruction.

1. Provide students with good reading material. Students should read well-written material that exhibits the writing style of the discipline under study. Each discipline has unique writing patterns (see Chapters 6 and 7). Reading materials should serve as models of writing in the content areas.
2. Clarify your expectations. Do you expect students to revise, edit, and rewrite their assignments, or will you accept the assignments as originally written? These guidelines can be varied from assignment to assignment. You may choose to focus at different times on such concepts as spelling, punctuation, grammar, organization, and smooth transitions.
3. Focus on the elements of writing that will refine your students' abilities to write expository content. Teach students to organize their writing. Their writing should include an introduction; it should focus on a few major points; it should provide relevant details and/or examples; and it should summarize the major points.
4. Provide skill development activities. Students should expand their vocabularies and practice expressing precise meanings. They should also practice writing cohesive sentences and paragraphs.

5. Give students authentic writing assignments that are motivating for them. Writing assignments should require students to express main ideas and concepts in their own language rather than filling in blanks or selecting multiple-choice responses. Ask students to write down their immediate reactions to a reading selection, to a movie, or to a television program. Give them an assignment that requires them to compare the ideas in their text with those presented in another source. Students may write letters to the editor of the local paper regarding an issue that concerns them. Give students problem-solving writing assignments. For example, identify a local issue and ask students to research the problem and to write their responses along with suggested solutions.

6. Keeping journals is a valuable writing experience in any content classroom. Students may write their own feelings, reactions, and experiences in their journals. Interactive journals wherein students react to class readings, lectures, and discussions are useful learning tools. The teacher may respond to the students' reactions and questions.

7. Use a "webbing" activity with students, during which students brainstorm words and ideas related to a topic. The teacher writes the words and ideas on the board, as in Example 3. When the web is completed, students may choose one portion of the web to write about. They should create a paragraph for each idea in the branch of the web.

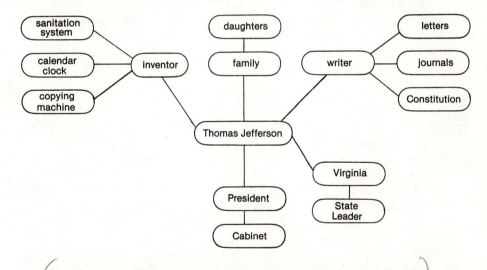

Visualization Strategies for Comprehension Development

Visualization is the process of forming mental images of the content that one is reading. Through visualization one's schemata are used to understand and remember content. Written language is translated into visual images that depict various elements of reading material: story settings, characters, story action, geographic areas, famous historical figures, scientific experiments, steps in mathe-matical problems, and problem-solving situations.

Teachers can help students create visual images by discussing the language an author has used. Activities that encourage the visualization of scenes, situations, or people help students learn to use their schemata to comprehend reading content. Students can practice visualization by forming mental images of places, people, things, and situations they have experienced: for example, a play in a football game, a place in the community, the school principal, or one's home. Visualization activities should be followed by discussion of the students' feelings and reactions to the images they have created.

Following are some visualization activities that can be used to increase content reading comprehension.

Activities

1. *Social Studies:* Develop a "You-Are-There" activity. The students might be asked to visualize Abraham Lincoln as he delivered the Gettysburg Address. They could discuss the sounds, smells, and emotions of the situation. Students could visualize a battle in a war they are studying, discussing the placement of various battle lines and giving descriptions of weapons and uniforms.
2. *Science:* As preparation for performing an experiment, students could be asked to visualize the steps of the experiment as well as its outcome.
3. When working with problem-solving activities in any subject, students can be asked to visualize alternative solutions that will help them work through the various ways of solving a problem.

SUMMARY

Reading comprehension, the primary goal of reading instruction, is especially important in teaching students to read content materials. In order to understand written language, readers use schemata, metacognitive skills, and vocabulary. They also use their understanding of language and the ways that authors organize and structure content. Reasoning plays a significant role in reading comprehension with particular stress on inferencing ability.

The instructional strategies for reading comprehension focus on developing schemata, activating schemata, metacognition, prediction, visualizing content, writing, and levels of reasoning. Schemata strategies are concerned with activating the schemata that will be most useful to readers as they predict information, ideas, and language in written content. Teaching strategies encourage students to develop and use schemata. Metacognitive skills are those skills that students use when they unconsciously search for understanding; when comprehension falters, they "debug" the process by rereading and rethinking selected portions of the text. Self-questioning strategies are especially important to metacognition. Students' writing can contribute to comprehension because students who write are more able to understand the ways that authors express ideas in written language. Comprehension is basically a thinking process; therefore readers who think about content as they read comprehend better. Reasoning about written language is developed through questions on various levels: literal, interpretive, critical, and creative.

SELF-TEST

1. What do we deal with when we examine reading comprehension? (a) An unimportant process (b) The product of the process (c) An observable process (d) A controversial process

2. What are schemata? (a) Organized stores of information and experience (b) Word recognition schemes (c) Printed letters (d) Purposes

3. According to this chapter, what is reading? (a) Identifying words (b) Processing information from print (c) A delegated process (d) A structured overview

4. Which of the following answers describes prediction as it relates to reading comprehension? (a) Print (b) Anticipating ideas, information, and language (c) Being able to spell the words that occur in a text (d) Random information

5. What is the purpose of activating schemata? (a) To improve readers' eye movements (b) To create entirely new cognitive structures (c) To help students relate their experiences to written content (d) To increase the number of pages read in an assignment

6. Which answer describes metacognition? (a) Knowing when you have comprehended (b) Knowing when you have not comprehended (c) Both *a* and *b* (d) Neither *a* nor *b*

7. What conditions are necessary for metacognition to occur? (a) Establishing a purpose and awareness of cognitive processes (b) Sampling and problem solving (c) Textual schemata, story grammar, and think time (d) Propaganda, think time, application, and experience

8. Why is writing a way of comprehending? (a) Because it is a mechanical process (b) Because it requires editing (c) Because it is a mode of language processing (d) Because it is not creative

9. What is one purpose of problem-solving activities? (a) To teach word recognition skills (b) To activate the reader (c) To teach schemata (d) To teach psycholinguistics

10. How can a preview guide help the reader? (a) It helps one relate personal experience to the reading content. (b) It makes the pictures easier to understand. (c) It makes reading some parts of the material unnecessary. (d) It tells the reader what pages to read.

11. What is the purpose of the structured overview in developing readiness for reading? (a) It helps the reader understand syntax. (b) It helps the reader fit

personal experience into a conceptual framework. (c) It structures the entire book for the student. (d) It helps the student recognize similarities and differences.

12. What type of meaning is understood at the interpretive level? (a) The meaning stated in the content (b) Evaluation of ideas read (c) Meanings that are not stated in the text (d) Application of ideas to new situations

13. What level of thinking is recognizing stated main ideas? (a) Literal (b) Interpretive (c) Evaluative (d) Creative

14. What information do readers use to make inferences? (a) Information stated in the selection (b) Experiential information (c) Neither *a* nor *b* (d) Both *a* and *b*

15. What level of thinking is making generalizations? (a) Literal (b) Interpretive (c) Evaluative (d) Creative

16. What is one of the aspects of textual schemata? (a) Semantics (b) Concepts (c) Paragraph structure (d) Phonics

17. Why do purposes for reading improve comprehension? (a) They are interesting. (b) They speed up reading. (c) They cause students to share ideas. (d) They focus the reader's thinking.

18. What levels of thinking are presented in this chapter? (a) Literal, chaining, critical (b) Literal, translation, evaluation, creative (c) Literal, interpretive, evaluative, creative (d) Literal, analytic, interpretive, creative

19. "What did the author say?" is a good question for what level of thinking? (a) Literal level (b) Inferential level (c) Critical level (d) Creative level

20. In what level of thinking is propaganda important? (a) Literal (b) Interpretive (c) Critical (d) Creative

21. Why should teachers allow students time to think? (a) Being given more time makes students think. (b) Being given more time enables students to answer questions better. (c) It is the polite thing to do. (d) It provides students with a break in the work routine.

THOUGHT QUESTIONS

1. How is prediction related to reading comprehension?
2. What are textual schemata? How do textual schemata function in reading comprehension?
3. Why is it important to be an active reader?
4. What is the relationship between reading comprehension and content reading?
5. How does metacognition relate to active reading?
6. Discuss the role of writing in comprehending content reading materials.
7. What strategies to aid comprehension can the teacher use before students read?

ENRICHMENT ACTIVITIES

1. Read an article in the local newspaper and write down all of the thinking processes that you use to understand what you are reading.
2. Read a chapter in a book of your choice and write a question at each level of thinking related to the chapter. Share your questions with your classmates.
3. Read a current best seller and write a brief paragraph that paraphrases the theme of the book. Have a classmate who has read the same book analyze your comprehension.
4. Visit a secondary classroom for the purpose of watching questioning procedures. What level of questions is used most? How much time are the students allowed for formulating answers?
5. Find examples of paragraphs in content area textbooks that follow organizational patterns illustrated in this chapter. Bring these examples to class to share and discuss.
6. Use the "key word" idea to analyze several paragraphs in a content textbook.
7. Select a chapter in a content textbook and make a plan to help other students comprehend the chapter, using the strategies suggested in this chapter.
8. Adapt one of the metacognitive activities in this chapter to your content area.
9. Create a list of writing ideas to use in your content area.
10. Examine the activities suggested in this chapter and plan ways to adapt them to your content area.

NOTES

1. R. C. Anderson and P. D. Pearson, "A Schema-Theoretic View of Basic Processes in Reading Comprehension," in *Handbook of Reading Research,* ed. P. D. Pearson (New York: Longman, 1984), pp. 255–291.

2. Ibid. K. Stanovich, "Toward an Interactive-Compensatory Model of Individual Differences in the Development of Reading Fluency," *Reading Research Quarterly,* 16 (1980), 32–71.

3. Anderson and Pearson, p. 255.

4. Jill Olshavsky, "Reading as Problem Solving: An Investigation of Strategies," *Reading Research Quarterly,* XII, No. 4 (1976–77), 654–674.

5. Richard Anderson, "Concretization and Sentence Learning," in *Theoretical Models and Processes of Reading,* ed. Harry Singer and Robert Ruddell (Newark, Del.: International Reading Association, 1976), pp. 588–596.

6. David Rumelhart, "Schemata: The Building Blocks of Cognition," in *Comprehension and Teaching: Research Reviews,* ed. John Guthrie (Newark, Del.: International Reading Association, 1981), pp. 3–26.

7. D. Durkin, "What Is the Value of the New Interest in Reading Comprehension?" *Language Arts,* 16 (1981), 515–544. M. Adams and B. Bertram, *Background Knowledge*

and Reading Comprehension, Reading Education Report No. 13 (Urbana, Ill: University of Illinois, Center for the Study of Reading, 1980). (ED 181 431).

8. P. D. Pearson, "A Context for Instructional Research on Reading Comprehension," in *Promoting Reading Comprehension*, ed. James Flood (Newark, Del.: International Reading Association, 1984), pp. 1–15.

9. E. Z. Rothkopf and M. J. Billington, "Goal Guided Learning from Text: Inferring a Descriptive Processing Model from Inspection Times and Eye Movements," *Journal of Educational Psychology*, 71 (1979), 310–327.

10. Rumelhart, pp. 3–26.

11. J. Bransford and M. Johnson, "Contextual Prerequisites for Understanding: Some Investigations of Comprehension and Recall," *Journal of Verbal Learning and Verbal Behavior*, 11 (1972), 717–726.

12. Marilyn Jager Adams and Allan Collins, "A Schema-Theoretic View of Reading," in *Theoretical Models and Processes of Reading*, ed. Harry Singer and Robert Ruddell (Newark, Del.: International Reading Association, 1986), pp. 404–425.

13. J. W. Pichert and R. C. Anderson, "Taking Different Perspectives on a Story," *Journal of Educational Psychology*, 69 (1977), 309–315.

14. Anderson and Pearson, pp. 255–291.

15. S. G. Paris and M. Lipson, "Metacognition and Reading Comprehension" (Research colloquium presented at the International Reading Association Annual Meeting, Chicago, Ill., 1982). A. Brown, J. Campione, and J. Day, "Learning to Learn: On Training Students to Learn from Texts," *Educational Researcher*, 10 (February 1981), 14–21.

16. J. Jaap Tuinman, "The Schema Schemers," *Journal of Reading*, 23 (February 1980), 414–419.

17. P. David Pearson and Dale D. Johnson, *Teaching Reading Comprehension* (New York: Holt, Rinehart and Winston, 1977), p. 44.

18. Margie Bowman, "A Comparison of Content Schemata and Textual Schemata or the Process of Parachuting," *Reading World*, 21 (October 1981), 14–22.

19. R. Oaken, M. Wiener, and W. Cromer, "Identification, Organization, and Reading Comprehension for Good and Poor Reading," *Journal of Educational Psychology*, 62 (1971), 71–78.

20. E. Rothkopf, "Writing to Teach and Reading to Learn: A Perspective on the Psychology of Written Instruction," in *The Psychology of Teaching Methods*, ed. N. Gage (Chicago: Univ. of Chicago Press, 1976), pp. 91–129.

21. P. David Pearson and Kaybeth Camperell, "Comprehension of Text Structures," in *Comprehension and Teaching: Research Reviews*, ed. John Guthrie (Newark, Del.: International Reading Association, 1981), pp. 27–55.

22. G. H. Bower, "Experiments on Story Understanding and Recall," *Quarterly Journal of Experimental Psychology*, 28 (1976), 511–534. P. W. Thorndyke, "Cognitive Structures in Comprehension and Memory of Narrative Discourse," *Cognitive Psychology*, 9 (1977), 77–110. C. J. Gordon, "The Effects of Instruction in Metacomprehension and Inferencing on Children's Comprehension Abilities" (Ph.D. dissertation, University of Minnesota, 1980).

23. T. Harris and R. Hodges, eds., *A Dictionary of Reading and Related Terms* (Newark, Del.: International Reading Association, 1981), p. 162.

24. A. Collins, J. Brown, and K. Larkin, "Inference in Text Understanding," in *Theoretical Issues in Reading Comprehension*, ed. R. Spiro, B. Bruce, and W. Brewer (Hillsdale, N.J.: Lawrence Erlbaum Associates, 1980), pp. 385–407.

25. R. C. Omanson, W. H. Warren, and T. Trabasso, "Goals, Inferential Comprehension, and Recall of Stories by Children," *Discourse Processes*, 1 (1978), 337–354.
26. Ibid.
27. W. Matthews et al., *Investigating the Earth*, 4th ed. (Boston: Houghton Mifflin Company, 1984), p. 46.
28. J. Bransford et al., "Differences in Approaches to Learning: An Overview," *Journal of Experimental Psychology: General*, 3 (1982), 317–398.
29. C. J. Gordon, "The Effects of Instruction in Metacomprehension and Inferencing on Children's Comprehension Abilities" (Unpublished doctoral dissertation, University of Minnesota, 1980).
30. T. E. Raphael and P. D. Pearson, *The Effects of Metacognitive Awareness Training on Students' Question Answering Behavior*, Technical Report II (Urbana, Ill.: University of Illinois at Urbana-Champaign, Center for the Study of Reading, 1982).
31. Ibid.
32. Matthews et al., p. 49.
33. J. H. Flavell, "Metacognitive Aspects of Problem Solving," in *The Nature of Intelligence*, ed. L. B. Resnick (Hillsdale, N.J.: Lawrence Erlbaum Associates, 1976), pp. 231–235.
34. Y. L. Bernice Wong, "Self-Questioning Instructional Research: A Review," *Review of Educational Research* 55, No. 2 (Summer 1985), 227–268.
35. Scott Paris and Meyer Myers, "Comprehension Monitoring, Memory and Study Strategies of Good and Poor Readers," *Journal of Reading Behavior*, 13 (Spring 1981), 5–22.
36. L. K. Cook and R. E. Mayer, "Reading Strategies Training for Meaningful Learning from Prose," in *Cognitive Strategy Research: Educational Applications*, ed. M. Pressley and J. R. Levin (New York: Springer-Verlag, 1983), pp. 87–131.
37. A. Brown, J. Day, and R. Jones, "The Development of Plans for Summarizing Texts," *Child Development*, 54 (1983), 968–979.
38. R. Horowitz, "Text Patterns: Part I," *Journal of Reading*, 28 (February 1985), 448–454.
39. S. Hoskins, "Text Superstructures," *Journal of Reading*, 29 (March 1986), 538–543.
40. D. Shannon, "Use of Top-Level Structure in Expository Text: An Open Letter to a High School Teacher," *Journal of Reading*, 28 (February 1986), 426–431.
41. Ibid.
42. S. Hoskins, "The Use of Top-Level Structure of Exposition by Entering College Freshmen" (Ph.D. dissertation, Texas Woman's University, Denton, Texas, 1983).
43. L. Brooks and D. Dansereau, "Effects of Structural Schema Training and Text Organization on Expository Prose Processing," *Journal of Educational Psychology*, 75, No. 6 (1983), 811–820.
44. R. Vacca and J. Vacca, *Content Area Reading* (Boston: Little, Brown and Company, 1986). J. Readence, T. Bean, and R. Baldwin, *Content Area Reading: An Integrated Approach* (Dubuque, Iowa: Kendall/Hunt, 1981).
45. Howard B. Wilder, Robert P. Ludlum, and Harriet McCune Brown, *This Is America's Story* (Boston: Houghton Mifflin Company, 1982), p. 238.
46. John Morton and Ronald Rezny, *Consumer Action* (Boston: Houghton Mifflin Company, 1978), p. 308.
47. Edward Rosenberg, Henry Gurney, and Vivian Harlin, *Investigating Your Health*, rev. ed. (Boston: Houghton Mifflin Company, 1978), p. 313.

48. Joseph Jackson and Edward Evans, *Spaceship Earth: Earth Science*, rev. ed. (Boston: Houghton Mifflin Company, 1980), p. 19.

49. Faith Hill and Jeffrey May, *Spaceship Earth: Physical Science*, rev. ed. (Boston: Houghton Mifflin Company, 1981), p. 102.

50. John T. Guthrie, "Paragraph Structure," *The Reading Teacher*, 33 (April 1979), 880–881.

51. Ibid, p. 881.

52. P. D. Pearson, "A Retrospective Reaction to Prose Comprehension," in *Children's Prose Comprehension: Research and Practice*, ed. C. M. Santa and B. L. Hayes (Newark, Del.: International Reading Association, 1981), pp. 117–132.

53. J. Cunningham and D. Moore, "The Confused World of Main Idea," in *Teaching Main Idea Comprehension*, ed. J. Bauman (Newark, Del.: International Reading Association, 1986), pp. 1–17.

54. H. Herber, *Teaching Reading in Content Areas*, 2nd ed. (Englewood Cliffs, N.J.: Prentice-Hall, 1978), p. 78.

55. B. Taylor and S. Berkowitz, "Facilitating Children's Comprehension of Content Material," in *Perspectives on Reading Research and Instruction*, ed. M. Kamil and A. Moe, Twenty-ninth Yearbook of the National Reading Conference (Washington, D.C.: National Reading Conference, 1980), pp. 64–68. M. Doctorow, M. Wittrock, and C. Marks, "Generative Processes in Reading Comprehension," *Journal of Educational Psychology*, 70 (1978), 109–118.

56. A. Palinscar and A. Brown, *Reciprocal Teaching of Comprehension Monitoring Activities*, Technical Report No. 269 (Champaign, Ill.: University of Illinois, Center for the Study of Reading, 1984).

57. Harris and Hodges, eds., op. cit.

58. William Gray and Bernice Rogers, *Maturity in Reading—Its Nature and Appraisal* (Chicago: University of Chicago Press, 1956), p. 48. Amiel T. Sharon, "What Do Adults Read?" *Reading Research Quarterly*, 9 (1973–74), 148–169. Buel Lyle, *Final Report: The Adult Performance Level Study* (Washington, D.C.: The U.S. Office of Education, 1977), p. 35.

59. Sharon, pp. 148–169.

60. Lyle, op. cit.

61. Frederick Davis, "Psychometric Research on Comprehension in Reading," *Reading Research Quarterly*, VII, No. 4 (Summer 1972), 628–678.

62. Richard Smith and Thomas Barrett, *Teaching Reading in the Middle Grades*, 2nd ed. (Reading, Mass.: Addison-Wesley, 1979), pp. 63–66.

63. Robert Ruddell, "Developing Comprehension Abilities: Implications from Research for an Instructional Framework," in *What Research Has to Say About Reading Instruction*, ed. S. Jay Samuels (Newark, Del.: International Reading Association, 1978), pp. 108–120.

64. Bertha Kingore and Ruth Kurth, "A Workshop for Teachers in Teaching Reading Comprehension," *Reading Teacher*, 35 (November 1981), 173–179.

65. B. Rosenshine, "Skill Hierarchies in Reading Comprehension," in *Theoretical Issues in Reading Comprehension*, ed. Rand Spiro, Bertram Bruce, and William Brewer (Hillsdale, N.J.: Lawrence Erlbaum Associates, 1980), pp. 535–554.

66. Ibid.

67. B. Davey, "Think Aloud—Modeling the Cognitive Processes of Reading Comprehension," *Journal of Reading*, 27 (October 1983), 44–47.

68. Philip McFarland et al. *Focus on Literature: Viewpoints* (Boston: Houghton Mifflin Company, 1978), pp. 244–253.

69. Gary Ryan, "The Influence of Readability of Text, Motivation and Intelligence on Critical Reading Comprehension of Secondary School Social Studies Students" (Ph.D. dissertation, University of Texas, 1979). Charles Curtis and James Shaver, "Slow Learners and the Study of Contemporary Problems," *Social Education*, 44 (April 1980), 302–309.

70. John P. Lunstrum, "Building Motivation Through the Use of Controversy," *Journal of Reading*, 24 (May 1981), 687–691.

71. David Ausubel, *Educational Psychology: A Cognitive View*, 2nd ed. (New York: Holt, Rinehart and Winston, 1978), p. 149.

72. Mary F. Heller, "How Do You Know What You Know? Metacognitive Modeling in the Content Areas," *Journal of Reading*, 29 (February 1986), 415–422.

73. Wong, 227–268. H. Singer and D. Donlan, "Active Comprehension: Problem-Solving Schema with Question Generation for Comprehension of Complex Short Stories," *Reading Research Quarterly*, 27 (1982), 901–908. M. Andre and T. H. Anderson, "The Development and Evaluation of Self-Questioning Study Technique," *Reading Research Quarterly*, 14 (1978–79), 606–623.

74. A. K. O. Hori, "An Investigation of the Efficacy of a Questioning Training Procedure on Increasing the Reading Comprehension Performance of Junior High School Learning-Disabled Students" (Unpublished master's thesis, University of Kansas, 1977).

75. W. E. Combs, "Sentence-Combining Practice Aids Reading Comprehension," *The Reading Teacher*, 21 (1977), 18–24.

76. Michael Kibby, "Intersentential Processes in Reading Comprehension," *Journal of Reading Behavior*, XII (1980), 299–312.

77. Richard Larson, "Sentences in Action: A Technique for Analyzing Paragraphs," *College Composition and Communication* (February 1967), 16–22.

78. H. Alan Robinson, *Teaching Reading and Study Strategies* (Boston: Allyn and Bacon, 1978), p. 111.

79. Ibid., p. 112.

80. L. Frase and B. Schwartz, "Effect of Question Production and Answering on Prose Recall," *Journal of Educational Psychology*, 67 (1975), 628–635; S. Ross and F. Divesta, "Oral Summary as a Review Strategy for Enhancing Recall of Textual Materials," *Journal of Educational Psychology*, 68 (1976), 689–695.

81. M. Andre and T. Anderson, pp. 606–623.

82. Mary Wilkins Freeman, "A New England Nun," in *Where We Live*, ed. Michael Spring (New York: Scholastic Book Services, 1976), pp. 111–120.

83. Norris M. Sanders, *Classroom Questions: What Kinds?* (New York: Harper and Row, 1966), p. 43.

84. Willavene Wolf, Charlotte S. Huck, and Martha L. King, *The Critical Reading Ability of Elementary School Children* (Columbus, Ohio: Ohio State University Research Foundation, 1967), pp. 20–21 (Project No. 5-1040 supported by the U.S. Office of Education).

85. Nila B. Smith, *Reading Instruction for Today's Children* (Englewood Cliffs, N.J.: Prentice-Hall, 1963), p. 274.

86. Morton and Rezny, Chapter 7.

87. C. H. Knoblauch and Lil Brannon, "Writing as Learning Through the Curriculum," *College English*, 45 (September 1983), 465–474. Janet Emig, "Writing as a Mode of Learning," *College Composition and Communication* (May 1977), 123–124.

88. Gloria Blatt and Lois Matz Rosen, "The Writing Response to Literature," *Journal of Reading*, 28, No. 1 (October 1984), 8–12.

SELECTED REFERENCES

Altick, Richard. *Preface to Critical Reading*. New York: Holt, Rinehart and Winston, 1960.

Baldwin, R. Scott, and John E. Readence. "Critical Reading and Perceived Authority." *Journal of Reading*, 22 (April 1979), 617–622.

Bauman, James F., ed. *Teaching Main Idea Comprehension*. Newark, Del.: International Reading Association, 1986.

Bromley, Karen D'Angelo. "Precis Writing: Promoting Vocabulary Development." In *Classroom Strategies for Secondary Reading*. 2nd ed. Ed. W. John Harker. Newark, Del.: International Reading Association, 1985, pp. 91–97.

Brown, Ann L. "Metacognitive Development and Reading." In *Theoretical Issues in Reading Comprehension*. Hillsdale, N.J.: Lawrence Erlbaum Associates, 1980, pp. 453–475.

Cunningham, James W. "An Automatic Pilot for Decoding." *The Reading Teacher*, 32 (January 1979), 420–424.

Cunningham, James W., Patricia M. Cunningham, and Sharon V. Arthur. *Middle and Secondary School Reading*. New York: Longman, 1981.

Daines, Delva. *Reading in the Content Areas: Strategies for Teachers*. Glenview, Ill.: Scott, Foresman and Company, 1982. Chapters 1, 6, and 8.

Davey, Beth. "Think Aloud—Modeling the Cognitive Processes of Reading Comprehension." *Journal of Reading*, 27 (October 1983), 44–47.

Donlan, Dan. "Using the DRA to Teach Literacy Comprehension at All Three Response Levels." *Journal of Reading*, 28 (February 1985), 408–415.

Earley, Margaret. *Reading to Learn in Grades 5 to 12*. New York: Harcourt Brace Jovanovich, 1984. Chapters 1, 3, and 12.

Estes, Thomas H. "The Nature and Structure of Text." In *Secondary School Reading*. Eds. Allen Berger and H. Alan Robinson. Urbana, Ill.: National Conference on Research in English, 1982, pp. 85–96.

Flood, James, ed. *Promoting Reading Comprehension*. Newark, Del.: International Reading Association, 1984.

Frager, Alan M., and Loren C. Thompson. "Conflict: The Key to Critical Reading Instruction." *Journal of Reading*, 28 (May 1985), 676–683.

Gordon, Christine J. "Modeling Inference Awareness Across the Curriculum." *Journal of Reading*, 28 (February 1985), 444–447.

Guthrie, John. "Paragraph Structure." *The Reading Teacher*, 33 (April 1979), 880–881.

Haggard, Martha Rapp. "An Interactive Strategies Approach to Content Reading." *Journal of Reading*, 29 (December 1985), 204–210.

Herber, Harold. *Teaching Reading in Content Areas*. 2nd ed. Englewood Cliffs, N.J.: Prentice-Hall, 1978.

Irwin, Judith W. *Understanding and Teaching Cohesion Comprehension*. Newark, Del.: International Reading Association, 1986.

Johnson, Dale D., and Bonnie von Hoff Johnson. "Highlighting Vocabulary in Inferential Comprehension Instruction." *Journal of Reading*, 20 (April 1986), 622–625.

Karlin, Robert. *Teaching Reading in High School: Improving Reading in the Content Areas.* 4th ed. New York: Harper and Row, 1984. Chapter 7.

Moore, David W., and John E. Readence. "Processing Main Ideas Through Parallel Lesson Transfer." *Journal of Reading,* 23 (April 1980), 589–593.

Poggi, Jeanlee M. "The Case of the Confused Tenth Grader: Solving the Mystery of a Higher Level Comprehension Problem." *Journal of Reading,* 28 (October 1984), 44–47.

Robinson, H. Alan. *Teaching Reading and Study Strategies.* 2nd ed. Boston: Allyn and Bacon, 1978. Chapters 6 and 7.

Rodriguez, Joan Hughes. "When Reading Less Can Mean Understanding More." *Journal of Reading,* 28 (May 1985), 701–705.

Sanders, Norris M. *Classroom Questions: What Kinds?* New York: Harper and Row, 1966.

Shepherd, David L. *Comprehensive High School Methods.* 3rd ed. Columbus, Ohio: Charles E. Merrill, 1982.

Slater, Charles. "Writing: The Experience of One School District." *Journal of Reading,* 26 (October 1982), 24–33.

Smith, Sharon Pugh. "Comprehension and Comprehension Monitoring by Experienced Readers." *Journal of Reading,* 28 (January 1985), 292–300.

Stevens, Kathleen C. "Can We Improve Reading by Teaching Background Information?" *Journal of Reading,* 25 (January 1982), 326–329.

Stewart, Oran, and Ebo Tei. "Some Implications of Metacognition for Reading Instruction." *Journal of Reading,* 27 (October 1983), 36–43.

Thomas, Ellen L., and H. Alan Robinson. *Improving Reading in Every Class: A Sourcebook for Teachers.* 3rd ed. Boston: Allyn and Bacon, 1982. Chapter 3.

Tonjes, Marian J., and Miles V. Zintz. *Teaching Reading/Thinking/Study Skills in Content Classrooms.* Dubuque, Iowa: Wm. C. Brown, 1981. Chapters 7 and 13.

Trosky, Odarka, S., and Clifford C. Wood. "Using a Writing Model to Teach Reading." *Journal of Reading,* 26 (October 1982), 34–41.

Whimbey, Arthur. "Reading, Writing, Reasoning Linked in Testing and Training." *Journal of Reading,* 29 (November 1985), 118–123.

Wolfe, Denny, and Robert Reising. *Writing for Learning in the Content Areas.* Portland, Maine: J. Weston Walch, 1983.

Wong, Bernice Y. L. "Self-Questioning Instructional Research: A Review." *Review of Educational Research,* 55 (Summer 1985), 227–268.

CHAPTER
F O U R

READING-STUDY SKILLS

OVERVIEW

In this chapter consideration is given to the development of additional skills that enhance both comprehension and retention of information contained in printed material. These skills are important in helping a student manage reading assignments in content area classes.

Study methods, such as SQ3R, EVOKER, SQRQCQ, REAP, and PANORAMA, are described, and their usefulness in different subject areas is discussed. Attention is given to the organizational skills of outlining, summarizing, and note taking, and to location skills related to use of the library and use of books.

Techniques to develop report-writing skills are considered, and ways to help students learn to read to follow directions are suggested. Consideration is given to helping students learn from the graphic aids (maps, graphs, tables, diagrams, and pictures) in their content area reading materials, as well as to helping students learn to adjust reading rate to fit their purpose and the material to be read. Two final topics of discussion are retention and test taking.

PURPOSE-SETTING QUESTIONS

As you read this chapter, try to answer these questions:

1. What are some study methods designed for use with content area reading selections?
2. What organizational skills are helpful to students who are reading material that is to be used later in some manner?

3. What location skills do secondary school students need in order to use the library? To use books?
4. How can a teacher prepare students for writing reports in content area classes?
5. How can you teach students to read to follow directions accurately?
6. What are the types of graphic aids found in textbooks?
7. What are some factors to consider in instruction related to reading rate?
8. What are some suggestions that can help students retain what they read?
9. How can teachers help students read tests with understanding?

KEY VOCABULARY

As you read this chapter, check your understanding of these terms:

PRST	map legend	bar graphs
SQ3R	map scale	line graphs
EVOKER	graphic aids	controlled reading projectors
SQRQCQ	latitude	tachistoscopes
REAP	pacers	skimmers
PANORAMA	longitude	skimming
guide words	map projections	scanning
cross references	circle or pie graphs	picture graphs (pictographs)
précis	paraphrase	PORPE

STUDY METHODS

Many methods of approaching study-reading have been developed. The one that is probably best known and most widely used, especially for social studies and science selections, is the SQ3R method, developed by Francis Robinson.[1] The steps in the SQ3R Method are Survey, Question, Read, Recite, Review. George Spache recommends use of a similar method that does not include prereading questions. This method is PRST[2]: Preview, Read, Summarize, Test. Except for the absence of a "Question" step, this procedure is carried out in essentially the same way as the SQ3R method. A study method that has been developed by Walter Pauk especially for use with prose, poetry, and drama is the EVOKER procedure.[3] EVOKER stands for Explore, Vocabulary, Oral reading, Key ideas, Evaluation, and Recapitulation. Since mathematics materials present special problems to readers, a special technique for studying mathematics has also been developed. This technique is called SQRQCQ.[4] The steps in SQRQCQ are Survey, Question, Read, Question, Compute, Question. Each of these methods will be considered in turn, as will two other general study methods, REAP[5] and PANORAMA.[6] The steps in the REAP strategy are Read, Encode, Annotate, and Ponder; the steps in the PANORAMA technique are Purpose, Adapting rate to material, Need to pose questions, Overview, Read and relate, Annotate, Memorize, Assess.

SQ3R

When SQ3R is applied to a content area reading selection, a variety of reading activities must be employed. These activities are discussed below.

1. **Survey**   During the survey step, the reader reads the chapter title, the introductory paragraph(s), the boldface and/or italicized headings, and the summary paragraph(s). The reader should at this time also inspect any graphic aids, such as maps, graphs, tables, diagrams, and pictures. This survey provides the reader with an overview of the material contained in the reading assignment and a framework into which he or she can organize the facts contained in the selection as reading progresses.

2. **Question**   During this step the reader is expected to formulate questions that he or she expects to find answered in the selection to be studied. The author may have provided purpose questions at the beginning of the chapter or follow-up questions at the end of the chapter. If so, the student may utilize these questions as purpose questions for the reading. If not, the reader can turn the section headings into questions and read to answer self-constructed questions.

3. **Read**   This is the step in which the student reads to answer the questions formulated in the previous step. The reading will be purposeful because the student has purpose questions in mind. Notes may be taken during this careful reading. Active involvement in the reading is important if the student is to obtain maximum benefit from it.

4. **Recite**   In this step, the student tries to answer the purpose questions formulated during the second step without referring to the book or any notes that he or she has made. This step helps to "set" the information in memory, so that it can be recalled at a later time.

5. **Review**   At this point the student reviews the material by rereading portions of the book or notes taken during the careful reading in order to verify the answers given during the previous step. This activity helps the student retain the material better; immediate reinforcement of ideas helps the student overcome the tendency to forget material shortly after reading it.

The SQ3R method, like other study techniques, seems to be learned best when taught in the situations where it is expected to be used. Ed Brazee compared the effect of *skill-centered* reading instruction (focusing on a skill apart from the situation in which it will be applied) with that of *content-centered* reading instruction (focusing on application of a skill for content learning) in social studies classes.[7] One group of students was instructed in the SQ3R study method and rate flexibility before, and separate from, their social studies lesson; the teacher was "teaching general reading skills, assuming that such general skills would 'automatically' transfer to the content area." With this group, "at no time did the instructors indicate that the reading skills might be effectively used in the context of each social studies lesson." The other group received instruction in the same two skills, but the skills were taught within the framework of the social studies material. The material itself determined the skills to be taught, a situation that was not present in the control group's instruction. The second group actually received less instructional time on the reading skills, yet that group showed greater improvement in both flexibility and the ability to use the survey part of SQ3R without specific instructions to do so. The difference in improvement between the two groups was greatest on the flexibility measure. Therefore, it seems that the reading skills involved in this study are more efficiently learned and utilized when taught in the context of content materials and during, rather than before, the content class.

EVOKER

This procedure should be applied when students are reading prose, poetry, and drama. It is a method for "close reading." The steps are as follows:

1. **Explore**   Read the entire selection silently to gain a feeling for the overall message.
2. **Vocabulary**   Note key words. Look up those words with which you are not familiar. Also look up unfamiliar places, events, and people mentioned in the selection.
   Oral reading   Read the selection aloud with good expression.
4. **Key ideas**   Locate key ideas in order to help you understand the author's organization. Be sure to determine the main idea or theme of the selection.
5. **Evaluation**   Evaluate the key words and sentences in respect to their contributions to developing key ideas and the main idea.
6. **Recapitulation**   Reread the selection.

SQRQCQ

This study method is suggested for use with statement problems in mathematics. The steps are discussed briefly below.

1. **Survey**   The student reads the problem rapidly in order to obtain an idea of its general nature.
2. **Question**   In this step, the student determines the specific nature of the problem. The student asks, "What is being asked in this problem?"
3. **Read**   The student reads the problem carefully, paying attention to specific details and relationships.
4. **Question**   At this point, the student must make a decision about the mathematical operations to be carried out and, in some cases, the order in which these operations are to be performed. The student asks what operations must be performed and in what order.
5. **Compute**   The student does the computation or computations decided on in the previous step.

6. **Question** The student checks the entire process and decides whether or not the answer seems to be correct. He or she asks if the answer is reasonable and if the computations have been performed accurately.

REAP

This study technique encourages students to demand meaning from the reading because it requires an overt response. Not only reading skills, but also thinking and writing skills, are sharpened by the use of this approach. The four steps of the technique are described below.

1. **Read** The student reads to find out what the writer is saying.
2. **Encode** The student translates the writer's message into his or her own language.
3. **Annotate** During this step, the student writes the message. Any one of several forms of annotations may be used. Heuristic annotations consist of quotations from the selections; they suggest the essence of the selections and stimulate responses. Summary annotations are brief restatements of the author's main ideas and relationships between them. A thesis annotation states the author's main premise or theme. A question annotation is a formulation of the question or questions that the annotator feels the author is answering in the selection. A critical annotation includes a statement of the author's thesis, a statement of the reader's reaction to this thesis, and a defense of the reader's stated reaction. An intention annotation states the author's purpose as it is understood by the reader. In a motivation annotation, the annotator speculates about the probable motives of the writer.[8] Probe annotations give emphasis to verification, consequence, and alternatives. Personal-view annotations answer the question, "How do personal experiences, views, and feelings stack up against the thesis or main idea?" Inventive annotations take a creative approach, drawing from other contexts or synthesizing ideas.[9]
4. **Ponder** The student thinks about the author's message. Discussion with others may be a part of this step.

PANORAMA

This technique consists of eight steps that are divided into three stages. The third stage may be omitted in some cases. The stages and their component steps are described briefly below.

Preparatory Stage
1. **Purpose** The reader decides why he or she is reading the material.
2. **Adapting rate to material** The reader decides how fast the selection should be read, holding in mind the need for flexibility of rate within the selection, depending upon the purpose of the reading.

3. **Need to pose questions**   This step is similar to the "Question" step in SQ3R. The reader converts headings of various types into questions to be answered as he or she reads the material.
   Intermediate Stage
4. **Overview**   This step is similar to the "Survey" step in SQ3R. The reader surveys the main parts of the book or article in order to develop an idea of the author's organization.
5. **Read and relate**   The reader uses the type of reading techniques necessary to meet his or her purposes. The reader relates his or her background of knowledge to the material being read and seeks answers to the questions posed earlier.
6. **Annotate**   Annotations may be made directly in the book, if this is permitted. If not, annotations can be made on separate paper. They may be made in outline form. Other ideas for annotation are mentioned in the discussion of the REAP technique.
   Concluding Stage
7. **Memorize**   The student utilizes outlines and summaries as aids to memorization. Acronyms are used as aids for remembering main points.
8. **Assess**   The student evaluates his or her efforts in relation to achievement of purposes previously stated and retention of the important parts of the material.

Reasons for Use

Students need to be told the advantages of using a good study method, so that they will be more likely to use one when they do independent reading. Delores Tadlock reports that students should also be told *why* a study method works. She points out in detail the ways in which SQ3R helps the readers overcome deficiencies in their information processing systems and causes them to utilize these systems more productively.[10]

Techniques for Teaching

In teaching the use of study methods, it is important that teachers provide students with opportunities to practice the methods before asking them to use the methods independently. The teacher should guide the students through use of each study method during a class period, using an actual reading assignment. At the teacher's direction, the students should be expected to perform each step in the chosen method. For example, with the use of SQ3R, all students should be asked to survey the material together, reading the chapter title, the introduction to the chapter, the boldface and/or italicized headings, and the chapter summary. At this time they should also be asked to inspect graphic aids within the chapter. Each of the other steps, in turn, would be carried out by all students simultaneously. This technique can be applied to any of the study methods described above.

ORGANIZATIONAL SKILLS

When participating in such activities as writing reports, secondary school students need to organize the ideas they encounter in their reading. Three helpful organizational skills are outlining, summarizing, and note taking.

Outlining

Teachers should help their students to understand that outlining is recording information from reading material in a way that makes clear the relationships between the main ideas and the supporting details. Before it is possible for the students to learn to construct an outline properly, they must have learned to identify main ideas and supporting details in reading selections. Information on how to help students locate main ideas and recognize related details is found in Chapter 3.

Readiness for formal outlining tasks may be developed by having students work with *arrays*, which are freeform outlines. When constructing arrays, students are required to arrange key words and phrases in ways that show the relationships set forth by the author. They can use words, lines, and arrows to do this. It is important to use a simple, familiar story for this activity so that the students can focus upon the logical arrangement of the terms, rather than worrying about the details of the story. Example 4.1 shows a story array for the familiar story "Johnny Appleseed."

EXAMPLE 4.1   STORY ARRAY ───────────────────

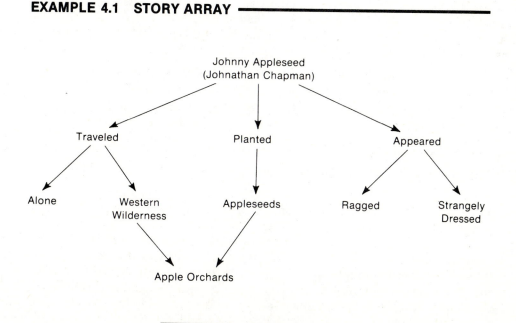

Teachers can guide students to learn how to make arrays by first supplying the words and phrases and then letting the students work in groups to complete the array. First the students read the selection; then they arrange the words and phrases appropriately, using lines and arrows to indicate relationships. The teacher questions students about positioning and direction of arrows, asking for reasons for the choices made. In addition, the teacher is available to answer the students' questions. Eventually, the students are expected to choose key words and concepts themselves and arrange them without the teacher's help. A thorough explanation of this approach and more information on developing outlining skills can be found in an article by T. Stevenson Hansell in the *Journal of Reading*.[11]

Two types of outlines that students may find useful are the sentence outline and the topic outline. Each point in a sentence outline is stated in the form of a complete sentence; the points in a topic outline are written in the form of key words and phrases. The sentence outline is generally easier to master because the topic outline involves an extra task—condensing main ideas, already expressed in sentence form, into key words and phrases.

The first step in making an outline is extracting the main ideas from the material and listing these main ideas beside Roman numerals in the order in which they occur. The next step is locating the details that support each of the main ideas and listing them beside capital letters below the main idea that they support. These details are indented to indicate subordination to the main idea. Details that are subordinate to these details are indented still further and preceded by Arabic numerals. The next level of subordination is indicated by lower case letters. Although other levels of subordination are possible, secondary school students will rarely have need of such fine divisions.

Following are some ideas about outlining that a teacher may wish to stress:

1. The degree of importance of ideas in an outline is shown by the numbers and letters used, as well as by indentation. Points that have equal importance are designated by the same number or letter style and the same indentation.
2. A topic should not be subdivided unless two points of equal value can be noted under the topic. (The student should not use a *I* without a *II* or an *A* without a *B*, for example.)
3. An outline should not incorporate unimportant or unrelated details.

A generic outline form may be helpful in demonstrating to students the proper form for an outline. Example 4.2 shows such a form.

Teachers can help students see how a textbook chapter would be outlined by showing them how the headings within the chapter indicate different levels of subordination. For example, in some textbooks the title for the outline would be the title of the chapter. Roman numeral headings would be centered headings in the chapter, capital letter headings would be side headings in the chapter, and Arabic numeral headings would be italic or paragraph headings in the chapter.

EXAMPLE 4.2   OUTLINE FORM ━━━━━━━━━━━━━━━

TITLE

I. Main idea
  A. Detail supporting I
  B. Detail supporting I
    1. Detail supporting B
    2. Detail supporting B
      a. Detail supporting 2
      b. Detail supporting 2
  C. Detail supporting I
II. Main idea
  A. Detail supporting II
  B. Detail supporting II
  C. Detail supporting II
    1. Detail supporting C
    2. Detail supporting C

One approach to helping students learn to outline their reading assignments is for the teacher to supply the students with partially completed outlines of the material and then ask the students to complete the outlines. The teacher can vary the difficulty of the activity by gradually leaving out more and more details until the students do the entire outline alone. In Example 4.3 a progression of assignments in outlining is suggested.

EXAMPLE 4.3   PROGRESSION OF OUTLINING ASSIGNMENTS ━━━

First Assignment

Title (Given by teacher)

I. (Given by teacher)
  A. (Given by teacher)
    1. (To be filled in by student)
    2. (To be filled in by student)
  B. (Given by teacher)
    1. (To be filled in by student)
    2. (Given by teacher)
      a. (To be filled in by student)
      b. (To be filled in by student)

II. (Given by teacher)
   A. (Given by teacher)
   B. (To be filled in by student)

Second Assignment

Title (Given by teacher)

I. (Given by teacher)
   A. (To be filled in by student)
   B. (To be filled in by student)
      1. (To be filled in by student)
      2. (To be filled in by student)
II. (Given by teacher)
   A. (To be filled in by student)
   B. (To be filled in by student)

Third Assignment

Title _____

I.
   A.
   B.
   C.
      1.
      2.
II.
   A.
      1.
         a.
         b.
      2.
   B.

_____

Outlining practice should probably be offered in every subject area because of the differences in organization of material among the disciplines. A standard form of outlining, used throughout the school, will decrease confusion among the students.

Summarizing

Summaries of reading assignments can be extremely valuable to secondary school students when they are studying for tests. The summaries have to be good ones to be helpful, however. In order to write a good summary, a student must restate what the author has said in a more concise form. The main ideas and essential supporting details of a selection should be preserved in a summary, but illustrative material and statements that merely elaborate upon the main ideas should not be included. The ability to locate main ideas is therefore a prerequisite skill for learning how to write good summaries. (Development of this skill is discussed in Chapter 3.)

A student must understand the material in order to write a good summary of it. He or she must comprehend the relationships between the main ideas appearing in the material and must record the material in such a way that these relationships are apparent.

The topic sentence of a paragraph is a good summary of the paragraph, if it is well written. Practice in finding topic sentences of paragraphs, therefore, is also practice in the skill of summarizing paragraphs.

Summaries of longer selections may be constructed by locating the main ideas of the component paragraphs and combining these ideas into a summary statement. Certain types of paragraphs can generally be disregarded when summaries of lengthy selections are being written. Introductory and illustrative paragraphs do not add new ideas and therefore are not helpful in constructing a concise overview of the material. Students who write summaries of their reading assignments may wish to compare their summaries with concluding or summary paragraphs written by the author to make sure that they have not omitted essential details.

When writing summaries, students should try not only to limit the number of sentences they use, but also to limit the number of words they use within sentences. Words that are not needed for conveying the meaning of the sentences can be omitted. For example,

Original sentence: A match, carelessly discarded by an unsuspecting tourist, can cause the destruction by fire of many acres of trees that will take years of work to replace.
Changed sentence: Carelessly discarded matches can result in extensive destruction of forested areas by fire.

Students can be given short passages with which to practice summarizing skills. The sample paragraph below could be used.

Voters in Hawk County defeated a proposed half-cent increase in sales tax on Tuesday. Their sales tax rate will continue to be 6 percent. The additional revenue from the tax would have been applied to educational needs in the county, if the measure had passed. Of 2,031 voters who cast ballots Tuesday, however, only 500 voted in favor of the increase.

Practice in summarizing is most effective if the material being summarized is taken from textbooks the students are currently using or from other material that they are expected to read in connection with classwork. The teacher may give the students a section of the textbook to read, along with three or four summaries of the material. The students can be asked to choose the best summary from those presented and asked to tell why the other summaries are not as good. This is good preparation for independent student writing of summaries.

Précis Writing

Karen Bromley and Laurie McKeveny[12] suggest the use of précis writing to enhance comprehension and recall of content material. Précis are concise paraphrases or abstracts of materials that retain the basic information and point of view of the original materials.

Students need to understand the purpose for précis writing, including vocabulary improvement and enhanced comprehension and retention. The teacher should demonstrate the process to the students, showing them how to analyze the original material, select main ideas for inclusion in their précis, reject nonessential material, and paraphrase the ideas through use of synonyms and restructuring of sentences. Encouraging the use of the thesaurus is a good technique.

Group composition of précis is a good beginning step. This can be done by having the students dictate as the teacher or one student records the précis. This is an application of the language experience technique described in Chapter 9.

Bromley and McKeveny suggest that models of acceptable précis be available so that students can compare the models to their own products, evaluate their efforts, and perhaps revise their work. They also suggest that students save their précis in folders for study prior to tests.

Note Taking

Taking notes on material read for classes can be a helpful memory aid. Well-constructed notes can make rereading of the material at a later time unnecessary and can thus save students time and effort. In order to take good notes, the students must think about the material they are reading; because of this, they will be more likely to remember the material when they need to use it. It is also true that the simple act of writing the ideas will help fix them in the students' memories.

Students should be encouraged to use a form of note taking that helps them most. Some may utilize outline form when taking notes on an assignment in a textbook. Others will wish to write a summary of the textbook materials. They need opportunities to practice both procedures. Ideas for practice are suggested in the two preceding sections of this text.

Notes for a research paper can be especially effective when made on index cards that can be later sorted into topics to be covered in the paper. If note cards are used, each one should include the source of information so that the paper can be well documented. Sample note cards are shown in Example 4.4. Some guidelines for note taking that may be helpful to students follow:

1. Key words and phrases should be used in notes.
2. Enough of the context must be included to make the notes understandable after a period of time has elapsed.
3. The bibliographical reference should be included with each note card or page.

EXAMPLE 4.4   NOTE CARDS ━━━━━━━━━━━━━━━━━━━━━

First reference from source:

> Fishel, Wesley R. "Indochina." *The World Book Encyclopedia*, 1978, X,
>   168.
>
>   Indochina includes the following countries: Cambodia, Laos, Vietnam.

Source previously used:

> Fishel, page 168
>
> A variety of racial and language groups are found in Indochina, resulting
> in a lack of uniformity and unity among the people.

Incomplete sentences:

> Fishel, page 169
>
> Khmer tribesmen—ancestors of present-day Cambodians—empire
> famous for art, architecture and government.

───────────────────

4. Direct quotations should be copied exactly and should be used sparingly.
5. Notes should differentiate clearly between direct quotations and reworded material.
6. Notes should be as brief as possible.
7. Use of abbreviations can make note taking less time consuming. Examples: ∴ for therefore; w/ for with; = for equals.

Teachers may be able to help their students learn to take good notes by "thinking through" a textbook assignment with them in class, emphasizing the points that should be included in a good set of notes. Students then can be encouraged to take notes on another assignment and compare them with a set of notes the teacher has constructed on the same material.

Another way to help students develop note-taking skills is the *Guided Lecture Procedure* (GLP), devised by Brenda Wright Kelly and Janis Holmes.[13] The steps in the GLP are as follows:

1. Before the lecture begins, the teacher writes the lecture objectives (maximum of four) in brief form on the chalkboard, accompanied by new terminology to be presented in the lecture.
2. Students copy this material from the board before the lecture begins. This gives them a purpose for listening.
3. The lecturer speaks for approximately thirty minutes while the students listen *without* taking notes.
4. The lecturer stops and gives the students approximately five minutes to write down all that they recall from the lecture. Students are encouraged to categorize and relate ideas.
5. Students are divided into small groups to discuss the lecture and organize their notes. The lecturer serves as an assistant during this phase, helping students find the answers they seek.
6. After the class, students reflect upon the material and the class activities. This step helps promote long-term memory.
7. Then students write from memory a narrative covering the main points of the lecture and conclusions drawn.

This procedure, which is excellent as a note-taking strategy, is also a study approach and, to a large degree, a teaching procedure. Teachers will find it helpful in many content classes.

LOCATION SKILLS

In order to take part in many study activities, students need to be able to locate specific reading material. The teacher can help students by showing them location aids that exist in libraries and books.

Libraries

Teachers may not wish to teach students location skills connected with the library because they feel that the librarian should perform this task. The librarian, however, may feel that he or she is not supposed to function as an instructor. Because of these conflicting viewpoints, students may receive no instruction in the use of the library, even though they are encouraged to use it for both reference work and recreational reading. This problem can be solved if teachers and librarians work cooperatively to help students develop the skills needed for effective library use.

The librarian can help by showing the students the location of books, periodicals, card catalogs, and reference materials (dictionaries, encyclopedias, atlases, *Readers' Guide to Periodical Literature,* and others) in the library; by explaining the procedures for checking books out and returning them; and by clarifying the rules relating to behavior in the library. The librarian can also demonstrate the use of the card catalog and the *Readers' Guide* and explain the arrangement of books in the library. (The Dewey Decimal System is the arrangement most commonly used in school libraries in the United States for classifying nonfiction books.) Posters may be constructed and displayed in the library to remind students of check-out procedures, library rules, and arrangement of books. A poster might, for example, list the major divisions of the Dewey Decimal System. These divisions are indicated below.

000–099:   Generalities
100–199:   Philosophy and Psychology
200–299:   Religion
300–399:   The Social Sciences
400–499:   Language
500–599:   Pure Sciences
600–699:   Technology (Applied Sciences)
700–799:   The Arts
800–899:   Literature
900–999:   General History and Geography[14]

Other posters that might be profitably displayed in the library could include samples of the different types of cards that are found in the card catalog. Sample cards are shown in Example 4.5.

EXAMPLE 4.5   CARD CATALOG CARDS

Subject Card:

```
    Animal Stories

A   Adams, Richard
    Watership Down
Rex Collings, Ltd. (c) 1972
```

Author Card:

```
A   Adams, Richard

    Watership Down
Rex Collings, Ltd. (c) 1972
```

Title Card:

```
Watership Down
A   Adams, Richard
        Watership Down
Rex Collings, Ltd. (c) 1972
```

Cross-Reference Card:

```
                    Zeus
                    see
              Greek Mythology
```

The librarian can be extremely helpful to the teacher. He or she may

1. help the teacher locate both printed and nonprinted materials related to current units of study.
2. help the teacher plan a unit on use of reference materials in the library.
3. help the teacher discover reading interests of individuals and specific groups of students.
4. alert the teacher to professional reading materials in his or her content area.
5. give presentations to the students on the availability and location of materials for a particular content area.
6. put materials on a particular content topic on reserve for a class.

Content area teachers will often want students to make use of the library. Simply telling them to do so is insufficient preparation for them. Students need guidance for each library assignment. If students are expected to use the card catalog to locate reference books or recreational reading selections, they should be reminded that the cards in the card catalog are filed alphabetically and that there are subject, author, and title cards for each book. A brief review of the Dewey Decimal System of classification may be advisable if nonfiction books are to be located.

If students seek material in popular magazines, the teacher might review or initially teach the use of the *Readers' Guide to Periodical Literature*, in which articles from approximately 160 popular magazines are indexed. Each article is indexed under the subject and the author's name. Sometimes an article also is included under the title. A pamphlet entitled *How to Use the Readers' Guide to Periodical Literature* is a useful source for the teacher.[15]

Social studies teachers may wish to teach students to use *The New York Times Index,* which is a subject index of articles from the *New York Times.* Since dates of the articles' publication are included, students may use this index as an aid to locating articles on the same subjects in local papers.

Teaching students how to locate material within informational books and special reference books (encyclopedias, dictionaries, almanacs, atlases) found in the library is also a concern of the content area teacher. Finding a book on a subject is useless if the student cannot then find within the book the information that is needed. Skills needed for this task are discussed below.

Books

Most informational books include special features that students can use to locate needed material. Content area teachers will find that explaining the functions of prefaces, tables of contents, indexes, appendixes, glossaries, footnotes, and bibliographies will be well worth the effort because of the increased efficiency with which the students will be able to use books.

Preface and/or Introduction

When a content area teacher presents a new textbook to secondary school students, he or she should ask them to read the preface and/or introduction to the book to obtain an idea about why the book was written and the manner in which the material is to presented. The teacher can then explain the function and importance of these book parts in books used for outside research reading.

Table of Contents

The table of contents of a textbook should also be examined on the day the textbook is distributed. The students can be reminded that the table of contents tells what topics the book includes and the pages on which these topics begin. They should also be led to understand that the table of contents makes it unnecessary to look through the entire book to find a particular section. A brief drill with the textbook can help to emphasize these points. Questions such as these can be asked:

1. What topics are covered in this book?
2. What is the first topic that is discussed?
3. On what page does the discussion about _____ begin? (This question can be repeated several times with different topics inserted in the blank.)

Indexes

Students need to understand that an index is an alphabetical list of the important items and/or names mentioned in a book, with the pages where each item or name appears. Many books contain one general index, but some have subject and author indexes as well as other specialized indexes (for example, a first-line index in a poetry or music book). Most indexes include both main headings and subheadings. Students generally need practice in using index headings to locate information within their books.

A preliminary lesson on what an index is and how to use it to locate information can be presented. Afterward, the teacher can use the student's own textbooks in teaching index use. The lesson idea shown in Example 4.6 can be modified for use with an actual index in a content area textbook. (The sample index is not from an actual textbook.)

EXAMPLE 4.6   SAMPLE INDEX AND QUESTIONS ───────

Sample Index

Absolute value, 145, 174–175
Addition
    of decimals, 101
    of fractions, 80–83
    of natural numbers, 15–16, 46–48
    of rational numbers, 146–148
    of real numbers, 170
Angles, 203
    measurement of, 206–207
    right, 204
Axiom, 241
Base
    meaning of, 5
    change of, 6–7

Index Questions

1. On what page would you look to find out how to add decimals? Under what main topic and subheading did you have to look to discover this page number?
2. On what pages will you find *base* mentioned?
3. What pages contain information about absolute value?
4. On what pages would you look to find out about measurement of angles? What main heading did you look under to discover this? What subheading did you look under?
5. Where would you look to find information about adding real numbers? Would you expect to find any information about real numbers on page 146? Why, or why not?
6. Is there information about addition of natural numbers on pages 46–48? Is information on this topic found on any other pages?

(The following questions could be incorporated into the lesson if an actual index were being used.)

7. Find the meaning for *base* and read it aloud. Did you look in the index to find the page number? Could you have found it more quickly by looking in the index?

_____

Appendixes

Students can be shown that the appendixes in textbooks and in other books contain information that they may find helpful. Bibliographies and tabular material may appear in appendixes. At times students may need to use this material, but they will not use it if they do not know where to find it.

Glossaries

Glossaries are often found in content area textbooks. Students can be taught that glossaries are similar to dictionaries but include only words presented in the books in which they are found. Glossaries of technical terms can be of much help to students in understanding a book's content. The skills needed for proper use of a glossary are the same as those needed for using a dictionary. (See Chapter 2 for further discussion of use of the dictionary.)

Footnotes

Footnotes tell the source or sources of information included in the text. If further clarification of the material is needed, a student may use the footnote as a guide to the original source.

Bibliographies

Bibliographies may refer students to other sources of information about the subjects discussed in a book. Students can be encouraged to turn to these sources for clarification of ideas and/or for additional information on a topic. The bibliography at the end of a chapter in a textbook is generally a list of references that the author(s) consulted when preparing the chapter and also references that contain additional information about the subject. Some books contain bibliographies that list books by a particular author or that list appropriate selections for particular groups. Bibliographies are extremely valuable aids for students doing assigned research activities.

Special Reference Books

Secondary school students are often called upon to find information in such reference books as encyclopedias, dictionaries, almanacs, and atlases. Unfortunately, many students have reached junior high or high school without being able to use such books effectively.

Important items related to effective use of reference books include:

1. Knowledge of alphabetical order (Most secondary school students will have mastered alphabetical order, but a few will need help.)
2. Knowledge that encyclopedias, dictionaries, and some atlases are arranged in alphabetical order
3. Ability to use guide words (knowing the location of guide words on a page, and understanding that they represent the first and last entry words on a dictionary or encyclopedia page)
4. Ability to use cross references (related primarily to use of encyclopedias)
5. Ability to use pronunciation keys (related primarily to use of dictionaries)
6. Ability to choose from several possible word meanings the one that most closely fits the context in which the word was found (related to use of dictionaries)
7. Ability to interpret the legend of a map (related to use of atlases)
8. Ability to interpret the scale of a map (related to use of atlases)
9. Ability to locate directions on maps (related to use of atlases)
10. Ability to determine which volume of a set will contain the information being sought (related primarily to use of encyclopedias)
11. Ability to determine key words under which related information can be found

Because encyclopedias, almanacs, and atlases are often written on extremely high readability levels, teachers should use caution in assigning work in these reference books. Students are not likely to profit from trying to do research in books written on a level they find frustrating. When students are asked to look up material in books that are too difficult for them to read with understanding, they tend to copy the material word for word instead of trying to extract the important ideas.

Kristina MacCormick and Janet Pursel conducted a study to determine the readability levels of three well-known encyclopedias: the *Academic American Encyclopedia*, the *Encyclopaedia Britannica*, and the *World Book*.[16] They applied the Fry Readability Graph to one hundred samples from each of the three encyclopedias and found an overall average readability of sixteenth grade for the *Encyclopaedia Britannica*, sixteenth grade for *Academic American Encyclopedia*, and eleventh grade for *World Book*. Some selections from each of the encyclopedias were appropriate for students reading at grade levels nine through twelve, but none were appropriate for grade levels eight or below in the *Encyclopaedia Britannica* or the *Academic American*. In these two encyclopedias, 88 percent and 90 percent, respectively, of the articles were at the college level, whereas only 44 percent of the articles in the *World Book* were at the college level. Teachers should be aware of the reading levels of encyclopedias they choose to assign to students in their content classrooms for work on reports.

A surprising number of junior high school students and a few high school students do not realize that, when you look up the name of a person in the encyclopedia, it will be alphabetized by the last name, not the first. A student who had to write a report on James Otis came to one of the authors of this text and proclaimed that James Otis was not in the encyclopedia. Puzzled, the author asked the student to show her how he had proceeded in looking for the name. He went to the "J" encyclopedia and began to look for "James." He seemed surprised when he was told that names are listed alphabetically according to *last* name, and then first name. Example 4.7 can be used as a diagnostic measure to determine whether students know how to look up people's names; when used in this way, it should be followed by appropriate explanations for those students who are unable to answer all the items correctly. This activity (or a similar one) may also be used as a reinforcement activity following such explanations. If the activity was used initially as a diagnostic instrument, it should be modified when used for reinforcement.

EXAMPLE 4.7 WORKSHEET ON USING THE ENCYCLOPEDIA ———

Directions: Pretend you have an encyclopedia whose volumes are arranged so that there is one volume for each letter of the alphabet. Look at the following names and decide which volume of the encyclopedia you would have to use to find each name. Write the letter of the volume in the space provided beside the name. When you finish, use the answer key to check your work. If you don't understand why you made your mistakes, ask the teacher for an explanation.

_____ Richard Nixon
_____ Marie Curie
_____ Clara Barton
_____ Martin Van Buren
_____ Martin Luther King
_____ Robert Louis Stevenson
_____ John Paul Jones
Answer key: N, C, B, V, K, S, J

Example 4.8 is an exercise that gives students practice in locating various types of information in the encyclopedia. To complete this activity (or one modeled on it), students decide which key words to look under in order to find certain information. For example, for "Education in Sweden" they would need to look first under Sweden and then find the section on education. When completed, this activity should be discussed in class to show students why they made the errors they made and how to approach the task correctly.

Because encyclopedias vary in content and arrangement, students should be taught to use several different sets. They should be asked to compare the entries in

EXAMPLE 4.8   WORKSHEET ON USING THE ENCYCLOPEDIA ———

Directions: Look up each of the following topics in the encyclopedia. On the line beside each topic, write the letter of the volume in which you found the topic and the page number on which the topic is discussed.

1. Tennis   _____
2. Solar system   _____
3. U.S. Constitution   _____
4. Lobster   _____
5. Oleander   _____
6. Sampan   _____
7. Education in Sweden   _____
8. Computer use in library systems   _____

several different sets on a specified list of topics. They may also be asked to compare different sets of encyclopedias on an overall basis, noting such features as type of index used, number of volumes, ease of reading, and date of publication.

Students frequently are not extremely familiar with dictionary content and usage. A few, but not a large number, have some trouble with alphabetical order. A much larger number have trouble with guide words and use of the pronunciation key, and many do not realize the variety of information that is found in a dictionary entry. Spending some time to familiarize students with dictionary use can pay good dividends in their future learning.

Example 4.9 shows a page from a dictionary that is recommended for use with grades nine through twelve and provides some instructional commentary that could be helpful to use with students who show a need for better understanding of the dictionary.

Similar dialogues to that in Example 4.9 can be held for other words until all of the features of the dictionary have been highlighted. For example, the teacher could read a sentence containing the word *knot* and have students decide which definition fit the context and why. Principal parts of verbs and degrees of adjectives should also be given attention.

Since dictionary skills are presented to students repeatedly during their school careers, even though they may not be thoroughly learned, they may seem to be boring to the students. The development of games, audiovisual presentations, and other motivational activities may enhance interest in the instruction. For example, paper-and-pencil scavenger hunts in the library might be fun for the students. They might be asked to find a book by Henry Melville (write down its name, call number, and location), the dictionary definition of *catamaran,* and the volume and page number of the *World Book Encyclopedia* that contains a discussion of catamarans. Each student or small group of students could have a different list.

EXAMPLE 4.9   DICTIONARY PAGE AND INSTRUCTIONAL COMMENTARY

knelt ● knotty   668

knelt (nĕlt) v. var. p.t. & p.p. of KNEEL.
Knes·set (knĕs'ĕt') n. [Heb. Kéneseth, assembly < kanas, he gathered.] The Israeli parliament.
knew (nōō, nyōō) v. p.t. of KNOW.
Knick·er·bock·er (nĭk'ər-bŏk'ər) n. [After Diedrich Knickerbocker, fictitious author of History of New York, by Washington Irving.] **1. a.** A descendant of the Dutch settlers of New York. **b.** A New Yorker. **2. knickerbockers.** Full breeches gathered and banded just below the knee.
knick·ers (nĭk'ərz) pl.n. [Short for KNICKERBOCKERS.] **1.** Long bloomers once worn as underwear by women and girls. **2.** KNICKERBOCKERS 2.
knick·knack (nĭk'năk') n. [Redup. of KNACK.] A trinket.
knife (nīf) n., pl. **knives** (nīvz) [ME knif < OE cnīf.] **1.** A cutting instrument having a sharp blade with a handle. **2.** A cutting edge: BLADE. —v. **knifed, knif·ing, knifes.** —vt. **1.** To use a knife on, esp. to cut, stab, or wound. **2.** Informal. To hurt, defeat, or betray by underhand means. —vi. To cut or slash a way with or as if with a knife. —**knif·er** n.
knife-edge (nīf'ĕj') n. **1.** The cutting edge of a blade. **2.** A sharp knifelike edge <felt the knife-edge of criticism> **3.** A metal wedge used as a low-friction fulcrum for a balancing beam or lever.
knight (nīt) n. [ME < OE cniht.] **1.** A medieval tenant giving military service as a mounted man-at-arms to a feudal landholder. **2.** A usu. high-born medieval gentleman-soldier raised by a sovereign to privileged military status after training as a page and squire. **3.** The holder of a nonhereditary dignity conferred by a sovereign in recognition of personal merit or services to the country. **4.** A member of an order or brotherhood designating its members knights. **5. a.** A zealous defender or champion of a principle or cause. **b.** A lady's devoted champion. **6.** A chess piece moved either two squares horizontally and one vertically or two vertically and one horizontally. —vt. **knight·ed, knight·ing, knights.** To raise (a person) to knighthood. —**knight'li·ness** n. —**knight'ly** adj.
knight errant (ĕr'ənt) n., pl. **knights errant. 1.** A knight of medieval romance who wandered in search of adventure. **2.** One given to adventurous or quixotic conduct. —**knight'-er'rant·ry** (nīt'ĕr'ən-trē) n.
knight·hood (nīt'hŏŏd') n. **1.** The rank, profession, or dignity of a knight. **2.** Behavior of or qualities worthy of a knight: CHIVALRY. **3.** Knights as a group.
Knight of Co·lum·bus (kə-lŭm'bəs) n. A member of a philanthropic fraternal society of Roman Catholic men.
Knight of Pythias n. A member of a secret philanthropic fraternal order.
Knights of the Round Table pl.n. The knights of the court of King Arthur in Arthurian legend.
Knight Templar n., pl. **Knights Templars.** A member of a 12th–14th cent. order of knights founded to protect pilgrims in the Holy Land during the Second Crusade.
knish (kə-nĭsh') n. [Yiddish < R.] Dough stuffed with potato, meat, or cheese and baked or fried.
knit (nĭt) v. **knit** or **knit·ted, knit·ting, knits.** [ME knitten < OE cnyttan, to tie in a knot.] —vt. **1.** To make by intertwining yarn or thread in a series of connected loops. **2.** To unite securely and closely. **3.** To draw (the brows) together in wrinkles: FURROW. —vi. **1.** To make a fabric or garment by knitting. **2.** To come or grow together securely. **3.** To come together in wrinkles or furrows. —**knit'** n. —**knit'ter** n.
knit·ting needle (nĭt'ĭng) n. A long, thin, pointed rod used for knitting.
knit·wear (nĭt'wâr') n. Knitted garments in general.
knives (nīvz) n. pl. of KNIFE.
knob (nŏb) n. [ME knobbe, prob. < MLG.] **1. a.** A rounded protuberance. **b.** A rounded dial. **2.** A prominent rounded hill or mountain. —**knobbed** adj. —**knob'by** adj.
knob·ker·rie (nŏb'kĕr'ē) n. [Afr. knopkierie: knop, knob (< MDu. cnoppe) + kieri, club < Hottentot kirri.] A short club with one knobbed end, used by South African tribesmen as a weapon.

knobkerrie
Three types of knobkerries

knock (nŏk) v. **knocked, knock·ing, knocks.** [ME knokken < OE cnocian.] —vt. **1.** To strike with a hard blow. **2.** To cause to collide. **3.** To produce by hitting <knocked a hole in the fence> **4.** To instill as if with blows <knocked some sense into their

heads> **5.** Slang. To criticize adversely: DISPARAGE. —vi. **1.** To strike a blow or series of blows. **2.** To collide. **3. a.** To make a clanking or pounding noise. **b.** To undergo engine knock. —**knock around (or about).** Informal. **1.** To be rough or brutal with: MALTREAT. **2.** To wander from place to place. **3.** To discuss or consider. —**knock back.** Informal. To gulp (an alcoholic drink). —**knock down. 1.** To disassemble into parts. **2.** To declare sold at an auction, as by striking a blow with a gavel. **3.** Informal. To reduce, as in price. **4.** Slang. To receive as wages: EARN. —**knock off.** Informal. **a.** To take a break or rest from: STOP. **b.** To cease work. **2.** Informal. To make, accomplish, or consume hastily or easily. **3.** Informal. To eliminate: deduct <knocked 15% off the bill> **4.** Slang. To kill. **5.** Slang. To hold up or rob. **6.** Informal. To copy the design or production of. —**knock out. 1.** To render unconscious. **2.** To defeat by knocking down to the canvas for a count of ten in boxing. **3.** Informal. To render useless or inoperative <power knocked out by a storm> **4.** Informal. To exert or exhaust (oneself or another). —**knock together.** To make or assemble quickly or carelessly. —**knock up. 1.** Chiefly Brit. To wake up by knocking at the door. **2.** To wear out: EXHAUST. —n. **1.** An instance of knocking. **2.** The sound of a sharp tap on a hard surface: RAP. **3.** A clanking, pounding noise made by an engine, esp. one in poor operating condition. **4.** Slang. A cutting, often petty criticism. —**knock cold.** To knock out. —**knock dead.** Slang. To affect strongly, usu. positively <a virtuoso piano performance that knocked us dead> —**knock for a loop.** Slang. To surprise greatly: ASTONISH. —**knock out of the box.** Baseball. To force the removal of (an opposing pitcher) by heavy hitting.
knock·a·bout (nŏk'ə-bout') n. A small sloop with a mainsail, a jib, and a keel but no bowsprit. —adj. **1.** Boisterous and rowdy. **2.** Appropriate for rough wear or use <knockabout clothes>
knock·down (nŏk'doun') adj. **1.** Forceful enough to knock down or overwhelm: POWERFUL <a knockdown punch> **2.** Designed to be assembled and disassembled easily and quickly <knockdown office furniture> —n. **1.** An act of knocking down. **2.** An overwhelming blow. **3.** A device or mechanism designed to be assembled and disassembled quickly and easily.
knock·down-drag·out (nŏk'doun-drăg'out') adj. Marked by roughness, violence, and acrimony.
knock·er (nŏk'ər) n. One that knocks, as a fixture for knocking on a door.
knock-knee (nŏk'nē') n. An abnormal condition in which one knee is turned toward the other or in which each is turned toward the other. —**knock'-kneed'** adj.
knock·off (nŏk'ôf', -ŏf') n. Informal. A usu. inexpensive copy, as of a garment <a knockoff of a designer original>
knock·out (nŏk'out') n. **1.** The act of knocking out or the state of being knocked out. **2.** The knocking out of an opponent in boxing. **3.** Slang. One that is very impressive or attractive.
knockout drops pl.n. Slang. A solution, as of chloral hydrate, put into a drink to render the drinker unconscious.
knock·wurst (nŏk'wûrst', -wŏŏrst') n. var. of KNACKWURST.
knoll¹ (nōl) n. [ME knolle < OE cnoll.] A small rounded hill or mound: HILLOCK.
knoll² (nōl) [ME knollen, prob. alteration of knellen, to knell < OE cnyllan.] Archaic. —vt. & vi. **knolled, knoll·ing, knolls.** To ring or sound mournfully. —**knoll** n.
knop (nŏp) n. [ME knoppe < OE cnop.] A decorative knob.
knot¹ (nŏt) n. [ME < OE cnotta.] **1. a.** A compact intersection of interlaced material, as cord, ribbon, or rope. **b.** A fastening made by tying together lengths of material, as rope, in a prescribed way. **2.** A decorative bow of ribbon, fabric, or braid. **3.** A unifying bond, esp. a marriage bond. **4.** A tight group or cluster <knots of spectators> **5.** A difficult problem. **6.** A hard node, esp. on a tree, at a point from which a stem or branch grows. **b.** The circular, often darker cross section of such a node as it appears crossgrained on a piece of cut lumber. **7.** A protuberant growth in living tissue. **8.** Naut. **a.** A division on a log line used to measure the speed of a ship. **b.** A unit of speed, one nautical mile per hour, approx. 1.15 statute miles per hour. **usage:** Knot is a unit of nautical speed with the built-in meaning of "per hour." Therefore, a ship would properly be said to travel at ten knots (not at ten knots per hour). **c.** A distance of one nautical mile. —v. **knot·ted, knot·ting, knots.** —vt. **1.** To tie in or fasten with a knot. **2.** To entangle. **3.** To cause to form knots. —vi. **1.** To become entangled. **2.** To form a knot. —**knot'ted** adj.
knot² (nŏt) n. [Orig. unknown.] A shore bird, Calidris canutus or C. tenvirostris, related to the sandpiper.
knot·grass (nŏt'grăs') n. **1.** A low-growing weedy plant, Polygonum aviculare, having tiny greenish flowers. **2.** A grass having jointed stems.
knot·hole (nŏt'hōl') n. A hole in lumber where a knot used to be.
knot·ty (nŏt'ē) adj. **-ti·er, -ti·est. 1.** Tied or snarled in knots. **2.** Covered with knots or knobs: GNARLED. **3.** Difficult to compre-

ā pat   ā pay   âr care   ä father   ĕ pet   ē be   hw which   ĭ pit
ī tie   îr pier   ō pot   ō toe   ô paw, for   oi noise   ōō took

Instructional Commentary

Notice the two words at the top of the page. These words are called guide words. The first word is *knelt.* Find it in the body of the dictionary page. Where is it? (Students indicate that it is the first word on the page.) The second word is *knotty.* Find it in the body of the dictionary page. Where is it? (Students indicate that it is the last word on the page.)

Look at the bottom two lines of the righthand column on this page and the lefthand column on the next page. (Only the first part of this is shown in the figure.) That is the pronunciation key. It has the special letter markings found in the phonetic respellings beside the entry words and a common word that has the sound each marking represents. The letter or letters that represent the sound are in bold print in the common word.

Find the word *knobkerrie* on this page. Look at its phonetic respelling in the parentheses following it. Notice that the first *k* does not appear in the respelling because it is not heard when the word is pronounced. Checking the pronunciation key, note that the *o* is pronounced like the *o* in *pot.* Looking again at the respelling, notice that the first syllable has the darkest, biggest accent mark, meaning that it gets the heaviest emphasis. Checking the pronunciation key once more, decide what sound the vowel in the second syllable has. (Students should decide that it sounds like the *e* in *pet.*) How strongly is the second syllable accented? (Students should say that it is accented less strongly than the first syllable, but more strongly than the third syllable.) How did you know? (Students should indicate that the size of the accent mark told them.) What does the final vowel in the word sound like? (Students should indicate that it sounds like the *e* in *be.*) Where did you look to find out? (Students should respond that they looked in the pronunciation key.)

Notice the *n.* just after the phonetic respelling. It tells you the part of speech of the word. What part of speech is *knobkerrie*? (If students cannot answer this question, point out the page in the dictionary that has the key to abbreviations and labels used.)

Look at the material in brackets following the *n.* It tells the etymology, or history, of the word. What does *Afr.* stand for? What does *MDu.* stand for? (If the students cannot answer immediately, refer again to the page of abbreviations.) Notice that the word is derived from words meaning "knob" and "club." Now read the definition. If, after reading the definition, you still could not decide what a knobkerrie was, you could study the illustration provided in the dictionary. Do all knobkerries look exactly alike? (After examining the illustration, students should be able to respond that they do not.)

REPORT WRITING

Content area teachers often assign reports to be written on topics related to the content area. Sometimes students are allowed to choose their own topics for reporting. In other instances, the teacher may ask each student to write on a predetermined topic. The process below can be followed to help students prepare good reports. The first step mentioned is not applicable if the teacher chooses the topic.

Step 1   Select a topic. The topic selected must be pertinent to the content area material being studied. It should be chosen because of its interest value for the reporter and for the rest of the class if the reports are to be shared. Ordinarily, students choose topics that are much too broad for adequate coverage. The teacher needs to help students narrow their topics so that the task of preparing the report is more manageable.

Step 2   Collect information on the topic. Students use the location skills discussed in previous sections of this chapter in order to collect information from a variety of sources. The organizational skill of note taking covered earlier is also essential for use at this point.

Step 3   Organize the material. Outlining the information collected is the main activity in this step. Material from the different sources used must be fused together at this time. Sequence and relationship of main ideas and details are important considerations in forming the outline.

Step 4   Write a first draft. Utilizing the outline just formulated and the notes compiled, the students write an initial draft of the report.

Step 5   Proofread the first draft. The students now read the first draft of the report to check for sentence and paragraph sense, cohesiveness of the information, appropriate usage, correct spelling, and proper punctuation. They check to make sure that all material is properly documented.

At this point, peer editing may be utilized. With this approach, the peer editor reads the report of his or her classmate carefully, answering questions provided by the teacher. Some sample questions might be as follows: Does the report have a title that accurately reflects its contents? Does the report have a good beginning that sparks interest in the topic? Is the sequence in which the information is presented logical? If not, what do you believe is wrong with it? Is enough information included? What questions remain to be answered by the report, in your opinion? Does the report have errors in mechanics (spelling, capitalization, punctuation, etc.)? If so, mark them for the author. Does the report have a conclusion that sums up the material adequately? Do you have any questions or suggestions for the author? After answering these questions, the editor returns the report and comments to the author, who revises the report, carefully considering the editor's comments. The editor may be asked to read and react to the report again before it is submitted to the teacher. Often two students work together, acting as peer editors for one another.

Step 6   Revise the report. The students make needed changes in the initial draft and rewrite the report in a form acceptable for submission to the teacher.

If word processing software and compatible microcomputers are available for report writing activities, revising the first draft is not likely to be as onerous a task as it may seem when the entire paper must be rewritten or retyped. As a result, use of word processing in report writing often results in superior end products.

The teacher can do much to help prepare students so they can perform effectively on an assigned written report. A procedure that a teacher might follow is described below.

1. Name a broad topic related to the course of study. Ask the students for suggestions as to how the topic could be narrowed to make it more manageable. Consider a number of acceptable topics that might be derived from the original topic.
2. Choose one of the acceptable narrowed topics. Take the students to the library and have them locate sources of information on the topic. Ask each of them to take notes from at least one source and to record bibliographical information. Remind them to make use of skimming and scanning techniques as they search for information. (See the section on "Techniques of Increasing Rate and Flexibility" later in this chapter.)
3. Return to the classroom. As a class, synthesize the notes into a single outline. (Use the chalkboard or overhead projector.)
4. Write the report from the outline as a whole-class or small-group activity, working as the scribe or assigning a student to be the scribe.
5. Have the students proofread the draft for content and mechanics.
6. Make needed changes in organization, spelling, and so forth, based upon the proofreading.

Essentially, the teacher who follows this procedure has walked the students through the steps of report writing before asking them to attempt it on their own. The students will know what to expect when they are assigned individual reports to write. Help with skills of note taking, outlining, summarizing information, and locating information should be a prerequisite for assignment of a written report. Help should also be given with footnote and bibliographic entries. A guide such as *Form and Style: Theses, Reports, Term Papers* (Houghton Mifflin, 1986) can be a valuable resource. Example 4.10 shows a sample page on footnote form from this useful guide. Some dictionaries, such as the *Houghton Mifflin College Dictionary* (see sample page in Example 4.9), also offer information on footnotes and bibliographic entries.

Some computer software has been developed to help students with basic research skills. The following programs from the Americana Software Library (Grolier Educational Corporation, New York) are examples: *The Americana Topic Finder and Research Planner*™ and *Note Card Maker*™. These programs are available for Apple II computers.

READING TO FOLLOW DIRECTIONS

Secondary school students are constantly expected to follow written directions both in the classroom and in everyday experiences. Teachers write assignments on the chalkboard and distribute duplicated materials that have directions written on them. Textbooks and workbooks in different content areas contain printed directions that students are expected to follow. This is particularly true of sci-

EXAMPLE 4.10   FORM AND STYLE GUIDE PAGE ———

NOTES

Books

Basic form
1 Jacob Bronowski, *The Ascent of Man* (Boston: Little, Brown, 1973), 57–67.

Two authors
2 James G. March and Herbert A. Simon, *Organizations* (New York: Wiley, 1958), 79.

More than three authors
3 Marion C. Sheridan et al., *The Motion Picture and the Teaching of English* (New York: Appleton–Century–Crofts, 1965), 37.

Two authors with same last name
4 Wilma R. Ebbitt and David Ebbitt, *Writer's Guide and Index to English*, 6th ed. (Glenview: Scott, Foresman, 1978), 67.

Pseudonym, real name supplied
5 J. Abner Peddiwell, Ph.D. [Harold Benjamin], *The Saber-Tooth Curriculum* (New York: McGraw-Hill, 1939), 78–85.

Author's name missing
6 [Dorothy Scarborough], *The Wind* (New York: Harper, 1925).

or

7 *The Wind* (New York: Harper, 1925), 27.

Group or corporation as author
8 Holiday Magazine, *Spain* (New York: Random House, 1964), 52.

Editor and author, emphasis on author
9 William C. Hayes, *Most Ancient Egypt*, ed. Keith C. Seele (Chicago: Univ. of Chicago Press, 1965), 5.

Translator and author, emphasis on translator
10 Suzette Macedo, trans., *Diagnosis of the Brazilian Crisis*, by Celso Furtado (Berkeley: Univ. of California Press, 1965), 147–53.

Two editors
11 Arthur S. Link and Rembert W. Patrick, eds., *Writing Southern History: Essays in Historiography in Honor of Fletcher M. Green* (Baton Rouge: Louisiana State Univ. Press, 1966), 384.

Examples of Note and Bibliography Forms

Source: William Giles Campbell, Stephen Vaughn Ballou, and Carole Slade, *Form and Style: Theses, Reports, Term Papers*, 7th ed. (Boston: Houghton Mifflin Company, 1986), p. 126.

ence, mathematics, and vocational education books, but it applies to all subject areas. Chapters 6 and 7 give examples of reading tasks in different subject areas that require students to follow directions. This section considers the general problem of following directions, especially in everyday activities.

Young people and adults alike need to be able to follow directions to accomplish a number of daily activities. Many people fail at a task either because they do not know how to read to follow directions or because they ignore the directions and try to perform the task without understanding the sequential steps that compose it. Almost everyone is familiar with the saying, "When all else fails, read the directions." This tendency to take printed directions lightly may have been fostered in the classroom. Teachers hand out printed directions and proceed to explain them orally. Teachers also often tell students each step to perform as they progress through the task, rather than asking the students to read the directions and point out which parts they need clarified. These actions promote a general disregard for reading directions.

There are many aspects of everyday activities that require us to follow directions: traffic signs, recipes, assembly and installment instructions, forms to be completed, voting instructions, and registration procedures, to name a few. A traffic sign gives a single direction that is vital for a person to follow in order to avoid bodily injury, misdirection, fines, or other penalties. The other activities mentioned above involve multiple steps to be performed. Failure to complete the steps properly may result in various penalties: inedible food, nonworking appliances, receipt of incorrect merchandise, and so forth.

Teachers are in an excellent position to show students the importance of being able to follow written directions. They are also in a position to show students techniques for reading directions with understanding.

Following directions requires two basic comprehension skills—the ability to locate details and the ability to detect sequence. Because each step in a set of directions must be followed exactly and in the appropriate sequence, reading to follow directions is a slow and deliberate task. Rereading is often necessary. The following procedure may prove helpful.

1. Read the directions from beginning to end to get an overview of the task to be performed.
2. Study any accompanying pictorial aids that may help in understanding one or more of the steps or in picturing the desired end result.
3. Read the directions, visualizing each step to be performed. Read with an open mind, disregarding your own preconceived ideas about the procedure involved.
4. Take note of such key words as *first, second, next, last,* and *finally.* Let these words help you picture the order of the activities to be performed.
5. Read each step again, just before you actually perform it.
6. Carry out the steps in the proper order.

Students will learn to follow directions more easily if the presentation of activities is scaled in difficulty from easy to hard. Teachers can start with one-step directions and then progress to two-step, three-step, and longer sets of directions as the proficiency of the students increases.

Some activities for developing skills in following directions are suggested below.

Activities
1. Give students a paragraph containing key direction words (*first, next, then, last, finally,* and so forth) and ask them to underline the words that help to show the order of events.
2. Prepare duplicated directions for Japanese paper-folding activities. Provide the students with paper, and ask them to follow the directions.
3. Make it a practice to refer students to written directions instead of telling them how to do everything orally. Ask the students to read the directions silently and then tell you in their own words what they should do.
4. Teach the meanings of words commonly encountered in written directions, such as *affix, alphabetical, array, estimate, example, horizontal, phrase,* and *vertical.* Some other words that might need attention are listed in an article by Helen Newcastle.[17]
5. Have the students follow directions in order to make something from a kit.
6. Use worksheets similar to those in Examples 4.11 and 4.12 to make a point about the importance of following directions.

EXAMPLE 4.11   WORKSHEET ON FOLLOWING DIRECTIONS ———

Questionnaire

Read all of this questionnaire before you begin to fill in the answers. Work as quickly as you can. You have five minutes to finish this activity.

Name _____

Address _____

_____

Phone Number _____

Age _____

What is your father's name? _____

What is your mother's name? _____

What is your mother's occupation? _____

Do you have any brothers? _____ If so, how many? _____

Do you have any sisters? _____ If so, how many? _____

Do you plan to go to college? _____ If so, where? _____

What career are you most interested in? _____

How many years of preparation past high school will be necessary if you pursue this career? _____

Who is the person that you admire most? ————————————————

What is this person's occupation? _____
After you have completed reading this questionnaire, turn the paper over and write your name on the back. Then give the paper to your teacher. You should have written nothing on this side of the page.

EXAMPLE 4.12   WORKSHEET ON FOLLOWING DIRECTIONS ——

Carefully follow the directions given in the sentences below:

1. Circle the numeral that stands for the largest number: 11, 52, 4, 16, 21, 32, 35, 15.
2. Underline the first and last numeral in this list: 2, 7, 1, 4, 3, 8.
3. Draw a line through the third word in this sentence.
4. Circle each word in this sentence that begins with the letters *th*.
5. Add 44 and 76. Take the result and subtract 10. Divide that result by 10. Place your answer on this line. _____
6. Circle every noun in this sentence.

Any exercises for improving the ability to understand details and detect sequence will also help students in their attempts to improve skills in following directions. See Chapter 3 for ideas in these areas.

GRAPHIC AIDS

Textbooks contain numerous graphic aids that are often disregarded by students because they have had no training in the use of such aids. Maps, graphs, tables, charts and diagrams, and pictures can all help students understand the textbook material better if they are given assistance in learning to mine the information from these graphic aids.

Edward Fry developed a taxonomy of graphic aids that he feels should receive instructional time.[18] Example 4.13 illustrates this taxonomy.

Maps

Maps may be found in social studies, science, mathematics, and literature textbooks, although they are most common in social studies textbooks. Since maps are generally included in textbooks to help clarify the narrative material, students need to be able to read maps in order to fully understand the material being presented.

EXAMPLE 4.13 AN ILLUSTRATED VERSION OF A TAXONOMY OF GRAPHS

1. Lineal

a. Simple   story

b. Multiple   history

c. Complex

     Hierarchy   organization

     Flow   computer

     Process   chemicals

     Sociogram   friendship

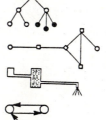

2. Quantitative

a. Frequency Polygon   growth

b. Bar graph   production

c. Scattergram   test scores

d. Status Graph   scheduling

e. Pie Graph   percentage

f. Dials   clock

3. Spatial

a. Two Dimensions
(single plane)   map   floor plan

b. Three Dimensions
(multiplane)   relief map   math shapes

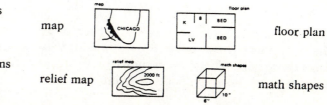

EXAMPLE 4.13   (continued)

4. Pictorial

  a. Realistic

  b. Semipictorial

  c. Abstract

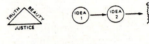

5. Hypothetical

  a. Conceptual

  b. Verbal

6. Near Graphs

  a. High Verbal Outline

Main Idea
a. Detail
b. Another detail

  b. High Numerical

Table	
25	4.2
37	6.1
71	7.3

  c. Symbols

$ ✠ 🚭

  d. Decorative Design

Source: Reprinted by permission of Edward Fry.

Some students may have received background in map-reading techniques in the elementary school, but many will not have had any structured preparation for reading maps. Therefore, secondary school students may vary greatly in their abilities to handle assignments containing maps. A survey of map-reading skills should be administered early in the school year by teachers who expect map reading to be an assigned activity at frequent intervals throughout the year. A sample map and some useful questions for surveying map-reading skills are shown in Example 4.14.

EXAMPLE 4.14   U.S. AIR AND WATER POLLUTION MAP AND MAP QUESTIONS

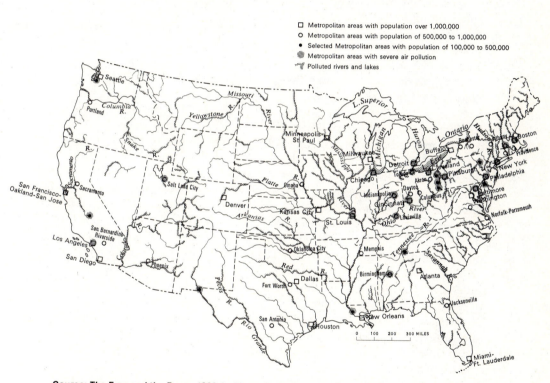

Source: *The Free and the Brave*, 1980, by Henry F. Graff. Courtesy of the Riverside Publishing Company.

Questions

1. What kind of information does this map supply?
2. What symbol indicates a metropolitan area with a population from 500,000 to 1,000,000?
3. What is the distance from Birmingham to Atlanta?
4. What lakes are shown on the northern boundary of this map?

5. What are possible reasons for the areas of severe air pollution shown on the map? The polluted rivers and lakes?

_____

After administering a survey of map-reading skills and evaluating the results, the teacher should systematically teach any of the following skills that the students have not yet mastered:

1. Locating and comprehending the map title
2. Determining directions
3. Interpreting a map's legend
4. Applying a map's scale
5. Understanding latitude and longitude
6. Understanding common map terms
7. Making inferences concerning the material represented on a map
8. Understanding projections

The first step in map reading should be examining the title of the map to determine what area is being represented and what type of information is being given about the area. Map titles are not always located at the tops of the maps, as students often expect them to be. Therefore, students may overlook the title unless they are alerted to the fact that they may need to scan the map to locate the title.

Next, the students should locate the directional indicator on the map and orient themselves to the map's layout. They should be aware that north is not always at the top of the map, although many maps are constructed in this manner.

Interpretation of the legend or key of the map is the next step in reading the map. The legend contains an explanation of each of the symbols used on a map. If a student does not understand these symbols, the map is incomprehensible.

In order to determine distances on a map, the student must apply the map's scale. Because it would be highly impractical to draw a map the actual size of the area represented (for instance, the United States), maps show areas greatly reduced in size. The relationship of a given distance on a map to the same distance on the earth is shown by the map's scale.

An understanding of latitude and longitude may be helpful in reading some maps. A system of parallels and meridians can enable a reader to locate places on a map using coordinates of degrees of latitude and longitude. Parallels of latitude are lines on a globe that are parallel to the equator. Meridians of longitude are lines that encircle the globe in a north-south direction, meeting at the poles.

There are many common map terms that students need to understand in order to comprehend maps. Among these terms are _latitude_ and _longitude_, of course, as well as _Tropic of Cancer, Tropic of Capricorn, North Pole, South Pole, equator, hemisphere, peninsula, continent, isthmus, gulf, bay_, and many others.

Teachers should encourage more than simple location activities with maps. They should ask students to make inferences concerning the material represented on maps. For example, for a map showing the physical features of an area (mountains, rivers, lakes, deserts, swamps, and so forth), the students might be asked to decide what types of transportation would be most appropriate. This type of activity is extremely important at the secondary level.

Students may need help in understanding different types of projections. Flat maps and globes can be compared to illustrate distortion. Inexpensive globes can be taken apart and flattened out to show one common type of projection.

It may be helpful to students to relate a map of an area they are studying to a map of a larger area that contains the original area. For example, a map of Tennessee can be related to a map of the United States. In this way, the position of Tennessee within the United States becomes apparent.

Many types of maps may be found in content area textbooks: road maps, relief maps, physical maps, vegetation maps, political maps, product maps, population maps, and weather maps. All of these maps require students to apply some or all of the map skills discussed above. Each type may require special explanation, because each may present a unique problem to the reader.

Further suggestions for working with map reading skills are given below.

Activities

1. Before presenting a chapter in a textbook that requires much map reading, ask students to construct a map of an area of interest to the class (for example, in a health or physical education class, a map of recreation facilities in the town). Help students draw the map to scale. (You may want to call upon a mathematics teacher to help with this aspect.) Make sure students include a title, a directional indicator, and a legend. This exercise will give students the opportunity for direct experience with the important tasks in map reading. It will also help prepare them to read the maps in their content textbook with a more complete understanding because their "map schema" will have been enlarged and activated. (See Chapter 3 for an explanation of schemata.)

2. When students encounter a map in a content area textbook, help them use the legend by asking questions such as the following:

Where is there a railroad on this map?
Where is the state capitol located?

Reprinted by permission of King Features.

Where do you find a symbol for a college?

Are there any national monuments in this area? If so, where are they?

3. Help students with map terminology by asking them to point out on a wall map such features as *gulf* and *peninsula* when these features are the pertinent ones in the content presentation.

Graphs

Graphs often appear in social studies, science, and mathematics books, and sometimes in books for other content areas. Graphs are used to make comparisons among quantitative data.

Types of Graphs

There are four basic types of graphs:

1. Picture graphs, which compare quantities using pictures
2. Circle or pie graphs, which show relationships of individual parts to the whole
3. Bar graphs, which use vertical or horizontal bars to compare quantities
4. Line graphs, which show changes in amounts

Picture graphs (or pictographs) Picture graphs are the easiest to read. Visualization of data is aided by use of this type of graph. The reader must remember, however, that only approximate amounts can be indicated by pictographs, making it necessary to estimate amounts when interpreting these graphs.

Circle or pie graphs Proportional parts of a whole can be shown most easily through use of circle or pie graphs. These graphs show the percentage of the whole that each individual part represents.

Bar graphs Bar graphs are useful for comparing the sizes of several items or the size of a particular item at different times. These graphs may be either horizontal or vertical.

Line graphs Line graphs can depict changes in amounts over a period of time. Line graphs have vertical and horizontal scales. Each point that is plotted on a line graph has a value on both scales.

Representative samples of each of these types of graphs and accompanying sample questions are shown in Examples 4.15, 4.16, 4.17, 4.18, and 4.19.

Graph-Reading Skills

Students can be taught to discover from the title of a graph what comparison is being made or information is being given; they can learn to interpret the legend of a picture graph and to accurately derive needed information from a graph.

EXAMPLE 4.15   SAMPLE PICTURE GRAPH AND QUESTIONS ——————

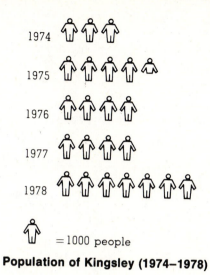

Population of Kingsley (1974–1978)

Questions

1. What does each symbol on this graph represent?
2. What time period does this graph cover?
3. During what year did Kingsley have the largest population?
4. Approximately how many people lived in Kingsley in 1976?

EXAMPLE 4.16   SAMPLE CIRCLE GRAPH AND QUESTIONS ——————

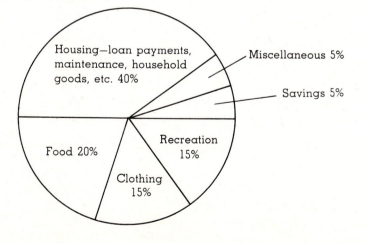

Monthly Budget

Questions

1. What kind of information does this graph contain?
2. What budget item consumes the most money?
3. What percentage of the budget is allocated for food?
4. What does the "Miscellaneous" category mean?

EXAMPLE 4.17 SAMPLE BAR GRAPH (VERTICAL) AND QUESTIONS

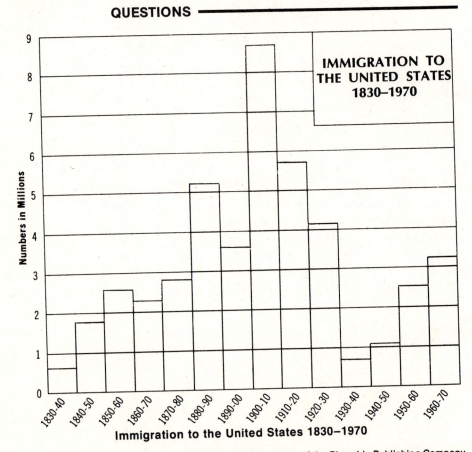

IMMIGRATION TO THE UNITED STATES 1830–1970

Immigration to the United States 1830–1970

Source: *The Free and the Brave*, 1980, by Henry F. Graff. Courtesy of the Riverside Publishing Company.

Questions

1. What is the topic of the bar graph?
2. How many people immigrated during the years 1910–20?
3. During what ten-year span did the largest number of people immigrate?
4. During what ten-year span did the smallest number of people immigrate?

EXAMPLE 4.18   SAMPLE BAR GRAPH (HORIZONTAL) AND QUESTIONS

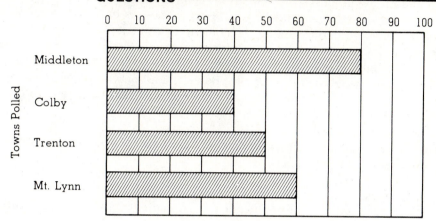

Percent of Voters for John Drew

Questions

1. What percentage of the voters from Middleton were for John Drew?
2. In which of the four towns was John Drew least popular?
3. In which of the four towns did John Drew have the most support?
4. In which town were 40 percent of the voters for John Drew?

Teachers can help students discover the following information about the graphs in their textbooks:

1. The purpose of the graph (Usually indicated by the title, the purpose becomes more evident when the accompanying narrative is studied.)
2. The scale of measure on bar and line graphs
3. The legend of picture graphs
4. The items being compared
5. The location of specific pieces of information within a graph (For example, finding the intersection of the point of interest on the vertical axis with the point of interest on the horizontal axis.)
6. The trends indicated by a graph (For example, does an amount increase or decrease over a period of time?)
7. The application of graphic information to actual life situations (A graph showing the temperatures for each month in Sydney, Australia, could be used for planning what clothes to take on a trip to Sydney at a particular time of the year.)

Edward Fry points out that "graphical literacy—the ability to both comprehend and draw graphs—is an important communication tool that needs more emphasis in the school curriculum." He urges teachers to include graphing in their assignments, perhaps taking a section of the content textbook or an outside reading and asking students to make as many graphs as they can to illustrate ideas in the material.[19] One of the best ways to help students learn to read graphs is to have them construct their own graphs. Below is a list of types of graphs students can construct to help them develop a graph schema that will enhance understanding of the graphs found in content area textbooks.

1. A picture graph showing the number of tickets each homeroom purchased for the senior prom
2. A circle graph showing the percentage of each day that the student spends in various activities (sleeping, eating, studying, and so forth)
3. A bar graph showing the number of outside readings that the student completed for English class during each grading period
4. A line graph showing the student's weekly quiz scores for a six-week period

EXAMPLE 4.19   SAMPLE LINE GRAPH AND QUESTIONS

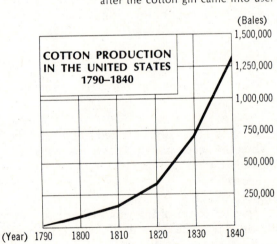

Describe the increase in cotton production that took place after the cotton gin came into use.

COTTON PRODUCTION IN THE UNITED STATES 1790–1840

Source: *The Free and the Brave,* 1980, by Henry F. Graff. Courtesy of The Riverside Publishing Company. Reprinted by permission.

Questions

1. What time period is depicted on this graph?
2. What does the vertical axis represent?
3. What does the horizontal axis represent?

4. What was the trend in cotton production over the years represented?
5. Did the invention of the cotton gin in 1793 have an effect on cotton production? Describe the effect.

(Note: If a teacher has students in the class who have directionality lags, the terms *vertical* and *horizontal* should be explained for them, since these terms are particularly difficult for these students.)

The teacher can construct graphs such as the ones in Examples 4.15, 4.16, 4.17, 4.18, and 4.19 and ask students to answer questions about them. Questions also can be asked about particular graphs in the students' textbooks.

Tables

Tables, which are found in reading materials of all subject areas, contain information arranged in vertical columns and horizontal rows. One problem that students have with reading tables is extracting the needed facts from a large mass of available information. The large amount of information provided in the small amount of space can confuse students unless the teacher provides a procedure for reading tables.

Like the titles of maps and graphs, the titles of tables contain information about their content. Also, since tables are arranged in columns and rows, the headings for these columns and rows can also provide information. Specific information is obtained by locating the intersection of an appropriate column with an appropriate row. A sample table is shown in Example 4.20. The questions that follow the table are presented as models for types of questions that teachers might ask about the actual tables in students' content textbooks.

EXAMPLE 4.20   SAMPLE TABLE AND QUESTIONS

Average Temperatures in Darby and Deal for June–December 1977
(in degrees)

		June	July	August	September	October	November	December
					Months			
Towns	Darby	70°	72°	75°	74°	65°	65°	60°
	Deal	68°	69°	71°	70°	65°	64°	58°

Questions

1. What type of information is located in this table?
2. What are the column and row headings? What are the subheadings?
3. What time period is covered by the table?

4. Which of the two towns had the lowest average temperatures over the time period represented?
5. What was the average temperature for Darby in October 1977?
6. In what month did Darby and Deal have the same average temperature?
7. What is the unit of measurement used in this table?

Example 4.21 is a table from a computer textbook. It offers a comparison of different generations of computers. It differs from the table in Example 4.20 in that there are no row headings, just column headings. Similar types of information are located in similar rows, however, making comparisons easier. Questions that might be asked concerning this table follow it.

EXAMPLE 4.21   TABLE FROM COMPUTER TEXTBOOK AND TABLE QUESTIONS

Computer Generations

First	Second	Third	Fourth
1946–1960	1960–1964	1964–1970s	1970s–1980s
Vacuum tubes	Transistors	Integrated circuits	Large-scale integrated circuits
Hundreds of computers in use	Thousands of computers in use	Tens of thousands of computers in use	Millions of computers in use
1000 circuits per cubic foot	100,000 circuits per cubic foot	10 million circuits per cubic foot	Billions of circuits per cubic foot
ENIAC, EDSAC, UNIVAC		Minicomputers developed	Microcomputers developed
	10 times faster than first generation	100 times faster than second generation	10 times faster than third generation
	Magnetic-tape storage	Disk storage	Floppy disks

Source: Barbara L. Kurshan, Alan C. November, and Jane D. Stone, *Computer Literacy Through Applications* (Boston: Houghton Mifflin Company, 1986), p. 81.

Questions

1. What type of information is located in this table?
2. What are the column headings?
3. What would be a good heading for each row, if the rows had headings?
4. In what time period were second generation computers manufactured?
5. How many fourth generation computers are in use?
6. To what generation of computers did UNIVAC belong?
7. How fast are fourth generation computers in relation to second generation computers?
8. What kind of storage did second generation computers use?

Charts and Diagrams

Charts and diagrams appear in textbooks for many different content areas. They are designed to help students picture the events, processes, structures, relationships, or sequences described by the text. At times they may be used as summaries of the text material.

Students must be made aware of the abstract nature of charts and of the fact that they often distort or oversimplify information. Interpretation of the symbols found in charts and understanding of the perspective used in diagrams are not automatic; teachers must provide practice in such activities.

The representative samples in Examples 4.22 and 4.23 show how visual aids can be used in textbooks.

EXAMPLE 4.22 SCIENCE CHART

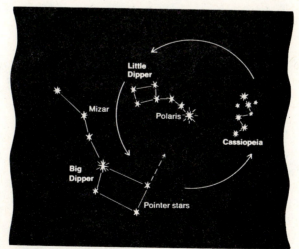

A line extended from the two bright stars at the "dipper" end of the Big Dipper points approximately to the North Star, Polaris.

Source: Joseph H. Jackson and Edward D. Evans: *SPACESHIP EARTH: Earth Science*, p. 72. Copyright © 1980 by Houghton Mifflin Company. Used by permission.

EXAMPLE 4.23   SCIENCE DIAGRAM

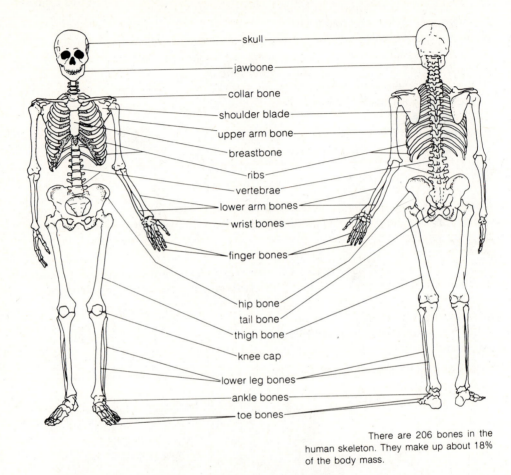

- skull
- jawbone
- collar bone
- shoulder blade
- upper arm bone
- breastbone
- ribs
- vertebrae
- lower arm bones
- wrist bones
- finger bones
- hip bone
- tail bone
- thigh bone
- knee cap
- lower leg bones
- ankle bones
- toe bones

There are 206 bones in the human skeleton. They make up about 18% of the body mass.

Source: James E. McLaren et al: *SPACESHIP EARTH: Life Science*, p. 113. Copyright © 1981 by Houghton Mifflin Company. Used by permission.

Numerous types of charts and diagrams are used in the various content areas: tree diagrams (English); flow charts (mathematics); process charts (science); and so on. Careful instruction in how to read such charts and diagrams must be provided for interpretation of content material. Another example of a diagram is a floor plan. See Chapter 7, page 288.

The teacher can point out that distortions are frequently found in textbook drawings. For example, when referring to the chart in Example 4.22, the teacher should tell students that the star symbols represent actual stars; that the lines connecting the stars are not visible but have been drawn to depict the shape of each constellation; that the solid arrows indicate the apparent rotation of the

EXAMPLE 4.24   SCIENCE TEXTBOOK ILLUSTRATION ——————

Source: Joseph H. Jackson and Edward D. Evans: *SPACESHIP EARTH: Earth Science*, p. 491. Copyright © 1980 by Houghton Mifflin Company. Used by permission.

constellations; and that the dashed arrow represents the pointer function of two stars in the Big Dipper. The teacher can also explain that some of the stars in the constellations are brighter than others and that some stars are so dim at times that they can barely be seen. Students can be helped to see that the diagrams in Example 4.23 are views of the human body's bone structure, which is not visible because it is covered by flesh and skin. The teacher can also identify the front and rear views and discuss differences between them. Diagrams such as this might also appear in health textbooks.

Pictures and Cartoons

Content area textbooks contain pictures that are designed to illustrate the material described and to interest students. The illustrations may be photographs that offer a realistic representation of concepts, people, and places, or they may be line drawings that are somewhat more abstract in nature.

Students frequently see pictures merely as space fillers, reducing the amount of reading they will have to do on a page. Therefore, the students may pay little attention to the pictures, although the pictures are often excellent sources of information.

Since pictures are representations of experiences, they may be utilized as vicarious means of adding to a student's store of knowledge. Teachers should help students extract information from textbook pictures by encouraging them to study the pictures before and after reading the text, looking for the purpose of each picture and its specific details. Studying pictures may help students understand and retain the information illustrated.

Example 4.24 depicts information about the birds referred to in a textbook. Because few students have had direct experiences with all of these birds, the vicarious experience gained from this picture is valuable.

EXAMPLE 4.25 SCIENCE TEXTBOOK CARTOON

Source: Joseph H. Jackson and Edward D. Evans: *SPACESHIP EARTH: Earth Science*, p. 511. Copyright © 1980 by Houghton Mifflin Company. Used by permission.

Cartoons are special types of pictures that contain special symbols. They often distort the things they represent in order to make a point. Students should be encouraged to read cartoons critically.

The cartoon in Example 4.25 can be used for an exercise in examining how a cartoon delivers a message: teachers can help the students connect the environmental issue involved with the situation depicted in the cartoon.

ADJUSTING RATE TO FIT PURPOSE AND MATERIALS

Study time will be used most efficiently if students are taught to vary their reading rates to fit their purposes and the materials they are reading. Making these adjustments, which is important for good comprehension, is known as *flexibility of rate.* Good readers adjust rates, thinking, and approaches automatically and are not aware that they make several changes when reading a single page.

Flexible readers are able to discriminate between important and unimportant ideas and to read important ideas carefully. They do not give each word, phrase, or paragraph equal attention but select the parts that are significant for understanding the selection. Familiar material is read faster than new material because familiarity with a topic allows the reader to anticipate ideas, vocabulary, and phrasing. A selection that has a lighter vocabulary burden, more concrete concepts, and an easily managed style of writing can be read more rapidly than material with a heavy vocabulary load, many abstract concepts, and a difficult writing style. Light fiction that is read strictly for enjoyment can and should be absorbed much faster than the directions for a science experiment; newspapers and magazines can be read more rapidly than textbooks; theoretical scientific content and statistics must be read more slowly than much social studies content.

When a student is looking for isolated facts, such as names and dates, he or she can scan a page for key words rather than read every word. When the purpose is to determine the main ideas or organization of a selection, a student can skim the material.

Students often think that everything should be read at the same rate. Thus, some of them read light novels as slowly and deliberately as they read mathematics problems. These students will probably never enjoy reading for recreation because they work so hard at reading and it takes so long. Other students move rapidly through everything that they read. In doing so, they generally fail to grasp essential details in content area assignments, although they "finish" reading all of the assigned material. Rate of reading should never be considered apart from comprehension. Therefore, the optimum rate for reading any material is the fastest rate at which an acceptable level of comprehension is obtained. Teachers who wish to concentrate upon improving their students' reading rates should include comprehension checks with all rate exercises.

Naturally, it is desirable for a person to read each type of material at the fastest possible speed that will meet his or her purposes. This speed will vary from an extremely slow rate for savoring the beauty of phrasing in a poem to a very rapid rate for getting a general overview of the news stories appearing on the front page of the paper.

Work on increasing reading rate should not be emphasized until basic word recognition and comprehension skills are thoroughly under control. Improvement in these skills often results in increased rate without any special attention to rate. For best results, flexibility of rate should be developed with the content materials students are expected to read. For research supporting this contention, see the discussion of Ed Brazee's study on the SQ3R method (pp. 135–136).

Factors Affecting Rate

There are many factors that influence the rate at which a person can read a particular selection. Some of these factors include the following:

1. Factors related to the material
   a. Size and style of type
   b. Format of the pages
   c. Use of illustrations
   d. Organization
   e. Writing style of the author
   f. Abstractness or complexity of ideas
2. Factors related to the reader
   a. Background of experiences
   b. Reading ability
   c. Attitudes and interests
   d. Reason for reading

Obviously, these factors will differ with each selection. Therefore, different rates will be appropriate for different materials.

Poor reading habits may greatly decrease reading rate. Poor habits include excessive vocalizing (forming each word as it is read); sounding out all words, both familiar and unfamiliar; excessive regressing (going back and rereading previously read material); and pointing at each word with the index finger. Concentrated attention to these problems can yield good results. Often secondary school students simply need to be made aware of the habits that are slowing them down and to be given some suggestions for practice in overcoming these habits. Using the machines cited in the next section of this chapter has proved to be helpful in correcting some of these problems.

Techniques for Increasing Rate and Flexibility

Many methods have been devised to help students increase or adjust their rates of reading. These approaches include the use of special machines, timed exercises, skimming and scanning exercises, and flexibility exercises.

Machines

Using machines to increase reading rate generally is not a responsibility of the content area teacher. However, the content area teacher may have students who, despite encouragement and teacher direction, read very slowly, in a word-by-word fashion, with many regressions. These students lack confidence in their ability to read and may claim that they cannot read more rapidly. The content teacher may refer these students to a reading laboratory or clinic for help by a reading teacher who uses rate machines to develop students' speed. Because they cannot regress as they read and are forced to move ahead through the material, students realize that they can indeed read more rapidly.

After rate increases have been achieved with the machines, the reading teacher and the content teacher can both help the students maintain their gains by using regular reading materials in timed situations. In choosing appropriate selections, the content teacher should avoid material that includes many small details (for example, a science experiment or a mathematics statement problem). Materials that present general background and recreational reading in the content area are more useful for this activity (for example, the story of a scientific discovery or the biography of a mathematician).

The machines commonly used for increasing rate are controlled reading filmstrip projectors; controlled reading motion picture projectors; tachistoscopes; pacers; and skimmers.

Controlled reading filmstrip projectors use sets of specially developed filmstrips. The stories printed on the filmstrips are exposed to the students one line at a time, or part of a line at a time, as a scanner moves across the line of print in a left-to-right sequence. The rate of presentation can be adjusted to fit the student or students using the material. Some of these films are accompanied by excellent books that emphasize comprehension through encouraging a preview of the material before the machine is used, programmed study of vocabulary, and checks for comprehension.

Films to increase rate are available for use with ordinary sixteen-millimeter motion picture projectors. The films let the reader view parts of a line in a left-to-right progression. The material that comes before and after the highlighted portion is obscured. The speed of the film can be varied in some cases by changing projector settings. The wide speed variations possible with the filmstrip projectors mentioned above are not possible with these films. Comprehension questions are included.

Tachistoscopes are devices that present printed materials for brief periods of time (for example, 1/100 of a second, one second, and so forth). Tachistoscopic attachments are available for use with filmstrip or slide projectors or with overhead projectors. Some are independent devices. Some have electronically controlled exposures, some have mechanically controlled exposures, and some have manually controlled exposures. Hand tachistoscopes can be constructed for individual use and are operated manually. These devices are designed to encourage students to take in more print in a single fixation and to shorten fixation time.

Pacers have arms, beams of light, or shades that move down the page of printed material from top to bottom at regulated speeds. The student tries to read below the moving bar or within the beam of light.

A skimmer has a bead of light that moves down the center fold of the book at a rapid rate to encourage the reader to keep up an appropriate rate when skimming. Only Educational Developmental Laboratories offers a machine of this type.

A newer machine has appeared upon the horizon recently. Computers have become involved in rate instruction as computer software has been developed to promote speed reading. Some is not very effective, but *Speed Reading: The Computer Course* (Bureau of Business Practices, Waterford, Connecticut) is one program that has received a very favorable review.[20] The program is available for the IBM PC and for the Apple. It includes techniques for broadening peripheral vision, looking for phrases, and focusing on key words in each lesson. Some comprehension skills are also given attention. Students keep records related to rate and comprehension and, thus, are able to compete with themselves in order to improve. Students can control the speed of materials presented.

Timed Readings

To help students increase their rate of reading material that does not require intensive study-reading, content teachers may use timed reading. As Brazee's study indicates (see pp. 135–136), such skills may be learned best in situations where they are actually used.

Content teachers may also refer students to the reading teacher for rate training. This can be especially effective if the content teacher reinforces the use of the skill in appropriate classroom situations (for example, when students are reading for general information).

Two types of timed readings are common: (1) reading for a fixed period of time and then counting the number of words read and computing the words read per minute and (2) reading a fixed number of words, computing the time elapsed while reading, and deriving a rate score in words per minute.

Timed readings should always be accompanied by comprehension checks. An extremely high rate score is of no use if the student fails to comprehend the material. Teachers should encourage rate increases only if comprehension does not suffer. Some students need help in basic reading skills before they will be able to participate profitably in these rate-building activities.

Graphs can be kept of timed rate exercises over a period of weeks or months. Seeing visible progress can motivate students to work on improving rate. Comprehension charts should also be kept in order to view rate increase in the proper perspective.

Timed readings are more satisfactory as rate-building exercises than machine-oriented exercises are. The main reason for this is that machines will not always be available to push students to read rapidly; eventually students must learn to operate without a machine for a crutch.

EXAMPLE 4.26   SKIMMING ━━━━━━━━━━━━━━━━━━━━━━━━━━━

Shown below is a view of how you might skim an article. Notice that you read all of the first and second paragraphs to get an overview. By the third or fourth paragraph you must begin to leave out material; read only key sentences and phrases to get the main ideas and a few of the details. Note also that, since final paragraphs often summarize, it may be worthwhile to read them more fully.

Skimming must be done "against the clock." That is, you must try to go as fast as you possibly can while leaving out large chunks of material. Be careful to avoid getting interested in the story since this might slow you down and cause you to read unnecessary detail. Skimming is work. It is done when you do not have much time and when you wish to cover material at the fastest possible rate.

Usually the first paragraph will be read at average speed all the way through. It often contains an introduction or overview of what will be talked about. Sometimes, however, the second paragraph contains the introduction or overview. In the first paragraph the author might just be "warming up" or saying something clever to attract attention. Reading a third paragraph completely might be unnecessary but ... . the main idea is usually contained in the opening sentence ... ... topic sentence ... . Besides the first sentence the reader should get some but not all the detail from the rest of the paragraph ... . names ... ... dates ... . This tells you nothing	... ... hence sometimes the main idea is in the middle or at the end of the paragraph. Some paragraphs merely repeat ideas ... . Occasionally the main idea can't be found in the opening sentence. The whole paragraph must then be read. Then leave out a lot of the next paragraph ... . to make up time ... . Remember to keep up a very fast rate ... . 800 w.p.m. ... ... Don't be afraid to leave out half or more of each paragraph ... . Don't get interested and start to read everything ... . skimming is work	... . Lowered comprehension is expected ... ... 50% ... . not too low ... ... Skimming practice makes it easier ... . gain confidence ... ... Perhaps you won't get anything at all from a few paragraphs ... . don't worry ... ... Skimming has many uses ... ... reports ... ... newspapers ... ... supplementary ... text ... ... The ending paragraphs might be read more fully as often they contain a summary. Remember that the importance of skimming is to get only the author's main ideas at a very fast speed.

Source: Reprinted by permission of Edward Fry.

Skimming and Scanning Techniques

Skimming and scanning are special types of rapid reading. Skimming refers to reading to get a general idea or overview of the material, and scanning means reading to find a specific bit of information. Skimming is faster than rapid reading of most of the words in the material because, when a person skims material, he or she reads selectively. Scanning is faster than skimming because only one bit of information is being sought. When scanning, a person runs his or her eyes rapidly down the page, concentrating on the particular information being sought.

Example 4.26 shows how you might go about skimming an article. Skimming techniques are used in the survey step of the SQ3R method discussed on pages 135–136. Teachers can help develop skimming skills as they work to teach this study method.

Other skimming activities include the following:

1. Give the students a short period of time to skim an assigned chapter and write down the main ideas covered.
2. Ask students to skim newspaper articles and match them to headlines written on the board. Have a competition to see who can finish first with no errors.
3. Give the students the title of a research topic and have them skim an article to decide whether it is pertinent. David Memory and David Moore developed a procedure for doing this that involves group activity: students skim a series of articles and then share their reactions.[21]

Scanning activities are easy to design. Some examples are:

1. Have the students scan a telephone book page to find a specific person's number.
2. Have the students scan a history chapter to find the date of a particular event.
3. Have the students scan a textbook to find information on a particular person.

By permission of Johnny Hart and Field Enterprises, Inc.

Students need to scan for key words related to the specific facts that they seek. An exercise in generating key words that are related to a specific topic may be beneficial.

Flexibility Exercises

Since not all materials should be read at the same rate, students need assistance in determining appropriate rates for different materials. The table in Example 4.27 shows three reading rates of a good reader, each of which is appropriate for a particular type of reading material.

EXAMPLE 4.27 RATE CHART ——————————————————————

Kind of Reading	Rate	Comprehension
Slow: *Study reading* speed is used when material is difficult or when high comprehension is desired.	200 to 300 w.p.m.	80–90%
Average: An *average reading* speed is used for everyday reading of magazines, newspapers and easier textbooks.	250 to 500 w.p.m.	70%
Fast: *Skimming* is used when the highest rate is desired. Comprehension is intentionally lower.	800 + w.p.m.	50%

Source: Reprinted by permission of Edward Fry.

———————————————

One type of flexibility exercise is to ask a series of questions such as the ones below and then discuss the students' reasons for their answers:

1. What rate would be best for reading a statement problem in your mathematics textbook?
2. Which could you read most quickly and still achieve your purpose—a television schedule, a newspaper article, or a science textbook?
3. Is skimming an appropriate way to read a science experiment?
4. What technique of reading would you use to look up a word in the dictionary?

RETENTION

Secondary school students are expected to retain much of the material they are assigned to read in their content area classes. Retention is demonstrated in different ways. When a student recognizes a word or a sound-symbol association learned previously, he or she exhibits retention of this information. If the student fails to recognize the previously learned information, retention is faulty for some reason. If a person who has learned a rule for decoding printed words is asked to state the rule and is able to do so, he or she can be said to have recalled it. Failure to recall the rule is evidence of lack of retention.

Use of study methods to enhance retention has already been discussed extensively in this chapter. Teachers can help students apply these techniques and others that will facilitate retention of material. Some suggestions that the teacher may offer include:

1. Always read study material with a purpose. If the teacher does not supply you with a purpose, set purposes of your own. Having a purpose for reading will help you extract meaning from a passage, and you will retain material that is meaningful to you longer.
2. Try to grasp the author's organization. This will help you to categorize concepts to be learned under main headings, which are easier to retain than small details and which facilitate the recall of these related details. In order to accomplish this task, outline the material.
3. Try to picture the ideas the author is attempting to describe. Visualization of the information being presented will help you remember it longer.
4. As you read, take notes on important points in the material. Writing information down can help you to fix it in your memory.
5. After you have read the material, summarize it in your own words. If you can do this, you will have recalled the main points, and the rewording of the material demonstrates your understanding. Sherrie Shugarman and Joe Hurst[22] describe paraphrase writing, or writing the material in one's own words, as a means to increase comprehension and recall. They suggest that students be allowed to consult with one another and with resource material in order to produce good paraphrases. They give ten suggestions for how teachers can incorporate paraphrase writing into their content area lessons, thereby helping students improve reading and writing abilities while learning content.
6. When you have read the material, discuss the assignment with a classmate or a group of classmates. Talking about the material facilitates remembering it.
7. Apply the concepts that you read about, if possible. Physical or mental interaction with the material will help you retain it.
8. Read assignments critically. If you question the material as you read, you will be more likely to remember it.
9. If you wish to retain the material over a long period of time, use spaced practice (a number of short practice sessions extended over a period of time) rather than massed practice (one long practice session). Massed practice facili-

tates immediate recall, but for long-term retention distributed practice produces the best results.

10. If you plan to recite the material to yourself or another student in order to increase your retention, do so as soon as possible after reading the material. Always check on your accuracy and correct any error immediately so that you will not retain inaccurate material.

11. Overlearning facilitates long-term retention. To overlearn something you must continue to practice it for a period of time after you have initially mastered it.

12. Mnemonic devices can help you retain certain types of information. (For example, remember that there is "a rat" in the middle of "separate.")

13. A variety of types of writing can improve retention. Judith Langer[23] reported the effects of different types of writing tasks on learning from reading in the content areas. Writing answers to study questions fostered recall of isolated bits of information. Essay writing produced more long-term and reasoned learning of a smaller amount of material. Notetaking fell somewhere in the middle, causing students to deal with larger chunks of meaning than did study questions, but not involving reorganization of material, as did essay writing.

Teachers can also facilitate student retention of material by offering students ample opportunities for review of information and practice of skills learned and by offering positive reinforcement for correct responses given during these practice and review periods. Class discussion of material to be learned will help to aid retention of the material. Emphasis on classifying the ideas found in the reading material under appropriate categories can also help.

TEST TAKING

Sometimes secondary school students fail to do well on tests, not because they do not know the material, but because they have difficulty reading and comprehending the test. Teachers can help by giving students suggestions about ways of reading different types of tests.

Essay tests often contain the terms *compare, contrast, trace the development, describe, discuss,* and many others. Teachers can explain what is expected in an answer to a question containing each of these terms and any other terms that they may plan to use. This will help prevent students from losing points because they "described" instead of "contrasted." For instance, if students are asked to compare two things or ideas, the teacher generally expects both likenesses and differences to be mentioned. If they are asked to contrast two things or ideas, differences are the important factors. If the students are asked to describe something, they are expected to paint a word picture of it. Sample answers to a variety of different test questions utilizing the special vocabulary may be useful in helping students understand what the teacher expects. An example follows:

Question: Contrast extemporaneous speeches and prepared speeches.
Answer: Extemporaneous speeches are given with little advance thought. Prepared speeches are usually preceded by much thought and research. Prepared speeches often contain quotations and paraphrases of the thoughts of many other people about the subject. Extemporaneous speeches can contain such material only if the speaker has previously become very well informed in the particular area involved. Assuming that the speaker has little background in the area, an extemporaneous speech would be likely to have less depth than a prepared speech, since it would involve only the speaker's immediate impressions. Prepared speeches tend to be better organized than extemporaneous speeches because the speaker has more time to collect thoughts and arrange them in the best possible sequence.

PORPE[24] is a technique developed by Michele Simpson to help students study for essay examinations. The steps in PORPE are as follows:

1. **Predict** Construct potential essay questions, based upon reading of the material. Use words such as *explain, criticize, compare,* and *contrast.* Focus on important ideas.
2. **Organize** Organize the information necessary for answering the questions.
3. **Rehearsal** Memorize material through recitation and self-testing. Space practice over several days for long-term memory.
4. **Practice** Write out in detail the answers to the questions that were formulated.
5. **Evaluate** Judge the accuracy and completeness of the answers.

Simpson suggests teaching this procedure through teacher modeling and a series of group and individual activities.

Objective tests must be read carefully. Generally, every word in an item must be considered. Teachers should emphasize the importance of considering the effect of words such as *always, never,* and *not,* as well as others of this general nature. Students need to realize that all parts of a true-false question must be true, if the answer is to be *true.* They also need to realize that all possible responses for a multiple-choice question need to be read before an answer is chosen.

Teachers can also help students do better on tests by offering the following useful hints:

1. When studying for essay tests:
   a. Remember that your answers should include main ideas accompanied by supporting details.
   b. Expect questions that cover the topics most emphasized in the course, since only a few questions can be asked within the limited time.
   c. Expect questions that are broad in scope.
   d. Consider the important topics covered, and try to guess some of the questions that the teacher may ask. Prepare good answers for these questions and try to learn them thoroughly. You will probably be able to use the points you learn in answers for the actual test, even if the questions you formulated were not exactly the same as the ones asked by the teacher.

2. When studying for objective tests:
   a. Become familiar with important details.
   b. Consider the types of questions that have been asked on previous tests, and study for those types. If dates have been asked for in the past, learn the dates in the material.
   c. If listing questions are a possibility, especially sequential listings, try preparing mnemonic devices to aid you in recalling the lists.
3. Learning important definitions can be helpful for any kind of test and can be useful in answering many essay questions.
4. Apply the suggestions listed in the section on "Retention."

When teachers construct tests, they need to take care to avoid making the test harder to read than the original material was. If this situation exists, a student may know the material required, but the readability level of the test may be so high that he or she is unable to comprehend the questions. The student may then make a low score on a test because of the teacher's poor test preparation, rather than because of the student's poor knowledge of the concepts involved.

Jason Millman, Carol Bishop, and Robert Ebel developed a list of test-wiseness principles that teachers can use when planning instruction in test-wiseness for objective achievement tests.[25] Irving McPhail developed strategies for teaching test-wiseness that have been used with inner-city high school students and others. He felt that this instruction could improve the validity of test results and help provide minorities with equal education, employment, and promotion opportunities.[26]

SUMMARY

Reading-study skills are skills that enhance comprehension and retention of information contained in printed material. They are helpful to students in managing their reading in content area classes.

Study methods such as SQ3R, PRST, REAP, and PANORAMA are applicable to a number of different subject areas, including social studies and science. EVOKER is a study method especially developed for use with prose, poetry, and drama; SQRQCQ is good for use with statement problems in mathematics.

Three helpful organizational skills needed by students who are participating in report writing are outlining, note taking, and summarizing. Also essential for good report writing are the skills of locating information in books and in the library. Teachers should carefully guide students through report-writing experiences.

The ability to follow written directions is vitally important to secondary school students. Teachers should plan activities to help students develop this important skill.

Content area textbooks are filled with graphic aids such as maps, graphs, tables, diagrams, and pictures. Teachers should give students guidance in interpreting these aids, so that the students will get the maximum benefit from their textbooks.

Other areas to which teachers should give attention are adjustment of reading rate to fit the purpose for which the reading is being done and the material to be read; retention of material read; and test-taking skills.

SELF-TEST

1. What does SQ3R stand for? (a) Survey, Question, Read, Recite, Review (b) Seek, Question, Read, Review, Report (c) Sequential Questioning, Read, React, Report (d) None of the above
2. For what content area is SQRQCQ designed? (a) English (b) History (c) Science (d) None of the above
3. Which statement below is true of outlining? (a) A main topic may have a single subdivision. (b) Indention helps to show the degree of importance of ideas in an outline. (c) Roman numeral headings are subordinate to capital letter headings. (d) None of the above
4. Which of the following are contained in the card catalog? (a) Subject cards (b) Author cards (c) Title cards (d) All of the above
5. Which of the following statements is *not* true? (a) Glossaries are found in many content area texts. (b) Skills needed to use glossaries are the same as those needed to use the dictionary. (c) Glossaries include mainly general vocabulary words. (d) None of the above
6. What should students know about guide words? (a) They represent the first and last entry words on a page. (b) They represent the first two entry words on a page. (c) They are found in the preface of the book. (d) None of the above
7. What should be avoided when written reports are assigned to students? (a) Organizational skills should be stressed before starting the process. (b) The teacher should guide the students through a report-writing experience before they are asked to write independently. (c) Use of a single source of information should be encouraged. (d) None of the above
8. Which skill(s) are involved in reading to follow directions? (a) The ability to locate details (b) The ability to detect sequence (c) Both of the above (d) Neither of the above
9. Which statement describes the legend of a map? (a) It is the history of the area represented in the map. (b) It contains an explanation of each of the symbols used on the map. (c) It is located in the top, left-hand corner of the map. (d) None of the above
10. What is a problem in reading charts? (a) They are generally filled with too much unimportant information. (b) They often over-simplify information. (c) Both of the above (d) Neither of the above
11. What is meant by flexibility of rate? (a) Reading all material as rapidly as possible (b) Varying reading rate to fit purposes and materials (c) Rapid reading without regard for comprehension (d) None of the above
12. Which factor(s) affect rate? (a) Size and style of type (b) Author's writing style (c) Reader's background of experiences (d) All of the above

13. What kind of rate machine has an arm that moves down a page of printed material from top to bottom at regulated speeds? (a) Tachistoscope (b) Controlled reading filmstrip projector (c) Pacer (d) None of the above
14. Which of the following represents the fastest reading rate? (a) Skimming (b) Study reading (c) Scanning (d) None of the above
15. Which of the following can improve retention? (a) Discussing the assignment with a classmate (b) Applying the concepts presented in the assignment (c) Reading the assignments critically (d) All of the above

THOUGHT QUESTIONS

1. Which of the study methods listed in this chapter is best for use in your content area? Why?
2. How can outlining help students to understand the material in the textbook for your content class?
3. What are helpful guidelines for note taking that you can share with students?
4. How can the librarian and content area teacher cooperate to teach library skills that students need for research activities?
5. What parts of a book do students need to be able to use effectively if they are going to locate needed information efficiently?
6. What are six steps in preparing written reports? How can the teacher prepare students for the report-writing activity?
7. What is a useful procedure for teaching students to read directions with understanding?
8. What graphic aids occur most commonly in your content area? What can you do to help students interpret them effectively?
9. What is the best setting in which to offer students instruction concerning flexibility of rate? Why is this so?
10. What are some techniques for helping students increase reading rate with acceptable comprehension?
11. How can you help your students retain as much of the material that they read in their content textbooks as possible?
12. Should you give attention to helping your students develop test-taking skills? Why, or why not?

ENRICHMENT ACTIVITIES

*1. Teach one of the study methods described in this chapter to a class of secondary school students. Work through it with them step by step.
2. Make a bulletin board display that would be helpful to use when teaching either outlining or note taking. Display it either in your college classroom or in a secondary school classroom.

*These activities are designed for in-service teachers, student teachers, or practicum students.

3. Make a set of sample card catalog cards for ten or more books. Plan a lesson on use of the card catalog. Teach this lesson to a group of your classmates. *Teach the lesson in a secondary school classroom, if possible.

4. Plan a lesson on use of the index of a secondary level textbook of your choice. Teach the lesson to a group of your classmates. *Teach the lesson in a secondary school classroom, if possible.

5. Collect materials that include directions that secondary level students often need to read. Discuss with your classmates how you could help the students learn to read these materials more effectively.

*6. Guide a group of secondary school students through the process of writing a group report.

7. Take a content area textbook at the secondary level and plan procedures to familiarize students with the parts of the book and with the reading aids the book offers.

8. Visit a secondary school library and listen to the librarian explain the reference materials and library procedures to the students. Evaluate the presentation, and decide how you might change it if you were responsible for it.

9. Collect a variety of types of maps. Decide which features of each map will need most explanation for students.

10. Collect a variety of types of graphs. Make them into a display that could be used in a unit on reading graphs.

11. Develop a procedure to help secondary school students learn to be flexible in their rates of reading. Use materials of widely varying types.

*12. Examine several of your old tests. Decide what reading difficulties they may present to your students. Isolate special words for which meanings may have to be taught.

13. Read Howard I. Berrent's article "OH RATS—A Note-Taking Technique," *Journal of Reading*, 27 (March 1984), 548–550. Try out Berrent's procedure on a chapter that you have been assigned to study. React to the effectiveness of the procedure for your study. Indicate whether you believe it would be as effective with secondary students and explain your reasons.

14. Read the following article: Victoria Chou Hare and Richard G. Lomax, "Readers' Awareness of Subheadings in Expository Text," in *Issues in Literacy: A Research Perspective*, ed. Jerome A. Niles and Rosary V. Lalik (Rochester, N.Y.: National Reading Conference, 1985), pp. 199–204. Report on the study to the class, giving your assessment of the implications of this study for secondary school teachers.

15. Read the following article: Lawrence B. Friedman and Margaret B. Tinzmann, "Graphics in Middle-Grade U.S. History Textbooks," in *Issues in Literacy: A Research Perspective*, ed. Jerome A. Niles and Rosary V. Lalik (Rochester, N.Y.: National Reading Conference, 1985), pp. 151–167. Analyze the graphic aids in one of your content texts in the way that Friedman and Tinzmann did in their study. Compare your results to theirs.

*These activities are designed for in-service teachers, student teachers, or practicum students.

NOTES

1. Francis P. Robinson, *Effective Study*, rev. ed. (New York: Harper & Row, 1961), Chapter 2.

2. George Spache, *Reading in the Elementary School*, 4th ed. (Boston: Allyn and Bacon, 1977), p. 299.

3. Walter Pauk, "On Scholarship: Advice to High School Students," *The Reading Teacher*, 17 (November 1963), 73–78.

4. Leo Fay, "Reading Study Skills: Math and Science," in *Reading and Inquiry*, ed. J. Allen Figurel (Newark, Del.: International Reading Association, 1965), pp. 93–94.

5. Marilyn G. Eanet and Anthony V. Manzo, "REAP—A Strategy for Improving Reading/Writing/Study Skills," *Journal of Reading*, 19 (May 1976), 647–652.

6. Peter Edwards, "Panorama: A Study Technique," *Journal of Reading*, 17 (November 1973), 132–135.

7. Ed Brazee, "Teaching Reading in Social Studies: Skill-Centered Versus Content-Centered," *Colorado Journal of Educational Research*, 18 (August 1979), 23–25.

8. Eanet and Manzo, "REAP," pp. 648–649.

9. Anthony V. Manzo, "Expansion Modules for the ReQuest, CAT, GRP, and REAP Reading/Study Procedures," *Journal of Reading*, 28 (March 1985), 498–502.

10. Dolores Fadness Tadlock, "SQ3R—Why It Works, Based on an Information Processing Theory of Learning," *Journal of Reading*, 22 (November 1978), 110–112.

11. T. Stevenson Hansell, "Stepping Up to Outlining," *Journal of Reading*, 22 (December 1978), 248–252.

12. Karen D'Angelo Bromley and Laurie McKeveny, "Précis Writing: Suggestions for Instruction in Summarizing," *Journal of Reading*, 29 (February 1986), 392–395.

13. Brenda Wright Kelly and Janis Holmes, "The Guided Lecture Procedure," *Journal of Reading*, 22 (April 1979), 602–604.

14. Melvil Dewey, *Dewey Decimal Classification and Relative Index* (Lake Placid Club, N.Y.: Forest Press, 1971).

15. *How to Use the Readers' Guide to Periodical Literature*, rev. ed. (New York: H. W. Wilson, 1970).

16. Kristina MacCormick and Janet E. Pursel, "A Comparison of the Readability of the *Academic American Encyclopedia*, the *Encyclopaedia Britannica*, and *World Book*," *Journal of Reading*, 25 (January 1982), 322–325.

17. Helen Newcastle, "Children's Problems with Written Directions," *The Reading Teacher*, 28 (December 1974), 294.

18. A version of this taxonomy appeared in Edward Fry, "Graphical Literacy," *Journal of Reading*, 24 (February 1981), 383–390.

19. Fry, pp. 388–389.

20. Bonnie E. Damm and Lawrence D. Chan, "Computer Software," *Journal of Reading*, 29 (January 1986), 373–374.

21. David M. Memory and David W. Moore, "Selecting Sources in Library Research: An Activity in Skimming and Critical Reading," *Journal of Reading*, 24 (March 1981), 469–474.

22. Sherrie L. Shugarman and Joe B. Hurst, "Purposeful Paraphrasing: Promoting a Nontrivial Pursuit for Meaning," *Journal of Reading*, 29 (February 1986), 396–399.

23. Judith A. Langer, "Learning Through Writing: Study Skills in the Content Areas," *Journal of Reading*, 29 (February 1986), 400–406.

24. Michele L. Simpson, "PORPE: A Writing Strategy for Studying and Learning in the Content Areas," *Journal of Reading*, 29 (February 1986), 407–414.

25. Jason Millman, Carol H. Bishop, and Robert Ebel, "An Analysis of Test-Wiseness," *Educational and Psychological Measurement*, 25 (Autumn 1965), 707–726.

26. Irving P. McPhail, "Why Teach Test Wiseness?" *Journal of Reading*, 25 (October 1981), 32–38.

SELECTED REFERENCES

Askov, Eunice N., and Karlyn Kamm. *Study Skills in the Content Areas*. Boston: Allyn and Bacon, 1982.

Beers, Penny G. "Accelerated Reading for High School Students." *Journal of Reading*, 29 (January 1986), 311–315.

Berger, Allen. "Increasing Reading Rate with Paperbacks." *Reading Improvement*, 9 (Winter 1972), 78–84.

Brazee, Ed. "Teaching Reading in Social Studies: Skill-Centered Versus Content-Centered." *Colorado Journal of Educational Research*, 18 (August 1979), 23–25.

Brunner, Joseph F., and John J. Campbell. *Participating in Secondary Reading: A Practical Approach*. Englewood Cliffs, N.J.: Prentice-Hall, 1978. Chapters 3 and 4.

Burmeister, Lou E. *Reading Strategies for Middle and Secondary School Teachers*. 2nd ed. Reading, Mass.: Addison-Wesley, 1978. Chapters 5 and 10.

Cheek, Earl H., and Martha Collins Cheek. *Reading Instruction Through Content Teaching*. Columbus, Ohio: Charles E. Merrill, 1983. Chapter 5.

Criscoe, Betty L., and Thomas C. Gee. *Content Reading: A Diagnostic/Prescriptive Approach*. Englewood Cliffs, N.J.: Prentice-Hall, 1984. Chapter 12.

Daines, Delva. *Reading in the Content Areas: Strategies for Teachers*. Glenview, Ill.: Scott, Foresman and Company, 1982. Chapters 5 and 7.

Dewey, Melvil. *Dewey Decimal Classification and Relative Index*. Lake Placid Club, N.Y.: Forest Press, 1971.

Eanet, Marilyn G., and Anthony V. Manzo. "REAP—A Strategy for Improving Reading/Writing/Study Skills." *Journal of Reading*, 19 (May 1976), 647–652.

Early, Margaret, and Diane J. Sawyer. *Reading to Learn in Grades 5 to 12*. San Diego, Calif.: Harcourt Brace Jovanovich, 1984. Chapter 14.

Edwards, Peter. "Panorama: A Study Technique." *Journal of Reading*, 17 (November 1973), 132–135.

Friedman, Lawrence B., and Margaret B. Tinzmann. "Graphics in Middle-Grade U.S. History Textbooks." In *Issues in Literacy: A Research Perspective*. Ed. Jerome A. Niles and Rosary V. Lalik. Rochester, N.Y.: National Reading Conference, 1985, pp. 151–167.

Fry, Edward. "Graphical Literacy." *Journal of Reading*, 24 (February 1981), 383–390.

Guthrie, John T. "Research: Context and Memory." *Journal of Reading*, 22 (December 1978), 266–268.

Hansell, T. Stevenson. "Stepping Up to Outlining." *Journal of Reading*, 22 (December 1978), 248–252.

Hare, Victoria Chou, and Richard G. Lomax. "Readers' Awareness of Subheadings in Expository Text." In *Issues in Literacy: A Research Perspective*. Ed. Jerome A. Niles and Rosary V. Lalik. Rochester, N.Y.: National Reading Conference, 1985, pp. 199–204.

Hoffman, James V. "The Relationship Between Rate and Reading Flexibility." *Reading World*, 17 (May 1978), 325–328.

How to Use the Readers' Guide to Periodical Literature. Rev. ed. New York: H. W. Wilson, 1970.

Karlin, Robert. *Teaching Reading in High School: Improving Reading in Content Areas*. 4th ed. New York: Harper and Row, 1984. Chapter 8.

Kelly, Brenda Wright, and Janis Holmes. "The Guided Lecture Procedure." *Journal of Reading*, 22 (April 1979), 602–604.

Kratzner, Roland R., and Nancy Mannies. "Building Responsibility and Reading Skills in the Social Studies Classroom." *Journal of Reading*, 22 (March 1979), 501–505.

Lamberg, Walter J., and Charles E. Lamb. *Reading Instruction in the Content Areas*. Boston: Houghton Mifflin, 1980. Chapter 5.

McAndrew, Donald A. "Underlining and Notetaking: Some Suggestions from Research." *Journal of Reading*, 27 (November 1983), 103–108.

MacCormick, Kristina, and Janet E. Pursel. "A Comparison of the Readability of the *Academic American Encyclopedia*, the *Encyclopaedia Britannica*, and *World Book*." *Journal of Reading*, 25 (January 1982), 322–325.

McPhail, Irving P. "Why Teach Test Wiseness?" *Journal of Reading*, 25 (October 1981), 32–38.

Memory, David M., and David W. Moore. "Selecting Sources in Library Research: An Activity in Skimming and Critical Reading." *Journal of Reading*, 24 (March 1981), 469–474.

Millman, Jason, Carol H. Bishop, and Robert Ebel. "An Analysis of Test-Wiseness." *Educational and Psychological Measurement*, 25 (Autumn 1965), 707–726.

Newcastle, Helen. "Children's Problems with Written Directions." *The Reading Teacher*, 28 (December 1974), 292–294.

Pauk, Walter. "The Art of Skimming." *Reading Improvement*, 2 (Winter 1965), 29–31.

––––––– . "On Scholarship: Advice to High School Students." *The Reading Teacher*, 17 (November 1963), 73–78.

––––––– . "Study Skills! That's the Answer!" *Reading Improvement*, 10 (Winter 1973), 2–6.

Putnam, Lillian R. "Don't Tell Them to Do It...Show Them How." *Journal of Reading*, 18 (October 1974), 41–43.

Robinson, Francis P. *Effective Study*. Rev. ed. New York: Harper and Row, 1961. Chapter 2.

Schachter, Sumner W. "Developing Flexible Reading Habits." *Journal of Reading*, 22 (November 1978), 149–152.

Schale, Florence. "Three Approaches to Faster Reading." *Reading Improvement,* 2 (Spring 1965), 68–71.

Schumm, Jeanne Shay, and Marguerite C. Radencich. "Readers'/Writers' Workshops: An Antidote for Term Paper Terror." *Journal of Reading,* 28 (October 1984), 13–19.

Shepherd, David L. *Comprehensive High School Reading Methods.* 3rd ed. Columbus, Ohio: Charles E. Merrill, 1982.

Smith, Carl B., Sharon L. Smith, and Larry Mikulecky. *Teaching Reading in Secondary School Content Subjects.* New York: Holt, Rinehart and Winston, 1978. Chapter 9.

Spache, George. *Reading in the Elementary School.* 4th ed. Boston: Allyn and Bacon, 1977.

Steiner, Kathy. "Speed Reading Revisited." *Journal of Reading,* 22 (November 1978), 172–176.

Tadlock, Dolores Fadness. "SQ3R—Why It Works, Based on an Information Processing Theory of Learning." *Journal of Reading,* 22 (November 1978), 110–112.

Taylor, Barbara. "Toward an Understanding of Factors Contributing to Children's Difficulty Summarizing Textbook Material." In *Issues in Literacy: A Research Perspective.* Ed. Jerome A. Niles and Rosary V. Lalik. Rochester, N.Y.: National Reading Conference, 1985, pp. 125–131.

Taylor, Karl K. "Teaching Summarization Skills." *Journal of Reading,* 27 (February 1984), 389–393.

Thomas, Keith J., and Charles K. Cummings. "The Efficacy of Listening Guides: Some Preliminary Findings with Tenth and Eleventh Graders." *Journal of Reading,* 21 (May 1978), 705–709.

Tonjes, Marian J., and Miles V. Zintz. *Teaching Reading/Thinking/Study Skills in Content Classrooms.* Dubuque, Iowa: Wm. C. Brown, 1981. Chapter 8.

Vacca, Richard. "Readiness to Read Content Area Assignments." *Journal of Reading,* 20 (February 1977), 387–392.

Vacca, Richard T., and Jo Anne L. Vacca. *Content Area Reading.* 2nd ed. Boston: Little, Brown and Company, 1986. Chapter 8.

CHAPTER
F I V E

THE DEMANDS AND COMMON
ELEMENTS OF CONTENT READING

OVERVIEW

This chapter examines the nature of expository and narrative writing and identifies some of the reading difficulties posed by the expository materials contained in content textbooks. In order to use textbooks as learning tools, students must be able to apply content reading skills. This chapter identifies content reading skills and abilities that help students meet the demands of textbooks. Applying these skills will help students learn content materials more effectively.

PURPOSE-SETTING QUESTIONS

As you read this chapter, try to answer these questions:

1. What are the differences between narrative writing and expository writing?
2. What are the characteristics of content materials that are most likely to create reading problems?
3. What are the common characteristics of content reading materials?

KEY VOCABULARY

As you read this chapter, check your understanding of these terms:

narrative	writing pattern (organization)
expository	readability
compact style	graphic aids

EXPOSITORY AND NARRATIVE CONTENT

There are fundamental differences between expository and narrative materials. The materials used for basic reading instruction in today's schools are largely of narrative content, whereas materials used for content area instruction are largely expository except for literature. In the elementary grades, students are more heavily exposed to narrative styles and patterns. This exposure prepares them to read literature, but not the other content materials. Understanding the differences between narrative and expository materials will help teachers understand the need for content reading instruction.

For many years, teachers assumed that students who could successfully read basal readers could read subjects such as science, social studies, and mathematics with equal success. Research and classroom experience have led educators to realize that reading in the content areas makes greater demands on the reader than reading narrative materials. If the student does not receive direct instruction in how to read various types of content material, he or she may tend to read all content materials in the same way as narrative material. This can defeat the learning process.

The problems involved in reading content area materials are complicated by the fact that we are living in an "information society" that is future oriented. John Naisbitt stated that this is a "literacy-intensive society" wherein we need basic reading and writing skills more than ever before.[1] He reported the following facts and predictions:

Between six thousand and seven thousand scientific articles are written each day. More powerful information systems and an increasing population of scientists means that data will double every twenty months.
In the future, editors won't tell us what to read: we will tell editors what we choose to read.

An information-based society that is multiplying information at the very rapid rate indicated by the preceding statements must have citizens that can use reading as a means of acquiring information. But the ability to organize information will be equally important. Otherwise, we will drown in a sea of disorganized information. Even today scientists complain of information pollution and charge that it takes less time to do an experiment than to research the literature to determine whether it has already been done.[2]

Students in today's schools are expected to read large amounts of material. Textbooks are frequently supplemented by outside reading from reference materials of many kinds. Students must be able to adjust to many types of content materials. They must learn to compare and contrast the ideas of several authors, to summarize content, and to draw conclusions based on their reading. Students in the past often studied only one textbook, but today's students may be inundated with books, newspapers, and magazines. Students must read widely, as well as organize and structure their reading so they can participate in class discussions and write reports.

THE DEMANDS OF CONTENT READING

One of the best ways to become acquainted with the demands of content reading is to examine both content materials and narrative materials. Compare and contrast the excerpts from secondary textbooks given in Examples 5.1 and 5.2. Example 5.1 is from a secondary literature book; Example 5.2 is from a secondary science book.

EXAMPLE 5.1   PASSAGE FROM A LITERATURE BOOK ─────────

You must hear, besides the first spring notes of the bluebird and the robin, four bird songs this spring. First (1) the song of the wood thrush or the hermit thrush, whichever one lives in your neighborhood. No words can describe the purity, the peacefulness, the spiritual quality of the wood thrush's simple "Come to me." It is the voice of the tender twilight, the voice of the tranquil forest, speaking to you. After the thrush (2) the brown thrasher, our finest, most gifted songster, as great a singer, I think (and I have often heard them both), as the southern mockingbird. Then (3) the operatic catbird. She sits lower down among the bushes than the brown thrasher, as if she knew that, compared with him, she must take a back seat; but for variety of notes and length of song, she has few rivals. I say *she*, when really I ought to say *he*, for it is the males of most birds that sing, but the catbird seems so long and slender, so dainty and feminine, that I think of this singer as of some exquisite operatic singer in a woman's rôle. Then (4) the bobolink; for his song is just like Bryant's bubbling poem, only better! Go to the meadows in June and listen as he comes lilting and singing over your head.

There are some birds that cannot sing: the belted kingfisher, for instance; he can only rattle. You must hear him rattle. You can do as well yourself if you will shake a "pair of bones" or heave an anchor and let the chain run fast through the hawse-hole. You then must hear the downy woodpecker doing his rattling *rat-ta-tat-tat-tat-tat* (across the page and back again), as fast as *rat-ta-tat* can *tat*. How he makes the old dead limb or fence-post rattle as he drums upon it with his chisel bill! He can be heard half a mile around.

Then high-hole, the flicker (or golden-winged woodpecker), you must hear him yell, *Up-up-up-up-up-up-up-up-up-up-up-up*—a ringing, rolling, rapid kind of yodel that echoes over the spring fields.

Source: Dallas Sharp: *The Year-Our-of-Doors.* Copyright © 1917 by Houghton Mifflin Company. Reprinted by permission.

─────────────────

EXAMPLE 5.2   PASSAGE FROM A SCIENCE BOOK ─────

Learning in Birds

Some of the songs that birds sing are short and simple, whereas others are quite complicated. Is a bird's song an example of an inborn behavior? Or must a bird learn the songs that its parents sing? The following experiments were conducted at Rockefeller University to study these questions.

A group of white-crowned sparrows was studied. As the adults reproduced, the individual offspring were placed inside sound-proof boxes so that they were isolated from each other as well as from their parents. The boxes were equipped with microphones and speakers. The microphones picked up the sounds made by each sparrow, and a recording was made. The speakers allowed the experimenters to play selected sounds to each sparrow.

The design of the experiments called for isolating the birds at various ages. Some birds were isolated as soon as they hatched, others when they were five days old, still others when they were ten days old, and some after they were ten days old. All the sparrows were kept in isolation until they were more than one hundred days old.

The sounds made by the birds were analyzed on an electronic machine called a *sound spectrograph,* which produced a chart called a *sound spectrogram.* Using the sound spectrograms, the experimenters could make accurate comparisons of sounds. The results of the experiments are below.

1. Sparrows that were isolated before they were ten days old did not produce songs that matched those of normal, adult sparrows.
2. Sparrows isolated after 50–100 days did produce songs similar to those of normal, adult sparrows.
3. Sparrows that were isolated before ten days of age that heard the tape-recorded songs of normal, adult birds sometime after they were ten days old, and before they were 50 days old, did reproduce normal adult songs.
4. Sparrows which did not hear normal, adult songs until after they were 50 days old failed to reproduce them, and their songs differed little or not at all from birds that heard no song after 10 days of age.

What conclusions can you draw from these experiments? Is the normal, adult song of the white-crowned sparrow an inborn or a learned behavior? What happens to young sparrows that are not raised with adults? How is age associated with learning?

Source: Walter A. Thurber, Robert E. Kilburn, and Peter S. Howell, *Exploring Life Science* (Boston: Allyn and Bacon, 1975), p. 89. Reprinted by permission of Allyn and Bacon, Inc.

─────────

Each of the passages explores the same topic, the songs of birds. The passage from the literature book describes the songs of birds in an easy-to-read manner that relates to the reader's own experience. The author uses vivid descriptive terms such as *purity, peacefulness, tender twilight, tranquil forest, gifted songster, dainty,* and *feminine.* The reader is carried along by the description of each of the various birds' songs. The birds are characterized with descriptive terms: the catbird is described as the "operatic catbird," and the brown thrasher is described as "our finest, most gifted songster."

The author of this passage is sharing with the reader his pleasure in the song of birds. He is also creating the mood of a June morning, which will encourage the reader to go out in search of the birds' songs. The reader is reading for the purpose of enjoying the mood created by the author's description. The mood and meaning of the selection are apparent to the reader. The reader does not have to analyze, synthesize, or reach a conclusion in order to understand.

The passage from the science textbook is written in compact style that includes very few descriptive words. It demands understanding of technical terms such as:

> inborn behavior
> experiment design
> electronic machine
> sound spectrograph
> sound spectrogram
> white-crowned sparrow

The reader must be able to read about the design of the experiments and then must synthesize the findings of the four studies to reach a conclusion regarding the singing of the sparrows. The reader's purpose is to reach an understanding of how birds learn to sing as a part of understanding a broader concept of inborn behavior. The reader must study the content carefully so that he or she will remember the information for future reference.

Examination of the passages in Examples 5.1 and 5.2 reveals some of the aspects of content reading materials that make this type of reading difficult for students. The following sections examine these aspects in greater detail.

Concepts

Content textbooks are designed to teach students the basic concepts of the various disciplines. The concepts of content area materials range from concrete to abstract. The difficulty in understanding concepts increases in direct proportion to the abstractness of the concept; the more abstract a concept is, the more difficult it is to learn. Content area writing abounds in abstract concepts, such as *freedom.* A simple definition of a concept like *freedom* does not teach the reader the concept; it is only after much experience with various types of freedom that the reader will begin to comprehend the concept. Content materials tend to include a larger number of unfamiliar, abstract concepts than do narrative materials. Content area concepts may be unrelated to the experience of the reader, while the concepts found in narrative reading are more often familiar.

Concepts found in curricular material are often developed in a pyramid fashion. Students are expected to understand and remember key concepts that will serve as a basis for later learning, although the author may not make an association between earlier and later concepts. For example, after reading the passage in Example 5.2, the student is expected to understand the concept of how birds learn to sing; this understanding will help the student understand inborn behavior and evaluate examples of inborn behavior. In this instance, the burden of learning is on the reader. The student who misses one concept cannot easily acquire later concepts. The student may be expected to develop an understanding of basic concepts almost entirely from reading.

Vocabulary

Concept development is linked to vocabulary development because one's vocabulary provides labels for the concepts one has acquired. Words are also an author's vehicle for expressing ideas; therefore, words are important to the reader. The vocabulary of the reading materials used in elementary schools is carefully controlled. Such material does not prepare the reader for the large number of important, unfamiliar words he or she will encounter in secondary textbooks. Content materials may introduce ten or more new words per page. These words are often not repeated; thus the reader is not given an opportunity to reinforce knowledge of the new words.

The vocabulary of content materials presents other problems for the reader; for instance, one of the difficult problems encountered in content materials is the extensive specialized vocabulary of the content fields. The technical vocabulary of a field may be entirely new to the reader, and the concepts on which the vocabulary is based may be unfamiliar and abstract. In science, a reader meets words like *solar, planet,* and *minerals;* in social studies, words such as *culture, longitude,* and *adaptation.* The abstractness of such words causes difficulty because the student remembers best words that represent concepts that are already meaningful to him or her.

A further aspect of the vocabulary problem in content materials is the use of common words in new and technical contexts. The fact that words such as *matter, composition, series,* and *mouth* have both general and specialized meanings may be confusing to the reader. For example, *mouth* may refer to an oral cavity in the face; it may refer to the natural opening of a river, harbor, or cave; or it may refer to the mouthpiece of a musical instrument. Words may shift meanings in a single selection, and the reader must be alert for these changes. Both technical and general vocabulary present major hurdles for the reader of content materials.

Writing Style

The style of writing used in content textbooks is demanding because it can be very compact. Each word is so important that the reader cannot skip words and maintain an understanding of the content read. The compactness of expository writing is the result of compressing a large number of ideas into a few lines of print. One paragraph in a social studies textbook may cover one hundred years of time, or a social studies textbook may devote only a paragraph to the presidency of Franklin Delano Roosevelt, while other books are devoted entirely to this subject. A paragraph cannot reveal character and provide insights for the reader in the same manner as a book. A paragraph in a science book may discuss a major discovery that is based on a number of concepts, and each sentence may include several important details. The author cannot explore each scientific principle in great detail because of the limitations of space.

Organizational Style

Writers of expository materials have special styles of organizing and expressing information. Knowledge in any discipline is more than a mere collection of facts: it is an understanding of an interrelationship of ideas. For example, authors can use types of organization, such as cause and effect and temporal order of events, to help readers understand the relationships among ideas. Students can comprehend more when they can identify the way expository materials are organized and can approach the content accordingly.

Narrative materials are organized around plot, theme, characterization, and setting. Because students generally are more familiar with this organization, they find it easier to read. Narrative content can be understood by following the events that unfold the plot. Also, readers' personal identification with the characters aids comprehension.

Readability and Comprehension

The teaching of any content area includes more than conveying information to students; it also involves teaching students how to read and comprehend their textbooks. The almost universal use of textbooks as instructional materials means that students must read textbooks effectively and efficiently in order to acquire the information they are expected to learn. Teachers who are aware of the readability levels of their content textbooks can identify the problem areas and intervene with strategies that will reduce reading comprehension problems.

Students typically experience more difficulty reading expository content than they do reading narrative content. Expository content like that found in content textbook materials is characterized by the intensity with which the information is presented and by interrelated concepts. Intensely written materials are ones in which concepts and ideas are stated in a terse manner with very little description. In addition, many ideas and concepts are presented in brief segments of text. Furthermore, these ideas and concepts are related to each other in such a way that missing or failing to understand one idea or concept prohibits comprehension of later text. Research indicates that compactness of ideas, terseness of writing style, complexity of concepts, and technical vocabulary are among the factors that hinder students' reading of textbooks. These factors also create more difficult readability levels, which can contribute to comprehension problems.[3]

Joyce Bryant found that more than one-half of the high school students she studied were assigned content area texts that were too difficult for them.[4] Linus Pauling contends that "today's chemistry textbooks, and probably the courses based on them as well, serve to turn interested students away from chemistry instead of attracting them into the field."[5] According to Pauling, elementary chemistry texts should not include any topic without also including a detailed, lucid, comprehensible discussion of that topic, he suggests that authors exclude any topic they do not know and understand. He also contends that many elementary chemistry textbooks are too long.

The complexity of comprehending a textbook is not fully revealed by a simple application of readability formulas because these formulas typically rely on average sentence and word length to determine "grade level." However, factors such as syntactic complexity of sentences, density of concepts, abstractness of ideas, text organization, coherence and sequence of ideas, page format, length of type line, length of paragraphs, intricacy of punctuation, and the use of illustrations and color also influence readability.[6] Therefore, we should consider these factors as well as readability formulas when matching students to textbooks. Readability formulas are discussed in Chapter 9.

Jill Wright and Dixie Spiegel found that teachers' judgment of the difficulty of a topic in biology was more predictive of students' performance than readability formulas were.[7] The teachers in their study considered the following factors when matching text materials to students:

> Vocabulary
> Sentence and paragraph structure
> Succinctness
> Concept load
> Concept depth
> Concreteness
> Interest

If we regard readability as a complex entity and use the preceding factors as well as readability formulas to measure it, we will experience greater success in matching students with content reading materials. Matching students with textbooks at appropriate levels of difficulty is a complex, difficult task. Teachers have many students reading at many different grade levels and usually reading in a single textbook, although the text is supplemented by a wide variety of materials. Cecelia Thompson and Patricia Davis identified this as a significant problem in teaching home economics.[8] Yet students who can read content comfortably tend to be more confident about learning content.[9] Robert Stevens and Barak Rosenshine found that the more time students spent on tasks with which they were highly successful, the greater their achievement gains.[10] Gerald Duffy found that students' attitudes toward both reading and school were improved when students were given materials they could comprehend successfully,[11] and Edward Glicking and David Armstrong found that success in reading led to more "on task" behavior and higher task completion rates.[12] The effects were maximized when the success rate on the reading task was between 93 and 97 percent.

Research has indicated that content textbooks present readability problems for many students. For example, Lawrence Hafner reported that social studies textbooks were consistently more difficult to read than their grade-level designation indicated.[13] Joseph Razek and his coworkers reported considerable readability variation among accounting books, and they found that teachers often assigned more difficult books before students were prepared to cope with them.[14] John Bradley, Wilbur Ames, and Judy Mitchell found that there was substantial intrabook readability variation in the history books they studied, and there was no clear progression of difficulty throughout the books.[15] Thus teachers can expect students to have more trouble with certain sections of a text than with others. The difficult parts can be anywhere in the book. It is helpful for teachers to identify the difficult sections and plan to use study guides and directed reading lessons for these areas.

Charles Peters studied the presentation of concepts in social studies textbooks and found that presenting concepts in a different style from that usually used in textbook writing increases reading comprehension.[16] Perhaps if the teacher chooses a textbook that has an interesting style and a comfortable readability level, students will comprehend expository materials more easily.

Research indicates that the nature of expository materials makes reading such materials a demanding task. It is important to examine the special instruction that teachers provide to help students deal with expository reading, particularly the materials that appear in content area textbooks. A number of studies made during the past forty years indicate that content reading instruction has generally not been available to students. Dolores Durkin studied both reading comprehension instruction and content reading instruction, again establishing that neither reading comprehension nor content reading instruction was provided for students.[17]

The inherent difficulty of content materials and the lack of instruction for reading them make it doubly difficult for students to comprehend them. Reading objectives include the expansion of knowledge and the solving of problems. In order to achieve these goals, readers must locate, evaluate, synthesize, and organize information. Students must understand and remember content for future reference. Reading for these purposes requires that students have a high level of understanding.

The characteristics of narrative and expository content are summarized below.

Narrative	Expository
1. Tells story; has characters, plot, theme, and setting	1. Provides information
2. Gives general description; repeats vocabulary frequently	2. Repeats specialized and technical vocabulary infrequently
3. Calls for character identification	3. Calls for interaction with subject matter

4. Holds attention by plot or description

4. Supports attention by form of presentation and organization

5. Uses single story or book

5. Uses supplementary materials, reference sources

6. Often contains concepts based on reader's experiences

6. Has unfamiliar abstract concepts that are concisely presented and developed in pyramid fashion

7. Has elaborate writing style

7. Has terse writing style

8. Offers entertainment

8. Presents material to expand knowledge and solve problems

9. Allows fairly rapid reading

9. Requires slower, more flexible reading rate

10. Conveys meaning through words

10. Widely uses graphic aids (pictures, graphs, charts, tables, maps)

11. Has varying readability level

11. Has high readability level

CONTENT AREA READING SKILL AND ABILITIES

Reading expository content such as that found in content textbooks requires the application of highly developed reading skills in very specific and often specialized ways within the various content area subjects. Although there are a few genuinely unique content skills (for instance, reading formulas in math and science, reading special symbols in math and music, or reading blueprints in industrial arts), the majority of skills necessary to content reading are basic reading skills with specialized applications and emphases.

The essential reading skills and abilities called upon in reading content materials are summarized in the following list:

1. Understanding special concepts and vocabulary
2. Identifying main ideas and supporting details
3. Locating facts or specific details
4. Organizing reading material by determining sequence, drawing conclusions, and finding cause-and-effect relationships
5. Locating information and using reference materials
6. Reading and interpreting graphic aids
7. Adjusting rate to purpose, difficulty, and type of content
8. Comprehending at the literal, inferential, critical, and creative levels
9. Developing the habit of extensive reading
10. Activating background knowledge and experience

Each of these skills is important within each content area; however, the actual application of each skill varies from subject to subject. For instance, although critical reading is important in all content areas, in social studies critical reading skills might be called into play in the evaluation of propaganda; in science these skills might be used to evaluate different experimental hypotheses. The content dictates the ways in which the skills need to be used.

The particular configuration of skills needed for proficient reading also varies from subject to subject. In other words, each content area emphasizes a somewhat different cluster of skills. For example, the ability to note causes and effects is probably needed more frequently in social studies and science than in other areas. Categorizing skills are often needed in reading science material, especially biology. The ability to cope with precise, compact writing is highly important both in mathematics and in certain forms of literature, such as poetry. Each content teacher must pay careful attention to the cluster of general reading skills important to his or her area and to the unique ways in which these skills are called into play by the particular materials.

Writing Patterns

The writing patterns used to structure expository content in individual subject areas do overlap considerably; but, again, each area has its own particular *grouping* of patterns and skills. These writing patterns are discussed fully in Chapters 6 and 7. The following section simply identifies the clusters of patterns most common to each area.

Social Studies
1. Cause-and-effect pattern
2. Definition or explanation pattern
3. Chronological or sequential events pattern (events in specific time sequence)
4. Comparison and/or contrast pattern
5. Question-and-answer pattern
6. Combination of patterns

Reading maps, graphs, charts, and pictures is associated especially with social studies. Students must integrate content from graphic aids with written content to understand social studies materials.

Science
1. Classification pattern
2. Experimental pattern
3. Definition or explanation pattern (often accompanied by diagrams)
4. Problem-solving pattern
5. Cause-and-effect pattern

The use of abbreviations and equations is also common in science materials.

Mathematics
1. Problem pattern (word or verbal problem)
2. Demonstration pattern
3. Graph and chart pattern

Special symbols, signs, and formulas are common elements in mathematics textbooks.

Literature
1. Fictional patterns (novels, novellas, short stories)
2. Nonfiction patterns (essays, criticism, true stories)
3. Poetry (narrative, descriptive, lyric)
4. Drama (tragedies, comedies, serious plays)

Literature differs from the other content areas discussed in this text because it includes both expository and narrative content. Students of literature must be prepared to use both narrative and expository reading skills.

Special Needs in Vocational-Technical Subjects

How-to-do-it directions abound in vocational-technical materials, as do diagrams, drawings, graphs, charts, and tables. These elements are also common in physical education, driver education, agriculture, art, and music. The reading demands of the vocational-technical areas, physical education, and the arts are complicated by the fact that each of these areas represents an amalgamation of written materials derived from various disciplines. For example, readers of industrial arts materials have to cope not only with technical terms unique to the subject, but also with directions that must be followed step-by-step and implemented; data reported in graphs, charts, and diagrams that must be interpreted and applied; scientific material written in the form of explanations of technical processes; scientific formulas for such things as paint and varnish; and mathematics content necessary for describing and measuring chemicals, wood, and the scale of blueprints. Thus, the written content can be quite complex. Listings of some of the reading demands for vocational-technical subject areas follow.

The use of technical terms, reference materials, directions, and graphs and charts is common to business education materials. In addition, business students must cope with demands such as the following:

Business Education
1. Mathematics (including symbols, signs, and formulas)
2. Thorough knowledge of punctuation, capitalization, and grammar
3. Proofreading

Home economics is a veritable complex of reading demands, including the following kinds of requirements:

Home Economics
1. Directions (recipes, patterns, labels)
2. Mathematics (especially with regard to measurement, fractions, budgeting)
3. Chemical data (as in food composition, detergents)
4. Reference materials (for problem solving, such as how to remove spots from clothing or stains from upholstery, or what to do with a problem child)
5. Critical reading (to evaluate products, problem solutions)

Agriculture is also a complex subject, due to the variety of disciplines that are brought together.

Agriculture
1. Mathematics (related to budgeting, estimating needs for seed and fertilizer)
2. Chemistry (as in soil composition, fertilizers)
3. Management (of livestock, soil, farm)
4. Graphs, charts, diagrams, pictures
5. Mechanical content (use of farm machinery)
6. Problem solving through reference materials (determining the best fertilizer to use, the best crops to plant)
7. Critical reading (to evaluate soil samples, livestock)

Much of the content in physical education can be explained orally to students, but reading also plays a significant role.

Physical Education
1. Diagrams
2. Directions (game rules, for example)
3. Narrative description of athletic events
4. Mathematics (scores, averages, handicaps)

On the surface music does not appear to require a great deal of reading, but in reality, music students must read quite a lot.

Music
1. Musical notes, special symbols, and special vocabulary
2. Biographical and other background information
3. Critiques
4. Research and reference materials
5. Media and media-related material (records, tapes, videotapes)

Art, like music, does not appear to require a great deal of reading, but underneath the surface appearance it also contains quite a lot of written material.

Art
1. Directions
2. Visualization requirements
3. Biography and other background information
4. Newspaper critiques and reviews of art shows
5. Location of information to solve problems

SUMMARY

Expository materials present some rather specific and difficult reading problems for students. They are different in several important aspects from the narrative materials that students have most commonly encountered in reading instruction. Factors such as technical vocabulary, abstract concepts, organizational patterns, readability level, and graphic aids create reading difficulties. Students' lack of experiential background and interest in content topics can limit comprehension. The demands placed on students by materials in content classes tend to be greater than the demands made by other reading materials. Students are expected to acquire concepts, remember facts, and learn independently from content materials.

Reading content materials involves highly developed essential reading skills such as understanding vocabulary and concepts; identifying main ideas and details; organizing information (especially in terms of sequence and cause and effect); utilizing graphic aids; adjusting rate; understanding at the literal, inferential, and critical levels; and reading related materials. The emphasis each of these skills receives and the relative importance of specific skills vary from content area to content area. Specific applications of these general skills also vary among subject areas. In addition, certain content areas require special content skills, such as the reading of formulas in math and science. All these skills will be considered—by content area—in Chapters 6 and 7.

SELF-TEST

1. Which of the following styles of writing is used in most content textbooks? (a) Expository (b) Narrative (c) Fictional (d) None of these
2. Which of the following factors represents(s) fundamental difficulties a student encounters when reading content materials? (a) Vocabulary (b) Language patterns (c) Printing (d) Both *a* and *b*
3. Which of the following phrases explains the pyramid development of concepts in content textbooks? (a) The content is written in the form of a pyramid. (b) The content teaches students how to understand pyramids. (c) Each concept developed depends upon previously developed concepts. (d) Concept development helps students measure pyramids.
4. Which type of vocabulary creates a comprehension problem for many students? (a) Technical vocabulary (b) Sight words (c) Spelling vocabulary (d) None of these
5. What does the term *compact style* mean as it relates to content materials? (a) Many ideas per sentence and paragraph (b) Smaller print used (c) Fewer pictures used (d) Lack of explanations
6. What is the main objective of content reading? (a) Entertainment (b) Expanding knowledge (c) Fulfilling teacher assignments (d) Completing the curriculum
7. Which of the following are graphic aids used in textbooks? (a) Maps (b) Graphs (c) Pictures (d) All of these
8. What word best describes the concepts usually presented in content textbooks? (a) Long (b) Abstract (c) Familiar (d) Funny

9. Why are the concepts presented in content materials difficult for students? (a) Students do not want to learn them. (b) They are not colorful. (c) They are abstract. (d) None of these

10. Why do writers of math, science, and social studies textbooks use different styles for organizing information? (a) To make the books interesting (b) Because they like to write in different ways (c) To best explain the knowledge of the discipline (d) To make reading easier

11. How many genuinely unique content reading skills are there? (a) Few (b) Many (c) Depends upon content area (d) None

12. Which is an example of a reading study skill common to any content area? (a) Rate adjustment (b) Location of information (c) Determining organization (d) All of these

13. In which subject area are cause-and-effect patterns probably most frequent? (a) Literature (b) Art (c) Social studies (d) Mathematics

14. Why are the reading demands of vocational-technical materials particularly complex? (a) Because these materials incorporate content from several disciplines (b) Because these subjects are not usually taught with textbooks (c) Because the students in these courses usually are illiterate (d) Because students in these classes are less motivated to read than students in other classes

THOUGHT QUESTIONS

1. Which of the content reading demands are the most important? Why?
2. Which of the reading demands of content materials is least important? Why?
3. Why do you think the readability of content materials is not controlled better?
4. Why is the content teacher the best qualified person to teach the skills necessary for reading his or her content materials?
5. What do you feel are the reading demands of the future? How can teachers and schools help students prepare for the reading demands of the future?

ENRICHMENT ACTIVITIES

1. Select a content textbook and a literature book at the same grade level and compare them on the following points: (a) Number of adjectives and adverbs (b) Abstract concepts (c) Types of organization of content

2. Visit a classroom at a secondary level and interview students regarding their reading interests. Compare their stated reading interests with the topics in their content textbooks.

3. Interview a good secondary school reader regarding the reading problems he or she encounters. Interview a student who is not a good reader regarding his or her reading problems. Compare the responses of the two students.

4. Use a readability formula to evaluate the readability level of a content textbook. (See Chapter 9.)

5. Select a content textbook and locate in the textbook an example of each reading demand cited in this chapter.

6. Select a paragraph from a content textbook and rewrite it in an easier-to-read fashion.

7. Discuss the following statements: (a) "The major problem in teaching any content area is the specialized vocabulary of that subject." (b) "There has been an overemphasis upon specialized vocabulary in the content areas."

8. Make a list of several of the words and definitions provided in the glossary of a content book. What information is needed to interpret the definitions? What other meanings must the reader know to understand the words in other contexts?

9. Begin to collect patterns of writing as classified in this chapter (and in Chapters 6 and 7) from content area textbooks. Try to find examples in which the same pattern is used in several subject areas. Also try to find an example in which the pattern occurs mostly in a single content area.

10. Find a representative passage from a content area textbook. Bring a copy of it to class for discussion purposes. List as many of the reading demands cited in this chapter as you can find in the selection. Cite the exact words, phrases, or sentences that illustrate each reading demand.

NOTES

1. John Naisbitt, *Megatrends* (New York: Warner Communications, 1984), p. 11.

2. Ibid., p. 17.

3. Rosalind Horowitz and S. Jay Samuels, "Reading and Listening to Expository Text," *Journal of Reading Behavior*, 17, No. 3 (1985), 185–198.

4. Joyce Bryant, "An Investigation of Reading Levels of High School Students with the Readability Level of Certain Content Textbooks with Their Costs" (Ph.D. dissertation, Florida State University, 1971).

5. Linus Pauling, "Throwing the Book at Elementary Chemistry," *The Science Teacher*, 40 (September 1983), 25–29.

6. Bernice Cullinan and Sheila Fitzgerald, "Background Information Bulletin on the Use of Readability Formulae," *Reading Today*, 2 (December 1984/January 1985), 1.

7. Jill Wright and Dixie Spiegel, "How Important Is Textbook Readability to Biology Teachers?" *The American Biology Teacher*, 46 (April 1984), 221–225.

8. Cecelia Thompson and Patricia Davis, "Readability: A Factor in Selecting Teaching Materials," *Illinois Teacher*, 15 (March/April, 1984), 156–160.

9. David Berliner, "Academic Learning Time and Reading Achievement," in *Comprehension and Teaching: Research Reviews*, ed. J. T. Guthrie (Newark, Del.: International Reading Association, 1981).

10. R. Stevens and B. Rosenshine, "Advances in Research on Teaching," *Exceptional Education Quarterly*, 2 (1981), 1.

11. G. Duffy, "Teacher Effectiveness Research: Implications for the Reading Profession," in *Directions in Reading: Research and Instruction*, ed. M. Kamil (Washington, D.C.: National Reading Conference, 1981).

12. E. Glicking and D. Armstrong, "Levels of Instructional Difficulty as Related to On-task Behavior, Task Completion, and Comprehension," *Journal of Learning Disabilities*, 11 (1978), 6.

13. Lawrence Hafner, *Developmental Reading in Middle and Secondary Schools* (New York: Macmillan, 1977), p. 200.

14. Joseph Razek, Gordon Hosch, and Daniel Pearl, "Readability of Accounting Textbooks," *Journal of Business Education*, 59 (October 1982), 23–26.

15. John Bradley, Wilbur Ames, and Judy Mitchell, "Intrabook Readability: Variations Within History Textbooks," *Social Education* (October 1980), 524–528.

16. Charles Peters, "The Effects of Systematic Restructuring of Material upon the Comprehension Process," *Reading Research Quarterly*, 11 (1975–76), 87–111.

17. Dolores Durkin, "What Classroom Observations Reveal About Reading Comprehension Instruction," *Reading Research Quarterly*, 14 (1978–79), 481–533.

SELECTED REFERENCES

Anders, Patricia. "Dream of a Secondary Reading Program? People Are the Key." *Journal of Reading*, 24 (January 1981), 316–320.

Berger, Allen, and H. Alan Robinson, eds. *Secondary School Reading: What Research Reveals for Classroom Practice*. Urbana, Ill.: National Conference on Research in English, 1982.

Bradley, John, Wilbur Ames, and Judy Mitchell. "Intrabook Readability: Variations Within History Textbooks." *Social Education* (October 1980), 524–528.

Cullinan, Bernice, and Sheila Fitzgerald. "Background Information Bulletin on the Use of Readability Formulae." *Reading Today*, 2 (December 1984/January 1985), 1.

Dupuis, Mary M., ed. *Reading in the Content Areas: Research for Teachers.* Newark, Del.: International Reading Association, 1984.

Elliott, Charles A. "The Music-Reading Dilemma." *Music Education Journal* (February 1982), 33–59.

Harker, John, ed. *Classroom Strategies for Secondary Reading.* Newark, Del.: International Reading Association, 1985.

Horowitz, Rosalind, and S. Jay Samuels. "Reading and Listening to Expository Text." *Journal of Reading Behavior*, 17, No. 3 (1985), 185–197.

Kresse, Elaine Campbell. "Using Reading as a Thinking Process to Solve Math Story Problems." *Journal of Reading*, 27 (April 1984), 598–601.

McCabe, Patrick. "The Effect Upon Comprehension of Mathematics Material Repatterned on the Basis of Oral Language." *Reading World*, 21 (December 1981), 146–154.

Naisbitt, John. *Megatrends.* New York: Warner Communications, 1984.

Thelen, Judith N. *Improving Reading in Science.* 2nd ed. Newark, Del.: International Reading Association, 1984.

CHAPTER
S   I   X

READING   IN   THE   CONTENT

AREAS: PART   1

OVERVIEW

Content textbooks are designed to teach students the basic concepts of the content area. Students must be able to understand content text materials in order to acquire these basic concepts. This chapter focuses on content reading materials in the areas of social science, science, mathematics, computer science, English (language arts), and foreign languages. Strategies for helping students develop word meanings, content understanding, and comprehension of writing patterns are presented. Study guides, process guides, and concept guides are among the strategies discussed.

PURPOSE-SETTING QUESTIONS

As you read this chapter, try to answer these questions:

1. What are the reading skills that you think are necessary in such fields as social studies, science, mathematics, computer science, English, and foreign languages? Make a list of skills for the content area in which you are most interested. As you read the chapter, check to see if your predictions are accurate.
2. What common writing patterns appear in these content areas?
3. Why is content reading comprehension important?
4. What strategies can a content teacher use to help students comprehend content materials?
5. Does each content area have unique reading strategies? To what degree can reading strategies be adapted from subject area to subject area?

KEY VOCABULARY

As you read this chapter, check your understanding of these terms:

writing patterns	chronological and sequential pattern
cause-and-effect pattern	comparison and/or contrast pattern
classification pattern	word (verbal) problems
experimental pattern	poetry
demonstration pattern	drama
definition or explanation pattern	fiction
problem-solving pattern	nonfiction
essays	editorial
computer literacy	

INTRODUCTION TO READING CONTENT MATERIAL

"The teaching of any content area includes more than merely conveying information to students through a lecture; it also includes teaching students how to read and comprehend their textbooks."[1] William Dea[2] estimates that over 75 percent of the learning at the secondary level is acquired through reading. Therefore, students must read textbooks effectively and efficiently. The teaching and reading strategies included in this chapter are designed to help content teachers guide students as they read content textbooks.

Each section of this chapter introduces teaching strategies. These strategies can be adapted to various types of content although the constraints of space prohibit demonstrating every strategy with each type of content.

SOCIAL STUDIES

Social studies classes are concerned with the study of human behavior. The area of social studies encompasses many academic disciplines.[3] Jack Fraenkel includes the following subjects under the social studies discipline: history, anthropology, geography, economics, political science, psychology, and sociology.[4] Social studies is at the core of the secondary school curriculum. One of the reasons students need to read social studies content is so they can become effective citizens of a democracy. To read social studies content effectively students must develop reading skills that will enable them to

1. Understand the ideas and viewpoints of others
2. Acquire and retain a body of relevant concepts and information
3. Think critically and creatively, thus developing attitudes and values and the ability to make decisions

In Chapter 3 we discussed four levels of reasoning: literal, inferential, critical, and creative. In developing comprehension of social studies and science content, the creative reasoning level is altered to become the level of *application*. Application, which involves elements of both critical and creative reading, uses knowledge that has been acquired from previous experience and reading in many different situations; the reader applies his or her knowledge to illustrate understanding of the material.

Critical reading is particularly important in social studies materials because all aspects of information on a topic cannot be included in a single textbook; each author selects information that supports and illustrates his or her point of view and purpose. Readers must use books, magazines, and newspapers to supplement the information offered by social studies texts in order to fully understand a topic. It is especially important to read critically when an author writes about not only *what* has happened but also *why* events have occurred. An author's biases are likely to appear when causes of events are explained. The author's point of view is affected by the following factors:

1. Author's age
2. Author's nationality
3. Author's religion
4. Author's political views
5. Author's race
6. Author's family history
7. Author's sex
8. Audience for whom author is writing[5]

Vocabulary

There are a large number of technical words and concepts in each content area. Specific words in the content area convey the basic concepts of the discipline. Social studies content is written to teach concepts, facts, and generalizations.[6] It includes a great deal of technical vocabulary, and students must learn the meanings of such words as *barriers, dominion, democracy, domestic, tyranny,* and *expansion* in order to understand social studies material. According to Wayne Herman, a student must comprehend 75 percent of the ideas and 90 percent of the vocabulary of a social studies selection to read it on an instructional level. This level of understanding is necessary for the student to learn and to avoid frustration.[7] Even higher levels of understanding and vocabulary knowledge are required to read social studies content fluently. These statements are true of other content areas as well.

Vocabulary activities should be used to help students learn word meanings and to enhance their recall of words. Through activities like those described in Chapter 2 and those that follow, word meanings are reinforced and recall is enhanced.

Activities
1. Give students practice exercises such as the following one: From the list of phrases below, choose a phrase that is associated with each of the words in the word list.[8]

Phrases

rules of conduct	control behavior
process	making and enforcing rules
power of making rules	power of enforcing rules
printed list of candidates	self-government
lawmaking branch	rights of the people
citizen's freedoms	indicate voter's choices
people's vote	power of political unit
choosing governing nation	

Word List

1. jurisdiction	6. autonomy
2. plebiscite	7. civil rights
3. law	8. legislature
4. govern	9. ballot
5. government	10. power structure

2. An activity called "Possible Sentences" encourages students to learn word meanings and to predict ideas they will encounter when reading content.[9] For this activity, use the following steps:

a. Identify important vocabulary in the reading selection and write the words on the chalkboard. Pronounce each word as you write it. The words below are taken from a social studies text chapter comparing democracy and communism.

democracy	civil rights
socialism	laws
capitalism	communism
legislature	welfare state

b. Ask each student to construct sentences for at least two of the words. Record these sentences on the chalkboard, underlining the important words. Continue eliciting sentences from the students as long as the sentences are creating new contexts.

Democracy means rule by the people.
The Communist form of government is based on the dictatorship of the Communist party.
Laws are made by the legislature.
Civil rights are the freedoms that people have that are guaranteed by the government.

c. Have students read their textbooks to verify the accuracy of the sentences they constructed.

d. After they read the text have the students evaluate each sentence using the text as a reference. Students may also use glossaries, dictionaries, and thesauruses. Have students modify the sentences if necessary.

e. Ask students to create additional sentences if they can think of any. The following are examples of sentences that might be provided by students:

The United States government is an example of a democratic government, while the Russian government is an example of a Communist government. Individual rights are more important under a democratic government than under a Communist government.

In a socialist system, the economy is controlled by the government. A welfare state is one in which the government is responsible for the welfare of the people.

3. The List-Group-Label lesson, originated by Hilda Taba,[10] uses categorization to help students develop and refine concepts. This activity also encourages students to relate content to past experiences. The following steps will help you develop this activity:

a. Give students a topic drawn from the materials they are studying. An appropriate topic could be "The Geography of Georgia."

b. Have students develop a list of words or expressions they associate with the topic. Record these words on the chalkboard until the list totals approximately twenty-five to thirty words.

Appalachian Mountains	Blue Ridge Mountains
The Piedmont	Atlantic Coast
Okefenokee Swamp	Stone Mountain
peanuts	shrimp
pecans	stone
lumber	peaches
tobacco	cotton
Savannah	Augusta
Callaway Gardens	Cyclorama
Altamaha River	Chattahoochee River
Savannah River	Atlantic Ocean

c. Have students group words from the large list, providing a label for each group.

Mountains	*Waterways*	*Products*
Blue Ridge Mts.	Atlantic Ocean	peanuts
Stone Mt.	Altamaha River	cotton
Appalachian Mts.	Chattahoochee River	tobacco
	Savannah River	lumber
		pecans
		peaches

Content

Social studies materials are written in an expository style, which is precise and factual. Example 6.1 illustrates this style of writing. As you read this example, note the lack of description. Also note the use of several technical terms that must be defined before the content can be understood. The reader must understand these technical terms and remember them for future reading of economics.

EXAMPLE 6.1   SOCIAL STUDIES CONTENT ⎯⎯⎯⎯⎯⎯⎯⎯⎯⎯

The Gross National Product

The dollar value of all the goods and services produced by an economic system in one year is called the **gross national product (GNP).** That is certainly one way of measuring how well an economic system does. When the economy suffers, the gross national product (or GNP for short) also suffers and goes down. On the other hand, if the economy is healthy, the GNP will rise.

The dollar value of all the goods and services produced by the system in one year gives you an idea of the system's size, if nothing else. In one recent year, the GNP of the United States was almost two trillion dollars. That figure represents the value of all of the goods and services produced in just one year by all of the business firms and individuals in our economic system. We not only produced more than any other country in the world, we also produced more than a hundred countries put together.

Because the GNP is an index of the health of the economy, it is used as a measure of growth. We can compare last year's gross national product with this year's. To make such comparisons not only easy but realistic, we should adjust for changes in the value of a dollar. We take one year and call that our *base year.* We say that the dollar of our base year is a **real dollar,** which means that it is a measure against which we will determine the value in purchasing power of the dollars of other years. For example, if we call 1967 our base year, the 1967 dollar becomes our real dollar. If in 1968 the real dollar can buy only 97¢ worth of goods or services, it is worth less than it was in 1967. If in 1968 the real dollar can buy $1.03 worth of goods or services, it is worth more than it was in 1967. In either event, we can measure the worth of the 1968 dollar against a constant: the real dollar of 1967. If we measure the GNP every year in terms of real dollars, our basis of comparison will remain the same.

Source: *General Business: Our Business and Economic World,* by Betty Brown and John Clow (Boston: Houghton Mifflin, 1982), pp. 142–143.

⎯⎯⎯⎯⎯⎯⎯⎯⎯⎯⎯⎯⎯

One of the most important strategies that content teachers can use to increase students' comprehension of social studies (and other) content materials is the study guide.[11] A study guide directs students through content materials, points out important ideas and concepts, and leads students in reasoning about the content. A study guide creates a point of contact between the student and the written material, showing readers how to comprehend content. Teachers should provide students with many opportunities for practicing reading with a study guide to make them independent in reading and understanding content.

The composition of a study guide is determined by the instructor's reasons for having students read the content material—and by the students' needs. A study guide may cover a chapter, a larger unit, or merely a part of a long chapter. If students are given a study guide to read before they read an assignment, they can respond to the questions and activities in the study guide as they read the content selection.

There are many ways to develop study guides. In this text there are examples of a number of different study guides that can be varied to fit particular selections. (Refer to Chapter 9 for a more detailed presentation of various kinds of study guides.) The important factor is that you, as a teacher, help students comprehend content. The following example of a study guide is based on a social studies concept that is related to Example 6.1.

EXAMPLE 6.2   SOCIAL STUDIES STUDY GUIDE

Vocabulary

Directions: Pay attention to the words in Column A—they are important for understanding of this selection. After reading the selection, draw a line from the word in Column A to its meaning in Column B.

Column A	Column B
Gross National Product	dollar value in the base year
Base year	value of goods and services for a given year
Real dollar	the year selected for comparison

Levels of Comprehension

Directions: Write short answers to the following questions.

Literal
1. How is Gross National Product computed?
2. What are the components of Gross National Product?
3. Why is the GNP considered an index of the health of an economy?

Applied
4. The value of goods and services is computed for the GNP. Which of the following are categorized as goods and which are categorized as services?
   TV repair bill, wool, house, steel, dentist's fee, lumber, draperies, dishes, lathe
5. What practical value does the GNP have for you as an individual?

Critical
Directions: Write a short essay to answer this question.
6. How could GNP be used as propaganda?

_____

A concept guide, which is another form of study guide, is essentially concerned with developing students' understanding of an important content concept. Concept guides may be developed in a number of different ways. Following is an example of a concept guide based on the chapter that contains the selection shown in Example 6.1. This concept guide would be completed by a student after he or she has read the chapter. Concept guides are a form of reasoning guides, which are presented and explained on page 409.

EXAMPLE 6.3   SOCIAL STUDIES CONCEPT GUIDE ————

Directions: Write a + before each term that is associated with Gross National Product, according to the information in your social studies textbook. Write a − before each word that is unrelated to the concept Gross National Product. Be prepared to explain and support your answer by using your textbook.

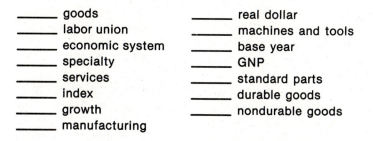

_____ goods   _____ real dollar
_____ labor union   _____ machines and tools
_____ economic system   _____ base year
_____ specialty   _____ GNP
_____ services   _____ standard parts
_____ index   _____ durable goods
_____ growth   _____ nondurable goods
_____ manufacturing

_____

Writing Patterns

A variety of writing patterns is used to structure the information and concepts that are the heart of social studies content. The major objective of content materials in this subject is to convey information. Like most expository content, this information is structured through main ideas and details that are commonly organized according to the following writing patterns:

1. cause and effect
2. chronological or sequential events
3. comparison and/or contrast
4. questions and answers
5. explanation or definition
6. a combination of patterns (The preceding patterns rarely exist in isolation and are usually used in combination.)

Knowing the patterns of writing in social studies content and practicing the strategies presented in this chapter should help students improve their reading comprehension. Above all, students should learn to use an organized approach in reading content materials and to follow the author's writing pattern.

Students should be given many opportunities for guided comprehension practice as they read the patterns of organization used in social studies materials. They should use the strategies introduced in this chapter with actual social studies content. Teachers can incorporate the strategies into study guides similar to those that are suggested here for teaching each pattern of writing.

Cause-and-Effect Pattern

Each area of social studies is concerned with chains of causes and effects: one cause results in certain effects that become causes of other effects. The passage in Example 6.4 is written in the cause-and-effect writing pattern.

EXAMPLE 6.4   CAUSE-AND-EFFECT PATTERN (SOCIAL STUDIES) ——

The British government should have learned a lesson from its experience with the Stamp Act. The American colonists had made it clear that they would resist any interference with what they considered their rights. But King George III and his ministers did not take kindly to having their plans blocked by a group of colonists across the Atlantic Ocean. In addition, the British government still felt it was necessary to raise money in America to help pay the cost of governing and protecting the colonies.

The Townshend Acts anger the colonists. Within a year after the repeal of the Stamp Act, Parliament passed new laws to regulate the colonies. These laws became known as the *Townshend Acts* because they were proposed by Charles Townshend (*town'* zend), a minister of the king. He was unfriendly to the colonists and his attitude was, "Let these Americans dare disobey these acts, and we shall see who is master."

Every one of the Townshend Acts angered the colonists. What were these acts, and why did the colonists object to them?

(1) Once again the Navigation Acts were to be strictly enforced. So that the British might look for smuggled goods, officers were to use general search warrants called *writs of assistance.* These writs (legal papers) would allow them to enter and search any house or building. The colonists were distressed to learn that their homes could be searched by any officer who had a writ of assistance.

(2) The Townshend Acts placed duties, or taxes, on a number of goods imported into the colonies. The list included such articles as lead, paper, paint, glass, and tea. The purpose of these duties was to raise money. The colonists were angry because this law seemed to tax them without their consent.

(3) The money raised from the duties was to be used to pay British officials in America, including the governors of royal colonies. The colonists objected

strongly to this plan, because it took away the right of their assemblies to control the salaries of colonial officials.

(4) Still another law forbade the New York Assembly to meet. This law was intended to punish the Assembly for not voting money to support British soldiers stationed in the colony. If such a thing could happen in New York, thought the colonists, might not all the colonies soon lose their assemblies?

Britain vs. The Colonists

Year	British Actions	American Actions
1763	Frontier closed by proclamation	Settlers ignore proclamation
1764	Navigation Acts enforced strictly	
1765	Stamp Act passed	Stamp Act Congress protests, British goods boycotted
1766	Stamp Act repealed	
1767	Townshend Acts passed	British goods boycotted
1768		↓
1769		
1770	Townshend Acts repealed, except for tea tax	Boston Massacre
1771		
1772		
1773	Cheap tea shipped to colonies	Boston Tea Party
1774	Intolerable Acts passed	First Continental Congress protests, British goods boycotted
1775	Troops raid Lexington and Concord	Minutemen resist

Source: Howard B. Wilder, Robert P. Ludlum, and Harriett McCune Brown: *This is America's Story,* pp. 144–146. Copyright © 1982 by Houghton Mifflin Company. Used by permission.

After students have read examples of cause-and-effect content in their textbooks and have learned to identify this organization, the teacher can use teaching strategies that will aid comprehension of this pattern. The cause-and-effect writing pattern can be understood best when students identify the causes and effects and relate causes with associated effects. The following strategies can be used with content text materials.

Activities
1. State some effects and ask students to identify the causes. Ask them to answer the question "Why did this happen?" after reading the material in Example 6.4.
   a. The colonists' objection to taxation was caused by _____
   _____ .

    b. The taxes levied on the colonists by the British were caused by _____

_____ .

2. State some causes and ask students to identify the effects. Have them answer the question "What did this fact cause?"
    a. The passing of the Townshend Acts caused _____ .
    b. The passing of the Intolerable Acts caused _____ .
3. Develop a chart like the one in Example 6.4 for another reading selection. This activity is especially important when the text does not provide such a chart.
4. Scramble the events in the "Causes" and "Effects" columns on a chart like the one in the example. Ask students to draw lines to correctly match causes and effects.

Definition or Explanation Pattern

The definition or explanation pattern is used to define or explain important concepts. The concept that is explained or defined serves as the main idea, and the supporting details constitute the elements of the definition or explanation. To comprehend this pattern of writing, the student must identify both the concept and the author's definition or explanation. This pattern is important to the reader because the knowledge included in the definition or explanation frequently serves as a basis for subsequent information on the topic.

One useful approach for helping students comprehend this pattern is to have them write a brief explanation or definition of a concept in their own words. Outlining is also a useful strategy for helping students with this pattern. Example 6.5 provides a sample of this pattern and an outline based on the passage presented.

EXAMPLE 6.5   DEFINITION OR EXPLANATION PATTERN
AND OUTLINE (SOCIAL STUDIES)

The Articles of Confederation are adopted after a long delay. Meanwhile, the states realized that a regular government was needed for the nation, and the members of Congress worked out a definite plan for such a government. The states were to be joined in a union known as the *Confederation.* The plan for this union was called the *Articles of Confederation.*

When the new plan was sent to the states for approval, it ran into trouble. At that time, about half the states had claims to large areas of land west of the Appalachian Mountains. (The map on page 212 shows the land claimed by the states.) Naturally these states wanted to keep their western lands, but the states that had no western claims did not agree. They were afraid of remaining forever small and weak in comparison with their large, strong neighbors. They believed that the western lands should be turned over to the United States, and refused to accept the Articles of Confederation until this was done. Finally the states claiming western lands agreed to give up their claims, and the Articles were approved. Because of this delay, the new government was not established until 1781, when the war was almost over.

What was the new government like? The government of the Confederation was not like our national government today. There was no President with power to carry out the laws and no Supreme Court to settle important disputes. To run the nation's business there was a Congress made up of representatives from each state. Whether large or small, each state was to have only one vote. And in most matters nine states had to agree before the Confederation could act.

The new government under the Articles of Confederation could (1) wage war and make peace, and organize an army and navy when needed; (2) control the relations of the United States with other nations; (3) regulate trade with the Indians and other Indian affairs; (4) arrange for carrying the mail; (5) borrow money to pay necessary expenses; and (6) ask each of the states to contribute money to pay the expenses of the Confederation.

Source: Howard B. Wilder, Robert P. Ludlum, and Harriett McCune Brown: *This Is America's Story*, pp. 210–211. Copyright © 1982 by Houghton Mifflin Company. Used by permission.

Outline

1. Articles of Confederation
   A. Adoption after long delay
      1. Purpose to join the states
      2. Western lands a problem
      3. Claims to western lands relinquished
      4. Confederation finally accepted 1781
   B. Nature of the government formed by Confederation
      1. Congress had equal representation for each state.
      2. Nine states had to agree for action.
      3. Could wage war
      4. Could establish foreign relations
      5. Could regulate trade
      6. Could provide for mail service
      7. Could borrow money
      8. Could collect money

Chronological or Sequential Events Pattern

In the chronological or sequential events pattern of writing, events are arranged in order of occurrence; thus a chronological pattern presents a sequence based on time and space. The teacher can help students develop a concept of time by having them consider time in relation to their own lives. Understanding time is necessary for comprehending social studies material, but memorization of dates has much less value than thinking about what one has read. Since indefinite time references, such as "in early days" or "in ancient times," may confuse the reader, the teacher should discuss with students the meanings of these terms.

The chronological pattern of writing is presented in Example 6.6.

EXAMPLE 6.6   CHRONOLOGICAL PATTERN (SOCIAL STUDIES) ———

Civil War

The war began in April, 1861, at Fort Sumter, South Carolina, where Federal troops were stationed on an island in Charleston harbor. Confederate forces opened fire after the Union garrison refused to surrender. Southern artillery soon pounded Fort Sumter into submission.

Four years later—after Bull Run, Shiloh, Gettysburg, and Appomattox—it was all over. Northern industrial might and doggedness overpowered Southern chivalry and heroism. In the modern world, then emerging, slavery had to be abolished once and for all, and Americans on both sides of the Mason-Dixon line today do not regret it. As of April, 1865, a reunited nation, forged in the fires of civil war, started patching its wounds and looking towards the future.

Source: From *Land of Progress*, by Irwin Unger and H. Mark Johnson. © Copyright, 1975, by Silver, Burdett & Ginn Inc. Used with permission.

Understanding of chronological patterns may be developed by using the following techniques.

Activities
1. Guide students to understand blocks of time. Seeking relationships among events helps students comprehend time. After reading the full text of the material extracted in Example 6.6, the student should understand that the twenty years prior to the Civil War was the period when the immediate causes of the war became apparent and that a great many factors that led to the war developed during that period. The war itself lasted from 1861 until 1865. It was followed by the Reconstruction period. Each of these three blocks of time are interrelated. A time line can help students understand blocks of time in a concrete way.

Civil War

April, 1861	April, 1865
War began	War ended
nation divided	nation reunited
some states left	beginning of
union	Reconstruction period

2. Relate a time sequence to a student's own experience with time and help the student develop a concept of the past, present, and future. The student can relate historic occurrences to his or her own lifetime and the lifetimes of his or her parents and ancestors. For example, the Civil War probably occurred in the lifetime of the great, great grandparents of present-day students.

Past	*Ancestors*
Civil War	great, great grandparents
World War I	great grandparents
World War II	grandparents
Korean Conflict	parents
Present	student
Future	descendants

Comparison and/or Contrast Pattern

When using the comparison and/or contrast pattern, an author explains social studies ideas by using likenesses and differences to develop understanding. Example 6.7 shows this writing pattern.

EXAMPLE 6.7   COMPARISON AND/OR CONTRAST PATTERN
(SOCIAL STUDIES)

Two new political parties develop. At the same time that the changes just described were taking place in American life, there was also a change in political parties. The Federalist Party died out soon after Monroe became President (page 238). For a few years there was only one political party, the Republican or Democratic-Republican. After Monroe left the presidency, however, the Democratic-Republican Party split into two parts. The friends and supporters of Andrew Jackson became known in the 1830's as the *Democratic Party.* Many of the same kinds of men who had supported Thomas Jefferson were members of the Democratic Party. It came to stand for low tariffs and states' rights (page 378), and opposed a strong federal government. Many Southerners and Westerners were Democrats.

Those who disliked "King Andrew I," as they called Andrew Jackson, formed a political party to oppose him and his beliefs. This party was called at first the National Republican Party but later became known as the *Whig Party.* It stood chiefly for high tariffs and a strong federal government. It included many men who had belonged to the Federalist Party in earlier years or who held the same beliefs. The Whig Party was strong in the East.

Source: Howard B. Wilder, Robert P. Ludlum, and Harriett McCune Brown: *This is America's Story,* pp. 336–337. Copyright © 1982 by Houghton Mifflin Company. Used by permission.

Understanding of the comparison and/or contrast pattern can be developed by using the following techniques.

Activities

1. The teacher and students may develop a chart to show comparisons and/or contrasts. The following chart is based on Example 6.7 and shows the contrast between the Democratic party and the Whig party.

Democratic Party	*Whig Party*
Opposed strong federal government	For strong federal government
For states' rights	Opposed states' rights
For low tariff	For high tariff

2. Using the example selection provided, the teacher may provide contrasts and ask students to locate comparisons; or the teacher may give the Democratic party's point of view and ask students to list the contrasting views of the Whig party.

Democratic Party	*Whig Party*
Believed in states' rights	
Believed in low tariff	

Question and Answer Pattern

Authors sometimes use a question and answer pattern to organize social studies materials. In this pattern, the author asks a question and then answers it. Readers should be able to recall the author's questions and identify his or her answers. Example 6.8 illustrates this style of writing.

EXAMPLE 6.8 SAMPLE QUESTION/ANSWER WRITING PATTERN (SOCIAL STUDIES)

Now, how accurate are these descriptions that we read? Did the people who wrote them tell the absolute truth? This is a difficult question to answer! Though everyone tries to be honest and accurate in describing what he sees, his feelings color his reporting. For example, a reporter who is sympathetic with workers conducting a strike will probably write an account of the strike which favors those workers. Another reporter who opposes the strike can be expected to offer a somewhat different version of the same event. By the same token, the activities of the President of the United States (whoever he may be) are generally presented with a note of approval by those writers who support him, and with a note of disapproval by his opponents. These slanted feelings or prejudices are called *bias,* a concept which will be dealt with throughout this unit.

Sources. Historians usually classify records as one of two types: primary or secondary sources. Eyewitness accounts of historical events are called primary sources. These sources consist of contemporary newspaper accounts, chronicles, letters, diaries, and speeches. Secondary sources, such as textbooks, are written by authors who study the primary sources and try to interpret and explain their true meaning. The texts' authors then present us with their version of history, in their own words. Both primary and secondary sources have built-in advantages and limitations for the student of history.

Which source—primary or secondary—would probably contain more historical data and information? Which source would probably be more free from bias or personal feeling? Is history what *actually* happened, or what people *think* happened? Is there any way to discover what *actually* happened? These are hard questions that historians must face.

Trying to find the truth of history by sifting through primary and secondary sources is no easy task. As you can imagine, you will encounter many different interpretations of historical figures, trends, and events, depending on the bias and viewpoint of the people reporting them.

Source: From *Land of Progress*, by Irwin Unger and H. Mark Johnson. © Copyright, 1975, by Silver, Burdett & Ginn Inc. Used with permission.

Combination Pattern

In writing that combines patterns the student can be asked to identify the types of writing patterns the author has used; the teacher then can use the techniques suggested for understanding the individual patterns to help the student comprehend the assigned selection.

Graphic Aids

Graphic aids are particularly meaningful in social studies materials, where readers must integrate graphic information with the written content. Graphic aids include maps, charts, pictures, graphs, and tables.

When a graphic aid is mentioned in the text, students should examine the aid, its caption, and any associated material. For instance, Example 6.1 refers to a graph and asks questions that are based on the graph. To answer the questions, students must look at the comparisons created in the graph.

The teacher should include instruction on graphic aids so that students will learn to read and interpret them and to combine this information with the ideas that are written in the text.

SCIENCE AND HEALTH

The goal of scientific study is to help people understand the world through investigation and explanation of natural phenomena. The goal of health education is to help people understand themselves.

The objective of health education is twofold: to help students understand both their physical bodies and their emotional growth and development.

Science education has two objectives for secondary students. The first objective is to develop scientific literacy—"the ability of an intelligent layman to read scientific literature and to understand its implications for the culture."[12] Scientific literacy enables the reader (and the consumer) to recognize that although science can solve many of our universal problems, in doing so it creates new problems. For example, the present environmental crisis was partially created by the same technology that gave the world a cleaner, whiter laundry.

The second objective is to introduce the field to young people who may be interested in pursuing scientific careers. Adolescence is a period of exploration during which students study many areas to find special interests that they may develop in the future.

All scientific content (including health education material) is written to convey concepts, details, generalizations, and theories. Many details are used in scientific writing, and readers must be able to relate these details to larger ideas in order to understand the concepts, generalizations, and theories. Scientific content frequently includes experiments and laboratory work, which require students to apply knowledge and to follow directions precisely.

In order to comprehend scientific material, students must learn to follow scientific thinking and writing style, which is generally terse with dense factual content. The reader must read slowly and thoroughly and pay careful attention to the concepts, details, generalizations, and theories in order to understand the exact meaning. Technical words and typical patterns of writing should be learned.

Study guides, concept guides, preview guides, directed reading activities, and SQ3R are some of the strategies that can be used to help students understand scientific and health education content.

Vocabulary and Concept Development

Many specialized, technical terms are used in science and health materials. Scientific vocabulary changes often because new discoveries add new technical terms and cause other terms to become obsolete. Example 6.9 shows an activity that is useful for teaching students scientific vocabulary. It is an entry from a student-constructed and illustrated dictionary of scientific terms.

The Frayer Model is useful for developing students' understanding of concepts. Many of the activities suggested in Chapter 2 are also helpful. Frederick Frayer,[13] making use of some of H. J. Klausmeier's research, developed a teaching model that clarifies concepts by giving students the essential and nonessential attributes of new concepts as well as examples and nonexamples of those concepts. Following is an application of the Frayer Model[14] to the scientific concept of adaptation. This model is equally useful with other types of content.

Concept: Adaptation

Essential Attributes
1. Improves chance of survival
2. Improves genetic selection
   Nonessential Attributes
1. Seasonal changes
2. Changes that do not contribute to survival
   Examples
1. Front legs of mole
2. Walrus tusks
3. Beak of black skimmer
   Nonexamples
1. Albinism
2. Human beings with six fingers

In addition to creating guides like the preceding to aid students' comprehension, teachers can create blank forms for students to complete as they read textbook selections.

EXAMPLE 6.9   ILLUSTRATED DICTIONARY OF SCIENTIFIC TERMS

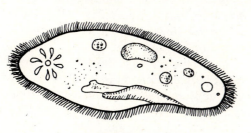

A paramecium is a one-celled animal that is found in the scum on pond water.

paramecium

Writing Patterns

The main ideas and supporting details in scientific materials are frequently organized into classification patterns; explanations of technical processes; cause-and-effect patterns; and problem-solving patterns. Another pattern used to structure scientific content is the experimental pattern.[15]

Classification Pattern

In the classification pattern, information is ordered under common headings and subheadings. The information sorted in this way may consist of living things, objects, or general ideas. This pattern is a type of outlining that shows a classification, the distinguishing characteristics of the members of the class, and examples. It is a form of the pattern that presents a main idea and supporting details: the classification represents the main idea, and the distinguishing characteristics and examples are treated as details.

To understand text material written in this pattern, students should identify the distinguishing characteristics of the classification and identify examples of members of the classification. Outlining is also a useful strategy. Example 6.10 shows a passage written in this pattern and an outline based on the passage.

EXAMPLE 6.10   CLASSIFICATION PATTERN AND OUTLINE ————

Nonvascular Plants

Multicellular Algae   simplest metaphytes are the multicellular plants called algae. These organisms do not have true roots, specialized leaves, or systems for transporting water and food. But they are multicellular and they photosynthesize.

Some algae, like *Spirogyra,* consist of filaments made up of cells attached in a row, and live in fresh water. Other algae are in the form of sheets of cells, like the seaweed called sea-lettuce. These algae are green in color, as you would expect.

There are other algae whose green color is hidden by other colors. These plants photosynthesize just as green plants do. However, their chlorophyll is covered up by other pigments that give them their red and brown colors. All of these plants live in the ocean. At some time during the life cycle of each there is a plant body that has an upright part as well as root-like structures.

The root-like structures serve to attach the plants to the bottom of the ocean or to rocks near the shore. The more upright portion is involved in photosynthesis and reproduction. The main plant body is made of cells joined together as branching filaments or flat blades. Some of these algae can be over 30 meters long. Others are tiny plants only a few millimeters high.

The most familiar types of brown algae are kelp and the seaweed *Fucus. Fucus* covers rocks in the intertidal zone; kelp lives attached to the ocean bottom in shallow water. Other seaweeds have a red color. A red alga common on both the Atlantic and Pacific coasts of North America is *Polysiphonia.* This organism is a mass of small, branching, delicate filaments.

Source: Earl D. Hanson, J. David Lockard, and Peter Jensch: *Biology: The Science of Life* (Boston: Houghton Mifflin Company, 1980), pp. 458–459.

Outline

I. Classification—Algae
    A. Distinguishing characteristics
        1. Multicellular plants
        2. Do not have true roots

  3. Do not have specialized leaves
  4. Do not have systems for transporting food and water
  5. Photosynthesize
 B. Classified by color
  1. Green
  2. Brown
  3. Red

Definition or Explanation Pattern

Although the definition or explanation pattern that is described in Chapter 3 occurs in all types of content materials, this pattern as it occurs in scientific content and health materials is particularly important for students to learn. The pattern may explain processes that are biological (the digestive process) or mechanical (the operation of an engine). It also may provide definitions for scientific terms, such as *atmosphere*. Diagrams usually accompany this kind of pattern, so the reader must incorporate written content information with the diagrams.

The information in the definition or explanation pattern is usually presented in a very dense style of writing; readers need to learn how to read this style in order to understand basic scientific information, principles, processes, and definitions. This style of writing requires a very slow rate of reading. Example 6.11 illustrates an explanation pattern that describes a process and includes a diagram.

EXAMPLE 6.11   EXPLANATION OF A PROCESS (SCIENCE)

Recombinant DNA

Scientists have recently learned how to transfer small segments of DNA molecules from the cells of one organism into the DNA of another organism. The new DNA segments are called **recombinant** (*ree KAHM buh nuhnt*) **DNA**. This transfer of bits of DNA is a remarkable achievement. Some scientists have wanted for a long time to find ways to improve the genetic make-up of organisms. Transferring DNA opens up a wide new world of research opportunities. This field of research is called **genetic engineering.** When you have seen how the transfer of DNA is accomplished, you might consider some of the possibilities and dangers of this line of research.

Transferring bits of DNA from one organism to another presented three major problems. First, scientists had to learn how to break DNA apart at specific points along the molecule. Second, they had to develop chemical methods for connecting the tiny segments of DNA with other DNA strands. And third, scientists had to find a way to insert the remodelled DNA molecules into living cells.

Scientists have been able to transfer DNA segments into certain types of bacterial cells. Bacteria contain small doughnut-shaped rings of DNA separate from

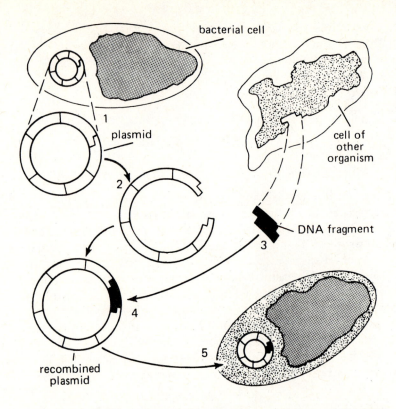

Figure 10-20 A diagram of DNA transfer from two separate organisms into a new host bacterial cell. **1.** A plasmid is taken from a bacterial cell. **2.** The plasmid's molecular ring is broken open, leaving space for a fragment of DNA from the other organism. **3.** DNA fragment is split off from the other cell. **4.** DNA fragment is added to complete the recombined plasmid. **5.** Completed plasmid is placed within a new host bacterial cell.

the bacterial "chromosome." These rings are called **plasmids** (*PLAZ mihds*); they are found floating free within each bacterial cell. Until it became possible to transfer DNA segments, scientists paid very little attention to the presence or function of plasmids. Now, however, plasmids play a key role in DNA transfer research. Look at Figure 10–20 for a description of how DNA segments are transferred from one organism to another.

Under the right conditions, the genetic instructions contained in the foreign fragment of DNA are followed in the bacterial cell. Therefore, a bacterial cell could serve as a sort of "biochemical factory" and produce large quantities of a desired substance. For instance, the hormone insulin is missing or in low supply in people who suffer from the disease diabetes. Normally, insulin is formed by cells of the pancreas. It might be possible to move the gene coding for insulin production from a pancreas cell to a bacterium that multiplies very rapidly. This bacterium may follow the genetic instructions for producing insulin. If so, its rapid growth would then provide an inexpensive source of large quantities of insulin.

Even if the host bacterial cell does not follow the inserted genetic instructions, DNA transfer can serve another useful purpose. Many such bacterial cells are not in any way disturbed by the presence of the foreign DNA fragment. As it divides, the cell will reproduce the foreign DNA fragment. Thus, scientists would be able to use a rapidly dividing bacterium and its dividing daughter cells to produce large quantities of a particular gene for study.

Source: Earl D. Hanson, J. David Lockard, and Peter Jensch: *Biology: The Science of Life* (Boston: Houghton Mifflin Company, 1980), pp. 294–295.

Techniques that will help students comprehend the explanation of a process follow.

Activities
1. Have students attempt to restate the explanation in their own words.
2. Have students reread the explanation to check their comprehension.
3. Have students study the sequence of steps in the process and attempt to explain the process by recalling the steps in sequence. For the passage in Example 6.11, the steps would be as follows:
   a. Plasmid is taken from bacterial cell.
   b. Plasmid's molecular ring is broken open.
   c. DNA fragment is split off from the other cell.
   d. DNA fragment is added to complete the recombined plasmid.
   e. Completed plasmid is placed in new host bacterial cell.
4. Mask the labels in a diagram such as that shown in Example 6.11 and have students insert appropriate labels.

Examples 6.12 and 6.13 also illustrate the definition or explanation writing pattern. In Example 6.12, the pattern explains and provides examples for the term *instinct;* in Example 6.13, the pattern explains and provides examples for the term *insomnia.*

EXAMPLE 6.12   EXPLANATION PATTERN (SCIENCE) ───────

Instinct and Behavior

In the experiment with squirrels already described, the scientist found that certain behavior did not have to be learned. The squirrels were born with the information that nuts were food and that they could try to crack them open. The squirrels, without learning by trial-and-error, also knew how to hide nuts or bury them in order to eat them in the winter. Scientists call this behavior that does not have to be learned **instinctive** (*ihn STIHNGK tihv*) **behavior**. Instinctive behavior is part of the nature of an animal. It is born with the animal.

Source: Earl D. Hanson, J. David Lockard, and Peter Jensch: *Biology: The Science of Life* (Boston: Houghton Mifflin Company, 1980), p. 57.

EXAMPLE 6.13   EXPLANATION PATTERN (HEALTH)

Insomnia (*ihn SAHM nee uh*), or having difficulty sleeping, takes several forms. Some people have a very hard time falling asleep, or they wake up much earlier than they want to. Others may not be able to sleep more than a few hours at a time without waking up. People who have insomnia sometimes feel that they don't sleep at all, but actually they drift in and out of sleep without realizing it. They probably get more sleep than they think they do.

Source: Edward Rosenberg, Henry Gurney, and Vivian Harlin: *Investigating Your Health*, rev. ed., p. 142. Copyright © 1978 by Houghton Mifflin Company. Used by permission.

The teacher may use the following techniques to help students read materials like those found in Examples 6.12 and 6.13.

Activities
1. Have students identify the main idea and supporting details in paragraphs that they read. For instance, a definition of the term *instincts* is the main idea of Example 6.12; a definition of *insomnia* is the main idea of Example 6.13.
2. Have students reread this pattern as many times as necessary to understand the information, principle, process, or definition that is being explained.
3. Ask students to suggest additional applications or examples. For Example 6.12 the student could list additional types of behavior that are instincts.

Cause-and-Effect Pattern

The cause-and-effect pattern, as it is presented in scientific or health materials, is illustrated by the passage in Example 6.14. The chart that follows is based on the passage. Students might create this type of chart themselves; or the activity could be varied so that the teacher supplies either the causes or effects and the students fill in the missing information in the appropriate column.

The following activities can be used to provide practice with the cause-and-effect and other writing patterns.

Activities
1. Writing (composition) can be used to reinforce reading comprehension in any content area or of any writing pattern. In the following paragraph, the student writer connected the earth science content he read to his own experiences.

The climate is the average pattern of weather in a place. The climate affects the habitat, which includes the water, rocks, soil, and air that all living things need. Since the plants and animals need certain things to live, they exist in places where the habitat provides the things they need to live. The kind of water, rocks, soil, and air that are available makes a difference in the kinds of plants and animals that live in that place. Woodpeckers and sapsuckers live in North Carolina because they eat the insects that live in the pine trees growing in this state.

EXAMPLE 6.14   CAUSE-AND-EFFECT PATTERN (BIOLOGY TEXT) AND CHART

Concentration and the Environment

Too many stimuli from the environment can cause confusion. Have you ever tried to concentrate in a place where people are talking or moving around? You may have learned to tune out certain distracting sights and sounds. Many animals have this ability to choose which stimulus they will respond to in the environment. This is called tuning out a stimulus.

Scientists call the mind's ability to select among stimuli "gating" because the process resembles a gate opening and closing to let in or keep out information. Scientists do not know exactly where and how messages are stopped. But it appears that what is allowed through the mind's "gate" depends on what the animal is doing or intends to do.

Scientists have also found that too much stimulation from the environment can interfere with learning. Experiments with animals, including humans, have shown that if there are too many distractions, they cannot be tuned out. The animals make many errors, learn more slowly, and become restless. On the other hand, an environment with too few stimuli also slows learning and results in drowsiness. The best condition for learning seems to be an environment with a moderate amount of stimulation.

Source: Earl D. Hanson, J. David Lockard, and Peter Jensch: *Biology: The Science of Life* (Boston: Houghton Mifflin Company, 1980), p. 53.

Chart

Cause	Effect
too many stimuli	cause confusion
distracting sounds	tune out
distracting sights	tune out
too much stimulation	interferes with learning
too many distractions	cannot tune out
cannot tune out distractions	errors, slow learning, restlessness
too few stimuli	slow learning, drowsiness
moderate stimulation	learning

2. Ask students to write questions about the content they read. For example,
   a. Why do some animals become extinct?
   b. If Guilford County became a desert, what animals would become extinct?

Study guides can be developed to help students read the cause-and-effect pattern. Example 6.15 illustrates the cause-and-effect pattern in health materials and presents a study guide built on the passage.

EXAMPLE 6.15   CAUSE-AND-EFFECT PATTERN (HEALTH) AND STUDY GUIDE

Being active is not just a way to improve an already healthy body—to become stronger or more attractive, for example. The fact is, if you are not regularly active, you don't just stay the same. Your health actually goes downhill.

Constantly inactive muscle fibers become smaller, and they store less energy. They exert less tension for a task, and they tire quickly. When inactive muscles are overworked, they often feel stiff and sore for a few days afterwards. Unused joints become stiff and less flexible, and can become sore if moved too far or too fast. A lack of stress regularly exerted by muscles makes bones eventually become softer and more easily broken.

The effect of regular exercise is to make muscles and joints stronger and more flexible. Tendons and bones also become harder and stronger. Well-used muscles do not tire as quickly as flabby muscles do, even though they do more work. This is because trained muscles can take up and use glucose and oxygen from the blood at a faster rate. They also get rid of waste products faster. And trained muscles are also more efficient at turning food energy into work.

Source: Edward Rosenberg, Henry Gurney, and Vivian Harlin: *Investigating Your Health,* rev. ed., p. 131. Copyright © 1978 by Houghton Mifflin Company. Used by permission.

Cause-and-Effect Study Guide

Directions: Read the assigned selection and identify all of the causes and effects in the selection. After reading the selection read the list of effects and the list of causes. Then place the letter of the cause in the blank before the effect with which it is associated.

Causes
a. smaller muscle fibers
b. overworked, inactive muscles
c. unused joints
d. regular exercise
e. trained muscles
f. lack of muscle stress

Effects

_____ 1. Less energy is stored.
_____ 2. Muscles tire easily.
_____ 3. The individual feels stiff and sore.
_____ 4. Muscles and joints become stronger.
_____ 5. Tendons and bones become harder, stronger.
_____ 6. Food energy is turned efficiently into work.
_____ 7. Bones become softer.

For additional teaching suggestions to use with this style of writing, see the cause-and-effect pattern in the section on social studies.

Problem-Solving Pattern

The problem-solving style of writing is used in scientific materials and health materials to describe a real or hypothetical problem and its actual or suggested solution. For example, a writer might use this style of writing to explain how a vaccine was developed for polio. Example 6.16 contains an illustration of this style of writing that was drawn from science content; Example 6.17 was taken from health content.

EXAMPLE 6.16   PROBLEM-SOLVING PATTERN (SCIENCE) ————

Unsolved Problems

In 1970, the greatest unsolved problem regarding ocean basins was their origin. By the 1980's, the development of the present basins was well established. Now the question is, "How many ocean basins have there been throughout Earth's history?" Clearly there have been more than we know today, but the puzzle requires many detailed studies of the ocean's rocks.

Have any deep-sea sediments ever formed into rocks that now occur on land? Certainly ancient rocks must have formed from such sediments, and marine geologists would like to examine them. They have not come from cores drilled in the sea floor. A geologist from the University of Hawaii believes she sampled some in the Solomon Islands in 1980. Her analysis is interesting, yet still incomplete.

Certain areas of the sea floor, far away from sources of sediment, have few deposits. Rocks are not covered with sediment, or are close to the surface of the sea floor. In 1981 oceanographers completed a study of these parts of the sea floor, and learned that they are as quiet as had been supposed.

Source: William Matthews, Chalmer Roy, Robert Stevenson, et al.: *Investigating the Earth*, 4th ed. (Boston: Houghton Mifflin Company, 1984), p. 211.

EXAMPLE 6.17   PROBLEM-SOLVING PATTERN (HEALTH)

Additives

The biggest problem with modern food technology—the one you hear about so often—concerns chemical **additives.** The average American and Canadian consumes over five pounds (about two and one-half kilograms) of food additives each year. Additives are added to food to prevent spoilage and to improve color, flavor, nutrition, or other food characteristics. So, for example, dry breakfast cereals usually come labeled "BHA and BHT added to reduce spoilage." (BHA and BHT stand for the chemical names.) Oranges are dyed a uniform orange color. Cereals and milk usually come with vitamin additives. And hams often have meat tenderizers as well as water injected into them. Even meats that are not injected or treated in a processing plant may contain high amounts of certain chemicals and hormones that were fed to the animals while they were alive. In all, over a thousand chemicals are added to our foods.

Source: Edward Rosenberg, Henry Gurney, and Vivian Harlin: *Investigating Your Health,* rev. ed., p. 167. Copyright © 1978 by Houghton Mifflin Company. Used by permission.

To teach students to read and understand the problem-solving style of writing, the teacher may use the following techniques.

Activities
1. Ask students to identify the problem in a passage and state it in their own words.
2. Ask students to locate the solution or solutions suggested by the author.
3. Ask students to prepare a problem and solution statement similar to the following:

   Problem: Why don't bacteria grow and divide in the region surrounding bread mold?

   Solution: Fleming found that mold gave off a chemical that killed the bacteria. He isolated the chemical and tested it against bacteria. He tested the chemical on animals with bacterial disease. He tested the chemical on diseased human volunteers.

Experimental Pattern

The experimental pattern of writing is frequently used in scientific materials because experiments are the basis of scientific knowledge and advancement. The reader must be able to read experiment directions and translate them into action. The reader must carry out the directions precisely and carefully observe the outcomes. The purpose of an experiment is comparable to a main idea, and experimental directions are comparable to details. Example 6.18 presents this pattern of writing.

EXAMPLE 6.18   EXPERIMENTAL PATTERN (SCIENCE)

Procedure

Place a glass beaker on your desk with two objects in it. This will represent the earth, which will hold only a certain size population.

Put a row of paper cups on your desk (ten should be enough). In the first cup, place two of the objects. In the second cup, place twice as many as in the first cup, or four objects. Write on the outside of the cups the number of objects that have been placed in each cup.

In cups 3 through 10, double the number of objects that are in the previous cup (that is, cup number 3 will contain 8 and cup number 4 will contain 16). Write the amount in each cup on the outside. Determine the height of the beaker with the two objects in it. What is the approximate volume (in percent) of the empty space in the beaker? Record this at 0 time. Make a table to record your data.

In 35 seconds, add the contents of cup 1 (that is, 2 objects) to the beaker and record in the table the total population and the approximate percent of the volume of the beaker that is empty. At 35-second intervals, add the contents of cups 2 through 10. Record your results.

Make a graph of your results, with population on the vertical axis and time on the horizontal axis.

Discussion

1. The human population of the earth is thought to have had a slow start, with early periods of doubling in size as long as 1 million years. The present world population is thought to be doubling every 37 years. How would the mathematical nature of this growth rate compare to your investigation?
2. The present world population is well over 4 billion people. To answer this question, assume that it is 4.5 billion. The earth's radius is about 6400 kilometers and about 7/10 of its surface is covered with water. What is the present density of human population in terms of people per square kilometer of land surface? (Area of a sphere $= 4\pi r^2$)
3. Assume that the present population growth rate will continue. What will the density per square kilometer be 37 years from now? 111 years? 1110 years?
4. Is space the only limiting factor in determining maximum human population? If not, describe others.

Source: William Matthews, Chalmer Roy, Robert Stevenson, et al.: *Investigating the Earth*, 4th ed. (Boston: Houghton Mifflin Company, 1984), p. 340.

Following are the steps a reader should use when reading an experiment.

1. Ask the following questions:
   a. What am I to find out?
   b. What materials are needed?

   c. What processes are used?

   d. What is the order of the steps in the experiment?

   e. What do I expect to happen?

2. Perform the experiment.

3. Observe the experiment.

4. Compare the actual outcomes with predicted outcomes. (Success or failure of an experiment is determined by the learning that takes place.)

Additional Skills

In addition to an understanding of technical terminology and the styles in which science materials are organized, the reader of science must have mathematics skills: he or she must know and be able to apply the abbreviations and equations that are found in scientific content. Example 6.19 contains scientific writing that requires readers to use these skills.

EXAMPLE 6.19 ABBREVIATIONS AND EQUATIONS IN SCIENCE CONTENT

Powers of Ten

In earth science it is often necessary to use very large and very small numbers. The area of the earth's surface is 361,000,000 square kilometers. A convenient shorthand for writing numbers like this one is to use powers of ten. For example:

Number			Equivalent Power of 10
1000	=		1×10^3
100	=		1×10^2
10	=		1×10^1
1	=		1×10^0
0.1	=	$\dfrac{1}{10^1}$	=	1×10^{-1}
0.01	=	$\dfrac{1}{10^2}$	=	1×10^{-2}
0.001	=	$\dfrac{1}{10^3}$	=	1×10^{-3}
0.0001	=	$\dfrac{1}{10^4}$	=	1×10^{-4}

Thus, 361,000,000 is the same as 3.61 times 100,000,000. Since this is 3.61 times $10 \times 10 \times 10 \times 10 \times 10 \times 10 \times 10 \times 10$ or 3.61 multiplied by 10 eight times, we call this 3.61×10^8.

$$\text{coefficient} \rightarrow 3.61 \times 10^{8 \swarrow \, exponent}_{\leftarrow \, base}$$

The **exponent** tells how many times to multiply by 10, which is called the **base**. To change a number from the usual long form to the standard form, move the decimal point to the left until you have a number between one and ten. The number of places that you moved the decimal point is the exponent, or power of ten. The **coefficient** is the number between one and ten used with the power of ten. In the example, the decimal point was moved eight places to the left, so the exponent is 8. The base is 10 since we are using the decimal number system. The coefficient is 3.61.

If the original long number is less than one, it can be written as a number between one and ten divided by ten to some power.

$$0.008 = 8 \times \frac{1}{1000} = 8 \times \frac{1}{10^3} = 8 \times 10^{-3}$$

That is, if you have to move the decimal point to the *right* to get a number between 1 and 10, the exponent has a negative sign.

Source: William Matthews, Chalmer Roy, Robert Stevenson, et al.: *Investigating the Earth*, 4th ed. (Boston: Houghton Mifflin Company, 1984), p. 521.

To help students learn and apply abbreviations and equations, teachers can use the following strategies. Abbreviations and equations must be practiced until the student has memorized those that are necessary for understanding.

Activities
1. Omit part of an equation and have the students fill in the missing parts. For example:

$$\text{Large Calories} = \frac{\text{Temp change} \times \text{wt of ?}}{1 \, ?}$$

2. Write an equation or formula and ask students to identify what it represents. For example:

$$\underline{\qquad\qquad} = \frac{\text{Temp change} \times \text{wt of } H_2O}{1000}$$

(The answer in this instance is *Large Calories*.)
3. Ask students to write out the words that are represented by a number of abbreviations.

Reading Science and Health Content

Many of the reading strategies discussed in this chapter and in other chapters are useful for helping students comprehend science and health content. Applications of some of these teaching strategies are demonstrated on the next few pages. Although these applications were developed for science and health content, they are equally valuable for the other content areas.

The directed reading lesson is a strategy devised to guide students through content and help them comprehend content on their own. (This activity is described fully in Chapter 9.) In the following example the directed reading lesson is applied to a biology textbook chapter entitled "Cells."

EXAMPLE 6.20   DIRECTED READING LESSON FOR SCIENCE ————

Motivation and Building Background

1. Show the students slides of plant and animal cells. Ask them to compare and contrast the slides. Write their responses on the chalkboard for future reference.

Skill Development Activities

2. Draw students' attention to the italicized words in the chapter. These words include *physiology, metabolism, membrane, nucleus,* and *vacuoles.* Discuss the meanings of these words. Ask students if they recognize familiar word roots.

Guided Reading

3. *Silent*—Have the students read the chapter silently. Tell them to think about these purpose questions as they read:
   a. How can we tell whether a cell is a plant cell or an animal cell?
   b. What is the cell theory?
   c. What is the physiology of a cell?

4. *Discussion*—Discuss the silent reading purposes first. Additional discussion questions such as the following can be used:
   a. What is meant by the metabolism of a cell?
   b. Did reading this chapter change any of your ideas about cells? How?
      Discuss the material that was written on the chalkboard in step one.
   c. Why must a cell be constantly taking in and getting rid of substances?
   d. How are cells related to tissues? How are tissues related to organs?

Follow-up Activities

5. Prepare slides of onion, frog blood, frog skin, sprouted onion. Compare various elements of these cells, including membrane, cell shape, nucleus, plastids, vacuoles. Ask students to observe the cells carefully and state generalizations regarding the comparisons and contrasts between plant and animal cells.

EXAMPLE 6.21   A STUDY GUIDE FOR A BIOLOGY CHAPTER ON CELLS

Introduction

This chapter tells us a great deal about plant and animal cells. It covers the basic structure of cells, the physiology of cells, and cell duplication. The three basic components of cell theory are included in this chapter.

Vocabulary

Directions: The chapter introduces many new terms that you will need to know in later chapters. Match each word in Column A with its correct meaning in Column B.

A	B
diffusion	study of biological function
physiology	random movement of molecules
nucleolus	boundary between a cell and its environment
mitosis	center of the cell
cell membrane	nuclear division
metabolism	chemical reactions in cells

Diagrams

Directions: Explain the process that is pictured in the two sets of diagrams that follow. How is the process pictured in *A* different from the process pictured in *B*? What is the cause of this difference?

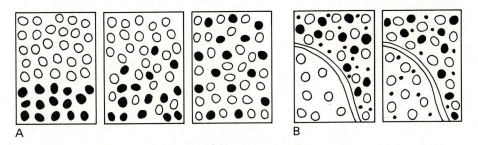

A   B

Levels of Comprehension

Directions: Place a check √ beside each item that is supported by information in this chapter.

Literal

_____ 1. Cells are units of structure in living organisms.

_____ 2. Cells are the units of function in living organisms.

_____ 3. Cells are too small to affect the total organism.

_____ 4. All cells come from pre-existing cells.

_____ 5. Cells can be made of synthetic materials in a laboratory.

Interpretive

_____ 6. Mitosis occurs differently in plant and animal cells.

_____ 7. Aging of cells can be stopped by controlling the environment.

_____ 8. Lack of a nucleus causes cells to age quickly.

_____ 9. The sequence of events in mitosis insures exact, equal division of the nuclear substance.

_____ 10. We know exactly why cells divide.

Directions: Write short answers to the following questions.

Critical

11. Will we ever be able to create synthetic life without using a pre-existing cell? Why or why not?

12. It we could create a cell, which aspect of cell theory would be violated?

Applied

13. What disease(s) occur when cell division does not follow the orderly process described in this chapter?

14. Identify some everyday uses of diffusion.

MATHEMATICS

The discipline of mathematics is used in many areas of work and study. "To most people, the abilities to read and to think mathematically are probably the two most valuable skills learned in school. Most quantitative information is encountered in written form, and it must be read to be understood.[16] Before students can solve a math problem, they must read it and understand what it is about. Researchers have established a high correlation between problem solving in mathematics and reading comprehension.[17]

We use mathematics in our lives in many ways: telling time, making change, banking, and computing income tax. Mathematics is the use of numbers, symbols, and words to express qualities, quantities, and relationships. The mathematics student must have good general reading skills in order to comprehend mathematical concepts, which are explained in written words; there is a high correlation between reading ability and mathematics achievement.

Words and Symbols

The field of mathematics requires that students think in terms of abstract ideas and symbols. Mathematics is a highly compressed system of language in which a single symbol may represent several words; for example, the symbol > represents the words *greater than*. Writing in mathematics is generally denser and contains more ideas in each line and on each page than writing in the other disciplines. Mathematics must be read slowly, with a step-by-step procedure.

In mathematics, words and symbols are mixed; comprehension depends not only on words and word relationships, but also on the relationships between words and symbols. The reader of mathematics must be able to read symbols, signs, abbreviations, exponents, subscripts, formulas, equations, geometric figures, graphs, and tables, as well as words.

Vocabulary study is essential in teaching students to read mathematics. Students must learn to read with precision; they cannot skip words or fill in meanings from context. It is important to understand the precise meaning of every word because reading a single word wrong may alter the meaning of an entire passage. The reader also must integrate the words into thought units and understand relationships among words. Some words, like *count, odd,* and *power,* have meanings in mathematics that are quite different from their meanings in everyday conversation.

Since mathematical terminology is so important, teachers should use a variety of vocabulary strategies in their instruction. For example, students can be asked to develop a dictionary of mathematical terms, adding each new term that is introduced in class. When creating these dictionaries, students should be encouraged to write meanings in their own words rather than to use standard dictionary definitions. Paraphrasing the meanings will help students understand and remember the terms.

Another method of developing definitions for mathematics is suggested by Richard Earle.[18] He suggests four types of definitions: formal definition, listing of characteristics, simulated examples, and real-life examples. Following are examples of each type of definition.

1. *Formal definition:* A square is a parallelogram that has four right angles and four sides of equal length.
2. *Listing of characteristics:* Several things are true about any square. It has only two dimensions—length and height. It has exactly four sides, all of which are straight lines of equal length. It has four interior angles, which total exactly 360 degrees. Each angle is a 90-degree angle.
3. *Simulated example:* Squares can be drawn on a chalkboard, cut from paper or other material, or pointed out in drawings or pictures.
4. *Real-life example:* These can be natural occurrences that exemplify square formulation or manmade objects that utilize squares as industrial, architectural, or decorative features. Natural occurrences used as examples might include the shape of a field; manmade objects might include a windowpane, a room, or a piece of furniture.

Students can use these approaches to defining mathematical terms when they devise their mathematics dictionaries. Teachers also can use these approaches to introduce terms before students read a mathematics assignment: after the teacher has identified the terms, students can define the new terms in the four different ways. Discussion and comparison of definitions will help students clarify their understanding of the new terms.

Another instructional approach to mathematical terms involves defining concept characteristics. The teacher prepares a worksheet for the students and asks them to identify the characteristics that describe each mathematical term on the worksheet.[19] This activity could be used after students finish reading a mathematics chapter. Following is a worksheet that illustrates this strategy.

EXAMPLE 6.22   MATHEMATICAL TERMS WORKSHEET ———————

Directions: Check the characteristics that describe the term.

A set

_____ is a collection of objects.
_____ has members.
_____ has common properties.
_____ includes dissimilar objects.
_____ can be an empty set.
_____ has fractional numbers.

Reading Mathematics

It is important for teachers to emphasize the fact that reading mathematics content is very different from reading a story. To read mathematics material effectively, the following procedures are recommended. Students should preread a section of the text at a moderate rate to get the general idea of the concept being introduced. Then they should read it more slowly, this time taking notes and copying definitions and the information they find printed in bold type. As they read, students should paraphrase the content and devise questions relating to the assignments. Finally, they should reread any passages that are unclear and write questions regarding information they need in order to clarify the material. They should give special attention to illustrations.[20]

A directed reading lesson gives students a guide that can help them understand mathematics texts. The following set of steps can be used for directing the reading of a math chapter.

1. *Introduce the new terms, using them in sentences.* Sentences from the text may be used. Give students an activity to help them learn the new terms, such as paraphrasing the meanings for a mathematics dictionary. Students may use their texts to help work out the meanings of the words.
2. *Ask students to preview the chapter and identify the topic.*
3. *Provide students with two or three silent reading purposes.* This step may be varied. If students have some background knowledge about the topic, they can help formulate silent reading purposes.

4. *Have students read the text silently.* Students should take notes on the content and should formulate questions while reading.
5. *Work any examples provided.* Students should ask questions if they do not understand an example.
6. *Discuss the silent reading purposes* and the questions formulated by the students in step 4.

Writing Patterns

The writing patterns that occur most frequently in mathematics are the problem pattern and the demonstration pattern. In addition, graphs and charts are used often.

Verbal Problems

Solving word problems (verbal problems) is a very sophisticated task. Many readers have significant difficulties reading and understanding word problems, which are mathematical situations that are stated in words and symbols. Even when they can read the words and sentences, they have difficulty choosing the correct process (operation) to solve the problem. J. Dan Knifong and Boyd Holtran found that 95 percent of the students they studied could read all the words correctly in word problems; 98 percent knew the situation the problem was discussing; 92 percent knew what the problem was asking; yet only 36 percent knew how to work the problem.[21]

Elaine Kresse recommends a technique similar to SQ3R for helping students solve story problems.[22] This approach to solving verbal problems helps students identify the appropriate process or processes for solving a problem. A mathematics reading technique similar to Kresse's follows. Immediately after the description of the technique, the process is modeled as it would be applied to the mathematics problem in Example 6.23.

Technique
1. *Survey* the problem out loud. Try to visualize the situation.
2. *Question* What is the problem asking me to find? This step gives students a purpose for reading the problem. It helps them know why they are reading.
3. *Question* What is the correct process? (addition, subtraction, division, etc.)
4. *Read the problem aloud.*
5. *Work the problem.*

Modeling the Reading and Solving Mathematics Process (as applied to Example 6.23)
1. *Survey* The question sentence in this problem is, "What was your average cost per mile to own and operate your car?" I see that the car was a used one that the owner bought for $4200.00 two years ago. Also I see that the person drove the car 17,500 miles. The expense record for the last two years is given in

the problem. This is the kind of problem that business people who travel have to figure out all of the time. They need this kind of information for their income tax records.

2. *Question*   What is this problem asking me to find? I have to determine the average cost per mile to own and run the car. This problem is an averaging task.

3. *Question*   What is the correct process? I will have to use two processes. I will add all of the expenses to figure out the total expenses. Then I will divide the total expenses into the total number of miles that the owner has driven over the last two years.

4. *Read the problem aloud*   The problem states, "You bought a used car two years ago for $4200.00. Since then, you have driven it 17,500 miles. You kept a record of all your car expenses." The car expense record follows. Then the problem continues, "What was your average cost per mile to own and operate your car?"

5. *Work the problem*   I am adding $360 + 65 + 66 + 200 + 480 + 4200 + 66 + 165 + 60 + 400 + 390 + 60. The total is $6512.00. Now I will divide $6512.00 by 17,500, which gives an answer of 37 cents per mile as the average cost per mile to own and operate the car.

Kresse recommends having students check their work by reasoning through the problem. Following is a model of this process.

1. *Question*   What processes did I use to solve the problem?
2. *Answer*   Addition and division
3. *Evidence*   I had to determine the average cost, and you add and divide to figure out average cost.
4. *Reasoning*   I added the expenses for operating the car and the cost of the car when the owner bought it. Then I divided that total by the number of miles the owner drove the car.

One of the reading difficulties that students experience when reading mathematics is realizing that the information they need to solve a problem is found in the wording of the problem. A study guide can help students reach this understanding. Example 6.23 contains a verbal problem and a reading guide based on the problem. The teacher would prepare the mathematics reading guide; students would complete it as they read a verbal problem. The guide shown here is based on a format suggested by James Riley and Andrew Pachtman.[23]

EXAMPLE 6.23 VERBAL PROBLEM (MATHEMATICS) AND READING GUIDE

Problem Solving: Driving a Bargain

You bought a used car two years ago for $4200. Since then, you have driven it 17,500 miles. You kept a record of all your car expenses.

Car Expense Record

1st Year		2nd Year	
Insurance	$360	License	$ 66
Tune-up	65	Repair brakes	165
License	66	Tune-up	60
Repair clutch	200	Insurance	400
Gas	480	Gas	390
		Repair muffler	60

PROBLEM: What was your average cost per mile to own and operate your car?

Solution Plan: Find the total of your car expenses. Figure the unit rate, in cents per mile, for your car.

Source: Bryce Shaw, Robert Kane, and Katherine Merseth: *Fundamentals of Mathematics: Skills and Applications,* 2nd ed. (Boston: Houghton Mifflin Company, 1986), p. 226.

Reading Guide

Part I: Facts of the Problem

Directions: Read the problem. Then in Column A check those statements that contain the important facts of the problem. You may refer to the problem to verify your responses. In Column B check the statements that will help you solve the problem.

A   B

_____   _____ 1. The car is two years old.

_____   _____ 2. You have driven the car 17,500 miles.

_____   _____ 3. You have a record of all car expenses.

_____   _____ 4. You found it necessary to repair the muffler.

_____   _____ 5. The problem asks for average cost per mile to own and operate your car.

_____   _____ 6. You paid $4200.00 for the car.

Part II: Mathematical Ideas and Interpretation

Directions: Check the statements that contain mathematical concepts related to the problem. You may go back to Part I to review your responses.

_____ 1. The total cost for insurance was $760.00.
_____ 2. Multiply dollars times 100 to get cents.
_____ 3. "Per" often suggests that division is necessary.
_____ 4. The total cost of repair and maintenance was $550.00.
_____ 5. To find the total expenses, add initial cost, first year expenses, and second year expenses.
_____ 6. Gasoline currently costs 98¢ a gallon.

Part III: Computation

Directions: Below are possible mathematical calculations. Check those that apply to this problem. You may refer to Part I and Part II to verify your responses.

_____ 1. ($760.00 + $550.00 + $132.00 + $870.00)/2
_____ 2. $760.00 + $550.00 + $132.00 + $870.00 + $1200.00
_____ 3. $4200.00 divided by 17,500
_____ 4. $4200.00 multiplied by 17,500
_____ 5. [($4200.00 + 1171.00 + $1141.00) ÷ 17,500] × 100

Part IV: Final Computation

Directions: Compute the answer.

_____

Another valuable approach to reading verbal problems was suggested by Richard Earle.[24] In this technique, the teacher uses a series of steps to guide students through the written language of the problem. The following steps are based on those suggested by Earle.

1. Read the problem quickly to obtain a general understanding of the problem. Visualize the problem. Do not be concerned with the numbers.
2. Examine the problem again. Identify the question you are asked to answer. This question usually comes at the end of the problem, but it may occur anywhere in the problem.
3. Read the problem again to identify the information given. This information will be stated in exact numbers or values.
4. Analyze the problem to see how the information is related. Identify any missing information and any unnecessary information.
5. Compute the answer.
6. Examine your answer. Label the parts of the solution to correspond with the question that the problem asks you to solve. Is your answer sensible?

Demonstration Pattern

The demonstration pattern is used to show students the development of processes and concepts. This writing pattern is usually accompanied by an example that illustrates the written material.

It is important that students understand the demonstration pattern because they need to be able to use the demonstrated process to work problems. Following are strategies that students can use while reading the demonstration pattern.

Activities

1. The student should work through the example to determine whether he or she understands the process. If the student does not compute the same answer as the example, he or she should work slowly through the example again, rereading each step carefully.
2. The reader should paraphrase the process in his or her own words.
3. The student should apply the process to other situations.

Example 6.24 shows the demonstration writing pattern.

EXAMPLE 6.24   THE DEMONSTRATION WRITING PATTERN ————

The Pythagorean Theorem

Objectives
1. Determine the geometric mean between two numbers.
2. State and apply the relationships that exist when the altitude is drawn to the hypotenuse of a right triangle.
3. State and apply the Pythagorean Theorem.

6-1   Geometric Means

Suppose r, s, and t are positive numbers with $\dfrac{r}{s} = \dfrac{s}{t}$. Then s is called the **geometric mean** between r and t.

Example 1
Find the geometric mean between the given numbers.
a. 3 and 7   b. 6 and 15

Solution

a. $\dfrac{3}{x} = \dfrac{x}{7}$ b. $\dfrac{6}{x} = \dfrac{x}{15}$

$\quad x^2 = 21$ $\quad x^2 = 90$

$\quad x = \sqrt{21}$ $\quad x = \sqrt{90} = \sqrt{9 \cdot 10} = \sqrt{9} \cdot \sqrt{10} = 3\sqrt{10}$

The symbol $\sqrt{}$ always indicates the positive square root of a number. In (b) above, the *radical* $\sqrt{90}$ could be *simplified* because the *radicand* 90 has the factor 9, a perfect square. When you write radical expressions you should write them in **simplest form.** This means writing them so that

1. No radicand has a factor, other than 1, that is a perfect square.
2. No radicand is a fraction.
3. No fraction has a denominator that contains a radical.

You should express answers involving radicals in simplest form unless you are asked to use decimal approximations.

Source: Ray C. Jurgensen, Richard Brown, and John Jurgensen: *Geometry* (Boston: Houghton Mifflin Company, 1985), p. 247.

Graphs and Charts

Graphs and charts are often used to represent mathematical concepts in math materials, as well as in other content textbooks, in newspapers, and in magazines. The graph in Example 6.25 appears in a mathematics textbook. The questions that follow can be used to guide students' reading of charts and graphs.

EXAMPLE 6.25   SAMPLE MATHEMATICS GRAPH AND QUESTIONS

Bar Graphs

A *bar graph* is a way to present information. Bars (rectangles) and a scale are used to compare quantities. Each quantity is represented by the length of a bar. To read a bar graph, use the scale to find the length of the bar.

A group of high school seniors were asked what they planned to do after graduation. The results are shown in the bar graph. How many plan to go to technical school?

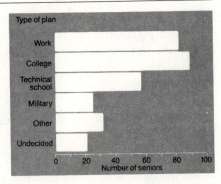

MODEL

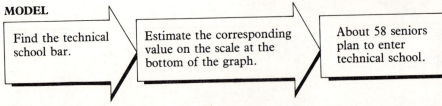

Find the technical school bar. → Estimate the corresponding value on the scale at the bottom of the graph. → About 58 seniors plan to enter technical school.

Source: Bryce Shaw, Robert Kane, and Katherine Merseth: *Fundamentals of Mathematics*, p. 238. Copyright © 1982 by Houghton Mifflin Company. Used by permission.

Questions

1. What is the title of this graph?
2. What type of graph is it?
3. What is being compared in this graph?
4. Who would find the information in this graph useful?
5. State a conclusion based on this graph.

Additional information on graph reading can be found in Chapter 4.

Additional Skills

Students of mathematics must learn to read the special symbols, signs, and formulas that are used in mathematics textbooks. Reading and understanding these is like learning a foreign language. Example 6.26 is a selection from a math textbook that contains special symbols, signs, and formulas.

Students should practice reading and translating the symbols, signs, and formulas that are used in mathematics textbooks, rewriting formulas in words to help themselves learn the necessary symbols.[25] Activities that require the matching of words and symbols help reinforce comprehension of symbols.

Teaching a Chapter of Mathematics Content

Mathematics teachers may wish to use the following strategies. They can develop student readiness for reading a chapter by introducing key terms and concepts, writing the terms on the chalkboard or on a handout sheet, and using them in sentences. Students may be asked to associate their ideas and previous experiences (brainstorm) with the terms. This introduction can be varied with some of the strategies introduced in Chapter 2.

After the concepts and vocabulary have been introduced, students may be given an advance organizer, a structured overview, a study guide, or a concept guide to use as they read through the selection. A directed reading lesson may be used instead of a study guide or concept guide.

After students have read the chapter, the teacher can monitor their comprehension by having them demonstrate their ability to apply the new concepts.

COMPUTER LITERACY

Computer literacy classes are becoming more prevalent at the junior and senior high school levels than ever before. They are generally concerned with familiarizing students with computers and terminology related to them and teaching students to use computers in a variety of ways. Topics such as the history of computing, careers in computing, the social impact of computers, applications of computers, and programming may be included in such courses.

EXAMPLE 6.26   SYMBOLS IN MATHEMATICS CONTENT

Circumference

The distance around a circle is called the **circumference** of the circle. You can use the diameter of a circle to find the circumference.

Circumference = $\pi \times$ diameter, or $C = \pi \times d$

The value of π is about 3.14. This value is the same for all circles.

MODEL

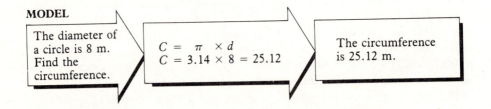

The diameter of a circle is 8 m. Find the circumference.

$C = \pi \times d$
$C = 3.14 \times 8 = 25.12$

The circumference is 25.12 m.

Because the diameter of a circle is twice the radius, the circumference can be expressed as follows:

Circumference = $2 \times \pi \times$ radius, or $C = 2 \times \pi \times r$

MODEL

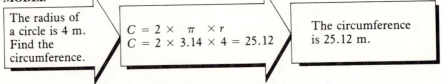

The radius of a circle is 4 m. Find the circumference.

$C = 2 \times \pi \times r$
$C = 2 \times 3.14 \times 4 = 25.12$

The circumference is 25.12 m.

Source: Bryce Shaw, Robert Kane, and Katherine Merseth: *Fundamentals of Mathematics*, p. 156. Copyright © 1982 by Houghton Mifflin Company. Used by permission.

The goal of computer literacy courses is generally to make students aware of the impact of computers on our society, to acquaint them with the equipment that is available, to give them experience in using some computer applications, and to teach them some basic programming skills. A computer literacy course may be a prerequisite for regular programming courses. Computer literacy courses also offer students an opportunity to decide if they would like to prepare for computer-related jobs.

The reading materials in computer literacy courses are quite varied. Students are usually asked to read from textbooks, handouts, computer displays, computer printouts, and computer magazines and journals. The content of these materials varies from expository discourse to program listings to narrative discourse.

Most of the material in computer literacy textbooks is expository in nature. It abounds with difficult vocabulary that represents abstract concepts likely to be unfamiliar to students, although with the current popularity of home computers, some students may have had prior exposure to some of the concepts. The expository discourse is generally interspersed with examples and graphic aids. The material is precise and factual. The idea density may be extremely high.

This expository material must be read slowly and carefully. Almost every statement may present an important idea that must be grasped in order to comprehend later material.

The material read from the computer screen may be either expository or narrative in nature. The narrative material would likely be the content of applications programs that students are asked to run. This type of material is unlikely to cause as many reading problems for students as expository material may cause.

The ability to read program listings is a specialized skill that requires use of logical thinking and knowledge of technical terminology. Programs are written in computer languages that are very different from regular English and must be learned in a manner similar to the learning of a foreign language. Every number, word, and punctuation mark in a computer program is important to the program's correct function and, therefore, is important to the comprehension of the program. Visualization of the effect that each line of the listing has on the program's operation is also important.

Vocabulary

Many specialized, technical terms are found in computer literacy materials— from the labels for the parts of the computer to the terminology used in writing programs. In this field there are many words that stand for very complex procedures. For example, the word *format* refers to the process of causing a diskette to be prepared for use in programming, word processing, or other activities that require disk storage.

EXAMPLE 6.27 SAMPLE ITEMS FOR A VOCABULARY
EXERCISE FOR COMPUTER LITERACY ─────

Directions: Choose the correct meaning for each underlined word, depending upon the context in which this sentence is found in your chapter.

1. Boot the program.
    a. kick
    b. start up
    c. footware
2. Boot the program.
    a. set of instructions for the performance of a specific task
    b. a public presentation
    c. a plan of action

Many words in computer literacy materials are multiple-meaning words that have a specialized meaning in this field. Examples of these words are *chip, hardware, program,* and *boot.* Example 6.27 contains sample items for a vocabulary exercise involving multiple-meaning words in computer literacy.

An exercise like that in Example 6.27 can be given to students before they read assigned material containing the vocabulary words. The teacher can instruct the students to look for the sample sentences as they read the assignment, to read the context of the sentences surrounding the sample sentences carefully, and to decide which definition the underlined words have in the specific context of the chapter. After students finish reading the selection, the teacher can conduct a class discussion of the meanings chosen, asking students to read parts of the chapter that they feel support their choices. Before students will be able to participate in a discussion of this type, the teacher will have to model the behavior of finding the supporting clues in the context and verbalizing them.

The computer field also abounds with abbreviations and acronyms. Examples include RAM, ROM, BASIC, CTRL, CAT, CRT, and DIR.

Another part of the vocabulary of computer use is concerned with control characters that send messages to the computer. In the popular word-processing language WordStar, for example, Control-B is the command used to tell the computer to format a paragraph. The command may appear in print as ˆB, adding a further difficulty to recognition of the term.

Writing Patterns

The writing patterns in computer literacy classes are much like those found in the areas of science and mathematics and include the definition or explanation of a technical process pattern; the classification pattern; the cause-and-effect pattern; and the problem-solving pattern. At times patterns are combined. Graphic aids are also used in abundance in computer literacy materials.

Definition or Explanation Pattern

This pattern may explain processes performed by the computer or processes followed by programmers in software development. It may also provide definitions for specialized terms in the computer field. This pattern may be accompanied by graphic aids, such as flow charts and pictures. The graphic aids must be understood in relation to the expository text that accompanies them.

The information presented in this pattern is usually densely packed with specific information that students need to acquire. For this reason, it should be read slowly and carefully, with much allowance for reflection on the meaning of each bit of information presented.

The passage in Example 6.28, taken from a computer literacy textbook, illustrates the definition pattern.

Note that in Example 6.28 the definition is given in words *and* graphic aids are also included to clarify the definition. The reader must correlate the written words with the diagrams in an attempt to understand the definition.

EXAMPLE 6.28   DEFINITION PATTERN IN A COMPUTER LITERACY BOOK ─────────

In designing a system, the systems analyst may use a special type of diagram called a **flowchart.** The flowchart is a tool that shows all the steps in a system in sequence. As you can see from the illustration, various-shaped symbols stand for input/output devices, memory or storage, and processing steps. Arrows, called **flowlines,** indicate the direction that each step in the sequence takes. A flowchart is a kind of problem-solving tool.

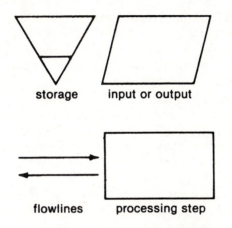

storage   input or output

flowlines   processing step

Source: June St. Clair Atkinson: *Help with Computer Literacy* (Boston: Houghton Mifflin Company, 1984), p. 58.

───────────────

After students have read material such as the passage in Example 6.28, have been given the meanings of all the different shapes used in flowcharts, and have been led through the flowcharts authors have developed for a specific function, the logical method of checking understanding would be to have the students develop flowcharts for simple, everyday tasks and explain their charts. This activity would not be appropriate for students who had read only the excerpt in Example 6.28, however, for not enough information is provided for full development of the process in this brief selection. Guidance through the process by the teacher would be imperative.

Classification Pattern

In the classification pattern, information is ordered under common headings and subheadings. Generally in this pattern, a classification is given and the distinguishing characteristics of the members of the class are explained. Examples of class members are also usually included.

For each classification described in this way, readers must be able to identify the important distinguishing characteristics and relate them to the examples. If the reader comprehends the material, he or she should then be able to recognize examples and nonexamples of class members.

Example 6.29 illustrates the classification pattern of writing.

EXAMPLE 6.29   CLASSIFICATION PATTERN IN A COMPUTER LITERACY BOOK AND STUDY GUIDE ⟶

Suppose, for instance, you want a printed copy as the end result. That's simple! You need a *printer.* But how do you want your printed material to look? How much will it cost? Is speed important? You can buy a printer that is relatively inexpensive but slow, or one that is expensive and fast. There are impact and nonimpact printers. It all depends on the results you want, whether in business or in your own home. The speed of printing is increasing so fast that most information about it is out of date as soon as it is printed!

An *impact printer* forces (impacts) a character against a ribbon and paper like a typewriter. Some of these so-called character printers are very much like typewriters. They can produce copy at speeds of 10 to 300 characters per second. A common type of impact printer is the ball-like unit originally introduced by IBM on the Selectric typewriter. This kind of typewriterlike printer is considered very slow as far as speed of output is concerned.

Another widely used printing element is the *daisy wheel.* As the illustration indicates, it looks like a daisy with a set of spokes, each spoke with a character at the end. A hammer mechanism strikes a character when it is in position for printing. Print quality of the daisy wheel is excellent at a rate of about 10 to 55 characters per second.

A *dot matrix printer* has wire ends that strike against the ribbon in a kind of grid, making a dot pattern. This dot pattern contrasts with the fully filled-in character made by the ball element or the daisy wheel. However, the matrix printer is faster and less expensive than the daisy wheel. It prints up to 330 characters per second.

A *chain printer* carries the characters on a loop chain. As the type moves across the paper, individual hammers strike the characters engraved on the chain links. Such a high-speed impact printer can print up to 3000 lines per minute.

Nonimpact printers do not use the method of striking a ribbon with a key or a wire end. Instead, they use heat, ink jets, or laser beams. One kind of heat-process printer requires specially coated paper. The color of the paper changes as the top layer is literally burned away, leaving the desired characters. Unfortunately the resulting print is not of very high quality. The heat-process printer can print from 160 to 220 characters per second.

Ink-jet printers fire a jet of charged ink through a magnetic field onto the paper. Such a printer is expensive, but it can print up to 60,000 lines per minute.

Laser beam printers, which burn images onto specially prepared paper, are also expensive and fast.

Source: June St. Clair Atkinson: *Help with Computer Literacy* (Boston: Houghton Mifflin Company, 1984), pp. 47–48.

Study Guide

Directions: Fill in the columns with the characteristics of the different types of printers.

Daisy Wheel	Dot-matrix	Chain	Heat-process	Ink-jet	Laser

Cause-and-Effect Pattern

In the cause-and-effect pattern, the results of particular actions by a computer programmer or operator may be revealed or the cause of particular computer output may be reflected upon. In the passage in Example 6.30 the effect of entering certain values as variables into a computer program is explained.

EXAMPLE 6.30   CAUSE-AND-EFFECT PATTERN

IN COMPUTER LITERACY ————————————

Variables

ROBOT 6 COMMANDS
U—move UP
D—move DOWN
R—move RIGHT
L—move LEFT
K—KICK

nU, nD, nR, nL, where "n" is a number, repeats the step "n" times.

S—STOP
CLEAR—end exercise
n(. . .) where "n" is a number, repeats everything inside the parentheses "n" times

"A," "B," "C" variable names.

Using the program that takes the robot to the ball and around it, you can understand that it is simple to make the robot circle the ball once, twice, or any number of times. You simply replace the number that controls the steps within parentheses. In some computer applications, a series of steps must be repeated, but the exact number of repetitions is not known in advance. Thus, some kind of "place holder" is put into the program at the spot where the number will be needed. This is called a variable.

This robot can handle the concept of a variable. Whenever the robot comes upon the letter "A," "B" or "C" in its program, it will stop and ask you for a number to replace that variable in the program. It then proceeds with the program. If the computer came upon A(R), for example, it would stop to ask for a value of "A." If you answered "10," it would then move the robot ten spaces to the right.

Source: Stephen M. Booth et al.: *Computer Discovery* (Chicago: Science Research Associates, 1981), p. 48.

To check for mastery of the information presented in the passage in Example 6.30, the teacher might use an activity such as the one below.

Directions: Fill in the effect upon the robot if you gave the response "3" to each of the following screen prompts:

	Prompt	*Effect*
1.	A(L)	
2.	A(U)	
3.	A(D)	

Problem-Solving Pattern

The problem-solving pattern may appear in computer science materials with descriptions of real or hypothetical questions and actual or suggested solutions. For example, the material may describe how reservations for tours were handled before and after computerization. A content study guide can be used with such material to help students focus on the information that they should be able to extract from the material and the applications of the information that they should try to make.

ENGLISH (LANGUAGE ARTS)

The language arts are concerned with communication between the sender and the receiver of a message. Both sender and receiver must have command of the English language in order to communicate effectively; therefore, study of the language arts is involved primarily with effective use and appreciation of the English language. English has the most varied content of all the content subjects. Study of English requires readers to work with grammar, composition, and many forms of literature—novels, short stories, poetry, biographies, autobiographies, newspapers, and magazines.

All too often, it is assumed that English teachers know more about teaching reading than other content teachers do. English teachers have been prepared to teach their content area, which includes reading literature; however, they generally have acquired skills in literary analysis rather than in reading instruction.

This section of the chapter focuses on the reading skills that teaching English content requires.

Vocabulary Development

Vocabulary development is an important aspect of English instruction because students who have at their command a large store of word meanings are better communicators. English teachers should encourage students to be interested in words and should motivate students to develop a large general vocabulary as well as the technical vocabulary relevant to the English content area.

Students can expand and enrich their general vocabulary through instruction and through reading literature. In English class they can be taught technical vocabulary words such as *pronoun, hyperbole, precis,* and *haiku.* Suggestions for teaching technical words are provided in Chapter 2 of this text.

A good program of vocabulary instruction helps students develop their vocabularies independently. There are a number of techniques teachers can use to help students broaden vocabulary: for example, establishing a word file; showing students a system for learning new words; studying word etymology; and studying the denotations and connotations of words.

The vocabulary file is often overlooked as a method for developing vocabulary because it doesn't seem very exciting, but it can be a very effective device. Each student keeps his or her own file of cards containing the new words that are encountered in reading. The word cards may take the following form (or any form that appeals to the teacher).

```
Word _____
Sentence in which found _____
Student definition _____
```

For the word file to be effective, the teacher must carefully evaluate the content at regular intervals, according to individual student abilities. Students may test each other in pairs, or they may construct crossword puzzles from their words for friends to complete. The teacher may evaluate an individual file by asking the student to build sentences from his or her words or by asking the student to place words in categories.

Students should be encouraged to make a point of systematically adding new words to their vocabularies. A helpful technique includes the following steps:

1. Look at the word.
2. Say the word.
3. Write the word with a synonym or brief definition.
4. Use the word in conversation or writing.

To say the word and write its meaning students may need assistance from the teacher or a classmate, but they should try first to find the meaning of the word by using context clues. If other help is not available, they can use a dictionary or thesaurus. After adapting this system or developing systems of their own, students will become more independent in acquiring vocabulary.

Studying the etymology of words motivates some students to learn more about words and to remember them. Through this kind of word study, students will learn that meanings of certain words have changed over time. For example, the word *nice* once meant "ignorant"—it was certainly not a compliment to be called "nice" in those days. As a result of being used daily over a period of years, the words in a living language gradually change in predictable ways. Following is a list of the ways in which words change.

1. *Amelioration*—The meaning of the word has changed so that the word means something better than it once did. For example, a person who was called *enthusiastic* was once considered a fanatic. Currently, enthusiasm is considered a desirable quality.
2. *Pejoration*—Pejoration indicates that the word has a more derogatory meaning than it did earlier in history. For example, a *villain* once was a feudal serf or a servant from a villa. Currently, a villain is considered to be a depraved scoundrel.
3. *Generalization*—Some words become more generalized in meaning. When generalization operates, the meaning of words is broadened. Once upon a time, a *picture* was a painting, but now a picture may be a print, a photograph, or a drawing. In fact a picture may not be a picture at all, because in art a picture may not have a distinct form.
4. *Specialization*—The opposite of generalization is specialization. In this case, word meanings become more specific than they were in the past. At one time, *meat* was any food, not just mutton, pork, or beef. The Chinese used the word *pork* to mean any kind of meat earlier in their history.
5. *Euphemism*—This term is assigned to an affectation used to achieve elegance, or the use of a more pleasant word for an unpleasant one. For example, a *janitor* is often called a "custodian" or "maintenance engineer," and a person does not die, but rather "passes away."
6. *Hyperbole*—This is an extreme exaggeration. For example, a man who is tired might say that he could "sleep for a year." Of course, he does not have a real desire to sleep so long. He is using exaggeration to make the point of his extreme fatigue. Many people currently use the word *fantastic* to describe almost everything, although fantastic means strange, wonderful, unreal, and illusory.

Examining reading selections for amelioration, generalization, specialization, pejoration, euphemism, and hyperbole can increase students' understanding of words. Activities such as the following can be used to develop word meanings through etymology.

Activities

1. Give students a list of words with instructions to determine the origin of each term and the type of changes that have occurred in its meaning. Words like the following could be used in this activity: *city, ghetto, manuscript, lord, stench.*

2. Ask students to identify the origins of the names of the months and/or the days of the week. For example, *October* is from the Latin *Octo* (eight), because it was the eighth month of the Roman calendar. *Monday* means "day of the moon."

3. Encourage students to determine the origins and meaning of their first names and surnames. For example, *Susan* means "lily." Many surnames are related to occupation or geographic origin. The surname *Butler* refers to a bottlemaker; the surname *Hatfield* means wooded field.

Word knowledge can be increased by exploring some of the unique characteristics of different types of words. Activities with acronyms, oxymorons, homonyms, and so forth will develop students' vocabularies. Following are definitions of some special types of words and strategies for teaching these words.

1. *Acronyms*—Words composed of the first letters or syllables of longer terms, such as *SNAFU*, which means "situation normal all fouled up." This is a Navy term coined during World War II.

2. *Oxymorons*—Two incongruous words used together, such as *cruel kindness* or *broadly ignorant.*

3. *Homonyms*—also known as *homophones*—Words that sound alike but are not spelled alike, such as *to, too, two; pare, pair; sum, some.*

4. *Heteronyms*—Words that have different pronunciations and meanings although they are spelled exactly the same, such as:

   Don't *subject* me to that experience.
   What is the *subject* of your book?

5. *Coined words*—Words invented to meet specific needs. Words are coined by using previously existing words and word parts. *Gerrymander, curfew, motel,* and *astronaut* are examples of coined words. Many product names are coined words: for example, *Pream, Tang, Jello,* and *Bisquick.*

The denotative and connotative meanings of words can be introduced through literature. *Denotation* is the literal definition of a word as defined by the dictionary. *Connotation* refers to the ideas and associations that are suggested by a term, including emotional reactions. For instance, the word *home* denotes the place where one lives, whereas it may connote warmth, love, and family. Readers must learn to recognize the connotations of words in order to comprehend a selection. By definition, *cunning* and *astute* are very similar, but when the word *cunning* is used to describe a person it usually implies an insult, whereas describing a person as *astute* is a compliment.

Students can look for examples of both connotative and denotative uses of words in the literary selections they read. In addition, the following activities will increase understanding.

Activities
1. In each pair select the word that you would prefer to use for describing yourself. Tell why you chose the word.
   a. *creative* or *screwball*
   b. *stolid* or *easy-going*
   c. *thrifty* or *tight*
   d. *enthusiastic* or *excitable*
   e. *fat* or *heavy-set*
   f. *conceited* or *proud*
2. Provide students with a list of words similar to the preceding list and ask them to write a plus (+) beside each positive word, a minus (−) beside each negative word, and a zero (0) beside each neutral word.

Figurative Language

Figurative language is connotative use of language. The author implies ideas through figurative language, and this expressive application of language makes written language more interesting to readers. You can refer to Chapter 2 for suggestions to aid instruction regarding figurative language.

Literature

The goal of teaching literature is to develop in readers a life-long interest in and appreciation for literature. Being unable to read in our culture is a devastating problem; an even worse situation occurs when individuals can read but never choose to. These are the people whom Francis Chase calls the "higher illiterates."[26] Having students read and respond to interesting literary selections helps teachers achieve their goals for teaching literature. When students read material that is related to their interests and background experience, they have the schemata that enable them to read with greater comprehension.

Novels and Short Stories

Reading novels and short stories is basic to the study of literature. The guidelines for responding to literature can be used with both novels and short stories. Both forms of literature are imaginative expressions of a writer's ideas: the author shares an experience with the reader by relating incidents through a story. The form of the novel permits an author to develop literary elements like characterization with greater depth than in the form of the short story.

Researchers have identified eight processes that are involved in a student's response to literature.[27] These processes are as follows:

1. *Description:* Students can restate in their own words what they have read.
2. *Discrimination:* Students can discriminate among different writings on the basis of type, author, theme, and so forth.
3. *Relation:* Students can relate to each other several aspects of a piece of literature. For example, students could discuss the relationship between a story's setting and plot or could compare the plots of two different stories.
4. *Interpretation:* Students can interpret the author's ideas and support these interpretations.
5. *Generalization:* Students can use what they have learned in one piece of literature to understand another piece of literature.
6. *Evaluation:* Students can apply criteria to evaluate a piece of literature. For example, they might evaluate the quality of the element of characterization.
7. *Valuing:* Students can relate literature to their own lives.
8. *Creation:* Students can respond to literature by creating their own art, music, writing, drama, or dance.

It is advisable to have students read straight through a literary selection. This helps them understand the entire plot, character development, setting, and theme. If the reading of a selection is broken into chapters or smaller parts, the reader does not have an opportunity to grasp the entire selection or the way the components of the selection fit together.

In addition to using the eight processes of responding to literature to guide instruction, the teacher should ask students to support answers with material from the selections they have read. Students may be asked to diagram story structure in the following manner.[28]

Title

Setting	*Theme*	*Plot*	*Characters*
Place	Symbols	Episode #1	Main character
Time	Incidents	Episode #2	Supporting
		Episode #3	character

A directed reading lesson like that in Example 6.31 is another way for teachers to help students read and understand novels and short stories. Directed reading lessons are discussed in detail in Chapter 9.

Following is a sample literature lesson.

EXAMPLE 6.31   DIRECTED READING LESSON: LITERATURE ————

Motivation and Building Background

1. Ask the students these questions: Do you know any good ghost stories? Have you ever sat around with a group of friends telling ghost stories? How did you feel later, particularly if you had to go some place alone? You probably felt the

way Ichabod Crane felt in this story after he listened to some ghost stories and rode home alone over country roads.

2. Tell the students that the story they are going to read is a ghost story. The characters in this story include a worthy pedagogue; a rantipole hero; a ripe, melting and rosy-cheeked maiden; and a contented farmer. After they read the story, they should try to name each of the characters listed.

Skill Development Activities

3. Have the students match a number of words from the story with their definitions.

words	definitions
continual reverie	German soldier
Hessian trooper	Bible study
spectre	constant daydream
psalmody	ghost

Guided Reading

4. *Silent*—Have the students read the story silently. Tell them to think about these purpose questions as they read: What factors created an atmosphere for the ghost to appear? What happened to Ichabod?

5. *Discussion*—After the students have read the selection, use these questions for further discussion:
   a. How would you characterize the residents of Sleepy Hollow?
   b. Is the setting important in this story? Why?
   c. Do you think Katrina was really interested in Ichabod? Why?
   d. How are Brom Bones and Ichabod Crane alike? How are they different?
   e. What was the point of view of this story?
   f. Do you agree with the old man about the purpose of this story? What do you think the purpose was?

Follow-up Activities

6. Have students write a paragraph telling what they would have done if they were Ichabod.

7. Ask students to read another story written by Washington Irving and compare it to the "Legend of Sleepy Hollow."

8. Have students draw a picture of the way they visualize Ichabod.

Nonfiction

Nonfiction writing is generally precise, factual, and objective, and frequently is used to develop concepts. Nonfiction content is usually organized into an introduction, a body, and a summary. The main ideas and details may be developed in a variety of ways, such as in patterns of explanation or definition, comparison/contrast, and sequential order. Since nonfiction is usually written to develop concepts, it includes technical vocabulary. (Refer to Chapter 3 for additional information about nonfiction.)

Poetry

Poetry is a condensed form of writing that expresses in a succinct fashion the writer's thoughts and emotions and stimulates the reader's imagination. Frequently, a poet can inspire a reader to appreciate familiar things and ideas in a new way. Poets use rhythm, rhyme, and imagery—and many other devices—to make a reader see or feel what they are expressing.

Teachers may use the following techniques with poetry:

1. Poems should be read aloud.
2. Poems should be read in their entirety for full appreciation of them.
3. Poems usually should be read twice in order to achieve full appreciation.
4. Prose and poetry on the same topic may be compared in order to understand the succinctness of poetry.

Drama

Drama is literature that is written to be acted. The writer intends for characters to speak the lines and for the audience to see the action. Drama includes stage directions that the reader must read in order to understand the story. The reader should pay attention to all information in parentheses and italics. The name of the speaker is printed before his or her lines; so the reader must be alert to the names of the speakers in order to follow the speeches and the action. In drama the characters are responsible for telling the story.

The following teaching procedures may be used for drama.

1. Ask the students to visualize the action.
2. Have the students read the speeches aloud to aid comprehension.
3. Have the students act out the described actions in order to arrive at a better understanding of the action.

Essays and Editorials

Essays, editorials, and position papers are expository forms of writing. Exposition is used to present information from a particular point of view. The author is usually trying to convince readers to accept his or her argument. Exposition contains a greater amount of information than fiction does. The strategies suggested in this chapter (and in Chapter 3) for guiding the reading of content materials aid the teacher in teaching exposition. Following are activities that teachers can use to help students comprehend expository materials.

1. Identify the author's purpose.
2. Identify the author's perception of his or her audience.
3. Identify the author's argument.
4. Identify the details the author uses to support his or her argument.

5. Identify the author's organization of details.
6. Identify the details that are emphasized.
7. Identify the sequence of details (chronological, and so forth).
8. Identify the author's attitude toward the topic and the audience.[29]

The preceding activities can be used for discussions and study guides.

Grammar and Composition

Textbooks are used in many language arts classes to teach grammar and composition. They explain the grammar and punctuation of the English language, using technical vocabulary words such as *complex sentences, interrogative,* and *adjective.* Frequently, these textbooks follow an expository pattern: a concept or idea is explained and illustrated, a definition or generalization is developed, and application exercises are provided. The many details that are packed into each page make rather uninteresting, though clearly presented, reading. Frequently the material is almost in outline form, requiring the reader to identify supporting details and main ideas. Some of the models and examples used in language arts textbooks have been written in a narrative style, so the reader must switch from expository to narrative style content. Example 6.32 shows content from a grammar and composition text. This content is written in a definition or explanation pattern.

EXAMPLE 6.32   CONTENT FROM A GRAMMAR AND COMPOSITION TEXT

Prepositional Phrases

A preposition is usually followed by a noun or a pronoun, which is called the **object of the preposition.** The preposition, the object, and the modifiers of that object form a *prepositional phrase.*

       prep.   *obj.*
There are deep cracks **in the moon's surface.** [The prepositional phrase consists of the preposition, *in,* the modifiers, *the* and *moon's,* and the object of the preposition, *surface.*]

 In some sentences the preposition comes *after* the object. This arrangement often occurs in questions, as in the following example.

   obj.   *prep.*
Which state are you **from?** [**Think:** From which state are you?]

 A prepositional phrase may have more than one object, as in the following sentence.

            prep. *obj.*   *obj.*
The moon's surface is covered **with rocks and dust.**

 Prepositional phrases usually act as modifiers. A prepositional phrase functions as an adjective if it modifies a noun or a pronoun. A prepositional phrase functions as an adverb if it modifies a verb, an adjective, or an adverb.

Used as an Adjective

prep. phrase

I still have to paint the other *side* **of the house.** [*Of the house* tells which side.]

Used as an Adverb

prep. phrase

Max *hit* the golf ball **into the pond.** [*Into the pond* tells where Max hit the ball.]

Source: Ann Brown, Jeffrey Milson, Fran Shaw, et al.: *Grammar and Composition: Second Course* (Boston: Houghton Mifflin Company, 1986), pp. 31–32.

Teachers can approach grammar and composition by teaching students the technical vocabulary and identifying details and main ideas. The outline approach that is used in some textbooks to present grammar content makes identification of details and main ideas a most important skill. To help students remember the text material, instruction should be given in paraphrasing and finding applications for content. Advance organizers, study guides, and concept guides are especially useful for teaching grammar and composition content.

FOREIGN LANGUAGE

The ability to read and speak foreign languages is a valuable skill in today's world due to increased travel and communication among the people of the world. Studying a foreign language has an additional value in that it helps students understand the culture of another country. Foreign language instruction should be approached through meaning-centered instruction, which results in the ability to use a language functionally.

Learning to read a foreign language is very similar to learning to read one's native tongue. Therefore, readiness is an important factor in reading a foreign language. The teacher must build a point of contact between the reader and the content he or she is reading. Students should be exposed to oral language to develop listening comprehension of the language they are learning. Listening comprehension precedes reading comprehension. Recordings and foreign language broadcasts on radio and television provide opportunities for students to develop listening comprehension.

Students should be taught the concepts and the vocabulary used in the selections they are preparing to read. Discussion and practice of common phrases and expressions are useful in developing readiness to read. The teacher should stress the use of context as an aid to understanding vocabulary in a foreign language. In addition, the teacher should provide purposes to guide the students' silent reading.

To become fluent in reading a foreign language, students need to read for global meaning rather than translating word by word through a page or passage. Students who have to stop several times on each line to check English equivalents are not actually reading because they are not able to access the ideas from the written language.[30] Students should have opportunities to listen to the language, speak the language, read the language, and write the language. These activities will help them learn both the semantics and the syntax of the language they are studying. Teachers can use the same methods in teaching students to read a foreign language that they use in teaching them to read English.

Following are some specific techniques useful for helping students develop comprehension of a foreign language.

Activities

1. Teach students to use a foreign language dictionary.
2. Encourage students to write their own ideas in the language being studied.
3. List words in English that are derived from the language studied.
4. Ask students to describe a basketball or football game in the language they are studying.
5. Provide students with direction cards written in English. Have the students state the directions in the foreign language. For example, directions for finding the children's department in a department store could be provided.
6. The above activity can be reversed with the directions printed in a foreign language and the students stating them in English.
7. Have students write in a foreign language an advertisement to sell an automobile.
8. Provide students with grocery advertisements and ask them to write the foreign word for each item in the advertisement.
9. Provide students with objects to categorize by form, function, color, or texture in the foreign language.

SUMMARY

This chapter focuses on reading strategies that are useful for helping secondary students read content materials in the areas of social studies, science and health, mathematics, computer science, English (language arts), and foreign languages. Study guides, concept guides, directed reading lessons, and pattern guides are useful for developing comprehension in each of these content areas.

Reading materials in each of the content areas are organized in unique ways, and they include technical vocabulary. Content in social studies is organized in patterns of cause and effect, definition and/or explanation, chronological order, comparison/contrast, question and answer, and combinations of these patterns. Science and health materials are organized through classification, definition and/or explanation, cause and effect, problem solving, and experiment. Mathematics content includes many details and is presented through written (verbal) problems, the demonstration pattern (of processes and concepts), and graphs and charts. Computer science content is organized in patterns of definition or explanation, classification, cause and effect, and problem solving. Language arts reading materials are probably the most diversified of those of all the content areas. These materials include narrative writing in literary selections and examples, and expository writing that is used for explaining concepts of grammar and composition. Foreign language reading requires the skills needed for reading English.

The content reading strategies presented in this chapter may be used before, during, and after reading to help students become more independent in their approaches to reading and comprehending content.

SELF-TEST

1. What level of vocabulary understanding should a student achieve in order to read social studies at an instructional level? (a) 50% (b) 25% (c) 75% (d) 90%
2. What style of writing is used in social studies content? (a) Fictional (b) Expository (c) Narrative (d) Stream of consciousness
3. Which pattern(s) of writing(s) are used in social studies content? (a) Comparison/contrast (b) Chronological (c) Cause and effect (d) All of these
4. Why are graphs and charts used in textbooks? (a) To make the text more interesting (b) To brighten the book (c) To make the text more difficult (d) To present information in a concise manner
5. Which of the following is the best example of a scientifically literate person? (a) One who enjoys reading science (b) One who reads a large amount of science (c) An intelligent, understanding reader of science (d) A professional scientist
6. Why should scientific content be read slowly? (a) The vocabulary is difficult. (b) There is a high concentration of information included in scientific content. (c) The teacher prefers it. (d) Both *a* and *b*
7. Which of the following styles of writing science materials is/are used in science textbooks? (a) Experiment (b) Explanation of a technical process (c) Classification (d) All of these
8. Why is mathematics considered abstract? (a) It is difficult. (b) The symbols represent ideas. (c) It is compactly written. (d) All of these
9. Which of the following factors contribute to the problems of reading mathematics? (a) One symbol may represent several words. (b) Mathematics is a difficult subject for many students. (c) Too many problems are introduced on a single page. (d) Too many examples are given.
10. What is the basic goal of language arts materials? (a) Understanding between the sender and the receiver of a message (b) Speaking clearly (c) Learning specialized vocabulary (d) Diagraming sentences
11. What is the purpose of computer literacy courses? (a) To familiarize students with computers (b) To familiarize students with the terminology related to computers (c) To teach students to use computers in a variety of ways (d) All of these
12. What kinds of written materials do computer science students read? (a) Novels and newspapers (b) Fiction and handouts (c) Textbooks, handouts, computer displays, and computer magazines and journals (d) None of the above

13. Why should foreign language teachers include the study of culture in their instruction? (a) To help students acquire vocabulary (b) To increase the number of words students have to memorize (c) To provide students with more examples (d) None of these
14. What language arts instructional methods are used in teaching students to read a foreign language? (a) English novels (b) Listening, speaking, reading, and writing the language (c) Listening to radio broadcasts of languages that belong to the same language family (d) Reading newspapers written in languages that belong to the same language family

THOUGHT QUESTIONS

1. How are social studies content and mathematics content alike? How are they different?
2. Why is critical reading important in social studies content?
3. Why do some students find mathematics content difficult to read?
4. How can teachers help students comprehend mathematics content?
5. What are the characteristics of science content?
6. How can the use of directed reading lessons and study guides lead to independent reading comprehension?

ENRICHMENT ACTIVITIES

1. Develop a directed reading lesson for a chapter in a social studies or science textbook.
2. Prepare a study guide for a chapter in a social studies or science textbook.
3. Prepare a study guide for a verbal problem in a mathematics textbook.
4. Develop a bibliography of trade books that could be used by students who are unable to read the textbook.
5. Prepare a cause-and-effect chart for a topic in a content area text.
6. Check professional journals such as *Social Education, Science Teacher, Mathematics Teacher,* and *English Journal* for articles dealing with reading of content material. Share your findings with the class.
7. Check the readability level of a textbook and/or supplementary material used for one of the subjects treated in this chapter.

NOTES

1. Yvonne Tixier y Vigil and James Dick, "Problems and Suggestions for Improving the Reading of Textbooks: A Social Studies Focus," *The High School Journal* (December/January 1984), 116–121.
2. W. A. Dea, "The Relationships Between Vocabulary Recognition and Higher Chapter Test Scores in United States History Classes" (Master's thesis, Whittier College, 1978).
3. Lee Ehman, Howard Mehlinger, and John Patrick, *Toward Effective Instruction in Secondary Social Studies* (Boston: Houghton Mifflin Company, 1974), p. 3.

4. Jack Fraenkel, *Helping Students Think and Value* (Englewood Cliffs, N.J.: Prentice-Hall, 1973), p. 83.

5. From *Land of Progress* by Irwin Unger and H. Mark Johnson. © Copyright, 1975, by Silver, Burdett & Ginn Inc. Used with permission.

6. Fraenkel, p. 93.

7. Wayne L. Herman, Jr., "Reading and Other Language Arts in Social Studies Instruction: Persistent Problems," in *A New Look at Reading in the Social Studies*, ed. R. Preston (Newark, Del.: International Reading Association, 1969), p. 5.

8. Vigil and Dick, p. 119.

9. D. W. Moore and S. V. Arthur, "Possible Sentences," in *Reading in the Content Areas: Improving Classroom Instruction*, ed. E. K. Dishner, T. W. Bean, and J. E. Readence (Dubuque, Iowa: Kendall/Hunt, 1981).

10. Hilda Taba, *Teacher's Handbook for Elementary Social Studies* (Reading, Mass.: Addison-Wesley, 1967).

11. Leslie McClain, "Study Guides: Potential Assets in Content Classrooms," *Journal of Reading*, 24 (January 1981), 321–325.

12. George G. Mallinson, "Reading in the Sciences: A Review of the Research," in *Reading in the Content Areas*, ed. James L. Laffey (Newark, Del.: International Reading Association, 1972), p. 145.

13. Frederick Frayer and H. J. Klausmeier, *A Scheme for Testing the Level of Cognitive Mastery*, Working Paper No. 16 (Madison: Wisconsin Research and Development Center for Cognitive Learning, 1969).

14. Judith N. Thelen, *Improving Reading in Science*, 2nd ed. (Newark, Del.: International Reading Association, 1984), p. 18.

15. Nila B. Smith, "Patterns of Writing in Different Subject Areas," *Journal of Reading*, 8 (October 1964), 34.

16. Stephen Krulik, "To Read or Not to Read That Is the Question!" *Mathematics Teacher* (April 1980), 248–252.

17. Ibid., p. 248.

18. Richard A. Earle, *Teaching Reading and Mathematics* (Newark, Del.: International Reading Association, 1976), p. 18.

19. Ibid., p. 20.

20. Margaret Henrichs and Tom Sisson, "Mathematics and the Reading Process: A Practical Application of Theory," *Mathematics Teacher* (April 1980), 253–256.

21. J. Knifong and B. Holtran, "A Search for Reading Difficulties Among Erred Word Problems," *Journal for Research in Mathematics Education*, 8 (May 1977), 237–230.

22. E. Kresse, "Using Reading as a Thinking Process to Solve Math Story Problems," *Journal of Reading*, 27 (April 1984), 598–601.

23. J. Riley and A. Pachtman, "Reading Mathematical Word Problems: Telling Them What to Do Is Not Telling Them How to Do It," *Journal of Reading*, 21 (March 1978), 531–534.

24. Earle, pp. 48–50.

25. Henrichs and Sisson, p. 254.

26. Francis Chase, "Demands on the Reader in the Next Decade," in *Critical Reading*, ed. Martha King, Bernice Ellinger, and Willavene Wolf (New York: Lippincott, 1967), pp. 1–3.

27. Charles Cooper and Alan Purves, *A Guide to Evaluation* (Lexington, Mass.: Ginn and Company, 1973).

28. John T. Guthrie, "Story Comprehension," *The Reading Teacher*, 30 (February 1977), 574–577.

29. Morris Finder, "Teaching to Comprehend," *Journal of Reading*, 13 (May 1970), 611–636.

30. John E. Carlson, "Reading in the Content Area of Foreign Language," in *Reading in the Content Areas: Research for Teachers*, ed. Mary M. Dupuis (Newark, Del.: International Reading Association, 1984), p. 23.

SELECTED REFERENCES

Bean, Thomas, Harry Singer, and Stan Cowan. "Analogical Study Guides: Improving Comprehension in Science." *Journal of Reading*, 29 (December 1985), 246–250.

Berger, Allen, and H. Alan Robinson, eds. *Secondary School Reading: What Research Reveals for Classroom Practice*. Newark, Del.: International Reading Association, 1982.

Blatt, Gloria T., and Lois Matz Rosen. "The Writing Response to Literature." *Journal of Reading*, 28 (October 1984), 8–12.

Cheyney, Arnold. *Teaching Reading Skills Through the Newspaper*. 2nd ed. Newark, Del.: International Reading Association, 1984.

Dupuis, Mary M. ed. *Reading in the Content Areas: Research for Teachers*. Newark, Del.: International Reading Association, 1984.

Gebhard, Ann O. "Teaching Writing in Reading and the Content Areas." *Journal of Reading*, 27 (December 1983), 207–211.

Gordon, Christine. "Modeling Inference Awareness Across the Curriculum." *Journal of Reading*, 28 (February 1985), 444–447.

Kresse, Elaine Campbell. "Using Reading as a Thinking Process to Solve Math Story Problems." *Journal of Reading*, 27 (April 1984), 598–601.

Lunstrum, John, and Bob Taylor. *Teaching Reading in the Social Studies*. Newark, Del.: International Reading Association, 1978.

Olson, Mary W., and Bonnie Longnion. "Pattern Guides: A Workable Alternative for Content Teachers." *Journal of Reading*, 25 (May 1982), 736–741.

Santeusanio, Richard P. *A Practical Approach to Content Area Reading*. Reading, Mass.: Addison-Wesley, 1983.

Shannon, Darla. "Use of Top-Level Structure in Expository Text: An Open Letter to a High School Teacher." *Journal of Reading*, 28 (February 1985), 426–431.

Siedow, Mary Dunn, David Memory, and Page Bristow. *Inservice Education for Content Area Teachers*. Newark, Del.: International Reading Association, 1985.

Simpson, Michele L. "PORPE: A Writing Strategy for Studying and Learning in the Content Areas." *Journal of Reading*, 29 (February 1986), 407–414.

Slater, Wayne H. "Teaching Expository Text Structure with Structural Organizers." *Journal of Reading*, 28 (May 1985), 712–718.

Strahan, David, and John Herlihy. "A Model for Analyzing Textbook Content." *Journal of Reading*, 28 (February 1985), 438–443.

Thelen, Judith N. *Improving Reading in Science*. 2nd ed. Newark, Del.: International Reading Association, 1984.

CHAPTER APPENDIX: USING NEWSPAPERS AND MAGAZINES

STRATEGIES

Teachers in every content area can use newspapers and magazines in their classes as instructional aids. They provide interesting, relevant, up-to-date information. Newspapers and magazines are excellent media to use for reading instruction because they are readily available, they treat a wide variety of subject matter, and they are highly motivating for secondary students because they focus on the present. Students who have been turned off by formal reading materials find newspapers and magazines more interesting and personally relevant. Newspapers have the added advantage of providing a fresh set of materials each day. Magazines enable students to pursue special interests in depth. Teachers can devise newspaper and magazine activities as enrichment for content text materials or as a substitute for the text for students who are unable to read the text. Following are suggested activities to use with newspapers, and a directed reading lesson based on work with newspapers.

Literal Reading Activities

1. Locate the main points in an article and the writer's supporting material for these main points.
2. Read the classified advertisements to find a job you would like to fill. Write a letter of application responding to the qualifications listed in the advertisement.
3. Ask specific literal questions related to news stories or advertisements, such as: "Who won the baseball game?" and "Which grocery has the cheapest coffee?"
4. Locate *who, where, when, why,* and *how* in a newspaper story.
5. List in sequence the steps of a how-to-do-it article.
6. Follow directions for making an item found in a newspaper or magazine.
7. Examine a newspaper to determine the percentage of space used for advertising.

Interpretive Reading Activities

1. Identify the point of view of an editorial.
2. Compare two editorials for likenesses, differences, and points of view.
3. Compare the treatment of a news event in a news story and in an editorial.
4. Find examples of an author's interpretation in a news story.
5. Ask questions such as the following:
   a. How does one reporter's writing differ from another reporter's writing?
   b. What can you learn about the author from the way he or she writes news stories?
6. State the effects you anticipate as the result of a news event. This exercise may be developed in the form of a chart such as the following:

News Event	Effects

Critical Reading Activities

1. Analyze articles, editorials, and advertisements for examples of fact and opinion.
2. Analyze the way connotations of words are used in newspapers to influence the reader.
3. Analyze for bias news stories related to controversial topics.
4. Evaluate the effectiveness of editorials in achieving their purposes.
5. Determine whether the writer of a news story is well informed.
6. Ask questions such as the following:
   a. Did the writer omit important information?
   b. Does the story fit with what the reader knows from past experience?
7. Analyze advertisements to find examples of various types of propaganda.
8. Analyze advertising to determine if it appeals to emotions or logic.

Creative Reading Activities

1. Write an advertisement for an item or service that is advertised in a newspaper or magazine.
2. Rewrite a news story to improve it.
3. Write a letter to the editor on a topic of concern.
4. Create a cartoon relating to a controversial issue or personality.
5. Write a review of a movie or a television show.
6. Dramatize a news story.

Flexible Rate Activities

1. Suggest the rates at which you feel various sections of newspapers or magazines should be read.
2. Make a list of the purposes you have for reading newspapers and magazines.
3. Skim news stories and advertisements for main ideas.
4. Scan the entertainment section to locate the time of the late showing of a movie.

Picture, Chart, Graph, and Map Activities

1. Learn to identify the different types of pictures used in newspapers, such as file photographs, on-the-spot photographs, and drawings.

2. Analyze the information provided in graphs, maps, and charts.
3. Discuss the value of pictures, graphs, maps, and charts for illustrating the news.

EXAMPLE 6.33   DIRECTED READING LESSON: FACT AND OPINION AND BIAS

Objectives
To identify fact and opinion in a news story
To identify bias in a news story
To suggest effects of a news event

Material
Articles from several newspapers relating to the Supreme Court ruling that allows lawyers to advertise routine legal services

Motivation and Building Background
Ask the students if they have heard any discussion or read anything about the Supreme Court ruling. Ask the students what they think about advertising by lawyers. Have them supply reasons.

Guided Reading
Silent—Present these purpose questions. Then allow sufficient time for silent reading of the selection.

Do the authors of these articles agree with your opinion?
Do the writers present any advantages or disadvantages of this advertising?
Do you think the writers are biased in their presentations of the story?

Discussion—Discuss the questions posed as silent reading purposes as well as the following questions:

Did the writers of these articles all have the same attitude regarding the topic?
Were they expressing fact or opinion? How do you know they were stating facts or opinions?
Why do you think the writers were biased, if they were?

Follow-up Activities
The class members may conduct a poll to determine how many people are opposed to this ruling and how many are in favor of the ruling. The class may analyze the reasons for voting yes or no.
The students may locate further information on the topic by reading additional newspapers and magazines.
The class may develop a chart of the effects of this ruling based upon their reading, discussion, and poll.

SOURCES OF NEWSPAPER TEACHING MATERIALS

The following materials are available from the sources cited.

1. American Newspaper Publishers Association (ANPA) Foundation, The Newspaper Center, Box 17407, Dulles International Airport, Washington, D.C. 20041.

   NIE Development Plan
   NIE Beginner's Kit
   Why NIE?
   Newspaper Test Sample Kit
   Workshop Workbook
   Using Newspapers to Teach Reading Skills
   The Newspaper as an Effective Teaching Tool
   Films About Newspapers

2. The Canadian Daily Newspaper Publishers Association (CDNPA), 321 Bloor Street East, Suite 214, Toronto, Ontario M4W1E7.

   Canadian Newspaper in Education Bibliography
   Effective Decision Making: A Survival Skill for Today's World
   A News Beginning
   Learning from Newspapers

3. International Reading Association, 800 Barksdale Road, PO Box 8139, Newark, Del. 19714–8139.

   Write for annual publications catalog.

CHAPTER
S E V E N

READING IN THE CONTENT
AREAS: PART 2

OVERVIEW

Vocationally oriented content areas are the focus of this chapter. Reading competence is as important for studying these content areas as it is for studying all other subjects. Students need both general reading skills and specific reading skills to understand industrial arts, business education, home economics, agriculture, physical education, driver education, art, and music. This chapter describes both of these types of skills and presents strategies for developing them.

PURPOSE-SETTING QUESTIONS

As you read this chapter, try to answer these questions:

1. Why do subjects such as industrial arts, business education, home economics, agriculture, physical education, driver education, and fine arts require reading competence?
2. What reading skills help students understand industrial arts, business education, home economics, and agriculture?
3. What reading skills increase comprehension of physical education and driver education?
4. What reading skills are required by fine arts subjects?
5. What strategies are useful for helping students comprehend vocational and technical materials?

KEY VOCABULARY

As you read this chapter, check your understanding of these terms:

vocational subjects   home economics
expository style   study guide
graphics   directed reading lesson
industrial arts   business education

VOCATIONAL AND TECHNICAL MATERIALS

Vocational and technical students must be able to read an author's words and language patterns, to recognize the organization of ideas, and to understand and integrate graphics with content. Because teachers should develop students' reading skills as they teach vocational and technical content materials, they must know how to help students read the specialized content in these subject areas.

Vocational and technical content, which is closely related to the world of work, is usually taught in a pragmatic fashion that demands practical application of textbook material. Reading plays an important role in the working world. Beatrice Levin states, "There are no areas in either the academic world or in the world of work in which reading does not play a crucial role."[1] She also points out that even at the lowest job level, a person has to be able to read directions and complete applications and forms required by the job.[2] William Diehl and Larry Mikulecky studied the reading requirements of one hundred occupations and found that almost 99 percent of the subjects reported reading each day at work. They reported that an average of 113 minutes a day was spent in work-related reading.[3]

The primary objective of teaching vocational and technical subjects is to educate workers who are careful, organized, effective, and efficient and have mastered occupational skills. Teachers also hope to foster in students positive attitudes toward work. In order to do this, instructors must not only acquaint students with particular content reading materials but must also develop in their students adequate reading skills, providing direct reading instruction so students can comprehend specialized materials. Because vocational and technical materials deal with students' direct interests and future goals, students are often motivated to read, desiring success in these work-related areas.

The range in reading achievement among secondary students who elect occupationally oriented subjects tends to be broader than it is among students who choose academic areas. Some students choose vocational subjects because they believe that they can avoid reading if they follow a vocational course of study.[4] Mikulecky examined the literacy demands, competencies, and strategies present in the daily reading of both students and workers. He found that students read less often in school than most workers do on the job, that students read less competently than workers, and that students face easier material, which they read with less understanding. The reading strategies employed by students may be less effective than those employed by workers.[5] Unfortunately for poor readers, there is no subject in the secondary curriculum that does not require reading skill, just as there are no jobs that do not require reading skill.

Reading is an integral part of technical and managerial jobs, which can be frustrating for people employed in those positions. A study by Phyllis Miller[6] showed that these workers spend, on the average, fifteen to twenty hours per week doing work-related reading. Many of the participants in Miller's study averaged fifteen pieces of reading material per day.[6] They read mainly the following types of materials:[7]

> technical pieces
> proposals
> manuals
> data sheets
> memos and attachments
> correspondence
> nontechnical pieces

People in these positions read to analyze problems, propose solutions, and carry out research. Managers and supervisors read to review, advise, assign, and develop organizational procedures and policy. However, the participants in this research reported that they were inefficient readers who were often frustrated by their work-related reading.[8]

ASPECTS OF VOCATIONAL READING

Since the amount of written material used in vocational subjects appears to be smaller than in other subjects, students and teachers may misjudge the level of reading required. Even brief vocational reading selections demand reading skill and precise, careful reading. The readability level of these materials averages tenth grade or above.[9] Vocational materials are written in an expository style that is concise and uses technical vocabulary. Readers must be able to follow directions and to apply ideas and words to actual situations.

Vocabulary

Each vocational subject includes a great deal of technical vocabulary as well as common vocabulary words that have special meanings. For example, the common word *credit* has a special meaning when used for bookkeeping, where it refers to a bookkeeping entry that shows money paid on an account. ("You may place this entry on the *credit* side of the ledger.") Technical vocabulary words usually represent concepts that are essential to know in order to read a particular subject with understanding. Fortunately for teachers of vocational subjects, the technical vocabulary terms usually represent concrete concepts, which are easier to teach than abstract ideas. For example, in home economics, *saute* is a word that represents a particular way of cooking food that can be demonstrated to students; in bookkeeping, *debit* represents a specific concept that can be concretely illustrated.

Unfortunately, there are also disadvantages related to the technical vocabulary of vocational subjects. Teachers cannot assume that students will be able to learn the precise meaning of a word by using context clues or a dictionary.[10] Technical material does not always contain enough clues to help a reader define a term, and many high school dictionaries do not include the technical terms that are used in vocational materials. These factors make vocabulary instruction very important in vocational subject areas.

Teaching Technical Vocabulary

Teachers should plan direct instruction for technical vocabulary. They can point out and define new terms before having students read a textbook assignment. They can also demonstrate the concrete meanings of many technical terms by showing students the objects or activities the words represent. Students can write the words in a notebook and develop a content dictionary for their own or class use.

Teachers or students can construct picture word cards that have a drawing and the word or words on one side and the definition on the other side. These cards can be used individually by students or by the entire class; they may be laminated for protection and displayed around the classroom. The teacher should give the students a quiz on these words every other week to check vocabulary development. Vocabulary evaluation strategies for teachers and additional suggestions for developing word meanings are presented in Chapter 2. Example 7.1 illustrates two possible picture word cards.

Following Directions

Every technical and vocational subject requires that the student read directions and translate them into action. The reader of industrial arts material must read directions for operating and repairing various pieces of equipment. The reader of home economics material must be able to follow the directions for baking a cake or constructing a garment. The business education student must read directions for operating business machines and for setting up bookkeeping systems.

Reading directions requires that the student read slowly and precisely. The student should be prepared to reread in order to achieve complete understanding. When reading directions, students should be guided by the following questions.

1. What am I trying to do? (What is the task?)
2. What materials are required?
3. Do I understand all of the terms (words) used in these directions?
4. What is the sequence of steps?
5. Have I omitted anything?

6. Am I ready to perform the task?
7. Was I successful in accomplishing the task?

These questions can be incorporated into study guides. Suggestions for developing study guides are included later in this chapter and in Chapters 6 and 9.

EXAMPLE 7.1 PICTURE WORD CARDS ───────────

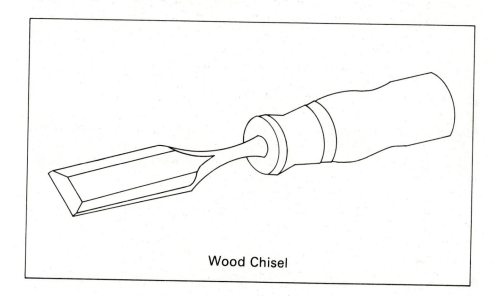

Wood Chisel

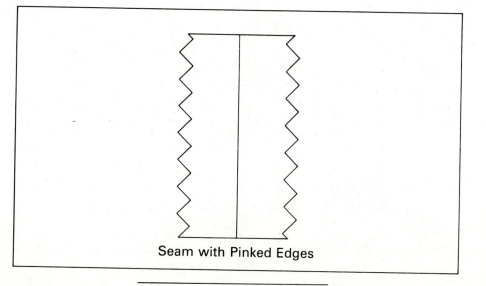

Seam with Pinked Edges

In vocational materials there is immediate feedback regarding how well a student has read directions; if directions are not followed properly, the result is a concrete, observable outcome. For example, if a student has failed to follow directions for operating a machine in the industrial arts shop, the machine will not work. That a student has failed to follow directions for baking a cake will be apparent when the cake is seen or eaten.

Teachers—or students—can develop an illustrated dictionary of terms for each subject area. This activity is useful for all vocational and technical subjects. Following is an example of an entry in an illustrated dictionary of terms for the subject area of woodworking.

EXAMPLE 7.2   ILLUSTRATED DICTIONARY OF TERMS ———

Term: vise
Pronunciation: vis
Definition: A vise is a tool with two jaws that are opened and closed by a screw. It is used to hold an object firmly while this object is worked on.
Sentence: A vise can be of a permanent type, which is bolted to a workbench or table, or it can be one of many clamp-on types.
Illustration:

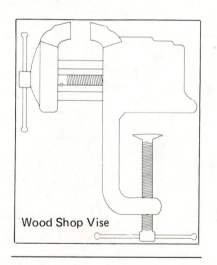

Wood Shop Vise

Example 7.3 is a set of directions from a home economics textbook. The reader could apply these questions and activities to this example.

1. What am I trying to do? (make a dessert pancake)
2. What materials are required? (1/3 cup flour, 1/4 teaspoon baking powder, 1/3 cup milk, 2 eggs, 2 tablespoons butter or margarine, 1 tablespoon confectioners' sugar, 4 lemon wedges)

3. Do I understand the terms? (combine, sifted, preheat, batter, lumpy, beat, sprinkle)
4. What is the sequence of steps? (1. preheat oven; 2. combine flour and baking powder; 3. beat in milk and eggs; 4. melt butter; 5. pour batter in skillet; 6. bake pancake; 7. sprinkle with sugar; 8. serve)
5. Have I omitted anything? (no)
6. Complete the steps.
7. Was I successful in accomplishing the task? (If the pancake looks appetizing and is tasty, the student has succeeded.)

EXAMPLE 7.3   DIRECTIONS FROM A HOME ECONOMICS BOOK ——

German Dessert Pancake

4 Servings

1/3 cup sifted all-purpose flour [*80 ml*]
1/4 teaspoon baking powder [*1.25 ml*]
1/3 cup milk [*80 ml*]
2 eggs, slightly beaten
2 tablespoons butter or margarine [*30 ml*]
1 tablespoon confectioners' sugar [*15 ml*]
4 lemon wedges

1. Preheat oven to 425 degrees F (218° C).
2. In small bowl, combine flour and baking powder.
3. Beat in milk and eggs, leaving batter a bit lumpy.
4. In a 10-inch (25-cm) skillet with heatproof handle, melt butter or margarine. When butter is very hot, pour batter in all at once.
5. Bake 15 to 18 minutes until pancake is golden.
6. Sprinkle with sugar. Serve hot with lemon wedges to squeeze over pancake.

Note: Strawberries may be served over the pancake instead of the lemon.

Source: Reprinted from TEEN GUIDE TO HOMEMAKING by J. Brinkley and V. Chamberlain, with permission of Webster/McGraw-Hill.

Graphics

Vocational and technical students are very often required to read a variety of graphic materials such as blueprints, drawings, cutaways, patterns, pictures, and sketches. They must be able to visualize these graphic materials and understand the three-dimensional aspects of the graphics. They must also be able to interpret the scales and legends that accompany many graphics in order to under-

EXAMPLE 7.4   FLOOR PLAN (INDUSTRIAL ARTS)

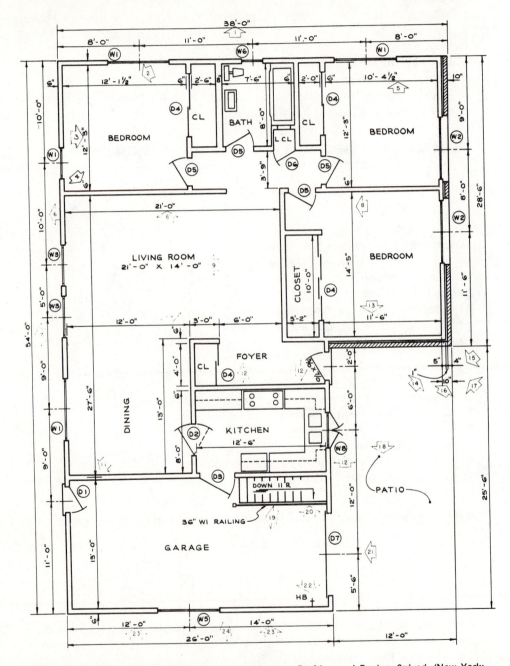

Source: Donald Hepler and Paul Wallach, *Architecture Drafting and Design*, 3rd ed. (New York: McGraw-Hill, 1977), p. 204.

EXAMPLE 7.5   SEWING DIAGRAM (HOME ECONOMICS)

STEPS IN THE UNIT CONSTRUCTION METHOD

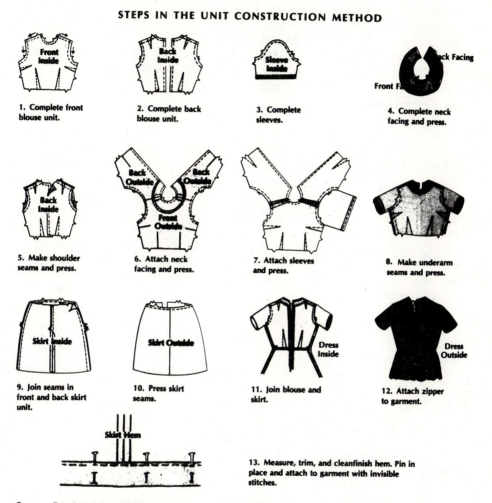

1. Complete front blouse unit.

2. Complete back blouse unit.

3. Complete sleeves.

4. Complete neck facing and press.

5. Make shoulder seams and press.

6. Attach neck facing and press.

7. Attach sleeves and press.

8. Make underarm seams and press.

9. Join seams in front and back skirt unit.

10. Press skirt seams.

11. Join blouse and skirt.

12. Attach zipper to garment.

13. Measure, trim, and cleanfinish hem. Pin in place and attach to garment with invisible stitches.

Source: Reprinted from TEEN GUIDE TO HOMEMAKING by J. Brinkley and V. Chamberlain, with permission of Webster/McGraw-Hill.

stand the textual materials they are reading. Examples 7.4 and 7.5 show two types of graphics that vocational students commonly encounter. Example 7.4 is from an architecture drafting and design text; Example 7.5 is from a home economics book.

To read the floor plan in Example 7.4 the student must be able to interpret both the scale of the drawing and special symbols such as the symbol (′) for feet, the symbol (″) for inches, and the symbol (×) for *by*. There are also several abbreviations for words that need to be interpreted correctly.

In reading the diagram in Example 7.5, the student must coordinate the text with the illustrations. Directions must be followed carefully and in sequence.

Teachers should give students many opportunities to convert written directions, drawings, and blueprints into models and actual objects. They can also have students match blueprints and diagrams with pictures of the finished products—an activity that will help students develop the ability to visualize written ideas. Having students prepare directions, diagrams, and blueprints for classmates to follow will help them become more adept at understanding these written materials themselves.

Rate

Readers of vocational and technical materials must adjust their reading rates according to purpose, type of content, and familiarity with the subject. Since vocational materials are often problem oriented and include many directions, they should be read slowly and precisely. Vocational students should learn to reread content until they fully comprehend it. Written directions are rarely understood well with only one reading and often need to be gone over many times to be followed successfully. It is important for students to realize that rereading is a normal, necessary procedure. Through problem-solving activities the teacher can give students practice in the skills of reading slowly and rereading.

Writing

Writing is another vehicle for helping students understand content materials. Both group and individual writing experiences are useful in content classrooms.[11] Writing can expand students' understanding of technical and vocational language and their ability to express ideas effectively. One teacher asked his students to write short paragraphs describing their shop activities for a day; then he asked the students to revise their paragraphs.[12] This exercise required the students to know technical vocabulary, sentence construction, paragraph organization, and sequencing.

Utilizing Motivation

Utilizing or building motivation is a responsibility of the teacher in vocational and technical education. Because students are often personally motivated to study these subjects, the students' interest will help make them want to read. Students frequently are able to read materials with higher readability levels than usual because of the nature of the reading content.[13] The classroom library should include periodicals, which provide information about new products, materials, and techniques. Periodicals also give general information about the various trades that is useful to students. Teachers can use these materials to develop their students' reading interests and understanding of the content area. This understanding will increase students' ability to predict content and, consequently, to comprehend content materials. Following are some suggestions for using motivation to increase comprehension of content materials.

1. Display books, magazines, and related materials that are appropriate to student interest and reading levels.
2. Suggest readings in magazines, newspapers, periodicals, and books.
3. Review and refer to relevant books.
4. Use learning activities such as field trips, movies, records, and radio and television programs to build background and to stimulate a desire for further information.
5. Provide time in class for reading materials related to class topics.
6. To develop interest and critical reading ability, compare and contrast the way two or more authors have treated a topic.
7. Encourage students to discuss their readings with each other.
8. Permit students to work together so that good readers can help poor readers.

The Textbook as a Reference

Teachers should make a particular effort to introduce the textbook to their students, since vocational textbooks frequently are used also as reference books. Students in vocational classrooms tend to ignore the textbook because they think it is unnecessary. Instruction that familiarizes the students with the wealth of information provided by the textbook will help them use it and other reference books more effectively to acquire knowledge and to solve problems.

Following are some questions that can be used at the beginning of the term to prepare students for reading their textbooks. The questions can be presented on a worksheet or on an overhead transparency. These questions are based on an industrial arts textbook, but they can be adapted to any subject area.

1. How many chapters are in this book?
2. Which chapter discusses floor plans?
3. On what page can scale drawings be found?
4. What is the copyright date of this book?
5. Is this a current book?
6. Who wrote this book?
7. Is the author qualified in this field? Why or why not?
8. Turn to page 205 in the glossary. What are *oleum spirits*?
9. How does the drawing on page 9 help you?
10. On what page or pages can you find information about different kinds of paint?

Reading Strategies

The demands of reading-to-learn and reading-to-do have been the focus of recent research. Thomas Sticht divided reading tasks into these two categories.[14] *Reading-to-learn* is a reading task in which an individual reads with the intention of remembering and applying textual information. *Reading-to-do* is a reading task in which an individual uses the material as an aid to do something else. In the latter situation, the materials often serve as "external memories," because the individual may refer to them to check information rather than to specifically learn the content. Sticht found that most on-the-job reading is a type of reading-to-do, which demands the following reading strategies.[15]

1. *Re-read/rehearse*, which involves repeating the information or reading it again.
2. *Problem solve/question*, which involves answering questions posed by the text and/or searching for the information necessary to solve a specific problem.
3. *Relate/associate*, which is associating new information with the individual's existing store of information.
4. *Focus attention*, which involves reducing the amount of information in some way, such as by underlining, outlining, or taking notes.

Having students read to solve problems is a good way to teach the preceding reading strategies. Before having students practice the strategies on their own, the teacher should present a content-based problem and explain to the students each of the steps as it relates to the problem. The problem and the associated strategies may be introduced through overhead transparencies, posters, or bulletin board displays. Problem-solving activities such as the following might be used:

1. Industrial arts—List the tools you need to build a chair.
2. Home economics—Prepare menus for nutritionally balanced meals for a week based on a budget of [$85].
3. Business—Set up an office mailing system for the [XYZ] Company.

The problem-solving writing pattern is common in vocational materials. These materials also include presentations of factual information and how-to-do-it directions. Reading instruction should focus on these types of content materials.

Directed reading lessons are also useful in helping vocational students learn to read textual materials. Following is an example of a directed reading lesson based on home economics content.

EXAMPLE 7.6   DIRECTED READING LESSON:
HOME ECONOMICS

Motivation and Building Background
1. Ask students the following questions: What kind of fabric is used in the clothing you are wearing today? What is your favorite kind of fabric? Here is a box of various types of fabric. Look at each piece and try to determine the contents of each piece of fabric.

Skill Development Activities

2. Discuss and pronounce each of the following vocabulary words. Be certain students have a concept for each type of fabric by giving them labeled samples of each to examine.

wool	brocade
synthetic fabric	lamé
satin	velvet
cotton	

Guided Reading

3. *Silent*—Provide students with *silent reading purposes* such as the following: How do you choose a suitable fabric to make a dress? How are synthetic fabrics different from natural fabrics? Have the students *read the lesson silently.*

4. *Discussion*—*Discuss* the silent reading purposes and ask discussion questions such as the following: Do you prefer natural or synthetic fabrics? Why? What are the advantages of natural fabrics? What kind of dress pattern would you choose for a brocade fabric?

Follow-up Activities

5. Have students reread as necessary to solve the problem of selecting an appropriate fabric for their next garment.

The teacher can also prepare study guides to help students comprehend vocational materials as they read. Example 7.7 shows a selection from an industrial arts textbook and includes a study guide based on the selection.

EXAMPLE 7.7   SAMPLE WRITING IN VOCATIONAL MATERIALS AND STUDY GUIDE

Painting and Enameling

Paint and enamel are protective and decorative coatings for the less expensive woods for which a transparent finish may not be desirable. Either paint or enamel can be used satisfactorily as a colorful finish on furniture and cabinets.

Paint is generally applied to exterior surfaces or to projects which are used out of doors. Enamel is suitable for interior trim and for projects used in the home. It comes in a gloss, a semigloss, or a dull (flat) finish. Enamel usually produces a harder finish than paint because varnish is an ingredient in enamel.

Both paint and enamel are available in many colors. Both can also be bought either in white or tinted with colors ground in oil. Each of the many paints and enamels has its own recommended thinner. Read the instructions on the container for the method of thinning and for the manufacturer's suggestions for applying.

Mixing and Applying Paint or Enamel

1. Prepare the surfaces for painting or enameling. They should be properly planed, scraped, and sanded.
2. Read the directions on the container before opening it. Each manufacturer of paint and enamel recommends how it should be mixed and applied. The container also specifies the drying time required.
3. If the directions call for a primer coat, apply it first.
4. Shake the can thoroughly. Remove the lid, and pour off some of the top liquid into another container.
5. Stir the base mixture with a paddle. Add the top liquid to the base mixture a little at a time, and stir them until they are thoroughly blended.
6. Add turpentine, linseed oil, or the thinner recommended on the can, if needed.
7. Select a suitable high-quality brush.
8. Dip the brush into the paint so that about three-fourths of the length of the bristles absorbs paint. Wipe the surplus paint or enamel on the edge of the can as you remove the brush.
9. Apply the paint or enamel to the surface with long, even strokes. A little practice helps to determine the proper amount to apply. It should cover the surface smoothly and evenly. Do not allow it to run.
10. Allow the coat to dry thoroughly according to the time given in the directions. Sand smooth with fine sandpaper. Wipe the surface with a clean cloth.
11. Apply a second and a third coat if needed. Do not sand the final coat, because it will dull the finish.

Source: Chris H. Groneman, *General Woodworking,* 5th ed. (New York: McGraw-Hill, 1976), pp. 247–248.

Study Guide

Introduction

This selection discusses the value of paint and enamel as finishing materials. Directions are given for preparing a surface for paint or enamel and applying that finish.

Vocabulary

Give examples for each of the following terms: paint, enamel, transparent, gloss, semigloss, dull, flat, tinted, sandpaper.

Levels of Comprehension

Directions: Put the following steps for painting in the correct sequence by numbering them. Refer to the text.

Literal
• Apply a primer coat first, if needed.

- Dip 3/4 of the length of the bristles into the paint. Wipe the surplus on the edge of the can.
- Prepare the surface by planing, scraping, and sanding.
- Read the directions on the container. Note drying time.
- Apply the paint or enamel with long, even strokes.
- Stir the paint or enamel.
- Shake the can.
- Apply a second and a third coat if needed.
- Allow to dry thoroughly, sand smooth with sandpaper, and wipe clean.

Directions: Write a short answer to each of the following questions.

Interpretive

1. Does varnish cause a hard finish? How do you know this?
2. Which coating—paint or enamel—is probably more waterproof? Why do you think this?
3. What would happen if you did not shake the can thoroughly?
4. Why does the author recommend a high-quality brush?
5. What might happen to a cabinet if you gave it only one coat of paint?

Applied

6. Give an example of an item that you would finish with enamel rather than paint. Why did you choose enamel for this item?
7. Give two examples of substances that could be used for thinning paint. What is the best way to choose the right thinner?
8. Can you mix paint and enamel? Why or why not?

After students complete a study guide like that in Example 7.7 and read the corresponding chapter, they should have an opportunity to discuss their answers and should be prepared to explain and support their answers by citing the text.

APPLICATIONS OF READING COMPREHENSION SKILLS

The sections that follow discuss how specific reading comprehension skills and strategies can be applied to particular subject areas. However, the skills and strategies that are demonstrated can be used interchangeably in the various subject areas. In addition, the strategies and activities included in Chapter 6 can be used with the content areas discussed in this chapter. Spatial limitations prohibit demonstrating each strategy with each type of content.

Industrial Arts

Industrial arts content includes materials that are written about machine operation, woodworking, auto mechanics, drafting, and radio and television repair. Obviously, these areas have large technical vocabularies that must be understood. Example 7.8 shows writing from a general woodworking text.

EXAMPLE 7.8   INDUSTRIAL ARTS CONTENT ———————————

Recognizing Good Design

Recognizing the factors that constitute good design helps create a well-designed product. When you go to a store to buy furniture, you look for certain characteristics. One of the first is *pleasing appearance.* Does the piece of furniture have a graceful or pleasing shape? Is the color suitable? Will it fit well with other furniture in the room? These are some of the questions that will help in determining whether or not the customer thinks the product being considered for purchase has a pleasing appearance.

You consider *function* when you decide whether the product or object fulfills the role for which it was originally planned and designed. If the design problem calls for a bookcase to hold 50 books, and there is room for only 30, the product will not do the job for which it was intended and is therefore not useful.

High-quality craftsmanship is essential to good design. No one wants to buy a piece of poorly constructed furniture. Tight joints, smooth finish, and precise cutting and fitting of parts are a few of the important considerations in selecting a well-designed and well-constructed product.

Source: Chris H. Groneman, *General Woodworking,* 5th ed. (New York: McGraw-Hill, 1976), p. 22.

———————————

Readers must understand the following essential words in order to understand the preceding selection:

joints	function
appearance	craftsmanship
finish	shape
surface decorations	

Many of the technical terms that are introduced in industrial arts classes are related to tools and equipment. Demonstrating and labeling tools and equipment clearly in the classroom can help students learn to recognize these terms when they appear in textbooks.

Demonstrating mechanical processes also can clarify printed textual explanations. For example, the teacher might illustrate the process of replacing the jets on a carburetor.

Many reading tasks in industrial arts courses involve the students' ability to read and implement directions. Students must know how to follow step-by-step directions for operating equipment, constructing furniture, or installing a carburetor. They must learn to follow the directions on "job sheets," which are used in industrial arts classes to assign daily work. Safety rules also are important reading content for industrial arts students. Teachers should prepare study guides to help students comprehend and carry out written instructions.

Example 7.9 presents a diagram taken from an automobile repair textbook. The diagram illustrates a "V" design compressor. Teachers should encourage students to study such diagrams carefully and to associate this type of illustration with the written textual material. To fully understand this particular diagram, students need to realize that it represents a cutaway section of a compressor and that the lines with letters identify the parts of the compressor. Industrial arts materials are often coordinated with illustrative designs.

EXAMPLE 7.9   INDUSTRIAL ARTS DIAGRAM

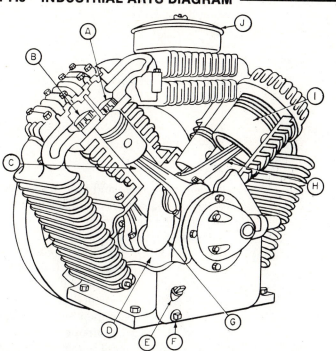

27-8. Cutaway of a two-stage "V"-design compressor: A. Intake valve assembly. B. Exhaust valve assembly. C. High-pressure connecting rod and piston assembly. D. Crankcase. E. Oil level dipstick. F. Crankcase oil drain. G. Crankshaft. H. Low-pressure connecting rod. I. Low-pressure piston. J. Air intake filter.

Business Education

Business education encompasses a wide variety of studies, including shorthand, typing, bookkeeping, computer courses, secretarial studies, general business, business mathematics, business law, management, economics, and business communications. Computer applications in business are extensive; therefore students who have basic computing skills can better compete for many of the jobs they want. Each of the courses in business education has considerable written content. According to Susan Heinemann, "Courses in business have traditionally relied heavily on reading as an important part of instruction."[16] People in business face increasing volumes of business transactions and the accompanying paper work.[17]

Business education students and people who work in the business world read many types of content. Following is a list of written materials that they commonly read.

manuals	directions
reference materials	reference materials
ledgers	memos
business letters	computer printouts
invoices	charts
directories	graphs
handbooks	labels
checklists	trade journals and professional magazines
reports	newspapers
textbooks	

"Many of the written materials used in business and industry are complex and have a high readability level. These materials are often filled with concepts, loaded with information, data-filled and combinations of these characteristics."[18] However, business education textbooks probably do not reflect the diversity apparent in business reading materials. Generally, these textbooks are academic in both content and format and fall into two categories: how-to-do-it manuals and informational books. Students must acquire the reading skills not only to read the textbooks that are often the basis of classroom instruction but also to read the other business materials that will be important to their employment.

Researchers who have examined the literacy requirements of various occupations found that business people read many types of materials like those listed in the preceding paragraph and that workers generally underestimated the reading demands of their occupations.[19] Workers engaged in work-related reading for approximately two hours per day. In all the occupations studied, the predominant reason for reading was reading to do work. Reading and study are basic tools for broadening one's knowledge in any field; therefore any ambitious student will find reading skills invaluable.

The reading tasks that confront business education students and people who work in business are summarized in the following list.

1. Reading and interpreting symbols such as the double lines under numbers that represent a final total in computation.
2. Reading directions/instructions and implementing them. Workers who have to stop others to ask for instructions or who complete tasks incorrectly slow down others and themselves.[20]

3. Identifying main ideas and details in textbooks, magazine articles, and newspaper articles.
4. Skimming and/or scanning to locate needed information. These skills may be used to locate materials needed to solve a problem or to prepare a report.[21]
5. Reading newspapers, magazines, and professional journals to learn about current trends in the business world.
6. Reading and implementing memos. Memos are organized differently than other types of written communication. Memos often inform workers of changes in existing practices or rules in a business situation; therefore, the receiver must read these communications and remember the details.
7. Reading and responding to business letters. Business letters are organized differently, use more technical vocabulary, and use different semantics than social correspondence. Thus they require different reading skills.[22]
8. Reading invoices to check accuracy.
9. Reading computer printouts to locate needed information. These printouts may be used to problem solve or as a basis for planning programs to meet specific needs.
10. Reading reference materials such as Coffin's Interest Tables,[23] financial handbooks, and handbooks of business mathematics. Students must interpret and apply the information obtained from these sources.
11. Reading and interpreting textbooks in order to complete class assignments that enable students to learn business skills.
12. Reading technical vocabulary. Researchers have identified both general and specific vocabulary lists for secretaries, account clerks, and others.[24]

The following word list includes the "Highest Frequency Words for Ten Occupations."[25] These one hundred words are those most frequently used by adults, according to a study of ten skilled and semiskilled occupations and training programs.

the	will	your	see
of	one	was	more
to	not	get	these
and	an	has	into
a	there	must	just
is	can	any	them
in	when	he	down
it	out	got	time
for	we	know	about
that	which	them	been
you	what	don't	some
be	do	each	business
or	up	air	how
on	pressure	check	its
are	two	that's	back
I	so	but	over

this	they	system	work
with	here	through	would
as	other	valve	temperature
by	okay	going	same
if	right	well	also
have	no	use	where
all	used	than	now
at	may	it's	only
from	should	go	like

Example 7.10 contains a selection from a business education textbook. Note the technical terminology, including *property tax, real estate, personal property tax, assessor, assessment, revenues, and tax base.* The preview guide also shown in Example 7.10 should be completed by students before they read the selection; it helps the readers anticipate the selection content, thus increasing comprehension. After students have completed the preview guide and read the chapter, they should have an opportunity to discuss and support their answers.

EXAMPLE 7.10   BUSINESS EDUCATION CONTENT AND
PREVIEW GUIDE

Property Tax

Local governments get a major share of their revenues from property taxes. This includes counties, cities, towns, townships, and school districts. About one-third of all revenues at this level comes from property tax. The state and federal governments have almost no revenue from this tax.

A **real estate property tax** is one on the value of land, and anything *on* the land such as houses, barns, garages, or other buildings. A second tax is the **personal property tax,** a tax applied to movable items such as automobiles, furniture, and machinery used by businesses. Because of the ease with which personal property can be hidden, the personal property tax is being used less and less. Real estate has thus become the most important property tax base and source of revenue for local communities.

The amount of real estate taxes is determined by first estimating the value of the property, and then multiplying the tax rate by the value. The amount at which the property is valued is called an **assessment,** and the government official who does the valuation is called an **assessor.**

Source: Betty Brown and John Clow: *General Business: Our Business and Economic World*, p. 231. Copyright © 1982 by Houghton Mifflin Company. Used by permission.

Preview Guide

Directions: Place a check mark under the *Yes* column if you believe the selection will support the statement. Place a check under the *No* column if you believe the text will not support the statement. After you read the selection, review your responses.

Yes   *No*

_____	_____	1. Property tax is levied upon real estate and personal property.
_____	_____	2. Property tax is not levied on any personal property that can be bought and sold.
_____	_____	3. Personal property tax is applied to movable items.
_____	_____	4. Taxpayers may be exempted from paying tax on the full value of a property if there is a mortgage on it.
_____	_____	5. Taxpayers find it difficult to avoid paying personal property tax.
_____	_____	6. The assessed value of a property is the basis for calculating the amount of tax.

Business students must learn to combine skimming and scanning with close reading. First, they should skim for the main idea or scan for specific information they need to solve a problem, to compose a letter or memo, or to write a report. Then they should carefully and accurately read the section or sections of content containing the information they need. Close reading is important because in many situations even a small error can have disastrous consequences. For example, a bookkeeping error can make a company appear profitable when it is actually losing money; a secretary's error in proofreading a business letter can change the entire meaning of an important communication; a tiny error in a computer program may result in a program that will not run. Business students should understand clearly how meaning is expressed through grammar, and they should concentrate on reading to identify details that convey meaning.[26]

Chapter 3 includes suggestions for teaching students how to read for details. Teaching strategies like preview guides, study guides, and directed reading lessons can help business education students refine vital skills. Each of these strategies can be applied to a specific area of business education and can focus on skills like following directions, solving problems, and locating information. In addition, a reading strategy like the following is helpful.

A Reading Strategy for Business Education Materials

Students who must read the many kinds of materials identified earlier in this section can improve their reading comprehension by using a strategy like PRC.[27] Its three phases are prereading, reading, and consolidation.

Prereading   The prereading phase of the business reading process is the limbering up part of the process. The reader surveys the reading material to identify the type of content (memo, letter, report, text, etc.) and to set the stage for remembering. During this phase, the reader identifies topics around which he or she can cluster the ideas that are in the selection. The reader also identifies the author's organization: knowing how the material is organized will help the reader pinpoint the main ideas when reading. During this phase the reader establishes questions that will guide her or his reading. Following are sample questions.

1. What does this selection tell me?
2. What is the main point?
3. What are the important details?
4. What questions will I be asked about this reading?

Reading   The reader reads carefully if close reading is necessary or scans if that is adequate. For example, if he or she is reading to gather data to write an important report, close reading is in order. However, if he or she is reading to locate specific pieces of information and those details are all that is needed from the content, then scanning is in order.

Consolidation   During this phase, the reader consolidates the information acquired from reading. Processing the information helps the reader organize it for long-term memory and for implementing the ideas when that is necessary. The reader may make notes to aid remembering. The reader should ask him- or herself questions like the following:

1. What is it that I don't understand?
2. How does this information relate to what I already know?
3. What other examples can I think of?
4. How does this information change or alter what I already know?
5. How can I implement this information?

Business education students must be able to read graphs, charts, tables, balance sheets, invoices, and tax forms. Example 7.11 shows a table from a business education textbook and sample questions that a teacher might use to help students comprehend a table such as this one. Refer to Chapter 4 for further suggestions about how to teach students to read tables.

EXAMPLE 7.11   BUSINESS EDUCATION TABLE AND QUESTIONS ——

The United States government publishes information about the average incomes of families. The information in the chart shows three average family budgets for a year. Each family has a total of four people, with two children ages 8 and 13.

Annual Budgets for Three U.S. Families (Family of Four, Living in City)

Item	Lower-Income	Middle-Income	Higher-Income
Food	$ 3,574	$ 4,609	$ 5,806
Housing	2,233	4,182	6,345
Transportation	856	1,572	2,043
Clothing & personal care	1,148	1,612	2,338
Medical care	1,065	1,070	1,116
Other personal expenses	515	956	1,578
Social security taxes, insurance contributions	1,221	1,883	2,456
Personal taxes	935	2,738	5,739
Total	$11,546	$18,622	$27,420

The cost of living varies from city to city and in different parts of the country, but these are average budgets. You will notice the breakdown of spending into various standard items. A comparison of the ways these families spend their incomes with your own may suggest some ways for you to stretch your budget. It often helps to compare your own habits with someone very much like you. Such a comparison may also throw light on how others set priorities.

Source: Betty Brown and John Clow: *General Business: Our Business and Economic World*, p. 107. Copyright © 1982 by Houghton Mifflin Company. Used by permission.

Questions

1. What amount is spent for transportation by the middle-income family?
2. How much difference is there between the personal taxes of the lower-income family and those of the higher-income family?
3. On which item are the differences greatest among the different income levels?
4. Compare the amount spent by your family on one item with the amount spent by the families in the table. To which level is your family closest? Does the comparison suggest any changes that your family should make in spending habits?

The gloss in Example 7.12 shows a section from a computer science textbook used in secondary computer science classes. The gloss identifies the reading tasks that a student would encounter when reading this section, found at the beginning of the textbook.

Home Economics

Home economics is a complex area of study; it includes child care, consumer economics, foods and nutrition, clothing and textiles, design, management, housing, home furnishings, and personal growth and development. Home economics students may be seeking either a vocation or an avocation.

EXAMPLE 7.12   GLOSS OF COMPUTER SCIENCE TEXT SHOWING

READING TASKS REQUIRED BY THE CONTENT ────

1-3 Communicating with the Computer

Identify
Main Idea →
The methods used to communicate with a computer are very important. The computer must receive instructions in a form that it has been programmed to accept and to which it can respond.

Detail →
Technical
language →
Mathematics →
The computer itself cannot understand a human language such as English. It is built (that is, its electronic circuits are arranged) to respond to instructions in *machine language*. Machine language is based on coding in the binary number system. (See the Computer Language Feature on page 64.) The binary number system uses only 0's and 1's to represent numbers. These digits — 0 and 1 — can easily be related to the electronic components of the computer, where the current (or switch) is either on (represented by 1) or off (represented by 0). Although the computer understands machine language, human beings sometimes have difficulty with it; an instruction telling an

Example →
Apple computer to add one number to another looks like this: 10101101 00001010 00000011 01101101 00000111 00000011 10001101 00001000 00000011.

Description →
Clearly, it would be easier for a human being to communicate in a familiar language like English. Of course, the computer does not understand English (a very complicated language, if you think about it), so a compromise was reached. Languages less complicated than English but easier for a programmer to work with than machine language were invented. In this book, you will learn to use the BASIC language to communicate with computers.

Acronym
Important
Idea →
BASIC (*B*eginner's *A*ll-purpose *S*ymbolic *I*nstruction *C*ode) was first developed in the early 1960's as a general purpose computer language. It was, and is today, a language that you can learn without having a strong technical or scientific background. BASIC is the most popular language used for microcomputers. Any computer language that a human can understand easily,

Comparison →

English	BASIC	Machine Language
Add two numbers.	LET X = A + B	10101101 . . .

English → BASIC → Machine Language

such as BASIC, is called a *high-level language*. Many other high-level computer languages have been developed. You can learn a little about Logo, Pascal, and others in the Computer Language features at the end of each chapter of this book.

Source: D. Myers, V. Elswick, P. Hopfensperger, and J. Pavlovich: *Computer Programming in Basic* (Boston: Houghton Mifflin Company, 1986), p. 8.

Students can learn home economics content more effectively with teacher assistance through strategies that include guided reading lessons, study guides, and preview guides. Study guides have proven to be valuable aids to comprehension and have, in fact, been requested by students. Dorothy Szymkowicz found that students learn best when they receive guided reading instruction.[28] Included in this section are examples of home economics content and sample teaching strategies.

Home economics content includes many technical terms: for example, *saute*, *parboil*, *top sirloin*, *topstitch*, and *French seam*. Example 7.13 presents a selection from a home economics textbook. Notice that the reader must understand the following terms: *warm-colored*, *cool-colored*, *color wheel*, *primary*, *secondary*, *monochromatic*, *analogous*, *complementary*, *tints*, and *shades*. The study guide that follows the selection will help students check their understanding of these terms and of the content.

EXAMPLE 7.13   HOME ECONOMICS CONTENT AND STUDY GUIDE ─

Colors

As you glance around the room, what things catch your eye first? Doesn't the bright red shirt catch your eye before the pale blue shirt nearby? Do you see the bright orange books on the shelf before you notice the green ones? Do the warm-colored objects seem to be closer and larger than the cool-colored objects? What does this tell you about the effect colors give when you wear them? The warm colors will cause you to be noticed. They will help you to feel cheerful, and they may make you appear larger than you are. The cool colors will cause you to blend into a group. They will help you to feel calm and will make you appear smaller than you really are.

Look at the color wheel on page 265. Pick out the *primary* colors of red, yellow, and blue. Colors made by combining two primary colors in equal amounts are called *secondary* colors. Orange, green, and violet are secondary colors. Each one appears on the color wheel between the two primary colors it is made from. All other colors are made from combinations of the primary and secondary colors. As you look at the wheel, you can see how red shades into red-violet, violet, and blue-violet as it moves toward blue. On the other side, red moves into red-orange and orange as it moves toward yellow.

Any three colors that are equally distant from each other on the color wheel form a triad. Red, yellow, and blue make up a triad, so do green, orange, and violet. What are some others?

A color scheme built around one color and its various values and intensities is called *monochromatic.* For example, the red-blue colors combined as plum, lilac, and pink can be worn together for a rich monochromatic effect.

Colors appearing next to each other on the color wheel and sharing a common hue are called *analogous,* or related, colors. Such colors as yellow, yellow-green, and green are analogous and can be combined to make an interesting color scheme.

Those colors directly opposite each other on the color wheel are called *complementary* colors. This means that if these color pigments are mixed together, they will produce gray, or will neutralize each other. They are opposites, or complements. When placed next to each other, each makes the other look brighter. Thus, green and red look much brighter when they appear together than when each color is used separately. Worn together in full strength, they can be too bright and distracting. However, when used in *tints* (lighter values of a color) and *shades* (darker values of a color), they can be pleasing.

Source: Reprinted from TEEN GUIDE TO HOMEMAKING by J. Brinkley and V. Chamberlain, with permission of Webster/McGraw-Hill.

Study Guide

Introduction

This selection discusses the characteristics of color, including the relationships among colors. These relationships include primary colors, secondary colors, triads, complementary colors, and analogous colors. Included are discussions of the ways color can fool the eyes and the effect color has on emotions.

Vocabulary

Find an example for each of the following terms:

primary color	tint
secondary color	shades
triad	monochromatic
analogous colors	complementary colors

Levels of Comprehension

Directions: Place a + beside each statement that is supported by the reading selection and a − beside each item that is not supported by the selection.

Literal

_____ 1. Warm colors make you feel calm.

_____ 2. A color scheme built around one color is monochromatic.

_____ 3. Complementary colors can neutralize each other.

_____ 4. Wearing green and red together has a soothing effect on the wearer.

_____ 5. All secondary colors are made by combining primary colors.

Interpretive

_____ 6. Emergency vehicles are often painted bright colors so they will attract attention.

_____ 7. Color harmony is created by pleasing combinations of color.

_____ 8. Special effects in decorating can be created by individuals who understand the effect that colors have on people.

———— 9. There are no set rules for creating color harmony.

———— 10. Large areas in the home should be covered with the color red.

———— 11. If we block off any color in the spectrum, the remaining colors form its complement.

Directions: Write short answers for the following questions.

Applied

12. Identify three ways in which you can use the ideas in this article for interior decorating.
13. What are your best colors? Why?
14. What color relationship is formed by your school colors?

————————————

Home economics students need to learn to read diagrams, patterns, drawings, graphs, and charts. They must be able to visualize the finished product of a pattern or of a floor plan and to read mathematical symbols and legends to understand the graphics. Example 7.14 shows a table from a home economics textbook and sample questions that might be used when a table such as this is presented. (Refer to Chapter 4 for the steps to use in reading tables.) Note that there are several levels of headings under the main headings of the table. Students must be able to read complicated, categorized material. Students must know how to use the different units of measure used for the nutrients, and they need to be able to read numbers expressed in decimals.

Home economics students should know how to interpret labels for specific information: for example, the labels on foods, fabrics, and cleaning products that tell exactly how much of the item is contained in the package. They must be able to determine from a label whether a certain product is suitable for their needs. When planning a special diet, the students may have to locate information about the amount of carbohydrates, fats, proteins, and other nutrients contained in a food. Example 7.15 is an illustration of label information.

Reading and applying directions are also important aspects of the study of home economics. The range and number of prepackaged products has expanded so greatly that we may be living in "the age of directions."[29] Today there are very few commodities without some type of directions attached: clothing has labels that provide washing and cleaning instructions, and food wrappers carry directions for preparation.

The directions used in home economics study and in prepackaged products for the home include technical vocabulary words that must be understood. Additionally, following directions precisely and in the proper sequence is necessary for achieving the desired outcome. Some directions are written very concisely and may omit words that are assumed to be understood. Directions require slow, precise, and careful readings. Unfortunately, many people tend to become overconfident when they see short and concise directions; this attitude seems to be a common failing and can lead to limited understanding.[30] Note the sequence and technical words in the directions in Example 7.16, taken from a home

EXAMPLE 7.14   HOME ECONOMICS TABLE AND QUESTIONS

FOOD COMPOSITION CHARTS

	Caloric Information				Nutritive Values								% U.S. RDA										
Milk	Calories	% Cal. from Protein	% Cal. from Carbohydrate	% Cal. from Fat	Protein g	Vitamin A IU	Vitamin C mg	Thiamin (B₁) mg	Riboflavin (B₂) mg	Niacin mg	Calcium mg	Iron mg	Calories G, 11-14	Calories G, 15-18	Calories W, 23-50	Protein	Vitamin A	Vitamin C	Thiamin (B₁)	Riboflavin (B₂)	Niacin	Calcium	Iron
Buttermilk, 1 cup (245 g)	88	43	55	2	8.8	Trace	2	0.10	0.44	0.2	296	Trace	4	4	4	20	—	3	7	26	1.0	30	—
Cheese, American, 1 ounce (28 g)	104	25	6	69	6.02	236	—	—	0.10	—	172	—	4	5	5	14	5	—	—	6	—	17	—
Cheese, Cheddar, 1 ounce (28 g)	113	26	2	72	6.9	237	1	0.01	0.1	0.1	202	0.1	5	5	6	15	5	1.6	0.6	6	0.5	20	0.6
Cheese, Cheddar, 1¼ ounce (35 g)	141	26	2	72	8.7	296	1	0.01	0.13	0.1	252	0.1	6	7	7	19	6	2	0.8	8	0.5	25	0.8
Cheese, Cottage, ½ cup (113 g)	120	55	11	35	15.4	192	0	0.03	0.28	0.1	106	0.3	5	6	6	34	4	0	2	16	0.5	11	1.7
Cheese, Swiss, 1 ounce (28 g)	103	33	2	66	8.0	206	—	—	0.09	—	268	—	4	5	5	18	4	—	—	5	—	27	--
Cocoa, ¼ cup (188 g)	182	13	34	41	7.1	300	2	0.08	0.34	0.4	221	0.8	8	9	9	16	6	3	5	20	2	22	4
Cream, Sour, 1 tablespoon (12 g)	25	14	15	70	Trace	100	Trace	Trace	0.02	Trace	12	Trace	1.0	1.2	1.3	—	2	—	—	1.2	—	1.2	—
Cream, Whipped, 1 tablespoon (8 g)	26	3	3	95	0.2	116	Trace	Trace	0.01	Trace	6	Trace	1.1	1.2	1.3	0.4	2	—	—	0.6	—	0.6	—
Half-and-Half, 1 tablespoon (15 g)	20	11	14	79	0.5	72	Trace	0.01	0.02	Trace	16	Trace	0.8	1.0	1.0	1.1	1.4	—	0.7	1.2	—	1.6	—
Ice Cream, Vanilla, ½ cup, ¼ pint (66 g)	138	8	38	53	2.7	346	1	0.03	0.13	0.1	82	0.1	6	7	7	6	7	1.7	2	8	0.5	8	0.6
Milk, 1 cup (244 g)	145	22	30	48	7.3	250	4	0.10	0.48	0.2	304	0.1	6	7	7	16	5	4	7	28	1.2	30	0.7
Milk, ¾ cup (183 g)	109	22	30	48	5.5	188	3	0.08	0.36	0.2	228	0.1	5	5	5	12	8	3	5	21	0.9	23	0.5
Milk, Chocolate, 1 cup (250 g)	213	17	50	35	8.5	325	3	0.08	0.40	0.3	278	0.5	9	10	11	19	7	5	5	24	1.5	28	3
Milk, Lowfat (2%), 1 cup (244 g) fortified with vitamin A	118	26	37	37	7.3	500		0.10	0.48	0.2	304	0.1	5	6	6	20	10	4	7	28	1.2	30	0.7
Milk, Skim, 1 cup (244 g) fortified with vitamin A	77	40	57	3	7.3	500	4	0.10	0.48	0.2	304	0.1	3	4	4	16	10	4	7	28	1.2	30	0.7
Milkshake, Chocolate, 1½ cups (349 g)	391	13	47	38	12.1	688	3	0.11	0.56	0.5	376	0.7	16	19	20	27	14	5	7	33	3	38	4
Yogurt, Strawberry, 1 cup (227 g)	225	17	72	9	92	90	5	0.07	0.4	0.22	290	0.2	9	11	11	20	1.8	8	5	24	1.1	29	1.1

Source: Reprinted from TEEN GUIDE TO HOMEMAKING by J. Brinkley and V. Chamberlain, with permission of Webster/McGraw-Hill.

Questions

1. What is the subject covered by this table?
2. How many calories from protein are found in a one-ounce serving of Swiss cheese?
3. How much iron is contained in one cup of skim milk?
4. What milk product has the largest amount of vitamin C?
5. How can you use the information in this table for meal planning?

EXAMPLE 7.15   FOOD LABEL INFORMATION ——————

NUTRITION INFORMATION
(PER SERVING)
SERVING SIZE = 1 OZ.
SERVINGS PER CONTAINER = 12

CALORIES	110
PROTEIN	2 GRAMS
CARBOHYDRATE	24 GRAMS
FAT	0 GRAM

PERCENTAGE OF U.S. RECOMMENDED DAILY ALLOWANCES (U.S.RDA)*

PROTEIN	2
THIAMINE	8
NIACIN	2

*Contains less than 2 percent of U.S. RDA for Vitamin A, Vitamin C, Riboflavin, Calcium, and Iron.

This is the minimum information that must appear on a nutrition label.

NUTRITION INFORMATION
(PER SERVING)
SERVING SIZE = 8 OZ.
SERVINGS PER CONTAINER = 1

CALORIES	560
PROTEIN	23 G
CARBOHYDRATE	43 G
FAT (PERCENT OF CALORIES 53%)	33 G
POLYUNSAT-URATED*	2 G
SATURATED	9 G
CHOLESTEROL* (20 MG/100 G)	40 G
SODIUM (365 MG/ 100 G)	830 M

PERCENTAGE OF U.S. RECOMMENDED DAILY ALLOWANCES (U.S. RDA)

PROTEIN	35
VITAMIN A	35
VITAMIN C (ASCORBIC ACID)	10
THIAMINE (VITAMIN B₁)	15
RIBOFLAVIN	15
NIACIN	25
CALCIUM	2
IRON	25

*Information on fat and cholesterol content is provided for individuals who, on the advice of a physician, are modifying their total dietary intake of fat and cholesterol.

A label may include optional listings for cholesterol, fats, and sodium.

Source: Reprinted from TEEN GUIDE TO HOMEMAKING by J. Brinkley and V. Chamberlain, with permission of Webster/McGraw-Hill.

economics textbook. Teachers can prepare students for reading the directions in home economics textbooks through directed reading lessons, study guides, and other instructional strategies. However, although students can learn strategies for reading directions in practice exercises, they must also be given opportunities to apply these strategies to actual content.

EXAMPLE 7.16   DIRECTIONS IN A HOME ECONOMICS TEXTBOOK —

Prepare the Pattern and Fabric for Cutting

Regardless of what you are making, you will follow the same general procedure in cutting out a garment. If you followed the plan in Book I, and made the suggested projects, you have already gone through the steps at least five or six times. By now you should be thoroughly familiar with them and be able to proceed automatically.

Check body measurements with your pattern and, if necessary, make pattern alterations.

Prepare fabric for grain perfection.

Check fabric carefully for one-way, match, diagonal, or any other feature that must be taken into consideration for correct cutting.

Pin pattern pieces to fabric according to cutting layout on the instruction sheet.

Cut out.

Transfer pattern markings to the fabric.

Source: Reprinted from HOMEMAKING FOR TEENAGERS, Book 2, Copyright 1972, by Irene McDermott, Jeanne L. Norris, and Florence Nicholas. Used with permission of the publisher, Bennett Publishing Company, Peoria, IL 61615. All rights reserved.

Home economics students must be able to read critically—for example, to evaluate a recipe for use. They must be able to compare and contrast the information provided regarding various products to determine which is most appropriate for their needs. The homemaker must read and evaluate information regarding sewing techniques or cooking procedures to determine which technique will make the work easier. New equipment that appears on the market must be evaluated for efficiency and cost: one must determine whether the cost of such equipment is worth the advantages it offers. One new piece of equipment that many homemakers have been evaluating is the microwave oven.

The home economics student reads newspapers, magazines, sewing books, and cookbooks. These materials frequently must be read in the same way reference books are read. The student should use the index to locate information, scan the text for the needed information, and read for details. The instructional strategies used by content teachers should direct students toward developing these skills.

Agriculture

Agriculture is a complex subject involving such diverse disciplines as science and mathematics. Science is involved when agriculture students learn about the care and feeding of livestock, as well as when they learn about planting and cultivating crops. Prospective farmers must also know mathematics for budgeting and accounting purposes. Management plays a pivotal role in the study of agriculture since farms are businesses. Because farming is mechanized, prospective farmers must develop some mechanical skills. In addition, conservation of natural resources is a significant aspect of agricultural study.

Students who study agriculture will read materials in the areas of science, mathematics, social science, geology, and auto mechanics. This wide variety of reading content creates a very real challenge for students: each of these content areas involves technical vocabulary and characteristic patterns of organizing content. These patterns include cause and effect, problem solving, comparison, experiment, directions, and chronological order. In addition, authors of agricultural content often use graphs, charts, diagrams, and pictures, which students must be able to interpret. Following are examples of agricultural content. Example 7.17 shows scientific content, and Example 7.18 shows content related to mathematics use. Example 7.19 shows a mapping activity based on the content in Example 7.17.

EXAMPLE 7.17   SCIENTIFIC CONTENT

What Are the Causes of Diseases Among Farm Animals?

A *disease* is considered in a broad sense to be any disorder of the body. (When the word is analyzed, it really means "lack of ease," which is probably its original meaning.)

Improper Feeding as a Cause of Diseases

Some diseases are caused entirely by improper feeding methods. The disease called *rickets,* in which the bones of an animal fail to develop properly, is due to improper amounts of certain minerals and vitamins. Young animals are sometimes born with enlargements in the throat region. This ailment, which is known as *goitre,* or "big neck," is caused by insufficient amounts of iodine in the ration of the mother animals during the period previous to the birth of the young. *Colic* in horses and *bloat* in cattle and sheep are usually caused by improper methods of feeding.

Animals may be poisoned by lead, which they can get through licking paint pails or freshly painted surfaces. They may also consume feeds that have a poisonous effect on their bodies. Poisonous weeds such as loco weed and white snakeroot are examples. The latter weed, if eaten by dairy cows, may injure not only the cows themselves but also the people who drink the cows' milk. Halogeton is a weed that has spread rapidly in semidesert areas; at times, it has caused the death of many sheep in some western states. Other plants that have a poisonous effect on livestock are alsike clover, when eaten wet; bouncing Bet, cocklebur, and corn cockle roadside plants; bracken fern, found in dry and abandoned fields; buttercup, when eaten green; larkspur; ergot; horse nettle; jimson weed; Johnson grass; nightshade; hemlock; milkweed; and wild cherry.

Ornamental plants toxic to goats include oleander, azalea, castorbean, buttercup, rhododendron, philodendron, yew, English ivy, chokeberry, laurel, daffodil, jonquil, and many members of the lily family. Even tomatoes, potatoes, rhubarb, and avocadoes contain toxic substances. Goats may also be harmed by toadstools, mushrooms, mistletoe, and milkweed.

Source: Alfred H. Krebs: *Agriculture in Our Lives,* 5th ed. (Danville, Ill.: The Interstate Printers and Publishers, Inc., 1984), p. 405.

EXAMPLE 7.18   CONTENT RELATED TO MATHEMATICS USE

Keeping Records for a Farm Business

In keeping farm business records, a farmer should select a good type of record book to use. Most state colleges of agriculture have developed farm record books that are quite easy to keep. Usually, directions are provided for keeping and summarizing these records. These record books may usually be purchased for a small sum from the state agricultural college or the county agricultural agent; or the high school agriculture teacher will help a farmer secure one. The most suitable record books provide for (1) figuring depreciation on machinery, buildings, and equipment; (2) making opening and closing inventories; (3) recording expenses and income; and (4) other items.

Some farmers obtain help in keeping and using records by attending adult-farmer classes sponsored by high school departments of vocational agriculture. Some join with other farmers in a farm record association and cooperatively employ a field supervisor who helps each farmer-member keep records and use them in improving the farm business.

Source: Alfred H. Krebs: *Agriculture in Our Lives,* 5th ed. (Danville, Ill.: The Interstate Printers and Publishers, Inc., 1984), p. 694.

Physical Education

Physical education is a popular area of study today, due to the increased amount of leisure time available to Americans. Also, the growing national interest in physical fitness has created a surge of interest in physical education in the schools. The content of physical education studies can be used to motivate reluctant

EXAMPLE 7.19   MAPPING ACTIVITY FOR CAUSE AND EFFECT IN AGRICULTURAL CONTENT ───────

IMPROPER FEEDING CAUSES DISEASE

Causes	Effects
Lack of iodine	goitre
Improper feeding methods	colic bloat
lead weeds ornamental plants	toxic (poison)

───────

readers; students who may not be interested in reading other materials often willingly read physical education materials.

Reading serves four purposes in physical education:

1. Physical education topics can motivate students to read, and reading can motivate students to become involved in athletics.
2. Students can learn game rules and signals by reading.
3. Reading can be used to increase and refine skills.
4. Reading can increase understanding of a sport and thus can increase the spectators' pleasure.

Physical education is frequently taught without textbooks, but students need reading skills even when they do not have textbooks. Students have to be able to read the rules and directions for playing games. Also, they may read books and magazines to improve techniques in various sports. For example, there are many books and magazine articles available to help people improve their golf swings and tennis strokes.

Reading physical education material requires a number of reading skills. There is extensive specialized vocabulary in this reading content. Each sport has a separate set of terms to be learned. (For example, *love, touchdown, foul,* and *guard.*) Notice that the word *love* from tennis and the terms *foul* and *guard,* which apply to several sports, are multiple-meaning terms for which students have other meanings in their everyday vocabularies.

The team and individual sports taught in physical education classes utilize much special equipment. In order to learn the names and functions of the various pieces of equipment, the students could illustrate each piece of equipment, label it, and describe its function. A notebook could be maintained for this purpose, with the equipment for each sport categorized and alphabetized.

Teachers may wish to develop inventories of terminology related to each sport studied. These inventories can be used both as preparation to introduce the sport and, after study, as a means to review students' understanding. Students may be asked to supply synonyms or to define terms in their own words and may develop an illustrated dictionary of sports terms. Following are examples of inventories of sports terms.

EXAMPLE 7.20   SPORTS TERM INVENTORIES

Directions: Define the following terms in your own words.

Tennis	*Basketball*
racket	dribble
backhand	field goal
forehand	foul
love	free throw
serve	jump ball
net	pass
game point	pivot
deuce	press
match	rebound
fault	shoot
double fault	traveling
volley	violation
lob	backboard
slice	division line
chop	restraining circle
overhead smash	basket

Example 7.21 shows a referee's hand signals. The reader of these diagrams has to translate the stick-figure drawings into actual actions, and he or she must associate the signal with its name and the rule it represents. This is a rather complex reading task. A study guide or directed reading lesson would help the reader in this situation.

High school physical education students can increase their understanding of content by writing game rules, directions, and suggestions for younger children. They may refine these materials and actually use them to teach games to elementary school children. They may choose to illustrate their written directions.

The teacher can help students develop critical reading skills by asking them to evaluate the strategies and/or equipment suggested by different authors. This is a good thinking activity, since different authors may suggest widely different approaches to a sport.

Reading can increase the enjoyment of spectator sports. As students read to learn more about the finer points of soccer, hockey, and professional football, they can increase their pleasure in watching these games.

EXAMPLE 7.21   DIAGRAM OF REFEREE'S HAND SIGNALS

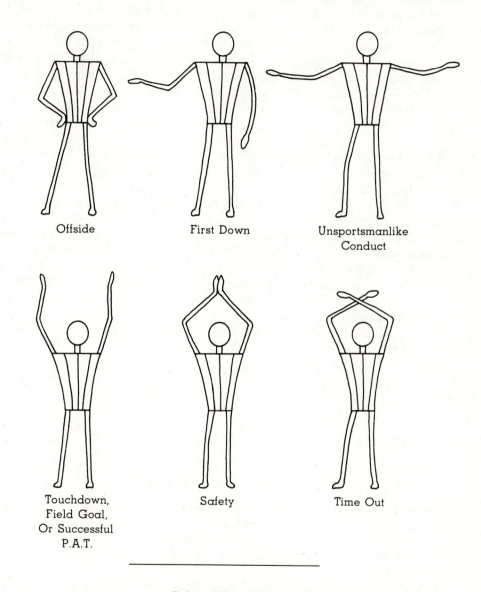

| Offside | First Down | Unsportsmanlike Conduct |

| Touchdown, Field Goal, Or Successful P.A.T. | Safety | Time Out |

Driver Education

Driver education classes are provided for secondary students to prepare them to drive safely, carefully, and effectively. Driver education courses usually include a section of theory that is taught with a textbook; this is followed by practical application of driving skills and actual driving practice. Most young people look forward with great anticipation to acquiring a driver's license, because a driver's license is one of the symbols of becoming an adult. For modern American teenagers, learning how to drive is a rite of passage into adulthood. Since driving is a very significant skill for young people, reading driver education content and related materials is very important for secondary students.

Readers of driver education content utilize skills similar to those needed for the other content areas. They must be able to interpret the following types of content: technical vocabulary, cause-and-effect relationships, directions, inferences, comparisons, pictures, diagrams, symbols, and mathematical material. In addition, readers must be able to read at the literal, interpretive, and critical levels. They must be able to visualize what they are reading so that they can translate words into action as they move from the textbook to actual driving practice.

Understanding the technical vocabulary used in driver education materials is essential to understanding the content and translating the content into action. The technical vocabulary of such materials usually represents concrete concepts relating to driving skill and automotive equipment. The student who has had little or no experience with an automobile is at a disadvantage because he or she has had no experience with the concepts represented by the words. This problem can be overcome by showing the student the object or process represented by the terms. Following are examples of the technical words found in driver education materials: *crosswalk, oversteering, intersection, collision, accelerator, right-of-way, regulatory signs, vehicle malfunction,* and *gauges.* (Refer to Chapter 2 for vocabulary teaching suggestions.)

In addition to the technical terms in driver education materials, the reader must be familiar with the writing patterns used to organize the content. Cause-and-effect writing is often used in helping the reader understand how to operate a vehicle. Example 7.22 provides a sample of cause-and-effect writing from a driver education textbook.

EXAMPLE 7.22 DRIVER EDUCATION CONTENT

Your Feelings and the Driving Task

Changes in the way you feel can affect the way you drive. Strong emotional feelings, such as joy or anger, can "blind" you and make you less alert. If your mind isn't alert, it can't do a good job. And if you fail to see problems, you won't be able to predict, decide, or execute. The driving task requires that your mind and body work together.

Drivers who feel great anger or sadness may act in ways they would not if all were well. If they're very angry or if they resent something that has happened, they may drive carelessly. Or if they're worried about being late, they may take chances they would not otherwise take.

Source: Jay Davis, Donn Maryott, and Warren Stiska: *In the Driver's Seat*, p. 22. Copyright © 1978 by Houghton Mifflin Company. Used by permission.

To comprehend written material, readers must be able to follow the author's organizational patterns. Activities like the following can be incorporated into driver education study guides.

Activities

1. Have students make a diagram of causes and effects. The following are based on the text in Example 7.22:

Causes	Effects
joy or anger	becomes "blind," less alert
lack of alertness	fails to predict, decide, execute
anger	becomes careless
worry about being late	takes chances

2. State the effects and ask students to identify the causes, as in this example:
   a. Cause: _____
      Effect: becomes careless
   b. Cause: _____
      Effect: takes chances

Another way that authors organize content in driver education materials is through directions. The passage in Example 7.23, taken from a driver education textbook, requires the student to read a set of directions in sequence. He or she must be able to translate these directions into action.

EXAMPLE 7.23   DIRECTIONS IN A DRIVER EDUCATION TEXTBOOK ▬

How to Change a Flat Tire

Every owner's manual has instructions for changing a tire. Advice on how to use the jack that comes with the car is often attached to the lid of the trunk. Before you have an emergency, practice changing a wheel in your driveway.

Never change a tire on the traveled portion of the road. Drive to a level place on solid ground well off the pavement. If you cannot pull off to a safe place, keep on driving with your flashers on until you can find such a place. Ruining a tire is better than being hit by a passing car.

Get all the passengers out of the car and follow the basic steps listed below:

1. Set the parking brake and put the gear-selector lever in PARK (in REVERSE for a manual-shift car.) Block the wheel diagonally opposite the flat. A block of wood or a large stone will do.
2. Remove the jack and spare tire from the trunk. Using the flat end of the lug wrench, pry off the wheel cover and place it near the flat.
3. Loosen each lug nut slightly about one turn.

4. Jack up the car until the flat is well clear of the ground. Make sure that the jack is straight and will not slip. Bumper jacks tend to be unstable.

5. Remove lug nuts and place them in the wheel cover where you can easily find them.

6. Pull off the flat tire and mount the spare. If necessary, use the lug wrench as a lever to help lift the wheel to the axle.

7. Replace the lug nuts. First tighten two opposite nuts firmly with your fingers to position the wheel correctly. Then tighten the remaining nuts with your fingers. Finally, lower the car until the wheel just touches the ground and tighten all lug nuts as securely as you can—first one and then the one opposite it.

8. Finish lowering the car and remove the jack. Do not replace the wheel cover. Put it in the trunk. Each time you see that wheel without its cover, you will be reminded to get the flat fixed. Driving without a spare is courting trouble.

Source: Jay Davis, Donn Maryott, and Warren Stiska: *In the Driver's Seat*, pp. 252–253. Copyright © 1978 by Houghton Mifflin Company. Used by permission.

Following are some strategies for teaching students to read directions in driver education materials. These activities can be incorporated into driver education study guides.

Activities

1. Present students with a set of directions from which a step has been omitted. Ask students to fill in the missing step. For example:
   a. Loosen each lug nut slightly.
   b. _____
   c. Remove lug nuts and place them in the wheel cover.

2. Give students a set of scrambled directions to put in the proper sequence. For example:
   Directions: Number in the correct order the following steps for changing a flat tire.
   ( ) Set the parking brake, and block the wheel opposite the flat.
   ( ) Jack up the car.
   ( ) Remove lug nuts.
   ( ) Remove the jack and spare tire from the trunk and pry off the wheel cover.
   ( ) Loosen each lug nut.
   ( ) Finish lowering the car and remove the jack.
   ( ) Replace the lug nuts.
   ( ) Pull off the flat tire and mount the spare.

In addition to reading organizational patterns, readers of driver education materials frequently must identify main ideas and details in order to understand the content. (Chapter 3 suggests a number of ways to help students read for main ideas and details.)

The content of driver education materials and the actual driving process both require the student to make predictions based upon inferences and comparisons. Observing traffic conditions and signs enables the driver to predict the road conditions he or she will encounter. Also, the driver can relate present conditions to past driving experiences in order to predict how to react to particular traffic situations. The reader must be able to make inferences and comparisons that are based on written information. Following is an example of a worksheet that teachers can use for helping their students develop skill in making predictions.

EXAMPLE 7.24 INFERENCE AND COMPARISON WORKSHEET (DRIVER EDUCATION) ———————————

1. *Inferences:* Inferences enable the driver to decide on appropriate actions. Read the following question and then answer it: if you are driving an automobile that is traveling at 45 miles per hour and you encounter a sign indicating a sharp curve with a sign below it saying 35 M.P.H., what inference should you make?

2. *Comparison:* It will help you as a driver to compare present conditions with previous experience. Read and answer the following comparison questions.
   a. How does driving a truck compare with driving an automobile?
   b. If you were driving through a snowstorm, what comparisons could you make that would help you decide how to drive?
   c. If you see a horse running toward the road, what should you do? What previous experiences can help you make your decision?

———————————

Readers of driver education materials and drivers both must be able to identify traffic signs. The excerpt from a driver education textbook in Example 7.25 shows a number of the most common traffic signs. The questions that follow can be used to ensure that the students understand the meanings of the road signs.

The reader of traffic signs should learn to identify them by color, size, and shape. Flash cards that show the various traffic signs are useful in helping students memorize these signs.

Driver education textbooks also include diagrams to help students understand various driving situations and related information. Example 7.26 shows a representative diagram from a driver education textbook.

The teacher can help students understand diagrams of driving situations by using these steps:

1. Give students diagrams of a stretch of road and a written description of a driving maneuver. Students should draw the vehicle in each of the major positions needed to complete the maneuver.
2. Give students a complete diagram and ask them to write the directions for completing the maneuver.

EXAMPLE 7.25 COMMON TRAFFIC SIGNS AND QUESTIONS

Symbolic Warning Signs

This group of signs uses both symbolic and written messages to warn drivers of hazards ahead.

HILL

SLIPPERY WHEN WET

FARM MACHINERY

CATTLE XING

PED XING

BIKE XING

DEER XING

R R

NO PASSING ZONE

Railroad Sign and
No Passing Pennant

These two signs are exceptions to the rule that warning signs are diamond-shaped. They warn drivers of railroad crossings and no-passing zones.

EXIT 25 M.P.H.

RAMP 30 M.P.H.

35 M.P.H.

Advisory Speed Signs

These signs recommend safe speeds in hazardous areas.

Source: Jay Davis, Donn Maryott, and Warren Stiska: *In the Driver's Seat*, p. 65. Copyright © 1978 by Houghton Mifflin Company. Used by permission.

Questions

1. Is a curve indicated by any of the signs? If so, draw a picture of the sign.
2. What is the meaning of the sign that has only a person pictured on it?
3. Which signs are concerned with animals?
4. Which signs indicate safe speeds in hazardous areas?

EXAMPLE 7.26   DRIVER EDUCATION DIAGRAM —————————

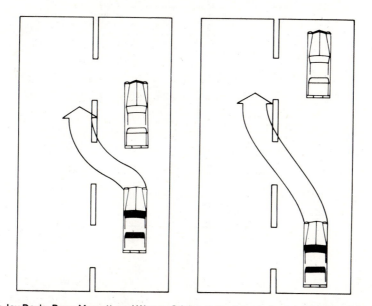

Source: Jay Davis, Donn Maryott, and Warren Stiska: *In the Driver's Seat*, p. 207. Copyright © 1978 by Houghton Mifflin Company. Used by permission.

Students must also be able to read and compute mathematical material in order to understand driver education content. Example 7.27 shows the type of mathematical skills required by driver education materials.

The teacher may help students use a diagram like the one in Example 7.27 in the following ways:

1. Ask students to explain the main idea of the chart.
2. Ask students to explain the significance of the information.
3. Ask students to explain how to apply this information to actual driving situations.
4. Ask students to state the stopping distance of snow tires on glare ice.

EXAMPLE 7.27   MATHEMATICS IN A DRIVER EDUCATION BOOK ——

STOPPING DISTANCES ON GLARE ICE AND ON LOOSELY PACKED SNOW

On glare ice at 25°F (about −4°C)

conventional tires ▭ 149 feet (about 45.4 m)

snow tires ▭ 151 feet (about 46 m)

studded tires
(front only, new) ▭ 120 feet (about 36.6 m)

studded tires
(front & rear, new) ▭ 103 feet (about 31.4 m)

chains ▭ 75 feet (about 22.9 m)

On loosely packed snow

conventional tires ▭ 60 feet (about 18.3 m)

snow tires ▭ 52 feet (about 15.9 m)

chains ▭ 38 feet (about 11.6 m)

In feet from 20 mph, not including reaction time.
Source: Nat'l Safety Council's Committee On Winter Driving Hazards

Source: Jay Davis, Donn Maryott, and Warren Stiska: *In the Driver's Seat*, p. 246. Copyright © 1978 by
Houghton Mifflin Company. Used by permission.

Teachers of driver education should encourage students to think at the literal, interpretive, and critical levels of reasoning. (Refer to Chapter 3 for a discussion of these levels.)

Art

Art students use and study the media of artistic expression more frequently than they use and study textbooks. The study of art does not involve as much textbook reading as many other content areas, and fewer textbooks are available in this subject area than in other areas. Nevertheless, art students need to have well-developed reading skills because they read many types of written content for a variety of purposes.[31] For example, they read to acquire information about artistic techniques, art history, and the lives of important artists. Following is a summary of the reading skills art students commonly use.

1. Reading for information. Art students often read about exhibitions, artists, and techniques. They read to identify art styles or movements. Reading for information involves identifying main ideas and supporting details.

2. Reading to follow directions. Art students must read and follow steps in sequential order. This kind of reading would occur when they read about such things as new media and new techniques or how to make a woodcut.
3. Reading to interpret charts and diagrams such as a color wheel. For example, art students may need to find complementary colors.
4. Reading critically. The art student uses this skill when evaluating reviews of art shows or the impact of a medium or a style.
5. Reading to implement information or directions acquired from reading. After reading about a particular medium, an art student may experiment with the medium or style.
6. Reading and organizing information for reports. Art students may be required to write a report on the life of an artist, a style of art, or ways of interpreting moods and feelings in art. This reading task requires that the reader identify main ideas and details.
7. Reading technical vocabulary related to art. This vocabulary includes words like *linear, hue,* and *perspective.*
8. Reading such materials as reference books, art history books, biographies, and magazines. The art student reads magazines like *Arts and Activities, School Arts, Popular Photography, and Craft Horizons* to obtain current information and ideas.

Study guides, preview guides, and vocabulary activities are particularly helpful to art students. In addition, many of the strategies presented in Chapters 2, 3, and 6 can be used to help art students develop appropriate reading skills. Examples of art reading activities follow. These activities include a vocabulary activity, a preview guide, and a study guide.

Activity: Art Vocabulary Game
Objective: To provide practice in associating words with colors.
Materials Needed: Set of cards with hues (as listed below), set of cards with color words

vermilion	cinnamon	burgundy
cerise	ocher	ecru
puce	sepia	ivory
indigo	magenta	

Directions for Activity: This game is one in which a student accumulates "books" (sets of two) of matching cards (color card plus hue card). The regular rules of a card game may be used. (This activity can be played by two or more people. The person who matches the most cards correctly within a specified period of time wins.)

Example 7.28 includes material from a textbook used for teaching art. As you read this brief selection, note the many technical words and expressions used (for example, *linear perspective, diminishing contrasts, hue, value, intensity of color, texture, achieve deep penetration, two-dimensional surface, infinite concept, at-mospheric perspective, pictorial composition, theme, picture plane, volume of deep space, softening edges of objects, scale,* and *middle ground*). Following the selection are two reading guides that are based on the passage.

EXAMPLE 7.28 ART CONTENT AND READING GUIDES ───────

Problem 1

In conjunction with linear perspective, artists of the past frequently used diminishing contrasts of hue, value, and intensity of color and texture to achieve deep penetration of space on a two-dimensional surface. This is known as the infinite concept of space or atmospheric perspective.

Create a pictorial composition based on the theme "Objects in Space." Conceive of the picture plane as the near side of a volume of deep space. Use the indications of space suggested in the opening paragraph, plus softening edges of objects as they are set back in depth. The human figure may be used to help suggest the scale of objects in space. Foreground, middle ground, and deep space may be indicated by the size of similar objects.

Source: Otto Ocvirk, Robert Bone, Robert Stinson, and Philip Wigg, *Art Fundamentals: Theory and Practice* (Dubuque, Iowa: William C. Brown Company, 1975), p. 114.

Preview Guide

Directions: Check *Yes* if you believe the reading selection supports the statement; check *No* if you believe the selection does not support the statement.

Yes　　No

_____ _____ 1. The infinite concept of space and atmospheric perspective are the same thing.

_____ _____ 2. Artists of the past used diminishing contrasts of hue, value, and intensity of color to achieve atmospheric perspective.

_____ _____ 3. Students should conceive of the picture plane as the far side of a volume of deep space.

_____ _____ 4. Trees are used to suggest scale.

Study Guide

Introduction

This selection poses a problem for art students to solve. If you have questions after you have read the problem, refer to books and articles in the bibliography on linear perspective.

Vocabulary

Provide an example for each of the following words: linear perspective, diminishing contrasts, hue, value, intensity, texture, two-dimensional surface, infinite concept, atmospheric perspective, pictorial composition, theme, picture plane.

Levels of Comprehension

Directions: Write a short answer to each question.

Literal
1. What does this selection ask you to do?
2. What concept is explained in the first paragraph?
3. What is the theme of the pictorial composition that the student is to create?

Interpretive
4. Why does the author suggest that a human figure may be used to suggest scale?
5. Will color play an important role in this composition?
6. What similar objects might be used to indicate foreground, middle ground, and deep space?

Applied
7. What materials will you need to complete this problem?
8. Can you create another composition that has the same title but uses a different object to show scale? If so, what could you use?

Music

Music students also generally have special interests and talents. According to Frank Tirro, "Music theory texts are almost in a class unto themselves. Very similar to an algebra text or a geometry problem book where each letter, number, and sign must be carefully considered, tasted, chewed, swallowed, and rechewed like a cow's cud."[32] Tirro points out that one does not read a music theory book; one grapples and struggles with it.[33]

To help secondary students with the task of reading music books, teachers may use the following strategies:

1. Anticipate students' problems before they read. Standardized reading tests and teacher-made inventories can provide data regarding students' reading skills. Observation of students' performance in reading music is very helpful.
2. Teach necessary vocabulary before students read a selection.
3. Develop and use illustrated dictionaries of musical terms.
4. Teach students how to study and prepare assignments. (See Chapter 3.) Demonstrating these techniques with music content can be helpful.

5. Use strategies such as study guides, directed reading lessons, structured over-views, preview guides, and vocabulary study to help students read and understand music content.

Music instruction often requires a high level of reading ability, including knowledge of notes, lyrics, and music theory. Students must be able to understand material that is written about music in order to interpret the music. Music students must be able to read and understand the following types of content:[34]

> expository and narrative materials about composers
> critiques, reviews, and descriptions of performances
> exposition—music history
> reporting—current events related to music
> references—research, reviews
> types of media—books, magazines, newspapers, scores
> records, tapes, and videotapes

Music students are expected to read and interpret a large number of musical terms such as *sonatina, spiritoso, andante,* and *allegretto.* In addition, special symbols are used in music books. These symbols aid the student in interpreting the music. Students must be able to recognize symbols for such elements as treble clef; bass clef; notes (whole, half, quarter, and so on); rests (varying values corresponding to note values); sharps; flats, crescendo; and diminuendo. The teacher must frequently demonstrate the musical terms and concepts. For example, the teacher might demonstrate *pianissimo* by playing a song softly and show *forte* by playing the same song loudly; or he or she might illustrate a *crescendo* followed by a *diminuendo.*

Charles Hicks points out that in instrumental music the reading process involves recognizing the notes, which represent pitch; the meter symbols, which indicate time; and various other interpretive and expressive markings. At the same time, an instrumentalist must physically manipulate valves, bows, slides, and keys.[35] Hicks suggests that teachers present the early stages of music reading as a problem-solving activity involving simple duple and triple meters. He suggests presenting all songs in the same key, emphasizing continuity and repetition, and using materials that have repeated patterns and a narrow range. He also recommends including familiar elements in each new activity.[36]

Example 7.29 includes a selection from a secondary school music textbook. Note that the student must read the words of the song, the notes, and specialized directions. In addition, the music student must coordinate all of the information he or she has read with his or her fingers and/or voice. A study guide based on the selection is also included in the example.

Often students have trouble reading the songs in music books, particularly when words are presented in syllabic form. The teacher may utilize several specific procedures to help:

1. Provide background information about the song.
2. Present the words of the song in poem form on a ditto sheet (to avoid confusion that may result from all the accompanying signs and symbols on a music sheet).
3. Discuss any words that may not be recognized or comprehended, as well as the overall meaning of the lyrics.
4. Cooperatively, the teacher and students should divide the words into syllables. A ditto sheet may again be prepared with words in this form.

After the musical aspects of the song are taught, the students can use the ditto sheet (with divided words) to sing from. Later, they may use the music books that contain the syllabicated words along with the notes and other symbols.

When preparing to perform a composition, music students must ask themselves a number of questions regarding the composition and their performance. Michael Tanner asked a saxophone player in a high school band to identify the questions he had before playing a piece of music, and he produced a list similar to the following:

1. What will playing this exercise show me?
2. What skill should I learn or develop?
3. From what I know about the composer, what does this piece tell me about him or her?
4. What mood is conveyed?
5. What is the key signature?
6. What is the meter (time signature)?
7. What rhythms does the composer use?
8. What intervals are used?
9. What form does the piece have?
10. How long are the phrases?
11. How did the composer want the piece played?
12. What dynamic markings are shown and why?
13. How many motives did the composer use?
14. Is this music challenging to play?
15. Can I play this successfully?
16. Do I want to play this piece?
17. Is this music too hard?
18. How can I play it better?
19. Would it help me if I heard this song played by someone else?
20. Would it help if I read the lyrics?[37]

The SQ3R study procedure can be applied to music as shown in the following paragraphs. SQ3R is applied to the music selection "Chumbara," presented in Example 7.29.

Survey Read the title. (*The title is "Chumbara."*) Who is the composer? (*Not identified*) What subtitles do you see? (*Canadian College Song*)

EXAMPLE 7.29   SELECTION FROM SECONDARY SCHOOL MUSIC TEXTBOOK AND STUDY GUIDE ────────

Source: Beth Landis and Lara Haggard, *Exploring Music* (New York: Holt, Rinehart and Winston, Publishers, 1968), p. 150.

Study Guide

Introduction

"Chumbara" is a Canadian college song that illustrates the use of nonsense words as lyrics. This music is versatile and is especially adapted for percussion instruments.

Vocabulary

Explain the meaning of each of the following terms or phrases: brightly, autoharp, chords C and C7, transposing to the key of C, percussion patterns, maracas, wood block.

Levels of Comprehension

Directions: Place a plus (+) beside statements that are supported by the selection and a minus (−) beside any statements that are not supported by the selection.

Literal

_____ 1. The tambourine, triangle, and sticks can be used to play an accompaniment for this song.

_____ 2. The ♩♩♩♩ pattern is suggested for the triangle.

_____ 3. The ♩♩♩♩ pattern is suggested for the maracas.

Interpretive

_____ 4. This song could be sung at a football rally.

_____ 5. Nonsense words are used in this song to make it hard to understand.

Directions: Write a short answer or follow the specific directions for each item below.

Applied

6. Can you think of another musical composition that is similar to this one?
7. What instruments (that are not mentioned) could be used to play this music?
8. Transpose this song to the key of C.
9. Make up your own patterns for different parts of the song.

Question Compose questions regarding the content to be read. For example:

> How should the song be played?
> In what key is the song written?
> What is a percussion pattern?
> How many counts does a half note get in this song?
> How is this song especially adapted for percussion instruments?

Read Read the selection to answer your questions. When reading music you may read the rhythms of the music to yourself to aid comprehension and retention.

Recite Answer the questions that you composed in the question step of this study process. Answer any other questions that occur to you.

Review Reread the content related to any questions that you could not answer. You may apply the content read by identifying examples of the same type of music. You could compare this selection to other college songs, other songs that use nonsense words, and/or other music adapted for percussion instruments.

Example 7.30 illustrates another type of content that music students read.

EXAMPLE 7.30 MUSIC TEXT

Structure of the Classical Sonata

Just as the Classical symphony is a sonata cycle for orchestra, the Classical sonata is a sonata cycle for piano, or for piano and another instrument. The number of movements in the cycle varies from three to four. The first movement is always in sonata form, although it is sometimes preceded by a slow introduction. The second movement may be in sonata, ternary, or theme and variations form. In a four-movement work, the third movement is generally a minuet and trio, while the last movement is in rondo or sonata form. Sonatas with only three movements omit the minuet.

Major Composers of Classical Sonatas

Haydn's most important works for piano are sonatas. Mozart too wrote sonatas for solo piano and sonatas for piano and violin. In the early years of the nineteenth century, Franz Schubert (1797–1828) also emerged as a major composer of solo piano sonatas. While many of their works are of fine quality, it is in the sonatas of Beethoven that the epitome of the genre is reached. His works form a bridge between Classical and Romantic styles and foreshadow many later nineteenth-century developments.

Beethoven: Piano Sonata in C Minor, Op. 13

One of Beethoven's finest and best-loved works is the *Piano Sonata in C Minor, Op. 13* (the "Pathétique"), which was published in 1799, quite early in his career. The work is in three movements.

First Movement: Grave; Allegro di molto e con brio; in Sonata Form The first movement begins with a slow, ominous introduction. This contrasts dramatically with the main part of the movement, which is marked Allegro and cast in sonata form. The structure of the sonata form is clear, but it is further clarified by the return of the slow introductory material between the exposition and the development, and again after the recapitulation. Dramatic contrasts of theme, key, and dynamics are much greater here than in piano works written earlier in the Classical period.

Listening Guide for Beethoven's *Piano Sonata in C Minor,* First Movement

Timbre:	piano
Melody:	dotted motive prominent in introduction; first theme stresses rising motion; second theme more lyrical
Rhythm:	duple meter; tempo of introduction Grave (very slow); main tempo of movement Allegro di molto e con brio (very fast, with spirit)
Harmony:	mainly minor mode; begins in C minor, modulates most significantly to E♭ major, ends in C minor
Texture:	mainly homophonic
Form:	sonata form preceded by slow introduction

Source: Daniel T. Politoske, *Music,* 2nd ed., © 1979, pp. 204, 205. Reprinted by permission of Prentice-Hall, Englewood Cliffs, New Jersey.

SUMMARY

Efficient reading is a prerequisite for successful learning. Unfortunately, some students enroll in vocational and technical courses because they believe the reading demands in these courses will be less rigorous than those in academic courses. Vocational and technical content is actually very demanding of the reader. Most vocational and technical content has a readability level of tenth grade or higher, which is above the reading level of many students who must read these materials.

The complexity of reading vocational and technical materials is increased by the fact that these materials usually include content from a variety of disciplines and subjects. For example, students in agriculture classes must read scientific content, mathematics content, ecology, directions, and material on auto mechanics, as well as graphs, charts, diagrams, and pictures. Home economics and music students also face a wide variety of reading content.

Vocational and technical reading materials are written and organized to impart information, provide directions, and give solutions to problems. Teachers should plan to use vocabulary strategies, advance organizers, study guides, preview guides, directed reading lessons, mapping, and SQ3R to help students comprehend these materials. Systematic reading instruction as a part of content instruction will improve students' achievement in these courses.

SELF-TEST

1. Why do vocational students need reading instruction? (a) So they can read vocational materials in class (b) So they can real well enough to get a job (c) Both *a* and *b* (d) Neither *a* nor *b*
2. Why do poor readers often choose to study vocational subjects? (a) The subjects are more abstract in nature. (b) The students think they will be required to do less reading. (c) The students want to learn to read. (d) None of the above

3. Vocational materials usually include three writing types. Which of the following is *not* one of the three? (a) Factual information (b) How-to-do-it material (c) Stories (d) Problem solving
4. The technical vocabulary of industrial arts, business education, and home economics is which of the following? (a) Often concrete so it can be illustrated and demonstrated (b) Hard to pronounce (c) Difficult to teach (d) Abstract
5. How must the reader of vocational materials read directions? (a) Quickly (b) Skip them (c) Precisely and carefully (d) Memorize them
6. Why do readers of vocational subjects have an advantage when they read directions? (a) The directions are short. (b) They are easy. (c) The reader receives feedback regarding the success of his or her reading. (d) Following directions is fun.
7. What factors do not influence the rate used by the reader of vocational materials? (a) Purposes for reading (b) Type of content (c) Familiarity with the subject (d) None of the above
8. Why is critical reading important to industrial arts students? (a) They must evaluate material on labels. (b) They must pronounce the words. (c) Both *a* and *b* (d) Neither *a* nor *b*
9. Which of the following references might a business education student use? (a) A shorthand book (b) Coffin's Interest Tables (c) *Encyclopaedia Britannica* (d) All of the above
10. Which of the following is *not* a reason for critical reading in home economics? (a) To evaluate new equipment (b) To evaluate the contents of food products (c) To select recipes (d) To read for pleasure
11. Which content area discussed in this chapter is not complicated by the number of different disciplines involved in its written content? (a) Mathematics (b) Industrial arts (c) Agriculture (d) Business education
12. What techniques can teachers use to help students read music more effectively? (a) Teach the sounds and rhythms students will encounter (b) Avoid the relationship between sight and sound (c) Read only the narrative portions of the music text (d) Read only the lyrics
13. Which of the following types of content are music students most likely to encounter? (a) Reviews and critiques of performances (b) Musical compositions (c) Music history (d) All of these

THOUGHT QUESTIONS

1. Why do the reading materials for vocational subjects give the impression that less reading is required in these areas?
2. How does the reading in vocational subjects compare with the reading in academic subjects?
3. What kinds of reading tasks does the reader of vocational subjects encounter?
4. What strategies can teachers use to help students comprehend vocational materials?

5. How would you respond to a colleague who states that it is not necessary for vocational students to read?
6. How many reading-to-do tasks can you identify in a vocational textbook?
7. Discuss the eclectic nature of agriculture and home economics. How can teachers effectively teach the variety of content in these subjects?

ENRICHMENT ACTIVITIES

1. Select a set of directions from a subject treated in this chapter and rewrite the directions in simpler language for poor readers.
2. Develop an annotated bibliography of materials that could constitute a classroom library in one of the subjects treated in this chapter. Indicate readability levels whenever possible.
3. Make a dictionary of terms for use in one of the areas treated in this chapter. You could use drawings and pictures from magazines, catalogs, and newspapers to illustrate the dictionary.
4. Collect pamphlets, magazines, newspapers, and library books that could be used to develop understanding of vocabulary and concepts in a subject treated in this chapter.
5. Select a section in a textbook on a subject treated in this chapter. Make a reading lesson plan for the selected section.
6. Prepare a presentation, describing how you would help teach a student to read one of the following: (a) an invoice or balance sheet; (b) a contract; (c) a tax form; (d) a physical education activity or game; (e) a critical review of art or music; (f) a specialized handbook; (g) a reference source.
7. Read several of the articles cited in the Selected References on one of the subjects treated in this chapter. Report to the class on the suggestions for teaching reading in this area.
8. Examine materials from industrial arts, business education, and home economics textbooks. Locate examples of the common reading problems.
9. Prepare a study guide for a selection from one of the subjects discussed in this chapter.
10. Prepare a vocabulary activity to teach new terms in a textbook chapter.
11. Use a readability formula and compute the readability level of a textbook for one of the content areas discussed in this chapter.

NOTES

1. Beatrice J. Levin, "Reading Requirements for Satisfactory Careers," in *Reading and Career Education*, ed. Duane Nielsen and Howard Hjelm (Newark, Del.: International Reading Association, 1975), p. 77.
2. Ibid., p. 78.
3. William Diehl and Larry Mikulecky, "The Nature of Reading at Work," *Journal of Reading*, 24 (December 1980), 221–227.

4. Howard Lee, "Dealing with Reading in Industrial Arts," *Journal of Reading*, 24 (May 1981), 663–666.

5. Larry Mikulecky, "Job Literacy: The Relationship Between School Preparation and Workplace Actuality," *Reading Research Quarterly*, 17 (1982), 400–419.

6. Phyllis A. Miller, "Reading Demands in a High-Technology Industry," *Journal of Reading*, 26 (November 1982), 109–121.

7. Ibid., p. 114.

8. Ibid., p. 109.

9. Andrew Clark, "Readability of Industrial Education Textbooks," *Journal of Industrial Teacher Education*, 16 (1978), 13–23. Barbara Stoodt and Susan Milhouser, "Reading Job-Related Materials." Unpublished research, Greensboro: University of North Carolina, 1979.

10. Michael Conroy, "Instructional Sheets for Students with Reading Difficulties," *Industrial Education*, 68 (November 1979), 32–34.

11. William Palmer, "Teaching Reading in Content Areas," *Journal of Reading*, 19 (October 1975), 43–51.

12. Ibid., p. 50.

13. Diehl and Mikulecky, p. 226.

14. Thomas Sticht, *Literacy and Vocational Competence* (Columbus, Ohio: National Center for Research in Vocational Education, 1978).

15. Ibid., p. 5.

16. Susan Turk Heinemann, "Can Job-Related Performance Tasks Be Used to Diagnose Secretaries' Reading and Writing Skills?" *Journal of Reading*, 23 (December 1979), 239–243.

17. Z. Quibble, "The Office of the Future and Its Impact on Employees," *Business Education Forum*, 32 (December 1977), 25–28.

18. B. Stoodt, *Literacy in an Information Age* (Greensboro, N.C.: Center for Creative Leadership, 1985).

19. Thomas Sticht, *Basic Skills in Defense* (Alexandria, Va.: Human Resources Research Organization, 1982). Miller, pp. 109–121. Mikulecky, pp. 400–419.

20. J. Banks, "Secretarial Survival Skills," *Business Education Forum*, 33 (December 1978), 45–48.

21. Ibid.

22. R. Pooley, *The Teaching of English Usage* (Urbana, Ill.: National Council of Teachers of English, 1974).

23. John E. Coffin, *The Teaching of English Usage* (Philadelphia: John C. Winston, 1953).

24. R. Rush, A. Moe, and R. Storlie, *Occupational Literacy Education* (Newark, Del.: International Reading Association, 1986), pp. 66–159.

25. Ibid., p. 65.

26. Pooley, op. cit.

27. Stoodt, p. 126.

28. Dorothy Szymkowicz, "Home Economics and Reading," in *Fusing Reading Skills and Content*, ed. H. A. Robinson and Ellen Thomas (Newark, Del.: International Reading Association, 1969), pp. 62–66.

29. Szymkowicz, p. 63.

30. Ibid., p. 64.

31. D. Daines, *Reading in the Content Areas: Strategies for Teachers* (Glenview, Ill.: Scott, Foresman and Company, 1982, p. 29.

32. Frank Tirro, "Reading Techniques in the Teaching of Music," in *Fusing Reading Skills and Content*, ed. H. Alan Robinson and Ellen Lamar Thomas (Newark, Del.: International Reading Association, 1969), pp. 103–107.

33. Ibid., p. 105.

34. Michael Tanner, "Reading in Music Class," *Music Education Journal* (December 1983), 41–45.

35. Charles E. Hicks, "Sound Before Sight: Strategies for Teaching Music Reading," *Music Education Journal* (April 1980), 53–67.

36. Ibid.

37. Tanner, pp. 41–45.

SELECTED REFERENCES

Brown, James M., and Gerald Yuh-Sheng Chang. "Supplementary Reading Materials for Vocational Students with Limited Reading Ability." *Journal of Reading*, 26 (November 1982), 144–149.

Clark, Andrew. "Readability of Industrial Education Textbooks." *Journal of Industrial Teacher Education*, 16 (1978), 13–23.

Conroy, Michael. "Instructional Sheets for Students with Reading Difficulties." *Industrial Education*, 68 (November 1979), 32–34.

Criscuolo, Nicholas P. "Creative Approaches to Teaching Reading Through Art." *Art Education* (November 1985), 13–16.

Daines, Delva. *Reading in The Content Areas: Strategies for Teachers*. Glenview, Ill.: Scott, Foresman and Company, 1982. Chapter 2.

Diehl, William, and Larry Mikulecky. "The Nature of Reading at Work." *Journal of Reading*, 24, (December 1980), 221–227.

Elliott, Charles A. "The Music-Reading Dilemma." *Music Education Journal* (February 1982), 33–34, 59.

Frager, Alan, and Loren Thompson. "Reading Instruction and Music Education: Getting in Tune." *Journal of Reading*, 27 (December 1983), 202–206.

Gillis, M. K. "Strategies for Mapping Content Texts." *Reading Education in Texas*, 1 (1985), 95–101.

Gottsdanker-Willekens, Anne E. "Functional Folders: Independent Applied Reading Materials." *Journal of Reading*, 25 (May 1982), 764–767.

Heinemann, Susan Turk. "Can Job-Related Performance Tasks Be Used to Diagnose Secretaries' Reading and Writing Skills?" *Journal of Reading*, 23 (December 1979), 239–243.

Hicks, Charles E. "Sound Before Sight: Strategies for Teaching Music Reading," *Music Education Journal* (April 1980), 53–67.

Horowitz, Rosalind, and S. Jay Samuels. "Reading and Listening to Expository Text." *Journal of Reading Behavior*, 17, No. 3 (1985) 185–197.

Lee, Howard, "Dealing with Reading in Industrial Arts." *Journal of Reading*, 24 (May 1981), 663–666.

Ley, Connie J. "Reading: Its Place in the Home Economics Classroom." *Illinois Teacher* (September/October 1978), 48–50.

McWilliams, Lana. "Riding and Reading." *Journal of Reading*, 22 (January 1979), 337–339.

Manzo, Anthony V., and Ula Price Casale. "Listen-Read-Discuss: A Content Reading Heuristic." *Journal of Reading*, 28 (May 1985), 732–734.

Mikulecky, Larry. "Job Literacy: The Relationship Between School Preparation and Workplace Actuality." *Reading Research Quarterly*, 17 (1982), 400–419.

Miller, Phyllis A. "Reading Demands in a High-Technology Industry." *Journal of Reading* (November 1982), 109–121.

Newson, Sarah. "Rock'n Roll'n Reading." *Journal of Reading*, 22 (May 1979), 726–730.

Noe, Katherine. "Technical Reading Technique: A Briefcase Reading Strategy." *Journal of Reading*, 27 (December 1983), 234–237.

Razek, Joseph, Gordon Hosch, and Daniel Pearl. "Readability of Accounting Textbooks." *Journal of Business Education* (October 1982), 23–26.

Slater, Wayne H. "Teaching Expository Text Structure with Structural Organizers." *Journal of Reading*, 28 (May 1985), 712–718.

Sticht, Thomas. *Literacy and Vocational Competence*. Columbus, Ohio: National Center for Research in Vocational Education, 1978.

Tanner, Michael. "Reading in Music Class." *Music Education Journal* (December 1983), 41–45.

Young, Edith M., and Leo V. Rodenborn. "Improving Communication Skills in Vocational Courses." *Journal of Reading*, 19 (February 1976), 373–377.

CHAPTER
E I G H T

ASSESSMENT PROCEDURES

OVERVIEW

A major purpose of this chapter is to assist the content area teacher in determining whether students possess the reading and study skills necessary to deal successfully with the course materials. To do this evaluation, the content teacher must be aware of the reading and study skills appropriate to the particular subject.

This chapter discusses six major assessment procedures: (1) norm-referenced tests of reading achievement; (2) aptitude tests; (3) criterion-referenced tests; (4) informal tests of reading achievement; (5) other informal tests; and (6) minimum competency tests. Each procedure is an important tool and serves certain purposes.

PURPOSE-SETTING QUESTIONS

As you read this chapter, try to answer these questions:

1. What are some representative norm-referenced reading tests, and how can test results be used to help a teacher plan an instructional program?
2. What are criterion-referenced tests?
3. What are some informal measures of reading achievement, and how can results of each be used to help a teacher plan an instructional program?
4. What types of questions and record-keeping systems may be utilized for observation checklists related to reading achievement?
5. What are some self-appraisal techniques to help students evaluate reading strengths and weaknesses?
6. What measures of attitudes toward reading are helpful to the teacher in individualizing the instructional program?

7. What is a "reading interest inventory," and how may the results be used by the teacher to enhance an instructional program?
8. What is the content of several minimum competency tests?

KEY VOCABULARY

As you read this chapter, check your understanding of these terms:

norm-referenced reading test aptitude tests
informal reading inventory reading expectancy
independent reading level test norms
graded word list instructional reading level
criterion-referenced tests frustration reading level
survey reading test group reading inventory
validity skills inventory or test
grade equivalent capacity (potential) reading level
percentile rank cloze test procedure
stanine reading autobiography
normal curve equivalents competency tests

NORM-REFERENCED TESTS

Content teachers may administer and interpret certain types of norm-referenced tests, especially survey achievement tests, to check student performance in a wide range of areas: reading, listening, language, mathematics, science, social studies, reference skills, and others. Test results indicate the relative achievement of the groups tested in these areas. Results can be used to determine how a student's performance on a test in one subject compares with his or her performance on other subtests in a battery. Teachers can learn also how a student's performance on a test compares with his or her earlier or later performance on the same test.

Norm-Referenced Tests of Reading Achievement

Norm-referenced reading tests yield objective data about reading performance. Ideally, they are designed so that each response to a test item is subject to only one interpretation. Authors of norm-referenced tests sample large populations of students to determine the appropriateness of test items, and they seek to verify the validity and reliability of test results so that schools can be confident that the tests measure what they are supposed to measure and do so consistently.

There are various types of norm-referenced reading tests:

1. Survey tests, which measure general achievement in a given area, such as reading

2. Study skills tests, which measure ability to utilize techniques essential for enhancing comprehension and retention, such as study methods, locating and organizing information, adjusting rate of reading, and so forth
3. Diagnostic tests, which analyze and locate specific strengths and weaknesses and may suggest causes

A bit more needs to be said about the validity and reliability of a test. A valid norm-referenced reading test represents a balanced and adequate sampling of the instructional outcomes (knowledges, skills, and so forth) that it is intended to cover. Validity is best judged by comparing the test content with the related courses of study, instructional materials, and educational goals of the class. Evidence about validity is nearly always given in the test manual of directions; such information may be checked against the impartial opinions of educational professionals and should be given a careful inspection to see if the test is designed to measure what one wants to measure.

The reliability of a test refers to the degree to which the test gives consistent results. One way of establishing reliability is to give the same test twice to a large group of pupils. If each student makes practically the same score in both testing situations, the test is highly consistent and reliable. If many students make higher scores in one testing situation than in the other, the test has a low reliability. Another method of measuring reliability is to compare students' scores on the odd-numbered items with their scores on the even-numbered items; if they are in the same rank order, or if they have a high correlation, the test is reliable. A third method of measuring reliability is to compare one form of a test to an equivalent form of the test. When measuring the level of achievement of an individual student, only a test of high reliability should be used as it is necessary to find his or her specific, not comparative, level of achievement. While a test of low reliability cannot be very valid, high reliability does not guarantee that a test is valid.

The most common ways in which results of norm-referenced tests are expressed are (a) grade scores or grade equivalents, (2) percentile ranks, and (3) stanines.

Grade equivalent indicates the grade level, in years and months, for which a given score was the average score in the referencing sample. For example, if a score of 25 has the grade equivalent of 8.1, 25 was the average score of pupils in the norm group who were in the first month of the eighth grade. If a pupil (not in the norm group) who is in the first month of the eighth grade were to take the same test and score 25 correct, his or her performance would be at "grade level," or average for his or her grade placement. If that pupil were to get 30 right, or a grade equivalent of 9.1, he or she would have done as well as the typical ninth grader in the first month. Similarly, a 6.3 grade equivalent for an eighth grader would mean that he or she is performing the way the average pupil in the third month of sixth grade would perform on that test.

Words of caution need to be offered at this point about grade equivalents. Grade equivalents do not indicate the appropriate grade placement for a student. For example, a score of 9.0 may indicate only that the student who is just beginning the ninth grade had 50 items correct; it does not mean that the student who had 50 items correct can necessarily read 9.0 grade level material. In fact, the grade score a student gets on a silent reading test usually tells you that material of that level is too difficult for the student, since many of these tests give frustration level (the level at which a reader cannot perform adequately) scores, not instructional level (the level at which a reader can function adequately with assistance) scores. Certainly a grade equivalent of 9.0 does not mean that a fifth-grade test taker can read as well as a ninth grader. Moreover, the grade equivalents from grade level to grade level (for example from 9.0 to 10.0) are partly hypothetical and are arrived at statistically, since tests are usually standardized at only one or two places within each grade. Due to these and other misinterpretations, some test publishers are beginning to discourage the use of grade equivalents. The Board of Directors of the International Reading Association, noting the serious misuses of grade equivalents, has recommended that grade equivalent interpretations be eliminated from tests.

Content area teachers need to understand percentile ranks, stanines, and normal curve equivalents in order to interpret and understand results of tests that they or others, such as special teachers of reading, have administered. These three ways to express test results are more acceptable than grade equivalents. Also, the use of local norms is more important than national norms, particularly if the local population of students differs significantly from the norming population.

Percentile rank expresses a score in terms of its position within a set of 100 scores. The percentile rank indicates the percent of scores of the norm group that are equal to or lower than the given score. Thus a result ranked in the 35th percentile is regarded as equivalent to or surpassing the results of 35 percent of the persons in the norm group. A student who scores in the 83rd percentile, as compared with the local school's norms, may only score in the 53rd percentile if his or her score is based on national norms.

A *stanine* ranks a test score in relation to other scores on that test. (The term is derived from the words *standard* and *nine*.) A stanine is expressed as a value from one to nine on a nine-point scale. Thus, the mean score of the standard population has a stanine value of 5. Verbal descriptions often assigned to stanines are as follows:

> stanine 9—highest performance
> stanines 7 and 8—above average
> stanines 4, 5, and 6—average
> stanines 2 and 3—below average
> stanine 1—lowest performance

Stanines and percentiles may be compared as follows:

Stanines	Percentiles
9	96–99
8	90–95
7	78–89

6	60–77
5	41–59
4	23–40
3	11–22
2	5–10
1	1–4

Normal curve equivalents (NCEs) are used in some states and school systems. NCEs are represented on a scale of 1–99 with a mean of 50. They have many of the characteristics of percentile ranks but have the additional advantage of being based on an equal-interval scale. This scale allows a meaningful comparison to be made between different achievement test batteries and/or different tests within the same test battery. For example, if a student receives an NCE score of 62 on the mathematics test of a battery and an NCE of 53 on the reading test of a test battery, it would be correct to say the mathematics score is 9 points higher than the reading score. Tables that show the conversions of test scores to NCEs are usually supplied by test publishers.

Readers interested in further study of basic measurement concepts can read L. R. Gay, *Educational Research: Competencies for Analysis and Applications*, 2nd ed., Columbus, Ohio: Charles E. Merrill, 1981.

A norm-referenced test that is selected for use should meet certain criteria. For example, a test is inappropriate if the sample population used to standardize it is significantly different from the class or group to be tested. A description of the norm population is usually contained in the test manual. Even a test that is based on populations of students from a wide variety of rural and urban centers, of various social, racial, and ability levels, and of different sexes and races is not always the most appropriate. Some publishers have begun to standardize tests according to a particular geographic region or a particular educational reference group. In many cases, local norms may be more appropriate to use.

In addition to measuring the skills it claims to measure (validity) and having subtests that are long enough to yield reasonably accurate scores, a test should not result in a chance score, with students obtaining high scores by luck, guessing, or other factors (reliability). The more reliable tests have a reliability coefficient of .90 with subtests above .75.

For readers who are interested in more detailed descriptions of particular tests, the following collections of reviews on reading tests are suggested.

O. K. Buros. *Mental Measurement Yearbook*. 8th ed. Highland Park, N.J.: Gryphon Press, 1978.

_____. *Reading Tests and Reviews*. Highland Park, N.J.: Gryphon Press, 1968.

_____. *Reading Tests and Reviews, II*. Highland Park, N.J.: Gryphon Press, 1975.

William Blanton, et al., eds. *Reading Tests for the Secondary Grades: A Review and Evaluation*. Newark, Del.: International Reading Association, 1972.

Daniel J. Keyser and Richard C. Sweetland, eds. *Test Critiques*. Kansas City, Mo.: Test Corporation of America, 1985.

In addition to these sources, articles dealing with testing often appear in the *Journal of Reading* and may prove useful.

Scores from two different kinds of norm-referenced reading tests cannot be easily compared since the tests probably differ in purpose, length, and difficulty. Even the results of the same test administered on successive days may vary, depending on the reliability of the test and other factors related to the student.

Survey Tests and Study Skills Tests

Of the three types of norm-referenced reading tests described earlier, the content teacher will have most direct contact with survey tests and study skills tests.

A survey test measures general achievement in a given area, such as reading. The results can show how well students are performing. By examining a student's score in relation to scores of others, the teacher obtains an impression of the student's reading achievement. Looking at a number of students' scores gives an indication of the range of reading achievement in the class.

Table 8.1   Range of Reading Scores in a Tenth-Grade Class

Grade Score	Number of Students
15.0–15.9	1
14.0–14.9	1
13.0–13.9	4
12.0–12.9	4
11.0–11.9	2
10.0–10.9	6
9.0– 9.9	2
8.0– 8.9	3
7.0– 7.9	5
6.0– 6.9	1
5.0– 5.9	1
	N = 30

For example, the distribution in Table 8.1 approximates the range of reading achievement scores for a tenth-grade class. A cursory examination of the distribution shows that one-third of the students are performing well below grade level, one-third within a year or two of grade level, and one-third well above grade level. A teacher who has this information at the beginning of the school year knows that it is necessary to make provisions for individual differences.

A single score on a survey test represents the student's overall achievement and does not reveal how the student will perform on specific reading tasks. However, some reading survey tests designed for secondary school students have separate sections on vocabulary, comprehension, and reading rate. Such tests yield separate scores for each section. A wise teacher will not merely be concerned with a student's total achievement score but will want to determine if the student is equally strong in all areas tested or if he or she is stronger in one area than another. Furthermore, a careful examination of student responses to individual test items might provide the teacher with information about more specific reading needs. One way to learn more from testing is to go over the test items with the student to see if he or she can explain his or her responses. It is possible that correct responses were reached in inappropriate ways or that a student guessed a number of the answers.

Some survey and reading achievement tests include:

1. *California Achievement Tests.* Forms E and F. Monterey, Calif.: California Test Bureau, McGraw-Hill, 1985. (Includes subtests on reading vocabulary, comprehension, reference skills, and content areas of language and mathematics. Level 17 for 6.6–7.9; Level 18 for 7.6–9.9; and Level 19 for 9.6–12.9.)
2. *Stanford Tests of Academic Skills.* Monterey, Calif.: CTB/McGraw-Hill, 1981. (Includes subtests on reading vocabulary and comprehension, and content areas of mathematics, spelling, English, social studies, and science. Level 1 for grades 8, 9, and 10; Level 2 for grades 11 and 12.)
3. *Comprehensive Test of Basic Skills.* Monterey, Calif.: CTB/McGraw-Hill, 1981. (Includes subtests on reading vocabulary, comprehension, reference skills, and content areas of spelling, language, mathematics, science, and social studies.)
4. *Gates-MacGinitie Reading Tests.* 2nd ed. Chicago: Riverside, 1978. (Includes subtests on vocabulary and comprehension. Level E for grades 7–9; Level F for grades 10–12.)
5. *Iowa Silent Reading Tests.* Rev. ed. San Antonio: Psychological Corporation, Harcourt Brace Jovanovich, 1973. (Includes subtests on vocabulary, comprehension, directed reading, and reading efficiency. Level 1 for grades 6–9; Level 2 for grades 9–14.)

Notice that the first three survey tests listed provide achievement measures in some of the content areas, whereas the last two tests provide information about reading achievement only. In addition to being interested in the results of the content subtests, content teachers should be concerned with the reading achievement level of students in terms of knowing what printed materials are appropriate for study. Reference skills tests measure the student's ability to utilize essential study techniques: study methods, locating and organizing information, adjusting rate of reading, and so forth. Such techniques are of major concern to content area teachers, since these skills are very important aspects of learning from texts. Using results from such tests, the content area teacher may wish to refer low-achieving students to the special teacher of reading who, in turn, could use the content textbook to help develop the students' comprehension, retention, and study skills. There are several norm-referenced study skills and study habits tests that are not a part of a norm-referenced achievement or reading survey test. One popularly used norm-referenced study habits test is *Survey of Study Habits and Attitudes* (Form H, grades 7–12; San Antonio: Psychological Corporation,

Harcourt Brace Jovanovich, 1967). Scores from this test identify students whose habits and attitudes may prevent them from taking full advantage of their educational opportunities.

A profile sheet from the *Iowa Silent Reading Test* is presented in Example 8.1 to give an indication of the content of the test and the recording of results.

EXAMPLE 8.1   IOWA SILENT READING TESTS

Iowa Silent Reading Tests

Level_____ [ISRT] Form_____

PUPIL PROFILE

Name_____

Teacher_____ School_____

School System_____

City and State_____

Date of Testing_____ Reference Group_____

DIRECTIONS: The Score Detail and Stanine Profile are designed to provide a graphic and convenient representation of each student's reading strengths and weaknesses as revealed by his ISRT scores. Detailed information on how to interpret the *Pupil Profile* is provided in the *Manual of Directions* under "Summarizing the Test Results." To enter the scores and other information, proceed as follows:

1. Enter the appropriate information at the top of the page, above the boxes. Make sure that the reference group is noted correctly.

2. In the Score Detail section, copy the scores for this student directly from his answer document or from the Class Record.

3. In the Stanine Profile section, circle the appropriate stanine number for each of the following: Reading Power, Directed Reading,* and Reading Efficiency. Then, circle the appropriate stanine numbers for Vocabulary and Reading Comprehension. Note that only this Stanine Profile appears on the third copy of the *Pupil Profile*; the third copy is designed for conveying information to parents. The parents' copy provides an explanation of the ISRT rationale and of the use and interpretation of stanines. If parent-teacher conferences are held, it would be helpful to remind parents of two important points. First, a difference of only one stanine between scores is not significant; these stanines are used simply to designate three performance levels: below average, average, and above average. Second, while the Reading Power stanine is the best single indicator of the student's general reading ability, stanines for Vocabulary and for Reading Comprehension are also provided.

4. If a Reading Survey was administered, enter the student's responses from his answer document or from the Class Record by writing the response letter under each question number. It will, of course, be necessary to refer to the Reading Survey questions in order to interpret the responses.

5. Finally, the Teacher Notes section at the bottom of the page should be used to record data from other tests or any other pertinent information that will enable a better understanding of the "whole picture" of the student's reading behavior. It may be desirable to remove the third copy intended for parents before entering information relevant only for in-school use.

*Reported for Levels 1 and 2 only. Level 3 has no Directed Reading test.

SCORE DETAIL

Reading Power				} =	Vocabulary (50 Items)				+	Reading Comprehension (50 Items)			
Raw Score	Standard Score	%-ile Rank	Stanine		Standard Score	%-ile Rank	Stanine	RS/Items Attempted		RS/Items Attempted	Standard Score	%-ile Rank	Stanine
								/		/			

Directed Reading* (44 Items)				Directed Reading Part A (24 Items)	Directed Reading Part B (20 Items)	Reading Efficiency (40 Items)				R-E Index
Raw Score	Standard Score	%-ile Rank	Stanine	RS/Items Attempted	RS/Items Attempted	RS/Items Attempted	Standard Score	%-ile Rank	Stanine	

STANINE PROFILE

TEST SCORE	STANINE		
	1 2 3 *Below Average*	4 5 6 *Average*	7 8 9 *Above Average*
Reading Power (Vocabulary + Reading Comprehension)	1 2 3	4 5 6	7 8 9
Directed Reading* (Part A + Part B)	1 2 3	4 5 6	7 8 9
Reading Efficiency	1 2 3	4 5 6	7 8 9
Vocabulary	1 2 3	4 5 6	7 8 9
Reading Comprehension	1 2 3	4 5 6	7 8 9
	Below Average	Average	Above Average

Reading Survey

Question: 1 2 3 4 5 6 7 8 9 10 11 12

Response: ___ ___ ___ ___ ___ ___ ___ ___ ___ ___ ___ ___

TEACHER NOTES:

Diagnostic Tests

Diagnostic reading tests are used most frequently by special teachers of reading. Content teachers find it helpful to have some basic information about this type of test in order to discuss such tests and test results with a special teacher of reading.

Diagnostic reading tests help to locate specific strengths and weaknesses and possibly suggest causes for them. Such tests often include subtests for comprehension, vocabulary, word identification skills, rate of reading, and the like. There are group diagnostic tests (such as the *Stanford Diagnostic Reading Test,* New York: Harcourt Brace Jovanovich, 1984) that are given by reading specialists or sometimes by classroom teachers. Individual diagnostic reading tests require experience and training on the part of the administrator.

Several *oral reading tests* are available for students at the secondary level. The oral reading tests, which must be given on an individual basis, require preparation for their administration. Presumably the kinds of errors a student makes when reading orally serve as a clue to the kinds of errors he or she makes when reading silently. This may or may not be true. But oral reading tests are valuable diagnostic tools for some students who are having serious reading problems. Oral reading tests usually check for accuracy of reading, comprehension, and rate.

When data from such tests are available, secondary school content teachers may find them helpful.

Aptitude Tests

Several group aptitude (general academic ability) tests used in the secondary school are listed below:

1. *Short-Form Test of Academic Aptitude.* Monterey, Calif.: California Test Bureau, McGraw-Hill, 1974. (For K–college level.)
2. *Cognitive Abilities Tests.* Multilevel ed. Chicago: Riverside, 1982. (For grades 3–13.)
3. *Otis-Lennon School Ability Test.* San Antonio: Psychological Corporation, Harcourt Brace Jovanovich, 1982. (Intermediate for grades 6–8; Advanced for grades 9–12.)

Most mental tests for secondary school students require reading. Results often place the poor reader in the dull-normal category, possibly underestimating his or her real ability. Such students should be measured by a test that does not require reading for a more valid assessment. The test must be individually administered and may require special training for administration.

Intelligence test scores are useful in identifying the underachiever. A student's score on a norm-referenced reading test only indicates present performance and not the performance of which the student may be capable. An intelligence test score can indicate a student's capability level, which can then be compared with his or her actual performance. Whether or not the student is performing up to capacity can be determined. One commonly used formula for finding this information, suggested by Guy Bond, Miles Tinker, and Barbara Wasson, is given below:[1]

$$\frac{IQ}{100} \; (\textit{years in school}) + 1.0 = \textit{Reading Expectancy}$$

Thus, a mid-year eighth grader who scored 150 on an intelligence test would have a reading capacity or expectancy of twelfth-grade level:

$$\frac{150}{100} \times 7.5 \quad + 1.0$$
$$(1.50 \times 7.5) + 1.0$$
$$(11.25) + 1.0$$
$$12.25$$

Because of the differences in students' backgrounds of experience and because of the limitations of norm-referenced tests, caution should always be exercised in the use of such formulas. Experience indicates that most formulas for predicting reading potential are least accurate for extremely good and extremely poor readers.

There is a second way to estimate a student's reading potential. The student's listening ability is a good indicator of the level at which he or she could be reading. The following test provides a measure of the student's listening comprehension:

Stanford Listening Comprehension Test (Grades 1.5–9.9; San Antonio: Psychological Corporation, Harcourt Brace Jovanovich, 1985)

(Informal measures of listening comprehension are also useful. See the section on the informal reading inventory later in this chapter.)

Intelligence or general academic ability tests and listening tests are used most often by the special teacher of reading.

CRITERION-REFERENCED TESTS

Criterion-referenced tests (CRTs) have become popular in recent years. While norm-referenced tests compare the test taker's performance with that of others, CRTs check the test taker against a given performance criterion as a predetermined standard. Thus a criterion-referenced test might read: "Given ten paragraphs at the ninth-grade reading level, the student can identify the main idea in eight of them." In short, a CRT indicates whether or not the test taker has mastered a particular objective or skill, rather than how well his or her performance compares with that of others. A norm-referenced test, on the other hand, may indicate that the student can identify the main idea of a paragraph better than 90 percent of the test takers his or her age.

The results of criterion-referenced tests can be used as instructional prescriptions (that is, if a student cannot perform the task of identifying the contraction for *cannot*, the need for instruction in that area is pointed out). These tests are therefore useful in day-to-day decisions about instruction.

CRTs have limitations and unresolved questions, however. For example, the level of success demanded is one issue. Often the passing level is set arbitrarily at

80 or 90 percent. There is no agreement as to the nature of mastery or how to measure it. And many criterion-referenced tests give the appearance that there are literally hundreds of separate reading skills that are important to the reading act. There is some question about whether CRTs can measure complex domains such as critical/creative reading skills, reading appreciation, or attitude toward reading. CRTs may also be questioned in terms of reliability and validity. Any type of test may measure only knowledge of rules rather than ability to use them, and a short set of items over a particular reading objective can be less than reliable, particularly in terms of individual measurement.

It seems likely that both criterion-referenced tests and norm-referenced tests will continue to be important tools, serving different purposes. In fact, both kinds of interpretation—individual and comparative—are offered by a number of tests, including the *Stanford Achievement Test* and the *Metropolitan Achievement Test*.

Below is a listing of some criterion-referenced tests.

1. *Fountain Valley Reading Skills Tests* (R. L. Zweig Associates, Inc., 20800 Beach Boulevard, Huntington Beach, Calif. 92648)
2. *MULTISCORE* (Riverside Publishing Company, 8420 Bryn Mawr Avenue, Chicago, Ill. 60631)
3. *Objectives-Referenced Bank of Items and Tests* (*ORBIT*) (CTB/McGraw-Hill Publishing Company, Del Monte Research Park, Monterey, Calif. 93940)
4. *Prescriptive Reading Inventory* (CTB/McGraw-Hill Publishing Co., Del Monte Research Park, Monterey, Calif. 93940)
5. *Reading Yardsticks* (Riverside Publishing Company, 8420 Bryn Mawr Avenue, Chicago, Ill. 60631)

The above listing includes CRTs that are related to reading programs. These will be utilized mainly by the special teacher of reading. However, content teachers may also make frequent use of certain CRTs. They may construct these measures themselves, using banks of behavioral criterion-referenced test items that are available for all subject areas from some state educational departments or from such places as Educational Testing Services, in Princeton, New Jersey. Teachers may choose appropriate items from such collections to construct tailor-made CRTs, or they may construct their own items, using sources such as Norman E. Gronland's *Preparing Criterion-Referenced Tests for Classroom Instruction* (New York: Macmillan, 1973). The teacher should construct items that assess the extent to which specific instructional objectives have been attained.

For many years, content teachers have been using their own criterion-referenced measures to assess the results of instruction. In such cases, definite instructional objectives are tested, and there is a definite standard of judgment or criterion for students' "passing." For example, here is an objective that is measured by six items on a test prepared by a teacher. The criterion for demonstrating mastery of this objective is set at five of six; that is, the student must answer five of six items correctly to show mastery.

EXAMPLE 8.2 CRITERION-REFERENCED TEST

Objective: Utilizing the information found on the content pages of the almanac
Directions: Find answers to the following:

1. Who were the fifteenth president and vice president of the United States?
2. Who holds the world record for high diving?
3. What was the Academy Award winner for the Best Picture of 1959?
4. What are the names of the Kentucky Derby winner of 1975 and the jockey who rode to victory?
5. Where is the deepest lake in the United States?
6. How many American League baseball teams have won the World Series since 1965?

Note that each question in Example 8.2 is related to the objective. The criterion level for "passing" must be determined by the teacher. Results give the teacher precise information concerning what each student can or cannot do; the test results can be used to improve classroom instruction. Thus, criterion-referenced tests are useful for planning further instruction.

INFORMAL TESTS

Informal tests (those not standardized against a specific norm or objective) are an invaluable aid to the content teacher. Although some are commercially available, many are constructed by the teachers themselves. These informal measures offer the content teacher ongoing assessment information about both the students' reading achievement and their nonreading behaviors and attitudes that may affect reading.

Informal Tests of Reading Achievement

There are several informal measures of reading achievement that can be useful to the teacher in revealing student reading achievement. Nine of these measures are discussed in the sections that follow: (1) vocabulary assessment, (2) assessment of background knowledge, (3) group reading inventory, (4) skills inventories, (5) informal reading inventories, (6) secondary reading inventories, (7) cloze procedure, (8) observation checklists, and (9) self-assessment techniques.

Vocabulary Assessment

As noted earlier in the listing of norm-referenced survey reading tests, there are several formal measures of this aspect of reading. In this section, we will focus on one informal diagnostic device.

The San Diego Quick Assessment is a graded word list that may be used to determine reading level and detect errors in word analysis. The information provided may be used to group students or to select appropriate reading materials for them. To administer this device, the teacher should follow the steps below.

1. Type each list of ten words on an index card.
2. Begin with a card that is at least two years below the student's grade level.
3. Ask the student to read the words aloud; if he or she misreads any on the initial list, drop to easier lists until no errors are made.
4. Encourage the student to attempt to read aloud the unfamiliar words so that the techniques the student uses for word identification can be determined.
5. Have the student read from increasingly difficult lists until he or she misses at least three words on a list.

The level at which a student misses no more than one out of ten words is his or her *independent reading level* (the level of material that he or she can read successfully without teacher aid). Two errors on a list indicates the *instructional level* (the reading level of the material to be used under teacher guidance). Three or more errors indicate that the level is too difficult for the student (called the *frustration level*).

Lists are available for preprimer level up to the eleventh grade; for practical purposes, only the lists for grades 4 through 11 are presented in Table 8.2.

Table 8.2   Graded Word List for Quick Assessment

Grade 4	Grade 5	Grade 6	Grade 7
decided	scanty	bridge	amber
served	business	commercial	dominion
amazed	develop	abolish	sundry
silent	considered	trucker	capillary
wrecked	discussed	apparatus	impetuous
improved	behaved	elementary	blight
certainly	splendid	comment	wrest
entered	acquainted	necessity	enumerate
realized	escaped	gallery	daunted
interrupted	grim	relativity	condescend
Grade 8	Grade 9	Grade 10	Grade 11
capacious	conscientious	zany	galore
limitation	isolation	jerkin	rotunda
pretext	molecule	nausea	capitalism
intrigue	ritual	gratuitous	prevaricate
delusion	momentous	linear	risible
immaculate	vulnerable	inept	exonerate
ascent	kinship	legality	superannuate
acrid	conservation	aspen	luxuriate
binocular	jaunty	amnesty	piebald
embarkment	inventive	barometer	crunch

Source: M. LaPray and R. Ross, "The Graded Word List: A Quick Gauge of Reading Ability," *Journal of Reading* 12 (January 1969): 305–307. Reprinted with permission of the authors and the International Reading Association.

This type of vocabulary assessment will give the content area teacher a rough estimate of the student's reading ability. Such data can be used to match the student with printed material of appropriate difficulty level in varying situations, such as independent reading or instructional reading. This is a particularly helpful device to administer to a student new to the class. One caution: this device gives information about the reader's ability to recognize words out of context—not his or her ability to comprehend material in which these words appear. Also, the use of graded word lists does not produce as accurate an estimate of the reading levels as can be obtained from other measures, such as informal reading inventories.

Assessment of Background Knowledge

Since the background knowledge of the students plays a vital role in their comprehension of reading material (see Chapter 3), it is wise to assess background knowledge about a topic before asking students to read about that topic. Background knowledge may be assessed through class brainstorming sessions concerning the topic, having students write down all the facts they know about the topic, and holding discussions concerning the students' prior experiences that relate to the topic. Oral methods of assessment may be better for poorer students because they may actually know more than their writing skills will allow them to express.

Group Reading Inventory (GRI)

The content teacher may administer a group reading inventory before asking students to use a particular text for study. A group reading inventory of content material may be given by having students read a passage of 1,000 to 2,000 words from their textbooks and asking certain types of questions. This procedure can give some indication of how well students will be able to read a particular textbook. Content books to be studied should be written on a student's instructional or independent level; trade and supplementary books should be on a student's independent level.

Usually the selection used in an inventory is chosen from an early part of the textbook. The teacher introduces the selection and directs the students to read it for the purpose of answering certain kinds of questions. As students read, the teacher writes the time on the chalkboard at 15-second intervals; each student writes down the last time recorded when he or she finishes reading the passage. Later, a words-per-minute score is computed by dividing the time into the total number of words in the passage. For example, if the passage is 1,000 words long and the student reads it in 4 minutes, the student would divide 4 into 1,000 to get a 250-words-per-minute score. When finished reading, the student closes the book and answers a series of questions on such things as

1. vocabulary (word meaning, word recognition, context, synonyms, antonyms, syllabication, accent, affixes)

2. literal comprehension (main ideas, significant details, sequence, following directions, and so forth)
3. interpretive comprehension (evaluative and inferential)

A sample group reading inventory from a secondary level history textbook is provided in Example 8.3. (Also see David Shepherd, *Comprehensive High School Reading Methods,* for other examples of group reading inventories.)

EXAMPLE 8.3   SAMPLE GROUP READING INVENTORY ———————

Name _____   Date _____

Motivation Statement: Read to find out why the Confederation Congress was unable to settle its foreign problems.

Selection: Dealing with Other Countries

The men who represent one country as it deals with other nations are called *diplomats.* Their work is called *diplomacy,* or the *foreign relations* of their country. The foreign relations of the Confederation were not very successful. Congress did not have the power to make the states or the people follow the agreements that it made with other countries. Under these conditions other nations had little respect for the United States.

The British had promised in the Treaty of Paris to leave the territory they had agreed was now part of the United States. Instead, they remained in their forts along the Great Lakes. They also used their Indian friends to keep settlers out of the Northwest Territory. There was much fighting between the frontiersmen and England's Indian allies.

Why did the English hold these forts? They hoped to keep their fur trade and the control it gave them over some Indian tribes. They even hoped to set up an Indian nation north of the Ohio River. Suppose the American government failed to last. Some British leaders thought that they could then move back into control of their former colonies. The reason they gave for keeping their grip on the Northwest was that the United States had not kept its treaty promise to help British creditors collect their debts in America.

In 1784 Congress tried to settle some of its problems with England. It sent John Adams to London. He tried to get the British to give up the forts on American soil and to increase trade with the United States. The British refused to give up the forts until American debtors had paid the money owed to British creditors since before the Revolutionary War. They refused to make any kind of trade treaty. Adams tried for three years, but could not get the British to change their minds.

Congress also tried to settle its troubles with Spain. In the Treaty of Paris, England had given Americans the use of the Mississippi River and the right to store their goods at New Orleans. This agreement was most important to the people who had moved into Kentucky and Tennessee. They had to use the Mississippi to get their goods to market. They also needed the right to deposit, or keep, their goods in New Orleans until a ship could load them for the trip across the ocean.

Spain held the lower Mississippi and New Orleans. Its rulers would not accept the agreement made by the British and Americans. They also hoped the new nation would not succeed so they could take part of it. Spanish officials urged the settlers south of the Ohio to secede, or take their territory out of the United States. They could then join the Spanish empire. Spain would give them the use of the Mississippi and New Orleans. Spain was still a strong nation. It proved this by getting Indians to attack the pioneers who settled near Spanish territory, and by holding onto Natchez, in American territory.

But Spain was willing to discuss such problems. In 1785 Don Diego de Gardoqui became the first Spanish minister to America. He and John Jay, the American Secretary of Foreign Affairs, soon began to bargain. By this time Spain had closed the lower Mississippi to American trade. Jay was told by Congress that he must get Spain to allow such trade. Don Diego was willing, but only if Spain would control the Mississippi, most of what is now Alabama and Mississippi, and parts of Tennessee, Kentucky, and Georgia. Spain claimed this land because it had held parts of it while fighting the British as allies of the United States during the Revolutionary War. Don Diego also asked that Spain should hold all lands south of the thirty-fifth parallel.

John Jay refused to accept such claims. He insisted that the United States would accept only the terms of the Treaty of Paris, which made the thirty-first parallel the boundary between Florida and the United States. Businessmen in the North and East wanted to build up their trade with Spain. In August, 1786, Congress changed its position. It told Jay that he could give up American rights on the Mississippi River for 25 years, if Spain would in turn agree to allow more American trade in Spanish ports. This would have helped the businessmen of New England, but would have hurt the farmers and settlers in the South and West. There was a bitter debate in Congress, and the men who represented seven of the states voted for this plan. This was two states less than the nine that had to agree before Congress could make a treaty. The talks between Spain and the United States then ended. The problems between the two countries were not settled until the Pinckney Treaty of 1795.

Relations with France were also poor. Thomas Jefferson became our minister to France. He wrote that the French showed him little respect. The leaders of the French government were angry because the United States could not repay its wartime debts. However, Jefferson did get them to agree to allow more trade by American ships.

The Confederation had no army, and could not do much about Indian attacks. It could not open up the Mississippi, build up trade with Europe, or make needed agreements with foreign governments. More people began to wonder why they had to have such a weak national government.

Source: Boyd Shafer et al., *A High School History of Modern America*, 3rd ed., pp. 104–105. Copyright 1977. By permission of LAIDLAW BROTHERS, A Division of Doubleday and Company, Inc.

Inventory Questions

Directions: Write a short answer to each question.

Vocabulary
1. What is meant by the term *diplomacy?*
2. Define *secede.* Define *allies.*
3. What is a synonym for the word *treaty?*
4. Divide the word *Confederation* into syllables.
5. Write the definition of the word *relations* as used in the passage.
6. What did the author mean by "keeping their grip on the Northwest"?

Literal Comprehension
1. What job did John Jay have in the Confederation government? (Detail)
2. Why did the English remain in forts along the Great Lakes? (Detail)
3. Why was the Treaty of Paris important to the people of Tennessee and Kentucky? (Detail)
4. List, in order, the sequence of steps in the discussion of problems with Spain. (Sequence)

Interpretive Comprehension
1. Do you agree with the directive of Congress to Jay in 1786? Why or why not? (Evaluation)
2. What do you think the people began to want from their national government? What makes you think this? (Inference)
3. Why did the U.S. under the Articles have so much difficulty in dealing with other nations? (Conclusion)

Materials are suitable for instructional purposes if the student can comprehend 75 percent of what he or she reads (answers six out of eight questions correctly). If students can comprehend 75 percent of what they read, their comprehension will increase if teachers introduce specialized vocabulary words, help with comprehension, teach a study method, and provide specific purposes for reading. Of course students have many different reading levels, depending upon their interests and the background information that they may possess on any specific topic. Thus, there is a need to apply a group reading inventory to texts in each specific content area. When the student comprehends 90 to 100 percent of what he or she reads (answers 9 questions out of 10 correctly), the material can be classified as being on his or her *independent* level. When the student comprehends 50 percent or less of what he or she reads (answers 5 questions out of 10 correctly), the material is on his or her *frustration* level. Students scoring 70 percent or below on a set of materials should be given an inventory on easier material; those who score 90 percent or above should be given an inventory on more difficult material.

Skill Inventories

A content teacher may want to know if students have developed the reading skills that are necessary to understand his or her content area. When a teacher is preparing to teach a particular chapter or unit that involves reading content area materials, he or she should be aware of the material that is going to be read and, hopefully, understood. To decide the level and amount of instruction needed to accommodate the varied differences among students, the teacher can prepare and administer to class members skill inventories that are based on a textbook chapter or unit, modeling them after the skill inventories presented in this section. On the basis of the results, the teacher will become more aware of what activities are needed to prepare students to read and understand the assigned materials. Activities suggested by such inventories are particularly good to use with students who are not profiting from their reading assignments and who may need special help and additional practice in the required skills.

Skill inventories may serve as a part of the total assessment program: that is, part of a test by a science teacher may require students to read a table or graph that appears in the text; questions about interpretation of a map that appears in the text might be used as a part of a social science teacher's chapter or unit test; symbol knowledge and diagram-reading ability might be included in a mathematics teacher's test; questions on vocabulary words may be used to check the special terms in a content chapter or unit; assignments in outlining or note taking or adjusting reading rate to purpose and difficulty may be included in tests by all content teachers. The ultimate purpose of skill inventories is that students master and comprehend the content found in their textbooks and in other printed materials used in the classroom. The following skills are common to all content areas.

1. Understanding and using parts of textbooks (table of contents, index, list of illustrations, appendices, bibliography, glossary)
2. Interpreting maps, tables, charts, graphs, diagrams, cartoons
3. Knowing specialized vocabulary
4. Using reference materials (encyclopedias, dictionaries, supplemental reference books)
5. Recognizing special symbols, formulas, and abbreviations

Other necessary general skills are using study methods, outlining, taking notes, and reading at a flexible rate. Of course, general comprehension skills are involved in all content areas, as suggested in the group reading inventory. The following items may be used to prepare skill assessments:

1. Parts of textbooks—Have students make use of different aids in their textbooks, such as preface, index, vocabulary lists, and appendices.
2. Maps, tables, charts, graphs, diagrams, cartoons—Use examples from the students' textbooks and ask students to answer questions you have prepared.

3. Specialized vocabulary—Use words from the glossaries of textbooks or supplemental materials.
4. Reference materials—Use the reference materials that are available for your content area and develop questions to see if students know the various reference sources and how to use them.
5. Symbols, abbreviations, and formulas—See if students can recognize the most frequently used symbols and abbreviations in the content material.

The following examples provide some sample reading skills tests. The examples deal with several different content areas.

EXAMPLE 8.4   USING PARTS OF A TEXTBOOK—SKILL INVENTORY

Directions: Below are two columns of words or phrases. Match the expression from the right-hand column with the one that means the same, or almost the same, thing in the left-hand column.

```
_____ Index
_____ Table of contents
_____ Bibliography
_____ Appendix
_____ Glossary
_____ Preface
_____ Title
_____ Copyright date
```

1. Name of book
2. Part of book giving additional information, such as notes and tables
3. Introduction
4. List of books for further reading
5. Alphabetical list of topics with the page on which each is found
6. Year when book was published
7. List in front of book with chapter headings or topics in sequence and page on which each begins
8. List of words with their meanings

Directions: Use your textbook to answer the following questions:

1. What is the title of your book?
2. When was it published?
3. Who wrote the book?
4. What are the titles of the first three chapters?
5. How are the chapters arranged or grouped?
6. On what page does Chapter 4 begin?
7. Find the meaning of the term _____ .
8. On what page is there a chart showing _____ ?
9. What does the map on page _____ tell you?
10. On what page does the book explain the construction of a _____ ?
11. What index entries are given for _____ ?

EXAMPLE 8.5 READING TABLES, MAPS, AND GRAPHS—SKILL INVENTORY

Tables

Directions: Look at the table below and answer the following questions.

Element	Symbol	Number of Protons	Number of Neutrons	Number of Electrons in Neutral Atoms
hydrogen	H	1	0	1
helium	He	2	2	2
lithium	Li	3	4	3
beryllium	Be	4	5	4
boron	B	5	6	5
carbon	C	6	6	6
nitrogen	N	7	7	7
oxygen	O	8	8	8
fluorine	F	9	10	9
neon	Ne	10	10	10
sodium	Na	11	12	11
magnesium	Mg	12	12	12
aluminum	Al	13	14	13

Source: Faith Fitch Hill and Jeffrey C. May, *SPACESHIP EARTH: Physical Science*, p. 382. Copyright © 1981 by Houghton Mifflin Company. Used by permission.

Questions

1. What is the symbol for helium?
2. What is the number of neutrons for carbon?
3. Ten is the number of protons for which element?
4. What is the number of electrons in neutral atoms for aluminum?
5. Which element has no neutrons?

Maps

Directions: Study the map below. Tell whether the statements about the map are true or false.

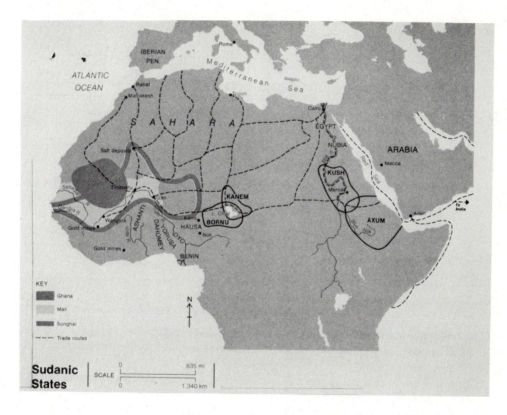

Source: Marvin Perry, *Unfinished Journey: A World History*, p. 221. Copyright © 1980 by Houghton Mifflin Company. Used by permission.

True or False

_____ 1. The Sahara is located south of the Iberian Peninsula.

_____ 2. The Senegal River intercepts the Gambia River.

_____ 3. One could sail from Mirot to Cairo on the Nile River.

_____ 4. It would be closer to take a land journey than to travel by sea from Rome to Tripoli.

_____ 5. Rabat is located on the coast of the Atlantic Ocean.

_____ 6. It would take longer to walk from the gold mines to Wangara than from the gold mines to Nok.

Graphs

Directions: Look at the graph and answer the questions about it.

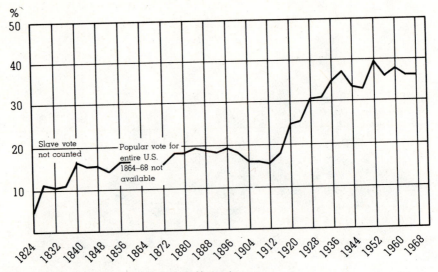

Source: Historical Statistics and Statistical Abstract.

Questions

1. Was there a steady growth of voters from 1824 to 1860?
2. Around what year was there a sudden increase in popular votes cast in presidential elections?
3. Does the graph show the percentage of voting-age citizens participating in presidential elections?
4. For what years are complete data not provided?
5. About what percentage of Americans voted in the 1972 presidential election?

EXAMPLE 8.6   USING REFERENCE SOURCES—SKILL INVENTORY

Directions: Answer the following questions (based on English classroom reference sources).

1. What library aid will tell you the library number of a book?
2. What is a biography?
3. What is the difference between fiction and nonfiction?
4. Explain what each circled numeral of this entry from *Readers' Guide to Periodical Literature* refers to.

① AIRPLANES
   ② Electra on public trial.   L. Davis   il   Flying
                       ⑦   ⑧   ⑨

68:   46—7$^+$ F'   61

③   ④   ⑤   ⑥

5. Describe the content of *Dictionary of American Biography.*
6. Describe the content of *Granger's Index to Poetry.*
7. Where could you find an alphabetical listing of words with synonyms and antonyms instead of definitions?
8. What information may be found in the *Reader's Encyclopedia?*
9. Where might you find short stories listed by title, author, subject?
10. What information may be found in the *Book Review Digest?*
11. What information may be found in *Cumulative Book Index?*
12. Where might you go to find the answer to the question, "Is Steinbeck's *The Grapes of Wrath* considered to be one of his better works?"

Directions: Find the following words in a dictionary and list the guide words and numbers of the pages on which they fall.

Word	Guide Words	Page Number
anachronism		
aphorism		
assonance		
denouement		
epigram		
foreshadowing		
irony		
soliloquy		

Directions: Use a set of encyclopedias, such as *The World Book.* Answer the following questions.

1. What is the purpose of an encyclopedia?
2. What are the meaning and purpose of the guide letter or letters on the cover of each volume?
3. What are the meaning and purpose of *guide words?*
4. What is meant by *cross reference?*
5. What is the purpose of the bibliographies at the ends of articles?
6. Where is the index located in the encyclopedia?

A vocabulary skill inventory would be used to check the specialized vocabulary of a content area as a part of the total assessment program (see Example 8.7). Vocabulary tests are usually administered at the start of each unit of study, providing the teacher with data about what is needed for vocabulary development activities.

EXAMPLE 8.7   VOCABULARY—SKILL INVENTORY

Directions: Explain the following terms concisely. (The source of these vocabulary items is Chapter 5, "Elections," in *American Government,* by Allen Schech and Adrienne Pfister, Boston: Houghton Mifflin, 1975.)

suffrage	closed primary
franchise	open primary
poll tax	plurality
suffragettes	presidential preference primary
literacy tests	favorite son
voting register	electoral votes
absentee ballot	electoral college
Australian ballot	office line ballot
party line ballot	caucus ballot
short ballot	

Directions: Divide each of the following words into syllables.

discriminations	residency
compulsory	nomination
convention	primary
candidates	delegates
expenditures	amendment
registration	

Directions: Rewrite each word phonetically.

majority	eligibility
precinct	candidates
registrars	campaign
strategy	qualification

Directions: Define the italicized words.

The word *primary* suggests a first election—a nominating election held sometime before a regular election. A person who runs in a primary election needs only a *plurality* to win his party's nomination. A run-off by the two persons with the most votes may be required if no candidate receives a *majority.*

In the *closed* primary, the voter receives only the ballot of his own party; this is different from the *open* primary.

The inventory in Example 8.8 checks symbol knowledge and diagram-reading ability. Skills in these areas are required by most content area textbooks. The inventory shown here is somewhat different from the other inventories—it is an actual page from a textbook, not a teacher-made instrument. However, its use—as a diagnostic tool—is similar to that of the other inventories.

EXAMPLE 8.8   SPECIAL SYMBOLS FOR FLOW CHARTING

1. The *oval* is used to signal the *start* or *end* of the instructions.
2. The *diamond* is used to tell you that a question is being asked. You should be able to answer the question with a *yes* or *no.* The diamond indicates a decision point.
3. The *rectangle* is used to tell you that some process must be carried out. The rectangle indicates a do-something point.
4. The *parallelogram* tells you to record or copy or remember something. If you were writing flow charts for giving instructions to a computer, you would be very careful to use enough of these. The computer is a quick accurate machine, but it is also absolutely without imagination. It needs to be told everything it must do, down to the smallest detail.
5. The *arrow* indicates the sequence of the steps in a flow chart. The arrow tells you which box to go to next.

Here is a flow chart for simplifying numerical expressions which contain parentheses. The flow chart on page 42 is referred to as "Procedure A."

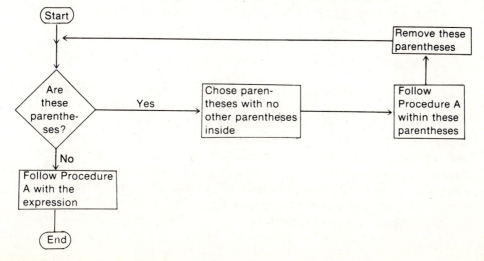

Exercises

Copy the flow chart on page 43 and number the parts as shown in the figure.

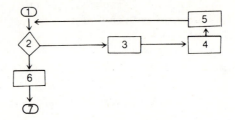

1. For each expression given, write the number of each step in the order which would be used to simplify the expression.
   Sample 10 − [2 − (1 + 1)] would use 1→2→3→4→5→
   2→3→4→5→6→7

   a. 3 − (5 − 4)
   c. 2 × [10 − (2 + 2)]
   e. 3 × 5
   g. 10 − (13 − (16 − (10 − 3)))
   h. 8 ÷ {[1 + (4 − 3) − 2] × 3 + 1} − 2

   b. 2 × 3 − 5 ÷ 4
   d. (2 + 5) × (4 − 2)
   f. (2 × (5 − 3) + 1) × 7

2. Using the flow chart of Exercise 1, what is the greatest number of steps there can be in simplifying an expression?

Source: William H. Nibbelink and Jay Graening, *Algebra 1,* Teacher's Annotated Edition (Columbus, Ohio: Charles E. Merrill, 1975), pages 43 and 44.

EXAMPLE 8.9 OUTLINING/TAKING NOTES—SKILL INVENTORY ——

Directions: Read the selection below. Outline what you have read as you would a reading assignment in your course. (Use one main idea and four subtopics.)

Signs of promise   The philosophes of the Enlightenment believed that humans were essentially good. They were confident that humans could improve themselves and society if they relied on reason. Two major developments in modern European history seemed to bear out their hopes. These were the French Revolution (1789–1799) and the Industrial Revolution which began in England about 1760.
   Inspired by the philosophes, reformers in France sought to advance liberty and equality. They ended the special privileges of the clergy and aristocracy, did away with absolutism, and established parliamentary government in France. During

the nineteenth century the ideas of the Enlightenment and the French Revolution spread throughout Europe and to other parts of the world. Reformers sought to imitate the achievements of the revolution. Many lands drew up constitutions, established parliaments, and granted equality under the law. In the tradition of the Enlightenment they established public education.

At the same time advances in science and technology were transforming the material conditions of life. New inventions dramatically improved the standard of living, opened up new opportunities, and gave people more leisure. Discoveries in medicine prolonged life.

In the nineteenth century most thinkers believed that they were living in an age of progress. They saw their age as a fulfillment of the dreams of the philosophes. And they expected that this progress would continue indefinitely.

Source: Marvin Perry: *Unfinished Journey*, p. 346. Copyright © 1980 by Houghton Mifflin Company. Used by permission.

EXAMPLE 8.10   ADJUSTMENT OF RATE TO PURPOSE AND DIFFICULTY—SKILL INVENTORY

Directions: Read this selection carefully. Try to comprehend the author's point of view and remember the main ideas, details, and what might be implied by the author. (A selection with appropriate questions would follow.)

Read as rapidly as you can to understand the main points. The questions for the selection will deal with the main events of the selection. (A selection and appropriate questions would follow.)

Scan the following selection to answer the questions. (Appropriate questions would precede the selection.)

A skills chart can be developed for recording the instructional needs of students. Skills charts include a list of skills and a list of students' names. The teacher places a check mark beside a skill by the name of a student who successfully achieves the skill. A glance at the chart will provide a clue as to which students need special help in developing a required skill. If most students need help with a particular skill, the teacher may plan a total class instructional session. If only certain students lack a skill, the teacher may set up a skill group to help students who need it. Skill groups are temporary groups in that they are dissolved when the members have accomplished the skill. Perhaps a skills file (collection of materials, equipment, and supplies) will provide the needed practice activities for some students.

A sample record-keeping chart is provided in Example 8.11.

Informal Reading Inventory (IRI)

There are published, commercial inventories to gauge a student's reading levels. They are compilations of graded reading selections with questions prepared to test the reader's comprehension. These types of inventories are often administered by the special or remedial reading teacher to students identified as problem readers.

EXAMPLE 8.11   SAMPLE SKILLS RECORD

Skills	Student Names		
1. Parts of textbook			
2. Interpretation of maps, tables, charts, diagrams etc.			
3. Specialized vocabulary			
4. Reference sources			
5. Special symbols/abbreviations			
6. Study methods			
7. Outlining/taking notes			
8. Flexibility of rate			

Key: Pupil Performance Code
I—needs introduction and teaching
R—needs review and reinforcement
S—satisfactory (regular instruction adequate)
M—has mastered (no more practice needed)

Two widely used inventories are:

1. Betty D. Roe, *Burns/Roe Informal Reading Inventory*. Boston: Houghton Mifflin Company, 1985 (For grades PP–12).
2. Jerry L. Johns, *Advanced Reading Inventory: Grades Seven Through College*. Dubuque, Iowa: William C. Brown, 1981.

The chief purpose of these inventories is to identify the independent, instructional, frustration, and capacity reading levels of the student. Such inventories are valuable in that they not only provide an overall estimate of the student's reading ability, but they make possible identification of the specific strengths and weaknesses of the reader. They are helpful in determining what books a student can read independently and how difficult assigned reading can be if it is to be used as instructional material. Although a reading specialist might give an entire series of inventory selections and locate all four of these levels, the content teacher may give a similar inventory based on textbooks used in a particular class to find out if students can benefit from those textbooks.

Although it is time consuming, it is possible for the teacher to construct and administer an informal reading inventory. The steps below are suggested:

1. Select a set of books (or other materials) used at various grade levels (as 7th, 8th, 9th, 10th, 11th, and 12th)—preferably a series used in the class.
2. From each book, select one passage to be used for oral reading and one passage to be used for silent reading (200 words or more each)
3. Make a copy of each of the passages from each book. (Later the student reads from the book. The teacher marks the errors on the copy.)
4. Make up approximately ten questions for each passage. The questions should be of various types, including:
   a. Main idea—Ask for the central theme of the selection.
   b. Detail—Ask for bits of information conveyed by the material.
   c. Vocabulary—Ask for meanings of words used in the passage.
   d. Sequence—Ask for a listing of events in order of their occurrence.
   e. Inference—Ask for information that is implied but not directly stated in the material.
   f. Cause and effect—Ask for related factors that establish a cause-effect relationship.
5. Direct the student to read the first passage orally. Mark and count his or her errors. Follow these directions for marking errors:
   a. Place *p* above each unknown word that must be supplied by the teacher.
   b. Underline each word or word part that is mispronounced, indicating given pronunciation above word.
   c. Circle each omitted word or word part.
   d. For insertion of words not in the text, place caret and word above where insertion was made.
   e. Use reversal mark ∿ to indicate reversals of word order or word parts.
   f. Use wavy underline to indicate repetition.
   Spontaneous corrections may be marked as well, although they should not be scored as errors. Mispronounced proper names and differences due to dialect should also not be counted as errors. Some teachers have found it effective to tape a student's oral reading, replaying the tapes to note the errors in performance.
   Then ask questions prepared for the oral reading. Count the number of questions answered correctly.
   Direct the student to read the second passage silently. Ask questions prepared for silent reading. Again, count the number of questions answered correctly.
6. Count the number of errors in oral reading. Subtract from the number of words in the selection. Then divide by number of words in the selection and multiply by 100 for the percent correct:

$$\frac{Number\ of\ words\ correct}{Number\ of\ words\ in\ selection} \times 100 = \%\ Correct$$

Total the number of correct answers to questions for both the oral and silent reading passages. Then divide by number of questions and multiply by 100 for the percent correct:

$$\frac{Number\ of\ questions\ right}{Number\ of\ questions\ asked} \times 100 = \%\ Correct$$

7. Read aloud to the student higher levels of material until you reach the highest reading level for which he or she can correctly answer 75 percent of the comprehension questions. (The highest level achieved indicates the student's probable *capacity*, or potential, reading level.)

The following chart will help the teacher in estimating the reading levels of the reader:

Level	Word Recognition		Comprehension
Independent	99%	and	90%
Instructional	95%	and	75%
Frustration	<90%	or	<50%
Capacity			75%

Various writers in the field suggest slightly differing percentages relative to independent, instructional, frustration, and capacity levels. Originally, the criteria to establish the levels were developed by Emmett Betts.[2] W. R. Powell and C. G. Dunkeld have suggested that the numerical standard used for determining the instructional level is too stringent, particularly at lower levels.[3] At the same time, Eldon Ekwall has presented evidence that the Betts criteria should be maintained, particularly if repetitions are counted as "errors."[4] Since the authors of this text do recommend counting repetitions as "errors," we have utilized the criteria as above. The set of criteria for the reading levels are basically those proposed by Johnson and Kress.[5]

Again, it should be pointed out that the informal reading inventory provides only an estimate of student reading levels; the teacher must use his or her professional judgment in interpreting the results. Further, reading at the instructional level can be achieved only if the reader receives instruction before and/or while reading selected materials at that level.

Secondary Reading Inventory (SRI)

Joseph Vaughan and Paula Gaus[6] suggest an alternate secondary reading inventory, which combines features of the group reading inventory and the informal reading inventory previously described. They suggest that five silent reading selections (fictional, factual, social studies, scientific, and problematic) be used from each of four reading levels (fifth-sixth, seventh-eighth, ninth-tenth, eleventh-twelfth). First the student is asked to rank the subject areas according to interest. The inventory would start at the fifth-sixth level, with the selection at the middle of the student's interest range. If the student's comprehension falls between 70 percent and 90 percent on the passage, the next higher level is administered until the student fails to meet the 70 percent comprehension criterion. On the highest level at which this criterion is met, the selections from the other interest areas are administered to find out the student's differing comprehension in the various types of selections.

Cloze Test Procedure

An alternative method of assessment that can provide information similar to that provided by the informal reading inventory is the cloze test procedure. This test is easy to construct, administer, and score. It takes much less time to administer than the informal reading inventory.

Again, the student is asked to read selections of increasing levels of difficulty and to supply words that have been deleted from the passage.

A sample cloze passage is given in Example 8.12.

EXAMPLE 8.12   SAMPLE CLOZE PASSAGE ————————

Rocks exposed to the atmosphere slowly change. Air, water, and materials _____ living things can react _____ minerals in rock to _____ or even
(1)   (2)   (3)
remove them.

_____ is the process by _____ rocks change to soil. _____ may result
(4)   (5)   (6)
from both _____ and physical action on _____ .
(7)   (8)

In a common form _____ chemical weathering, minerals containing
(9)

_____ are broken down. Iron _____ to moisture and air _____ a red-brown
(10)   (11)   (12)

coating or _____ . The iron combines with _____ and becomes a new
(13)   (14)

_____ , iron oxide (rust). Similar _____ occur in rocks exposed _____ air
(15)   (16)   (17)

and water. Some _____ are more easily changed _____ than others. In the
(18)   (19)

_____ of air and moisture, _____ , for instance, changes to _____
(20)   (21)   (22)

minerals. Quartz, however, is _____ to chemical changes.
(23)

Physical _____ acting on rocks cause _____ *weathering.* In mechanical
(24)   (25)

weathering, _____ are broken down by _____ forces as windblown
(26)   (27)

sand, _____ water, and temperature changes _____ cause rocks to

(28)   (29)

shrink _____ expand.

(30)

    Plants also weather _____. Simple plants called lichens _____ grow on

(31)   (32)

unweathered rocks. _____ the lichens weather the _____, other types of

(33)   (34)

plants _____ themselves. Plants remove chemicals _____ developing soil.

(35)   (36)

Living and _____ plants may also add _____ such as acids to _____. Besides

(37)   (38)   (39)

their chemical effects, _____ roots may act upon _____ physically. Some

(40)   (41)

plant roots _____ work their way into _____ and crevices and split _____

(42)   (43)   (44)

apart. Plants also have _____ great effect on soil _____ it is formed.

(45)   (46)

Soil _____ might otherwise be carried _____ by wind or water _____ be

(47)   (48)   (49)

held in place _____ a dense mat of plant roots.

(50)

Answers:

1. from, 2. with, 3. alter, 4. Weathering, 5. which, 6. It, 7. chemical, 8. rocks, 9. of, 10. iron, 11. exposed, 12. develops, 13. rust, 14. oxygen, 15. substance, 16. changes, 17. to, 18. minerals, 19. chemically, 20. presence, 21. feldspar, 22. clay, 23. resistant, 24. forces, 25. mechanical, 26. rocks, 27. such, 28. moving, 29. that, 30. and, 31. rocks, 32. can, 33. As, 34. rocks, 35. establish, 36. from, 37. decaying, 38. chemicals, 39. rocks, 40. plant, 41. rocks, 42. can, 43. cracks, 44. rocks, 45. a, 46. after, 47. which, 48. away, 49. can, 50. by.

Source: Norman Abraham et al., *Interaction of Earth and Time*, 2nd ed. (Chicago: Rand McNally Co., 1976), pp. 262–265.

Following are the steps used for constructing, administering, and scoring the cloze test:

1. Select a set of materials typical of those used in your classroom. Select a passage of about 250 words. It should be one the students have not read previously.
2. Delete every fifth word until you have about fifty deletions. Replace the deleted words with blanks of uniform length. No words should be deleted in the first sentence.
3. Ask the student to fill in each blank with the exact word that has been deleted. Allow time to complete the test.
4. Count the number of correct responses. Do not count spelling mistakes as wrong answers; do not count synonyms as correct answers.
5. Convert the number of right responses into a percentage.

The following criteria may be used in determining levels:

Accuracy	*Reading Level*
57% or greater	Independent reading level
44–57%	Instructional reading level
Below 44%	Frustration level

A student who achieves a percentage of accuracy at or above the instructional level is asked to complete the next higher level cloze test until that student reaches his or her highest instructional level. The teacher can probably assign instructional reading of tested material to any student who makes a score of between 44 and 57 percent on that material. A score of 57 percent or better on any passage means the teacher can use the material from which the passage was taken for independent reading. A score of less than 44 percent accuracy on a passage would indicate that the material from which the passage was taken is probably not suitable for that particular student.

Readers who wish to know more about the cloze procedure should refer to the references cited in Thought Question 8 at the end of this chapter. Another source that answers frequently asked questions about the cloze procedure is John Bormuth's "The Cloze Readability Procedure," in *Elementary English*, 45 (April 1968), 429–436. These references explain the research that supports the following statements:

a. Scores on cloze readability tests correlate with scores on conventionally designed comprehension tests.
b. Cloze difficulties of passages correlate with the difficulties of the passages as determined by conventional tests.
c. The traditional, fifth-word deletion pattern appears to be the best pattern.
d. For test purposes, there is no advantage in giving credit for synonyms when the purpose is to differentiate among students.
e. The established level criteria are comparable to scores judged as instructional, independent, or frustration level on conventional comprehension tests.

An alternative cloze has been proposed by Arnold Burron and Amos Claybaugh.[7] They suggest that when constructing a cloze for content materials, a passage of 520 words should be selected, with every tenth word deleted, due to the denseness of concepts and technical language.

Another modification of the cloze has been proposed by Richard Baldauf and others for lower secondary English-second-language students.[8] This is a "matching" cloze: students select from the five words randomly ordered in the margin and copy the correct ones into the five blank spaces for one set of sentences of the passage, continuing this procedure for other sections of the passage.

To obtain very specific information about students' use of particular types of context clues a teacher may wish to delete specific categories of words in specific contexts, rather than every nth word.[9] For example, only nouns or only adjectives might be deleted. Of course the modification would make determination of reading levels according to the criteria indicated on page 369 inappropriate.

According to Peter Johnston, a cloze test does not present "a normal reading task because often one must hold an empty slot in memory until one can locate information to fill it and construct a meaning for the segment. This places quite a demand on short-term memory, and there are search skills involved."[10]

A caution about the use of the cloze procedure needs to be provided here. Students should be given an explanation of the purpose of the procedure and a few practice passages before a cloze test is used for assessment. Students need to be encouraged to use the information contained in the material surrounding a blank in order to make a decision about what word to place in the blank or they may simply guess without considering all of the available clues. Some students exhibit anxiety with this form of test, and some practice may help alleviate this anxiety.

The cloze test is informal and provides only an approximation of a student's ability to read selected materials. Once again the teacher must be guided by his or her professional judgment in interpreting test scores.

Observation Checklist

It has been mentioned that careful teacher judgment must enter into decisions about a student's reading ability. In the classroom, the teacher has the opportunity to see each student perform every day and to become aware of the level and nature of each student's performance. The teacher should keep questions such as the following in mind as he or she observes each student:

1. Does the student approach the assignment with enthusiasm?
2. Does he or she apply an appropriate study method?
3. Can he or she find answers to questions of a literal type (main idea, details, sequence, and so forth)?
4. Is he or she reading below the surface (answering interpretive and critical level questions)?
5. Can he or she ascertain the meanings of new or unfamiliar words? What word recognition skills are used?
6. Can he or she use locational skills in the book?
7. Can he or she use reference skills for various reference sources?
8. Is he or she reading at different rates for different materials and purposes?

Observation of reading behaviors can and should take place continuously in the classroom. Every reading activity the students engage in, whether instructional or recreational, provides a possible source of diagnostic information.

Observations will be more directed if a systematic record of observations is kept. One of the values of such a record is that it provides information for planning instruction. Patterns of student development will become apparent over a period of days and weeks. Consistent and new needs will be noted. Growth of the student and other changes will be more evident.

When a student gives an oral report, or reads orally, the teacher has the opportunity to observe the following:

Oral report	*Oral reading*
pronunciation	methods of word attack
general vocabulary	word recognition problems
specialized vocabulary	rate of reading
sentence structure	phrasing
organization of ideas	peer reactions
interests	

Observation may suggest a need for an individual interview with the student. In this conference, a teacher can learn whether a student has successfully completed a given assignment and can assess the student's attitudes toward reading, school, and self, as well as his or her relations with other students. The student may divulge the uses he or she has for reading.

Self-assessment

Self-appraisal techniques can be used to help students evaluate their own reading strengths and weaknesses. Such techniques include:

1. *Discussion*. Self-assessment may focus upon a single topic, such as word recognition, meaning of vocabulary, comprehension, study skills, or problems in reading a particular textbook. With guiding questions from the teacher, the students can discuss, orally or in writing, their strengths and weaknesses in regard to the particular topic.
2. *Structured interview or conference*. After the student has written a reading autobiography (see page 373), such questions as the following may be asked:
   a. How do you figure out the pronunciation or meaning of an unknown word?
   b. What steps are you taking to develop your vocabulary?
   c. What do you do to get the main ideas from your reading?
   d. Do you use the same rate of reading in most of your assignments?
   e. What method of study do you use most?
   f. How do you organize your material to remember it?
   g. What special reference books have you used lately in the writing of a report?
   h. How do you handle graphic aids that appear in the reading material?
   i. How do you study for a test?
   j. What could you do to become an even better reader?

3. *Self-rating checklist.* A sample checklist is provided in Example 8.13. It deals with several broad areas. Similar checklists could be prepared that focus upon particular skills, such as reading to follow directions.

EXAMPLE 8.13 SELF-RATING CHECKLIST

Name _____   Date _____

Subject _____

Please rate yourself on these items:

	Good	Average	Need Help
1. Pronouncing and knowing the meaning of most of the words in your content book	____	____	____
2. Using parts of textbooks	____	____	____
3. Using the dictionary	____	____	____
4. Using strategies to help increase vocabulary	____	____	____
5. Answering questions that call for critical thinking	____	____	____
6. Being flexible in reading rate	____	____	____
7. Knowing a good study method	____	____	____
8. Outlining, summarizing, and taking notes	____	____	____
9. Locating materials in books and reference sources	____	____	____
10. Writing a report	____	____	____
11. Following printed directions	____	____	____
12. Interpreting graphic aids	____	____	____
13. Remembering material	____	____	____
14. Test taking	____	____	____

Other Informal Measures

In addition to testing and measuring reading achievement, informal assessment tools can be used by the content teacher to measure such nonreading behaviors as attitudes and interests. Each of these behaviors can directly or indirectly affect a student's reading achievement.

Attitude

A student's affective response to reading selections critically affects his or her becoming a reader. Therefore, some kind of measure of the student's attitudes toward reading experiences is an important aspect of the total assessment program.

Reading takes many forms and means many different things to different students; a student might enjoy reading the sports page but be bored or even dislike reading a library book to complete an English assignment. Whether or not a student likes "reading" depends on what he or she is reading and for what purpose.

Therefore, perhaps the most valid measure of a student's attitude toward reading would be his or her responses to individual selections. A scale such as the one presented in Example 8.14 could be given to students after they have read particular selections.

EXAMPLE 8.14   RESPONSE SCALE ───────────

Directions: Rate the selection you have just read by circling the appropriate letter for each item.

A = strongly agree; B = agree; C = disagree; D = strongly disagree

1. I enjoyed reading this selection.	A	B	C	D
2. This selection was boring.	A	B	C	D
3. This selection held my attention.	A	B	C	D
4. I disliked reading this selection.	A	B	C	D

Students are not expected to respond positively to all their reading experiences, but if the majority of their responses indicate negative attitudes toward reading, something is amiss. A profile of individual scores may be kept as an ongoing assessment of each student's attitude toward reading. Content teachers should be concerned about the attitudes of students toward reading material; students who have negative attitudes toward the material may not comprehend well and will probably need additional motivation for reading. An assessment near the beginning of the school term should be valuable to content teachers.

To make a more comprehensive study of the student's reading, some authorities suggest the use of the reading autobiography—a developmental history of a student's reading experiences. Some accounts give details concerning the student's early reading experiences, when and how he or she was taught, range and variety of his or her reading, home background, and use of available resources. Other autobiographies reveal the writer's attitude, special reading interests, and perhaps reading difficulties. Sometimes they include the writer's ideas about ways to overcome the difficulties that he or she has recognized.

Other attitude assessment instruments include one prepared by Larry D. Kennedy and Ronald S. Halinski. It is a seventy-item instrument, in which students respond to statements according to a four-point scale—Strongly Agree,

Agree, Disagree, and Strongly Disagree. A copy of the instrument may be found in the *Journal of Reading*, 18 (April 1975), 518–522, in the article entitled "Measuring Attitudes: An Extra Dimension." A second instrument can be found in Thomas H. Estes, "A Scale to Measure Attitude Toward Reading," *Journal of Reading*, 15 (November 1971), 135–138. Also see the following article: Kenneth L. Dulin and Robert D. Chester, "A Validated Study of the Estes Scale Attitude Scales," *Journal of Reading*, 18 (October 1974), 56–59.

Interests

Interest is often the key that unlocks effort. Consequently, a study of students' reading and other interests is an important part of the teaching procedure. The dynamic force of interest should be fully used; so the teacher should plan ways to motivate the student and show how a subject is related to his or her personal life.

Studies have been conducted on the reading interests of students. One guide is *Books and the Teen-age Reader* by G. Robert Carlsen (New York: Bantam Books, 1980). It is, of course, helpful to know the stages of interest development through which students frequently progress from early adolescence. However, the subject-matter teacher is interested in more than a knowledge of the interests of students in general. The teacher needs to know the specific interests of a student in order to capitalize upon them in recommending materials.

One of the ways to learn a student's reading interests is through observation in daily classes. The teacher notes the books the student chooses to read, the degree of concentration and enjoyment with which he or she reads them, his or her eagerness to talk about them, and the desire to read more books of a similar nature or books by the same author.

More detailed information about reading interests may be obtained from an interest inventory. An inventory should include both general interests and reading interests. A sample inventory is presented in Example 8.15.

EXAMPLE 8.15 GENERAL AND READING INTERESTS INVENTORY —

Name: _____   Grade: _____   Age: _____

General Interests
1. What do you like to do in your free time?
2. What are your favorite TV shows?
3. What are your favorite hobbies?
4. What games or sports do you like best?
5. What clubs or other groups do you belong to?
6. Do you have any pets? If yes, what?
7. What is your favorite type of movies?
8. What is your favorite school subject?
9. What is your most disliked school subject?
10. What kind of work do you want to do when you finish secondary school?

Reading
1. How often do you go to the public library?
2. What are the favorite books that you own?
3. What things do you like to read about?
4. Which comic books do you read?
5. Which magazines do you read?
6. What are some books you have liked?
7. What part of the newspapers do you read most frequently?
8. Do you like to read?

MINIMUM COMPETENCY TESTS

Another type of testing procedure, essentially criterion-referenced, is the assessment of minimum competency. Due to an increased concern with the quality of education today, many states have adopted some kind of minimum competency test.[11] Some states require the student to "pass" a minimum competency test in order to graduate from high school. Such tests are basically of two types: one is a "survival skills" reading test, asking the student to read a schedule, a medicine bottle label, or the like; the other type is the "basic skills" test. Both tests assess specific skills and are scored on the basis of a specific cutoff point, but there is frequent disagreement as to what cutoff point should be set for "passing."

The trend toward competency assessment has created much concern and controversy. Local school systems or state departments of education have to consider many questions: What competencies should be assessed? How should they be measured? Where should the "passing" cutoff point be placed? What should be done for those who "fail" the test?

Whatever skills are selected as "minimum," they must be taught in a functional manner.[12] That is, they should be those skills that are needed and used by readers for reading informational sources and those skills that the reader feels there is a purpose for learning. As one example, employment notices in the classified section of the newspaper are generally most relevant to those who are trying to enter the job market. Additionally, instructional activities for functional reading should focus upon comprehension. Remember all the strategies suggested in earlier chapters dealing with ways to make printed materials more understandable to students.

There are widely different practices in the field of competency testing. For example, certain local school systems have developed minimum basic reading objectives and tests for secondary school students. In other situations, the state departments of education have established objectives and have prepared tests that are administered at specified grade levels. Such instructional objectives as the following are commonly included on such tests: identifying main ideas and details; finding sequence and cause-and-effect patterns; making inferences; following written directions; using an index and table of contents; using a dictionary;

extracting information from graphic aids; and interpreting and completing common forms. In some secondary schools, a commercially available standardized survey reading test (such as *Gates-MacGinitie Reading Test: Survey*) has been selected as the assessment instrument. Other schools have utilized commercially available standardized reading tests that measure survival reading skills or basic skills as a basis for high school graduation requirements.

Two other tests frequently used in competency testing are as follows:

Performance Assessment in Reading (PAIR). California Test Bureau/McGraw-Hill, Del Monte Research Park, Monterey, Calif. 93940. 1978.
Reading/Everyday Activities in Life (R/EAL). Westwood Press, 76 Madison Avenue, New York, N.Y. 10016.*

The cutoff point for "passing" depends upon the arbitrary judgment of the local school system or the state department of education. In the same way, there is a lack of uniformity in "preventive" or "follow-up" plans with students who are poor achievers or do not obtain a required score. In some situations, "nonpassing" students are assigned to a remedial reading class in high school. Credit for the English requirement may be given when a student successfully completes the class. The student may be assigned to a reading class throughout high school, depending upon improvement.

Beyond the educational or reading issues, legal questions have been raised about the general competency testing movement. Basically, the concerns revolve around such topics as

Selection of competencies tested
Time provided for a phase-in period prior to implementation
The match between the content of competency tests and the instructional program
Culturally biased test items
Provision for multiple testing opportunities
Applicability to special education students
Establishment of "passing" score
Appropriateness of remedial programs for "nonpassers"[13]

A position on minimum competencies in reading was adopted by the Board of Directors of the International Reading Association in 1979 as follows:

---

*For a brief review of the commercially available tests of functional literacy cited in this section, see Patricia Anders, "Tests of Functional Literacy," *Journal of Reading*, 24 (April 1981), 612–619. Other references dealing with the many issues of competency testing include Cecelia Algra's "Meeting the Challenge of a Minimum Reading Graduation Requirement," in *Journal of Reading*, 21 (February 1978), 392–402. The entire issue of the October 1978 *Journal of Reading* is devoted to the topic of competency testing. Also, see Mary K. Monteith, "Minimum Competencies, Minimal Competency Testing: Reading and Language," *Journal of Reading* (May 1978), 750–753.

No single measure or method of assessment of minimum competencies should ever be sole criterion for graduation or promotion of a student. Multiple indices assessed through a variety of means, including teacher observation, student work samples, past academic performance, and student self-reports, should be employed to assess competence.

Furthermore, every effort should be made through every possible means to remediate weaknesses diagnosed through tests. Retention in grade or non-promotion of a student should be considered as only one alternative means of remediation and one that should be considered only when all other available methods have failed.

For these reasons, the Board of Directors of the International Reading Association is firmly opposed to the efforts of any school, state, provincial or national agency which attempts to determine a student's graduation or promotion on the basis of any single assessment.[14]

The Minimum Competency Programs and Reading Committee of the International Reading Association (IRA) conducted a survey in 1983 and 1984 that was designed to investigate the extent and nature of minimum competency testing and programs in reading in the United States.[15] Twenty-nine states indicated that minimum competency testing in reading is required, and two others reported that plans to implement such a program were then in motion. Nineteen states reported no plans to implement competency testing in reading. Only fifteen of the states linked minimum competency to graduation. Since Jeanne Chall[16] found that forty-two states were planning to implement competency testing in 1979, it appears that interest in this approach is waning somewhat.

The IRA Committee's study[17] also produced the information that twenty-two of the twenty-nine states with minimum competency programs require remedial help for those who need it. However, only fifteen of these states reported that funding was provided for such programs. Linda Gambrell notes that "the present trend appears to be toward testing across several grade levels and providing remediation across several grade levels for students who fail rather than using minimum competency testing results as a criterion for retention or graduation."[18]

Although W. J. Popham and others[19] concede that "it is still too early to tell whether most competency testing programs are having good or bad effects," they describe four programs (instituted in Detroit, Maryland, Texas, and South Carolina) that have resulted in positive influences on student learning.

SUMMARY

Teachers at the secondary school level often need to interpret norm-referenced reading test results to learn about individual students' reading abilities and about the range of reading abilities within the classroom. Results from other tests such as general academic ability tests (often called mental or intelligence tests) also are helpful for revealing students' capability levels.

Perhaps more useful to content teachers are informal tests, including the *San Diego Quick Assessment*, for finding the general reading level of a student; the group reading inventory (GRI), which gives an indication of how well students read a particular textbook; the informal reading inventory, which provides an overall estimate of a student's reading ability and points out some strengths and weaknesses; and the cloze procedure, which provides the teacher with two types of information—an overall view of the student's reading ability and the appropriateness of text material for the student.

The type of assessment measure used most frequently by secondary school content teachers is the skill inventory, which provides information about whether students have developed the specific reading skills necessary to understand content material in the teacher's particular area.

Since careful judgment enters into decisions about the level of each student's performance, the classroom teacher must carefully observe students as they perform daily tasks with printed materials. Beyond that, teachers can help students utilize self-appraisal techniques as a way of evaluating their strengths and weaknesses in handling printed materials.

Student attitude toward the reading experiences in the content classroom is an important aspect of the overall assessment program. Besides observation and discussion, there are teacher-made devices, self-evaluation devices, and other instruments available to show attitude. Similarly, since interest is often the key that unlocks effort, content teachers who know the general and reading interests of students can plan ways to motivate the students and can capitalize upon these interests when selecting and using materials.

The minimum competency test is relevant for all secondary school teachers who wish to develop in their students basic reading competencies that relate to their particular subject matter. Being familiar with some common competency tests gives teachers clues about minimum essential skills and how these skills can be utilized in the content classroom.

SELF-TEST

1. What type of norm-referenced test measures general achievement in reading? (a) Survey (b) Diagnostic (c) Oral (d) Study skills
2. What feature about a norm-referenced test is assessed when the results on one form of a test are compared with results of an equivalent form of the test? (a) Validity (b) Reliability (c) Population (d) None of these
3. What does one call expressing test scores in terms of position within a set of 100 scores? (a) Grade equivalent (b) Percentile rank (c) Stanine (d) Median score
4. What would be the reading capacity or expectancy of a mid-year seventh grader who scores 90 on an intelligence test? (a) 4.6 (b) 6.8 (c) 5.2 (d) None of these
5. What reliability coefficient should subtests have to be of much use? (a) Above .50 (b) Above .65 (c) Above .75 (d) .80
6. What level is usually indicated by the score achieved on a norm-referenced silent reading test? (a) Independent (b) Instructional (c) Frustration (d) Each of these

7. If a student misses no more than one of ten words on a list of graded words, what level does this represent? (a) Independent (b) Instructional (c) Frustration (d) Capacity

8. What classification may be given material on a group reading inventory that was read with a comprehension score of 50 percent or less? (a) Independent (b) Instructional (c) Frustration (d) Capacity

9. For which skills common to all content areas can sample skill inventories be prepared? (a) Parts of a textbook (b) Reference sources (c) Specialized vocabulary (d) All of the above

10. What is (are) the chief purpose(s) of an informal reading inventory? (a) Identifying reading levels (b) Analyzing oral reading errors (c) Providing an exact assessment of reading ability (d) Both *a* and *b*

11. In using cloze test procedures as recommended in this text, which words are deleted in content material? (a) Every fifth (b) Every eighth (c) Every tenth (d) None of these

12. What would be perhaps the most valid measure of a student's attitude toward reading? (a) Reaction to specific selections (b) A reading autobiography (c) "Incomplete sentences" (d) None of these

13. What technique may be utilized in self-appraisal by students? (a) Discussion (b) Conference (c) Checklist (d) All of these

14. Which type of score is the NCE most similar to? (a) Grade equivalents (b) Stanines (c) Percentiles (d) None of these

15. Which is the least desirable way of expressing test results? (a) Percentile ranks (b) Stanines (c) Grade equivalents (d) Scale scores

16. What type of score uses the specific content skills or objectives measured by the test as a reference point? (a) Norm-referenced score (b) Criterion-referenced score (c) Anticipated achievement score (d) Normal curve equivalents

17. What type of measure is available for minimum competency testing? (a) Norm-referenced tests (b) Criterion-referenced tests (c) Both of these (d) Neither of these

THOUGHT QUESTIONS

1. What do you consider to be the major strengths and weaknesses of each of the major assessment procedures discussed in this chapter?

2. Which way of reporting results of norm-referenced tests do you think is the most helpful? Why?

3. The "reading expectancy" concept has been criticized by several reading authorities. Read about this controversy and discuss it with others. Then prepare a statement about this way of estimating potential and identifying underachievers. Justify your statements.

4. What are some of the major strengths and weaknesses of CRTs?

5. In what ways may a group reading inventory be useful to a content area teacher?

6. Which reading skill inventory do you think would be most helpful to you as a content area teacher? Why?

7. Why might secondary teachers prefer the cloze test procedure to the informal reading inventory?

8. Consider these questions about the cloze procedure: "Why choose a selection of about 250 words?"; "Why delete every fifth word?"; "Why must the replacement be the exact word?"; "How were the percentages/levels established?" Research these questions and report your findings. Two helpful resources are Michael C. McKenna and Richard D. Robinson, *An Introduction to the Cloze Procedure*, An Annotated Bibliography, rev. ed. (Newark, Del.: International Reading Association, 1980), and Eugene A Jongsma, *Cloze Instruction Research: A Second Look* (Newark, Del.: International Reading Association, 1980).

9. Do you think a self-assessment checklist would help you learn more about a student's reading of a content area textbook? If so, prepare a self-rating checklist that would be most appropriate in your classroom.

10. How would you revise the general and reading interests inventory to be most appropriate to your specific content area?

11. Do you agree with the position of IRA on the use of minimum competency test results? Why or why not?

ENRICHMENT ACTIVITIES

1. Secure a copy (and manual) of a norm-referenced reading test of each of these types: survey and study skills. Study these tests and report on them to your peers. Use this outline for evaluation.

    I. Test Overview
      A. Title
      B. Author(s)
      C. Publisher
      D. Date of publication—original, revised
        1. Manual
        2. Test
      E. Level and forms
        1. Grade level
        2. Individual or group
        3. Number of forms available
      F. Administration time
      G. Scoring—hand or machine scorable
      H. Cost
        1. Question booklets—consumable or not
        2. Answer sheets
        3. Manual

    II. Evaluation of Subtests and Items
       A. Description of subtests
         1. Given meaningful name—describe test adequately
         2. Is each subtest long enough to provide usable results?
         3. Is sequential development of each subtest logical and transition smooth?
       B. Author's purpose, reflected in selection of items
       C. Scoring ease and usability of tables
       D. Directions—clarity and level of language appropriate to grade level
       E. Design—format, currentness, printing, legibility, pictures
       F. Readability
   III. Evaluation of Reliability and Validity
       A. Norming population
         1. Size
         2. Age, grade, sex
         3. Range of ability
         4. Socioeconomic level
         5. Date of administration
       B. Validity
         1. Content validity
           a. Face validity
           b. Logical or sampling validity
          2. Empirical validity
           a. Concurrent
           b. Predictive
         3. Construct validity
           a. Construct and theory of which construct is a part clearly defined
           b. Discriminant or convergent validity evidence
           c. Significant difference found in performance between groups that have varying degrees of this trait?
         4. Does reported validity appear adequate in relation to author's stated purpose? Why or why not?
*2. If feasible, administer a norm-referenced reading rate test to a student and interpret the results.
  3. Calculate the reading expectancy level, given the following data:
    a. IQ of 80; mid-year (6.5) seventh grader
    b. IQ of 90; mid-year (10.5) eleventh grader
    c. IQ of 120; mid-year (8.5) ninth grader
*4. Administer the San Diego Quick Assessment to a student. Share your findings about reading level with peers.

---

*These activities are designed for in-service teachers, student teachers, and practicum students.

*5. Prepare a group reading inventory, using content area reading materials. Administer your inventory to a student, record your results, and share the findings with the class.

6. Using a textbook of your choice, develop at least ten sample questions on each of the book parts listed. (If a particular book part is not included in your text, select examples from supplemental materials.)
   a. Preface, Introduction, or Foreword
   b. Table of Contents
   c. Index
   d. Appendix
   e. Glossary
   f. Unit or Chapter Introduction and/or Summary

*7. Prepare a reading skills inventory for a content area textbook. Administer it to a student, record your results, and share the findings with the class.

*8. Secure a published IRI and administer it to a student. Report the results to the class.

*9. Prepare an IRI using content area reading materials. Administer it to a student, record the results, and share your findings with the class.

*10. Prepare a cloze procedure test for a passage of content area reading material. Administer it to a student. Report the results to the class.

11. If feasible, visit a secondary school classroom. Use the observation checklist on page 370 to note the reading pattern of a student.

*12. Prepare a self-appraisal checklist of some aspect of reading (see sample on study skills, Example 8.13). Administer to a student and report your findings to the class.

*13. Administer an interest inventory to a student. What information may be utilized in the instructional program?

*14. Prepare an interest check on one topic of study in your content area. If feasible, administer it to a student.

*15. If possible, administer a criterion-referenced test to a group of secondary students. Also, prepare a criterion-referenced test, using content area reading materials.

16. Secure a copy of a minimum competency reading test. Study it and report on it to your peers.

NOTES

1. Guy L. Bond, Miles A. Tinker, and Barbara B. Wasson, *Reading Difficulties: Their Diagnosis and Correction*, 4th ed. (Englewood Cliffs, N.J.: Prentice-Hall, 1979), p. 62.

2. Emmett A. Betts, *Foundations of Reading Instruction* (New York: American Book Company, 1946).

3. W. R. Powell, "Reappraising the Criteria for Interpreting Informal Reading Inventories," in *Reading Diagnosis and Evaluation*, ed. J. DeBoer (Newark, Del.: Inter-

*These activities are designed for in-service teachers, student teachers, and practicum students.

national Reading Association, 1970). William R. Powell and C. G. Dunkeld, "Validity of the I R I Reading Levels," *Elementary English*, 48 (October 1971), 637–642.

4. Eldon E. Ekwall, "Should Repetitions Be Counted As Errors?" *The Reading Teacher*, 27 (January 1974), 365–367.

5. Marjorie S. Johnson and Roy A. Kress, *Informal Reading Inventories* (Newark, Del.: International Reading Association, 1965).

6. Joseph L. Vaughan, Jr., and Paula J. Gaus, "Secondary Reading Inventory: A Modest Proposal," *Journal of Reading*, 21 (May 1978), 716–720.

7. Arnold Burron and Amos L. Claybaugh, *Using Reading to Teach Subject Matter: Fundamentals for Content Teachers* (Columbus, Ohio: Charles E. Merrill, 1974), pp. 50–51.

8. Richard B. Baldauf, Jr., et al., "Can Matching Cloze Be Used with Secondary E S L Pupils?" *Journal of Reading*, 23 (February 1980), 435–440.

9. Peter H. Johnston, *Reading Comprehension Assessment: A Cognitive Basis* (Newark, Del.: International Reading Association, 1983), p. 63.

10. Ibid., pp. 62–63.

11. Chris Pipho, "Minimum Competency Testing in 1978: A Look at State Standards," *Phi Delta Kappan*, 60 (May 1978), 585–588. This entire issue is devoted to minimum competency testing. See also W. James Popham and Stuart C. Rankin, "Minimum Competency Tests Spur Instructional Improvement," *Phi Delta Kappan*, 62 (May 1981), 637–639.

12. Linda B. Gambrell and Craig J. Cleland, "Minimum Competency Testing: Guidelines for Functional Reading Programs," *Journal of Reading*, 25 (January 1982), 342–344.

13. Shirley Boes Neill, "A Summary of Issues in the Minimum Competency Movement," *Phi Delta Kappan*, 60 (February 1979), 452–453.

14. *The Reading Teacher*, 33 (October 1979), 54–55.

15. Linda B. Gambrell, "Minimum Competency Testing and Programs in Reading: A Survey of the United States," *Journal of Reading*, 28 (May 1985), 735–738.

16. Jeanne S. Chall, "Minimum Competency in Reading: An Informal Survey of the States," *Phi Delta Kappan*, 60 (January 1979), 351–352.

17. Gambrell, pp. 736–737.

18. Ibid., p. 737.

19. James W. Popham et al., "Measurement-Driven Instruction: It's on the Road," *Phi Delta Kappan*, 66 (May 1985), 628–634.

SELECTED REFERENCES

Allington, Richard, and Michael Strange. *Learning Through Reading in the Content Areas.* Lexington, Mass.: D. C. Heath and Company, 1980. Chapters 4 and 5.

Blanton, William E., Roger Farr, and J. Jaap Tuinman. *Reading Tests for the Secondary Grades.* Newark, Del.: International Reading Association, 1972.

———, eds. *Measuring Reading Performance.* Newark, Del.: International Reading Association, 1974.

Burmeister, Lou E. *Reading Strategies for Middle and Secondary School Teachers.* 2nd ed. Reading, Mass.: Addison-Wesley, 1978. Chapter 4.

Burron, Arnold, and Amos Claybaugh. *Using Reading to Teach Subject Matter: Fundamentals for Content Teachers.* Columbus, Ohio: Charles E. Merrill, 1974. Chapters 2 and 3.

Cheek, Earl H., Jr., and Martha Collins Cheek. *Reading Instruction Through Content Teaching.* Columbus, Ohio: Charles E. Merrill, 1983. Chapter 4.

Early, Margaret, and Diane J. Sawyer. *Reading to Learn in Grades 5 to 12.* San Diego, Calif.: Harcourt Brace Jovanovich, 1984. Chapter 6.

Estes, Thomas, and Joseph L. Vaughan. *Reading and Learning in Content Classrooms: Diagnostic and Instructional Strategies.* Boston: Allyn and Bacon, 1978.

Friedman, Myles I., and Michael D. Rowls. *Teaching Reading and Thinking Skills.* New York: Longman, 1980. Chapter 11.

Johnson, M. S., and R. A. Kress. *Informal Reading Inventories.* Newark, Del.: International Reading Association, 1965.

Johnston, Peter H. *Reading Comprehension Assessment: A Cognitive Basis.* Newark, Del.: International Reading Association, 1983.

Jongsma, Kathleen S., and Eugene A. Jongsma. "Test Review: Commercial Informal Reading Inventories." *The Reading Teacher* (March 1981), 697–705.

Karlin, Robert. *Teaching Reading in High School: Improving Reading in Content Areas.* 4th ed. New York: Harper and Row, 1984. Chapter 4.

Lamberg, Walter J., and Charles E. Lamb. *Reading Instruction in the Content Areas.* Boston: Houghton Mifflin Company, 1980. Chapters 8 and 9.

Robinson, H. Alan. *Teaching Reading and Study Strategies: The Content Areas.* Boston: Allyn and Bacon, 1978. Chapter 3.

Schell, Leo M. "Test Review: California Achievement Tests: Reading." *Journal of Reading,* 23 (April 1980), 624–628.

Shannon, Albert J. "Effects of Methods of Standardized Reading Achievement Test Administration on Attitude Toward Reading." *Journal of Reading,* 23 (May 1980), 684–686.

Shepherd, David L., *Comprehensive High School Reading Methods.* Columbus, Ohio: Charles E. Merrill, 1978. Chapters 6 and 7.

Tonjes, Marion J., and Miles V. Zintz. *Teaching Reading/Thinking/Study Skills in Content Classrooms.* Dubuque, Iowa: Wm. C. Brown, 1981. Chapter 4.

Tullock-Rhody, Regina, and J. Estill Alexander. "A Scale for Assessing Attitudes Toward Reading in Secondary Schools." *Journal of Reading,* 23 (April 1980), 609–614.

Vacca, Richard T., and Jo Anne L. Vacca. *Content Area Reading.* 2nd ed. Boston: Little, Brown and Company, 1986. Chapter 3.

Valmont, William J. "Creating Questions for Informal Reading Inventories." *The Reading Teacher,* 25 (March 1972), 509–512.

Vaughan, Joseph, Jr., and Paula J. Gaus. "Secondary Reading Inventory: A Modest Proposal." *Journal of Reading,* 21 (May 1978), 716–720.

CHAPTER
N I N E

ADJUSTING READING
ASSIGNMENTS TO FIT
ALL STUDENTS

OVERVIEW

Not all students are alike in their ability to handle printed instructional material, and the instructional material itself may not be what teachers assume it is in terms of difficulty. For these reasons, teachers have a tremendously important task to perform in adjusting their reading assignments to fit all students. Teachers know that not all students read at the same level, but teachers do not always know whether a given student in class can read at the level on which the textbook is written; in fact, they may not know what this level actually is. In order to match students with reading materials that are appropriate for them, teachers need to understand the factors that influence readability and how to use readability formulas and other measures for determining the difficulty of materials.

The variety of reading achievement levels within a classroom makes it important for teachers to have knowledge of how and when to group students for motivation and differentiated assignments. Also, if assignments truly are to fit all students, teachers need to understand means of differentiating assignments by using study guides, directed reading approaches, alternate textbooks, rewritten materials, language experience materials, and computer applications. Teaching units can be used as a vehicle for this differentiation, and selection aids can help the teacher locate materials on different topics and levels.

PURPOSE-SETTING QUESTIONS

As you read this chapter, try to answer these questions:

1. How is an understanding of the readability levels of textbook materials important to a teacher?
2. What are some types of groups that a teacher might wish to form within a classroom?
3. What is the purpose of a study guide?
4. Under what circumstances would a teacher wish to locate alternate textbooks or printed materials for use in his or her classroom?
5. Is it possible for classroom teachers to rewrite textbook materials at lower readability levels?
6. How can a teacher use language experience materials at the secondary level?
7. How can the computer be used to adjust assignments?
8. What four basic types of activities are a part of a teaching unit?
9. What selection aids are available to help secondary school teachers locate appropriate books for the readers in their classes?

KEY VOCABULARY

As you read this chapter, check your understanding of these terms:

directed reading approach
high interest, low
   vocabulary materials
language experience
   materials
multilevel materials
readability

readability formula
simulation programs
structured overview
student tutorial groups
study guides
teaching units
trade books
word processing programs

READABILITY OF PRINTED MATERIALS

When educators refer to the readability of printed materials that students are asked to read, they mean the reading difficulty of these materials. Selections that are very difficult to read are said to have high readability levels; those that are easy to read are said to have low readability levels.

Many factors influence the difficulty of printed materials. Some of these are vocabulary, sentence length, sentence complexity, abstract concepts, idea organization, size and style of print, format, reader interest, and reader background. Of the factors identified, two are directly related to the uniqueness of the reader: interest and background. A piece of literature may be of great interest to one student and yet have little appeal for another. A reader's areas of interest may be related to his or her background of experience. This background enables a reader to understand easily that material for which vocabulary and concepts have been experienced directly or vicariously by the individual.

Although all of the other factors mentioned obviously have some effect on difficulty, vocabulary and sentence length have been found by researchers to be the most important factors to use in predicting readability.

Table 9.1   Readability Formulas

	Characteristics Measured	
Formula	Vocabulary difficulty	Sentence difficulty
Dale-Chall Readability Formula[a]	Percentage of "hard words"	Average sentence length
Flesch "Reading Ease" Formula[b]	Average number of syllables per 100 words	Average sentence length
SMOG Grading Formula[c]	Polysyllabic word count for 30 sentences	
Fry Readability Graph Formula[d]	Average number of syllables per 100 words	Average number of sentences per 100 words

[a] Edgar Dale and Jeanne S. Chall, "A Formula for Predicting Readability," *Educational Research Bulletin* 27 (January 21, 1948): 11–20, 28; also Edgar Dale and Jeanne S. Chall, "A Formula for Predicting Readability: Instructions," *Educational Research Bulletin* 27 (February 18, 1948): 37–54.
[b] Rudolf Flesch, *The Art of Readable Writing* (New York: Harper and Row, 1949).
[c] Harry G. McLaughlin, "SMOG Grading—A New Readability Formula," *Journal of Reading* 12 (May 1969): 639–646.
[d] Edward Fry, "A Readability Formula that Saves Time," *Journal of Reading* 11 (April 1968): 513–516, 575–578; also Edward Fry, *Fry Readability Scale (Extended)* (Providence, R.I.: Jamestown Publishers, 1978).

Readability Formulas

Various formulas have been developed to measure the readability of printed materials. Most contain measures of vocabulary and sentence difficulty. Some of the most frequently used formulas are listed in Table 9.1.

The Dale-Chall Readability Formula is a well-validated formula, but it is relatively difficult and time consuming to use. Therefore, few secondary classroom teachers are likely to choose it as a regular teaching tool, although they can learn to use it with practice and may want to do so in special situations that need a highly valid formula. A number of samples of approximately 100 words each are used for computing readability with this formula. A word from a sample that is on the 3,000-word Dale list (words known by 80 percent of fourth graders) or a word that is an acceptable variation of a word on the list is considered easy; if the sample word is not on the list, it is considered hard. The sample scores are averaged, and a correction table is provided with which to determine the grade score for a selection. Powers, Sumner, and Kearl have revised the formula in order to modernize it.[1]

The Flesch "Reading Ease" Formula is also somewhat complex. When using the Flesch Formula, one must count the number of sentences in the sample, treating each independent unit of thought as a sentence, and must compute the average sentence length. After having determined the "Words per Sentence" and "Syllables per 100 Words" figures, one can use a chart prepared by Flesch to determine the "Reading Ease" score.[2] The Flesch "Reading Ease" Formula was recalculated at the same time that the Dale-Chall Formula was recalculated.[3] This formula is obviously time consuming for teachers to use; therefore it may not be chosen by secondary classroom teachers for use on a routine basis.

The SMOG Grading Formula requires the user to count each word of three or more syllables in each of three ten-sentence samples. The approximate square root of the number of such polysyllabic words is calculated (by taking the square root of the nearest perfect square); to this figure the number three is added to give the SMOG Grade. This formula takes less time to calculate than the Dale-Chall and Flesch formulas, and it may be chosen for use by some secondary teachers. It produces a score that reflects an independent reading level, meaning that a student reading at the indicated level could read the tested material with complete understanding.

The Fry Readability Graph is another relatively quick readability measure. To use the graph, one needs to select three 100-word samples and to determine the average number of sentences and the average number of syllables per 100 words. (The number of sentences in a 100-word sample is determined to the nearest tenth of a sentence.)[4] Using these figures, it is possible to use the graph to determine the approximate grade level of the selection. Fry's Graph and the instructions for using it are reprinted in Figure 9.1. The Fry Graph reflects an instructional reading level, the level at which a student should be able to read with teacher assistance. The authors of this text have found that, in many cases, secondary classroom teachers are more comfortable with this formula than with the other three formulas discussed here. For that reason, it is presented in more detail. There is no implication that it is superior to the other three, and teachers should use their own judgment in choosing a formula for personal use.

Some educators prefer to use the more lengthy formulas, which, they feel, are more accurate. Considering the number of factors that formulas fail to take into account, however, no formula can provide more than an approximation of level of difficulty. For this reason, the quick formulas should not be scorned. Determination of the relative difficulty levels of textbooks and other printed materials can be extremely valuable to a teacher. It has been demonstrated that estimating reading difficulty by using a formula produces much more consistent results than estimating without the aid of a formula.

If you are daunted by the prospect of counting syllables, words, sentences, and unfamiliar words, and your school has a computer or a microcomputer, you can use one of these valuable aids to save you time and effort in calculation.[5] Although a school's main-frame computer may not be available to teachers for such projects, in many cases microcomputers are.

Figure 9.1   Fry Readability Graph

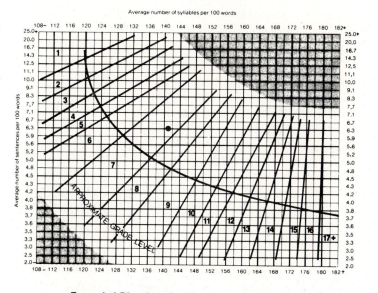

Average number of syllables per 100 words

Average number of sentences per 100 words

APPROXIMATE GRADE LEVEL

Expanded Directions for Working Readability Graph

1. Randomly select three (3) sample passages and count out exactly 100 words each, beginning with the beginning of a sentence. Do count proper nouns, initializations, and numerals.
2. Count the number of sentences in the hundred words, estimating length of the fraction of the last sentence to the nearest one-tenth.
3. Count the total number of syllables in the 100-word passage. If you don't have a hand counter available, an easy way is to simply put a mark above every syllable over one in each word, then when you get to the end of the passage, count the number of marks and add 100. Small calculators can also be used as counters by pushing numeral 1, then push the + sign for each word or syllable when counting.
4. Enter graph with *average* sentence length and *average* number of syllables; plot dot where the two lines intersect. Area where dot is plotted will give you the approximate grade level.
5. If a great deal of variability is found in syllable count or sentence count, putting more samples into the average is desirable.
6. A word is defined as a group of symbols with a space on either side; thus, *Joe, IRA, 1945,* and *&* are each one word.
7. A syllable is defined as a phonetic syllable. Generally, there are as many syllables as vowel sounds. For example, *stopped* is one syllable and *wanted* is two syllables. When counting syllables for numerals and initializations, count one syllable for each symbol. For example, *1945* is four syllables, *IRA* is three syllables, and *&* is one syllable.

Note: This "extended graph" does not outmode or render the earlier (1968) version inoperative or inaccurate; it is an extension. (REPRODUCTION PERMITTED—NO COPYRIGHT)

Degrees of Reading Power

The Degrees of Reading Power (DRP) test is a relatively new criterion-referenced test published by the College Entrance Examination Board to measure students' reading ability at different levels of difficulty. DRP units can also be used to measure readability of printed materials. By measuring both the student's reading ability and the readability of printed materials in the same units, the idea is to produce a match between student and material that is more accurate than matching by many other means available.

DRP units are based on cloze research done by John Bormuth. As Ronald Carver explains, "The DRP-Difficulty of a passage is an inverted cloze score predicted from (a) average word length in letters, (b) average sentence length in words, (c) percentage of easy words in the passage."[6] The College Entrance Examination Board's *Readability Report* lists DRP scores for many materials that are used in schools.[7] In addition, the College Entrance Examination Board will calculate DRP readability scores for any material sent to them, for a fee. Carver has studied the DRP-Difficulty scale and found it to be reliable and valid. He has also provided a table to be used to convert DRP-Difficulty scores to grade equivalent scores.[8] However, Carver has also done research that indicates that the DRP test is not valid for matching students and materials, due to internal inconsistency in the DRP system.[9]

John Bormuth[10] agrees that the DRP system overestimates the difficulty of easy material for younger readers and underestimates the difficulty of hard materials for older readers. He attributes this tendency, which is common to readability estimates, to the fact that the DRP formula, and other existing formulas, do not take into account background knowledge of the students and the level of background knowledge that authors assume in their readers. This conclusion offers a caution to all users of formulas to consider the students with whom the text is being used and the assumptions of the text's authors.

Cautions and Controversy

All teachers should be familiar with at least one formula so that they can check the printed materials used in their classes. Then perhaps students will not be asked so frequently to read textbooks or supplementary materials that are too difficult for them to comprehend. However, because of the limitations of the available formulas, teachers should always combine results obtained from the formulas with judgment based upon personal experience with the materials and knowledge of the abstractness of the concepts presented, the organization and writing style of the author, the interests of the students in the class, the backgrounds of experience of the students, and other related factors such as size and style of print and format of the material. Because sampling procedures suggested by several formulas result in limited samples, teachers should be very cautious in accepting calculated grade levels as absolutes.

Readability formulas do not have any measure for abstractness or unfamiliarity of concepts covered. Familiar words, such as "run" and "bank," do not always have their familiar meanings. A social studies text might discuss a "run on the banks," which would present a less familiar situation than "fast movement along the shore of a stream," which may be the meaning that comes to mind immediately.

Authors may organize materials clearly, or they may have very poor organization, and the clarity of their writing styles may vary immensely, with some choosing to construct sentences in less common ways and others choosing familiar sentence structures. Readability formulas contain no measures for organization or style.

Factors within a student help determine the readability of particular material for that person. If material is of high interest to a student, he or she may find the material easier to read because of high motivation to read it. Another person with similar reading skills may find the material uninteresting and, thus, much more difficult to read. Likewise, readers who have had much experience related to the topic being read will find the material easier to read than those who have had little experience with the topic. No formula has the power to foresee interest and background of particular readers.

Formulas also have no measures for such mechanical features as size and style of type and format of the printed material. Print that is too small or too large may adversely affect readability, and some styles of print make reading the material harder than do other styles. Additionally, closely packed print, unrelieved by sufficient white space, can make reading more difficult.

Other Methods of Readability Assessment

Formulas may be used to determine which materials should be reasonable to use with a given group of readers. However, there are other means of determining if material is actually appropriate for specific students. Some of these are discussed below.

Checklists

A checklist approach to assessing readability has been presented by Judith Irwin and Carol Davis.[11] Their excellent 36-item checklist is based on accepted psychological research and includes many considerations not covered by readability formulas. Items check understandability—relationships between the student's conceptual and experiential background and the textual material, concept development in the material, syntax, irrelevant details, implicit connectives, suggested resources, and readability level from formula. Items also check learnability—organizational features, reinforcement activities, and motivational procedures.

Phrase Analysis

Another system for assessing comprehensibility has been developed by Charles Clark.[12] It is called the PHAN (phrase analysis) system and considers such factors as reference cohesion, connectives, and vocabulary. Number of phrases between pronouns and their referents and number of phrases between connected information, number of inferences the reader must make, and number of potentially difficult phrase concepts are counted. Using the three totals obtained, passages having the same numbers of phrases can be compared as to comprehensibility. Higher totals reflect more difficult material. Since the PHAN system does not yield grade-level scores, Clark suggests its use in conjunction with other readability assessments, including formulas.

A Questioning Procedure

Suzanne Clewell and Anne Cliffton[13] decided upon the characteristics of a comprehensible text and then composed a list of questions that teachers should ask about a textbook in an attempt to determine its comprehensibility. The questions are arranged under the headings of textual aids, content, coherence, types of discourse, and language and style. Teachers can use the questions to make decisions related to text adoptions and instructional procedures to use with texts that have already been adopted.

User Involvement Techniques

Some techniques involve trying out representative portions of the material on prospective users. These techniques take into consideration reader interest, reader background, author's writing style and organization, abstractness of concepts, and, except for the cloze test, also may include format and print size and style. Three of these techniques are cloze tests, group reading inventory selections, and informal reading inventory selections. (See Chapter 8 for a more detailed discussion of these three techniques.)

Cloze tests[14] involve systematic deletion of every fifth word in a 250-word passage and substitution of blanks of uniform length for these words. Students are asked to fill in the blanks. Only exact words are scored as acceptable. Scores of 44–57 percent correct indicate instructional level material for the students; lower scores indicate material that is too difficult; higher scores indicate material suitable for independent use by the students. Larry Chance[15] found the cloze procedure to be a quick and reliable way to determine the readability of specific material for individual students. He also verified that subject matter teachers find it easy to construct cloze tests and use them for determining readability.

Group Reading Inventories[16] and Informal Reading Inventories[17] consist of representative passages chosen from the textbook in question, 1,000–2,000 words long for group reading inventories and approximately 200 words long for informal reading inventories. The passages are accompanied by carefully prepared sets of comprehension questions. See the discussions in Chapter 8 for question types, examples, and explanations. Comprehension scores of 75 percent to 90 percent on either measure are considered indicative of instructional level material; higher scores are indicative of independent level material; and scores below 50 percent are indicative of material that is too hard. Scores between 50 percent and 75 percent could be at times instructional and at times frustration level. Teachers should use other indicators, such as signs of student restlessness when reading, frowning, and so forth, to help determine whether the material is actually too hard. The informal reading inventory also includes a word recognition indicator of difficulty level: 95–99 percent accuracy signaling the instructional level; 99–100 percent signaling the independent level; and less than 90 percent signaling the frustration level. Both word recognition and comprehension criteria must be met for a passage to be considered independent or instructional with an informal reading inventory; but, if either frustration level criterion is met, the passage is considered to be too difficult.

Reactions of Teachers

Criscuolo, Vacca, and LaVorgna surveyed the attitudes of content area teachers toward selected reading skills and teaching strategies.[18] They asked these teachers to indicate how much sense each activity made to them. Readability formulas made sense to 70 percent of the teachers. The cloze procedure made sense to only 30 percent. Teachers may need in-service training to help them understand the cloze procedure better and to ensure that they know the limitations of readability formulas so that they will not rely on them too heavily and fail to consider other factors such as those listed in the section on "Cautions and Controversy" (pp. 390–391).

Studies of Textbooks

Unfortunately, studies have shown that secondary level textbooks in various curriculum areas tend to have high readability levels in relation to the reading abilities of the students who are expected to read them. Evidence also indicates that there is a wide variability of difficulty within single texts and that many texts do not have a gradation of difficulty from the beginning to the end. Following are some representative studies that illustrate the problem:

1. Keith Kennedy studied the readability of several high school biology textbooks using the Fry Readability Graph. Most of the textbooks in his study were designed to be used in an introductory course usually taught in the tenth grade. Of fifteen textbooks examined, only one was found to have a readability level of more than one grade level above the tenth grade, but four of the books had some parts that were written on levels well above tenth grade, some even as high as college readability level.[19] Considering the fact that not all tenth graders read on a tenth-grade level, even more of the texts may have been inappropriate for a given group of students.

2. Ann Howe and Margaret Early found that a ninth-to-tenth grade reading level was necessary to handle the Intermediate Science Curriculum Study Level I Textbook. The reading levels of the seventh and eighth grade students in their study ranged from 2.5 to 10.5, indicating that the Level I text was too difficult for many of the students.[20]

3. Peggy Elliott and Clyde Wiles studied the difficulty of math textbooks by giving a cloze test from an eighth-grade mathematics text to ninety-one certified mathematics teachers. They found that 27 percent of the teachers scored in

the instructional or frustration level on the test; that is, 27 percent of the teachers got 55 percent or fewer responses correct.[21] If mathematics teachers are not all reading at an independent level in an eighth-grade mathematics textbook, it seems unlikely that a majority of eighth graders would be doing so.

4. Calfrey Calhoun and Barbara Horner compared the readability of first-year bookkeeping texts with the reading levels of the students enrolled in the book-keeping classes. They used the Flesch Readability Formula and the Nelson-Denny Reading Test. Of the seventy-three students who participated in the study, twenty-four read below tenth-grade level, and sixteen read above twelfth-grade level. The difficulty levels for the texts were as follows: thir-teenth- to sixteenth-grade for two texts and tenth- to twelfth-grade for two texts. A significant number of the chapters in all of the textbooks had a read-ability level above the expected range of the students.[22]

5. B. K. Clark discovered that the reading levels of a sample of eighth-grade stu-dents ranged from grade six to grade twelve. Their textbooks for social studies and science were written at tenth- and eleventh-grade levels, respectively.[23] Obviously, not all of the students were adequately served by these texts.

6. J. B. Kahle found four popular high school science texts to have college read-ability levels, according to the SMOG, FOG, and Dale-Chall formulas.[24]

7. J. M. Bradley and others found a range of readability scores from fourth grade to college level for samples from American history texts designed for use at the junior high level. The readability levels varied greatly within single texts. The Fry readability graph was used to determine these scores.[25]

Teachers must be aware that the readability of almost all textbooks will vary from section to section, possibly because some sections present more complex con-cepts and thus include more difficult vocabulary and sentence structure. English teachers should be aware that literature anthologies often vary widely in read-ability from selection to selection because they contain material written by a number of different authors who have varying writing styles.

Even if textbooks are labeled properly for the intended grade placement (that is, the text says grade nine and is written on a ninth-grade difficulty level), many students in that grade will be unable to benefit from them. Many students in the ninth grade are unable to read with understanding material written on that level. Many ninth-grade students read anywhere from one to five grade levels below their placement, and a few are even further behind than that! This situation ob-viously presents a difficult problem for the teacher working with this variety of abilities. Furthermore, the teacher will have some students who are reading one to five (and possibly more) grades above their ninth-grade placement. A textbook may be adequate for teaching subject-matter concepts to these better students, but it may seem so elementary that more challenging supplementary materials will need to be provided to avoid boredom on the part of the gifted students.

Finding challenging materials for gifted students is generally not a difficult task. Difficulty often does arise, however, when teachers are confronted with textbooks that are too difficult for their students. Available materials at lower readability levels are often designed for younger children and may, therefore, seem childish to older students. Some possible solutions are to use alternate textbooks written on an appropriate maturity level; to find fiction or nonfiction trade books that cover the material at a lower readability level; to use books from high-interest, low-vocabulary series; or to rewrite the text material at a lower readability level. These solutions and several others are discussed later in this chapter.

Teachers may be encouraged by G. W. Jorgenson's findings that classroom behavior became better as material became less difficult.[26] This alone may be reason enough to incorporate readability measures to match students with textbooks.

GROUPING FOR MOTIVATION AND DIFFERENTIATED ASSIGNMENTS

Teachers who know the results of reading tests administered to their students (see Chapter 8 for a discussion of testing) and know the readability levels of the textbooks to be used can readily determine if the textbooks are appropriate, too easy, or too difficult for each student in the class. An illustration of grouping procedures based on such information is given in the following case.

Case: Ninth-Grade Science Class

Mrs. Jones is a ninth-grade science teacher. After using the Fry Readability Formula, she discovers that the science textbook assigned to her class has a readability level of ninth grade. Examination of norm-referenced reading test results for the students in her class reveals this information:

Reading grade level (Instructional)	Number of students
11	3
10	5
9	10
8	9
7	4
6	2
5	1
	34

Using the science textbook itself, she administers a cloze test to the class to help her confirm that those students reading at a ninth grade, or above, instructional level can in fact handle this textbook.

In order to have optimum utilization of the textbook, Mrs. Jones divides her class into instructional groups. Group A includes the eight students with instructional reading levels of grades 10 and 11. These students are able to read the textbook independently, without the teacher's constant supervision. They can set their own purposes for reading most of the time, or at least work cooperatively with the teacher on purpose setting.

Group *B* includes the ten students reading at a ninth-grade level, who can profit from the textbook with the aid of the teacher. Mrs. Jones needs to prepare them carefully for the reading, setting purposes for them or helping them set their own purposes. As they proceed with the reading, she needs to be available to help them with any difficulties they might have.

Group *C* includes the sixteen students reading at levels ranging from grade five to grade eight. These students would be frustrated by the reading demands of the textbook and need to have alternate reading material of some type. Mrs. Jones provides rewritten material, alternate textbooks, and supplementary library books. Obviously, the span of reading levels within Group *C* is too great for all of the students to use identical materials all of the time. Rewritten text material at the fifth-grade level is utilized by the entire group. Alternate texts are chosen to fit each student's reading level, as are supplementary library books. The things learned by each individual from the various sources are synthesized through group discussion and individual presentations of summary statements. Mrs. Jones elicits these statements through the use of the language experience approach (discussed later in this chapter).

Group *C* is able to utilize the textbook to a limited degree. For instance, all members of the group can study the graphic aids offered in the textual material. In addition, at times the nine students reading on the eighth-grade level use a limited portion of the written text with extensive help from the teacher.

Whole class discussion follows the study of a topic by the three individual groups. The poorer readers are able to contribute to the discussion, having studied the subject from material that they can understand. They learn more from the whole class discussion because the better readers have gained more insights into the overall subject through their superior ability to do critical reading. As the better readers discuss the concepts presented in the material, these concepts are clarified for others in the class.

This illustration of grouping procedure is an example of *achievement grouping,* or grouping students on the basis of their general (achieved) ability to read material of certain levels with understanding.

There are other types of grouping within a class which may facilitate differentiation of assignments or provide motivation for completing assignments. These include *needs groups, student tutorial groups, partnerships, interest groups, research groups,* and *friendship groups.* Each type is discussed below:

1. *Needs groups*—Some students in a class may have trouble with basic reading skills, which may impede their understanding of the content of the subject area textbook. For example: some students may have difficulty determining main ideas. This will make study of any subject area difficult. Some students may not be able to read to follow directions. Work in science, mathematics, art, and vocational subjects will suffer greatly. Some students may be unable to read maps adequately. Social studies and, possibly, science classes often require students to be able to handle map-reading tasks in order to completely understand the material. Some students may not be able to recognize common

prefixes and suffixes. This skill is very important in many science and mathematics classes. The examples could go on and on.

A teacher may form needs groups, each consisting of students who lack a particular skill. The needs group members may not all be from the same achievement group (or at the same reading level) because many of the best students have gaps in their reading skill development corresponding to those of poorer students. The teacher can use materials specially designed to aid students in applying needed skills to the content area involved. A needs group can be assembled when the remainder of the class is involved in other purposeful activity, such as doing research, working on a study guide, or doing supplementary reading from library books.

Needs groups are formed when a need becomes apparent to the teacher; they are disbanded when that need has been met. Some students will require only one or two meetings to achieve the desired goal. Others will need more time. No student should be retained in a needs group after he or she has mastered the needed skill.

2. *Student tutorial groups*—While the teacher is busy working with one group of students (either an achievement group or a needs group), another group of students can be assisted by a classmate who has achieved mastery in the particular area. Student tutors must be given explicit instructions as to their responsibilities. They must know exactly what they should and should not do to help classmates. (For example, if a tutor merely tells other students answers, which might be considered help by the classmates, he or she would not bring about the results desired by the teacher.) Student tutors can be particularly helpful in supervising the completion of study guide assignments, which are discussed later in this chapter on pages 400–409.

Student tutorial groups generally prove beneficial to both the tutor and the "clients." The student tutor often achieves a more complete understanding of the material in attempting to explain it to classmates or in attempting to clarify students' incomplete concepts or to correct their misconceptions. Being placed in the position of student tutor is also an ego-satisfying situation. While the tutor benefits from his or her experience, classmates generally improve their skills. Some of them may be able to express their difficulties more easily to a fellow student than to a teacher, and the student tutor may be able to explain ideas in the students' own language more adeptly than the teacher.

When student tutorial groups are used, the teacher must be careful to choose students who can work together. Some students tend to be more disruptive when in the presence of certain other classmates. Such combinations should be avoided, for they cannot possibly result in the desired outcomes. It should be clearly understood by all of the group members that any disruptive behavior will result in immediate termination of the group engaged in such behavior.

Roles in student tutorial groups should not be static; that is, one or two students should not always be tutors while the others are always in the role of clients. As many different students as possible should be allowed to function in the role of tutor. There should, of course, be the limitation that no student can act as a tutor in a situation where he or she is not competent.

3. *Partnerships*—When two (or possibly more) students have nearly attained mastery of a skill or when they have marginal competence to complete an assigned task, the teacher may decide to set up a partnership grouping. In such a grouping, the students are presented a task (for example, a study guide) to be completed and are allowed to pool their resources in order to complete it successfully. Each individual is likely to accomplish more in a partnership than working alone at a task, and success is a strong positive reinforcement for the activity or skill involved. Being successful also tends to motivate the students to continue to try in successive reading tasks.

Teachers must be as careful in choosing students for partnerships as in choosing students for tutorial groups. Disruptive partnerships should be immediately dissolved. Setting a very specific task and a time limit for the partners to complete it may help a partnership remain task oriented. Partners may work together while the teacher is involved with other groups.

4. *Interest groups*—When units are being taught in the content areas, many possibilities for additional student reading are available, often more than the teacher wishes to utilize. In such cases the teacher may allow class members to choose areas of interest for supplementary reading. The students who choose the same area may be formed into an interest group, asked to read individually in the area of interest, and brought together to discuss with the other group members the material read. The group may be charged with the responsibility of reporting its findings to the whole class through a formal report, a panel discussion, a dramatization, or some other means. Individual group members may be on different achievement levels in reading since they can read materials designed for their own individual levels and then can contribute their findings to the group as a whole.

Interest groups are motivational because the students are allowed to pick their own subjects for reading. They help to avoid the stigma that is sometimes attached to members of low achievement groups because they provide an opportunity for these students to be mixed with students from other groups.

5. *Research groups*—Research groups are similar to interest groups in that a group of students read independently about a particular topic, discuss it together, and share their findings with the class as a whole. These groups are different from interest groups in that the topics and group members are assigned by the teacher. The teacher may deliberately mix students with varying strengths and weaknesses to capitalize upon each group member's strengths and to enable students with specific weaknesses to learn from those with corresponding strengths. The groups may need to be closely monitored to ensure that these results are achieved. Research groups do not have the built-in motivation for reading content that interest groups do. They do, however, provide an intermingling of students from varying achievement levels.

6. *Friendship groups*—At times, class members can be allowed to work on certain assignments with friends of their choice. This type of grouping is motivational and may be highly beneficial for some students. Other students may be unable to conduct themselves properly under such conditions. Friendship groups should be used with discretion.

All teacher-assigned groups should be flexible. In achievement groups, for example, some students may experience sudden spurts in attaining reading skills and should be transferred to higher groups. Other students, because of extensive absences, emotional difficulties, or other reasons, may fall behind the group in which they have been placed. These students should be moved to a lower group, at least temporarily. In needs groups, students are included and dismissed as their needs are detected and met. Student tutorial groups, partnerships, and research groups last only until the assigned task is completed.

Grouping will not be necessary for all assignments in a content classroom. Obviously, all students will be able to function together when doing many non-reading tasks or reading tasks that are easy enough for all participants. Grouping is most important when students are asked to complete reading assignments because, as has been shown earlier in this text, all students cannot perform reading tasks at the same levels. As illustrated by the case presented earlier, members of different achievement groups (as determined by standardized reading test scores and a readability formula or by one of the informal assessment measures) should be given differentiated reading assignments. One group may read the textbook independently, perhaps in conjunction with a teacher-made study guide or with a list of purposes constructed by the students themselves. Another group may use the textbook as the teacher guides them through a directed reading lesson. Still another group may use only the pictures and graphic aids in the actual text while reading lower-difficulty material on the topic; this lower-difficulty material might have been located by the teacher or it might be textual material that the teacher has rewritten to a lower difficulty level. Tapes, films, filmstrips, and other audio-visual aids may also be used to present material to these students (and to the entire class). After a whole-class discussion of the material covered, the teacher may develop a summary in language experience style and use it for reading material with this group in subsequent study sessions. All of these approaches are discussed later in this chapter.

As the teacher works with the achievement groups, he or she may discover the need to form needs groups, student tutorial groups, or partnership groups for students who lack the mastery of a specific skill. If all students in the class lack such mastery, whole-class instruction on the skill may be in order.

Especially when a unit approach to teaching is being used in the class, the teacher may find it effective to form some interest groups or research groups or may decide to utilize friendship groups for motivational purposes. Research groups may be formed to capitalize upon the special abilities of various class members, and assignments should take varying reading levels into consideration.

Ned Ratekin and others[27] found from observations in classrooms that the Grade 8 and 11 English and mathematics teachers in their study did not use small-group instruction, whereas social studies teachers spent 4 percent of the time in small-group instruction and science teachers spent 12 percent. Instructional strategies involving student interaction, shared predictions, and verification activities can be best carried out in small-group situations. The teachers in the observational study relied heavily on lecture-discussion and monitoring students working individually.

READING APPROACHES FOR USE WITH CONTENT MATERIALS

Two effective ways to guide reading assignments are through use of study guides and directed reading approaches. These techniques may be used separately or, at times, concurrently.

Study Guides

A study guide is a "set of suggestions designed to lead the student through a reading assignment by directing attention to the key ideas in a passage and suggesting the application of skills needed to read a passage successfully."[28] The set of suggestions may take one of several forms. Some of these have already been presented in earlier chapters in the context of helping students with specific content reading assignments. The discussions below expand on this presentation and offer alternative forms of study guides.

Process and Content Guides

Robert Karlin suggested two types of study guides that may be helpful for students: process guides and content guides.[29] A *process guide* gives students ideas about how to read content material to gain information. It focuses on the skills necessary to understanding the material. A *content guide* leads students to particular information by offering purpose questions and comprehension questions. A process question or statement of the type generally found in process guides offers guidance or suggestions about *how* to read to determine information. A content question, such as those found in content guides, deals with *what* information is being sought.

Actually, these two types of guides can be synthesized into a single study guide that sets purposes for reading and provides aids for interpretation of the material. These guides are particularly valuable when the teacher employs grouping in the content class. They can be designed in such a way that the different groups have differentiated assignments, or separate guides can be prepared for different groups and can call for use of reading materials on different difficulty levels. Each small group of students can sit together, work through the study guide individually, and then discuss their answers with each other. During the discussion, the group members will try to reconcile any differences they discover in their answers. A whole-class discussion may follow the small-group sessions. All class members will have something to contribute from their learning during the guided reading or during their ensuing group discussion.

Handling material this way causes the students to think about the material that they are reading; critical thinking is necessary when small groups try to reach a consensus about certain answers. Thinking is also necessary later when the different groups perceive how all of their findings fit together. Retention of material is aided by the act of critically thinking about it.

Example 9.1 shows a science selection followed by a study guide. The content of this selection is also typical of health and home economics textbooks. The study guide incorporates aspects of process guides and content guides into a single document.

EXAMPLE 9.1   SCIENCE SELECTION AND STUDY GUIDE ————————

Food Additives: A Danger, a Safeguard, or Both?

Every day suppliers deliver tons of food items to grocery stores all over the country. Most of this food has traveled hundreds of miles from farms and processing plants. Food can take days, weeks, or even months to reach your table. Did you ever wonder what kept food from spoiling on its journey?

Since many foods travel long distances before reaching the market, certain chemicals are added to prevent spoilage during shipment and storage. Other chemicals, or food additives, improve texture, prevent caking, or provide extra vitamins and minerals. Some additives make foods look more appealing by adding colored vegetable dyes.

Even though government agencies test foods and additives to be sure they are safe, some research indicates that certain food additives can cause cancer in laboratory animals.

Nitrites and nitrates are common additives in meat, fish, and poultry. At first, these chemicals were added because their interaction with bacteria made the food look fresher longer. Later, scientists found that nitrites act as preservatives. They slow down the growth of bacteria that cause botulism, a food poisoning that is often fatal.

A committee supported by the National Academy of Sciences reported in December, 1981, that the cancer risk to humans from nitrites is small but genuine. The committee recommended that the amounts of nitrites added to foods be lowered, but that enough be added to protect against botulism. One way to safely add nitrites to food is to also add vitamins C and E. Other methods to prevent botulism without adding nitrites are being tested. These methods include using ionizing radiation, which kills bacteria, adding nonpoisonous chemicals such as potassium sorbate, and adding bacteria that lower the meat's pH, inhibiting the growth of botulism bacteria.

Additives can be both helpful and harmful. If you want to eliminate additives from your diet, you might have to give up many foods. For instance, you might have to limit your diet to foods which can be grown in your part of the country. You might also have to prepare many foods "from scratch." On the other hand perhaps the inconvenience and forgoing of certain foods would be safer for us all in the long run. More information is needed before definite conclusions can be drawn.

Analysis

1. What standards or criteria would you set for the use of food additives?
2. Look at labels and find out what additives are in some of your favorite foods.

Source: From *Scott, Foresman Biology*, p. 556, by I. L. Slesnick, et al. Copyright © 1985 by Scott, Foresman and Company. Reprinted by permission.

Study Guide

Overview Questions: What are the positive and negative aspects of food additives? How do you feel about eating foods containing additives?

1. Read the first paragraph to find out how long it may take food items to arrive at their final destinations. What does the author mean by the phrase "to reach your table"?
2. Read the second paragraph to find out what food additives are. (Two context clues are there to help you.)
3. What are five different uses of food additives?
4. Read the third paragraph to find out the effect that food additives may have on laboratory animals.
5. Read the fourth paragraph. It tells two advantages of using nitrites and nitrates as additives. What are they?
6. What is a preservative? (Think about the root word of preservative and use the meaning of this word to help you decide.)
7. What is botulism? (Use the context to help you answer.) Why would you want to avoid botulism?
8. Read the fifth paragraph. Is the cancer risk to humans from nitrites real? What word tells you so?
9. How can nitrites safely be added to food?
10. What are some methods being tested to prevent botulism without adding nitrites?
11. Read the last paragraph. If you wanted to avoid additives, what two things might you have to do and why? What does it mean to prepare food "from scratch"? (The words do not mean what they usually do.)

The study guide in Example 9.1 could be used for all students who can read the textbook, with or without teacher assistance; however, if a teacher wanted to reduce the length of the guide, he or she could assign some questions to both groups and divide other questions between the groups. For example, all students might complete items 1, 2, 4, 5, 8, and 11, which would provide some guidance through the entire selection. The other questions could be divided between the groups as the teacher thinks appropriate, although the process items might be best used with the instructional group. The teacher may work closely with the instructional-level group members as they discuss their assigned questions and may monitor the independent-level group less intensively. A group that cannot handle the text material should be given another reading assignment in order to learn the content or related content. This group should have its own study guide, geared to its assignment. The whole-class discussion that should follow the small-group sessions with the guides would help all of the students clarify their concepts and see relationships between ideas.

Looking carefully at the study guide in Example 9.1, one can see the instructional intent of the teacher. First, overview questions are presented. These questions are designed to focus on the understandings that students are expected to have gained when the entire selection has been read. They give purpose to the reading of an entire selection, often require critical and/or creative reading abilities, and lead to more complete comprehension. The remainder of the guide provides a series of questions and guidance statements that are arranged sequentially in the order in which they are needed in the reading. The students are expected to read the first numbered item, read the selection to find the answer to that question or use the skill suggested, and then repeat the process with the next question or guidance statement.

There is a reason for each question and statement. Following is a brief analysis of the reasoning behind the questions and statements in the study guide in Example 9.1. The numbers refer to the items in the study guide.

1. The first statement gives a purpose for reading the first paragraph. (*Content guidance*) The accompanying question requires the student to think about an expression that takes interpretation to understand. (*Content guidance*)
2. The first statement gives a purpose for reading the paragraph. (*Content guidance*) The parenthetical comment offers process guidance.
3. The question focuses the student's attention on a list of important details. (*Content guidance*)
4. The statement focuses on important information in the paragraph (*Content guidance*) and the cause-and-effect relationship expressed. (*Process guidance*)
5. The question focuses upon important information in the paragraph. (*Content guidance*)
6. The question focuses on word meaning, and the parenthetical information focuses on how to determine word meaning through structural analysis. (*Process guidance*)
7. The first question focuses on word meaning, and the parenthetical information focuses on how to determine word meaning through context clues. (*Process guidance*) The second question asks for higher-order thinking about the material read. (*Content guidance*)

8. The first question focuses upon an understanding that should be gained from the reading. (*Content guidance*) The second question guides the students to consider the importance of a word's meaning in determining the answer. (*Process guidance*)
9. The question focuses on important information given in the paragraph. (*Content guidance*)
10. The question focuses on important information given in the paragraph. (*Content guidance*)
11. The first question (which has two parts) focuses on important information given and asks the student to make inferences related to this information. (*Content guidance*) The second question asks for the meaning of a figurative expression, which requires interpretation. (*Content guidance*) The parenthetical comment warns the students that the meaning is not a literal one. (*Process guidance*)

Three-level Guides

A three-level study guide is one in which the student is guided toward comprehension at the literal level (understanding ideas that are directly stated), the interpretive level (reading between the lines), and the applied level (reading to use information to solve problems).[30] This type of guide can be especially useful with literature selections. The guide in Example 9.2 is designed for use with the short story "The Man Without a Country," by Edward Everett Hale.

EXAMPLE 9.2 THREE-LEVEL STUDY GUIDE

Directions: Check the statement or statements under each level that answer the question.

Literal—What did the author say about Phillip Nolan?

_____ 1. Phillip Nolan said, "I wish I may never hear of the United States again!"
_____ 2. Phillip Nolan never actually met Aaron Burr.
_____ 3. The court decided that Nolan should never hear the name of the United States again.
_____ 4. Nolan was placed on board a ship and never allowed to return to the United States.
_____ 5. Nolan was often permitted to go on shore.
_____ 6. Nolan did not intentionally make it difficult for the people who were supposed to keep him from knowing about his country.

Interpretive—What did the author mean by his story?

_____ 1. Nolan never seriously regretted having denied his country.
_____ 2. Nolan spoke against his country without realizing how much it had meant to him.
_____ 3. Nolan never really missed hearing about his country.

Applied—How can the meaning be applied to our lives?

_____ 1. People should consider the consequences of their actions before they act.

_____ 2. People can live comfortably away from home.

_____ 3. Punishment is not always physical; it may be mental.

_____

The student is guided through reading at the three levels of comprehension, building from the literal level of comprehending what is stated directly, to the interpretive level of inferring meanings, and finally to the level of applying the material to his or her own life. This type of guide is given to the students before they read the material so that they may use it to direct and focus their reading. As Herber points out, "To use the statements following the reading of the selection does not guide their reading; rather it merely tests their recall."[31] You want to *guide* their reading, not test it.

James Riley emphasizes the value of these three-level guides in stimulating the comprehension process.[32] He offers an extensive example of how such guides can be utilized in a content classroom. In his example, a three-level guide was presented with a poem to several small groups. The students in each group examined the statements and then looked in the poem for evidence supporting each statement. They discussed these statements in their groups as the teacher listened to the group interaction. The teacher then questioned the groups about their responses to each of the statements that might have caused difficulty or controversy, asking for the supporting evidence from the poem. When insufficient support was offered, the teacher asked for further explanation. If there were widely differing views presented in the small-group discussion, the teacher asked about any disagreement that existed. Riley points out that the teacher tried "to *recognize* students' responses, to *infer processes* underlying those responses, and to *value* students' initial responses as ones to build upon" and to encourage "the students to *generalize* their attempts at understanding the material to similar situations."[33] Teachers can and should do all these things when using any study guide, not just three-level guides.

Preview Guides

A preview guide is designed to help students relate what they are about to read to their own experiential backgrounds. Although in its simplest form the preview guide may be a request to, for example, "list everything you already know about word processing," it is likely to be more structured. In one form of the guide, the student is asked to place a check mark by the statements that are substantiated by the reading. They may also be asked to make revisions in statements that were proven wrong and put question marks beside items that were not addressed by the reading. All three types of items should be brought out in class discussion.

In more structured forms of the guide, statements or questions about the material to be read can be presented. Before they have read the material, students can be asked to indicate whether they believe the statements are true or false, or they can be asked to answer the questions. After completing the reading, they should check the accuracy of the answers they gave. Example 9.3 shows a preview guide of the more structured form.

EXAMPLE 9.3 PREVIEW GUIDE ━━━━━━━━━━━━━━━━━━━━

Directions: Before you read the chapter, answer the following question to the best of your ability by placing check marks beside your chosen responses. After you finish reading the chapter, check the accuracy of your responses.

What functions are possible with word processing software that are not possible with a standard typewriter?

_____ 1. Straight typing of sentences
_____ 2. Deleting a word in a paragraph after the paragraph is typed
_____ 3. Typing the material with one set of margins and then changing the margins without retyping
_____ 4. Underlining
_____ 5. Moving material from one paragraph to another without retyping
_____ 6. Setting up typed material in tabular form
_____ 7. Inserting material in the middle of a paragraph without retyping the paragraph
_____ 8. Copying a paragraph to another section of a document without retyping
_____ 9. Inserting material at the end of a selection without retyping the paragraph
_____ 10. Using footnotes with superscripts

Pattern Guides

A pattern guide focuses on the organizational pattern of the text.[34] If a text is organized according to a cause-and-effect pattern, for example, the guide would highlight causes and effects. Some possible focuses for pattern guides other than cause and effect are sequence, comparison/contrast, and categorization. Chapters 5, 6, and 7 provide information about organizational patterns frequently found in various subject areas. Below is a comparison/contrast guide for a selection from a biology text.

EXAMPLE 9.4 COMPARISON/CONTRAST GUIDE ━━━━━━━━━━

Directions: Read the selection about flowers and animal pollinators and then fill in the chart below to help you compare and contrast flowers pollinated by bees and moths with flowers pollinated by birds.

Flowers Pollinated by Birds	Flowers Pollinated by Bees	Flowers Pollinated by Moths
Usually red or yellow		
Petals fused into a		
long tube that holds		
nectar		

Flowers and Animal Pollinators: Made for Each Other

With rapidly beating wings the hummingbird hovers over the flower. Its long bill plunges deep inside the flower to gather the sweet nectar. As the bird flies away, its head is covered with a dusting of pollen from the flower's stamens. When the hummingbird visits the next flower, the pollen on its head will be brushed off to pollinate the flower.

Because flowering plants cannot move about as animals do to accomplish fertilization, they rely on other means of transferring pollen. Many flowers are pollinated by birds or insects. Scientists are taking an interest in studying the amazing adaptations of flowers that allow certain animals to pollinate them.

Birds have a poor sense of smell, but have excellent vision. So bird-pollinated flowers rely on color to attract their pollinators. Birds' eyes are most sensitive to the red end of the spectrum, so bird-pollinated flowers are usually red or yellow. Bird-pollinated flowers include hibiscus, red columbine, and fuchsia. Bird-flower petals are usually fused into a long tube that holds large quantities of nectar. When a bird inserts its long bill to reach the nectar, pollen is brushed off the stamens onto its head or breast.

Bee-pollinated flowers are usually brightly colored blue or yellow since bees' vision is most sensitive to this end of the spectrum. Bee-pollinated flowers also give off a sweet scent since bees are attracted to sweet or minty odors. Bee-pollinated flowers are usually open only during the day when bees are flying. Many bee-pollinated flowers have at least one protruding petal that serves as a landing platform for the bees. The nectar is usually hidden deep in the flower, but many flowers have *nectar guides* that point the way to the nectar. In violets and irises the nectar guide is a series of lines; in Turk's-cap lilies it is a cluster of spots in the center of the flower. Petunias and morning glories have a star-shaped pattern that surrounds the nectar opening.

But some nectar guides are not visible to humans. Bees can see them because their eyes are sensitive to ultraviolet light. To the human eye the marsh marigold flower appears solid yellow. But to the bee, only the center of the flower appears yellow. The outer part of the flower reflects a mixture of yellow and ultraviolet light called *bee purple.*

Moth-pollinated flowers are generally white or pale yellow, and are easily visible at dusk or night when moths are most active. Many moth flowers are open only during late afternoon or evening. Moth flowers have a strong, sweet scent and include orchids, evening primroses, and night-blooming cactuses. Since moths hover while feeding, moth-pollinated flowers do not have landing platforms.

The relationship between flowers and their animal pollinators is beneficial to both organisms. The animals secure food and the flowers get pollinated. Many scientists think that flowers and their animal pollinators coevolved to suit each other's needs.

Source: From *Scott, Foresman Biology*, p. 376, by I. L. Slesnick, et al. Copyright © 1985 by Scott, Foresman and Company. Reprinted by permission.

Analogical Guides

Thomas Bean and others[35] suggested the use of analogical study guides for science instruction. An example of such a guide on cell structure and function relationships is shown in Example 9.5. In this example, Bean and others compared the parts of a cell and their functions to the parts of a factory. They offered three steps for construction of these guides: "(1) Analyze the reading assignment for appropriate concepts. (2) Create appropriate analogies in a complete or skeletal guide. (3) Instruct students in the use of analogies as reading and retrieval cues."

EXAMPLE 9.5   CELL STRUCTURE-FUNCTION ANALOGICAL STUDY GUIDE

Structure	Main Functions	Analogy (comparing the cell to a factory)
cell wall	support; protection	factory walls
cell membrane	boundary, gatekeeper	security guards
cytoplasm	site of most metabolism	the work area
centrioles	cell reproduction	?
chloroplasts	photosynthesis	snack bar
endoplasmic reticulum	intracellular transport	conveyor belts
golgi bodies	storage, secretion	packaging, storage, and shipping
lysosomes	intracellular digestion	clean-up crew
microfilaments	movement	?
microtubules	support; movement	?
mitochondria	cellular respiration	energy generation plant
nucleus	control; heredity	boss's office, copy machine
ribosomes	protein synthesis	assembly line
vacuoles	storage	warehouses

Source: Thomas W. Bean, Harry Singer, and Stan Cowan, "Analogical Study Guides: Improving Comprehension in Science," *Journal of Reading*, 29 (December 1985), 249. Reprinted with permission of the authors and the International Reading Association.

Reasoning Guides

There is a type of guide that may be used to help develop post-reading reasoning skills. Herber calls it a reasoning guide, and says that it "can be thought of as an applied-level guide standing alone."[36] This guide may look exactly like the applied-level portion of a three-level guide, but it would be used *after* students have read the selection. It may also have a format that differs somewhat from the statements in the applied level of the guide in Example 9.2. For example, rather than having a list of statements, it could have a list of words, as in Example 9.6.

EXAMPLE 9.6   REASONING GUIDE ─────────────────

Directions: Each of the words below may have something to do with the story "The Man Without a Country." If you think a particular word applies in any way to the story or to a person or event in the story, place a check on the line before the word. Be ready to tell your reason for checking each word.

_____ treason	_____ thoughtlessness
_____ disowned	_____ court-martial
_____ considerate	_____ confined
_____ punishment	_____ prisoner
_____ courage	_____ kindness
_____ isolation	_____ suffering
_____ loyalty	_____ shrine
_____ harsh	_____ compassion
_____ repentant	_____ reconciled

Directed Reading Lessons

A directed reading lesson is a method for guiding students through the reading of a textbook selection. It is used most often with basal reader selections but can be adapted for use with content area selections. Directed reading approaches vary from source to source in the number of steps involved, but the following components are present in all of the plans:

1. Motivation and building of background
2. Skill development activities
3. Guided reading of the story
   a. Silent reading
   b. Discussion and oral reading (when appropriate)
4. Follow-up activities

The first step—*motivation* and *building of background*—consists of the following elements: a discussion of background concepts needed to understand the selection and of the relationship of content to the background experiences of the students; some discussion of difficult vocabulary; and a preview of the selection to see what type of information will be presented. The teacher may wish to help build background by using films, filmstrips, slides, still pictures, models, or other visual aids. These aids ordinarily generate some motivation to study the passage. Discussion of the way the content relates to their own lives can also be motivational for the students. Research has shown that developing students' background in a topic before they read about it can improve the students' comprehension of material on that topic.[37]

The structured overview, explained in Chapter 2, is a technique for developing readiness to read that can be used in a directed reading lesson. Richard Barron developed this technique;[38] it involves using a graphic arrangement of terms that apply to the important concepts in the passage.

To introduce a reading assignment, the teacher can show the students a structured overview and explain why the terms are arranged in the order chosen. He or she can encourage students to participate in the discussion and to contribute any information they might have. Then, as the assignment is carried out, the teacher and students continue to relate new information to the overview, which provides a framework for understanding the content. Example 9.7 shows a sample structured overview in the area of atomic structure.

Other examples of structured overviews may be found in *Teaching Reading and Mathematics* by Richard A. Earle (Newark, Del.: International Reading Association, 1976) and *Improving Reading in Science* by Judith Thelan (Newark, Del.: International Reading Association, 1976). Both are part of the IRA Reading Aids Series, Peter B. Messmore, review editor.

EXAMPLE 9.7   STRUCTURED OVERVIEW

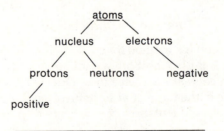

Students are more likely to benefit from structured overviews if they actively participate in the construction. For example, they can be given vocabulary terms on slips of paper and can be encouraged to place them in a logical arrangement, showing relationships. The teacher can then see what initial information the students have and can correct any erroneous impressions. The activity could be repeated after the assignment has been studied to assess the comprehension of the interrelated concepts presented.

Structured overviews, such as the one illustrated in Example 9.7, chapter overviews, and even chapter summaries all may be used by teachers as advance organizers for students who are about to read material in a textbook. Advance organizers are materials given to the students to read before reading a chapter assignment: approaching a selection in this way helps the students to grasp the author's organization and to read the body of the text purposefully. If a structured overview does not seem to be the best approach for guiding the reading, and if no chapter overview is provided to point out main ideas and important concepts, the teacher may direct the students to read the end-of-chapter summary before they read the chapter. If there is no summary of the chapter, the teacher may wish to provide a list of main points and important concepts, in simplified terms, as an advance organizer.

Previewing the selection—reading the title, the introduction, the boldface headings, and the summary—will give students a framework into which they can fit the ideas they gain through reading. A brief examination of graphic aids—pictures, maps, graphs, and diagrams—may also be helpful.

The second step—*skill development activities*—includes direct teaching of vocabulary, word recognition skills, comprehension skills, and study skills. The skills taught should be those the students will need to use when reading the selection; for example, if the students need to read a map in the story, a map-reading lesson would be in order.

Difficult vocabulary words that are not clearly explained by the context may need to be presented prior to the lesson. Vocabulary words that have appropriate context clues should *not* be presented; students should use their reading skills to determine the meanings of these words. Students also should be alerted to and encouraged to use the glossaries included in many content area textbooks.

The third step—*guided reading of the selection*—includes both setting purposes for reading and actually reading. Purposes for reading may be developed in different ways. They may be in the form of questions constructed by the teacher. (In this case, a study guide might be used to guide the reading.) They may be questions that have been formulated by the students themselves, perhaps based on the boldface headings picked out during the preview of the selection. Or, they may be predictions about what the selection offers, based on clues from the title and illustrations. If the purpose is in the form of a prediction, students would read to confirm or deny their hypotheses. Russell Stauffer believes that this type of purpose setting is likely to encourage students to think as they read.[39]

Once the purposes have been set, the students read to fulfill them. The initial reading should be silent. Silent reading always precedes oral reading unless a reading teacher is testing for word recognition skills. The content teacher usually does not ask students to read orally unless they have had a chance to read the selection silently first. There are several reasons for this:

1. Reading silently gives the reader an opportunity to decode unfamiliar words without being subject to embarrassment in front of his or her peers.

2. Reading silently allows the reader to become familiar with the phrasing patterns before he or she reads them aloud.
3. Most reading at the secondary level should be done silently because silent reading is more prevalent than oral reading in everyday situations.

After the silent reading, students may discuss the answers to the purpose questions or to additional discussion questions, perhaps reading orally to verify some of them. Any oral rereading that is done should be purposeful. Purposeful oral rereading would include reading to prove a point, reading to appreciate the beauty of the language (especially in poetry), and reading to interpret characterization (in a play where different people are reading various parts). Many directed reading lessons at the secondary level do not include an oral reading component.

The fourth step—*follow-up activities*—includes enrichment activities related to the lesson and designed to further develop the topic. Examples might be reading additional books on the same topic or by the same author, illustrating an event or concept from the story, constructing a model, writing a story related to the content, conducting an experiment, or otherwise applying concepts presented in the reading assignment.

Movement through a sequence of steps such as those described above may sound time consuming, but in actuality teaching a lesson in this format will probably involve no more time than a teacher would typically spend on a section of a content text. Furthermore, after the students have been led through the above steps, they will be more likely to understand the material. They will also be more likely to retain the material because they have had adequate preparation for the lesson and have read the material with a purpose in mind.

Example 9.8 shows a directed reading lesson used with a section of a vocational textbook.

EXAMPLE 9.8   VOCATIONAL SELECTION AND DIRECTED
READING LESSON ——————————————

Following a Troubleshooting Chart

Many manufacturers of small engines provide a troubleshooting chart in their service manual. The troubleshooting chart is a guide the mechanic can follow in locating a problem. The chart usually lists the problems starting with the ones that occur most frequently. The possible causes are listed under each problem. The things the mechanic must do to repair the problem are listed next to each cause. When using a troubleshooting chart, the mechanic should follow each of the recommended steps. It sometimes helps to check off each step as it is finished. A troubleshooting chart is provided in this unit for most of the common small engines. It is always best, however, to find and use the chart designed for the exact engine on which you are working.

Troubleshooting Chart for Small Two- and Four-Stroke Engines

Cause	Remedy
Engine Fails to Start or Starts with Difficulty	
On-Off switch Off	Turn switch to On.
No fuel in tank	Fill tank with clean, fresh fuel.
Shut-off valve closed	Open valve.
Obstructed fuel line	Clean fuel screen and line. If necessary, remove and clean carburetor.
Tank cap vent obstructed	Open vent in fuel tank cap.
Water in fuel	Drain tank. Clean carburetor and fuel lines. Dry spark plug points. Fill tank with clean fresh fuel.
Engine over-choked	Close fuel shut-off and pull starter until engine starts. Reopen fuel shut-off for normal fuel flow.
Improper carburetor adjustment	Adjust carburetor.
Loose or defective magneto wiring	Check magneto wiring for shorts or grounds; repair if necessary.
Faulty magneto	Check timing, point gap, and, if necessary, overhaul magneto.
Spark plug fouled	Clean and regap spark plug.
Spark plug porcelain cracked	Replace spark plug.
Poor compression	Overhaul engine.
Engine Noises	
Carbon in combustion chamber	Remove cylinder head or cylinder and clean carbon from head and piston.
Loose or worn connecting rod	Replace connecting rod.
Loose flywheel	Check flywheel key and keyway; replace parts if necessary. Tighten flywheel nut to proper torque.
Worn cylinder	Replace cylinder.
Improper magneto timing	Time magneto.
Engine Misses Under Load	
Spark plug fouled	Clean and regap spark plug.
Spark plug porcelain cracked	Replace spark plug.
Improper spark plug gap	Regap spark plug.
Pitted magneto breaker points	Clean and dress breaker points. Replace badly pitted breaker points.
Magneto breaker arm sluggish	Clean and lubricate breaker point arm.
Faulty condenser (except on Tecumseh Magneto)	Check condenser on a tester; replace if defective.
Improper carburetor adjustment	Adjust carburetor.
Improper valve clearance (four-cycle	Adjust valve clearance. engines)
Weak valve spring (four-cycle engine)	Replace valve spring.

Troubleshooting Chart for Small Two- and Four-Stroke Engines (continued)

Cause	Remedy
Reed fouled or sluggish (two-cycle engine)	Clean or replace reed.
Crankcase seals leak (two-cycle engine)	Replace worn crankcase seals. Some two-cycle engines have no lower seal. Check bearing surface of bottom half of crankcase.

Engine Lacks Power

Cause	Remedy
Choke partially closed	Open choke.
Improper carburetor adjustment	Adjust carburetor.
Magneto improperly timed	Time magneto.
Worn piston or rings	Replace piston or rings.
Lack of lubrication (four-cycle engine)	Fill crankcase to the proper level.
Air cleaner fouled	Clean air cleaner.
Valves leaking (four-cycle engine)	Grind valves.
Reed fouled or sluggish (two-cycle engine)	Clean or replace reed.
Improper amount of oil in fuel mixture (two-cycle engine)	Drain tank; fill with correct mixture.
Crankcase seals leaking (two-cycle engine)	Replace worn crankcase seals. Some two-cycle engines have no lower seal. Check bearing surface of crankshaft.

Engine Overheats

Cause	Remedy
Engine improperly timed	Time engine.
Carburetor improperly adjusted	Adjust carburetor.
Air flow obstructed	Remove any obstructions from air passages in shrouds.
Cooling fins clogged	Clean cooling fins.
Excessive load on engine	Check operation of associated equipment. Reduce excessive load.
Carbon in combustion chamber	Remove cylinder head or cylinder and clean carbon from head and piston.
Lack of lubrication (four-cycle engine)	Fill crankcase to proper level.
Improper amount of oil in fuel mixture (two-cycle engine)	Drain tank; fill with correct mixture.

Engine Surges or Runs Unevenly

Cause	Remedy
Fuel tank cap vent hole clogged	Open vent hole.
Governor parts sticking or binding	Clean and if necessary repair governor parts.
Carburetor throttle linkage or throttle shaft and/or butterfly binding or sticking	Clean, lubricate, or adjust linkage and deburr throttle shaft or butterfly.

Engine Vibrates Excessively

Cause	Remedy
Engine not securely mounted	Tighten loose mounting bolts.
Bent crankshaft	Replace crankshaft.
Associated equipment out of balance	Check associated equipment.

Source: Jay Webster: *Small Engines: Operation and Service* (Chicago, Ill.: American Technical Publishers, 1981, pp. 145–147.

Directed Reading Lesson

Motivation and building background

1. Discuss the meaning of troubleshooting.
2. Have the students give examples of situations in which they have practiced troubleshooting.
3. Explain that troubleshooting charts can make location of problems easier.

Skill development activities

4. Go over appropriate steps to use in table reading, since the troubleshooting chart is a form of table. Remind students to check the title of the table to see what is covered and then to check the headings of the columns and/or rows. Tell them that subheadings should also be examined. Finally, explain that they can locate the information they need by finding the intersection of the appropriate column and row.
5. Have students examine the following words that will appear in the lesson: *improper, improperly, obstructed, obstructions, lubrication, remove, reopen, regap, replace, over-choked, overheats,* and *unevenly.* Ask them to decide what the root word is for each listed word. Talk about the meanings of the root words, prefixes, suffixes, and inflectional endings involved. Explain that these same word parts will appear again and again in their reading in this content area.
6. Review scanning techniques.

Guided reading

7. Silent reading—Have students silently read the introductory material and scan the chart to find answers to the following questions:
   a. If the engine misses under load, what is the first possible cause to consider?
   b. If the engine is surging or running unevenly and you discover that the carburetor throttle linkage is binding or sticking, what is the remedy?
   c. If the engine lacks power and a partially closed choke is not the problem, what is the next possible cause to consider?
   d. Name, in order, the three likely causes of the engine vibrating excessively.
   e. If the engine vibrates excessively and a bent crankshaft is found, what remedy should be used?

   (Charts such as the one in this selection are rarely read word-for-word, but are scanned for needed information.)
8. Discussion and oral reading—Ask some students to read aloud their answers to each of the questions given. Discuss how they rapidly located the answers. Then discuss the content concepts covered by the questions. Ask additional questions that can be answered by scanning the chart. Have students compete to locate each answer first.

Follow-up activities

9. Show the students a lawnmower with a two- or four-stroke engine that is malfunctioning. Let them troubleshoot the problem in small groups. Then have each group share its answer with the rest of the class.

Example 9.9 shows another directed reading lesson, which is based on an eighth-grade English textbook.

EXAMPLE 9.9 ENGLISH SELECTION AND DIRECTED READING LESSON

The Life of a Word

Our language constantly changes to meet our needs. We adopt words from other languages and maintain their meanings. We adapt words from languages by altering their meanings slightly. Sometimes we completely change the meaning of a word when we take it for our own. Words have origins and histories, many of which are fascinating. The study of words is called **etymology.**

Consider the word *canary,* which originally comes from the Latin word for *dog, canis.* What do dogs and canaries have in common? The Romans named a group of Islands off northwest Africa, Canaria Insula, or Dog Island, because of all the dogs that they found there. Songbirds also inhabited the islands. Later, when the birds were exported to Europe, they were called canaries, after their home, the Canary Islands.

Another word that got its name from a place is *mayonnaise.* According to a legend, the town of Mahón on the island of Minorca in the Mediterranean once had a shortage of milk products. Consequently, the usual cream sauces could not be made. One chef began experimenting with eggs and oil. The result was a sauce that took the name of the city, Sauce Mahónnaise. Eventually, the word changed to *mayonnaise.*

Word change is unpredictable. For instance, the word *silly* in Old English was *seely,* meaning "blessed." The Normans were considered *seely,* because they had idle time for hunting and playing. Over time, *seely* came to mean "idle." In contrast, the word *knight* was originally the Anglo-Saxon word for youth, *cniht.* Later, it came to mean "servant," then "servant of a noble." Finally, the meaning was elevated to mean a person who served a noble with great chivalry and daring.

Many dictionaries give whole or partial etymologies. Some dictionaries list the early meanings of a word before its current meanings. Check your dictionary for its etymologies. You may also want to look at the *Oxford English Dictionary* which provides extensive etymologies.

Practice

A. Create your own etymology for each of these words: *mathematics, study, gymnasium, vacation.* What are their real etymologies?
B. What is the etymology for the name of your state, the month of your birth, and the days of the week?

Source: Shirley Haley-James and others: *Houghton Mifflin English* (Boston: Houghton Mifflin Company, 1986), p. 417.

Directed Reading Lesson

Motivation and building background

1. Ask the students if they know what a *villain* is. After discussing its current meaning, tell them that it originally meant "a person from a villa" and that its meaning has changed for the worse.
2. Ask the students if they know what *nice* means. After discussing its current meaning, tell them that it once meant "ignorant" and that its meaning has changed for the better.
3. Ask the students if they know any words that have come from place names or names of people. Let them name as many as possible. Be ready to provide some examples for them, such as *pasteurization.*

Skill development activities

4. Remind students that words presented in bold-face print are important words for which to know meanings.
5. Review types of context clues that are often found in textbooks. Give special attention to definition clues, since there is a definition clue for the word *etymology* in the assignment.
6. Review the meaning of *-logy* (the study of). Have students name and define words ending in *-logy* (*biology, geology,* and so forth).
7. Review the meaning of the word part *un-* (not). Have students name and define words with this part (*unhappy, unwanted*).
8. Review the meaning of the word part *-able* (able to be). Have students name and define words with this part (*workable, marketable*).

Guided reading

9. Silent reading—Have students read the selection silently for the following purposes:
   a. Determine the meaning of the word *etymology.*
   b. Find two words whose names have come from the names of places.
   c. Determine the meaning of *unpredictable.*
   d. Find a word that had a negative meaning change over the years.
   e. Find a word that had a positive meaning change over the years.
10. Discussion and oral reading—Choose some students to read aloud and discuss the parts related to the silent reading purposes, especially if the students find the purpose questions difficult to answer. As H. Alan Robinson points out, "Oral rereading of difficult ideas often assists in understanding."[40]

Follow-up activities

11. Have the students do the two practice activities at the bottom of the selection and discuss their results in class.
12. Have the students list five words that they find that have interesting etymologies. Have a class discussion of the words.

In their observational study, Ned Ratekin and others[41] observed that eighth- and eleventh-grade teachers spent little time on readiness activities for textbook reading. In fact, the teachers spent only 20 percent of their time providing any kind of guidance for learning from textbooks. Science teachers used guidance materials slightly more frequently than mathematics, social studies, and English/language arts teachers. That all of these teachers spent so little time on readiness activities may be related to the fact that the teachers, not the textbooks, appeared to be the primary sources of information for the students. The students were not expected to learn concepts from the texts.

ADJUSTMENTS FOR TEXTBOOK USAGE

If a content teacher finds that some of the students in a class are unable to benefit from the textbook designated for the class because of the book's readability, he or she can make several possible adjustments. These include the use of alternate textbooks, supplementary readings, rewritten materials, language-experience materials, computer applications and other audio-visual aids.

Alternate Textbooks or Supplementary Readings

One obvious solution to the problem of an assigned textbook's high readability would be locating alternate textbooks or supplementary reading materials with lower readability levels. Sometimes this is a practical solution. In some cases, it may be difficult to secure an adequate supply of alternate materials. Many times, however, teachers overlook the possibilities of such materials even when they are readily available.

An ideal situation, of course, would be to have several textbooks that cover identical content but that are written on varying difficulty levels. For poorer readers at the secondary level, Science Research Associates has produced material of this type on the subject of career education. *The Job Ahead: A Career Reading Series* includes books that are written at three levels of reading difficulty (Grades 3, 4, and 6) but that all cover the same material.[42] The information is presented in a story format and thus probably has more appeal for poorer readers. A teacher's manual accompanies the textbooks, and there are workbooks also designed for the three different reading levels. The skills covered in the workbooks are all practical ones related to the stories and to real-life needs of teenagers. Unfortunately, such multilevel materials are not as prevalent or available as one might hope.

Although multilevel textbooks covering identical material with identical formats may not be available, teachers should not discard the idea of using textbooks at different levels. Many textbooks on the same subject (biology, chemistry, plane geometry, algebra, American history, civics, health, and so forth) are produced by various publishers. One publisher may include in a health text designed for eighth graders many of the same topics that another publisher includes in the health text designed for seniors in high school. A teacher assigned to use the health textbook from the second publisher might acquire some health textbooks from the first publisher to use with the students who cannot read the textbook designated for the course. This possibility becomes even more appealing if the lower-level textbook does not have "eighth grade" printed on it to label it as material for younger students. (Many textbooks have ceased to carry such designations.) When there are common topics in the two textbooks, part of the class could be assigned reading in one text and part in another. The reading, which of course would be done for specified purposes, could then be followed by class discussion, with both groups taking an active part.

Another possibility that should not escape the teacher's consideration is use of material that comes from different publishers but is designed for the same grade. As we have already mentioned, a textbook for a particular grade may not really be written on that grade level. By checking the readability of various publishers' products, a teacher may find a textbook that is considerably easier than the one being used, although it has been written for the same grade level and subject.

In some content fields attempts are being made to provide high interest, low vocabulary materials for use as regular basal materials. High interest, low vocabulary materials contain concepts appropriate to mature readers but have simplified vocabulary and sometimes simplified sentence structure. As George Mason pointed out, "High interest—low vocabulary books written especially for remedial readers are a relatively recent development and the term 'high interest—low vocabulary' is even more recent," even though the need for such books has been felt by educators since the late 1920s and some of these books have been available since then.[43] Willis Uhl wrote in 1937 of "the rather widespread movement of offering easy reading materials for upper grade and high-school pupils."[44] Actually, the movement does not appear to have been very widespread, as witnessed by the fact that Strang, McCullough, and Traxler in 1955 were still pointing out the need for such materials.[45] As mentioned earlier in this chapter, evidence shows that in classrooms today many books are being used that have fairly high difficulty levels. However, publishers are also becoming aware of the need for simplified materials for older students and are responding to this need. The *Scholastic World History Program* is an example of a move in this direction.[46] This program is a four-book series on world history that is written at a sixth- to eighth-grade level of difficulty but is designed for use at any grade level in secondary school world history programs.

Materials such as these can be purchased to supplement standard textbooks and can be used by the students in the class whose reading levels are lower than the readability level for which the class textbook is written. Study guides may be supplied by the teacher for both regular textbooks and for high interest, low vocabulary books, and class discussion of a topic can tie together the information students learn from both sources.

High interest, low vocabulary text materials for secondary school students are available from many publishers. Some examples are presented in Appendix A of this chapter.

If alternate textbook materials are unavailable, a teacher can still find supplementary material for those who cannot manage the reading in the textbook.

Trade books (library books) of various levels of readability are available on almost any topic covered in the school curriculum. Some publishers (for example, Follett) have made available information on the readability levels of many of the trade books that they produce. If such information is not readily available, the teacher can apply readability measures, following the procedures discussed earlier in this chapter.

Trade books are not the only available useful materials. Pamphlets produced by government agencies; newspaper articles, editorials, and other features; copies of political platforms of candidates; popular magazines; and a variety of other materials can be used. The teacher should probably check the readability of the portion of this supplementary material earmarked for the poorer readers. He or she should keep in mind that material that carries a high enough interest factor for the students may be readable even if it is on a slightly more difficult reading level than students can ordinarily manage.

The supplementary materials suggested above should not be limited to use with poorer readers. On the contrary, better readers will benefit greatly from having exposure to various points of view, different methods of presentation, and additional information, even though they may use the textbook as the basis for their studies.

Teachers need to be aware that all reading difficulties in content areas will not necessarily disappear magically simply because the student has a book "on the correct level." Regardless of the reading level of the book, students need guidance in approaching content area reading tasks.

Testing Considerations

If a teacher goes to the trouble of collecting reading materials on a variety of levels for each topic covered in class and then matches the reading assignments to the individual students, how is he or she going to test the students on this material? Teachers must take several things into consideration when composing tests for students who have to read different materials. For example:

1. The teacher should start by listing the concepts that he or she wishes to transmit to all of the students.
2. The teacher then can choose diverse materials that cover these concepts at different levels.
3. The teacher should give special attention in class discussion to any concepts that are not clearly covered in some levels of the materials assigned. Language experience materials (see pages 423–424) could be developed from such discussions to cover these key concepts. Language experience materials in this case would be the class discussion as recorded by the teacher and distributed to the students to study.
4. The teacher should compose tests of items covering those important concepts that have been treated either in all of the assigned printed material or in class discussion.

Rewritten Materials

If teachers find that there is not enough supplementary reading material available in their content areas, they should not assume that poorer readers have to struggle with the assigned textbook. Secondary school teachers *can* successfully rewrite textbook materials to lower difficulty levels. One of the authors of this text has experimented with this activity in a course entitled "Teaching Reading in the Secondary School."[47] All participants in the course were in-service classroom teachers, and the results were excellent: using selections from history, English, literature, and science textbooks, teachers managed to lower the reading difficulty two to four grade levels. Most of the teachers also said that the experience was eye opening and enjoyable, and several continued rewriting activities after the class ended. Rewritten material enables many students to learn more from content reading assignments.

In an earlier portion of this chapter, it is mentioned that vocabulary and sentence difficulty are the two most significant indicators of readability. Rewriting a selection to a lower readability level primarily involves simplifying the vocabulary and sentence structure contained in the material. Easier synonyms can be substituted for difficult words, and teachers can simplify sentences by shortening them or by changing compound and complex sentences into simple sentences. An example of how this can be accomplished follows.

Original sentence: The ancient Phoenicians were the undisputed masters of the sea; they were also adept at business matters, keeping scrupulous records of all transactions that took place during their extensive excursions.

Rewritten material: The Phoenicians who lived in the year 1000 B.C. were the best sailors of their time. People from other nations did not doubt that Phoenicians were masters of the sea. They were also good at the business deals that took place during their long trips over the seas. They kept careful records of those deals.

Although the rewritten material contains more words, the vocabulary and sentence structure have been simplified. Easier synonyms or explanations have been substituted for words that might have offered problems for poor readers: *ancient, undisputed, adept, scrupulous, transactions, extensive, excursions.* A thirty-one word sentence was simplified by being broken down into four sentences, ranging from seven to eighteen words in length.

Example 9.10 shows a selection rewritten by an education student, Paula King. The bracketed material indicates the readability sample taken from the passage. The italicized words within the brackets are the unfamiliar words in the passage. The bracketed passage from the original is 100 words long; the bracketed passage from the rewritten material is 108 words long. When the Dale-Chall Readability Formula was applied to the two samples, the original selection was found to be written on a ninth- to tenth-grade level, while the rewritten selection was found to be on a fifth- to sixth-grade difficulty level.

Although it has been argued that rewriting does not inevitably result in better comprehension, there is evidence that it is effective in some situations. Frederick Duffelmeyer rewrote selections from the comprehension section of the *Nelson-*

EXAMPLE 9.10   REWRITING A SELECTION AT A LOWER READABILITY LEVEL

Original Selection

How Are Fair Trials Guaranteed?

*No distant place for trial. [The *Constitution* protects the *individual* in that it *forbids* a *trial* to be held at a great *distance* from the *scene* of the *crime.* Unless the *accused* person asks for a *trial* in another *judicial district,* he cannot be removed from the *community* where the *crime* was *alleged* to have been *committed.*

*No treason trial for politics. The people in the United States are free from *unreasonable prosecution* for *treason.* In a *dictator-ruled* country, the *dictator* can charge his *opponents* with *treason* if they do not agree with him. At times *dictators* have ordered large numbers of people to be put to death without *trial.*] Our Constitution prevents the bringing of a charge of treason merely for political purposes by this provision: "Treason against the United States, shall consist only in levying War against them, or in adhering to their Enemies giving Aid and Comfort."

Citizens of the United States cannot be convicted of treason without positive proof. The Constitution provides that no person can be convicted of treason without at least two witnesses to the same treasonable act, or unless the person confesses in open court.

Source: Robert Carter and John M. Richards, *Of, By, and For The People* (Westchester, Illinois: Benefic Press), pp. 205–206.

Rewritten Selection

How Are Fair Trials Guaranteed?

No distant place for a trial

[The *Constitution* of the United States protects the *individual.* It does not allow a *trial* to be held too far away from the *scene* of the *crime.* Sometimes the person charged with the *crime* asks to be tried in another place. If not, he cannot be removed from the *community* where the *crime* was supposed to have taken place.

No treason trial for politics

The people of the United States are free from unfair *prosecution* for *treason.* *Treason* is the act of trying to overthrow the government. Some countries are ruled by an all-powerful ruler or *dictator.* At times these rulers have ordered large numbers of people to death without a fair hearing.] Our Constitution does not allow this to happen. The Constitution states two acts considered to be treason. One is going to war against the United States. The other is giving aid or comfort to the enemy.

Citizens of the United States cannot be convicted of treason unless there is no question about the act. Two persons must actually see the person commit treason or the person must admit the act in an open court.

*Note: Subheadings were not counted in word count.

Denny Reading Test, substituting concrete nouns for abstract nouns and full verbs for verb-nominalizations.[48] Poor readers comprehended the revised passages better than the original passages, but average or better readers did not.

Language Experience Materials

It has been suggested earlier in this chapter that the teacher make differentiated assignments for students who have different levels of reading ability, following these assignments with class discussions to which all groups contribute. This class or large-group discussion period offers an excellent opportunity for use of language experience materials that can be beneficial to all students, but especially to the poorer students.

Language experience materials are materials written in the students' own words. In the elementary school, language experience stories are often developed by a group of students who have had a special common experience. In the secondary school, experience materials may be written by a group of students who have read about a common topic and wish to summarize their findings. The teacher can record all significant contributions on the chalkboard as they are offered. At the conclusion of the discussion, the teacher and students together can organize the contributions in a logical order (chronological, cause-effect, and so forth). The teacher can then have duplicates of the group-composed material made and can give them to the students on the following day.

The members of the groups who are able to handle the textbook with ease may file the experience material to use for review for subsequent tests. A group that is unable to handle the textbook presentation may use the material more extensively. For example, the teacher may meet with this group and guide the members through the reading of the material by using purpose questions. The students are likely to succeed in reading this material because they have seen the content written on the board in the words of fellow students. Having heard a discussion of the content, the students will find it easier to apply context clues as they read. Any technical vocabulary or multiple-meaning words can be located and discussed thoroughly. These words may be written in a special notebook with accompanying pronunciations and definitions and a reference to the experience material in which they occurred. A booklet made up of experience material can serve as a reference source for these words when they are encountered again. The booklet is also used by this group in studying for tests on the material.

Experience materials may also be developed by individuals and groups who wish to record the results of scientific experiments or the periodic observation of some natural phenomena. These materials may be shared by the rest of the class in oral or written form. Such activities are extremely valuable for students who are not able to gain much information from a textbook that is too difficult for them.

Some Uses of the Computer in Adjusting Assignments

Some computer utility programs are available that teachers can use when constructing drill-and-practice materials and word search puzzles. These materials can serve as special assignments for students who need a particular type of practice or a different level of practice material from that currently available. The *MECC Teacher Utilities, Vol. 1* (Minnesota Educational Computer Consortium), is available for the Apple computer for the construction of drill-and-practice materials, word search puzzles, and tests. The *Author I* program, available for the TRS-80 computer, helps the teacher prepare drill-and-practice materials and tests. The PILOT language is a good authoring language for lesson construction. This language is available for a wide variety of computers.[49] A program called Co-Pilot (Apple Computer, Inc.) is available to help teachers learn to use PILOT to develop instructional materials.

Word processing programs can be used to prepare simpler materials for students to read, study guides, or tests. The preparation of such materials is made easier with a good word processing program [e.g., WordStar (MicroPro), Apple Writer (Apple Computer, Inc.), Bank Street Writer (Scholastic), Magic Slate (Sunburst Communications, Inc.)] because correction of errors, editing, and formatting changes may be made quickly, easily, and neatly without redoing a complete document. Word processing software can also be helpful when recording language experience materials, such as those mentioned in the previous section. If a large monitor is available, the material can be directly entered on the computer, rather than on the chalkboard, and can easily be modified according to suggestions given during class discussion, resulting in a well-organized, neat handout that can be printed and duplicated for the students' use.

Students may use the computer to write their own accounts about subjects under study and may edit them with teacher assistance, using the easier word processing programs. Teaching proofreading and editing skills can be made much easier when the students realize that changes can be made without recopying entire documents. Even organization of paragraphs can be easily changed with block moves. Therefore, report-writing efforts can be greatly improved, and students can take more pride in their well-developed products.

The teacher can use simulation programs, which simulate real events, to add high-interest reading material to the curriculum. Students can use these programs in independent study activities. The *Oregon Trail* program (Minnesota Educational Computer Consortium) may be used to enrich the reading in a history class; *Ecological Simulations 1 & 2* (Creative Computing) and *Three Mile Island* (Muse Software) can be used in a science class; *Sounds Abound* (Houghton Mifflin), in an accounting class; and *In Search of the Most Amazing Thing* (Spinnaker), in a class in which study skills are being taught. Any of a variety of interactive fiction story programs can be used as recreational reading in an English class. Jay Blanchard and George Mason feel that *In Search of the Most Amazing Thing* may start a trend in study skills/adventure programs.[50]

Because writing and reading skills go hand-in-hand, the many writing skills programs that are available may also enhance reading skills. Students who are involved in producing written products seem to do better at analyzing the written products of others.

Other Audio-Visual Materials

A classroom teacher may find that one of the best ways to help poorer readers gain access to important content information is through the use of supplementary audio-visual materials. Such materials may include computers, as well as audiotapes, videotapes and films, and filmstrips.

Audiotapes

If the teacher feels that certain textbook material is essential in its unchanged form (for example, a poem or a beautifully worded essay), he or she may wish to tape the passage and set up a listening station for students who cannot read the selection themselves. The teacher or a particularly good reader from the class may be the reader on the tapes. (If a class member makes the tapes, it would be wise for the teacher to preview the tapes before releasing them for general use.) If students who are unable to read the text for themselves follow along in the book as they listen to the tapes, they may pick up some sight vocabulary as they absorb the content. Some publishers offer commercial tapes to accompany their material. (See the Educational Activities, Inc., listing in the high interest, low vocabulary appendix to this chapter for some examples.) Pendulum Press offers *Read Along* tapes to accompany Shakespearean plays, other classics, and a history series. Bowmar/Noble Publishers has tapes to accompany some texts, such as the *Our Nation's Heritage* programs and the *Reading Incentive Series.*

John Tyo studied the use of tape-recorded social studies textual material for poor readers in junior high school.[51] One group of subjects listened to tapes of assignments while reading along. The other group read without tapes. The comprehension of the group using the tapes was significantly greater than that of the group that did not use tapes, as measured by a cloze test of the content.

Sometimes the tapes of textbook selections may be used by students who can handle reading the textbook assignments but who learn best through the auditory mode, rather than the visual mode. Students can also use these tapes as an alternate way to study for tests on material previously read.

Videotapes and Films

Videotapes of various topics of study can be used to illustrate text materials for the poorer readers. For example, if students are expected to read about the process of pasteurization in their textbooks, a videotape or film depicting the process can be shown before students read the material, thereby supplying background information and visual images for students to put with the words. Videotapes or films may also help bring a literary selection to life. For example, a videotape of a storyteller telling "The Monkey's Paw" or a film of Shakespeare's *A Midsummer Night's Dream* could be shown to either the poorer readers or the entire class before these works are studied. By giving poor readers advance knowledge of the plot and characters and a chance to adjust to the type of language used, teachers will prepare these students for interaction with the rest of the class in class discussion. In the case of the Shakespearean play, the entire class may benefit greatly from the opportunity to hear the unfamiliar language patterns spoken aloud. (This becomes a readiness activity).

Filmstrips and Illustrations

Some concepts covered in class may be covered also in filmstrips, which, like videotapes and films, can help poorer readers by supplying background information about text material and presenting visual images to go with new terms.

Some publishers offer filmstrips of literary selections that can be used to give poorer readers background and motivation for reading the selections. Pendulum Press has filmstrips in its *Illustrated Classics Series*, its *Shakespeare Series*, and its *Basic Illustrated History of America Series*, among others. These series include books illustrated in a style that resembles that of a comic book (dialogue attached to characters) but has typeset lettering and uncluttered pages. Students respond well to these books. Bowmar/Noble Publishers also has filmstrips to accompany some materials, notably the *Reading Incentive Program*.

DEVELOPING TEACHING UNITS

A teaching unit is a series of interrelated lessons or class activities organized around a theme, a literary form, or a skill. A unit generally involves four basic types of activities:

1. Introduction of the unit
2. Development of the unit
3. Organization of findings
4. Culmination activities

Each of these activities is explained below.

Introduction of the Unit

The students are introduced to the unit's theme or central idea, the literary form to be explored, or the skill to be developed. Through class discussion and/or pretests, the teacher determines the extent to which the students' background of experience in the area can contribute to the unit. The teacher discusses with the students what they already know about the area of consideration; he or she helps them to evolve questions that they need to answer and to identify areas in which they need clarification. During this discussion, the teacher helps the students relate the area of study to their own personal experiences or needs. The teacher may supply motivation for participating in the unit activities by showing a film or filmstrip or by playing records or tapes related to the area.

Development of the Unit

The teacher begins teaching the unit by presenting core instructional material to the whole class. This material will probably consist of the textbook material and supplementary material that the teacher has carefully chosen for students who cannot benefit from reading the textbook because of its difficulty level. The teacher may develop directed reading lessons for both the textbook material and the supplementary material.

During the first step of some of the directed reading lessons, the teacher may use structured overviews to develop readiness for reading. Next, using techniques presented in Chapters 2, 3, and 4, he or she may teach needed vocabulary, comprehension, and study skills that are vital to the understanding of the particular passages involved. As a part of the directed reading lesson, teachers may guide the actual student reading of the material by means of a study guide. All the students can join what they have learned through class discussion and language experience activities. The follow-up activities will be included among the independent assignments of different research groups that the teacher now forms.

After the core instructional presentation, the teacher assigns areas of concern to the students or allows them to choose areas in which they have particular interest. Students form several small groups that are attempting to answer specific questions or clarify specific areas of concern. The teacher may meet with each group to discuss the possible reference sources that are available: textbooks, library books (fiction and nonfiction), encyclopedias, other reference books, magazines, newspapers, original documents (such as *The Declaration of Independence*), films, filmstrips, and a variety of other audio-visual aids.

The teacher must be alert to the variety of reading abilities within the group and must help the group members expend their efforts in fruitful ways, making available books and reference aids on a number of different levels. A review of such study skills as using the card catalog, using encyclopedias, outlining, taking notes, skimming, and scanning may be helpful for some members of each research group. (See Chapter 4 for a discussion of these skills.) Needs groups encompassing members from all of the research groups may be formed for these purposes. (See the discussion of grouping on pages 395–400.)

Each member of each research group will be responsible for collecting data. Differentiated assignments within the groups may be developed by the teacher or by group leaders, who are guided by the teacher.

Organization of Findings

The research groups meet after ample time has been allowed for individual members to collect data. Each group then reviews the information collected from the various sources, discusses and attempts to resolve differences of opinion, and welds the findings into a coherent report. The report may be oral or written and may be accompanied by audio-visual aids such as charts, tables, maps, graphs, pictures, filmstrips, or tapes. It may be in the form of an oral report, a panel discussion, a skit, a more complete dramatization, a mural, and so forth.

Culmination Activities

At the end of the unit study, the different research groups present their findings in a variety of ways. The class critically examines the information that is presented, merges it with the core of information learned from the textbook and supplementary materials, and determines if the purposes of the unit have been met. If the class feels that not all of the original purposes have been met, the members may regroup to attempt to finish the task.

The teacher should help the students relate the findings to their individual lives. An activity that immediately applies the findings would be beneficial because it would emphasize the relevance of the unit.

Table 9.2 presents the steps in unit development.

Table 9.2 Unit Development

Introduction	Development	Organization of Findings	Culmination
1. Build background and motivation 2. Connect unit to students' experiences	1. Core lessons presented through a directed reading approach (Use of structured overviews, teaching of needed skills, study guides, language experience approach) 2. Research groups 3. Needs groups	1. Discussion 2. Oral or written reports	1. Merging of information from diverse sources 2. Evaluation of effort 3. Application of information

Sample Unit Ideas

A unit in health might be arranged around such a theme as "The Four Basic Food Groups." A discussion of the theme could make apparent the background knowledge that the group has concerning the theme. A film or filmstrip on the topic could clarify the composition of each of the four basic food groups. Four research groups could be set up, one for each food group. Additional groups might be formed to study fad diets.

Each group studying a basic food group could investigate the importance of the foods in its group, setting out to answer these questions: What are the benefits from eating these foods? What are the problems that could result from not eating them? Groups on fad diets could weigh the benefits and dangers of these diets. A variety of sources should be available, including current paperbacks, newspaper articles, and magazine articles concerned with nutrition and dieting. Textbooks and reference books, such as encyclopedias, should also be utilized.

The group reports could take a variety of forms: one possibility would be to have a student describe what happened when he or she went on a fad diet. In the whole-class discussion following the group reports, relationships among the reports should be emphasized. For example, the fad diets that sometimes have bad results often leave out some of the basic food groups.

A unit in literature might be developed around a type of literature, such as "Tall Tales of the United States." The opening discussion could include an attempt to define "tall tales" and opportunities for the students to name tall tales with which they are familiar. The teacher might use a film, filmstrip, or tape during the introductory stage to clarify the nature of tall tales. Different groups could be formed to read tall tales about different superhuman individuals, for example, Old Stormalong, Paul Bunyan, Mike Fink, and Pecos Bill. Other groups could concentrate on tall tales of other types such as Washington Irving's "Rip Van Winkle" and "The Legend of Sleepy Hollow" or Mark Twain's "The Celebrated Jumping Frog of Calaveras County." As a culminating activity each student could write a tall tale of the general type that he or she has read. The tales could be shared in oral or written form with the rest of the class.

SUMMARY

In order to adjust reading assignments to fit all students, teachers need to know the difficulty levels of classroom reading materials so that they can match the materials to the students' reading levels. The difficulty levels can be determined by using readability formulas or other readability measures in conjunction with teacher judgment.

Assignments can be adjusted more readily if a teacher utilizes a number of grouping procedures in the classroom. Study guides, directed reading approaches, alternate textbooks, supplementary reading, rewritten materials, language experience materials, computer applications and other audio-visual aids can all be used to differentiate assignments. Teaching units are a natural vehicle for differentiated assignments.

SELF-TEST

1. Which statement is incorrect? (a) Textbooks placed at grade nine often are written at a tenth-grade readability level or above. (b) Content textbooks tend to be written by reading specialists. (c) Literature anthologies often vary widely in readability from selection to selection. (d) Many students in any given grade are unable to read at grade level.

2. What are the two factors that researchers have found to be the most useful in predicting readability? (a) Vocabulary and sentence length (b) Vocabulary and reader background (c) Sentence length and abstract concepts (d) Idea organization and format

3. What is true of student tutorial groups? (a) The tutor is allowed to plan his or her own lessons. (b) The tutor does not benefit from the activity, although the "clients" do. (c) One or two especially good students should always act as tutors. (d) None of the above.

4. What should teachers who use groups within their classes remember? (a) Needs groups should continue for a minimum time period of a semester. (b) All groups should be flexible. (c) Both *a* and *b* (d) Neither *a* nor *b*

5. Which statement is true of study guides? (a) They are not helpful for poor readers. (b) They are useful when the teacher is employing grouping with the content class. (c) They can be designed to help students focus on particular information by offering purpose questions. (d) Both *b* and *c*

6. Which kind of guide is designed to help students relate what they are about to read to their own experiential backgrounds? (a) Content (b) Pattern (c) Preview (d) Reasoning

7. Which statement is true of structured overviews? (a) They involve a graphic arrangement of terms that apply to the important concepts in the passages. (b) They contain a list of purpose questions. (c) They cannot be used with mathematics materials. (d) All of the above

8. Which one of the following is *not* a step in a directed reading approach? (a) Motivation and building background (b) Oral reading, paragraph by paragraph, without specific purposes (c) Skill development activities (d) Guided reading of the story, silent and oral

9. If secondary school students cannot read the textbooks assigned for their classes, what can the teacher do? (a) The teacher can rewrite the material to a lower difficulty level. (b) The teacher can find an alternate textbook or other alternate printed material. (c) The teacher can tape portions of the textbook for student use. (d) All of the above are possibilities.

10. Which statement is true of language experience materials? (a) They consist of the students' own words. (b) They are inappropriate for use above ninth grade. (c) They must be developed in small groups. (d) All of the above

11. For what purposes can word processing programs be used? (a) To prepare simpler materials for students to read (b) To prepare study guides (c) To allow students to write their own accounts about subjects under study (d) All of the above

12. Which statement is true if teaching units are utilized? (a) Separate lessons are unrelated. (b) Research groups can be profitably employed. (c) All students engage in identical activities. (d) None of the above

THOUGHT QUESTIONS

1. Why is it helpful for a content area teacher to know how to use a readability formula? Are there some readability formulas that would be more appropriate for you to use in your particular situation? Why, or why not?

2. Do readability formulas provide absolute grade level values? Why, or why not?

3. What are some measures other than readability formulas that could be used to test readability? Why would you use, or not use, one of these methods instead of a formula?

4. What are some types of groups that you might choose to use in your classroom? What advantages would there be to using these groups?

5. What can study guides do to enhance the learning of students in your content area classes?

6. How can structured overviews be used in a content area class? What are the advantages of using them?

7. What are the steps in a directed reading approach? How does each step enhance the learning of the content of the textbook?

8. What procedures might you follow in locating alternate textbooks to use with readers for whom the assigned textbook is not appropriate? Are there sources other than textbooks that you might utilize also? If so, what are they?

9. If you decide to rewrite materials to a lower readability level, what factors should you take into account in your rewriting?

10. How can tapes and films be used to further content learning when not all students can manage the textbook?

11. How are language experience materials helpful to both poor and good readers in content classrooms?

12. What are some ways that the computer can be used to adjust assignments?

13. How does unit teaching lend itself to differentiation of assignments?

ENRICHMENT ACTIVITIES

1. Apply the Fry Readability Graph Formula to a 100-word sample from the science textbook selection in Example 9.4. Start counting your 100-word sample with the first paragraph, which begins: "With rapidly beating...."

After you have completed the formula application, check your answer against the answers obtained by your classmates.

2. Construct a study guide that could be used with the English selection found in Example 9.9. Discuss your guide with your classmates.

*3. Construct a study guide for a secondary level textbook that you are currently using. Try it with your students and report to the class concerning the results.

4. Write out a plan for a directed reading lesson for the science selection in Example 9.1. Discuss your results with your classmates.

*5. Write out a plan for a directed reading lesson for a section of a textbook that you are currently using. Try it with your students and report to the class concerning the results.

6. Choose a topic and locate printed materials, both textbook and nontextbook, on a variety of difficulty levels that could be used by students when studying this topic.

7. Take a selection of about 500 words from a secondary level textbook of your choice and rewrite it to a lower difficulty level by simplifying vocabulary and sentence structure. Use the Fry Readability Graph Formula to test the original passage and rewritten passage.

8. Learn to use a readability formula other than Fry's formula. Test a passage of a secondary level textbook of your choice using this formula, and then test the passage using the Fry formula. Discuss with your classmates the results of your activity.

*9. Try using a language experience activity with students in one of your secondary classes. Report the results to your college class.

*10. Plan a unit from your chosen subject area. Try it with students in your class. Decide how you could improve the unit if you were to teach it again.

11. Arrange the vocabulary terms at the beginning of the chapter in the form of a structured overview. You may need to add some terms. Explain your arrangement to the class.

12. Select four articles on the topic of readability formulas from the Selected References at the end of this chapter or from other sources. Compare and contrast the viewpoints represented in a two- or three-page paper. Conclude with your own viewpoint.

NOTES

1. R. D. Powers, W. A. Sumner, and B. E. Kearl, "A Recalculation of Four Adult Readability Formulas," *The Journal of Educational Psychology*, 49 (April 1958), 99–105.

2. Rudolph Flesch, *The Art of Readable Writing* (New York: Harper and Row, 1951), p. 5.

3. Powers, Sumner, and Kearl, op. cit.

*These activities are designed for in-service teachers, student teachers, or practicum students.

4. Edward Fry, *Reading Instruction for Classroom and Clinic* (New York: McGraw-Hill, 1972), p. 231.

5. Dorothy H. Judd, "Avoid Readability Formula Drudgery: Use Your School's Microcomputer," *The Reading Teacher*, 35 (December 1981), 7–8. Philip P. Gross and Karen Sadowski, "FOGINDEX—A Readability Formula Program for Microcomputers," *Journal of Reading*, 28 (April 1985), 614–618. Joseph C. Kretschmer, "Computerizing and Comparing the Rix Readability Index," *Journal of Reading*, 27 (March 1984), 490–499.

6. Ronald P. Carver, "Measuring Readability Using DRP Units," *Journal of Reading Behavior*, 17, No. 4 (1985), 304.

7. *Readability Report: 1983–84 Academic Year* (New York: College Entrance Examination Board, 1983).

8. Carver, *op cit.*, pp. 303–316.

9. Carver, "Is the Degrees of Reading Power Test Valid or Invalid?" *Journal of Reading*, 29 (October 1985), 34–41.

10. John Bormuth, "A Response to 'Is the Degrees of Reading Power Test Valid or Invalid?' " *Journal of Reading*, 29 (October 1985), 42–47.

11. Judith Westphal Irwin and Carol A. Davis, "Assessing Readability: The Checklist Approach," *Journal of Reading*, 24 (November 1980), 124–130.

12. Charles H. Clark, "Assessing Comprehensibility: The PHAN System," *The Reading Teacher*, 34 (March 1981), 670–675.

13. Suzanne F. Clewell and Anne M. Cliffton, "Examining Your Textbook for Comprehensibility," *Journal of Reading*, 27 (December 1983), 219–224.

14. For more on the cloze procedure, see Wilson L. Taylor, "Recent Developments in the Use of Cloze Procedure," *Journalism Quarterly*, 33 (Winter 1956), 42–48, 99, and J. R. Bormuth, "Cloze Test Readability: Criterion Reference Scores," *Journal of Educational Measurement*, 5 (Fall 1968), 189–196.

15. Larry Chance, "Use Cloze Encounters of the Readability Kind for Secondary School Students," *Journal of Reading*, 28 (May 1985), 690–693.

16. For more on the group reading inventory, see David L. Shepherd, *Comprehensive High School Reading Methods*, 3rd ed. (Columbus, Ohio: Charles E. Merrill, 1982), pp. 153–163.

17. For more on informal reading inventories, see Emmett A. Betts, *Foundations of Reading Instruction* (New York: American Book Company, 1946); M. S. Johnson and R. A. Kress, *Informal Reading Inventories* (Newark, Del.: International Reading Association, 1965); and William J. Valmont, "Creating Questions for Informal Reading Inventories," *The Reading Teacher*, 25 (March 1972), 509–512.

18. Nicholas P. Criscuolo, et al., "What Reading Strategies Make Sense to Content Area Teachers?" *Reading World*, 19 (March 1980), 265–271.

19. Keith Kennedy, "Determining the Reading Level of Biology Textbooks," *The American Biology Teacher*, 41 (May 1979), 301–303.

20. Ann C. Howe and Margaret Early, "Reading and Reasoning in ISCS Classes," *Science Education*, 63 (January 1979), 15–23.

21. Peggy Gordon Elliott and Clyde A. Wiles, "The Print Is a Part of the Problem," *School Science and Mathematics*, 80 (January 1980), 37–42.

22. Calfrey C. Calhoun and Barbara Horner, "Readability of First-Year Bookkeeping Texts Compared with Students' Reading Level," *Business Education Forum*, 30 (October 1975), 20–21.

23. Dixie Lee Spiegel and Jill D. Wright, "Biology Teachers' Use of Readability Concepts When Selecting Texts for Students," *Journal of Reading*, 27 (October 1983), 28.

24. Ibid.

25. J. M. Bradley, W. S. Ames, and J. N. Mitchell, "Intrabook Readability: Variations Within History Textbooks," *Social Education*, 44 (1980), 524–528.

26. G. W. Jorgenson, "Relationship of Classroom Behavior to the Accuracy of the Match Between Material Difficulty and Student Activity," *Journal of Educational Psychology*, 69 (1977), 24–32.

27. Ned Ratekin et al., "Why Teachers Resist Content Reading Instruction," *Journal of Reading*, 28 (February 1985), 432–437.

28. Theodore L. Harris and Richard E. Hodges, eds. *A Dictionary of Reading and Related Terms* (Newark, Del.: International Reading Association, 1981), p. 313.

29. Robert Karlin, *Teaching Reading in High School: Improving Reading in Content Areas*, 4th ed. (New York: Harper and Row, 1984), pp. 145–149.

30. See Harold L. Herber, *Teaching Reading in Content Areas*, 2nd ed. (Englewood Cliffs, N.J.: Prentice-Hall, 1978), for an excellent discussion of three-level guides.

31. Ibid., p. 44.

32. James D. Riley, "Statement-Based Guides and Quality of Teacher Response," *Journal of Reading*, 23 (May 1980), 715–720.

33. Ibid., p. 720.

34. Thomas H. Estes and Joseph L. Vaughan, Jr., *Reading and Learning in the Content Classroom* (Boston: Allyn and Bacon, 1978), pp. 161–167.

35. Thomas W. Bean, Harry Singer, and Stan Cowan, "Analogical Study Guides: Improving Comprehension in Science," *Journal of Reading*, 29 (December 1985), 246–250.

36. Harold L. Herber, p. 124.

37. Kathleen C. Stevens, "Can We Improve Reading by Teaching Background Information?" *Journal of Reading*, 25 (January 1982), 326–329.

38. Richard F. Barron, "The Use of Vocabulary as an Advance Organizer," in *Research in Reading in the Content Areas: First Year Report*, ed. Harold Herber and Peter Sanders (Syracuse, N.Y.: Syracuse University Press, 1969), pp. 29–39.

39. Russell G. Stauffer, *Teaching Reading as a Thinking Process* (New York: Harper and Row), 1969.

40. H. Alan Robinson, *Teaching Reading and Study Strategies: The Content Areas*, 2nd ed. (Boston: Allyn and Bacon, 1978), p. 243.

41. Ned Ratekin et al., pp. 432–437.

42. Herman R. Goldberg and Bernard Greenberger, *The Job Ahead: A Career Reading Series* (Chicago: Science Research Associates, 1977).

43. George E. Mason, "High Interest—Low Vocabulary Books: Their Past and Future," *Journal of Reading*, 24 (April 1981), 603.

44. Willis L. Uhl, "The Materials of Reading," in *The Teaching of Reading: A Second Report*, Part I, ed. Gertrude M. Whipple. Thirty-sixth Yearbook of the National Society for the Study of Education (Bloomington, Ill.: Public School Publishing Co., 1937), p. 228.

45. Mason, p. 605.

46. *Scholastic World History Program* (New York: Scholastic Book Services, 1976).

47. Betty D. Roe, "Teacher Prepared Material for Slow Readers," *Journal of Reading*, 15 (January 1972), 277–279.

48. Frederick A. Duffelmeyer, "The Effect of Rewriting Prose Material on Reading Comprehension," *Reading World*, 19 (October 1979), 1–11.

49. Jay S. Blanchard and George E. Mason, "Using Computers in Content Area Reading Instruction," *Journal of Reading*, 29 (November 1985), 112–117.
50. Ibid.
51. John Tyo, "An Alternative for Poor Readers in Social Science," *Social Education*, 44 (April 1980), 309–310.

SELECTED REFERENCES

Allington, Richard, and Michael Strange. *Learning Through Reading in the Content Areas.* Lexington, Mass.: D. C. Heath, 1980. Chapters 1, 6, and 9.

Bean, Thomas W., Harry Singer, and Stan Cowan. "Acquisition of a Topic Schema in High School Biology Through an Analogical Study Guide." In *Issues in Literacy: A Research Perspective.* Ed. Jerome A. Niles and Rosary V. Lalik. Rochester, N.Y.: National Reading Conference, 1985.

———. "Analogical Study Guides: Improving Comprehension in Science." *Journal of Reading*, 29 (December 1985), 246–250.

Blanchard, Jay S., and George E. Mason. "Using Computers in Content Area Reading Instruction." *Journal of Reading*, 29 (November 1985), 112–117.

Bormuth, John. "A Response to 'Is the Degrees of Reading Power Test Valid or Invalid?'." *Journal of Reading*, 29 (October 1985), 42–47.

———. "Cloze Test Readability: Criterion Reference Scores." *Journal of Educational Measurement*, 5 (Fall 1968), 189–196.

Bradley, J. M., W. S. Ames, and J. N. Mitchell. "Intrabook Readability: Variations Within History Textbooks." *Social Education*, 44 (1980), 524–528.

Burmeister, Lou E. *Reading Strategies for Middle and Secondary School Teachers.* 2nd ed. Reading, Mass.: Addison-Wesley, 1978. Chapters 2, 3, and 5.

Calhoun, Calfrey C., and Barbara Horner. "Readability of First-Year Bookkeeping Texts Compared with Students' Reading Level." *Business Education Forum*, 30 (October 1975), 20–21.

Campbell, Anne. "How Readability Formulae Fall Short in Matching Student to Text in the Content Areas." *Journal of Reading*, 22 (May 1979), 683–689.

Carver, Ronald P. "Is the Degrees of Reading Power Test Valid or Invalid?" *Journal of Reading*, 29 (October 1985), 34–41.

———. "Measuring Readability Using DRP Units." *Journal of Reading Behavior*, 17, No. 4 (1985), 304.

Chance, Larry. "Use Cloze Encounters of the Readability Kind for Secondary School Students." *Journal of Reading*, 28 (May 1985), 690–693.

Cheek, Earl H., Jr., and Martha Collins Cheek. *Reading Instruction Through Content Teaching.* Columbus, Ohio: Charles E. Merrill, 1983. Chapter 8.

Clark, Charles H. "Assessing Comprehensibility: The PHAN System." *The Reading Teacher*, 34 (March 1981), 670–675.

Clewell, Suzanne F., and Anne M. Cliffton. "Examining Your Textbook for Comprehensibility." *Journal of Reading*, 27 (December 1983), 219–224.

Craig, Linda C. "If It's Too Difficult for the Kids to Read—Rewrite It!" *Journal of Reading*, 21 (December 1977), 212–214.

Criscuolo, Nicholas P., and others. "What Reading Strategies Make Sense to Content Area Teachers?" *Reading World*, 19 (March 1980), 265–271.

Davey, Beth. "Using Textbook Activity Guides to Help Students Learn from Textbooks." *Journal of Reading*, 29 (March 1986), 489–494.

Dillner, Martha H., and Joanne P. Olson. *Personalizing Reading Instruction in Middle, Junior and Senior High Schools: Utilizing a Competency-Based Instructional System*. 2nd ed. New York: Macmillan Company, 1982. Chapter 8.

Donlan, Dan. "Using the DRA to Teach Literary Comprehension at Three Response Levels." *Journal of Reading*, 28 (February 1985), 408–415.

Dreyer, Lois Goodman. "Readability and Responsibility." *Journal of Reading*, 27 (January 1984), 334–338.

Duffelmeyer, Frederick A. "The Effect of Rewriting Prose Material on Reading Comprehension." *Reading World*, 19 (October 1979), 1–11.

Elliott, Peggy Gordon, and Clyde A. Wiles. "The Print Is a Part of the Problem." *School Science and Mathematics*, 80 (January 1980), 37–42.

Estes, Thomas H., and Joseph L. Vaughan, Jr. *Reading and Learning in the Content Classroom*. Boston: Allyn and Bacon, 1978.

Fitzgerald, Gisela G. "How Many Samples Give a Good Readability Estimate? The Fry Graph." *Journal of Reading*, 24 (February 1981), 404–410.

Forgan, Harry W., and Charles T. Mangrum. *Teaching Content Area Reading Skills*. 2nd ed. Columbus, Ohio: Charles E. Merrill, 1981. Modules 1–3.

Fry, Edward. "Fry's Readability Graph: Clarifications, Validity and Extension to Level 17." *Journal of Reading*, 21 (December 1977), 242–252.

Gold, Patricia Cohen. "The Directed Listening-Language Experience Approach." *Journal of Reading*, 25 (November 1981), 138–141.

Gross, Philip P., and Karen Sadowski. "FOGINDEX—A Readability Formula Program for Microcomputers." *Journal of Reading*, 28 (April 1985), 614–618.

Herber, Harold L. *Teaching Reading in Content Areas*. 2nd ed. Englewood Cliffs, N.J.: Prentice-Hall, 1978.

Hittleman, Daniel R. "Readability, Readability Formulas, and Cloze: Selecting Instructional Materials." *Journal of Reading*, 22 (November 1978), 117–122.

Howe, Ann C., and Margaret Early. "Reading and Reasoning in ISCS Classes." *Science Education*, 63 (January 1979), 15–23.

Irwin, Judith Westphal, and Carol A. Davis. "Assessing Readability: The Checklist Approach." *Journal of Reading*, 24 (November 1980), 124–130.

Johnson, M. S. and R. A. Kress. *Informal Reading Inventories*. Newark, Del.: International Reading Association, 1965.

Judd, Dorothy H. "Avoid Readability Formula Drudgery: Use your School's Microcomputer." *The Reading Teacher*, 35 (October 1981), 7–8.

Karakalios, Sue M., Marion J. Tonjes, and John C. Townes. "Using Advance Organizers to Improve Comprehension of a Content Text." *Journal of Reading*, 22 (May 1979), 706–708.

Karlin, Robert. *Teaching Reading in High School: Improving Reading in Content Areas*. 4th ed. New York: Harper and Row, 1984. Chapter 5.

Kennedy, Keith. "Determining the Reading Level of Biology Textbooks." *The American Biology Teacher*, 41 (May 1979), 301–303.

Kretschmer, Joseph C. "Updating the Fry Readability Formula." *The Reading Teacher*, 29 (March 1976), 555–558.

––––––. "Computerizing and Comparing the Rix Readability Index." *Journal of Reading*, 27 (March 1984), 490–499.

Lamberg, Walter J., and Charles E. Lamb. *Reading Instruction in the Content Areas*. Chicago: Rand McNally College Publishing Company, 1980. Chapters 7 and 9.

McClain, Leslie J. "Study Guides: Potential Assets in Content Classrooms." *Journal of Reading*, 24 (January 1981), 321–325.

Mason, George E. "High Interest—Low Vocabulary Books: Their Past and Future." *Journal of Reading*, 24 (April 1981), 603.

Nelson, Joan. "Readability: Some Cautions for the Content Area Teacher." *Journal of Reading*, 21 (April 1978), 620–625.

Olson, Mary W., and Bonnie Longnion. "Pattern Guides: A Workable Alternative for Content Teachers." *Journal of Reading*, 25 (May 1982), 736–741.

Ratekin, Ned, and others. "Why Teachers Resist Content Reading Instruction." *Journal of Reading*, 28 (February 1985), 432–437.

Riley, James D. "Statement-Based Reading Guides and Quality of Teacher Response." *Journal of Reading*, 23 (May 1980), 715–720.

Robinson, H. Alan. *Teaching Reading and Study Strategies: The Content Areas*. 2nd ed. Boston: Allyn and Bacon, 1978. Chapter 4.

Roe, Betty D. "Teacher Prepared Material for Slow Readers." *Journal of Reading*, 15 (January 1972), 277–279.

Shantz, Marie. "Read-ability." *Language Arts*, 58 (November/December 1981), 943–944.

Shepherd, David. *Comprehensive High School Reading Methods*. Columbus, Ohio: Charles E. Merrill, 1978. Chapters 6 and 7.

Singer, Harry, and Dan Donlan. *Reading and Learning from Text*. Boston, Mass.: Little, Brown and Company, 1980. Chapters 4, 8, and 9.

Spiegel, Dixie Lee, and Jill D. Wright. "Biology Teachers' Use of Readability Concepts When Selecting Texts for Students." *Journal of Reading*, 27 (October 1983), 28–34.

Stevens, Kathleen C. "Can We Improve Reading by Teaching Background Information?" *Journal of Reading*, 25 (January 1982), 326–329.

Taylor, Wilson L. "Recent Developments in the Use of Cloze Procedure." *Journalism Quarterly*, 33 (Winter 1956), 42–48, 99.

Trapini, Fred, and Sean Walmsley. "Five Readability Estimates: Differential Effects of Simplifying a Document." *Journal of Reading*, 24 (February 1981), 398–403.

Tutolo, Daniel J. "The Study Guide—Types, Purpose, and Value." *Journal of Reading*, 20 (March 1977), 503–507.

Tyo, John. "An Alternative for Poor Readers in Social Science." *Social Education*, 44 (April 1980), 309–310.

Valmont, William J. "Creating Questions for Informal Reading Inventories." *The Reading Teacher*, 25 (March 1972), 509–512.

CHAPTER APPENDIX A: HIGH-INTEREST, LOW-VOCABULARY MATERIALS

Bowmar/Noble Publishers, Inc.:
United States Government, by J. R. Reich and Michael S. Reich. A comprehensive government text for below-average readers in grades 7–12.

Charles E. Merrill:
1. *Reading for the Real World.* Reading level, grades 4–7.5; grade level, grades 7–10.

Educational Activities, Inc.:
1. *Mythology Alive,* by Ronald A. Feldman and Lynn B. Goldman. Reading level, grades 3–4; grade level, grades 7–12. Books, cassettes, dittos.
2. *Biographies from American History,* by Michael Harrison, Alice Keener, and Deborah O'Brien-Smith. Reading level 2–3; interest level, all ages. Idiom controlled. Books, cassettes.

Follett Publishing Company:
1. *Skills for Understanding Maps and Globes,* by Kenneth Job and Lois Weiser. Reading level, grades 4–5; grade level, grades 7–12.
2. *American History,* 5th ed., by Jack Abramowitz. Reading level, grades 5–7; grade level, grades 8–12.
3. *Civics,* 5th ed., by Grant T. Ball and Lee J. Rosch. Reading level, grades 6–7; grade level, grades 8–12.
4. *World History,* 3rd ed., by Jack Abramowitz. Reading level, grades 6–8; grade level, grades 9–10.
5. *The Adventures of Primero Dinero,* by Steve Jackstadt and Yukio Hamada. Reading level, grades 5–7; grade level, grades 7–12.
6. *Superheroes of Macroeconomics,* by Steve Jackstadt. Reading level, grades 6–8; grade level, grades 7–12.
7. *Foundations of Freedom,* by Jack Abramowitz. Reading level, grades 6–8; grade level, grades 7–12.
8. *The American Nation: Adventure in Freedom,* by Jack Abramowitz. Reading level, grades 4–7; grade level, grades 7–8.
9. *Follett Coping Skills Series.* Reading level, grade 3.5; grade level, grade 9–Adult. Sixteen titles.

Frank E. Richards Publishers:
1. *Your Government and You,* by John H. Hoek.
2. *Meeting Basic Competencies in Reading,* by Eileen L. Corcoran.
3. *The World Around Us,* by Helen Prevo.
4. *Useful Science,* by Jerry J. Danley.

Globe Book Company
1. *Exploring United States History,* by John R. O'Connor et al. Reading level, grades 7–8; grade level, senior high.
2. *Minorities U.S.A.,* revised edition, by Milton Finkelstein et al. Reading level, grades 5–6; grade level, intermediate through senior high.
3. *Exploring World History,* by Sol Holt and John R. O'Connor. Reading level, grades 5–6; grade level, senior high.
4. *Inquiry: Western Civilization,* by Sidney Schwartz and John R. O'Connor (five softcover texts). Reading level, grade 7; grade level, junior and senior high.
5. *Exploring a Changing World,* revised edition, by Melvin Schwartz and John R. O'Connor. Reading level, grade 7; grade level, junior high.
6. *Exploring the Urban World,* by John R. O'Connor et al. Reading level, grades 5–6; grade level, junior and senior high.
7. *Unlocking Social Studies Skills,* by John R. O'Connor and Robert M. Goldberg. Reading level, grades 5–6; grade level, junior and senior high.
8. *Science Workshop,* by Seymour Rosen (twelve books). Reading level, grades 4–5; grade level, junior and senior high.
9. *Pathways in Science,* revised edition, by Joseph M. Oxenhorn (twelve books). Reading level, grades 5–6; grade level, junior high.
10. *Pathways to Health,* by J. Keogh Rash. Reading level, grades 4–5; grade level, junior high.
11. *Exploring Metrics,* by Frank D. Mark. Reading level, grades 3–4; grade level, middle school and above.
12. *The World of Vocabulary,* revised edition, by Sidney J. Rauch et al. (seven books). Reading level, grades 2–7; grade level, junior and senior high.
13. *An Edgar Allen Poe Reader,* adapted by Ollie DePew. Reading level, grades 6–7.
14. *Tales Worth Retelling,* adapted by Herzl Fife. Reading level, grades 5–6.
15. *Language Workshop: A Guide to Better English,* revised edition, by Robert R. Potter. Reading level, grades 4–5; grade level, senior high.
16. *Spell It Out: Reading/Spelling Workshop,* by Phillip Trocki (four books). Reading level, grades 3–7; grade level, junior and senior high.

Houghton Mifflin Company
1. *New Directions in Reading,* by Jo M. Stanchfield and Thomas G. Gunning (ten books). For less successful readers in grades 4–12.

Janus Publications:
1. *Job Application Language,* by Jim Richey.
2. *Reading and Following Directions,* by Winifred Ho Roderman.
3. *Supermarket Language,* by Jim Richey.
4. *Using the Want Ads,* by Wing Jew and Carol Tandy.

McGraw-Hill:
Challenges to Science: General Science for Tomorrow's World, by William L. Smallwood. Reading level, grade 6–6.5; grade level, junior and senior high.

Scholastic Magazines and Book Service:
1. *Action,* edited by Mel Cebulash. Reading level, grades 2–3; grade level, grades 7–9.
2. *Scope,* edited by Katherine Robinson. Reading level, grades 4–6; grade level, grades 8–12.
3. *Search,* edited by Eric Oatman. Reading level, grades 4–6; grade level, grades 8–12.

Steck-Vaughn Company:
1. *Wonders of Science,* by Joan S. Gottleib. Reading level, grades 2–3; grade level, grades 7–12.
2. *Living in America Series,* by Thomas A. Rakes, Annie De Caprio, and J. Ralph Randolph (four titles). Reading level, grades 3–6; grade level, mature learner.
3. *America's Story,* by Vivian Bernstein. Reading level, grades 2–3; grade level, older students in elementary and secondary grades.
4. *Health and You,* by Vivian Bernstein. Reading level, grades 2–3. Health program for students with learning disabilities who are reading below grade level.
5. *World History and You,* by Vivian Bernstein. Reading level, grade 4; grade level, older students in elementary and secondary grades.
6. *Panorama Reading Series.* Reading level, grades 2–4; grade level, junior and senior high.
7. *Reading for Winners,* by Norman Schacter and John K. Whelan. Reading level, grades 4–6; grade level, junior and senior high.
8. *Superstars Series,* by Randall C. Hill. Reading level, grades 4–6; grade level, junior and senior high.

Sullivan Associates:
Programmed Math for Adults. Reading level, grades 2–5; interest level, twelve years and older.

CHAPTER APPENDIX B: SELECTION AIDS

There are a number of selection aids that can help secondary school teachers locate appropriate books for the variety of readers in their classes. Following is a list of some of the especially useful aids:

Agee, Hugh. *High Interest—Easy Reading: For Junior and Senior High School Students*. 4th ed. Urbana, Ill.: National Council of Teachers of English, 1984.

Books for the Teenager, 1985 Annual. New York: New York Public Library, 1985.

Brewton, J. E., Sara W. Brewton, and G. Meredith Blackburn III. *Index to Poetry for Children and Young People*. New York: H. W. Wilson Company, 1983.

Carlsen, G. Robert. *Books and the Teenage Reader: A Guide for Teachers, Librarians, and Parents*. 2nd rev. ed. New York: Harper and Row, 1980.

Dole, Janice A., and Virginia R. Johnson. "Beyond the Textbook: Science Literature for Young People." *Journal of Reading*, 24 (April 1981), 579–582.

Donelson, Kenneth. "200 Adolescent Novels Worth Reading: 1972–1977." *Illinois English Bulletin*, 65 (Fall 1977).

Eble, Mary, and Jeanne Renton. "Books Unlimited: A School-Wide Reading Program." *Journal of Reading*, 22 (November 1978), 123–130.

Fader, Daniel N. *The New Hooked on Books*. Rev. ed. New York: Berkley Medallion Books, 1981.

Halpern, Honey. "Contemporary Realistic Young Adult Fiction: An Annotated Bibliography." *Journal of Reading*, 21 (January 1978), 351–356.

Junior High School Library Catalog. 4th ed. New York: H. W. Wilson Company, 1980.

Metzner, S. *World History in Juvenile Books: A Geographical and Chronological Guide*. New York: H. W. Wilson Company, 1973.

School Library Journal. New York: R. R. Bowker. Published monthly September through May.

Senior High School Library Catalog. 12th ed. New York: H. W. Wilson Company, 1986.

Spache, George. *Good Reading for Poor Readers*. Rev. ed. Champaign, Ill.: Garrard Press, 1978.

Stanford, Barbara Dodds, and Karima Amin. *Black Literature for High School Students*. Urbana, Ill.: National Council of Teachers of English, 1978.

Stensland, A. E. *Literature by and About the American Indian: An Annotated Bibliography for Junior and Senior High School Students*. 2nd ed. Urbana, Ill.: National Council of Teachers of English, 1979.

Stroud, Janet G. "The Handicapped in Adolescent Fiction." *Journal of Reading*, 24 (March 1981), 519–522.

"Teens Pick Favored Reading in Iowa Books for Young Adults Poll." *Phi Delta Kappan*, 59 (September 1977), 51.

Tway, Eileen, ed. *Reading Ladders for Human Relations*. 6th ed. Washington, D.C.: American Council on Education, 1981.

Vugrenes, David E. "North American Indian Myths and Legends for Classroom Use." *Journal of Reading,* 24 (March 1981), 494–496.

Walker, Elinor. *Doors to More Mature Reading.* 2nd ed. Chicago: American Library Association, 1981.

Wilton, Shirley M. "Juvenile Science Fiction Involves Reluctant Readers." *Journal of Reading,* 24 (April 1981), 608–611.

CHAPTER
T E N

THE READING PROCESS

OVERVIEW

Understanding why and how to use a procedure enables teachers to plan and implement effective instruction. This chapter aims to develop understanding of the reading process by exploring current theoretical constructs of reading and examining the factors that are related to developing reading competence. Both a skills approach and a psycholinguistic approach to reading are presented to help teachers conceptualize the reading process. Because physical factors, intellectual factors, emotional factors, language factors, home factors, and educational factors each play an important role in the development of competent readers, these elements are also discussed in this chapter.

PURPOSE-SETTING QUESTIONS

As you read this chapter, try to answer these questions:

1. How are a skills explanation of the reading process and a psycholinguistic explanation alike?
2. How does prediction operate in the reading process?
3. What is the relationship of each of the following factors to reading competence: physical factors, home factors, educational factors, intellectual factors, emotional factors, language factors?

KEY VOCABULARY

As you read this chapter, check your understanding of these terms:

Gray-Robinson skills model	comprehension	content reading
psycholinguistic model	reaction	study skills
prediction	assimilation	
perception	miscues	

THEORETICAL CONSTRUCTS OF READING

This discussion focuses on two popular influential reading models: the Gray-Robinson model and the psycholinguistic model. The *Gray-Robinson model* is essentially a *skills* model, because it identifies the reading skills required to perform each component of the model. The *psycholinguistic model* of reading is based on the relationships among language, thought, and the learning process.

The Gray-Robinson Model

The Gray-Robinson model was developed by William S. Gray and later modified by Helen M. Robinson.[1] This model incorporates five major components of reading: perception, comprehension, reaction, fusion (assimilation), and rate. Each of these components is equally important to our understanding of the reading process.

Perception refers to the reader's ability to identify a word and to associate meaning with the printed symbol. Word perception skills include memory (sight words), contextual analysis, phonic analysis, structural analysis, and dictionary usage. *Comprehension* concerns the reader's understanding of ideas stated by the author. Understanding of both literal and implied ideas is important in comprehension. Literal ideas are directly stated, but implied ideas are unstated, and the reader must read "between the lines" to discover what the author means to say. For example, the author may have written sarcastically or metaphorically. To understand the complete message of the author's words, the reader must recognize the author's purpose, assumptions, generalizations, and conclusions. The *reaction* aspect of the Gray-Robinson model is directed to critical reading or evaluation of content. The reader asks, "What do I think?" or, "How can I apply this knowledge?" To achieve this deeper level of understanding, a reader must also read *beyond* the lines (read creatively). *Assimilation* concerns a reader's integration of ideas acquired from reading and understanding with previously acquired information that has been stored in memory. *Rate* refers to the adjustment of reading speed to the type of content, the reader's purpose, and the reader's familiarity with the content.

The Psycholinguistic Model

The psycholinguistic model of reading is based on the work of Kenneth Goodman and Frank Smith, who explain reading as a psycholinguistic process.[2] According to the psycholinguistic model, a reader's eyes move across the line of print, picking up minimal cues that enable the reader to anticipate words, ideas, and sentences. The reader's knowledge of language and understanding of content help in this process; for example, the reader would predict a verb in the sentence, "Susan _____ the tennis ball." When a word is anticipated incorrectly, the reader's understanding goes awry. This indicates that the reader needs to regress to pick up additional cues for word identification. Psycholinguists are concerned with the processing of units of meaning as a basis for identifying words rather than with the one-by-one decoding of phonemes.

Goodman uses the term *miscues* to describe reading errors that, he believes, occur because of a mismatch between the reader's language and the book language.[3] This mismatch leads to a breakdown in the reader's anticipation system. However, miscues that do not change the meaning of content should not be considered errors. Following is an example of a reader's miscues that have been inserted in a sentence.

dad   car

John's f~~ather~~ handed him the auto~~mo~~bile keys.

These miscues probably occurred because the reader uses "dad" and "car" in oral language, thus creating the expectation that these words would occur in this sentence. However, these particular miscues did not result in a meaning change.

Psycholinguists have contributed the following ideas to our understanding of the reading process:

1. Reading ability is based on language competence.
2. Reading is not a precise process.
3. Reading is a meaning-centered process. To anticipate meaning, efficient readers utilize chunks of print, their own language, and experience. Thus, overall understanding is more important than word-by-word accuracy and decoding.
4. Context is an extremely important factor in reading. Context helps the reader identify the meanings of individual words.

A Combination Construct

Both the Gray-Robinson model and the psycholinguistic model help us to understand the reading process, but any single model or theoretical construct seems to fall short of explaining the entire process. Many of the existing models are partial explanations that are concerned with specific aspects (such as psycholinguistics) or levels (such as beginning reading). Because individual students learn to read in different ways, it appears very unlikely that a single explanation of the reading process can be devised that will encompass all of the individual differences that exist in people and written language.

A single theoretical construct of reading is not sufficiently comprehensive to explain the complex process of reading. The following compilation of basic concepts, which have been extrapolated from current models of reading, reflect the philosophy of this book.

1. Reading is an active process that should be directed toward obtaining meaning.
2. Both word identification and comprehension are important components of reading. Competent readers have fluency in word recognition that permits

them to devote their entire attention to comprehension. Unfortunately, students who lack this competence must apply word identification skills in order to perceive words and to achieve comprehension. Therefore, word identification is an important component of the reading process.

3. Reading is not a precise process, because it is characterized by the reader's efforts to obtain the author's meaning.

4. Prediction plays an important role in reading and should be a part of the instructional program. The reader's language, experience, and concepts permit the reader to predict the author's ideas, words, and sentences.

5. An author uses language, concepts, and experience to shape and organize written content; written content can enhance or detract from comprehension.

6. Students who have acquired basic competence in reading should have opportunities to read many different types of content for many different purposes.

FACTORS CORRELATED WITH READING COMPETENCE

Theoretical constructs help teachers understand the reading process. When teachers combine this understanding with a recognition of the factors that are correlated with reading competence, they can plan effective instruction. John Carroll states that "reading is an intellectual activity involving the whole physical, intellectual, perceptual, and spiritual life and growth of the individual."[4] This all-encompassing definition of reading suggests the complexity of the factors that are involved in a student's learning to read. These factors include language, thinking, emotions, physical development, experiential and family background, and educational experiences. The role of each of these factors is discussed in the following sections.

Physical Factors

Much of all that is learned is experienced first through the sense organs. Sensory experience is the basis of perception: through sensory experience an individual perceives and interprets information. Cognition (thinking) is based on perception. When sense organs are impaired, reading efficiency may be reduced because sensory information is prevented from reaching the brain. Fortunately, a reduction in the sensory input from one source does not usually disable a reader; other sources of sensory information can compensate for the weakness. A deficiency in any single sense organ rarely prevents a student from developing reading competence.

Vision

Vision is a significant factor in reading because the reading process begins with seeing. The two eyes must coordinate, move along the lines of print, and send perceptual messages to the brain. The reader must have clear, accurate images of letters and words; if the images are not accurate, letters and words that are similar in configuration may be confused. Thus, the reading process would be impaired. Perceiving letters, words, and sentences with the eyes is a basic part of the reading process.

Visual Acuity   Visual acuity is "the sharpness of seeing which is the result of the clarity of the image falling on the retina, the sensitivity of the retina and the nervous system, and the keenness of perception."[5] The role that visual acuity problems play in reading has not been clearly delineated by research, although Helen Robinson's classic study of reading failure produced the conclusion that approximately 50 percent of the disabled readers in the study had visual or visual-perceptual problems.[6] This study also indicated that no single factor was the cause of a reading problem. Apparently, although vision may be one of several factors that cause a reading problem, with the exception of total blindness, vision is generally not the single cause of a reading problem.

Visual screening tests are used by teachers to determine if referral to a vision specialist is in order. Vision can be tested with the Snellen Chart (American Optical Company), a wall chart that has rows of letters that gradually decrease in size from the top row to the bottom. The subject reads the letters from twenty feet away. However, only nearsightedness can be detected with this test. A more useful test is the Keystone Vision Screening Test for Schools (Keystone View Company). This instrument can be used to screen for nearpoint and farpoint acuity, usable binocular vision, eye posture and binocular imbalance, binocular depth perception, and color discrimination. When students show signs of visual difficulties on screening instruments, they should be referred to an opthalmologist (a medical specialist in eye problems) or an optometrist (a nonmedical eye specialist) for diagnosis.[7]

A teacher may also discover need for visual referral through observation of students engaged in school activities. Those who squint or close or cover an eye when reading, rub their eyes a great deal, lose their places when reading, or hold the book in an unusual position may need diagnosis. Reddened eyes, excessive tearing of the eyes, complaints of blurred vision or double vision, and excessive blinking are other signs of possible trouble.[8] Teachers are in a good position to discover such problems because they spend much time looking at their students' eyes as they stand in front of the class.

Visual Perception   Visual perception refers to the ability to interpret visual symbols. People concerned with adolescent reading should realize that visual perception is as important as visual acuity. "Visual perception is the extraction of information about things, places, and events in the visible world; the process of seeing such characteristics of things as shape, color, size, distance, etc., and identifying them meaningfully."[9] An element of visual perception is visual discrimination, which is the skill of seeing likenesses and differences in the physical characteristics of letters and words.

Visual discrimination is a significant factor in learning to read because in the English language many letters and words look very much alike: for example, *b* and *d*, or *was* and *saw*. There are many commercial materials and tests available for analyzing visual discrimination, but most of these materials are designed for primary-school children. Although visual perception skills correlate positively with reading achievement at the primary levels, as a youngster grows older the relationship between visual perception and reading achievement diminishes. Thus, visual perception is not the most significant factor in reading achievement of secondary students.

Hearing

Hearing influences reading achievement because readers often make an association between the oral pronunciation of a word and the printed word. This association can be inhibited by hearing problems. Speech development is also dependent on hearing acuity and is closely related to reading skill. Chidren who are hearing impaired show definite difficulty in acquiring reading skills.

Auditory Acuity   Auditory acuity is the physical ability to hear both the loudness and pitch of sound. Impaired hearing may be the result of physical damage to the inner ear, the middle ear, or the ear drum. Loss of hearing may be caused by a collection of wax in the ear canal or by brain damage. Research indicates that there are more cases of impaired auditory acuity among disabled readers than among average readers.[10] The ability to hear sounds pitched at different levels and at varying degrees of loudness is related to reading skill.

Auditory screening tests are used to determine if referral to a specialist is needed. An audiometer, such as that produced by Beltone Electronics Corporation, is an electronic device used to screen a person's hearing threshold for a series of frequencies at different decibel levels. *Frequency* refers to highness or lowness of pitch, and *decibels* are units for measuring intensity (or loudness) of sounds. Each ear is tested separately. When students show signs of hearing difficulties, based on an audiometer test, they should be referred to an audiologist (a nonmedical hearing specialist) or an otologist or otolaryngologist (both medical specialists in hearing disorders) for diagnosis.[11]

A teacher may also detect students' hearing problems through observation of the students in class. Teachers can screen students for auditory acuity by noting the following symptoms in their behavior:

1. Frequent requests that information be repeated
2. Poor articulation
3. Opening the mouth when listening
4. Tilting the head when listening
5. Poor spelling
6. Poor phonics skills
7. Apparent inattentiveness
8. Complaints of noises in the ears

9. Drainage or discharge from the ears
10. Frequent colds
11. Unnatural voice in oral reading

Students with allergies may suffer periodic hearing malfunctions. Both auditory acuity and auditory discrimination (discussed in the next section) may be affected.

Auditory Perception   While auditory acuity is a physical attribute, auditory *perception* is a mental process. Auditory perception enables the listener to screen out unimportant sounds and to attach meaning to the sounds that are heard. In order to achieve good auditory perception, the listener must separate important sounds from background noise and properly sequence the sounds heard. Taped instruction, using earphones, can be helpful for students who have difficulty screening out external auditory stimuli.

Auditory discrimination is an element of auditory perception and refers to the ability to hear likenesses and differences in the sounds of letters and words. This is an important skill because many words in the English language sound somewhat alike. For example, the listener must discriminate carefully to hear the difference between *run* and *fun*.

Experts differ in the importance they place on auditory perception as it relates to reading achievement, but there are two facts about auditory discrimination that are significant. First, the older a student is, the less likely it is that poor auditory discrimination is a significant factor in reading disability. Second, auditory discrimination plays a more important role when the student is involved in an instructional program that relies heavily on phonics or oral reading.

General Health

Reading is a complex task and can be arduous; therefore, good general health is important for young readers. Good general health enables a reader to be alert, to concentrate, and to participate in classroom activities. Any physical condition that decreases a student's vitality creates fatigue and makes it difficult for the student to be attentive. Poor health also may interfere with school attendance. If the student is absent when important skills are taught, he or she may miss presentation of the skills required for subsequent learning and consequently may fall farther and farther behind in reading.

Intellectual Factors

The level of a person's intelligence is related to his or her reading progress at all academic levels. G. L. Bond and E. B. Wagner found that the correlation between intelligence and reading success is closer in the higher grades than in lower grades.[12] This closer relationship may be the result of the nature of the reading skills required by more sophisticated reading materials. In the higher grades, reading is a complex act that requires reasoning, abstract analysis, synthesis, and various comprehension skills that are related to greater demands on mental ability.

Intelligence is the product of interaction between a person's environment and his or her innate potential, which is determined by genetic inheritance. One's intelligence is frequently assessed during diagnostic procedures that are used to determine whether the person's full reading potential is being achieved. Traditionally, students who did not read as well as their intelligence indicated they could were considered disabled readers. A secondary student who was reading two or more years below his or her reading potential was considered disabled. However, some members of the reading profession now believe that any student who cannot read well enough to learn from a textbook should be considered a disabled reader.

Individually administered intelligence tests, such as the Wechsler Adult Intelligence Scale (WAIS), generally are considered more valid than group tests. When a test is given to an individual, the examiner can motivate the student and note any behavior that casts doubt on the validity of the results. The WAIS does not require that the student read in order to complete the test; group intelligence tests require reading ability, thus penalizing disabled readers and confounding test results. A group intelligence test may cause a disabled reader to appear unintelligent, when the real problem is *reading* rather than intelligence.

Poor readers often experience problems in the testing situation (both group and individual) because they have had negative experiences with school and testing situations. They may be frightened of tests and become tense while taking a test. One should keep in mind that intelligence-testing situations may be influenced by the student's general health, emotional outlook, fear of the testing situation, and cultural factors.

There is another confounding factor that teachers should be aware of. As stated earlier, intelligence is the product of the interaction between an individual's genetic inheritance and his or her environment. Because reading is itself a part of one's environment, the amount that a person reads can affect his or her intellectual development. Reading provides vicarious experience and expands a person's store of information. It enlarges the reader's range of knowledge, develops interests, and increases vocabulary.

In a sense, a vicious circle can exist. The less one reads, the less one's vicarious experiences, knowledge, and vocabulary (factors in intelligence testing) may be developed. Thus, an inexperienced reader may test at a lower intelligence level, have a resultant lower reading potential—and ultimately not be *expected* to read as fluently or as much! Some teachers tend to view intelligence test scores as static figures; they have high expectations for students with high intelligence test scores and lower expectations for students with low scores. Thus, the intelligence test score may become a self-fulfilling prophecy for the student, as students tend to achieve in accordance with teacher expectations. However, for all the reasons described above, intelligence scores should be put in perspective and should not be used to limit a student's achievement.

Emotional Factors

A student's emotional state is a significant factor in the ability to read. Because reading is a highly valued skill in this literate society, failure to develop reading skill may have strong emotional impact on the student. The precise relationship between emotions and reading is difficult to ascertain, but it is apparent that emotional maladjustment may cause, result from, or accompany reading disability. Furthermore, the relationship between emotions and academic achievement is circular: each affects the other. A person's self-concept, which is one of the most important dimensions of emotional development, is very significant in reading success or failure.

Stanley Krippner studied causal factors of reading disability and found that "almost all children with reading disability have some degree of emotional disturbance, generally as a result of academic frustration."[13] Albert Harris and Edward Sipay reported similar results from a fifteen-year study of disabled readers; they found that nearly 100 percent of the disabled readers exhibited some kind of emotional maladjustment.[14]

A large number of poor readers manifest symptoms of emotional maladjustment that indicate poor personal and social adjustment, as well as failure to deal with the demands of school life. The emotional symptoms exhibited by disabled readers range from aggression to the opposite extreme of passive withdrawal. Emotional maladjustment as it is related to reading is manifested in characteristics such as the following:

poor self-concept	lack of motivation
self-consciousness	timidity
anxiety	aggression
disorganization	nervousness
social isolation	apathy
impulsiveness	immaturity
instability	withdrawal
inattention	hypertension

The above characteristics may function either as causes or effects of reading problems; whatever the relationship, they function to impede progress in learning to read.

Emotional maladjustment of secondary students is often the result of their inability to learn to read successfully in elementary school. Failure to learn to read at an acceptable level creates a vicious cycle of overall failure and having negative self-concepts; this cycle must be broken by a remedial reading program. Many students will become better adjusted as they experience success in reading; however, some secondary students may need special counseling from a guidance counselor, school psychologist, or a psychiatrist in order to achieve emotional health.

In addition to the emotional problems that accumulate for maladjusted students, young people frequently are rejected by teachers who react negatively to emotional problems. James Hake studied both good and poor readers and found that negative teacher reaction was a factor in the emotional problems of disabled readers.[15] Obviously, teacher rejection further complicates a student's reading problem.

Self-concept

Self-concept is the most important single aspect in the emotional development of human beings. The self-concept is the set of attitudes and beliefs that an individual holds about him- or herself. Self-concept is defined by Paul Berg as "the individual's understanding of the expectations of society and his peers; and the kind of behavior which the individual selects as a style of life."[16] A self-concept is the product of an individual's interactions with family, friends, and teachers. The actions of others toward an individual tell that person what he or she is like. Experiencing success or failure causes students to see themselves as successes or failures and to act accordingly. Students who continually fail to please the adults in the environment will begin to feel inferior and subsequently will develop poor self-concepts. Interaction with the people in one's environment provides one with a view of self and a base for self-appraisal.

Students with poor self-concepts believe that they cannot succeed in difficult tasks, and they tend to give up easily. Many of these students lack the motivation to start a task or to persist until the task is completed. A student's level of aspiration is based on a concept of self; if a person does not aspire to learn, that individual will be unable to learn. Unfortunately, some students do not learn to read because they believe they cannot learn to read.

Research has further established that self-concept is an important factor in reading achievement. Studies by William Padelford and by Maxine Cohn and Donald Kornelly show that a positive relationship exists between reading achievement and self-concept.[17] E. Zimmerman and G. W. Allebrand studied the personalities of good and poor readers and found that good readers possess more feelings of personal worth, belonging, personal freedom, and self-reliance.[18]

Language Factors

Language is an intellectual factor and is the basic medium for communication. Language is necessary for obtaining knowledge and skills. Written language is the content of reading; an author attempts to communicate with the reader through language, and the reader uses his or her own language to reconstruct the author's meaning. If the discrepancy between the writer's language and the reader's language is too large, communication may be inhibited.

Language interference with reading can come from two sources. The first source is the existence of a developmental lag in language, or a delay in its maturation. Since listening and speaking precede reading, the student whose language maturity lags is likely to experience difficulty in reading. The second source of language interference is an individual's dialect.

Some students come from homes where a dialectal variant of English, called *nonstandard English*, is spoken. Speaking a divergent dialect has great potential for interfering with a child's acquisition of reading skills in this country, because most written material in the United States is in *standard* English.

However, a number of researchers who have explored the question of whether dialect actually interferes with the process of learning to read have found that speaking a dialect is *not* a deterrent.[19] Richard Venezky and Robin Chapman found that dialect interference could arise indirectly through the teacher's failure to understand various dialects or through textbook authors' failure to limit the semantics and syntax of their materials. These researchers suggest limiting the semantics and syntax of textbooks to a common core of language that could be taught orally within a reasonable period of time prior to initiating reading instruction.[20]

The majority of disabled readers at the secondary level can comprehend standard English, even though they may have missed an important source of language learning through the reading of standard English. Although secondary students are older and more experienced than beginning readers, they continue to need opportunities for oral language development.

Teachers should become familiar with their students' dialects and try to create a bridge between dialect usage and standard English. Certain classroom activities can be developed that encourage students to paraphrase dialect into standard English. Students also might be asked to write a dictionary that provides the standard English equivalents of dialect expressions.

Home Factors

One of the most important influences on a student's reading development is the home environment. Language (as discussed above) is only one of the factors influenced by the home. Although it is difficult to establish a causal relationship between home factors and reading disability, many characteristics closely related to reading *success* are influenced by the home environment. A home that provides love, understanding, and a sense of security provides the best possible background for a student. In contrast, parental neglect makes a student feel insecure and unloved; parental indifference to a child's learning problems can create anxiety in the student.

Research on the relationship of home factors to reading disability is limited. Bruce Peck and Thomas Stackhouse studied families of both problem readers and readers without problems. They found two important factors in the families of problem readers: an atmosphere of closed communication and the fact that these students had learned "how not to learn."[21] Byron Callaway, Bob Jerrolds, and Wayne Gwaltney found that students who rated highest in reading and language achievement came from homes with the greatest amounts of reading material.[22] Parents' reading to their children, modeling reading for their children, and encouraging their children to read are actions that have positive effects on reading.[23]

Students with homes where parents provide good nutrition, opportunities for adequate rest, and a stable environment will have advantages in a learning situation. Students from homes where reading materials are available and reading skills are valued by the parents also have an advantage in school. Parents who provide a broad experiential background for their children help to enable them to read textual materials with understanding. Unfortunately, many young people experience environments that do not enhance development of reading skills. Children from these homes tend to

1. Move more frequently
2. Have background experiences different from that reflected in the textbooks
3. Speak nonstandard English
4. Have fewer magazines and newspapers in the home
5. Not value reading
6. View reading as a feminine activity
7. Have poor nutrition
8. Have less rest[24]

Achievement motivation is highly related to reading success. Research indicates "that parents can foster the development of achievement motivation in their children by: (a) holding high expectations and evaluating their performance carefully and (b) being involved in the achievement-related activities of their children."[25] Middle-socioeconomic status (SES) parents have been found to be more likely to fulfill these requirements than lower-SES parents.[26]

Lower-SES parents tend to have lower occupational aspirations for their children than do middle-SES parents. If the students also have this lowered aspiration level, they may not see school as having high utility for them.[27]

Lower-SES parents also tend to provide poorer problem-solving strategies for their children and have less confidence that their children can perform learning tasks than do middle-SES parents. They may see the school as an institution over which they have little control.[28] Thus, interaction and cooperation with school personnel is probably less likely to occur with them than it is with middle-SES parents.

An important deficit in the background of many students from lower socioeconomic homes is the lack of experience needed to read and understand textbooks. Experience is necessary for conceptual development; students who lack basic experience also lack the basic concepts necessary for reading comprehension. The experience that a student brings to the written page is as important in successful reading as what is written on the page.

Educational Factors

Unfortunately, schools, teachers, and instructional materials can and do contribute to reading problems. Any school policy or instructional practice that prevents adjustment of instruction to individual needs hinders student progress in acquiring reading skills. Regard for individual differences is a necessary concern in secondary schools.

Regard for individual differences does not necessarily mean totally individualized instruction. A report from the California State Department of Education showed that in higher-achieving schools classes were divided for instruction into several groups working at different paces; in lower-achieving schools, instruction was more frequently offered on a completely individualized basis. This report also showed that students in the higher-achieving schools were perceived by observers to be more engaged in their work, which could be related to the fact that students working with a teacher or other adult are generally engaged more of the time than those working alone, and there is generally more independent work with a totally individualized approach than with grouping.[29] J. Brophy has reported that "across a large number of studies, investigators have found that (1) students who receive much of their instruction from the teacher do better than those expected to learn on their own or from each other and (2) students learn to read most efficiently when teachers use systematic instruction, monitor student responses, and give students feedback about their performance."[30] Barak Rosenshine and Robert Stevens point out that use of computers and good educational software may provide feedback and monitoring similar to that provided by a teacher and may, therefore, provide higher engagement levels for students working alone.[31]

Research has shown the advantage of academic focus and task orientation for students. Student time spent on reading activities and on using texts, workbooks, and instructional materials has been found to correlate positively with achievement gain. Teachers in classrooms with high achievement gains have been found to emphasize regular homework, weekly tests, grading student work, and maintaining quiet classes.[32] These results lead to the conclusion that carefully planned and focused instruction will yield better achievement gains than incidental and casual instruction.

Research also supports an instructional model that focuses on demonstration of the new skill, guided practice with teacher feedback, and monitored independent practice. During guided practice, helping the student arrive at the correct answer or repeating the initial explanation seems to be the best way to handle incorrect answers. Giving hints, asking simpler questions, and reminding the student of the process needed to arrive at the answer are all good approaches.[33]

Teacher criticism of students, shouting, and ridicule have been shown to be negatively related to achievement gain, although criticism that specifies desirable alternatives has been shown to have a positive correlation with achievement gain.[34] These findings support treating students with consideration.

Peer tutoring can help both the tutor and the student being tutored make academic gains. Tutors should have training for the task and close supervision, and the tutoring should take place over a long period of time.[35]

School policy in many school systems today supports promotion by age rather than by achievement (this is sometimes called social promotion). When this policy is combined with rigid curriculum policies, it contributes greatly to the reading disability of secondary students. Students are passed from grade to grade without achieving adequate reading skills, but the curriculum is not adjusted to the lower reading skill levels of the students. Furthermore, many teachers mistakenly feel that a student whose grade placement is eighth grade should read eighth-grade materials.

Reading curricula and reading materials are generally not designed for students whose maturation lags behind that of the average student. Basic reading skills are introduced in the primary grades and reinforced in the intermediate grades, but students who do not grasp basic skills at the appropriate levels often do not have another chance at them unless they receive remedial instruction.

The reading curricula in many schools are deficient in providing for the development of study skills and content reading skills. The reading materials used to develop reading skills in elementary schools may be composed largely of story materials instead of the nonfiction materials necessary for developing study and content reading skills. This lack in curricula and materials results in students who are expected to use reading skills that they have not been taught.

To add to the problem, the reading curriculum of a school often ends at the sixth-grade level, even though many students have not attained reading maturity by the sixth grade. Some students referred to reading clinics could make progress in public schools if secondary reading programs were provided. The lack of such programs forces secondary students to seek help outside the public school system.

Some school systems attempt to meet individual needs by using test scores as a basis for assigning instructional materials to students. Unfortunately, this is not always a viable approach because test scores may reflect the frustration rather than the instructional level of the student. Instructional materials assigned on the basis of test scores may be too advanced for the reader. Furthermore, most tests are based on narrative materials, while secondary students must read content books as well to complete their assigned work, and the tests often contain only single sentences and paragraphs for the students to read, a task not closely comparable to the reading of extended passages in content textbooks.

One of the greatest problems in secondary schools is the lack of teacher preparation for teaching reading. The colleges, universities, and state departments of education have failed to provide adequate teacher preparation in the area of reading. Most elementary teachers have had a three- to five-quarter-hour course in reading, whereas most secondary teachers have had no course work at all in reading. Teachers at all levels need courses in basic reading, diagnostic reading, and content reading, if they are to meet student needs.

Because they are not well prepared, many secondary teachers do not realize that they should provide instruction in the specialized reading skills required by the disciplines they are teaching. Indeed, some teachers take reading for granted; they are not aware of the skills their students need. Teachers have a responsibility to prepare students for reading assignments and to give a clear purpose for each assignment. If secondary teachers are educated to address the various factors involved in the reading process, some of the educational factors that increase reading disability will be eliminated.

SUMMARY

Knowledge and understanding of the reading process enables teachers to develop effective reading instruction. Looking at both a skills model and a psycholinguistic model can increase our understanding of the reading process. A skills model provides an understanding of the discrete skills that lead to competent reading ability. The work of psycholinguists has led to recognition that reading is based on language, reading is not a precise process, reading is meaning centered, and context is extremely important in reading.

This text recommends that components of both a skills approach and a psycholinguistic approach be included in a theoretical construct of reading. This model approaches reading as an active process characterized by the reader's efforts to understand written language. The reader uses previous experience, language, and concepts to anticipate an author's meaning. Because authors use their own language, concepts, and experience to shape written content, readers must develop an understanding of these factors.

Reading ability is related to a number of factors: physical, intellectual, emotional, language, home, and educational. Each of these factors can enhance or interfere with the development of reading ability.

SELF·TEST

1. Which of these statements about the Gray-Robinson model is/are true? (a) It identifies the reading skills required to perform each component of the model. (b) It is psycholinguistically based. (c) It incorporates the components of perception, comprehension, reaction, fusion, and rate. (d) Both *a* and *c*

2. To what does the term *perception* refer? (a) A person's beliefs (b) Ability to identify a word and associate meaning with the printed symbol (c) Evaluation of content (d) None of the above

3. Which of these statements about the psycholinguistic model of reading is/are true? (a) It is based on the work of Goodman and Smith. (b) It encompasses the belief that the reader's proficiency with language enables the reader to anticipate the words, phrases, and sentences on the page. (c) It encompasses the idea that a reader picks up minimal clues from the page of print and uses them for prediction. (d) All of the above

4. What are miscues? (a) Goodman's term for reading errors (b) Words that are skipped when minimal cues are used (c) Both of the above (d) Neither of the above

5. Which of the following ideas is/are based on psycholinguistic theory? (a) Reading ability is based on language competence. (b) Reading is not a precise process. (c) Context is an extremely important factor in reading. (d) All of the above

6. What are some physical correlates of reading competence? (a) Vision (b) Hearing (c) General health (d) All of the above
7. What is visual discrimination? (a) Ability to see (b) Ability to see likenesses and differences in the physical characteristics of letters and words (c) Ability to relate past experiences to words that are seen (d) None of the above
8. What is auditory perception? (a) Ability to hear (b) Ability to hear likenesses and differences in sounds (c) Ability to hear high and low sounds (d) Ability to interpret the sounds one hears
9. For which students are visual perception skills most closely related to reading achievement? (a) Elementary students (b) Secondary students (c) All students (d) No students
10. How are emotions related to reading disability? (a) They are a cause of reading disability. (b) They are a result of reading disability. (c) Both of the above (d) Neither of the above
11. What percentage of disabled readers have emotional problems? (a) 100 percent (b) 75 percent (c) 50 percent (d) 65 percent
12. Some students do not learn to read because they believe they cannot learn to read. This statement (a) Is untrue (b) Reflects the relationship of self-concept to reading (c) Reflects a condition that can be cured only by a psychiatrist (d) None of the above
13. How do parents influence their children's reading achievements? (a) By providing a rich background of experience (b) By genetic planning (c) By making their children go to school (d) Not at all
14. What educational factors influence reading achievement? (a) Teachers (b) Reading materials (c) Instructional practices (d) All of the above

THOUGHT QUESTIONS

1. What are the five major components of reading incorporated in the Gray-Robinson model of the reading process, and with what is each component concerned?
2. According to the psycholinguistic model of the reading process, how does reading occur?
3. What aspects of the combination construct of the reading process presented in this book come from the Gray-Robinson model and what aspects come from the psycholinguistic model?
4. What are six factors involved in a student's development of reading ability, and how is each one important?

ENRICHMENT ACTIVITIES

1. Read a journal article favoring a skills model of the reading process and an article favoring a psycholinguistic model. Compare the stands taken and react to the content.

2. Administer a Peabody Picture Vocabulary Test to a student. Then compare the results of this test with your observation of the student to evaluate the student's intellectual level.
3. Obtain a copy of a local school's curriculum guide. Analyze the philosophy and approach described in the guide and determine whether it is a skills approach or a psycholinguistic approach.
4. There are many similarities between a skills approach and a psycholinguistic approach. Identify as many similarities as you can.
5. Visit a classroom during an oral reading session and identify as many miscues as you can. If possible, tape the session.
6. Interview a secondary remedial reading teacher. Ask this person to identify the major correlates of reading disability that exist among his or her students.

NOTES

1. Helen M. Robinson, "The Major Aspects of Reading," in *Reading: Seventy-Five Years of Progress*, ed. H. Alan Robinson (Chicago: University of Chicago Press, 1966), pp. 22–32.

2. Kenneth S. Goodman, "Reading: A Psycholinguistic Guessing Game," in *Theoretical Models and Processes of Reading*, ed. Harry Singer and Robert B. Ruddell, 2nd ed. (Newark, Del.: International Reading Association, 1976), pp. 497–508. Frank Smith, *Understanding Reading*, 2nd ed. (New York: Holt, Rinehart and Winston, 1978), pp. 1–10.

3. Goodman, pp. 497–508.

4. John Carroll, "Nature of the Reading Process," in *Theoretical Models and Processes of Reading*, 2nd ed., ed. Harry Singer and Robert B. Ruddell (Newark, Del.: International Reading Association, 1976), p. 10.

5. Theodore Harris and Richard Hodges, eds., *A Dictionary of Reading and Related Terms* (Newark, Del.: International Reading Association, 1981), p. 347.

6. Helen Robinson, *Why Pupils Fail in Reading* (Chicago: University of Chicago Press, 1946), p. 220.

7. Margaret Ann Richek et al., *Reading Problems: Diagnosis and Remediation* (Englewood Cliffs, N.J.: Prentice-Hall, 1983), pp. 48, 54.

8. *Educator's Checklist: Observable Clues to Classroom Vision Problems* (Duncan, Okla.: Optometric Extension Program Foundation, 1968).

9. Harris and Hodges, p. 348.

10. James Evans, "Auditory and Auditory-Visual Integration as They Relate to Reading," *The Reading Teacher*, 22 (April 1969), 652–629.

11. Margaret Ann Richek et al., pp. 45, 53.

12. G. L. Bond and E. B. Wagner, *Teaching the Child to Read*, 4th ed. (New York: The Macmillan Company, 1966), p. 63.

13. Stanley Krippner, "Etiological Factors in Reading Disability of Academically Talented in Comparison to Pupils of Average and Slow Learning Ability," *The Journal of Educational Research*, 61 (February 1968), 275–279.

14. Albert J. Harris and Edward R. Sipay, *How to Increase Reading Ability*, 7th ed. (New York: Longman, 1980), p. 316.

15. James Hake, "Covert Motivations of Good and Poor Readers," *The Reading Teacher*, 22 (May 1969), 731–738.

16. Paul C. Berg, "Reading: The Learner's Needs and Self-Concepts," *Florida Reading Quarterly*, 4 (June 1968), 2–8.

17. William Padelford, "The Influence of Socio-economic Level, Sex and Ethnic Background Upon the Relationship Between Reading and Self-Concept" (Ph.D. dissertation, University of California, 1969). Maxine Cohn and Donald Kornelly, "For Better Reading—A More Positive Self-Image," *The Elementary School Journal*, 70 (January 1970), 199–201.

18. E. Zimmerman and G. W. Allebrand, "Personality Characteristics and Attitudes Toward Achievement of Good and Poor Readers," *Journal of Educational Research*, 50 (September 1965), 29–31.

19. Victoria Seitz, *Social Class and Ethnic Group Differences in Learning to Read* (Newark, Del.: International Reading Association, 1977), p. 21. Paul Jay Melmed, "Black English Phonology: The Question of Reading Interference," in *Language Differences: Do They Interfere?* (Newark, Del.: International Reading Association, 1973), pp. 70–85. William H. Rupley and Carol Robeck, "ERIC/RCS: Black Dialect and Reading Achievement," *The Reading Teacher*, 31 (February 1978), 598.

20. Richard L. Venezky and Robin S. Chapman, "Is Learning to Read Dialect Bound?" in *Language Differences: Do They Interfere?*, ed. James L. Laffey and Roger Shuy (Newark, Del.: International Reading Association, 1973), pp. 62–69.

21. Bruce B. Peck and Thomas Stackhouse, "Reading Problems and Family Dynamics," *Journal of Reading Disabilities* (October 1973), 506–511.

22. Byron Callaway, Bob Jerrolds, and Wayne Gwaltney, "The Relationship Between Reading and Language Achievement and Certain Sociological and Adjustment Factors," *Reading Improvement*, 11 (Spring 1974), 19–26.

23. Allen Wigfield and Steven R. Asher, "Social and Motivational Influences on Reading," in *Handbook of Reading Research*, ed. P. David Pearson (New York: Longman, 1984), pp. 430–432.

24. Barbara D. Stoodt, "A Summary of Home Factors That Are Associated with Reading Disability." Unpublished manuscript, Greensboro, N.C., 1977.

25. Wigfield and Asher, p. 428.

26. Ibid.

27. Ibid., pp. 429–430.

28. Ibid., p. 429.

29. Barak Rosenshine and Robert Stevens, "Classroom Instruction in Reading," in *Handbook of Reading Research*, ed. P. David Pearson (New York: Longman, 1984), p. 749.

30. Ibid., p. 746.

31. Ibid., p. 752.

32. Ibid.

33. Ibid., pp. 758–769.

34. Ibid., p. 769.

35. Wigfield and Asher, p. 442.

SELECTED REFERENCES

Bowman, Margie. "A Comparison of Content Schemata and Textual Schemata or the Process of Parachuting." *Reading World*, 21 (October 1981), 14–23.

Brophy, J. *Recent Research on Teaching*. East Lansing, Mich.: Institute for Research on Teaching, Michigan State University, 1980.

Cleland, Craig. "An Information-Processing Model of Cognitive Development." *Reading World*, 20 (December 1980), 142–145.

Coehring, Donald, and Mark Aulls. "The Interactive Nature of Reading Acquisition." *Journal of Reading Behavior*, 11 (Spring 1979), 27–40.

Conley, Mark W. "A Teacher's Schema for Reading Instruction." In *Issues in Changing Perspectives on Research in Reading/Language Processing and Instruction*. Ed. Jerome A. Niles and Larry A. Harris. Rochester, N.Y.: The National Reading Conference, 1984, pp. 132–136.

Duffy, Gerald G. "Models of Reading Have Direct Implications for Reading Instruction: The Negative Position." In *Issues in Literacy: A Research Perspective*. Ed. Jerome A. Niles and Rosary V. Lalik. Rochester, N.Y.: The National Reading Conference, 1985, pp. 398–401.

Educator's Guide to Classroom Vision Problems. Duncan, Okla.: Optometric Extention Program Foundation, 1968.

Emans, Robert. "Reading Theory: Bringing Points of View Together." *Journal of Reading*, 22 (May 1979), 690–697.

Emmer, E., C. Evertson, J. Sanford, B. Clements, and M. Worsham. *Organizing and Managing the Junior High Classroom*. Austin, Tex.: Research and Development Center for Teacher Education, University of Texas, 1982.

Friedman, Myles I., and Michael D. Rowls. *Teaching Reading and Thinking Skills*. New York: Longman, 1980. Chapter 2.

Garner, Ruth. "Verbalization of Schemata Over Time: Investigation of Changes for Fifth Graders and Adults." In *Reading Research: Studies and Applications*. Ed. Michael Kamil and Alden Moe. Clemson, S.C.: The National Reading Conference, 1979, pp. 86–90.

Myer, Valerie, Donald Keefe, and Gail Bauer. "Some Basic Principles of the Reading Process Required of Literacy Volunteers." *Journal of Reading*, 29 (March 1986), 544–548.

Newman, Harold. "Psycholinguistics and Reading: A Dissenting Point of View." *Reading World*, 19 (May 1979), 368–383.

Richaudeau, Francois. Translated by Yvonne V. Basista. "The Reading Process in 6 Diagrams." *Journal of Reading*, 28 (March 1985), 504–512.

Richek, Margaret Ann, Lynne K. List, and Janet W. Lerner. *Reading Problems: Diagnosis and Remediation*. Englewood Cliffs, N.J.: Prentice-Hall, 1983. Chapter 3.

Robinson, Helen. "The Major Aspects of Reading." In *Reading: Seventy-five Years of Progress*. Ed. H. Alan Robinson. Chicago: University of Chicago Press, 1966. Chapter 3.

Rosenshine, Barak, and Robert Stevens. "Classroom Instruction in Reading." In *Handbook of Reading Research*. Ed. P. David Pearson. New York: Longman, 1984, pp. 745–798.

Singer, Harry. "A Century of Landmarks in Reading and Learning from Text at the High School Level: Research, Theories, and Instructional Strategies." *Journal of Reading*, 26 (January 1983), 332–342.

_____. "Models of Reading Have Direct Implications for Reading Instruction: The Affirmative Position." In *Issues in Literacy: A Research Perspective*. Ed.

Jerome A. Niles and Rosary V. Lalik. Rochester, N.Y.: The National Reading Conference, 1985, pp. 402–413.

Singer, Harry, and Robert Ruddell, eds. *Theoretical Models and Processes of Reading.* 2nd ed. Newark, Del.: International Reading Association, 1976.

Stallings, J., M. Needles, and N. Stayrook. *How to Change the Process of Teaching Basic Reading Skills in Secondary Schools.* Menlo Park, Calif.: SRI International, 1979.

Thompson, G. Brian. "Commentary: Toward a Theoretical Account of Individual Differences in the Acquisition of Reading Skills." *Reading Research Quarterly,* 16 (1981), 596–600.

Tovey, Duane R. "A Psycholinguistic Analysis of Reading Activities." *Reading World,* 17 (December 1977), 125–134.

Wigfield, Allen, and Steven R. Asher. "Social and Motivational Influences on Reading." In *Handbook of Reading Research.* Ed. P. David Pearson. New York: Longman, 1984, pp. 423–452.

Zintz, Miles V. *The Reading Process: The Teacher and the Learner.* Dubuque, Iowa: William C. Brown, 1980. Chapter 1.

CHAPTER
E L E V E N

SECONDARY SCHOOL READING

PROGRAMS

OVERVIEW

This chapter considers different types of secondary school reading programs: total-school reading programs, special English sections and units, remedial reading classes, reading laboratories, and reading improvement classes. The total-school organization for reading is much more comprehensive than the other plans, which are often combined so that two or more are initiated at the same time.

Any school reading program, regardless of its complexity, requires special planning. Responsibility for execution of the various aspects of the program must be assigned. Cooperation of staff members is essential, as is in-service training for these people. Program goals and instructional techniques must be determined cooperatively by the involved personnel, and materials for the program must be chosen carefully.

PURPOSE-SETTING QUESTIONS

As you read this chapter, try to answer these questions:

1. What are necessary activities related to the development of a total-school reading program?
2. In what two ways have English classes been utilized for reading instruction?
3. What are some techniques that should be used in working with remedial readers?
4. What are some skill areas considered in reading improvement classes?

5. What are some types of equipment that may be found in reading laboratories?
6. What are some questions that a teacher should ask about materials being evaluated for use in a secondary school reading program?

KEY VOCABULARY

As you read this chapter, check your understanding of these terms:

controlled reader   pacer
corrective instruction   reading achievement test
developmental instruction   reading laboratory
diagnostic test   remedial instruction
flexibility of rate   remedial reader
in-service training   tachistoscope

TOTAL-SCHOOL PROGRAMS

A total-school reading program is one in which all school personnel cooperate and all students are offered reading instruction according to their needs. Reading instruction is offered in special reading classes and clinical settings and is a priority in content area classes as well. The skills are taught as their use is required; therefore, the instruction is meaningful to the students because they see a direct application for it. Developmental instruction is offered to students who are progressing satisfactorily in the building of reading skills, and corrective and remedial instruction are offered to students who are experiencing difficulties. In such a program all aspects of reading are included:

1. Developmental reading is taught.
2. Content area reading is taught.
3. Recreational reading is encouraged.
4. Remedial reading is offered.

Implementing a total-school reading program is a difficult, demanding assignment, but the energy invested in it is well spent. The process of implementation can be diagrammed as shown on page 465.

Figure 11.1 shows a sequence of activities through which a school's staff can move in developing a total-school reading program. The sequence shows movement from defining a reading philosophy to evaluating the program. Throughout the entire sequence, constant in-service training of one type or another is offered to the staff involved in the program development. Suggestions provided during in-service activities will be most helpful if they can be implemented immediately. Therefore, the training sessions should be offered when a need for the particular information is current. Results of each step in the sequence provide input, which may affect subsequent in-service sessions, for the director(s) of the in-service training.

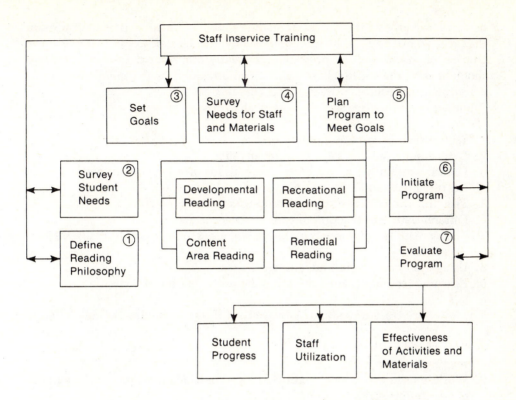

Figure 11.1   Implementation of a School Reading Program

Staff In-service Training

A first glance at this plan of implementation may result in the reaction that in-service training is being overemphasized. Careful consideration, however, reveals that this is not the case. Many secondary teachers (in some schools, most teachers) have little background knowledge concerning the nature of the reading act; the reading skill needs of students, available formal tests of reading progress, informal measures of reading achievement, reading interests and tastes of adolescents, and other topics related to helping secondary students progress in reading. In addition to this lack of knowledge, some of the teachers feel hostile to the idea of teaching reading skills. They often fail to analyze the situation carefully enough to realize that helping their students read the subject matter with more understanding will help these students learn subject matter concepts more effectively.

The first in-service training sessions should be designed to help the school's staff members recognize not only the need for reading instruction in the school but also the benefits to them as subject matter specialists if this need is adequately met. These sessions may involve selling the idea of a total-school program. Both teachers and administrators may need convincing, for many administrators have had no more background in the area of reading than the subject matter specialists on the faculty have had. If the attempts to convince the staff are not effective, the chances of success for the program are greatly diminished. In-service sessions should involve the entire school staff—administrators, faculty members from al¹ departments, media specialist(s), and guidance personnel.

Subsequent in-service sessions may deal with such topics as

1. Setting realistic program objectives
2. Determining reading skill needs of students
3. Locating and using appropriate materials for meeting student needs
4. Learning techniques for teaching specific skills
5. Teaching directed reading lessons in content areas
6. Differentiating instruction in content area classes
7. Fitting reading assignments in the content areas to the reading achievement of the students
8. Using the library to full advantage
9. Learning techniques for evaluating the program's effectiveness

The in-service training may take a variety of forms, including the following:

1. Workshops in the school, conducted by the school's reading consultant or reading teacher
2. Workshops in the school, conducted by an outside expert on the topic under consideration
3. Reading conferences and conventions
4. Demonstration lessons
5. Faculty planning sessions (teachers working together to plan implementation of the program in their special areas using the resources available in the school)
6. University courses

In-service sessions that involve "hands on" activities seem to be more successful with teachers than straight lecture sessions. Peggy Stier's article in the *Journal of Reading* on in-service programs describes one way to give secondary content area teachers some "hands on" in-service sessions that can transfer into their classroom teaching.[1] Any in-service session should include practical suggestions of immediate usefulness in addition to necessary theoretical background. Demonstrations of techniques, handouts, and displays of useful materials are more effective than mere "pep talks."

Reading Committee

Although staff members need to believe in the concept of a schoolwide program and need to be willing to cooperate in implementing the program, much planning can be done by a small staff group and submitted to the entire staff for input, endorsement, and implementation. This planning group is sometimes referred to as the reading committee. It should be composed of people with the ability and enthusiasm to offer effective guidance of the program. A good composition for such a committee might be the principal, the reading consultant, all special reading teachers, a representative from each department, the media specialist, a guidance counselor, and perhaps a school board member or representative from a parent group (PTA or PTO). The principal may choose to chair the committee or may appoint a knowledgeable person such as the reading consultant to act in that capacity.

Patricia Anders offers five justifications for having a reading committee that has representatives from each content area within a school:[2]

1. The committee allows working relationships between the reading specialist and other faculty members to be developed in a natural and efficient way.
2. The committee facilitates the reception of feedback on old practices and new ideas related to the reading program.
3. Committee members from specific departments may be more able to communicate ideas to their department members because the department members are more willing to listen to them than to a reading specialist.
4. Reading specialists can share their expertise in reading while relying on the content teachers on the committee to share knowledge about the processes involved in learning content area concepts.
5. All faculty members—content area teachers and the reading specialist—share the responsibility for the total-school reading program.

Defining Reading Philosophy

The reading committee may elicit ideas from the other members of the staff concerning the nature of reading, the reading abilities that are necessary for comprehending printed material in the respective subject areas, the importance of recreational reading, and other similar areas. These ideas should be integrated with carefully researched published materials. The committee may then produce a statement of the school's reading philosophy and share the results with the entire staff. Representative statements from such a document might include:

1. Reading is the process of getting meaning from printed symbols.
2. Secondary school students need reading instruction, although the type of instruction needed may differ from student to student.
3. Students need help in learning to read printed materials before they can read these materials to learn concepts.
4. Special reading skills are needed in order to read certain content area materials with understanding.

Surveying Student Needs

The idea of starting a total-school reading program may come about because of low student scores on standardized reading achievement tests, or it may come about because various faculty members have detected reading deficiencies in their students. If test results have inspired the effort, these results may be used as a beginning for surveying student needs. Reading achievement tests generally reveal the students' accomplishments in broad areas of reading skills (comprehension, vocabulary, rate). If an achievement test in reading has not previously been administered, the reading committee will probably wish to choose an appropriate test and make arrangements for its administration. After broad areas of difficulty have been identified, the committee may wish to choose either standardized or informal diagnostic measures for administration in order to pinpoint specific skill difficulties. Measures of reading interests and attitudes toward reading also may be used at this time to help the staff clarify the needs of the students.

Setting Goals

When embarking upon a new endeavor such as an all-school program, it is helpful to have some goals in mind. The reading committee may formulate a list of goals for the program and submit them to the rest of the faculty for input and approval. All faculty members need to feel that they have a part in deciding upon goals, because these goals will have a great deal of influence over each teacher's classroom activities. Some goals that might be stated include the following:

1. All students will be offered an opportunity to develop and refine their basic reading skills through special reading classes.
2. All students will be helped to develop reading skills specific to particular content areas during the content area classes.
3. Each student will be offered reading assignments that are appropriate to his or her reading achievement level.
4. All students will be encouraged to read for recreation in a variety of interest areas.
5. All students will be given opportunities to utilize the resources of the school's media center.
6. All students who classify as remedial readers will be given special instruction by a qualified specialist.

Surveying Needs for Staff and Materials

The reading committee can take the list of goals for the school's program and analyze the needs of the school relative to meeting these goals. For example, the committee may discover that another qualified reading teacher will be needed if each student classified as a remedial reader is to receive special help. It may not be possible to meet such a need at mid-year, and the complete implementation of the remedial portion of the program may have to be postponed; however, the program goal will at least clarify the need for specialized staff in the coming year.

If each student in the school is going to be offered an opportunity to develop and refine basic reading skills, the committee may find that rooms must be set aside for reading laboratories. These laboratories should be staffed by reading teachers and equipped with reading materials and equipment suitable for use by students who are reading on a wide variety of levels and need help with a variety of different skills. Once again, the committee may find that complete implementation is not immediately possible, but a beginning can be made, and future plans can include the needed changes.

Taking into account the amount of money available for implementing the program, the committee members may study catalogs of materials and equipment, may preview or examine available items, and may choose the items needed most to implement the program. The committee may continue to preview promising materials even after the program goes into full operation, or the reading consultant and reading teachers may assume that responsibility at some time in the process. Naturally, all staff members should be encouraged to suggest appropriate materials, especially those related closely to particular disciplines.

Planning a Program to Meet Goals

When the committee has obtained information about the skill needs of the students and the goals of the program, specific plans for a program can be made. Plans may center around the four major aspects of reading instruction—developmental reading, content area reading, recreational reading, and remedial reading.

Developmental Reading   Basic reading skills are often taught in developmental reading classes that are staffed by a reading teacher; these skills are also taught in remedial classes and, as needed for understanding the content, in content classes. Developmental reading classes frequently feature group instruction. However, some programs are individualized: teachers often assign materials on different levels to different students or make use of individual student contracts. The individualized programs often utilize a laboratory setting. Skills that usually receive attention in developmental reading classes include study skills, vocabulary building, general comprehension, critical reading, appreciation, and rate. The developmental reading classes also may go beyond basic skills instruction and offer help with special reading problems in the content areas, in cooperation with the content area teachers, who also will stress such assistance. In order to teach these skills, instructors generally use lectures, workbooks, and mechanical equipment.

Presentation in lecture form of material on how to improve reading skills is likely to elicit questions from the students, and the ensuing discussion can be valuable to the class as a whole. In addition, some students are auditory learners—they learn better those things that they have heard. Lecture-demonstration combinations are especially effective for helping students acquire techniques for increasing rate of reading.

Most developmental reading programs make use of workbooks or worktexts either as the basic texts for the programs or as supplementary materials. Many programs use a number of different workbooks, and instructors assign appropriate sections to individual students. Following are some important considerations concerning the selection of workbooks for a class:

1. Does the book include information about development of reading skills as well as exercises designed for practice of such skills? (If you intend to lecture on development of skills yourself, you may want only exercises. If the student is expected to learn some techniques of skill improvement through reading, the textbook should probably contain a balance of exercises and instructional material.)
2. Does the book cover all of the skill areas that you wish to cover in your class? (If you wish to use a basic text, you should choose one that covers all of the skill areas in which you are interested. If you are using the book as a supplement to other materials, check to be sure that the skills covered are ones for which you need further material.)
3. Are purposes indicated for each textbook assignment? (If not, you will need to provide purposes for the assignments to gain maximum benefit from the material.)
4. Are answers to the exercises included in the workbook? (If you wish the students to use the book independently, answers should be included.)
5. Are the reading selections ones that students consider interesting and relevant? (Lack of relevance of selections can result in decreased student enthusiasm for course activities.)
6. Does the book contain charts and/or graphs that are designed to help the student keep a record of his or her progress? (Such visible signs of progress serve as motivation for future effort. If the book does not include such aids, you may want to devise some for your students.)
7. Are the directions for the activities clear? (Vague directions may result in students following incorrect procedures. As a result, no learning may occur, or the students may learn an incorrect response.)
8. Is the workbook durable? (Students become understandably irritated by books that fall apart in the middle of a course.)

Some people think that a reading program should be built entirely upon mechanical devices. Although mechanical devices definitely can contribute to a reading program, they are not essential to the development of a good program. They seem to function primarily as motivational devices for the students.

Many types of hardware are utilized in reading programs. Some of them include (1) controlled reading devices, (2) tachistoscopes, (3) reading accelerators or pacers, and (4) tape recorders (often with listening stations). (See Chapter 4 for additional discussion of rate improvement devices.)

Controlled reading devices are used widely in secondary reading programs. They include filmstrip projectors that project a reading selection onto a screen at varying rates; filmstrip viewers with built-in screens; and motion picture projectors that utilize special films.

Tachistoscopes are devices that expose letters, words, or phrases for selected periods of time (one second, one-half second, and so forth). They may be operated by hand, or they may be automatic. Simple ones may be made from cardboard or paper with slots cut out to expose only the printed material you wish the student to view. Tachistoscopic attachments are available for filmstrip projectors and can be utilized with special filmstrips.

Reading accelerators or *pacers* are each equipped with a movable bar that moves down a page of print. The bar can be set to move at varying speeds. The student attempts to stay ahead of the bar as he or she reads the material.

Tape recorders are often used to allow students to listen to instruction on how to improve reading skills. Commercial sets of tapes are available, or the teacher may construct his or her own tapes covering skills needed most by a particular group. Tape recorders may be used in conjunction with any of the skills included in the program.

Controlled readers, tachistoscopes, and reading accelerators or pacers are ordinarily utilized to help students build reading speed. The printed material accompanying the controlled reading filmstrips is also designed to aid in vocabulary development and comprehension.

Since the various devices for increasing rate are adjustable to speeds appropriate for different individuals, these devices can contribute to individualization of a program. Group use of projected controlled reading materials, however, may cause teachers to neglect individual differences. The rate chosen may frustrate some students if it is too fast and may bore others if it is too slow for them. Controlled reading devices in general can help individuals realize that it is possible for them to read faster. However, the skills so acquired must be transferred from reading with machine aid to reading without artificial assistance before the student will have truly acquired a useful reading technique.

In a study of the kinds of reading courses taught in junior and senior high school, nearly half of the sixty-one respondents from across the United States indicated that developmental reading was offered in their schools, and more than a third indicated that accelerated reading courses were also offered.[3]

Content Area Reading   All of the basic reading skills discussed earlier—vocabulary skills, general comprehension skills, critical reading skills, study skills, appreciation skills, and rate skills—are important in content area reading because they are necessary to the understanding of content material. A good content teacher will teach all of these general skills at times when students need them to understand the particular content that is being presented. Thus, the skills are taught as a means to the end of better content understanding. The developmental reading teacher, on the other hand, has as his or her main goal the teaching of the reading skills themselves.

As explained and highlighted in Chapters 5, 6, and 7, each content teacher is especially concerned with the specific applications and clusters of skills that are particular to his or her content area. For instance, the social studies teacher will be very attentive to the cause-and-effect and sequential events patterns of organization, whereas the science teacher must be especially concerned with the classification pattern and the following of directions. Although the special reading teacher will also work on these skills, it is the content teacher who can observe the students' ability or inability to perform a particular skill within the actual content materials and can provide instruction as needed to facilitate the learning of the content. Since content area teachers may have had no previous training in helping students with reading skills, these teachers may need in-service training to help them prepare for these tasks.

Recreational Reading   Recreational reading is reading purely for pleasure. Many secondary school students today do not read recreationally. Outside distractions, such as movies, television, and readily available cars, are partially responsible for the fact that many young people do not read for pleasure. Also, students may not have adult role models who read for pleasure and may never have been exposed to enjoyable reading materials that stimulate personal interests. All teachers and other school staff members—principals, librarians, and guidance counselors—can help to encourage recreational reading. They can provide reading materials and information about reading materials and can act as positive role models by reading recreationally themselves in the presence of students.

Fran Newman[4] suggested the development of a readers' club to encourage students to read in their free time. The club can meet during lunch to discuss interesting books. Members can rate the books read and develop a list of recommended books. The club can be billed as being for students who love to read, but, if activities are interesting enough (book parties, guest authors, and so forth), others will be tempted to join also.

Recreational reading courses are sometimes offered by schools, but they are offered less frequently than remedial and developmental courses.[5]

Remedial Reading   Remedial instruction is generally designed for those students who read two or more years below the level at which they could be expected to read with understanding. Such instruction is given by a reading specialist in a special reading class or a reading laboratory. In most cases the student-teacher ratio for a remedial program is lower than that for a developmental program, and each student is given more individual attention by the teacher.

Diagnosis of needs for remedial readers is generally quite extensive, with both formal and informal diagnostic measures being utilized. Attitude, interest, and personality inventories are frequently used to supplement the reading test information, and counseling personnel are often involved in the testing and advisement of the student. See Chapter 8 for discussion of formal and informal tests that may be used.

Teachers strive to use high interest, low vocabulary materials with remedial readers. Care must be taken to avoid choosing materials obviously written for much younger readers. When high interest, low vocabulary materials are not available, teachers often resort to rewriting materials to lower difficulty levels or to using the language experience approach described in Chapter 9.

Due to repeated failures in the past, remedial students often enter reading programs with extremely poor self-concepts. Counseling, along with help in improving reading skills, may be needed for these students.

Remedial programs are generally individualized as much as staffing will allow. To offer more individual and small-group help than a single teacher can manage, schools often use aides in addition to the regular instructor. The diagnosis and prescription for each remedial student is done by the reading teacher. Then the teacher shows each aide how to conduct help-sessions with a specific student or a small group of students. Aides are shown how to help students use the printed materials and equipment prescribed in the students' individual programs; how to offer encouragement and reassurance; how to help the subjects correct poor reading habits; how to monitor attendance; and how to keep the reading teacher apprised of either positive or negative changes in the subjects' reading. While aides work with individuals and small groups, the reading teacher is free to offer intensive individual and small-group help to students who have problems that the aides are not qualified to handle. The instructor also must continuously monitor the activities of the aides.

Remedial reading instruction needs to be as practical as possible. The students need to be able to see how it is going to help them cope with real-life needs. Therefore, reading instructors would do well to confer with each student about his or her personal concerns and to try to tailor the remedial program to reflect the perceived needs of the individual.

Remedial students often need initial instruction in, or reteaching of, basic word recognition and comprehension skills. Therefore, decoding skills, vocabulary building, and comprehension are generally stressed in remedial programs, whereas little attention is given to rate. The basic skills are necessary prerequisites to programs for increasing rate, but in a remedial program some attention may be given to developing flexibility of rate. Peggy Flynn suggests that attention to skimming skills can be highly beneficial for students who have been indoctrinated with the idea that every word must be read, even if the students are remedial students who need much help with the basic skills. She describes a program in which the students' enthusiasm for the skimming exercises seemed to lead to widespread improvement.[6]

Remedial courses made up 74 percent of the reading courses described by respondents from sixty-one schools across the nation. Remedial courses were more numerous than any other type of course in each grade from grade six to grade twelve.[7]

More discussion of remedial reading may be found in the section on Special Reading Classes later in this chapter (pages 479–481).

Case Study: Total School Reading Plan

The way one school developed plans to meet specific goals is shown in the sample case described below.

Introduction

The school's faculty has recognized the fact that all of the students in the school can improve their basic reading skills in some way. They wish to offer possibilities for improvement to accelerated readers (students reading above grade level) as well as average readers (students reading on grade level) and retarded readers (students reading below grade level). They realize that many students have the capacity to read much better than they are reading, even though they are reading at grade level or above, and that some students reading below grade level are making satisfactory progress when their capacity levels are taken into consideration.

Area One: Developmental Reading

To meet the basic skills needs of the students, the faculty decides to include in each ninth-grade student's schedule one semester of reading instruction. Since there are approximately 200 ninth graders in the school, about 100 students are assigned to reading classes each semester. A special reading teacher is designated to teach five classes of approximately 20 students each semester. Because the students within each class vary greatly in reading achievement and needs, the class is conducted as a laboratory with individual and small-group instruction, rather than whole-class instruction. The teacher studies test results for each student and plans an individual course of study for each one, based upon the student's current achievement level and needs. If several members of a class have similar needs, the teacher plans small-group sessions. Otherwise, the students work independently with materials on appropriate reading levels and meet regularly with the teacher for teacher-pupil conferences concerning the assignments. During the conferences the teacher sometimes gives specific skill instruction, but conferences are also used to help students choose reading materials from a pool of appropriate ones, to check on word recognition and comprehension skills, and to help students plan ways to share their reading experiences with their classmates.

On Friday of each week, five or more of the students share with the rest of the class something that they have read. The sharing takes a number of forms: oral reading of epi-

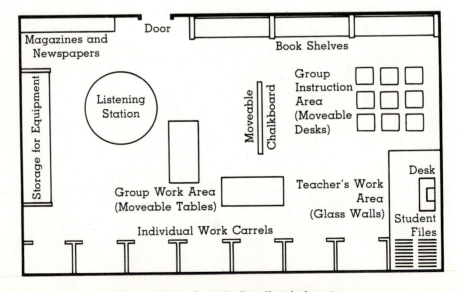

Figure 11.2   Sample Reading Laboratory

sodes from a book, illustrations of scenes from a book, panel discussions presented by several students who have read the same book, skits presented by students who have read the same book, and many others.

The reading laboratory is arranged in the following way:

The room includes seven carrels in which students can carry on individual work with a minimum of distraction, a listening station where up to eight students can listen to an audio presentation over headsets at the same time, two large tables at which small groups of students can work on common projects, a group instruction area in which up to nine students can receive small group instruction from the teacher, and a glassed-in teacher's work area where the teacher can conduct individual conferences privately without having to leave the classroom totally unsupervised.

Plans are made to develop a second reading laboratory for students in the tenth, eleventh, and twelfth grades who are developmental readers but feel a desire to work to improve their basic reading skills and are willing to attend the laboratory during their regularly assigned study periods or free periods. This second laboratory has to be postponed until the second year of the program because another qualified reading teacher will be needed to provide specialized help for the students.

Area Two: Content Area Reading

The reading committee members identify reading skills that they feel are vital for content understanding in many content areas. Then they arrange for inservice training sessions to help the content teachers learn to teach these skills in their subject areas, when needed. Each month of the year has a particular skill emphasis. At the beginning of each month, inservice training for the selected skill is offered to the teachers for whom the training is appropriate. This approach is taken to gradually introduce the content teachers to the application of appropriate skill instruction of different types, since inservice training about, and application of, instruction in all reading skills at once is thought to be too overwhelming to content teachers to be effective. Once they learn a technique, they are expected to continue to use it in all subsequent months as it is needed. Teachers who already have the skills being taught in a particular inservice session are not required to attend, although they are encouraged to do so to refresh their memories and perhaps pick up some new angles on presentation. Sometimes these teachers are enlisted to help with the inservice presentations.

The skill areas identified are vocabulary building, prefixes and suffixes, study methods, main ideas, following directions, locating information in textbooks, locating information in the library, developing flexibility of rate, sequence, context clues, drawing conclusions and making inferences, reading maps, reading tables, reading charts, reading graphs, detecting propaganda, recognizing fact and opinion, and detecting the author's motives or bias. During the first year, the faculty has chosen the following nine skills for emphasis: study methods, prefixes and suffixes, identifying main ideas, detecting sequence, using context clues, following directions, developing flexibility of rate, locating information in textbooks, and reading maps.

The content area teachers also learn how to teach directed reading lessons in their respective content classes. They learn to utilize study guides to direct the silent reading portions of the directed reading lessons.

The job of the media specialist is defined as helping the teachers locate appropriate materials for use in their subject areas. These materials include books, magazines, and pamphlets written on a variety of reading levels. The teacher attempts to match the materials to the students' abilities.

The reading consultant is available to offer help to content area teachers in planning for the teaching of reading skills related to each content area. The consultant is available to teach demonstration lessons in the content area classes when the content area teachers request such help.

Area Three: Recreational Reading

All content area teachers are encouraged to make students aware of materials available for leisure-time reading in their respective disciplines. The English teachers have decided to make available one day a week during their classes for recreational reading and the sharing of books and other materials read for pleasure. In addition, all students are encouraged to make use of the media center during their free periods.

A reading club has been formed during the homeroom-club period. The reading consultant and special reading teacher sponsor the club. Members read books on areas of mutual interest and discuss the books with fellow club members.

Area Four: Remedial Reading

The faculty has decided that all students reading two years or more below capacity level should be offered individual or small-group (ten or fewer students) assistance by a qualified reading specialist. For ninth graders, this instruction is in addition to the special reading class in basic skills and is offered during the semester when the basic reading class is not scheduled. For tenth through twelfth graders, instruction is offered two days a week during the study period. No student is forced to enroll in the remedial course, but conferences are held with students who need help, and they are invited to take part.

Initiating the Program

Initiating a total-school program is a difficult undertaking. For this reason, some schools initiate such a program gradually. One possible method of gradual initiation might take place over a two-year period, as shown in Table 11.1. Another approach might be to initiate the program one or more grade levels at a time over a period of years.

Table 11.1   Plan for Initiating Program

	Developmental Reading	Content Reading	Recreational Reading	Remedial Reading
1st year	9th-grade, developmental classes	Content teachers teach study methods; use DRA; emphasize vocabulary	Media center Reading clubs	9th-grade remedial classes (voluntary)
2nd year	9th-grade classes plus voluntary 10th–12th-grade classes	Content teachers learn and emphasize, when applicable, a reading skill each month	Media center English class time Reading clubs	9th–12th grade remedial classes (voluntary)

Evaluating the Program

A total-school reading program must constantly be evaluated in a variety of ways. Evaluation can be considered in three areas—student progress, staff utilization, and effectiveness of activities and materials.

1. Student progress can be evaluated through standardized and informal achievement tests, as well as through teacher observation. Teacher observation may serve to help evaluate progress in areas rarely covered by tests. For example, students' attitudes toward, and interests in, reading can often be detected through observation, whereas tests may give no information about these areas. If progress has been unsatisfactory, reasons for the situation must be investigated.
2. The staff members need to look at the functions that are being performed by different people to determine whether there is unwarranted overlap of responsibility, inadequate coverage of some area or areas by qualified personnel, or insufficient staff to handle the needs of the students in some areas (perhaps remedial reading). If any inadequacies are detected, the staff members need to make plans to alleviate the problems in the future.
3. Teachers can keep records of the activities and materials that seem to be most effective in meeting the objectives of the program. Use of ineffective activities and materials should be discontinued, and the advice of the reading consultant should be sought about other possible approaches to the students' problems.

A program should be evaluated regularly throughout the school year, not only at the end of the year, although the end of the year is generally one good checkpoint for evaluation. Periodic evaluation sessions can help keep teachers aware of the need for continuous assessment of progress toward program goals.

Needs Assessment

A school's evaluation of its established reading programs can take the form of a "needs assessment." Basically, a needs assessment is an attempt to measure the gap between "what is" and "what should be." Such an evaluation overlaps program planning, implementation, and periodic checkups by internal or external personnel. It is presented below as an isolated phase only for ease of exposition. The following items suggest the components of a needs assessment.

1. *Student Performance*—What is the present reading level of students? What specific types of reading problems are the students having? What are the reading potentials of students? What may be the reasons for underachievement, if this exists? What reading attitudes and interests exist?
2. *Personnel*—Who are the personnel involved in the reading program, including classroom teachers and reading teachers? What are their training, experience, abilities? What other personnel are available (psychologists, speech and hearing therapists, guidance counselors, and so forth)?

3. *Present Reading Program*—What are the locations of the reading classroom, reading laboratory, and so forth? What basic pattern or type of reading program exists? What time is provided for reading instruction? What use is made of reading specialists? What in-service program in reading is provided for specialists and classroom teachers? What is the present reading evaluation program? What record-keeping patterns are maintained?
4. *School Plant*—What are the size, location, and resources of the school library? What reading resources and materials are available in the classrooms or elsewhere in the building?
5. *Fiscal Resources*—What money is available to the reading program from the local school budget? From other sources?
6. *Professional Resources*—What use is made of specialized clinics, reading centers, college and university departments, private reading specialists, and others? What consultant help is available from sources such as these?

SPECIAL ENGLISH SECTIONS AND UNITS

In some schools, special sections of English are designated as classes for students who have reading difficulties. In these classes English teachers instruct the students in reading skills rather than in grammar and composition skills.

Donald Meints describes a task system that has been used to individualize instruction in reading in sections of Corrective Reading/English in one high school.[8] With this system, students are responsible for completing seven types of activities each week: reading skills, silent reading, writing, listening, word games and puzzles, cloze passages, and group activities. For a passing grade, ten tasks, each taking about twenty minutes, must be completed each week. Two tasks that involve reading skills, two that involve silent reading, and two group activities must be completed, as well as one task of each of the other four types. The reading skills tasks are keyed to individual needs as assessed by diagnostic tests. This approach certainly has positive features, because it takes into account the need for individualization of instruction in a class of students with diverse strengths and weaknesses.

However, one problem with these programs has been that the students object to being placed in the special classes. Another common problem may be even more serious. Some English teachers have no training in teaching reading skills because their teacher preparation programs did not include the techniques of teaching reading. These teachers may lack the abilities to identify the skill deficiencies of the students and to help students acquire these skills. These teachers often resent being asked to perform a function for which they lack sufficient training. With reluctant students *and* reluctant teachers, these classes are likely to be ineffective.

Many English teachers assigned to such special sections take the responsibility very seriously. They take reading courses from a nearby university, study professional literature, and attend conferences. These teachers can do a great deal of good for their students, if they can find effective ways to motivate the students

Some schools include reading units as a part of *all* English classes, instead of designating certain classes as special English classes. For example, using a special reward system, English teachers in a Minnesota junior high school taught students to use the SQ3R method when reading English, social studies, and science materials. This instruction, although carried out in the English classes, was part of a total-school reading program. Content teachers in the school also utilized the method in their classes.[9]

Although such reading study skills as outlining, summarizing, and note taking fit into the English curriculum fairly well, and some interpretive and critical reading skills are given attention as literature is taught, the inclusion of special reading units only in English classes should not be considered a comprehensive attack on the reading needs of the student population. English classes should not be expected to solve the entire school's reading problems, especially if the English teachers have not had special training in identifying reading needs or in teaching reading skills. Even if teachers know how to approach teaching the comprehension skills needed in literature study, it is unlikely that they will be equipped to handle a student with severe word recognition difficulties.

The three types of classes discussed next—remedial reading classes, reading improvement classes, and reading laboratory sessions—may be in the English department of a secondary school. They may be offered as options to English classes to fulfill the English requirements for graduation.

SPECIAL READING CLASSES

In some schools, students who are identified through testing procedures as remedial readers are assigned to special reading classes, whereas students who classify as corrective or developmental readers receive no outside help. In other schools, developmental and corrective readers are offered direct reading instruction in "reading improvement classes" or in reading laboratories.

Remedial Reading Classes

Different schools define remedial readers in different ways. A common definition for a remedial reader is a student who reads at a level two years behind where he or she should be reading.

Many teachers translate this definition into "a student who is reading two years below grade level." These teachers overlook the fact that not all students have the ability to read up to grade level and that some students who read two years below grade level are doing as well as can be expected, according to their capacities. Remedial readers should always be defined in terms of capacity level rather than in terms of grade placement level. If a large gap exists between capacity level and reading achievement level, there is a good chance for rapid student progress with adequate instruction. If the gap is small, little progress may result, even with excellent teaching, because the student is already performing at close to his or her potential.

Ideally, remedial reading classes should be small, and the work should be conducted in small groups and on a one-to-one basis. Each remedial reader will require a great deal of individual attention. Diagnostic tests must be given to each reader to determine specific areas of strength and weakness. Many of these tests are designed to be administered individually. After a student's weaknesses have been detected, a program that overcomes these weaknesses and that capitalizes on the student's strengths must be developed. Several students with the same needs may be helped together, but students should not be forced into group activities that are not appropriate for their personal needs. Individualization of assignments requires careful planning. Judith Ivarie describes a system for planning each student's weekly assignments on an individual matrix so that both teacher and student can see at a glance what needs to be done and what has been accomplished.[10] Such a system provides both structure for the student and a record of progress.

The students must be helped to recognize their specific reading needs and must understand how each activity used in the remedial work can help to overcome their difficulties. A teacher who develops good rapport with a student at the outset of the remedial instruction will find it easier to communicate with the student about needs and how to overcome problems than will a teacher who thinks only of lesson presentation and ignores the influence of the student's attitude. When students recognize the goals they are working for, they are generally much more receptive to techniques designed to help achieve these goals.

In many cases, a remedial reader has never had success in reading activities. Since success is a powerful motivator, the remedial reading teacher should plan some activity that is designed to allow the student to experience success with each session. Progressing through the instruction in a series of small steps will make success more likely.

Remedial readers need to have indications of progress. Graphing their comprehension scores from week to week may help them to see that they are improving as they apply themselves to their reading activities. Keeping a record of books read and satisfactorily reported on to the teacher gives another visible sign of progress.

Remedial readers often lack interest in conventional "reading resource room" activities because they have been exposed to these activities so often throughout their school years. "Secondary level remedial reading programs, then, must provide more than competent teachers, boxes and shelves of materials, and instruction based on the diagnosed needs of each student if they are to succeed. They must also capture the interest of the students and involve students actively in the learning process."[11]

Voluntary remedial reading classes seem to produce more impressive results than required classes. Subjects may resent being placed unwillingly in a remedial reading course; they may become sullen and noncommunicative and resist all of the reading teacher's attempts to help.

Dara Bass describes an elective program for remedial reading instruction that was utilized by Paducah Tilghman High School in Kentucky. This program made available to students several different reading courses: two "warm up" study skills and reading rate courses; a vocabulary course; two courses stressing basic comprehension skills; an individualized reading skills course based upon skill areas in which students felt deficient; and an individualized reading course that was based on adventure literature and emphasized comprehension. The elective program drew many more students than had previously taken reading courses in the reading laboratory. Gains in reading level of students who had been reading at least two years below grade level and had exhibited high absence rates averaged one year and two months, as compared with the average gain of two months by students referred to the reading laboratory during the previous year.[12]

Other formats for remedial instruction include New York City's Reading Improvement Through Art Project[13] and the District of Columbia's Special Education TV Reading Program.[14]

Students should probably be given credit for a remedial reading class, which is, in fact, as much a skill development class as an English composition class or a speech class. Students get credit for English composition and speech—why not for remedial reading? The credit may serve as added incentive to some students to do well. At the least, students will not resent being required to work at a task they would not have chosen without credit.

Since improvement is the aim of remedial reading classes, these classes are a means to an end—not an end in themselves. Ideally, students will overcome their reading deficiencies through participation in these classes and will move on into more developmental reading activities and full participation in the regular reading assignments for content classes. Placement in a remedial reading class should not constitute a "life sentence" to such classes.

Reading Improvement Classes

"Reading improvement classes" is a term that is often applied to developmental reading classes offered in the secondary school, although remedial programs, as described in the previous section, are sometimes also included under this title. In this section, only developmental classes will be considered.

Realizing that every reader has areas of reading in which he or she could improve if given the opportunity and assistance, many schools have initiated reading improvement classes for developmental readers. Developmental readers at the secondary level generally have good backgrounds in word recognition skills and general comprehension skills of a literal nature. In many cases, however, they have much room for improvement in interpretive, critical, and creative reading skills as well as in reading/study skills.

Evaluative instruments should be used to determine the skill profiles of the various members of a developmental reading class. Since these profiles will differ, grouping within the class and offering some individualized help will be necessary. Approaching any reading class with a "shotgun approach"—requiring the same activities of all students—wastes valuable instructional time and bores students who do not need help in the chosen skill.

Reading improvement classes often focus extensively on developing rate with comprehension. Mechanical devices such as tachistoscopes, pacers, and controlled readers are often used, in addition to timed readings. Flexibility of rate is another topic commonly included in such programs. Students who have a firm foundation in basic word recognition and comprehension skills are ready for some emphasis on rate, but the basic skills should be emphasized first.

Recreational reading is also frequently emphasized in these classes. Time in class is often utilized for recreational reading activities, and teachers may use many motivational techniques to encourage reading for pleasure, both in class and outside of class.

Reading improvement classes can be slightly larger than remedial classes, since the students generally require less one-to-one attention. In most programs, however, no more than twenty students are placed in a class of this type because of the diversity of needs that the teacher is trying to meet.

Some reading improvement classes are required; others are voluntary. Voluntary classes generally accomplish larger mean gains in reading achievement.

Some reading classes offer credit toward graduation; others do not. As in the case of remedial classes, it seems logical to offer some credit for the skill-developing reading class if credit is to be offered for English composition and speech, two other communication skills classes.

Ellen Farrell[15] described a junior high reading class that was based on sustained silent reading (SSR), a procedure in which students read self-selected material silently, while the teacher also reads. Some techniques other than SSR were also used in the class, including vocabulary development activities and discussion and writing of reports on material read. Students were graded on vocabulary tests, class reading, number of books read and reported on, and special forms of book reports. Most students in the program (90 percent) gained between one and two years on a standardized reading test during the year. The remaining students gained either less than one year or more than two. Farrell further noted that by May all students were reading above grade level.

Penny Beers[16] designed and implemented an advanced developmental reading class for ninth-grade college preparatory students who needed help in study skills, test-taking skills, and critical reading skills. Part of the class time was devoted to improving rate of reading. Not only were different rates discussed, but flexibility of rate was emphasized.

Reading Laboratories

Many secondary schools have established reading laboratories for improving reading skills. Although reading classes as described in the previous two sections can be held in a reading laboratory, reading laboratories are not usually bound to class organization, and the pupils work more independently than in a typical class situation. Reading laboratories are generally equipped with a wide variety of materials and equipment designed to be used individually by students. The laboratory instructor administers diagnostic instruments and plans a special program for each student that the student can follow independently to overcome his or her weaknesses. Many of the materials are self-scoring. Rate machines are usually available and sometimes other machines are utilized. Programmed materials are valuable also. The laboratory instructor is available to help students when needed.

It is important for the lab instructor to monitor the students' activities and progress constantly. If this is not done, a student can become locked into an unsuitable program that is not challenging enough or is frustrating.

Reading laboratory sessions may be required or voluntary, and attendance in the laboratory may be either scheduled or offered at the convenience of the students. Each school must make decisions about these points according to the needs of the student population and the available staff.

Elizabeth Webber[17] described how one senior high school in Ohio implemented flexible planning and scheduling in the use of the reading laboratory. Sometimes individual students who are having difficulty reading are assigned to attend the reading lab on a daily basis. At other times the reading laboratory instructor and content area teachers work together to identify weaknesses in a skill area, and the reading lab teacher schedules a lab session one or two days a week during the content class time to work with students on these weaknesses. One half of the students attend the lab while the rest attend the content class, and the two groups exchange places on alternate days. In still other cases, the content class and the reading lab are scheduled during consecutive periods, with the students in the content class attending reading lab following their content class. The content teacher and the lab instructor work together to plan work on skills that the students lack. Still another option is for the entire content class to attend reading lab instead of the content class one day each week. One additional option is available. The content teacher may ask the lab instructor to develop a particular skill in a limited time frame, perhaps several consecutive days.

COMBINATION PROGRAMS

Some schools that do not have total-school reading programs utilize a combination of two or more of the other programs. A typical combination is of remedial reading classes and reading improvement classes. A reading laboratory may house either remedial reading courses or reading improvement courses or both, or in a different situation the laboratory might be available for *independent* work by students. In this case, regular reading classes of one or both types are held elsewhere in the school or special "English" sections or units are utilized. In *all* cases and combinations, even when not part of a centralized total-school reading program or when partially covered within another setting such as "English" classes, content area reading instruction—within each content room—should be a priority.

CHOOSING MATERIALS FOR A SECONDARY SCHOOL
READING PROGRAM

A wide variety of reading materials is available for use in secondary school reading programs. Some materials are printed; others are audio-visual. Some are intended to teach skills; others are designed primarily to offer practice in skills already taught. Selection of the best materials for a particular situation is of primary importance. The burden of selection should not rest upon one individual; instead, materials should be chosen through the cooperative efforts of a variety of people, including school administrators, reading consultants, special reading teachers, and content area teachers.

Following are some of the questions that should be asked about materials being considered:

1. Is the philosophy behind the material sound?
2. Is the material designed to teach the skills the students in this school need?
3. Is the material appropriate to the maturity levels of the students with whom it is to be used? (This criterion is particularly important when choosing materials for secondary school students. Childish material should be avoided.)
4. Is the material appropriate to the backgrounds of experience of the students for whom it is intended?
5. Is the material interesting to the students who will be using it?
6. Are provisions made to encourage application of skills taught by the material to reading situations outside the reading class, including reading in the content areas?
7. Is the material free from role stereotypes (of different nationalities, ethnic groups, sexes)?
8. Is the material up-to-date?
9. Is proper emphasis given to all components of the reading process?
10. Does the material provide for continuous diagnosis of reading difficulties?
11. Does the material include an adequate teacher's manual?
12. What kinds of written material are covered? Poetry? Prose? Nonfiction? Fiction?
13. Does the material have a good format? (Easy-to-read print, adequate margins, good quality paper, and so forth)
14. If the material is audio-visual, can it be operated independently by the students?
15. Is the material easy to use with students?
16. Is audio-visual material technically acceptable (good sound, color, and so forth)?
17. Does multilevel material make provisions for placing students appropriately within a sequence?
18. Are all directions clearly given in written or oral form?
19. Does the material have available pretest and post-test activities?
20. Is the material adaptable to groups of students with different needs?

21. Does the material suggest follow-up activities to help reinforce the skills presented?
22. Has the material been field tested? With what results?
23. Has research shown this material to be effective in teaching skills?
24. Is the cost of the material reasonable?

Dallas Cheek[18] lists a number of documents that can be helpful in choosing good supplementary materials for secondary classrooms in a *Journal of Reading* article. He suggests sources concerned with selection of print materials for content classrooms of various types, for reading classrooms, for student interest, and for avoidance of sex and minority bias. The materials he cites are all ERIC documents that are readily available to teachers.

In another *Journal of Reading* article, Kenneth C. Krause[19] provides suggestions for choosing computer software that works. Some of his suggestions are similar to those Cheek makes for application to any material purchased. In addition, Krause recommends not buying software without trying it first and inquiring about the following concerns: existence of a warranty on the software, possibility of using portions of the material without using the entire program, availability of a management or record-keeping system, possibility of making a printout from the program's management system, possibility of controlling rate of presentation, and policy on obtaining upgrades of the program.

RESEARCH FINDINGS

James F. Baumann[20] reviewed the research on reading programs that are effective. The research shows that the presence of a strong instructional leader is very important. Teachers who are effective accept primary responsibility for student achievement and expect their students to learn. Effective teachers have clearly formulated instructional objectives and can communicate the objectives to their students. They provide frequent opportunities for their students to experience success, keep instruction at a brisk pace, have minimal transition time between activities, set unambiguous rules, have an ability to prevent misbehavior, and monitor their students' progress. These teachers are well prepared for teaching and engage in direct instruction.

Effective programs allot enough time to reading instruction to allow students time to learn, and the time on task is high in these programs. The classrooms have warm, nonthreatening atmospheres. Achievement is greater when the students work in homogeneous groups.

SUMMARY

Reading programs in secondary schools may fall under several different classifications: total-school reading programs, special "English" sections and units, remedial reading classes, reading improvement classes, and reading laboratories.

The total-school reading program is the most comprehensive type, since it involves all school personnel in a cooperative effort. Much in-service training is necessary for the program's implementation, and it is important to have a carefully chosen reading committee. All aspects of reading are considered in a total-school reading program: developmental reading, content area reading, recreational reading, and remedial reading. Other types of programs do not involve all school personnel and are much less comprehensive. Frequently, two or more of these less extensive programs are implemented simultaneously in a school.

Choice of materials for a secondary reading program is important and should be the result of the cooperative efforts of all personnel involved with the school's reading program.

SELF-TEST

1. What is true of a total-school reading program? (a) Developmental reading is taught. (b) Content area reading is taught. (c) Remedial reading is offered. (d) All of the above

2. If a total-school reading program is to be established, when should in-service training sessions be held? (a) Only at the beginning of the planning period (b) Only at the end of the planning period (c) Only after implementation of the program (d) Throughout the process of planning and implementation

3. Who should be involved in in-service sessions? (a) Administrators (b) Faculty members from all departments (c) Media specialists (d) All of the above

4. Which statement is true of a school reading committee? (a) It should be composed of only the school's reading teachers. (b) It should be composed of people who can offer effective guidance to the school's reading program. (c) It should never include an administrator. (d) It should never include faculty members from departments other than English.

5. Which statement is true of reading achievement tests? (a) They are of little use when planning a total-school reading program. (b) They generally pinpoint specific skill difficulties. (c) They generally reveal the student's accomplishments in broad areas of reading skills. (d) None of the above

6. Which statement is true of recreational reading? (a) It is unimportant for inclusion in a school's reading program plans. (b) It can be encouraged through reading clubs. (c) It is not a concern of content area teachers. (d) None of the above

7. What should evaluation of a total-school reading program include? (a) A measure of student progress (b) Consideration of staff utilization (c) Consideration of the effectiveness of activities and materials (d) All of the above

8. Why are English teachers often chosen to teach reading in special "English" classes? (a) They are well-prepared to do so by their teacher-preparation programs. (b) Other faculty members perceive English and reading as being closely related. (c) Both *a* and *b* (d) Neither *a* nor *b*

9. Which statement is true of reading instruction offered as special units in "English" classes? (a) It constitutes a comprehensive attack on the reading needs of the student population. (b) It is useless to most students. (c) It is useful for developing some types of reading skills. (d) None of the above

10. How are remedial readers defined? (a) Students who are reading at levels two or more years behind where they should be reading (b) Books for students reading below grade level (c) Students who dislike reading (d) None of the above

11. What do remedial readers need? (a) Much individual attention (b) To see some evidence of progress (c) Both *a* and *b* (d) Neither *a* nor *b*

12. Which statement is true of developmental readers at the secondary level? (a) They generally have a good background in word recognition skills. (b) They often need help with critical reading skills. (c) They often need help with reading/study skills. (d) All of the above

13. Which statement is true of reading laboratories? (a) They are generally set up to allow much independent work by the students. (b) They need to have a lab instructor present at all times. (c) Both *a* and *b* (d) Neither *a* nor *b*

14. Who should choose materials for a secondary school reading program? (a) The administrator (b) The special reading teacher (c) The content teacher (d) All three of the personnel mentioned above, plus the reading consultant

15. What does research indicate about effective reading programs? (a) The teachers expect their students to learn. (b) The instruction is kept at a brisk pace. (c) There is a strong instructional leader. (d) All of the above

THOUGHT QUESTIONS

1. List and elaborate upon the steps you would follow if you were given the assignment of planning the initiation of a total-school reading program. Which steps would you be able to handle alone? For which steps would you need assistance? What people could supply the expertise you would need in helping you to set up the program?

2. After a total-school reading program has been initiated, what evaluation procedures should be utilized to determine its effectiveness? When should evaluation of the program take place? Who should be responsible for the evaluation?

3. Can sufficient reading instruction for all students in a secondary school be provided through special "English" classes? Why?

4. How do remedial reading classes differ from developmental reading classes? Why do these differences exist?

5. Should remedial classes be elective or required? Why?

6. Should students receive credit toward graduation from remedial reading classes? Why, or why not?

7. What are some advantages of reading laboratories for improving reading skills?

8. What is the best procedure for choosing materials for use in a secondary school reading program?

ENRICHMENT ACTIVITIES

1. List the duties that a member of a school reading committee might be expected to perform. Compare your list with the lists your classmates have developed. Discuss differences of opinion.

*2. Report to the class on the provisions for reading instruction in your school.

*3. Check with your principal and fellow teachers about reading problems of students in your school. After identifying the two most common problems perceived by the educators in your school, write a plan for solving each problem. Share your findings and your plan.

*4. Draw a plan for a reading laboratory that would be adaptable to the needs of your school.

5. Make a list of reading skills that might be taught in a developmental reading class. Check the ones that could be taught by a content area teacher. Discuss your list with your classmates.

6. With a group of your classmates, design a total-school reading program. Include physical plant needs, materials and equipment needs, staff needs, organizational plans, and staff responsibilities.

*7. Choose a reading program described in one of the articles in the Selected References and analyze the possibilities for utilization of all or part of the program in your school.

8. Examine some reading material that could be used in a secondary school reading program. Ask yourself the questions presented in the section of this chapter entitled "Choosing Materials for a Secondary School Reading Program." Share your evaluation with your teacher and classmates.

NOTES

1. Peggy F. Stier, "Inservice Program Helps Teachers Learn by Doing," *Journal of Reading*, 22 (November 1978), 131–133.

2. Patricia L. Anders, "Dream of a Secondary Reading Program? People Are the Key," *Journal of Reading*, 24 (January 1981), 316–320.

3. M. Jean Greenlaw and David W. Moore, "What Kinds of Reading Courses Are Taught in Junior and Senior High School?" *Journal of Reading*, 25 (March 1982), 535.

4. Fran Newman, "Let's Join the Readers' Club!" *Journal of Reading*, 25 (April 1982), 693.

5. Greenlaw and Moore, p. 535.

6. Peggy Flynn, "Speed Is the Carrot," *Journal of Reading*, 20 (May 1977), 683–687.

*These activities are designed for in-service teachers, student teachers, or practicum students.

7. Greenlaw and Moore, p. 535.

8. Donald W. Meints, "The Task System in an Individualized Reading Class," *Journal of Reading*, 20 (January 1977), 301–304.

9. Paulette M. Gruber, "Junior High Boasts Super Stars," *Journal of Reading*, 16 (May 1973), 600–603.

10. Judith J. Ivarie, "Programming for Individualization in the Junior High School," *Journal of Reading*, 20 (January 1977), 295–300.

11. Fran Lehr, "New Approaches to Remedial Reading Programs at the Secondary Level," *Journal of Reading*, 24 (January 1981), 350.

12. Lehr, "New Approaches," pp. 350–351. Dara Bass, "Focus on Dropouts—A New Design in Elective Reading," *New Directions, New Dimensions: Practical Progress in Reading* (Frankfort, Ky.: Kentucky State Department of Education, Division of Program Development, 1975). (ED 130 228).

13. Lehr, pp. 350–351. Sylvia K. Corwin, "Assumptions, Implications and Consequences of New York State Education Department of Validation of 'Reading Improvement Through Art' (RITA)" (Paper presented at the American Educational Research Association Annual Meeting, Boston, Mass., April 1980). (ED 184 094).

14. Lehr, pp. 350–351. District of Columbia Public Schools, *Special Education TV Reading Program, Final Report* (Washington, D.C., 1979). (ED 182 730).

15. Ellen Farrell, "SSR as the Core of a Junior High Reading Program," *Journal of Reading*, 26 (October 1982), 48–51.

16. Penny G. Beers, "Accelerated Reading for High School Students," *Journal of Reading*, 29 (January 1986), 311–315.

17. Elizabeth A. Webber, "Organizing and Scheduling the Secondary Reading Program," *Journal of Reading*, 27 (April 1984), 594–596.

18. Dallas H. Cheek, "Secondary Reading Materials: Selection Criteria for the Classroom Teacher," *Journal of Reading*, 26 (May 1983), 734–736.

19. Kenneth C. Krause, "Choosing Computer Software that Works," *Journal of Reading*, 28 (October 1984), 24–27.

20. James F. Baumann, "Implications for Reading Instruction from the Research on Teacher and School Effectiveness," *Journal of Reading*, 28 (November 1984), 109–115.

SELECTED REFERENCES

Anders, Patricia. "Dream of a Secondary Reading Program? People Are the Key." *Journal of Reading*, 24 (January 1981), 316–320.

Ball, Howard G. "Standards for Materials Selection." *Journal of Reading*, 20 (December 1976), 208–211.

Baumann, James F. "Implications for Reading Instruction from the Research on Teacher and School Effectiveness." *Journal of Reading*, 28 (November 1984), 109–115.

Beers, Penny G. "Accelerated Reading for High School Students." *Journal of Reading*, 29 (January 1986), 311–315.

Berger, Allen, and H. Alan Robinson, eds. *Secondary School Reading: What Research Reveals for Classroom Practice*. Urbana, Ill.: National Conference on Research in English, 1982.

Burmeister, Lou E. *Reading Strategies for Middle and Secondary School Teachers.* 2nd ed. Reading, Mass.: Addison-Wesley, 1978. Chapter 12.

Cheek, Dallas H. "Secondary Reading Materials: Selection Criteria for the Classroom Teacher." *Journal of Reading,* 26 (May 1983), 734–736.

Corwin, Sylvia K. "Assumptions, Implications and Consequences of New York State Education Department of Validation of 'Reading Improvement Through Art' (RITA)." Paper presented at the American Educational Research Association Annual Meeting, Boston, Mass., April 1980. (ED 184 094)

District of Columbia Public Schools, Washington, D.C. *Special Education TV Reading Program.* Final Report 1979. (ED 182 730)

Farrell, Ellen. "SSR as the Core of a Junior High Reading Program." *Journal of Reading,* 26 (October 1982), 48–51.

Flynn, Peggy. "Speed Is the Carrot." *Journal of Reading,* 20 (May 1977), 683–687.

Gove, Mary K. "Getting High School Teachers to Use Content Reading Strategies." *Journal of Reading,* 25 (November 1981), 113–116.

Greenlaw, M. Jean, and David W. Moore. "What Kinds of Reading Courses Are Taught in Junior and Senior High School?" *Journal of Reading,* 25 (March 1982), 534–536.

Gudaitis, Michael S. "A Reading Course Outline for the College Bound Student." *Journal of Reading,* 19 (April 1976), 575–576.

Henry, Claire. "The Administration Helps Teachers Make the Difference." *Journal of Reading,* 20 (March 1977), 508–512.

Ivarie, Judith J. "Programming for Individualization in the Junior High School." *Journal of Reading,* 20 (January 1977), 295–300.

Jeffers, Pearl B. "Guidelines for Junior High Reading Programs." *Journal of Reading,* 15 (January 1972), 264–266.

Karlin, Robert. *Teaching Reading in High School: Improving Reading in Content Areas.* 4th ed. New York: Harper and Row, 1984. Chapter 1.

Krause, Kenneth C. "Choosing Computer Software that Works." *Journal of Reading,* 28 (October 1984), 24–27.

Kummer, Robert. "Reading as an Elective." *Journal of Reading,* 19 (April 1976), 575–576.

Lamberg, Walter J., and Charles E. Lamb. *Reading Instruction in the Content Areas.* Boston: Houghton Mifflin Company, 1980. Chapters 2 and 19.

Larson, Janet J., and Helen Ireland Guttinger. "A Secondary Reading Program to Prevent College Reading Problems." *Journal of Reading,* 22 (February 1979), 399–403.

Lehr, Fran. "New Approaches to Remedial Reading Programs at the Secondary Level." *Journal of Reading,* 24 (January 1981), 350.

Meints, Donald W. "The Task System in an Individualized Reading Class." *Journal of Reading,* 20 (January 1977), 301–304.

Peters, Charles W. "How to Get More Comprehensive Reading Programs at the Secondary Level." *Journal of Reading,* 20, No. 6 (March 1977), 513–519.

Professional Standards and Ethics Committee. *Guidelines for the Professional Preparation of Reading Teachers*. Newark, Del.: International Reading Association, May 1978.

Rauch, Sidney J. "Administrators' Guidelines for More Effective Reading Programs." *Journal of Reading*, 17 (January 1974), 297–300.

Rossman, Jean F. "How One High School Set Up a Reading Program for 500 Students." *Journal of Reading*, 20 (February 1977), 393–397.

Shannon, Albert J. "Monitoring Reading Instruction in the Content Areas." *Journal of Reading*, 28 (November 1984), 128–134.

Shepherd, David L. *Comprehensive High School Reading Methods*. 3rd ed. Columbus, Ohio: Charles E. Merrill, 1982. Chapter 15.

Siedow, Mary Dunn, David Memory, and Page Bristow. *Inservice Education for Content Area Teachers*. Newark, Del.: International Reading Association, 1985.

Singer, Harry, and Dan Donlan. *Reading and Learning from Text*. Boston: Little, Brown and Company, 1980. Chapters 15 and 16.

Sloan, Charles A., and James E. Walker. "Perceptions of and Practices in Middle/Junior High School Reading Instruction." *Journal of the Association for the Study of Perception*, 14 (Fall 1979), 16–21.

Smith, Richard J., Wayne Otto, and Lee Hansen. *The School Reading Program: A Handbook for Teachers, Supervisors, and Specialists*. Boston: Houghton Mifflin Company, 1978. Chapters 9 and 10.

Stier, Peggy F. "Inservice Program Helps Teachers Learn by Doing." *Journal of Reading*, 22 (November 1978), 131–133.

Webber, Elizabeth A. "Organizing and Scheduling the Secondary Reading Program." *Journal of Reading*, 27 (April 1984), 594–596.

Wood, Phyllis Anderson. "Judging the Value of a Reading Program." *Journal of Reading*, 19 (May 1976), 618–620.

APPENDIX: SELF-TEST ANSWERS

Chapter 1

1. a	3. d	5. b	7. c
2. c	4. a	6. d	8. d

Chapter 2

1. b	5. d	9. c	12. c
2. a	6. b	10. a	13. b
3. b	7. a	11. a	
4. a	8. d		

Chapter 3

1. b	6. c	11. b	16. d
2. a	7. a	12. c	17. c
3. b	8. c	13. d	18. a
4. b	9. b	14. b	19. c
5. c	10. a	15. c	20. b

Chapter 4

1. a	5. c	9. b	13. c
2. d	6. a	10. b	14. c
3. b	7. c	11. b	15. d
4. d	8. c	12. d	

Chapter 5

1. a	5. a	9. c	13. c
2. d	6. b	10. c	14. a
3. c	7. d	11. a	
4. a	8. b	12. d	

Chapter 6

1. c	5. c	9. a	13. d
2. b	6. d	10. a	14. b
3. d	7. d	11. d	
4. d	8. b	12. c	

Chapter 7

1. c	5. c	8. a	11. a
2. b	6. c	9. d	12. a
3. c	7. d	10. d	13. d
4. a			

Chapter 8	1. a	6. c	10. d	14. c
	2. b	7. a	11. a	15. c
	3. b	8. c	12. a	16. b
	4. b	9. d	13. d	17. c
	5. c			

Chapter 9	1. b	4. b	7. a	10. a
	2. a	5. d	8. b	11. d
	3. d	6. c	9. d	12. b

Chapter 10	1. d	5. d	9. a	13. a
	2. b	6. d	10. c	14. d
	3. d	7. b	11. a	
	4. a	8. d	12. b	

Chapter 11	1. d	5. c	9. c	13. c
	2. d	6. b	10. a	14. d
	3. d	7. d	11. c	15. d
	4. b	8. b	12. d	

INDEX

STUDENT RESPONSE FORM

Many of the changes made in this edition of *Secondary School Reading Instruction: The Content Areas* were based on feedback and evaluations of the earlier edition. Please help us respond to the interests and needs of future readers by completing the questionnaire below and returning it to: College Marketing, Houghton Mifflin Company, One Beacon Street, Boston, MA 02108.

1. Please tell us your overall impressions of the text.

	Excellent	Good	Adequate	Poor
a. Was it written in a clear and understandable style?	___	___	___	___
b. Were difficult concepts well explained?	___	___	___	___
c. How would you rate the frequent use of illustrative Examples?	___	___	___	___
d. How comprehensive was the coverage of major issues and topics?	___	___	___	___
e. How does this book compare to other texts you have used?	___	___	___	___
f. How would you rate the activities?	___	___	___	___
g. How would you rate the study aids at the beginning and end of each chapter?	___	___	___	___

2. Please comment on or cite examples that illustrate any of your above ratings.

_____

_____

_____

3. Were there any topics that should have been included or covered more fully?

_____

_____

_____

4. Which chapters or features did you particularly like? _____

_____

_____

5. Which chapters or features did you dislike? _____

_____

_____

6. Which chapters taught you the most? _____

_____

_____

7. What changes would you like to see in the next edition of this book? _____

_____

_____

8. Is this a book you would like to keep for your classroom teaching experience?
   _____ Why or why not? _____

_____

_____

9. Please tell us something about your background. Are you studying to be a
   secondary school classroom teacher or a reading specialist? Are you inservice
   or preservice? Are you an undergraduate or graduate student? _____

_____

_____